SECOND EDITION

RACE, ETHNICITY, and GENDER

*To Kaya O'Brien-James, Benjamin Healey, and
Caroline Healey, in the hope that the issues of our world will be resolved in theirs.*

SECOND EDITION

RACE, ETHNICITY, and GENDER
Selected Readings

EDITORS

Joseph F. Healey
Christopher Newport University

Eileen O'Brien
University of Richmond

PINE FORGE PRESS
An Imprint of Sage Publications, Inc.
Los Angeles • London • New Delhi • Singapore

For information:

Pine Forge Press
A Sage Publications Company
2455 Teller Road
Thousand Oaks, California 91320
E-mail: order@sagepub.com

Sage Publications Ltd.
1 Oliver's Yard
55 City Road
London EC1Y 1SP
United Kingdom

Sage Publications India Pvt. Ltd.
B 1/I 1 Mohan Cooperative Industrial Area
Mathura Road, New Delhi 110 044
India

Sage Publications Asia-Pacific Pte. Ltd.
33 Pekin Street #02-01
Far East Square
Singapore 048763

Printed in the United States of America.

Library of Congress Cataloging-in-Publication Data

Race, ethnicity, and gender : Selected readings / [edited by] Joseph F. Healey,
Eileen O'Brien. — 2nd ed.
    p. cm.
Includes bibliographical references and index.
ISBN 978-1-4129-4107-5 (pbk.)
    1. Minorities—United States. 2. United States—Race relations. 3. United States—Ethnic relations. 4. Racism—United States. 5. Ethnicity—United States. 6. Minority women—United States. 7. Sex role—United States. I. Healey, Joseph F., 1945- II. O'Brien, Eileen, 1972-
E184.A1R277 2007
305.800973—dc22

                            2006034890

This book is printed on acid-free paper.

07   08   09   10   11   10   9   8   7   6   5   4   3   2

Acquisitions Editor:	Benjamin Penner
Editorial Assistant:	Camille Herrera
Production Editor:	Sarah K. Quesenberry
Copy Editor:	Jennifer Withers
Proofreader:	Kevin Gleason
Typesetter:	C&M Digitals (P) Ltd.
Indexer:	Juniee Oneida
Cover Designer:	Janet Foulger
Marketing Manager:	Jennifer Reed

CONTENTS

PREFACE TO THE SECOND EDITION

As we worked on this second edition, immigration policy in the United States was all over the news. The national anthem was being sung in the Spanish language, and protest marches occurred across the nation. Media outlets included discussions of how to better address economic changes spawned by globalization, what would become of the United States with the growth of its "nonwhite" population, and whether racial or ethnic profiling was even justified in the wake of the so-called "war on terror." While in the 1990s discussions of race and ethnicity seemed to center upon the war on drugs, police brutality, and other issues central to African Americans, the lenses of the first decade of the 21st century widened to include Middle Eastern Americans, Arab Americans, Muslim Americans, Latino Americans, and Asian Americans in particular. Immigration and terrorism pressed discussions of these groups, whether implicit or explicit, more upon the front page, and we could not ignore the centrality of these political, economic, and cultural shifts as we compiled these significant changes to the second edition of this reader. Moreover, we understood discussions of such issues to be incomplete without taking into account gender; the meaning of immigration policy for predominantly male agricultural workers becomes quite different from its meaning and impact on predominantly female "sex slaves." Likewise, unmistakably gendered ideology, whether stated or unstated, could not be ignored in how such debates were framed. Fundamentalist terrorists' reactions against modernity included a backlash on feminism, just as an ethic of care and mothering became a political issue for mothers demanding immigration amnesty for their families. We knew our new edition should incorporate gender not just when readings were readily available, but rather consistently in every chapter.

Readers will find new selections in each and every chapter, plus an entirely new chapter, since the first edition. The most revamped chapters, in name at least, are Chapters 9 and 11. The new chapter added to Part III on "New Americans" (Chapter 9) includes readings on immigrants in American society (Philip Martin and Elizabeth Midgely), Middle Eastern Americans (Amir Marvasti and Karyn D. McKinney), and the white supremacy and patriarchy of domestic and global terrorists (Michael S. Kimmel). The final chapter, "Antiracist and Feminist Solutions" (Chapter 11), has also been renamed to take into account the heightened focus on gender since the last edition which has been infused not only here but throughout the book. A selection on the connections between antiracism and feminism (Eileen O'Brien and Michael P. Armato), another on comparable worth policy, which tackles gender and race inequality in earnings (Ronnie Steinberg and Jennifer Hickman), and a checklist on how to monitor sexist and racist behavior (Chris Crass) are all newly included in Chapter 11.

While the remaining nine *chapter titles* may appear similar since the first edition, the *content* of all the remaining chapters have nonetheless changed in some way, some rather significantly. For example, two of the readings contained in Chapter 4 are new— one on affirmative action (Fred L. Pincus) and another on the race, class, and gender dimensions of school shootings (Michael S. Kimmel). These were strategically chosen to address news items that may have hit home personally for many college students, but in a way that goes beyond the average news reporting to engaging the sociological imagination. Additionally, all of the chapters in Part III (aside from the entirely new Chapter 9) have one new reading apiece: Chapter 6 includes a piece on Native American women by Charon Asetoyer, Chapter 7 has an essay on Latinos and Asians' racial middle ground by Eileen O'Brien, and Chapter 8 contains a report on South Korean sex slaves in the United States and Canada by Salim Jiwa. New readings were chosen to address gender, more current issues, or both whenever possible.

Throughout our revision process, we kept an eye toward what would work best with students and keep them engaged. To frame the entire book, Part I remains relatively consistent, with an important change to Chapter 1—a reading on the construction of racial, ethnic, and gender categories themselves. This reading by Karen Rosenblum and Toni-Michelle Travis provides many excellent examples that will resonate with students and set up a distinctly sociological lens on these social statuses early on, pointing out that categories can and do change over time, and were put into place as social and political, not biological, creations. To Chapter 2 ("Assimilation and Pluralism") we have added one reading by Anthony DePalma from the highly acclaimed *New York Times* collection *Class Matters* that puts human faces on the "old" versus "new" immigrants by profiling one Greek's and one Mexican American's economic prospects in the restaurant business. Along with this reading, we have also added a powerful piece by Eugenia Kaw on cosmetic surgery among Asian American women, to explore how the toll of assimilation to the majority culture can have a distinctly different impact on non-majority women. While gender is an important component of this reading, we wrote new discussion questions for all the new readings which asked students to continue using their critical thinking skills even when gender was not an explicit agenda of the particular author in question. For instance, since DePalma's reading profiles two male immigrant stories, we ask students to consider how gender has structured their experiences.

Other important components that we retain, corresponding with the first author's *Diversity and Society* text, are the narrative portrait and current debate sections. These are another way we work to capture student interest and critical thinking in the reader. Most of the chapters now include two narrative portraits instead of one, so students can get a clearer sense of the diversity of experiences even within the particular category upon which the chapter is focused. Several of these narrative portrait couplings also highlight gender differences between authors. We also feature some new current debates, as well as some fresh new perspectives within the debates begun in the first edition. For instance, a new current debate in Chapter 6 considers the question, "Are Indian Sports Team Mascots Offensive?"—a question that we have found can engage even the most disengaged college students in our classrooms, and for many a question never before considered. Other new current debate questions get at the heart of recent conversations in the public media about immigration: one about whether "Hispanization" threatens American culture, and another about whether using "English only" or bilingualism should be the way we deal with our language differences. Three other current debate questions include new authors' perspectives since the last edition.

We have selected all readings with careful attention to what will keep the students engaged with the most critical and cutting edge questions in the field, as well as some classic readings that many instructors have found invaluable in helping students to grasp the useful lens that sociological analysis lends to racial, ethnic, and gender relations. In our experiences, the classroom that engages questions of race and gender inequalities is one of the rare times students have to speak openly and honestly about such issues, and thus has the potential to be a place of transformative power and social change. It is our sincere hope that this reader provides instructors and students with some of the tools to be able to help their classrooms live up to that potential.

Available on the book's accompanying website, http://www.pineforge.com/das2, are *Public Sociology Assignments*. Although not all sociologists would endorse a call for activism and involvement, the study of American race relationships will, for many people, stimulate an impulse to address social problems directly and personally. These *Public Sociology Assignments* were developed for students, to facilitate involvement in their communities and provide them with the possibility of making a positive difference in the lives of others.

PREFACE FROM THE FIRST EDITION

Relations between ethnic and racial groups in U.S. society today are fairer and more open than they have ever been before. This may not be saying much, however, given a national history that features slavery, segregation, attempted genocide, racist immigration restrictions, and unrelenting political, economic, legal, and sexual assaults on minority group members. The improvements in group relations during the past several decades are real and should be celebrated: they have opened up opportunities for millions of people and have moved us closer to the ideal of a truly color-blind society. However, we cannot mistake these improvements for final resolutions. As real as the progress has been, many long-standing minority group problems and grievances remain, and they are joined by new issues with great regularity.

Even as we acknowledge the improvements, it is clear that the minority group issues that remain are complex and difficult to resolve. They range from affirmative action to immigration policy, from discrimination in the criminal justice system to urban poverty and welfare reform, and from racism in the classroom to residential segregation. Furthermore, they affect virtually every aspect of the social system, from the halls of the Supreme Court to the meanest back alleys of our cities and towns. Solutions are not obvious and, indeed, there are no guarantees that the society will be able to address the issues honestly, let alone resolve them successfully. It is certain, however, that we will never succeed in building a truly open multigroup society unless we confront the problems openly and examine them critically.

This book is intended to help students understand and analyze the minority group issues that permeate our society. It emerges from decades of teaching and interacting with students and a continual monitoring of their responses to information, perspectives, and arguments. While the book presents no final answers or easy solutions, it will help students develop their understanding by presenting crucial background information and a variety of perspectives on the issues.

The book is divided into four parts. Part I introduces basic concepts and perspectives, and Part II presents an overview of the development of dominant-minority relations in the United States. Part III, the bulk of the text, is organized by minority group and examines a variety of issues for each group. Part IV presents some of the best contemporary thinking on anti-racist strategies for the present and for the future.

The chapters include three sections. The "Narrative Portraits" present the insights and experiences of the victims of racism and racial oppression and are intended to personalize the concepts used in the text and to give them a human face. The "Readings" present the views of a variety of leading scholars and analysts and represent some of the most important thinking and research currently being conducted. The readings were selected not only for their importance but also for their accessibility to students and for their diversity of approach and perspective. Finally, the "Current Debates" section presents opposing views on current issues, including affirmative action, reparations, and immigration policy. These selections are intended to help students develop their own thinking and come to a fuller understanding on these issues.

This reader has a companion textbook, *Diversity and Society* by Joseph F. Healey, also available from Pine Forge Press. The chapters in this reader have been designed to parallel the chapters in the text and to extend its analysis and broaden its perspective. Both books emphasize the diversity of the minority group experience and, especially, the ways in which that experience has been mediated and shaped by gender. In combination or singly, these texts present an analysis that is comprehensive, diverse, cogent, contemporary, and highly accessible to students.

ACKNOWLEDGMENTS

First and foremost, we thank our students, who, over the years, have helped us identify the approaches, ideas, and readings that would be most helpful for teaching a subject matter that is often complex, misunderstood, and emotionally charged. We also thank our colleagues for their support and guidance. Joe would like to thank Iris Price of Christopher Newport University for her invaluable assistance. Eileen would like to thank three special members of her family: her partner, Kendall, her daughter, Kaya, and her great-grandmother, Essie, for understanding the strange life of an academic—that even though she did not have to "go to work," she had work to do—and for helping her carve out the space and the child care necessary to be able to do that.

A reader like this is a horse of a different color; there are so many different parts to coordinate and put together, and we could not have done it without the persistent prodding and organizational skills of Camille Herrera and Ben Penner. We are also grateful to Ben and Camille for gathering external reviews of the first edition, and to all the anonymous reviewers who offered numerous suggestions and reading titles/topics, many of which are incorporated here, that have definitely helped us to create a stronger, and timely, second edition.

For permission to reprint from the following, grateful acknowledgment is made to the publishers and copyright holders.

Narrative Portraits

Chapter 1: "Developing a Racial Identity," Lawrence Hill. From *Black Berry, Sweet Juice: On Being White in Canada* by Lawrence Hill. Copyright © 2001 by Lawrence Hill. Reprinted by permission of the author, and HarperCollins*PublishersLtd*. All rights reserved.

"Kaffir Boy," Mark Mathabane. Reprinted with the permission of Scribner, an imprint of Simon & Schuster Adult Publishing Group, from *Kaffir Boy* by Mark Mathabane. Copyright © 1986 by Mark Mathabane.

Chapter 2: "Choosing a Dream: Italians in Hell's Kitchen," Mario Puzo. From *Visions of America* edited by W. Brown and A. Ling, pp. 56–57. Copyright © 1993 by Mario Puzo. Reprinted by permission of Donadio & Olson, Inc.

"Always Running: La Vida Loca," Luis Rodriguez. From *Always Running—La Vida Loca, Gang Days in L.A.* by Luis J. Rodriguez. (Curbstone Press, 1993). Reprinted with permission of Curbstone Press. Distributed by Consortium. Pp. 83–84.

Chapter 3: "Narrative of the Life and Adventures of Henry Bibb" Henry Bibb, edited by Gilbert Osofsky from *Puttin' on Ole Massa: The Slave Narratives of Henry Bibb, William Wells Brown, and Solomon Northup*. Copyright © 1969. Harper and Row. Reprinted with permission of Marcia Osofsky, Ph.D.

"Life as a Slave Girl," Harriet Jacobs. Reprinted by permission of the publisher from *Incidents in the Life of a Slave Girl, Written by Herself* by Harriet A. Jacobs, edited and with an introduction by Jean Fagen Yellin, pp. 27–30, Cambridge, MA.: Harvard University Press. Copyright © 1987, 2000 by the President and Fellows of Harvard College.

Chapter 4: "Death on the City Pavement," Richard Wright. From *12 Million Black Voices* by Richard Wright. New York: Thunder's Mouth Press, 1988.

Chapter 5: "A Black Man Ponders His Ability to Alter Public Space," Brent Staples. Reprinted by permission of the author. Brent Staples writes editorials for *The New York Times* and is author of the memoir, *Parallel Time: Growing Up in Black and White*.

"The Mulatto Millennium," Danzy Senna. Copyright © 1998 by Danzy Senna. Reprinted with the permission of The Wylie Agency, Inc.

Chapter 6: "Lakota Woman," Mary Crow Dog. From *Lakota Woman* by Mary Crow Dog. Copyright © 1990 by Mary Crow Dog and Richard Erdoes. Reprinted with permission of Grove/Atlantic, Inc.

"Talking to the Owls and Butterflies," John Lame Deer. Reprinted with permission of Pocket Books, an imprint of Simon & Schuster Adult Publishing Group from *Lame Deer Seeker of Visions* by John (Fire) Lame Deer and Richard Erdoes. Copyright © 1972 by John (Fire) Lame Deer and Richard Erdoes.

Chapter 7: "Americanization Is Tough on Macho," Rose Del Castillo Guibault. *The San Francisco Chronicle*, August 20, 1989. Copyright © 1989. Reprinted with permission via Copyright Clearance Center.

"The Island Travels With You," Judith Ortiz Cofer. From "The Myth of the Latin Woman: I Just Met a Girl Named Maria," in *The Latin Deli: Prose and Poetry* by Judith Ortiz Cofer. Copyright © 1993 by Judith Ortiz Cofer. The University of Georgia Press, pp. 148–154.

Chapter 8: "We Were Just Japs," Joseph Kurihara. From *The Spoilage* by Thomas Swaine and Richard S. Nishimoto. Copyright © 1946 University of California Press. Reprinted with permission.

Chapter 9: "Life in the Enclave." "Ho Yang, from China, 1920," is reprinted from *American Mosaic: The Immigrant Experience in the Words of Those Who Lived It* by Joan Morrison

Readings

France Winddance Twine and Kathleen M. Blee. Copyright © 2001 by France Winddance Twine and Kathleen M. Blee. Reprinted by permission of New York University Press.

"Abolish the White Race by Any Means Necessary," Noel Ignatiev and John Garvery. From *Race Traitor* by Noel Ignatiev and John Garvey. Copyright © 1996. Reproduced by permission of Routledge/Taylor and Frances Group, LLC.

"Being an Ally," Paul Kivel. Excerpts from *Uprooting Racism: How White People Can Work for Racial Justice* by Paul Kivel. Published by New Society Publishers, revised edition 2002. Reprinted with permission.

"Commitment to Combat Racism," Judith Katz. Excerpts from *White Awareness: A Handbook of Anti-Racism Training* by Judith Katz. Published by University of Oklahoma Press, 1978. Reprinted by permission.

"Tools for White Guys Who Are Working for Social Change," Chris Crass. Reprinted with permission of the author.

Current Debates

Chapter 1: "The Dominance of Black Athletes is Genetic," Jon Entine. From *Taboo: Why Black Athletes Dominate Sports and Why We're Afraid to Talk About It.* Copyright © 1999 by Jon Entine. Reprinted by permission of PublicAffairs. A member of Perseus Books, L.L.C.

"The Argument for Genetic Differences is Deeply Flawed," Kenan Malik. Originally titled "Yes, Nature Does Help to Explain African Sporting Success: If You Think That's Racist, Your Idea of Race is Wrong," from *New Statesman*, 129: 13–18. September 18, 2000. Copyright © New Statesman. All rights reserved. Reprinted with permission.

Chapter 2: "English Only Will Speed the Assimilation of Immigrants," Mauro Mujica. Originally titled "Official English Legislation: Myths and realities," from *Human Events*, 59, July 28, 2003. Copyright © 2003 Human Events Inc. Reprinted with permission.

"Bilingualism Should Be Encouraged," Aida Hurtado and Luis A. Vega. Originally titled "Shift Happens: Spanish and English Transmission between Parents and Their Children," from *Journal of Social Issues*, 60 (1): 137–155. Copyright © 2004. Reprinted with permission of Blackwell Publishing Ltd.

Chapter 3: "Slavery Created African American Culture," Stanley Elkins. From *Slavery: A Problem in American Institutional and Intellectual Life* by Stanley Elkins. Copyright ©1959, 1968, 1976 by University of Chicago Press. Reprinted by permission of The University of Chicago Press and the author.

"African American Culture Was Created by an Interplay of Elements from Africa and America," William Piersen. From *From Africa to America: African American History from the Colonial Era to the Early Republic, 1526-1790* by William D. Piersen. New York: Twayne, 1996.

Chapter 4: "Affirmative Action Casts Suspicions on Legitimate Black Achievement and Depicts African Americans as Incapable," Thomas Sowell. Originally titled "How

Chapter 9: "Immigration Is Harmful," Peter Brimelow. From *Alien Nation* by Peter Brimelow. Copyright © 1995 by Peter Brimelow; Maps & Illustrations copyright © 1995 by John Grimwade. Used by permission of Random House, Inc. and The Wylie Agency.

"Immigration Is Not Harmful," Reynolds Farley. Originally titled "New Americans" from *The New American Reality: Who We Are, How We Got There, Where We Are Going* by Farley Reynolds. Copyright © 1996 Russell Sage Foundation, 112 East 64th Street, New York, NY 10021. Reprinted with permission.

"We Need to Reframe the Immigration Debate," George Borjas. From *Heaven's Door: Immigration Policy and the American Economy* by George J. Borjas. Copyright © 1999 Princeton University Press. Reprinted by permission of Princeton University Press.

Chapter 10: "The Need to Understand Whiteness," Richard Dyer. From *White: Essays on Race and Culture* by Richard Dyer. Copyright © 1987. Reprinted by permission of Routledge.

"Symbolic and Involuntary Ethnicity," Mary Waters. Originally titled "Optional Ethnicities: For Whites Only?" from *Origins and Destinies: Immigration, Race and Ethnicity in America*, 1st ed., edited by Sylvia Pedraza and Rueben Rumbaut, Copyright © 1996. Reprinted with permission of Wadsworth, a division of Thomson Learning: www.thomsonrights.com. Fax 800-730-2215.

PUBLISHER'S ACKNOWLEDGMENTS

Pine Forge Press gratefully acknowledges the contributions of the following reviewers:

Von Bakanic
College of Charleston

Thomas Calhoun
Southern Illinois University Carbondale

Addrain S. Conyers
Southern Illinois University Carbondale

Elizabeth M. Esterchild
University of North Texas

Richard J. Harris
University of Texas at San Antonio

Diana L. Hayes
Georgetown University

P. Rafael Hernández-Arias
DePaul University

Ezekiel Kalipeni
University of Illinois at Urbana-Champaign

Kathleen Odell Korgen
William Paterson University

Augustine Kposowa
University of California, Riverside

Myriam Mekelburg
L.A. Mission College

Angela M. Orend
University of Louisville

Seth Ovadia
Bowdoin College

Peggy A. Shifflett
Radford University

S. Rowan Wolf
Portland Community College

Part I

An Introduction to the Study of
Minority Groups in the United States

1

Diversity in the United States

Questions and Concepts

This chapter introduces several concepts crucial to the study of dominant-minority relations in the United States. The selections emphasize prejudice and racism but also call attention to the widely misunderstood concept of race.

The concept of race is addressed in several places. First, the Narrative Portrait by Lawrence Hill presents the efforts of a person of mixed black-white heritage to grapple with issues of identity and status in a world where people have traditionally been regarded as *either* black or white. His thoughts are consistent with the view, widely held among social scientists, that race is a *social construction:* a way of thinking about ourselves and others that is socially determined and a reflection of our experiences in a highly race-conscious society. Race is important because we are trained to think it's important, not because of some essential quality inherent in the concept.

Second, the reading by Rosenblum and Travis explores the processes by which we construct social categories like race, sex, class, and ethnicity. The authors argue that so-called racial and gender differences lie more in the cultural and social perceptions we acquire during socialization than in the nature of the phenomena themselves. In other words, group boundaries are created by a social process, not by some "natural" quality of the groups themselves, and we come to regard these boundaries as important because of our socialization, not because of anything inherent in the group.

Finally, the biological and social realities of race are explored in the Current Debate. Why do African American (and African) athletes dominate in so many sports? Jon Entine's answer to this question assumes that race is a meaningful biological reality and that the dominance of African American athletes is, in some sense, "natural." Kenan Malik, on the other hand, questions not only Entine's logic and assumptions but the reality of the concept of race itself.

The concepts of prejudice and racism are addressed from a number of perspectives. The Narrative Portrait by Mark Mathabane recounts an incident from his childhood in South Africa during the days of apartheid. In this memoir, we see how prejudice (and the perception that race is a biological reality) is carefully taught in a highly racist society and how prejudicial thinking can be reinforced even by people who believe that they are trying to combat it. The reading by Yetman distinguishes among prejudice, discrimination, and racism—concepts that are at the core of the sociological analysis of dominant-minority relations. Researchers Van

Ausdale and Feagin explore how these concepts are used by young children in their interactions with each other. Again, we see the results of race-conscious thinking and careful training in prejudice.

Please visit the accompanying website to Race, Ethnicity, and Gender, second edition for the *Public Sociology Assignments* at http://www.pineforge.com/das2.

QUESTIONS TO CONSIDER IN THIS CHAPTER

1. Is race *merely* a social construction? Is the biology of race completely irrelevant? How about gender? Is it also merely a social construction? How do gender and race differ (if at all) in this regard?

2. What are prejudice, racism, and discrimination? How are these concepts linked to each other? How do they differ? Make sure you can explain and

describe each concept and cite examples from your own experience.

3. How are prejudice and racism taught? What roles do parents and significant others such as teachers, siblings, and friends play? Do we merely acquire the prejudiced views from our social environment or are we more active in the process? How?

NARRATIVE PORTRAIT

THE SOCIAL CONSTRUCTION OF RACIAL IDENTITY

Traditionally, in the United States, race has been seen as a set of fixed, unchanging, unambiguous categories. Perhaps the most powerful example of this perception was the "one-drop rule" that has been used to determine racial identity, especially in the South. The rule was simple: any trace of black ancestry—a single drop of African-American blood in your veins—meant that you were black.

In contrast to this rigid perception, the increasing numbers of cross-group marriages and "mixed race" individuals reminds us that race is subjective and negotiable, not fixed and permanent. That is, racial identity is a definition of self that is constructed during socialization and negotiated and developed in interaction with parents, siblings, peers, and others in the community. Race is not permanent or fixed, and social conceptions can change independent of the biological realities. New racial categories can emerge as the social conception of race changes. For example, professional golfer Tiger Woods has (tongue in cheek) made up his own racial category—Cablasian—to acknowledge his <u>C</u>aucasian, <u>Bl</u>ack, and <u>Asian</u> ancestry.

Although the newer, less rigid view of group membership might be growing in strength, the tradition of categorical thinking still has an enormous impact on the way people of mixed racial heritage are regarded by others and how they think about themselves and their place in the larger society. Some of these conflicts are illustrated in this selection from writer Lawrence Hill, the son of a black father and a white mother. His parents were involved in the U.S. civil rights struggle in the 1950s and 1960s but opted to move to the more tolerant racial climate of Canada to raise their children. Mr. Hill was raised in a suburb of Toronto and rarely encountered other children of color. In the passage below, he remembers some of the issues related to his multiracial status and the problem of finding a place for himself even in the mild Canadian racial atmosphere. He also reflects on the more certain racial identity of his parents, the difference between black and white racial identities, and provides something of an outsider's view on U.S. race relations.

DEVELOPING A RACIAL IDENTITY

Lawrence Hill

As a child, my experience of race, including my racial identity, was shaded quite differently from that of my parents. They were both born and raised in the United States, and their racial identities were clearly delineated all their lives. The America of their youth and early adulthood was replete with laws that banned interracial marriages and upheld segregation in every domain of public life. . . . In the United States, there was never any doubt that my father was first and foremost a black man. Or that my mother was a white woman. And there is no question that, had my siblings and I been raised in the United States, we would have been identified . . . as black. . . .

When I was growing up, I didn't spend much time thinking about who I was or where I fit in. I was too busy tying my shoelaces, brushing my teeth, learning to spell, swinging baseball bats and shooting hockey pucks. But once in a while, just as my guard was down, questions of my own identity would leap like a cougar from the woods and take a bite out of my backside.

I found that race became an issue as a result of environmental factors. The average white kid growing up in a white suburb didn't have to think of himself as white. Gradually, my environment started talking to me and making me aware that I could never truly be white. There's nothing like being called "nigger" to let you know that you're not white.

Learning that I wasn't white, however, wasn't the same as learning that I was black. Indeed, for the longest time I didn't learn what I was—only what I wasn't. In the strange and unique society that was Canada, I was allowed to grow up in a sort of racial limbo. People knew what I wasn't—white or black—but they sure couldn't say what I was . . . .

These days, I think of the factors that contributed to my sense of identity, and of how malleable that sense of identity was and still is. There were days when I went straight from my exclusive, private boys' high school to family events populated by black relatives or friends. . . . I bounced back and forth between studying Latin . . . and revering black American cultural icons, but who exactly was I? . . .

Today in Canada, black people still contend with racism at every level of society. And yet, the way my children will define themselves, and be defined by others, remains up for grabs. Racial identity is about how you see yourself, about how you construct a sense of belonging, community, awareness and allegiance.

To this date, I have mostly seen myself as black. . . . My siblings and I learned early that you can have a white parent and still be considered black, but you can never have a black parent and be considered white. It ain't allowed. You'll be reminded of your "otherness" more times than you can shake a stick at it. This is one of the reasons why I self identify as black. Attempts at pleasant symmetry, as in "half-white, half-black," trivialize to my eye the meaning of being black. . . .

The suburb of [Toronto in which I was raised] became as suffocating for [me as the U.S. had been for my parents]. There were no blacks in my school, on my street. Because I looked so different from everyone else, I feared that I was ugly. I worried about having frizzy hair, big ears, a big nose and plump lips. When I looked in the mirror, I felt disgust. None of the people I admired looked the least bit like me. Listening to my father's [stories] . . . instilled in [me and my siblings] a measure of black pride. . . . I had to find . . . ways to connect [to Black traditions and cultural icons]. So I ate up every bit of black writing that I could find. Langston Hughes, Ralph Ellison, Richard Wright . . . James Baldwin. Eldridge Cleaver . . . . I read Alex Haley's Autobiography of Malcolm X, and had to struggle through the section of Malcolm X's life when he ardently believed that white people were the devil incarnate. I knew this to be false. My mother was white, and she was no devil.

Without knowing exactly what I was doing, I was forming my own sense of blackness and my own connection to the black Diaspora. . . . Slowly, I was developing a sense of myself.

SOURCE: "Developing a Racial Identity" from *Black Berry, Sweet Juice: On Being White in Canada* by Lawrence Hill. Copyright © 2001 by Lawrence Hill. Reprinted by permission of the author, and HarperCollins*Publishers Ltd.* All rights reserved.

NARRATIVE PORTRAIT

THE CULTURAL SOURCES OF PREJUDICE

Kaffir Boy, Mark Mathabane's (1986) best-selling memoir of growing up in racist South Africa, provides abundant illustrations of the importance of culture and conformity in developing individual prejudice. Prior to recent social and political reforms, South Africa was the most rigidly race-conscious and segregated society on earth. Black South Africans were kept economically and politically powerless and were used as a source of cheap labor for the benefit of white South Africans. White South Africans of even modest economic means were able to afford domestic help (cooks, gardeners, maids, etc.) or other amenities because of this system of exploitation and discrimination.

This elaborate system of racial privilege was stabilized in part by a strong, government-sanctioned ideology of antiblack prejudice and racism. Black and white South Africans had little contact with each other except in situations in which the black person was clearly subordinate. What "knowledge" the white community had of blacks came from constrained, lopsided interactions or from the racist content of their culture. For example, the idea that blacks are inferior was taught in school as part of the official curriculum.

In the following passage, Mathabane recalls a day when he went to work with his grandmother, a gardener for an affluent white family named Smith. Clyde Smith was roughly the same age as Mark and clearly demonstrates the results of being socialized in a culture in which racism is both "normal" and government supported. Note that Mrs. Smith challenges her son's attitudes with antiracist values and beliefs—even blatantly racist cultures are not monolithic in their commitment to bias. How does she also reinforce racial inequality in her actions and words?

KAFFIR BOY

Mark Mathabane

"This is Mrs. Smith's house," Granny remarked as she led me up a long driveway of a beautiful villa-

type house. . . . We went to a steel gate at the back of the yard, where Granny rang a bell.

"I'm here, madam," she shouted through the gate. . . . A door creaked open, and a high-pitched woman's voice called out, "I'm coming, Ellen." . . . Presently the gate clicked open, and there appeared a short, slender white woman. . . . "I'm just getting ready to leave for tennis," she said to Granny.

"Madam, guess who I have with me today," Granny said with the widest smile. . . .

"My, what a big lad he is! . . . Is he really your grandson, Ellen?" The warmth in her voice somehow reduced my fears of her; her eyes shone with the same gentleness of the Catholic Sisters at the clinic.

"Yes, madam," Granny said proudly; "this is the one I've been telling you about. This is the one who'll some day go to university." . . .

"I believe you, Ellen," said Mrs. Smith. "He looks like a very smart pickaninny." . . .

Toward early afternoon Mrs. Smith returned. She called me to the car to remove several shopping bags from the backseat. . . . As we were talking, a busload of white schoolchildren stopped in front of the house and a young boy [Mrs. Smith's son, Clyde] alighted and ran up the driveway. . . ."Who is he, Mother?"

"That's Ellen's grandson. . . . Now run along inside and change and . . . then maybe you can play with pickaninny."

"I don't play with Kaffirs," the white boy declared. "At school they say we shouldn't."

"Watch your filthy mouth, Clyde," Mrs. Smith said, flushing crimson. "I thought I told you a million times to leave all that rubbish about Kaffirs in the classroom." . . .

Turning to Granny, . . . Mrs. Smith said, in a voice of someone fighting a losing battle, "You know, Ellen, I simply don't understand why those damn uncivilized Boers from Pretoria teach children such things."

"I agree, madam," Granny said, "All children, black and white, are God's children." . . .

"I'm afraid you're right, Ellen," Mrs. Smith said, somewhat touched. . . .

Shortly, Clyde emerged. . . . He called to me. "Come here, pickaninny. My mother says I should show you around."

I went.

I followed him around as he showed me the things his parents regularly bought him. . . . I couldn't understand why his people had to have all the luxuries money could buy, while my people lived in abject poverty. . . . We finally came to Clyde's playroom. The room was roughly the size of our house, and was elaborately decorated. . . . What arrested my attention were the stacks of comic books on the floor and the shelves and shelves of books. Never had I seen so many books. . . .

Sensing that I was in awe of his magnificent library, Clyde said, "Do you have this many books in your playroom?"

"I don't have a playroom."

"You don't have a playroom," he said bug-eyed. "Can you read? . . . My teachers tell us that Kaffirs can't read, speak or write English like white people because they have smaller brains, which are already full of tribal things. My teachers say you're not people like us, because you belong to a jungle civilization.* That's why you can't live or go to school with us, but can only be our servants."

"Stop saying that rubbish," Mrs. Smith said angrily as she entered the room. . . ."How many times have I told you that what your teachers say about black people is not true?"

"What do you know, Mama?" Clyde retorted impudently, "you're not a teacher. Besides, there are textbooks where it's so written."

*In South Africa, Kaffir is a derogatory term for blacks, roughly equivalent to nigger.

SOURCE: Reprinted with the permission of Scribner, an imprint of Simon & Schuster Adult Publishing Group, from *Kaffir Boy* by Mark Mathabane. Copyright © 1986 by Mark Mathabane.

READINGS

In this section, we examine the development and application of many key concepts related to the understanding of diversity in the United States. The first reading, "Prejudice, Discrimination, and Racism," examines in depth three concepts that are often confused and used interchangeably in everyday language, yet have very distinct and specific meanings in the sociological study of majority-minority relations. The author, Norman Yetman, begins by introducing sociologist Robert K. Merton's typology of prejudice (attitudes and feelings) and discrimination (behavior) and stressing the differences between the two. Discrimination is often motivated by prejudice, of course, but it can also be the result of social pressure and conformity. Likewise, prejudice does not always result in discrimination, for the same social reasons.

Yetman also reminds us that prejudice and discrimination are not simply psychological in nature. Thus, simply educating people to be "more open-minded" as a strategy of prejudice reduction is hardly enough to eliminate inequality, although many well-meaning Americans seem to think so. Driving home these distinctions, Yetman then develops a definition of racism that has both ideological and behavioral components and concludes by exploring the differences between attitudinal discrimination and institutional discrimination, providing many examples of each. Incidents with high media exposure, such as the beating of Rodney King and the refusal to serve black customers in places like Denny's restaurants, serve as examples of attitudinal discrimination. Institutional discrimination, on the other hand, refers to policies and practices that are not nearly as obvious in their intent. Examples such as jury selection from only registered voters, job referrals by word of mouth, and different penalties for crack and powder cocaine users alerts us to how covert and far-reaching the dynamics of prejudice, discrimination, and racism are in the United States.

The second selection, "Using Racial and Ethnic Concepts: The Critical Case of Very Young Children," takes us into a research setting where the concepts of prejudice, discrimination, and racism are put into practice be some of the seemingly most innocent citizens—preschool-aged children. Using the method of participant observation, authors Debra Van Ausdale and Joe R. Feagin investigate how young children negotiate racial and ethnic boundaries on their own terms with each other, rather than in response to any adult pre-formulations. This essay presents numerous firsthand examples of how children use racial and ethnic concepts to include each other as well as control each other, and also to demarcate their own and others' identities. Far from innocently parroting words they might overhear from adults, these children are quite savvy at putting racial and ethnic dividing lines into practice. Also interesting are the adult reactions to children's racial transgressions, since the adults are quick to deny that the children learned it from them. Thus, society at large has already given the children clear messages about who the in-groups and out-groups are in their communities, and they have learned these lessons well enough to begin putting them into practice, even at such young ages.

Rosenblum and Travis argue that race and gender—categories that we tend to see as "natural," unambiguous, and unchanging—are profoundly social, negotiable, and dynamic. The authors demonstrate the value of a "constructionist" approach to the social categories that people tend to accept as part of their everyday realities. By questioning the "essentialism" of these categories, they challenge us to critically examine our perceptions and assumptions of the world. They also demonstrate the ways in which categories and group names change in response to political pressures and group conflict. Rosenblum and Travis show that matters of group membership and the labels that are attached to groups—or that groups attach to themselves—are profoundly social processes that reflect the distribution of power and resources in the larger society.

Prejudice, Discrimination, and Racism

Norman Yetman

Prejudice and discrimination are important elements in all majority-minority relations. The term *prejudice* derives from two Latin words, *prae* "before" and *judicum* "a judgment." It denotes a judgment before all the facts are known. According to Gordon Allport, *prejudice* is "an avertive or hostile attitude toward a person who belongs to a group, simply because he (or she) belongs to that group, and is therefore presumed to have the objectionable qualities ascribed to the group" (Allport 1958:8). Prejudice thus refers to a set of rigidly held negative attitudes, beliefs, and feelings toward members of another group.

Prejudice often involves an intense emotional component. Thus, many white Americans consciously and rationally reject the myths of African American inferiority but react emotionally with fear, hostility, or condescension in the presence of African Americans. The forms of prejudice range from unconscious aversion to members of the out-group to a comprehensive, well-articulated, and coherent ideology, such as the ideology of racism.

Discrimination, on the other hand, involves unfavorable treatment of individuals because of their group membership. Prejudice and discrimination should not be equated. Prejudice involves attitudes and internal states, whereas discrimination involves overt action or behavior. Discrimination may be manifested in a multitude of ways: mild slights (such as Polish jokes); verbal threats, abuse, and epithets; intimidation and harassment (such as threatening phone calls); defacing property with ethnic slurs, graffiti, or symbols; unequal treatment (such as refusing to hire or promote qualified applicants); systematic oppression (such as slavery); or outright violence (vandalism, arson, terrorism, lynching, pogroms, massacres).

. . . Attitude surveys conducted in the United States since the 1940s have shown a significant decline in antiblack prejudice; increasingly, white Americans have come to support broad principles of racial integration and equal treatment in public accommodations, employment, public transportation, schools, housing, and marriage. For example, in 1942, 32 percent of whites agreed that whites and blacks should attend the same schools; by 1982, this figure was 90 percent. When asked in 1958 whether they would object to sending their children to schools in which half the children were black, nearly half (47 percent) responded affirmatively; by 1997, this figure had declined to 12 percent. In 1944, 45 percent thought that blacks should have as good a chance as whites to get any kind of job; and by 1972, 97 percent agreed. The percentage approving integration in public transportation rose from 46 percent in 1942 to 88 percent in 1970. Moreover, whites have indicated increasing willingness to participate personally in desegregated settings. In 1958, four-fifths of whites said they would move if blacks moved into their neighborhood "in great numbers"; in 1997, those indicating they would move declined to 12 percent. Finally, whereas only 4 percent of whites said they approved of interracial marriages in 1958, more than three-fifths (61 percent) expressed their approval in 1997 (Schuman, Steeh, and Bobo 1985; Hochschild 1995; Gallup Poll Social Audit 1997). These changes are a result of two factors. First, they reflect attitude changes among individuals over their lifetimes. Second, younger people generally exhibit less racial prejudice than their elders, and as younger, more tolerant cohorts have replaced older, more prejudiced ones, overall racial prejudice has declined (Firebaugh and Davis 1988).

However, among white Americans, the same striking agreement on how to combat discrimination or segregation does not appear. Although today white Americans endorse broad principles of nondiscrimination and desegregation in important areas of American life, they are much less likely to support policies for translating these principles into practice. For example, despite the strong support among white Americans for the principle of integrated education, the percentage of whites who felt that the federal government should ensure that black and white children attend the same schools declined between the 1960s and 1980s. Moreover, widespread white opposition was raised to busing as a means of desegregating schools (Schuman, Steeh, and Bobo 1985).

The substantial gap between white people's support for broad principles of equality and their support for specific programs to implement these principles indicates the complexity of racial attitudes. The relationship between prejudicial attitudes and discriminatory behavior is equally complex. Prejudice does not always produce discrimination, although it has frequently been treated as the cause of discrimination. An individual, however, may be prejudiced without *acting* in a discriminatory manner. In recent years it has become less fashionable to express racial prejudice publicly. Overt forms of discrimination, such as exclusion from public accommodations, jobs, and colleges and universities—behaviors that in the past were tolerated by most whites—are now often prohibited by law and condemned by public opinion.

The distinction between prejudice and discrimination and the interrelationship between these two phenomena were first systematically developed by Robert Merton (1949) in his classic article, "Discrimination and the American Creed." "Prejudicial attitudes," Merton argued, "need not coincide with discriminatory behavior." Merton demonstrated the range of possible ways in which prejudice and discrimination interact by distinguishing among four types of individuals:

1. The unprejudiced nondiscriminator—the all-weather liberal

2. The unprejudiced discriminator—the fair-weather liberal

3. The prejudiced nondiscriminator—the fair-weather bigot

4. The prejudiced discriminator—the all-weather bigot

The unprejudiced nondiscriminator consistently adheres to the American creed of equality for all in both belief and practice. The unprejudiced discriminator, on the other hand, internalizes and may even articulate the ideals of the American creed but may acquiesce to group pressures to discriminate. Similarly, the prejudiced nondiscriminator conforms to social pressures not to discriminate despite harboring prejudices toward ethnic minorities. Finally, the prejudiced discriminator is, like the unprejudiced nondiscriminator, consistent in belief and practice, rejecting the American creed and engaging in personal discrimination.

Merton's discussion was critical to the recognition that whether prejudice becomes translated into discriminatory behavior depends on the social context. From this perspective it becomes impossible to understand the dynamics of majority-minority relations by examining prejudice alone; prejudice is most appropriately considered not as a causal factor but as a dependent variable. As Richard Schermerhorn has cogently suggested, prejudice "is a product of situations, historical situations, economic situations, political situations; it is not a little demon that emerges in people because they are depraved" (Schermerhorn 1970:6).

Thus, discrimination is much more likely to occur in a social setting in which acts of ethnic and racial bias are accepted or are not strongly condemned. This principle was underscored in a study undertaken at Smith College, where in 1989 racial tensions erupted after four black students received anonymous hate messages. Researchers asked students how they felt about these incidents. Before a student could answer, a confederate, arriving at the same time, would respond by strongly condemning or strongly justifying the incidents. The researchers found that the students' opinions were strongly influenced by the opinions they heard expressed by the confederates. Hearing others express strongly antiracist opinions produced similar sentiments, whereas students who first heard expressions more accepting of racism offered "significantly less strongly antiracist opinions" (Blanchard, Lilly, and Vaughn 1991:105). Clearly, the social climate affects whether personal prejudices are translated into discriminatory acts; to explain the dynamics of ethnic and racial relations fully, it is necessary to analyze the historical, cultural, and institutional conditions that have preceded and generated them.

During the past quarter century, the conceptualization of American race relations has undergone several significant changes. These changes have been profoundly influenced by the changing nature of race relations in the United States. Before the advent of the Black Protest Movement during the 1950s, social scientists focused their attention primarily on racial attitudes, because prejudice was thought to be the key to understanding racial and ethnic conflict. This perception of the essential dynamics of race relations is perhaps best illustrated in Myrdal's classic *An American Dilemma,* in which he defined race prejudice as "the whole complex of valuations and beliefs which are behind discriminatory behavior on the part of the majority group . . . and which

are contrary to the egalitarian ideals in the American Creed" (Myrdal 1944:52). This model of race relations was predicated on the assumption that racial conflict in the United States was a problem of ignorance and morality that could best be solved by changing—through education and moral suasion—the majority's prejudicial attitudes toward racial minorities. "A great majority of white people in America," Myrdal wrote, "would be better prepared to give the Negro a substantially better deal if they knew the facts" (Myrdal 1944:48).

The black protest era of the 1950s and 1960s challenged the assumption that change in the patterns of racial inequality in American society could be brought about through a reduction in prejudicial attitudes alone. Sociologists and social activists focused increasingly on the dynamics of discrimination and sought means of eliminating discriminatory behavior. The numerous forms of direct protest, such as nonviolent sit-ins, boycotts, and voter registration drives, were tactics designed to alter patterns of discrimination. In keeping with this emphasis on discrimination were the legislative efforts undertaken to secure enactment of the Civil Rights Act of 1964, which outlawed discrimination in public accommodations and employment, and the 1965 Voting Rights Act, which provided federal support to ensure that African Americans had the right to vote throughout the South.

However, the greatest racial unrest of the black protest era occurred after these legislative victories had been achieved. Whereas the earlier civil rights phase of the Black Protest Movement had been directed primarily against public discrimination and especially its manifestations in the South, the outbreak of urban riots in northern cities focused attention on the nature of racial inequalities affecting African Americans throughout the entire nation. For several summers during the late 1960s, the nation was torn with racial strife. Parts of cities were burned, property damage ran into the millions of dollars, and the toll of dead—primarily, although not exclusively, blacks—numbered almost a hundred (National Advisory Commission on Civil Disorders 1968:116). In July 1967 President Lyndon Johnson appointed a national commission (the Kerner Commission) to investigate the causes of these urban riots. In 1968 the commission issued its report, which concluded the following:

> What white Americans have never fully understood—but what the Negro can never forget—is that white society is deeply implicated in the ghetto. White society condones it. . . . Race prejudice has shaped our history decisively in the past; it now threatens to do so again. White racism is essentially responsible for the explosive mixture which has been accumulating in our cities since the end of World War II. (National Advisory Commission on Civil Disorders 1968:203)

RACISM

Especially because the Kerner Commission concluded that the ultimate responsibility for the racial disorders of the 1960s should be attributed to "white racism," the term has been widely invoked to explain racial inequalities and conflict in American society. However, the term is extremely imprecise and ambiguous. This imprecision enabled President Johnson, who had created the Kerner Commission, to ignore its findings, and his successor, Richard Nixon, to condemn and deny them. Consequently, the term *racism* is in urgent need of clarification.

First, *racism* is a general term, subsuming several analytically distinct phenomena—prejudice and several forms of discrimination. Stokely Carmichael and Charles Hamilton distinguished between individual racism and institutional racism:

Racism is both overt and covert. It takes two closely related forms: individual whites acting against individual blacks and acts by the total white community against the black community. . . . The second type is less overt, far more subtle, less identifiable in terms of specific individuals committing the acts. But it is no less destructive of human life. . . . When white terrorists bomb a black church and kill five black children, that is an act of individual racism, widely deplored by most segments of the society. But when in that same city, Birmingham, Alabama—five hundred black babies die each year because of the lack of proper food, shelter, and medical facilities, and thousands more are destroyed and maimed physically, emotionally, and intellectually because of the conditions of poverty and discrimination in the black community, that is a function of institutional racism. (Carmichael and Hamilton 1967:41)

However, as I will note more fully later, prejudicial attitudes are causal factors in Carmichael and Hamilton's conceptualization of institutional racism. Moreover, they do not distinguish between psychological and sociological factors in its operation.

Another problem in the use of the word *racism* is that although it lumps together all forms of racial oppression, it is not sufficiently inclusive. It does not encompass majority-minority situations based on criteria other than race—criteria such as religion, tribal identity, ethnicity, or gender. Therefore, in the following discussion, I have analytically distinguished the terms *racism, prejudice,* and *discrimination.*

The term *racism* has traditionally referred to an *ideology*—a set of ideas and beliefs—used to explain, rationalize, or justify a racially organized social order. There are two essential parts of racism: its content and its function. Racism is distinguished from ethnocentrism by insistence that differences among groups are biologically based. The in-group is believed to be innately superior to the out-group, and members of the out-group are defined as being "biogenetically incapable of ever achieving intellectual and moral equality with members of the ingroup" (Noel 1972:157). Howard Schuman has offered a commonly accepted definition of racism:

> The term racism is generally taken to refer to the belief that there are clearly distinguishable human races, that these races differ not only in superficial physical characteristics, but also innately in important psychological traits, and finally that the differences are such that one race (almost always one's own, naturally) can be said to be superior to another. (Schuman 1969:44)

Racism's primary function has been to provide a rationale and ideological support —a moral justification—for maintaining a racially based social order. In other words, the assertion of the innate "natural" superiority or inferiority of different racial groups serves to justify domination and exploitation of one group by another. As Manning Nash has written, "no group of [people] is able systematically to subordinate or deprive another group of [people] without appeal to a body of values which makes the exploitation, the disprivilege, the expropriation, and the denigration of human beings a 'moral' act" (Nash 1962:288). In addition, not only does an ideology of racism provide a moral justification for the dominant group of their positions of privilege and power, but it also discourages minority groups from questioning their subordinate status and advancing claims for equal treatment.

. . . As noted before, there has been a substantial decline in professions of racist attitudes among white Americans in the past half century; especially since 1970, white Americans have increased their approval of racial integration (Schuman, Steeh, and Bobo 1985; Gallup Poll Social Audit 1997). In 1942 only 42 percent of a national sample of whites reported that they believed blacks to be equal to whites in innate intelligence; since the late 1950s, however, around 80 percent of white Americans have rejected the idea of inherent black inferiority. The Kerner Commission was therefore misleading in lumping all white antipathy toward blacks into the category of racism.

Rather than believing that African Americans are genetically inferior, whites often employ a *meritocratic ideology* to explain the substantial gap that continues to separate black and white income, wealth, and educational attainment. The basic element in a meritocratic ideology is the assumption of equality of opportunity—that all people in the United States have equal chances to achieve success, and that inequalities in the distribution of income, wealth, power, and prestige reflect the qualifications or merit of individuals in each rank in society. In other words, in a meritocratic society, all people are perceived to have an equal opportunity to succeed or fail—to go as far as their talents will take them—and the system of social ranking that develops is simply a "natural" reflection of each person's abilities or merit. Affluence is perceived as the result of the personal qualities of intelligence, industriousness, motivation, and ambition, while the primary responsibility for poverty rests with the poor themselves. Therefore, in this aristocracy of talent, those in the upper strata deserve the power, prestige, and privileges that they enjoy, while those lower in the social ranking system are placed according to their ability. Such a belief system is not inherently racist, but rather is a general judgment about human nature that can be applied to all sorts of human conditions or groups. However, it can have racist effects when it is used to explain racial inequalities in the United States without recognizing or acknowledging the external disabilities (such as prejudice and discrimination) that racial minorities experience. Thus, by this definition, African Americans are still considered inferior people; otherwise, they would be as well-off as whites.

(See Hochschild 1995 for an excellent discussion of the conflicting perceptions of whites and blacks regarding opportunity in American society.)

If the term *racism* referred merely to the realm of beliefs and ideology and not to behavior or action, its relevance for the study of race relations would be limited. To restrict the meaning of racism to ideology would be to ignore the external constraints and societally imposed disabilities—rooted in the power of the majority group—confronting a racial minority. If one group does not possess the power to impose its belief system on another, ethnic stratification cannot occur (Noel 1968). During the late 1960s and 1970s, when critics charged that the ideology of Black Power was "racism in reverse," African American spokespersons responded that their critics failed to consider the components of differential power that enabled the ideology of white supremacy to result in white domination:

> There is no analogy—by any stretch of definition or imagination—between the advocates of Black Power and white racists. Racism is not merely exclusion on the basis of race but exclusion for the purpose of subjugating or maintaining subjugation. The goal of the racists is to keep black people on the bottom, arbitrarily and dictatorially, as they have done in this country for over three hundred years. (Carmichael and Hamilton 1967:47)

Recently Feagin and Vera (1995) have taken a similar stance against the contention that "black racism" is equally as critical an issue as white racism. They contend that "black racism does not exist" because

> Racism is more than a matter of individual prejudice and scattered episodes of discrimination. There is no black racism because there is no centuries-old system of racialized subordination and discrimination designed by African Americans

to exclude white Americans from full participation in the rights, privileges and benefits of this society. Black (or other minority) racism would require not only a widely accepted racist ideology directed at whites but also the power to systematically exclude whites from opportunities and rewards in major economic, cultural, and political institutions. (Feagin and Vera 1995:ix-x)

Therefore, the crucial component of a definition of racism is behavioral. Racism in its most inclusive sense refers to actions on the part of a racial majority that have discriminatory effects, preventing members of a minority group from securing access to prestige, power, and privilege. These actions may be intentional or unintentional. This broader conception of racism therefore entails discrimination as well as an ideology that proclaims the superiority of one racial grouping over another.

As noted earlier, *discrimination* refers to the differential treatment of members of a minority group. Discrimination in its several forms comprises the means by which the unequal status of the minority group and the power of the majority group are preserved. In the ensuing discussion, I distinguish between *attitudinal* discrimination, which refers to discriminatory practices attributable to or influenced by prejudice, and *institutional* discrimination, which cannot be attributed to prejudice, but instead is a consequence of society's normal functioning. Both of these types can be further elaborated according to the sources of the discriminatory behavior. In reality, these types are at times interrelated and reinforce each other. Seldom is discrimination against a minority group member derived from one source alone.

ATTITUDINAL DISCRIMINATION

Attitudinal discrimination refers to discriminatory practices that stem from prejudicial attitudes. The discriminator either is prejudiced or acts in response to the prejudices of others. Attitudinal discrimination is usually direct, overt, visible, and dramatic. Despite increasing white acceptance of principles of nondiscrimination and racial segregation, ethnic minorities, especially African Americans, continue to be confronted with incidents of attitudinal discrimination. . . . [Joe] Feagin distinguished five categories of . . . discrimination: avoidance, rejection, verbal attacks, physical threats and harassment, and physical attacks. Despite increasing verbal acceptance by whites of the principles of nondiscrimination and racial integration, African Americans have been confronted with attitudinal discrimination in almost every public aspect of their lives. Many of these discriminatory acts appear trivial, insignificant, and unimportant to white observers: a white couple's crossing the street to avoid walking past a black male, a "hate stare," receiving poor service at restaurants, stores, and hotels. Many whites also trivialize discrimination that takes the form of racial and ethnic slurs and epithets. Incidents of this kind are seldom reported in the press, yet they are demeaning realities to which minorities of all social classes are consistently exposed.

Much more dramatic incidents of discrimination are reported almost daily in the news media. For example, the brutal beating of Rodney King, a black motorist, by members of the Los Angeles Police Department in 1991 was captured on videotape, was widely publicized, and drew widespread attention to the vulnerability of blacks to police harassment. The subsequent acquittal of four police officers who had been videotaped beating him unleashed the most destructive American urban disorders of the twentieth century. Yet the King incident was only one of 15,000 complaints of police brutality filed with the federal government between 1985 and 1991 (Lewis 1991). Moreover, during the 1980s and 1990s hundreds of incidents of discrimination, intimidation, harassment, and

vandalism as well as physical attacks against racial and religious minorities were reported. These included the burning of over 65 black churches in 1995 and 1996 alone; although investigators concluded that there was no evidence of an organized national racist conspiracy, they did find that racial hatred was a motive in most cases (Sack 1996; Butterfield 1996).

Similarly, cases of racial discrimination in education, in housing, in public accommodations, and in the workplace continue to be widely reported. Some of the most widely publicized cases of discrimination in the workplace and in public accommodations involved nationally prominent corporations—Denny's, Shoney's, Avis, Circuit City, and Texaco (*Time* 1987; Ehrlich 1990; U.S. Commission on Civil Rights 1990; Jaffe 1994; Feagin and Vera 1995; Eichenwald 1996; Myerson 1997). Yet these cases were among only the most widely publicized; between 1990 and 1993 the Equal Employment Opportunity Commission (EEOC), the federal agency responsible for enforcing civil rights laws in the workplace, resolved an average of 4,636 cases in favor of individuals charging racial discrimination. In most instances, however, discrimination is extremely difficult to prove, and the burden of filing charges and the recourse to legal remedies are so cumbersome and time-consuming that many people are discouraged from pursuing them. Nevertheless, by 1995 the EEOC had a back log of about 100,000 cases charging racial discrimination in employment alone (Kilbom 1995; Myerson 1997).

Thus, despite the enactment of antidiscrimination legislation and contrary to white perceptions that discrimination has been eradicated and that, as a consequence of affirmative action programs, minorities receive preferential treatment in hiring, recent "bias studies" have demonstrated that African Americans and Hispanics continue to experience discrimination.

In a study of employment discrimination, for example, pairs of white and black men with identical qualifications applied for 476 jobs advertised in Washington and Chicago newspapers. Whereas 15 percent of the white applicants received job offers, only 5 percent of the black applicants did. Moreover, white applicants advanced further in the hiring process and in the Washington area were much less likely to receive rude, unfavorable, or discouraging treatment than were their black counterparts. These findings were similar to an earlier study of the hiring experiences of Hispanics and Anglos in Chicago and San Diego in which whites were three times as likely both to advance further in the hiring process and to receive job offers as were Hispanic applicants (Turner, Fix, and Struyk 1991).

What are the consequences of these continuing encounters with attitudinal discrimination? In his study involving interviews with African Americans throughout the United States, . . . Feagin found that despite antidiscrimination legislation and changing white attitudes, even middle-class blacks remain vulnerable to discrimination and that incidents of discrimination against them are far from isolated. Instead, they are *cumulative;* that is, a black person's encounters with discrimination are best described as a "lifelong series of such incidents."

The cumulative impact of constant experiences of discrimination—what writer Ellis Cose (1993) has characterized as "soul-destroying slights"—and the energy expended in dealing with them was clearly articulated by one of the respondents in Feagin's study:

> . . . if you can think of the mind as having one hundred ergs of energy, and the average man uses fifty percent of his energy dealing with the everyday problems of the world—just the general kinds of things—then he has fifty percent more to do creative kinds of things that he wants to do. Now that's a white person. Now a black

person also has one hundred ergs: he uses fifty percent the same way a white man does, dealing with what the white man has [to deal with], so he has fifty percent left. But he uses twenty-five percent fighting being black, [with] all the problems of being black and what it means. Which means he really only has twenty-five percent to do what the white man has fifty percent to do, and he's expected to do just as much as the white man with that twenty-five percent. . . . So, that's kind of what happens. You just don't have as much energy left to do as much as you know you really could if you were free, [if] your mind were free.

Anthony Walton, an African American who grew up in a comfortable middle-class home in the Chicago suburbs, has referred to these "petty, daily indignities that take such a toll on the psyches of American blacks" as a "black tax," "the tribute to white society that must be paid in self-effacement and swallowed pride" (Walton 1996:7).

Attitudinal discrimination does not always occur in so virulent or so direct a manner. It may be manifested less dramatically merely by the acceptance by members of the dominant group of social definitions of traditional subordinate group roles. Malcolm X, the charismatic black protest leader who was assassinated in 1965, recalled how his well-intentioned white high school English teacher, Mr. Ostrowski, was bound by cultural norms concerning the "proper" caste roles for blacks:

> I know that he probably meant well in what he happened to advise me that day. I doubt that he meant any harm. . . . I was one of his top students, one of the school's top students—but all he could see for me was the kind of future "in your place" that almost all white people see for black people. . . . He told me, "Malcolm, you ought to be thinking about a career. Have you been giving it any thought?". . . The truth is, I hadn't. I have never figured out why I told him, "Well, yes, sir, I've been thinking I'd like to be a

lawyer." Lansing certainly had no lawyers—or doctors either—in those days, to hold up an image I might have aspired to. All I really knew for certain was that a lawyer didn't wash dishes, as I was doing.

Mr. Ostrowski looked surprised, I remember, and leaned back in his chair and clasped his hands behind his head. He kind of half-smiled and said, "Malcolm, one of life's first needs is for us to be realistic. Don't misunderstand me, now. We all here like you, you know that. But you've got to be realistic about being a nigger. A lawyer—that's no realistic goal for a nigger. You need to think about something you can be. You're good with your hands—making things. Everybody admires your carpentry shop work. Why don't you plan on carpentry? People like you as a person—you'd get all kinds of work." (Malcolm X 1966:36)

Here we should recall Merton's distinction between the prejudiced discriminator and the unprejudiced discriminator. According to the definition advanced earlier, discrimination involves differential treatment of individuals because of their membership in a minority group. The term has traditionally referred to actions of people who arbitrarily deny equal treatment (for example, equal opportunity to obtain a job or to purchase a home) to minority group members because of their own personal prejudices. Such is the behavior of the prejudiced discriminator or all-weather bigot.

But discrimination can occur without the discriminator's necessarily harboring prejudices. As Merton points out, an unprejudiced discriminator—the fair-weather liberal—can discriminate simply by conforming to existing cultural patterns or by acquiescing to the dictates of others who are prejudiced. Such discrimination can be attributed to the actor's conscious or unconscious perception of the negative effects that nondiscriminatory behavior will have. An employer or a realtor may genuinely disclaim any personal prejudice for having refused a minority group member a job or home. Perhaps the person felt constrained by the negative sanctions of peers, or by the fear of alienating customers. In this case, the discriminatory actor's judgment would be based on the prejudicial attitudes of a powerful reference group. Although the heart and mind of the actors in our hypothetical situations may be devoid of any personal prejudice, nevertheless, the consequences—no job, no home—for the minority-group applicant are no different than if they were old-fashioned, dyed-in-the-wool bigots.

. . .

INSTITUTIONAL DISCRIMINATION

Both forms of attitudinal discrimination just defined are ultimately reducible to psychological variables: the actor is prejudiced, defers to, or is influenced by the sanctions of a prejudiced reference group or the norms of a racially biased culture. Institutional discrimination, on the other hand, refers to organizational practices and societal trends that exclude minorities from equal opportunities for positions of power and prestige. This discrimination has been labeled "structural" by some scholars (*Research News* 1987:9). Institutional or structural discrimination involves "policies or practices which appear to be neutral in their effect on minority individuals or groups, but which have the effect of disproportionately impacting on them in harmful or negative ways" (Task Force on the Administration of Military Justice in the Armed Forces 1972:19). The effects or consequences of institutional discrimination have little relation to racial or ethnic attitudes or to the majority group's racial or ethnic prejudices.

The existence of institutional inequalities that effectively exclude substantial portions of minority groups from participation in the dominant society has seldom been considered under the category of discrimination. According to J. Milton Yinger, discrimination is "the persistent application of criteria that are arbitrary, irrelevant, or unfair by *dominant standards,* with the result that some persons receive an undue advantage and others, *although equally qualified,* suffer an unjustified penalty" (Yinger 1968:449, italics added). The underlying assumption of this definition is that if all majority-group members would eliminate "arbitrary, irrelevant, and unfair criteria," discrimination would, by definition, cease to exist. However, if all prejudice—and the attitudinal discrimination that emanates from it—were somehow miraculously eliminated overnight, the inequalities rooted in the normal and impersonal operation of existing institutional structures would remain. Therefore, the crucial issue is not the equal treatment of those with equal qualifications but rather is the access of minority-group members to the qualifications themselves.

Consider the following additional examples of institutional discrimination:

• An employer may be genuinely willing to hire individuals of all races but may rely solely on word-of-mouth recommendations to fill job vacancies. If Hispanics had previously been excluded from such employment, they would be unlikely to be members of a communications network that would allow them to learn about such vacancies.

• Jury selection is supposedly color-blind in most states, with jurors randomly selected from lists of registered voters. However, because they are more likely to be poor and geographically mobile (and thus ineligible to vote), blacks are less frequently selected as jurors. Similarly, a recent study found that, because a disproportionate number of black males are in prison or have been convicted of a felony, 14 percent of black men—nearly 1.5 million of a total voting age population of 10.4 million—are ineligible to vote, thus substantially diluting African American political power (Butterfield 1997).

• City commissions are often selected on either an at-large or a district basis. In at-large elections, all voters select from the same slate of candidates. By contrast, when elections are conducted on a district basis, the city is divided into geographically defined districts, and a resident votes only for candidates within his or her district. When an ethnic or a racial group constitutes a numerical minority of a city's population, its voting power is likely to be diluted and its representation in city government is likely to be lower than its proportion of the population under an at-large system of voting. Thus, under an at-large system, a city with a population that is 40 percent black could have no black representation on the city commission if voting followed racial lines. Because of patterns of residential segregation, this situation would be much less likely in a system organized on a district basis.

• In Minnesota a judge ruled unconstitutional a law that punished possession of crack more severely than possession of comparable amounts of powdered cocaine. Testimony indicated that crack is used mainly by blacks, whereas whites are much more likely to use cocaine. Although there was general agreement that the Minnesota legislature had enacted the penalties for the two crimes without any intent of targeting a specific minority group, the judge contended that the absence of racial prejudice or negative intent in the law's enactment was less relevant in considering the constitutionality of the crack law than whether enactment affected blacks disproportionately and thus had the practical effect of discriminating against them. "There had better be a good reason for any law that has the practical effect of disproportionately punishing members of one racial group. If crack was significantly more deadly or harmful than cocaine that might be a good enough reason. But there just isn't enough evidence that they're different enough to justify the radical differences in penalties" (London 1991).

The issue of racial disparities in sentencing for crack and powdered cocaine has become a hotly contested part of the national debate over mandatory federal sentences for drug offenses, where blacks were 90 percent of those convicted in Federal court crack offenses but only 30 percent of those convicted for cocaine. Studies show that the physiological and psychoactive effects of crack and powdered cocaine are similar, and the independent U.S. Sentencing Commission recommended that Congress scrap laws that establish dramatically harsher sentences (by a ratio of 100 to 1) for possession of crack than for possession of cocaine. Nevertheless, in 1995 both the Clinton Administration and Congress refused to modify the disparate sentences given for possession of the two drugs, and in 1996 the Supreme Court rejected the argument that the dramatic racial differences in prosecution and penalties for crack possession reflected racial discrimination. However, the consequence of these decisions was to reinforce and maintain the dramatically disproportionate number of African Americans under the control of the criminal justice system (Morley 1995; Jones 1995; Greenhouse 1996; Wren 1996).

Institutional discrimination is central to two important recent interpretations of inequalities in American life that focus on opportunities in two institutions in American life—the economy and education. In a series of books—*The Declining Significance of Race* (1978a), *The Truly Disadvantaged* (1987), and *When Work Disappears* (1996), William Julius Wilson has identified several broad social structural factors that have dramatically transformed the economic opportunity structure for African

Americans. He contends that the overall economic and social position of the inner-city poor has deteriorated in the past quarter century not only because of attitudinal discrimination but also because of impersonal structural economic changes—the shift from goods-producing to service-producing industries, increasing labor market segmentation, increased industrial technology, and the flight of industries from central cities—that have little to do with race. Earlier in the twentieth century, relatively uneducated and unskilled native and immigrant workers were able to find stable employment and income in manufacturing. Today, however, deindustrialization has created an economic "mismatch" between the available jobs and the qualifications of inner-city residents. On the one hand, manufacturing jobs, which in the past did not require highly technical skills, have either been mechanized or have moved from the inner cities to the suburbs, the sun belt, or overseas. Unskilled blacks in central cities are especially vulnerable to the relocation of high-paying manufacturing jobs. On the other hand, the jobs now being created in the cities demand highly technical credentials that most inner-city residents do not have. The economic opportunities of the African American urban poor, who lack the educational and occupational skills necessary for today's highly technological jobs, are therefore rapidly diminishing. The result is extremely high levels of unemployment.

These broad structural changes have triggered a process of "hyperghettoization" in which the urban poor are disproportionately concentrated and socially and economically isolated. As many stable working-class and middle-class residents with job qualifications have moved from inner-city neighborhoods, the stability of inner-city social institutions (churches, schools, newspapers, and recreational facilities) has been undermined, and the social fabric of neighborhoods and the community has deteriorated. As Wilson argues . . . , "A neighborhood in which people are poor but employed is different from a neighborhood in which people are poor and jobless."

Although the lack of educational and occupational skills among the African American urban poor reflects a historical legacy of attitudinal discrimination, institutional factors—the broad structural changes in the economy that were just mentioned—play a crucial role in sustaining black economic inequality. Even if all racial prejudice were eliminated, inner-city African Americans would still lack access to high-paying jobs that provide security and stability for both families and the black community (Wilson 1987; 1996).

Similar impersonal factors play a critical role in creating and sustaining dramatic racial disparities in educational opportunities. In his powerful book, *Savage Inequalities,* Jonathan Kozol (1991) has focused on the dramatic differences in the quality of public education in poor and in wealthy school districts in the United States and on the way in which these differences—these "savage inequalities"— affect educational opportunity. Focusing on the vast disparities in the quality of facilities, programs, and curricula that typically distinguish inner-city and suburban schools, Kozol contends that what is most glaringly apparent are the dramatic financial inequities among schools serving poor and affluent students, often in neighboring school districts; schools attended by poor students are invariably the most poorly funded, while those attended by students from affluent backgrounds have the highest per-pupil expenditures. Kozol reports that a study

[o]f 20 of the wealthiest and poorest districts of Long Island [New York], for example, matched by location and size of enrollment, found that the differences in per-pupil spending were not only large but had approximately doubled in a five-year period. Schools in Great Neck, in 1987, spent

$11,265 for each pupil. In affluent Jericho and Manhasset the figures were, respectively, $11,325 and $11,370. In Oyster Bay the figure was $9,980. Compare this to Levittown, also on Long Island but a town of mostly working-class white families, where per-pupil spending dropped to $6,900. Then compare these numbers to the spending level in the town of Roosevelt, the poorest district in the county, where the schools are 99 percent non-white and where the figure dropped to $6,340. Finally, consider New York City, where in the same year, $5,590 was invested in each pupil—less than half of what was spent in Great Neck. The pattern is almost identical to that [in the Chicago and many other metropolitan areas] (Kozol 1991:120).

The principal source of these glaring financial inequities is the mechanism—local property taxes—that traditionally has been used to fund public schools. Reliance upon local property taxes to fund public schools, although perhaps initiated as public policy with no racial considerations in mind, has, given the history of racial residential segregation in American society, created dramatically different educational opportunities for white and for minority children. Recently these disparities have increased at precisely the same time that cities have undertaken extensive urban redevelopment programs; by offering tax abatements to businesses and corporations that locate in central city locations, the tax bases from which inner-city schools are funded lose an estimated $5 to $8 billion annually (Lewin 1997). Kozol contends that, because states require school attendance but allocate their resources inequitably, they "effectively require inequality. Compulsory inequity, perpetuated by state law, too frequently condemns our children to unequal lives" (Kozol 1991:56).

Similarly, in an analysis of school desegregation within and between American cities and their suburbs, David James (1989) has shown that the state, by creating political boundaries that separate school districts and by refusing to accept interdistrict desegregation, has been instrumental in creating school segregation, thereby reinforcing patterns of social inequality. Suburban rings surrounding major American cities tend to have multiple school districts, and black suburbanites tend to be concentrated in areas close to the central cities. Therefore, because the Supreme Court has ruled that racial segregation *within* school districts is unconstitutional but that segregation *between* districts is not, whites can avoid living in school districts with large proportions of black students. They are able to implement a form of attitudinal discrimination precisely because the structure of school districts (in many instances created without racial intent) provides such opportunities.

Institutional discrimination, although not intended to victimize racial groups directly, is thus more subtle, covert, complex, and less visible and blatant than attitudinal discrimination. Because it does not result from the motivations or intentions of specific individuals, but rather from policies that appear race-neutral, institutional discrimination is more impersonal than attitudinal discrimination, and its effects are more easily denied, ignored, overlooked, or dismissed as "natural," inevitable, or impossible to change. Nevertheless, institutional discrimination has the same discriminatory consequences for minority group members. In examining institutional discrimination, therefore, it is more important to consider the *effect* of a particular policy or practice on a minority group than it is to consider the *motivations* of the majority group.

REFERENCES

Allport, Gordon W. 1958. *The Nature of Prejudice.* Garden City, NY: Doubleday.

Blanchard, Fletcher A., Teri Lilly, and Leigh Ann Vaughn. 1991. "Reducing the Expression of Racial Prejudice." *Psychological Science.* 2.

Butterfield, Fox. 1996. "Old Fears and New Hope: Tale of Burned Black Church Goes Far Beyond Arson." *New York Times.* July 21.

_____. 1997. "Many Black Men Barred From Voting, Study Shows." *New York Times.* January 30.

Carmichael, Stokely and Charles Hamilton. 1967. *Black Power: The Politics of Liberation in America.* New York: Vintage.

Cose, Ellis. 1993. *The Rage of a Privileged Class.* New York: HarperCollins.

Ehrlich, Howard J. 1990. *Campus Ethnoviolence and Policy Options.* Baltimore: National Institute against Prejudice and Violence.

Eichenwald, Kurt. 1996. "Texaco Executives, on Tape, Discussed Impeding a Bias Suit." *New York Times.* November 4.

Feagin, Joe R. and Hernan Vera. 1995. *White Racism: The Basics.* New York: Routledge.

Firebaugh, Glenn and Kenneth E. Davis. 1988. "Trends in Antiblack Prejudice 1972–1984: Region and Cohort Effects." *American Journal of Sociology.* 94.

Gallup Poll Social Audit. 1997. *Black/White Relations in the United States.* Princeton, NJ: The Gallup Organization. June.

Greenhouse, Linda. 1996. "Race Statistics Alone Do Not Support a Claim of Selective-Prosecution, Justices Rule." *New York Times.* May 14.

Hochschild, Jennifer L. 1995. *Facing Up to the American Dream: Race, Class and the Soul of the Nation.* Princeton: Princeton University Press.

Jaffe, Amy Myers. 1994. "At Texaco, The Diversity Skeleton Still Stalks the Halls." *New York Times.* December 11.

James, David R. 1989. "City Limits on Racial Equality: The Effects of City-Suburban Boundaries on Public-School Desegregation, 1968–1976." *American Sociological Review.* 54.

Jones, Charisse. 1995. "Crack and Punishment: Is Race the Issue?" *New York Times.* October 25.

Kilborn, Peter T. 1995. "A Family Spirals Downward in Waiting for Agency to Act." *New York Times.* February 11.

Kozol, Jonathan. 1991. *Savage Inequalities: Children in America's Schools.* New York: HarperCollins.

Lewin, Tamar. 1997. "Seeking to Shield Schools from Tax Breaks." *New York Times.* May 21.

Lewis, Neil A. 1991. "Police Brutality Under Wide Review by Justice Department." *New York Times.* March 15.

London, Robb. 1991. Judge's Overruling of Crack Law Brings Turmoil." *New York Times.* January 11.

Malcolm X. 1966. *The Autobiography of Malcolm X.* New York: Grove Press.

Merton, Robert K. 1949. "Discrimination and the American Creed." In Robert MacIver, ed., *Discrimination and the National Welfare.* New York: Institute for Religious and Social Studies and Harper and Row.

Morley, Jefferson. 1995. "Crack in Black and White." *Washington Post.* November 19.

Myerson, Allen R. 1997. "As U.S. Bias Cases Drop, Employees Take Up Fight." *New York Times.* January 12.

_____. 1997. "At Rental Counters, Are All Drivers Created Equal?" *New York Times.* March 18.

Myrdal, Gunnar. 1944/1962. *An American Dilemma: The Negro Problem and Modern Democracy.* New York: Harper and Row.

Nash, Manning. 1962. "Race and the Ideology of Race." *Current Anthropology.* 3:3.

National Advisory Commission on Civil Disorders. 1968. *Report.* Washington, DC: Government Printing Office.

Noel, Donald L. 1968. "A Theory of the Origin of Ethnic Stratification." *Social Problems.* 16.

Noel, Donald L. 1972. *The Origins of American Slavery and Racism.* Columbus, OH: Charles E. Merrill.

Research News. 1987. "The Costs of Being Black." 38.

Sack, Kevin. 1996. "Burnings of Dozens of Black Churches Across the South Are Investigated." *New York Times.* May 21.

Schermerhorn, Richard A. 1970. *Comparative Ethnic Relations: A Framework for Theory and Research.* New York: Random House.

Schuman, Howard. 1969. "Sociological Racism." *Transaction.* 7.

Schuman, Howard, Charlotte Steeh, and Lawrence Bobo. 1985. *Racial Attitudes in America: Trends and Interpretations.* Cambridge, MA: Harvard University Press.

Task Force on the Administration of Military Justice in the Armed Forces. 1972. *Report.* Washington, DC: U.S. Government Printing Office.

Time. 1987. "Racism on the Rise." February 2.

Turner, Margery Austin, Michael Fix, and Raymond J. Struyk. 1991. *Opportunities Denied, Opportunities Diminished: Discrimination in Hiring.* Washington, DC: The Urban Institute.

U.S. Commission on Civil Rights. 1990. *Intimidation and Violence: Racial and Religious Bigotry in America.* Washington, DC: U.S. Government Printing Office.

Walton, Anthony. 1996. Mississippi: *An American Journey.* New York: Knopf.

Wilson, William Julius. 1978. *The Declining Significance of Race: Blacks and Changing American Institutions.* Chicago: University of Chicago Press.

Wilson, William Julius. 1987. *The Truly Disadvantaged: The Inner City, the Underclass, and Public Policy.* Chicago: University of Chicago Press.

Wilson, William Julius. 1996. "Work." *The New York Times Magazine.* August 18.

Wilson, William Julius. 1996. *When Work Disappears: The World of the New Urban Poor.* New York: Knopf.

Wren, Christopher S. 1996. "Study Poses a Medical Challenge to Disparity in Cocaine Sentences." *New York Times.* November 20.

Yinger, J. Milton, 1968. "Prejudice: Social Discrimination." In D. L. Sills, ed., *International Encyclopedia of the Social Sciences.* New York: Macmillan.

DISCUSSION QUESTIONS

1. What is the difference between prejudice and discrimination? Why have declining degrees of prejudice in American society not resulted in the elimination of discrimination? Given the realities, what kinds of efforts might be more effective in reducing discrimination than the current civil rights measures described in this chapter?

2. What are the key components of a definition of racism and why has there been so much confusion about developing this definition? Given this definition, blacks can be prejudiced or discriminate, but there cannot be "black racism." Why?

3. The examples of institutional discrimination given in the reading are difficult to identify and change. How would you restructure employment practices, jury selection, and educational funding procedures so that they are no longer discriminatory in the ways described by Yetman?

USING RACIAL AND ETHNIC CONCEPTS:
THE CRITICAL CASE OF VERY YOUNG CHILDREN

Debra Van Ausdale and Joe R. Feagin

Since the 1930s social science has examined children's attitudes toward race. . . . The literature clearly demonstrates that racial identification and group orientation are salient issues for children (Ramsey 1987).

. . . Most research focuses on children over five years of age; very young children are rarely studied. . . .

Researchers have rarely sought children's views directly, beyond recording brief responses to tests. Few have interviewed children or made in-depth, long-term observations to assess social attitudes, limiting the ability to investigate more fully the nature of children's lives. . . . An emphasis on psychological testing is often coupled with the notion that children have limited understandings of race and ethnicity (Goodman 1964; Katz 1976; Porter 1971). Children are typically assumed to have temporary or naive views about social concepts until at least age seven. Prior to that age, children's use of concepts differs from that of adults in form and content.

Little attention has been devoted to how children create and assign meaning for racial and ethnic concepts. . . .

We provide data indicating that racial concepts are employed with ease by children as young as age three. Research based on the conception of children as incapable of understanding race (Menter 1989) presents an incorrect image of children's use of abstractions. Drawing on Willis (1990) and Thorne (1993), we suggest that notions of race and ethnicity are employed by young children as integrative and symbolically creative tools in the daily construction of social life.

THE RESEARCH APPROACH

. . . Our data come from extensive observations of 58 three-, four-, and five-year-old children in a large preschool in a southern city. The school employed a popular antibias curriculum (Derman-Sparks 1989). Over an 11-month period in 1993, we systematically observed everyday interactions in one large classroom containing a very diverse group of children. The center's official data on the racial and ethnic backgrounds of children in the classroom are: White = 24, Asian =19, Black = 4, biracial = 3, Middle Eastern = 3, Latino = 2, and other = 3.

Children's racial and ethnic designations, which were given by parents, were supplemented with information that we gained through classroom observation of a few children with mixed ethnic identities. We use a shorthand code to describe the racial and ethnic backgrounds of the children. For example, Rita is described as (3.5: White/Latina), indicating that she is three and one-half years old, was initially registered as White, but was later discovered to have a Latino heritage. Michael is listed as (4: Black), indicating that he is four years old, was registered as Black, and that no additional racial or ethnic information was revealed through further observation. This code attempts to illustrate the complex identities of many of the children. In a few cases we have used a broad designation (e.g., Asian) to protect a child's identity. . . .

Like the children and teachers, the senior author (hereafter Debi), a White woman, was usually in the classroom all day for five days a week. As observer and playmate, Debi watched the children and listened to them in their free play and teacher-directed activities. Over 11 months Debi observed 370 significant episodes involving a racial or ethnic dimension, about 1 to 3 episodes per day. When children mentioned racial or ethnic matters, Debi noted what they said, to whom they spoke, and the context of the incident. Extensive field notes were entered immediately on a computer in another room when the children were otherwise occupied. This was done to preserve the details of any conversations and the accuracy of the data.

Using an approach resembling that of the "least-adult role" (Corsaro 1981; Mandell 1988),

Debi conducted extensive participant observation. When children or adults asked, Debi identified herself as a researcher, and she consistently assumed the role of a nonauthoritarian observer and playmate. She was soon accepted as such by children and teachers, and the children spoke freely, rarely ceasing their activities when she was present. Children's interactions with her differed from their interactions with teachers and parents. Our accounts make clear Debi's natural, nonsanctioning role in discussing racial and ethnic matters initially raised by the children. In no case did Debi ask predetermined questions. Racial and ethnic issues arose naturally. Although Debi sometimes asked questions that might have been asked by other adults, she never threatened the children with a sanction for their words or actions. Thus, our interpretations of children's attitudes and behavior evolved gradually as Debi observed the children in natural settings.

We began with the assumption that very young children would display no knowledge of racial or ethnic concepts and that any use of these concepts would be superficial or naive. Our data contradicted these expectations.

Using Racial and Ethnic Concepts to Exclude

Using the playhouse to bake pretend muffins, Rita (3.5: White/Latina) and Sarah (4: White) have all the muffin tins. Elizabeth (3.5: Asian/Chinese), attempting to join them, stands at the playhouse door and asks if she can play. Rita shakes her head vigorously, saying, "No, only people who can speak Spanish can come in." Elizabeth frowns and says, "I can come in." Rita counters, "Can you speak Spanish?" Elizabeth shakes her head no, and Rita repeats, "Well, then you aren't allowed in."

Elizabeth frowns deeply and asks Debi to intercede by telling her: "Rita is being mean to me." Acting within the child-initiated framework, Debi asks Rita, "If only people who speak Spanish are allowed, then how come Sarah can play? Can you speak Spanish, Sarah?" Sarah shakes her head no. "Sarah can't speak Spanish and she is playing," Debi says to Rita, without suggesting she allow Elizabeth in. Rita frowns, amending her statement: "OK, only people who speak either Spanish or English." "That's great!" Debi responds, "because Elizabeth speaks English and she wants to play with you guys." Rita's frown deepens. "No," she says. Debi queries, "But you just said people who speak English can play. Can't you decide?" Rita gazes at Debi, thinking hard. "Well," Rita says triumphantly, "only people who speak two languages."

Elizabeth is waiting patiently for Debi to make Rita let her play, which Debi has no intention of doing. Debi then asks Rita: "Well, Elizabeth speaks two languages, don't you Elizabeth?" Debi looks at Elizabeth, who now is smiling for the first time. Rita is stumped for a moment, then retorts, "She does not. She speaks only English." Debi smiles at Rita: "She does speak two languages—English and Chinese. Don't you?" Debi invites Elizabeth into the conversation. Elizabeth nods vigorously. However, Rita turns away and says to Sarah, "Let's go to the store and get more stuff."

Language was the ethnic marker here. Rita defined rules for entering play on the basis of language—she was aware that each child not only did not look like the others but also spoke a different language. . . . Here we see the crucial importance of the social-cultural context, in particular the development of racial and ethnic concepts in a collaborative and interpersonal context. Defending her rules, Rita realized her attempts to exclude Elizabeth by requiring two languages had failed. This three-year-old child had created a social rule based on a significant understanding of ethnic markers. The final "two languages" rule did not acknowledge the fact that Sarah only spoke English. Rita's choice of language as an exclusionary device was directed at preventing Elizabeth from entering, not at maintaining a bilingual play space.

Exclusion of others can involve preventing associations with unwanted others, as in Rita's case, or removing oneself from the presence of unwanted others, as in this next instance. Carla (3: White) is preparing herself for the resting time. She picks up her cot and starts to move it. The head teacher, a White woman, asks what she is doing. "I need to move this," explains Carla. "Why?" asks the teacher. "Because I can't sleep next to a nigger," Carla says, pointing to Nicole (4.5: African/biracial) on a cot nearby. "Niggers are stinky. I can't sleep next to one." Stunned, the teacher's eyes widen, then narrow as she frowns. She tells Carla to move her cot back and not to use "hurting words." Carla looks amused and puzzled but complies. Nothing more is said to the children, but the teacher glances at Debi and shakes her head.

Three-year-old Carla's evaluation of the racial status of another young child was sophisticated and showed awareness not only of how to use racial epithets but also of the negative stigma attached to black skin. Like most children we observed, Carla was not the unsophisticated, naive child depicted in the mainstream literature. She used material (e.g., the epithet) that she undoubtedly had learned from other sources, probably in interaction with other children or adults, and she applied this material to a particular interactive circumstance.

Later, after the children have been wakened and have gone to the playground, the center's White director approaches Debi and says, "I have called Carla's parents and asked them to come to a meeting with me and Karen [the teacher] about what happened." Neither Debi nor the director feel a need to clarify what he is referring to, as he adds: "If you want to attend I would really like to have you there. Karen will be there too." Debi tells him she will attend.

"I suppose this is what you're looking for," he continues with a smile. "Well, no, not exactly," Debi replies, "but of course it is worth nothing, and I am interested in anything that the kids do with race." "Well," he shot back, "I want you to know that Carla did not learn that here!"

Although the observed children rarely used explicit racial slurs, the director's remark about the origin of Carla's epithet is typical of the responses adults gave when children at the center used negative terms. The center's staff was extremely interested in limiting children's exposure to prejudice or discrimination and used a multicultural curriculum to teach children to value diversity. The center's adults often seemed more concerned with the origins of child-initiated race-relevant behaviors than with the nuanced content or development of those behaviors.

The meeting with Carla's parents was informative. Carla's mother is biracial (Asian and White), and her father is White. Both parents are baffled when told of the incident. The father remarks, "Well, she certainly did not learn that sort of crap from us!" The teacher immediately insists that Carla did not learn such words at the center. Carla's father offers this explanation: "I'll bet she got that ["nigger" comment] from Teresa. Her dad is really red," When Debi asks what he means, the father responds, "You know, he's a real redneck." Then the director steps in: "It's amazing what kids will pick up in the neighborhood. It doesn't really matter where she learned it from. What we need to accomplish is unlearning it." He suggests methods for teaching Carla about differences and offers her parents some multicultural toys.

The reactions of the key adults illustrate the strength of adult beliefs about children's conceptual abilities. Their focus was on the child as imitator. The principal concern of teacher, parents, and administrator was to assure one another that the child did not learn such behavior from them. Thus adults reshape their conceptions as children do, collaboratively. Acting defensively, they exculpated themselves by suggesting someone else must be responsible. The director ended the blaming by attributing the source of the child's behavior to neighborhood—a diffuse, acceptable enemy—and initiated the task of unlearning.

USING RACIAL AND ETHNIC CONCEPTS TO INCLUDE

The children also used racial and ethnic understandings and concepts to include others—to engage them in play or teach them about racial and ethnic identities.

. . .

Jewel (4: Asian/Middle Eastern) uses her knowledge of different languages to draw an adult into a child-initiated game. Jewel, Cathie (4: White), and Renee (4.5: White) are trying to swing on a tire swing. Rob, a White college work-study student, has been pushing them but leaves to perform another task. Jewel starts to chant loudly, "Unche I, Unche I!" (an approximation of what she sounded like to Debi). The other girls join in, attracting Rob's attention. He begins to push the girls again. With a smile, he asks, "What are you saying?" Jewel replies, "It means 'pants on fire'!" All three girls roar with laughter. Rob smiles and urges Jewel, "Say it again." She begins to chant it again, now drawing Rob into the play. Rob asks, "Tell me some more." Jewel shakes her head, continuing to chant "Unche I!" and to laugh. Rob persists, asking Jewel to teach him how to "talk." Jewel obliges, making up new chants and repeating them until the others get them, then changing the words and repeating the behavior again. Cathie and Renee are delighted. The playing continues for a while, with the girls chanting and Rob pushing them on the swing.

Later, Debi learned that Jewel had developed sophisticated ethnic play around her understanding of language. When Jewel translated

"Unche I" as "pants on fire," Rob accepted this and the game continued. Several weeks later, however, Debi heard Jewel's mother greet her daughter at the door by saying "Unche I!" It seemed strange that a mother would say "pants on fire" to greet her child, and Debi noted the incident in her field notes. Some time later, when Debi presented this scene to graduate students in a seminar, one student laughed, informing her that as far as he could tell Jewel was saying her own name. The phrase meant "Jewel."

Jewel's use of her native name illustrates Willis's (1990) notion of symbolic creativity among children. Jewel was able to facilitate and increase interaction with an adult of another cultural background by choosing word symbols that intrigued the adult. As the interaction continued, she elaborated on that symbol, creating a new world of ethnic meanings that accomplished her goal. She successfully shaped an adult's actions for some time by catching his attention with language she realized he did not understand. This required that she understand his perspective and evaluate his knowledge of language, activities requiring considerable interpretive capability.

USING RACIAL AND ETHNIC CONCEPTS TO DEFINE ONESELF

The use of racial and ethnic concepts to include or exclude others is often coupled with the use of these concepts to describe and define oneself. For most children, racial and/or ethnic identity is an important aspect of themselves, and they demonstrate this in insightful ways in important social contexts.

Renee (4.5: White), a very pale little girl, has been to the beach over the weekend and comes to school noticeably tanned. Linda (4: White) and Erinne (5: biracial) engage her in an intense conversation. They discuss whether her skin would stay that color or get darker until she became, as Linda says, "an African American, like Charles" (another child). Renee denies she could become Black, but this new idea, planted in her head by interaction with the other children, distresses her. On her own initiative, she discusses the possibility with Debi and her mother, both of whom tell her the darker color is temporary.

Renee was unconvinced and commented on her racial identity for weeks. She brought up the issue with other children in many contexts. This linking of skin color with racial identity is found in much traditional literature on children's racial understandings (Clark and Clark 1940). But this racial marking was more than a fleeting interest, unlike the interest mainstream cognitive theorists might predict for such a young child. Renee reframed the meaning of skin color by questioning others on their thoughts and comparing her skin to others'.

Corinne (4: African/White) displays an ability to create meaning by drawing from her personal world. Corinne's mother is Black and is from an African country; her father is a White American. Corinne speaks French and English and is curious about everything at the center. She is a leader and often initiates activities with other children. Most children defer to her. One day Corinne is examining a rabbit cage on the playground. A teacher is cleaning out the cage and six baby bunnies are temporarily housed in an aluminum bucket that Corinne is holding. Three bunnies are white, two are black, and one is spotted black and white.

As Corinne is sitting at a table, Sarah (4: White) stuck her head into the bucket. "Stop that!" Corinne orders. Sarah complies and asks, "Why do you have the babies?" "I'm helping Marie [teacher]," says Corinne. "How many babies are there?" Sarah asks Corinne. "Six!" Corinne announces, "Three boys and three girls." "How can you tell if they're boys or girls?" Sarah questions. "Well," Corinne begins, "my daddy is White, so the white ones are boys. My mommy is Black, so the black ones are girls." Sarah counts: "That's only five." The remaining bunny is black and white. "Well, that one is like me, so it's a girl," Corinne explains gently. She picks up the bunny and says, "See, this one is both, like me!" Sarah then loses interest, and Corinne returns to cooing over the bunnies.

This four-year-old's explanation incorporates an interesting combination of color, race, and gender. While her causal reasoning was faulty, she constructed what for her was a sophisticated and reasonable view of the bunnies' sexes. She displayed an understanding of the idea that an offspring's color reflects the colors of its parents, a knowledge grounded in her experience as a biracial child. Strayer (1986) underscores how children develop appropriate attributions regarding situational determinants. Corinne's use of parental gender to explain the unknown gender of the bunnies was an appropriate explanation of how bunnies got certain colors. Skin color was a salient part of her identity, and it was reasonable in her social world to assume that it would be salient for the identity of others, even animals.

. . .

Racial and ethnic understandings involve many aspects of one's culture. Jie (4.5: Asian/ Chinese) brought her lunch of homemade Chinese dishes to school. When David, a White student employee, asks her what she has, she replies. "I brought food for Chinese people." Pointing to containers of Chinese food, she explains, "Chinese people prefer Chinese food." When David asks for a taste, she hesitates. "Well," she offers, "you probably won't like it. You're not Chinese." Here are the beginnings of explanations for differences between racial and ethnic groups.

Jie demonstrated not only that she recognized the differences between racial and ethnic groups, but also that she understood the socially transmitted view that physical differences are accompanied by differences in cultural tastes and behavior. Her interaction with the adult revealed a strong understanding of her culture by referring to her food as "for Chinese people" and wondering if non-Chinese people would enjoy it. Her explanation indicated that she was aware of what is *not* a part of her culture as much as what *is* a part of it, and that it is possible that outsiders would not enjoy Chinese food.

. . .

USING RACIAL AND ETHNIC CONCEPTS TO DEFINE OTHERS

We observed many examples of children exploring the complex notions of skin color, hair differences, and facial characteristics. They often explore what these things mean and make racial and/or ethnic interpretations of these perceived differences. Mindy (4: White) insists that Debi is Indian. When queried, Mindy replies that it is because Debi is wearing her long dark hair in a braid. When Debi explains that she is not Indian, the child remarks that maybe Debi's mother is Indian.

These statements show not only awareness of the visible characteristics of race and ethnicity but also insight into how visible markers are passed from generation to generation. They demonstrate a child's ability to grasp salient characteristics of a racial and/or ethnic category not her own and apply them to others in a collaborative and evolving way.

In another episode, Taleshia (3: Black) approaches the handpainting table. Asked if she wants to make a handprint, she nods shyly. A child with dark brown skin, Taleshia scans the paint bottles and points to pale pink. Curious about her preference, Debi asks, "Taleshia, is this the color that looks like you?" Taleshia nods and holds out her hand. Behind her, Cathie (3.5: White) objects to Taleshia's decision. "No, no," Cathie interjects, "She's not that color. She's brown." Cathie moves to the table. "You're this color," Cathie says and picks out the bottle of dark brown paint. Cathie is interested in helping Taleshia correct her apparent mistake about skin color. "Do you want this color?" Debi asks Taleshia. "No," she replies, "I want this one," touching the pink bottle. Regarding Taleshia with amazement, Cathie exclaims, "For goodness sake, can't you see that you aren't pink?" "Debi," Cathie continues to insist, "you have to make her see that she's brown." Cathie is exasperated and takes Taleshia by the arm. "Look," she instructs, "you are brown! See?" Cathie holds Taleshia's arm next to her own. "I am pink, right?" Cathie looks to Debi for confirmation. "Sure enough," Debi answers, "you are pink." "Now," Cathie continues, looking relieved, "Taleshia needs to be brown." Debi looks at Taleshia, who is now frowning, and asks her, "Do you want to be brown?" She shakes her head vigorously and points to pale pink, "I want that color."

Cathie is frustrated, and trying to be supportive, Debi explains that "Taleshia can choose any color she thinks is right." Cathie again objects, but Taleshia smiles, and Debi paints her palm pink. Then Taleshia makes her handprint. Cathie stares, apparently convinced that Taleshia and Debi have lost touch with reality. As Taleshia leaves, Cathie takes her place, remarking to Debi, "I just don't know what's the matter with you. Couldn't you see that *she is brown!*" Cathie gives up and chooses pale pink for herself, a close match. Cathie makes her handprint and says to Debi, "See, I am *not* brown."

Taleshia stuck to her choice despite Cathie's insistence. Both three-year-olds demonstrate a strong awareness of the importance of skin color, and their views are strongly held. This example underscores the importance of child-centered research. A traditional conceptualization of this Black child's choice of skin color

paint might suggest that the child is confused about racial identity. If she chose pink in the usual experimental setting (Clark and Clark 1940; Porter 1971), she would probably be evaluated as rejecting herself for a preferred whiteness. Debi had several other interactions with Taleshia. The three-year-old had, on other occasions, pointed out how pale Debi was and how dark her own skin was. She had explained to Debi that she was Black, that she thought she was pretty, and that pink was her favorite color. One possible explanation for her choice of pink for her skin color in the handpainting activity relies on Debi's knowledge of Taleshia's personality, family background, and previous interactions with others. Taleshia may have chosen pink because it is her favorite color, but this does not mean that she is unaware that most of her skin is dark. Another explanation for Taleshia's choice of skin color representation is that, like other African Americans, Taleshia's palms are *pink* while most of her skin is very dark. Perhaps she was choosing a color to match the color of her palms, a reasonable choice because the task was to paint the palms for handprints. The validity of this interpretation is reinforced by another episode at the center. One day Taleshia sat down and held Debi's hands in hers, turning them from top to bottom. Without uttering a word, she repeated this activity with her own hands, drawing Debi's attention to this act. The three-year-old was contrasting the pink-brown variations in her skin color with Debi's pinkish hand color. This explanation for the child's paint choice might not occur to a researcher who did not pay careful attention to the context and the child's personal perspective. Taleshia's ideas, centered in observations of herself and others, were more important to her than another child's notions of appropriate color. Far from being confused about skin color, she was creating meaning for color based on her own evaluations.

Using Racial Concepts to Control

The complex nature of children's group interactions and their solo behaviors demonstrates that race and ethnicity are salient, substantial aspects of their lives. They understand racial nuances that seem surprisingly sophisticated, including the power of race. How children use this power in their relationships is demonstrated in two further episodes.

Brittany (4: White) and Michael (4: Black) come to Debi demanding that she resolve a conflict. Mike tearfully demands that Debi tell Brittany that he "does too have a white one." As he makes this demand, Brittany solemnly shakes her head no. "A white what?" Debi asks. "Rabbit!" he exclaims. "At home, in a cage." Brittany continues shaking her head no, infuriating Mike. He begins to shout at the top of his lungs, "I do too have a white one!" Debi asks Brittany, "Why don't you think he has a white rabbit at home?" "He can't," she replies, staring at Mike, who renews his cries. Debi tries to solve the mystery, asking Mike to describe his bunny. "She white," he scowls at Brittany. "You do not," she replies. Mike screams at her "I DO TOOO!" Debi hugs Mike to calm him and takes Brittany's hand. Brittany says, "He can't have a white rabbit." Debi asks why, and the child replies, "Because he's Black." Debi tells Brittany, "He can have any color bunny he wants." Mike nods vigorously and sticks his tongue out at Brittany, who returns the favor. "See," he says, "you just shut up. You don't know." Brittany, who is intensely involved in baiting Mike, shakes her head, and says "Can't." She sneers, leaning toward him and speaking slowly, "You're Black." Mike is angry, and Debi comforts him.

Then Debi asks Brittany, "Have you been to Mike's house to see his bunny?" "No," she says. Debi asks, "Then how do you know that his bunny isn't white?" Debi is curious to find out why Brittany is intent on pestering Mike, who is usually her buddy. "Can't *you* see that he's Black?" she gazes at Debi in amazement. Debi replies, "Yes, of course I can see that Mike is Black, but aren't we talking about Mike's rabbit?" Debi is momentarily thrown by the child's calm demeanor. Brittany again shakes her head slowly, watching Debi for a reaction all the while. "Mike is Black." she says, deliberately forming the words. She repeats, "He is Black." Debi tries again, "Yes, Mike is Black and his bunny is white," now waiting for her response. Brittany shakes her head. "Why not?" Debi tries. "Because he is *Black*," Brittany replies with a tone suggesting that Debi is the stupidest person she has ever met. "Have you been to his house?" Debi asks her again. She shakes her head no. "Then," Debi continues, "how do you know that his bunny isn't white?" "I know," Brittany replies confidently. "How?" Debi tries one last time. "He can't have just any old color rabbit?" Debi asks. "Nope." Brittany retorts firmly, "Blacks can't have whites."

Brittany insisted that Mike could not own a white rabbit because he is Black. She "knew" it and belabored this point until he was driven to seek adult intervention. His plea for intercession was unusual because he is a large boy who was normally in charge of interactions with peers. In this instance, however, he was driven to tears by Brittany's remarks. "Blacks can't have whites" was her social rule. The power of skin color had become a tool in Brittany's hands that she used to dominate interaction with another child.

Brittany's ideas are strong—she creates a similar confrontation with a different child a week later. In this later case, Brittany and Martha (3.5: Black/White) are discussing who will get to take which rabbit home. Martha states that she will take the white one. Brittany again starts the "Blacks can't have whites" routine that she so successfully used with Michael. Martha becomes upset, telling Brittany she is stupid. This scene lasts about 10 minutes until it escalates into shouting, and Joanne, a teacher, breaks up the fight. Neither girl will explain to Joanne what the trouble is. They both just look at her and say "I don't know" when Joanne asks what is going on. Joanne tells them that friends don't yell each other. When the teacher leaves, Martha takes a swing at Brittany, who runs away laughing and sticking out her tongue.

Thus Brittany engaged two Black children in heated interactions based on skin color. In the classical Piagetian interpretation, she would be seen as egocentric and resistant to other interpretations. Contesting her social rule on skin color creates a disequilibrium for her that would somehow be worked out as she seeks a rational, adult perspective on skin color. However, an interpretive analysis underscores the crucial collaborative context. Brittany's use of racial concepts involves her in intimate interaction with two other children. When a teacher got involved, Brittany stopped, and she and her victim refused to offer an explanation. In the first episode Brittany was willing to engage Debi, who was not a sanctioning adult, in a detailed discussion, taking valuable playtime to explain her reasoning. When confronted by a teacher, Brittany withdrew, refusing to disclose what was going on between her and the Black girl. Brittany had created a tool to dominate others, a tool based on a racial concept coupled with a social rule. In addition, all three children were highly selective about the adults with whom they shared their racially oriented views and behavior.

In another encounter, this time among three children, a White child demonstrates her knowledge of broader race relations, demonstrating her grasp of race-based power inequalities. During playtime Debi watches Renee (4: White) pull Ling-mai (3: Asian) and Jocelyn (4.5: White) across the playground in a wagon. Renee tugs away enthusiastically. Suddenly, Renee drops the handle, which falls to the ground, and she stands still, breathing heavily. Ling-mai, eager to continue this game, jumps

from the wagon and picks up the handle. As Ling-mai begins to pull, Renee admonishers her, "No, no. You can't pull this wagon. Only *White Americans* can pull this wagon." Renee has her hands on her hips and frowns at Ling-mai. Ling-mai tries again, and Renee again insists that only "White Americans" are permitted to do this task.

Ling-mai sobs loudly and runs to a teacher complaining that "Renee hurt my feelings." "Did you hurt Ling-mai's feelings?" the teacher asks Renee, who nods, not saying a word. "I think you should apologize," the teacher continues, "because we are all friends here and friends don't hurt each other's feelings." "Sorry," mutters Renee, not looking at Ling-mai, "I didn't do it on purpose." "OK," the teacher finishes, "can you guys be good friends now?" Both girls nod without looking at each other and quickly move away.

This interaction reveals several layers of meaning. Both children recognized the implications of Renee's harsh words and demands. Renee accurately underscored the point that Ling-mai, the child of Asian international students, was neither White nor American. Her failure to be included in these two groups, according to Renee's pronouncement, precluded her from being in charge of the wagon. Ling-mai responded, not by openly denying Renee's statements, but by complaining to the teacher that Renee had hurt her feelings. Both children seem knowledgeable about the structure of the U.S. and global racial hierarchy and accept the superior position accorded to Whites. The four-year-old child exercised authority as a White American and controlled the play with comments and with her stance and facial expressions. Our findings extended previous research on young children's knowledge of status and power (Corsaro 1979; Damon 1977) by showing that children are aware of the power and authority granted to Whites. The children were not confused about the meanings of these harsh racial words and actions.

ADULT MISPERCEPTIONS

... Adults tend to control children's use of racial and ethnic concepts and interpret children's use of these concepts along prejudice-defined lines. Clearly, the social context of children's learning, emphasized in the interpretive approach, includes other children and adults, but our accounts also demonstrate the way in which children's sophisticated understandings are developed without adult collaboration and supervision.

Jason (3: White) and Dao (4: Chinese) have developed a friendship over a period of several weeks, despite the fact that Dao speaks almost no English and Jason speaks no Chinese. The two are inseparable. The adults at the center comment on the boys' relationship, wondering aloud about their communication. Yet the boys experience little trouble in getting along and spend hours engaged in play and conversation.

As this friendship develops, Jason's mother, several months pregnant at the time, comes to the head teacher with a problem. "Jason has begun to talk baby talk," she informs the teacher. "Oh, I wouldn't worry about it," the teacher reassures her. "Kids often do that when their mom is expecting another baby. It's a way to get attention." Jason's mother seems unconvinced and asks the teachers to watch for Jason's talking "gibberish" and to let her know about it.

Jason and Dao continue their friendship. Teachers remark on their closeness despite Dao's extremely limited command of English. One afternoon, Dao and Jason are playing with blocks near Debi. Deeply involved, they chatter with each other. Debi does not understand a single word either of them are saying, but they have no difficulty cooperating in constructing

block towers and laugh together each time a tower collapses. Jason's mother arrives to take him home. He ignores her and continues to play. The head teacher joins the scene and begins a conversation with Jason's mother. When Jason finally acknowledges his mother's presence, he does so by addressing her with a stream of words that make no sense to the nearby adults.

"See, see? That's what I mean," Jason's mother says excitedly. "He talks baby talk. It's really getting bad." The teacher remarks that perhaps after the baby's arrival this will disappear. Debi, after a moment's thought, says to Jason, "Honey, would you say that again in English?" Jason nods and responds, "I want to check out a book from the library before we go home." The teacher and Jason's mother look at him and then at Debi. "Oh, my goodness!" the teacher exclaims, "How did you know to ask him that?" Debi gestures toward the boys and says, "It seemed reasonable. They talk all the time." "That's amazing," Jason's mother shakes her head. "What language do you think they are speaking?" she asks Debi. "I don't know," Debi responds. "I don't understand a word of it. Maybe it's invented."

With the cooperation of Dao's father, who listened in on the boys, Debi finally determined that Jason had learned enough Chinese from Dao and Dao had learned enough English from Jason to form a blended language sufficient for communication. What adults thought was "baby talk"—and what was thought by the teacher to be jealousy toward an unborn sibling—was an innovative synthesis of two languages formed by young children maintaining a cross-ethnic friendship. This is a normal human phenomenon and, if the boys were adults, would likely have been interpreted as a pidgin language—the simplified language that develops between peoples with different languages living in a common territory.

One of the powerful ethnocultural definers of Dao's social life was his inability to speak English, which caused him grief because it kept him from following his teachers' directions promptly. He experienced difficulty in creating friendships, for most other children were not patient enough to accommodate him. Dao was a quiet and cautious child, particularly when teachers were nearby. Jason's ability to develop a language in interaction with Dao was empowering for Dao: the language was the cement that bonded the boys together. The boys' collaborative actions were not only creative, but also reveal one of the idealized (at least for adults) ways that human beings bridge ethnic and cultural differences. The boys were natural multiculturalists.

CONCLUSION

Through extensive observation, this study has captured the richness of children's racial and ethnic experiences. The racial nature of children's interactions becomes fully apparent only when their interactions are viewed over time and in context. Close scrutiny of children's lives reveals that they are as intricate and convoluted as those of adults.

Blumer (1969:138) suggests that any sociological variable is, on examination, "an intricate and inner-moving complex." Dunn (1993) notes that children's relationships are complex and multidimensional, even within their own families. In the case of Jason and Dao, for example, the interactions were not only complex and incomprehensible to adults, but also evolved over time. By exploring the use of racial concepts in the child's natural world, instead of trying to remove the child or the concepts from that world, we glean a more complete picture of how children view and manipulate racial and ethnic concepts and understandings.

For most children, racial and ethnic issues arise forcefully within the context of their interaction with others. Most of the children that we observed had little or no experience with people from other racial or ethnic groups outside of the center. For these very young children, who are having their first extensive social experiences outside the family, racial and ethnic differences became powerful identifiers of self and other. . . .

To fully understand the importance of children's racial and/or ethnic understandings, the nuanced complexity and interconnected nature of their thinking and behavior must be accepted and recognized. Measures of racial and ethnic awareness should consider not only children's cognitive abilities but also the relationships that children develop in social situations.

. . .

Regarding the racial and ethnic hierarchy, young children understand that in U.S. society higher status is awarded to White people. Many understand that simply by virtue of their skin color, Whites are accorded more power, control, and prestige. Very young children carry out interactions in which race is salient. Racial knowledge is situational, and children can interact in a race-based or race-neutral manner, according to their evaluations of appropriateness. In children's worlds race emerges early as a tool for social interaction and quickly becomes a complex and fluid component of everyday interaction.

The behaviors of the children in this preschool setting are likely to be repeated in other diverse settings. The traditional literature accepts that children display prejudice by the time they arrive at school, but offers no explanation about the acquisition of this prejudice beyond it being an imitation of parental behavior. We expect continuity of children's racial and ethnic categories across settings, for children reveal a readiness to use their knowledge of race and ethnicity.

The observed episodes underscore problems in traditional theories of child development. When children fail cognitive tasks framed in terms of principles such as conservation and reciprocity, researchers often conclude that children lack the cognitive capability to understand race. However, surveys and observations of children in natural settings demonstrate that three-year-old children have constant, well-defined, and negative biases toward racial and ethnic others (Ramsey 1987). Rather than insisting that young children do not understand racial or ethnic ideas because they do not reproduce these concepts on adult-centered cognitive tests, researchers should determine the extent to which racial and ethnic concepts— as used in daily interaction—are salient definers of children's social reality. Research on young children's use of racial and gender concepts demonstrates that the more carefully a research design explores the real life of children, the more likely that research can answer questions about the nature of race and ethnicity in children's everyday lives.

REFERENCES

Blumer, Herbert. 1969. *Symbolic Interactionism: Perspective and Method*. Englewood Cliffs, NJ: Prentice Hall.

Clark, Kenneth B. and Mamie P. Clark. 1940. "Skin Color as a Factor in Racial Identification and Preference in Negro Children." *Journal of Negro Education* 19:341–58.

Corsaro, William A. 1979. "We're Friends, Right?" *Language in Society*. 8:315–36.

———. 1981. "Entering the Child's World: Research Strategies for Field Entry and Data Collection in a Preschool Setting." Pp. 117–46 in *Ethnography and Language in Educational Settings*, edited by J. Green and C. Wallat. Norwood, NJ: Ablex.

Damon, William. 1977. *The Social World of the Child*. San Francisco, CA: Jossey-Bass.

Derman-Sparks, Louise. 1989. *Anti-Bias Curriculum: Tools for Empowering Young Children*. Washington, DC: National Association for the Education of Young Children.

Goodman, Mary E. 1964. *Race Awareness in Young Children*. New York: Crowell-Collier.

Holmes, Robyn M. 1995. *How Young Children Perceive Race*. Thousand Oaks, CA: Sage.

Katz, Phyllis A. 1976. "The Acquisition of Racial Attitudes in Children." Pp. 125–54 in *Towards the Elimination of Racism*, edited by P. A. Katz. New York: Pergamon.

Mandell, Nancy. 1988. "The Least-Adult Role in Studying Children." *Journal of Contemporary Ethnography* 16:433–67.

Menter, Ian. 1989. "'They're Too Young to Notice': Young Children and Racism." Pp. 91–104 in *Disaffection from School? The Early Years*, edited by G. Barrett. London, England: Falmer.

Porter, Judith D. R. 1971. *Black Child, White Child: The Development of Racial Attitudes*. Cambridge, MA: Harvard University.

Ramsey, Patricia A. 1987. "Young Children's Thinking about Ethnic Differences." Pp. 56–72 in *Children's Ethnic Socialization: Pluralism and Development*, edited by J. S. Phinney and M. J. Rotheram. Newbury Park, CA: Sage.

Strayer, Janet. 1986. "Children's Attributions Regarding the Situational Determinants of Emotion in Self and Others." *Developmental Psychology* 22:649–54.

Thorne, Barrie. 1993. *Gender Play: Girls and Boys in School*. New Brunswick, NJ: Rutgers University Press.

Willis, Paul. 1990. *Common Culture: Symbolic Work at Play in the Everyday Cultures of the Young*. Buckingham, England: Open University Press.

SOURCE: From *American Sociological Review*, vol. 61, no. 5 (October 1996). Reprinted by permission of the American Sociological Association.

Discussion Questions

1. There is a T-shirt that reads: "No Child Is Born a Racist." Based on the analysis presented in this reading, do you think that this statement is true? Is prejudice an inborn personality trait, a case of children mimicking adults, or is it the result of a complex combination of social factors? If the latter is true, what are the social causal factors for children?

2. On the one hand, we see these children enacting boundaries that seem cruel. On the other hand, we see them breaking barriers that most adults never get past. How can both be happening at the

same time? What does this tell us about prejudice and discrimination?

3. Why do you think adults attribute blame to someone else when their child has made a racial slur? Would the adults engage in this type of behavior if the child had been reprimanded for any other type of misbehavior? What kind of "unlearning" approach would be most effective for children? Is "We don't say that word" enough? What do you think needs to happen to enable children to unlearn negative stereotypes at this early age?

Constructing Categories of Difference

Karen Rosenblum and Toni-Michelle Travis

Race, sex, and class may be described as "master statuses." In common usage "status" means prestige, but in most social science literature status is understood as a position within a social structure, for example, a kinship or occupational status. Any individual simultaneously occupies a number of statuses, but their master status "in most or all social situations, will overpower or dominate all other statuses.... Master status influences every other aspect of life, including personal identity" (Marshall, 1994:315).

We argue that there are important similarities in how the master statuses like race and sex operate.... This is not to say that these master statuses operate identically, or that people in these categories have had interchangeable experiences. The past and present circumstances of African American, Latino, and Asian American men and women are distinctive on innumerable counts; they cannot easily be compared to the experience of white women.... The impact of race and sex... unfolds quite differently in the upper, middle, working, and poor classes. Nonetheless, there

are also important similarities in the way these master statuses are currently constructed and in their impact on individual lives....

The Essentialist and Constructionist Orientations

The difference between the constructionist and essentialist orientations is illustrated in the tale of the three umpires:

> Social psychologist Hadley Cantril relates the story of three baseball umpires discussing their profession. The first umpire said, 'Some are balls and some are strikes, and I call them as they are.' The second replied, 'Some's balls and some's strikes, and I call 'em as I sees 'em.' The third thought about it and said, 'Some's balls and some's strikes, but they ain't nothing 'till I calls 'em' (Henshel and Silverman, 1975:26).

The first umpire takes an essentialist position. In arguing that "I call them as they are," he indicates his assumption that balls and strikes are entities that exist in the world independent of his perception of them. For this umpire, "balls" and "strikes" are distinct, easily identified, mutually exclusive categories, and he is a neutral and relatively powerless observer of them. In all, he "regards knowledge as objective and independent of mind, and himself as the impartial reporter of things 'as they are'" (Pfuhl, 1986:5). For this essentialist umpire, balls and strikes exist in the world; he simply observes their presence.

Thus, the essentialist orientation presumes that the items in a category all share some "essential" quality, their "ball-ness" or "strikeness." For essentialists, the categories of race, sex, . . . and social class identify significant, empirically verifiable similarities among and differences between people. From the essentialist perspective, for example, racial categories exist apart from any social or cultural processes; they are objective categories of essential difference between people.

Though somewhat removed from pure essentialism, the second umpire still affirms that there is an independent, objective reality, though it is one which is subject to *interpretation*. For him, balls and strikes exist in the world, but individuals might have different perceptions of which is which.

The third umpire, who argues "they ain't nothing till I call 'em," is unabashedly constructionist. He argues that "conceptions such as 'strikes' and 'balls' have no meaning except that given them by the observer" (Pfuhl, 1986:5); balls and strikes do not exist until an umpire names them as such. While the essentialist presumes an external world with distinct categories existing independent of observation, the constructionist argues that reality cannot be separated from the way that a culture makes sense of it. From the constructionist perspective *social* processes determine that one set of differences is more important than another, just as social processes shape our understanding of

what those differences *mean*. The constructionist assumes that "essential" similarities are conferred and created rather than intrinsic to the phenomenon, that the way that a society identifies its members tells us more about the society than about the individuals so classified. Thus, the constructionist perspective treats classifications such as race as socially constructed through political, legal, economic, scientific, and religious institutions. Although individuals do not on their own create such classifications, macro-level social processes and institutions do. . . .

Few of us have grown up as constructionists. More likely, we were raised as essentialists who believe that master statuses such as race or sex encompass clear-cut, immutable, and in some way meaningful differences. From an essentialist perspective, one simply *is* what one *is*: someone with African ancestry is black, and a person with male genitalia is male even if he does not feel like a male. It is fairly unsettling to have these bedrock classifications questioned which is what the constructionist perspective does.

However, not all of us have grown up as essentialists. Those from mixed racial or religious backgrounds are likely to be familiar with the ways in which identity is not clear cut. They grow up understanding how definitions of self vary with the context; how others try to define one as belonging in a particular category; and how in many ways, one's very presence calls prevailing classification systems into question. For example, being asked "What are you?" is a common experience among mixed-race people. Such experiences make evident the social constructedness of racial identity.

Still, few of us are likely to take either an essentialist or constructionist perspective exclusively. . . . Our own perspective as authors has been constructionist. Nonetheless, we have sometimes had to rely on essentialist terms we ourselves find problematic. The irony of simultaneously questioning the idea of race, but still talking about "blacks," "whites," and "Asians" . . . has not escaped us. . . .

Further, . . . master statuses are not parts of a person that can simply be broken off from one another like the segments of a Tootsie Roll (Spelman, 1988). Each of us is always simultaneously all of our master statuses, and it is that complex package that exists in the world. . . . Indeed, even the concept of master status suggests that there can be only one dominating status, though we would reject that position. . . .

Discussions about racism and sexism generate the intensity they do partly because they involve the clash of essentialist and constructionist assumptions. . . .

NAMING AND AGGREGATING

Classification schemes are by definition systems for *naming* categories of people; thus constructionists pay special attention to the names people use to refer to themselves and others—particularly the points at which new names are asserted, the negotiations that surround the use of particular names, and those occasions when categories of people are grouped together or separated out.

Asserting a Name

The issues surrounding the assertion of a name are similar whether we are talking about individuals or categories of people. A change of name involves, to some extent, the claim of a new identity. For example, one of our colleagues decided that she wanted to be called by her full first name, rather than by its abbreviated version because the diminutive had come to seem childish to her. It took a few rounds of reminding people that this was her new name, and with most that was adequate. One telling example was provided by a young woman who wanted to keep her "maiden" name after she

married. Her fiancé agreed with her decision, recognizing how reluctant he would be to give up his name were the tables turned. When her prospective mother-in-law heard of this possibility, however, she was outraged. In her mind, a rejection of her family's name was a rejection of her family: she urged her son and his fiancé to reconsider getting married. (We do not know how this story ended.)

Thus, the assertion of a name can yield some degree of social conflict. On both the personal and a societal level, naming can involve the claim of a particular identity and the rejection of others' power to impose a name. All of this applies to individual preferences. For example, is one Chicano, Mexican American, Mexican, Latino, Hispanic, Spanish-American, or Hispaño; Native American, American Indian, or Sioux; African American or black; girl or woman; Asian American or Japanese American; gay or homosexual? This list does not begin to cover the full range of possibilities; or include geographic and historical variations.

> Geographically, *Hispanic* is preferred in the Southeast and much of Texas. New Yorkers use both *Hispanic* and *Latino*. Chicago, where no nationality has attained a majority, prefers *Latino*. In California, the word *Hispanic* has been barred from the *Los Angeles Times,* in keeping with the strong feelings of people in the community. Some people in New Mexico prefer *Hispaiio.* Politically, *Hispanic* belongs to the right and some of the center, while *Latino* belongs to the left and the center. Historically, the choice went from *Spanish* or *Spanish-speaking* to *Latin American, Latino,* and *Hispanic* (Shorris, 1992:xvi-xvii).

Thus, determining the appropriate name by which to refer to a category of people is no easy task. It is unlikely that all members of the category prefer the same name; the name members use for one another may not be acceptable when used by those outside the group; nor is it always advisable to ask what name a person prefers. We once saw an old friend become visibly angry when asked whether he preferred the term "black" or "African American." "Either one is fine with me," he replied, "*I* know what *I* am." To him, such a question indicated that he was being seen as a member of a category rather than as an individual.

As we have said, on both the individual and collective level naming may involve a redefinition of self, an assertion of power, and a rejection of others' ability to impose an identity. For this reason, social movements often claim a new name, just as those who continue to use the old name may do so as a way to indicate opposition to the movement. For example, in the current American setting, we may be in the midst of a change from "black" to "African American." "Black" emerged in opposition to "Negro" as the Black Power movement of the Black Panthers, Black Muslims, and the Student Nonviolent Coordinating Committee (SNCC) came to distinguish itself from the more mainstream Martin Luther King wing of the civil rights movement (Smith, 1992).

The term "Negro" had itself been born of a rejection of the term "colored" that dominated the mid- to late-nineteenth century. The term "African" had preceded "colored," and was used as late as the 1820s. Led by influential leaders such as W. E. B. Du Bois and Booker T. Washington, "'Negro' was seen as a 'stronger' term [than "colored"] . . . despite its association with racial epithets. 'Negro' was defined to stand for a new way of thinking about Blacks" (Smith, 1992:497–8).

On the same grounds, president of the National Urban Coalition Ramona H. Edelin, proposed in 1988 using "African American" instead of "black." The campaign to adopt the term, led by Coalition spokesman Jessie Jackson, met with immediate success among black leaders and now both terms are in use (Smith, 1992).

Ironically, the phrase "people of color" is emerging now as a reference encompassing all non-white Americans. White students unfamiliar with the historical background of "colored" will sometimes use that term interchangeably with "people of color." Unaware of the historical distinction, they are surprised by the anger with which they are met.

Each of these changes—from "Negro" to "black" to "African American"—was first promoted by activists as a way to demonstrate their commitment to change and militance. . . . [Similarly], the women's movement has asserted "woman" as a replacement for "girl." The significance of these two terms is revealed in the account of a student who described a running feud with her roommate. The student preferred the word "woman" rather than "girl," arguing that the application of the word "girl" to females past adolescence was insulting. Her roommate, who was also female, just as strongly preferred the term "girl" and just as regularly applied it to the females she knew. Finally, they tried to "agree to disagree," but each of them had such strong feelings on the matter it was clear they could not be roommates much longer.

How could these two words destroy their relationship? It appears that English speakers use the terms "girl" and "woman" to refer to quite different qualities. "Woman" (like "man") is understood to convey adulthood, power, and sexuality; "girl" (like "boy") connotes youth, powerlessness, and irresponsibility (Richardson, 1988). Thus, the two roommates were asserting quite different places for themselves in the world. One claimed adulthood; the other saw herself as not having achieved that. This is the explanation offered by many females: It is not so much that they like being "girls," as that they value youth and/or do not yet feel justified in calling themselves "women." Yet this is precisely the identity the women's movement has put forward: "We cannot be girls any more, we must be women."

The Negotiation and Control of Names

While individuals and social movements may assert a name for themselves, government agencies also control access to such categorizations. Still, these agencies are not impervious to social movements and social change. The recent history of U.S. Census Bureau classifications offers an example of the negotiation of a categorization system.

Census classifications and census data are significant for a variety of reasons. The census determines the apportionment of seats (among states) in the U.S. House of Representatives, and it affects the distribution of federal monies to states, counties, and cities for "everything from feeding the poor to running mass transit systems" (Espiritu, 1992:116). Since the census is conducted only once every ten years, its results shape policy for a decade.

Most important to our discussion, events in the 1960s and 1970s elevated the importance of census data:

> . . . The proliferation of federal grants programs and the cities' increasing dependence upon them tended to heighten the political salience of census statistics. Such formulas often incorporated population size, as measured or estimated by the Census Bureau, as a major factor. By 1978 there were more than one hundred such programs, covering a wide range of concerns, from preschool education (Headstart) to urban mass transportation. . . . [T]he single most commonly used data source was the decennial census (Choldin, 1994:27–8).

The census offered an important source of information by which the courts, Congress, and local entities could gauge the extent of discrimination. "Groups had to prove that they had been discriminated against in order to qualify for federal help under the Voting Rights Act. . . . To receive help in the form of an affirmative action plan from the newly established Equal Employment Opportunity Commission, each minority had to demonstrate its disproportionate absence from certain categories of employment" (Choldin, 1986: 406). As legislation raised the stakes involved in census data, disputes regarding its structure escalated. In response, the Census Bureau—for the first time ever—established minority committees to advise the government on the content and implementation of the 1980 census (Choldin, 1986).

On the Hispanic Advisory Committee, representatives argued strongly that the census "differentially undercounted" the Hispanic population, i.e., that the census missed more Hispanics than it did those in other categories. Undercounting primarily affects those who are low-income, non-English speaking, and live in inner cities—those who are poor often lack stable residences and are thus difficult to reach; those who cannot read English cannot answer the questions (only in 1990 did the census provide for Spanish-language surveys); those who are illegal immigrants may be unwilling to respond to the questionnaire. (The Constitution requires a count of all the people in the United States, not just those who are legal residents.)

While the Census Bureau might use birth and death records to determine the undercount of blacks, representatives on the Hispanic Advisory Committee pointed out that the Latino undercount could not be determined by this method since birth and death records did not record Hispanic ancestry. As a way to correct for an undercount, the advisory committee argued for the introduction of a Spanish/ Hispanic origin *self-identification* question in the 1980 census. Thus, negotiation produced a new census category. . . .

Thus, while many treat census classifications as if they were fixed categorizations grounded in scientifically valid distinctions, that is not the case as even the Census Bureau admits: "The concept of race as used by the Census Bureau reflects self-identification, it does not denote any clear-cut scientific definition of biological stock . . . the categories of the race item include both racial and national origin or sociocultural groups" (U.S. Bureau of the Census, 1990). Indeed, the federal guidelines that regulate research and policy-making in health, education, employment, civil rights compliance, school desegregation, and voting rights are similarly clear that the classifications "should not be interpreted as being scientific or anthropological in nature" (Overbey, 1994).

Still, when we consider "official counts" of the population, we risk believing that what is counted must be real. While the Census Bureau and other federal agencies operate from explicit constructionist premises, the data they produce may be used toward an essentialist worldview in which racial categories are presumed to reflect real and abiding differences between people. Indeed, the Census Bureau [made a change to the 2000 Census that allowed people to check more than one race box for the first time].

The Spanish/Hispanic origin question provides an example of the negotiation of a categorization. By contrast, assignment to the category "Native American" was not initially open to negotiation by those it affected: Native Americans were not allowed to define who was included within that classification, only the federal government could do that.

Historically, federal definitions relied on the idea of "blood quantum," which was a measure of how much of one's ancestry could be traced to Native Americans. This standard was established in the 1887 General Allotment Act, which redistributed collectively held reservation land as individually deeded parcels. In order to qualify for a land parcel, Native Americans had to document that they possessed one-half or more Native American ancestry. . . . Despite an ongoing debate about abandoning blood quantum, the standard persists for access to federal and some state services (one-quarter ancestry is now the usual requirement). Though individual tribes now define their own criteria for tribal membership, many still rely on the blood quantum standard.

Aggregating and Disaggregating

The naming or labeling processes we have described serve both to aggregate and disaggregate categories of people. On the one hand, the federal identification of categories of disadvantaged Americans collapsed various national-origin groups into four headings—Hispanics, Native Americans, Blacks, and Asian or Pacific Islanders (Lowry, 1982). Thus, Puerto Ricans, Mexican Americans, and Cuban Americans all became "Hispanic" in some way. On the other hand, the groups which comprised these aggregates had historically regarded one another as different and thus the aggregate category was likely to "disaggregate" or decompose back into its constituent national-origin elements.

While one might think that "Hispanic" or "Asian American" are terms used for self-identification, that does not appear to be often the case. In the U.S. "Mexicans, Puerto Ricans, and Cubans have little interaction with each other, most do not recognize that they have much in common culturally, and they do not profess strong affection for each other" (de la Garza, et al., 1992:14). Thus, it is not surprising that a survey of the Latino population concludes that "respondents do not primarily identify as members of an Hispanic or Latino community. . . . [Rather, they] overwhelmingly prefer to identify by national origin . . ." (de la Garza, et al., 1992:13). While members of these groups share common positions on many domestic policy issues, they do not appear to share a commitment to Spanish language maintenance, common cultural traditions, or religiosity (de la Garza, et al., 1992). In short, the category "Latino/Hispanic" exists primarily, but not exclusively, from the perspective of non-Latinos.

The same can be said about the aggregate census category "Asian or Pacific Islander," which encompasses about fifty different nationalities. While the classification "Hispanic" offers at least a commonality in Spanish as a shared language in the country of origin, "Asian American" encompasses groups with unique languages, cultures, and religions; different racial groupings; and several centuries of congenial and/or hostile contact with members of other groups with whom they now share the category "Asian American." In all, the category "Asian American" aggregates on the basis of geography rather than any cultural, racial, linguistic, or religious commonalities. "Asian Americans are those who come from a region of the world that *the rest of the world* has defined as Asia" (Hu-Dehart, 1994).

Aggregate classifications like "Latino," "Hispanic," or "Asian American" were not simply the result of federal classifications, however. These terms were first proposed by student activists following the lead of the Black Power and Civil Rights movements, and they continue to be used, although by a small proportion of people. As Yen Le Espiritu describes . . . , college students coined the pan-ethnic identifier Asian American in response to "the similarity of [their] experiences and treatment." As we saw earlier, when participants in social change movements forge new social identities and alliances, they also assert new names for themselves. In all, people use both aggregating pan-ethnic terms like "Asian American" and disaggregating national origin identifiers like Japanese American—each is used at particular moments, for particular reasons.

For two categories, however, Native and African Americans, the submerging of differences into an aggregate classification was the direct result of conquest and enslavement.

The "Indian," like the European, is an idea. The notion of "Indians" was invented to distinguish the indigenous peoples of the New World from Europeans. The "Indian" is the person on shore, outside of the boat. . . . There [were] hundreds of cultures, languages, ways of living in Native America. The place was a model of diversity at the time of Columbus's arrival. Yet Europeans did not see this diversity. They created the concept of the "Indian" to give what they did see some kind of unification, to make it a single entity they could deal with, because they could not cope with the reality of 400 different cultures (Mohawk, 1992:440).

Conquest made "Indians" out of a heterogeneity of tribes and nations distinctive on linguistic, religious, and economic grounds. It was not only that Europeans had the unifying concept of "Indian" in mind—after all, they were sufficiently cognizant of tribal differences to generate an extensive body of tribally specific treaties. It was also that conquest itself—encompassing as it did the usurpation of land, the forging and violation of treaties, and the implementation of policies that forced relocation and concentration—structured the life of Native Americans along common lines. While contemporary Native Americans still identify themselves by tribal ancestry, just as those called Asian American and Latino identify themselves by national origin, their shared experience of conquest also forged the common identity reflected in the aggregate name, Native American.

Similarly, the capture, purchase, forced and often fatal relocation of Africans, and their experience of being moved from place to place when they were sold as property, created the category now called African American. This experience forged a single people from those who had been culturally diverse; it produced an "oppositional racial consciousness," i.e., a unity-in-opposition (Omi and Winant, 1994). "Just as the conquest created the 'native' where once there had been Pequot, Iroquois, or Tutelo, so too it created the 'black' where once there had been Asante or Ovimbundu, Yoruba or Bakongo" (Omi and Winant, 1994:66). . . .

Every perspective on the social world emerges from a particular vantage point, a particular social location. Ignoring who the "us" is in the boat risks treating that place as if it were anywhere and nowhere, as if it were just the view "anyone" would take. Historically, the people in the boat were European, contemporarily they are white Americans. As Ruth Frankenberg frames it . . . , in America "whites are the nondefined definers of other people," "the unmarked marker of others' differentness." Failing to identify the "us" in the boat, means that "white culture [becomes] the unspoken norm," a category that is powerful enough to define others while itself remaining invisible. Indeed, as Frankenberg argues, those with the most power in a society are best positioned to have their own identities left unnamed, thus masking their power.

The term androcentrism describes the world as seen from a male-centered perspective. By analogy, one may also describe a Eurocentric perspective. To some extent, regardless of their sex [or] race, all Americans operate from an andro- [and] Euro- perspective since these are the guiding assumptions of the culture. Recognizing these as historically and culturally located perspectives makes it possible to evaluate their adequacy.

DICHOTOMIZATION

As we have seen, many factors promote the construction of aggregate categories of people. Often aggregation yields dichotomization, that is, the sense that there are two and only two categories, that everyone fits easily in one or the other, and that the categories stand in opposition to one another. . . . In contemporary American culture we [often separate the world into] "us" and "them"—as if people could be sorted into two mutually exclusive, opposed groupings.

Dichotomizing Race

Perhaps the clearest example of dichotomization is provided by the "one-drop rule. . . ." The one-drop rule describes the set of social practices whereby someone with any traceable African heritage is judged to be "black" by both American blacks and whites. . . . In American society this rule is applied only to blacks—no other category of people is defined by only "one drop." This is not simply an informal social practice; it was a principle reaffirmed in 1986 by the Supreme Court in *Jane Doe v. the State of Louisiana*. . . .

The one-drop rule explains why some American racial classifications are so confounding to many immigrant and even native-born Americans. . . . In contemporary American culture, assignment to the status of black is not based on appearance or even the preponderance of racial heritage. Rather, social custom and law hold that a person with as little as 1/32 African ancestry is black. The American one-drop rule precisely denied the possibility of being mixed; instead, it defined a child born to black and white parents as black.

While the black/white dichotomy may well be the most abiding and rigidly enforced racial distinction in American society, different regions and historical periods have also produced their own splits: In the southwest the divide has been between Anglos and Latinos; in parts of the west coast it is between Asian Americans and whites. Still, each of these distinctions is embedded in the country's historic dichotomy of "whites" and "non-whites." That distinction was stressed early in the nation's history: "Congress's first attempt to define American citizenship, the Naturalization Law of 1790, declared that only free 'white' immigrants could qualify" for citizenship (Omi and Winant, 1994:81). That position was reaffirmed in 1922, when the Supreme Court held that a Japanese immigrant could not become a naturalized U.S. citizen because he was not white, a position the Court reiterated a year later in terms of Asian Indians (Espiritu, 1992; Takaki, 1993). In this way, needed labor could be recruited to the country, while minimizing the risk that immigrants would become permanent residents and an economic threat (Steinberg, 1989). Not until 1952 were all immigrants eligible for naturalization, though the children of immigrants born on U.S. soil were always considered U.S. citizens.

Thus, while three racial categories—"white," "Negro," and "Indian"—were identified throughout the nineteenth century (Omi and Winant, 1994), all were located within the white/non-white dichotomy. In 1854, the California Supreme Court in *People v. Hall* held that blacks, mulattos, Native Americans, and Chinese were "not white" and therefore could not testify for or against a white man in court (Takaki, 1993:205–6). (Hall, a white man, had been convicted of killing a Chinese man on the testimony of one white and three Chinese witnesses; the Supreme Court overturned the conviction.) By contrast, Mexican residents of the Southwest territories ceded to the United States in the 1848 Treaty of Guadalupe Hidalgo "were defined as a white population and accorded the political-legal status of 'free white persons'" (Omi and Winant, 1994). As historian David Roediger argues, even European immigrants were initially treated as non-white, or at least not-yet-white. In turn, they lobbied for their own inclusion in American society on the basis of the white/non-white distinction.

[Immigrants struggled to] equate whiteness with Americanism in order to turn arguments over immigration from the question of who was foreign to the question of who was white. . . . Immigrants could not win on the question of who was foreign. . . . But if the issue somehow became defending "white man's jobs" or "white man's government" . . . [they] could gain space by deflecting debate from nativity, a hopeless issue, to race, an ambiguous one. . . . After the Civil War, the new-coming Irish would help lead the movement to bar the relatively established Chinese from California, with their agitation for a "white man's government," serving to make race, and not nativity, the center of the debate and to prove the Irish white (Roediger, 1994:189–90).

Thus, historically "American" has meant white, as many Asian Americans are casually reminded when they are complimented for speaking such good English—a compliment which presumes that someone who is Asian could not be a native-born American. . . . Novelist Toni Morrison would describe this as a story about "how American means white":

> Deep within the *word* "American" is its association with race. To identify someone as South African is to say very little; we need the adjective "white" or "black" or "colored" to make our meaning clear. In this country it is quite the reverse. American means white and Africanist people struggle to make the term applicable to themselves with . . . hyphen after hyphen after hyphen (Morrison, 1992:47).

Because American means white, those who are not white are presumed to be recent arrivals and are regularly told to go "back where they came from." In short, in America we appear to operate within the dichotomized *racial* categories of American/non-American—these are racial categories, because they effectively mean white/non-white.

But what exactly *is* race? First. we need to distinguish race from ethnicity. Social scientists define ethnic groups as categories of people who are distinctive on the basis of national origin, language, and cultural practices. As Robert Blauner explains, . . . "members of an ethnic group hold a set of common memories that make them feel that their customs, culture, and outlook are distinctive." Thus, racial categories encompass diverse ethnic groups; e.g., in America the racial category "white" encompasses ethnic groups such as Irish, Italian, and

Polish Americans. Unfortunately, many fail to recognize ethnic distinctions among people of color. For example, not all American blacks are African American, some are Haitian, Jamaican, or Nigerian; African American is an ethnic group identification that does not encompass all American blacks.

Returning to the concept of race, the term most likely first appeared in the Romance languages of Europe in the Middle Ages where it was used to refer to breeding stock (Smedley, 1993). A "race" of horses, for example, would describe common ancestry and a distinctive appearance or behavior. "Race" appears to have been first applied to humans by the Spanish in the sixteenth century in reference to the New World populations they discovered. It was later adopted by the English, again in reference to people of the New World, and generally came to mean "people," "nation," or "variety." By the late eighteenth century, "when scholars became more actively engaged in investigations, classifications, and definitions of human populations, the term 'race' was elevated as the one major symbol and mode of human group differentiation employed extensively for non-European groups and even those in Europe who varied in some way from the subjective norm" (Smedley, 1993:39).

Though elevated to the level of science, the concept of race continued to reflect its origins in animal husbandry. Farmers and herders had used the concept to describe stock bred for particular qualities; scholars used it to suggest that human behaviors could also be inherited. "Unlike other terms for classifying people . . . the term 'race' places emphasis on innateness, on the inbred nature of whatever is being judged" (Smedley, 1993:39). Like animal breeders, scholars also presumed that appearance revealed something about potential behavior, that among humans race signified something more than just difference of color. Just as the selective breeding of animals entailed the ranking of stock by some criteria, scholarly use of

the concept of race involved the ranking of human "races" along a variety of dimensions. Thus, differences in skin color, hair texture, and the shape of head, eyes, nose, lips, and body were developed into an elaborate system for classifying humans into discrete categories. These categories were then ranked as to their merit and potential for "civilization." Although the conquered peoples of the world were the objects of this classification system, they did not participate in its invention.

The idea of race emerged among all the European colonial powers (although their conceptions of it varied), but only the British in North America (and South Africa) constructed a system of rigid, exclusive racial categories and a social order *based on race*, a "racialized social structure" (Omi and Winant, 1994).

> [S]kin color variations in many regions of the world and in many societies have been imbued with some degree of social value or significance, but color prejudice or preferences do not of themselves amount to a fully evolved racial world view. There are many societies, past and contemporary, in which the range of skin color variation is quite large, but all such societies have not imposed on themselves worldviews with the specific ideological components of race that we experience in North America or South Africa (Smedley, 1993:25).

This racialized social structure—which in America produced a race-based system of slavery and later a race-based distribution of political, legal, and social rights—was an historical first. "Expansion, conquest; exploitation, and enslavement have characterized much of human history over the past five thousand years or so, but none of these events before the modern era resulted in the development of ideologies or social systems based on race" (Smedley, 1993:15). While differences of color had long been noted, social structures had never before been built on those differences.

Thus, it is not surprising that scientists have assumed that race difference involves more than simply skin color or hair texture and have sought the biological distinctiveness of racial categories—but with little success. In the early twentieth century, anthropologists looked to physical features such as height, stature, and head shape to distinguish the races, only to learn that these are affected by environment and nutrition. Later, the search turned to genetic traits carried in the blood, only to find that those cannot be correlated with conventional racial classifications. Even efforts to reach a consensus about how many races there are or what specific features distinguish them from one another are problematic.

If our eyes could perceive more than the superficial, we might find race in chromosome 11: there lies the gene for hemoglobin. If you divide humankind by which of two forms of the gene each person has, than equatorial Africans, Italians and Greeks fall into the "sickle-cell race"; Swedes and South Africa's Xhosas (Nelson Mandela's ethnic group) are in the healthy hemoglobin race. Or do you prefer to group people by whether they have epicanthic eye folds, which produce the "Asian" eye? Then the !Kung San (Bushmen) belong with the Japanese and Chinese. . . . [D]epending on which traits you pick, you can form very surprising races. . . . How about blood types, the familiar A, B, and O groups? Then Germans and New Guineans, populations that have the same percentages of each type, are in one race; Estonians and Japanese comprise a separate one for the same reason. . . . The dark skin of Somalis and Ghanaians, for instance, indicates that they evolved under the same selective force (a sunny climate). But that's all it shows. It does *not* show that they are any more closely related in the sense of sharing more genes than either is to Greeks. Calling Somalis and Ghanaians "black" therefore sheds no further light on their evolutionary history and implies—wrongly—that

they are more closely related to each other than either is to someone of a different "race." . . . If you pick at random any two "blacks" walking along the street, and analyze their 23 pairs of chromosomes, you will probably find that their genes have less in common than do the genes of one of them with that of a random "white" person [because the genetic variation within one race is greater than the average difference between races] (Begley, 1995:67, 68).

In all, the primary significance of race is as a *social* concept: We "see" it, we expect it to tell us something significant about a person, we organize social policy, law, and the distribution of wealth, power and prestige around it. From the essentialist position, race is assumed to exist independent of our perception of it; it is assumed to significantly distinguish people from one another. From the constructionist perspective, race exists because we have created it as a meaningful category of difference between people.

Dichotomizing Sex

First, the terms "sex" and "gender" require clarification. "Sex" refers to females and males, i.e., to chromosomal, hormonal, anatomical, and physiological differences. By contrast, "gender" describes the socially constructed roles associated with sex. Gender is learned; it is the historically specific acting out of "masculinity" and "femininity." . . .

While the approach may be unsettling, sex can be understood as a socially created dichotomy much like race. As developmental geneticist Anne Fausto-Sterling and anthropologist Walter Williams make clear, Western culture has an abiding commitment to the belief that there are two and only two sexes and that all individuals can be clearly identified as one or the other (Kessler and McKenna, 1978). [But] sex refers to a complex set of attributes—anatomical, chromosomal, hormonal, physiological—that may sometimes be inconsistent with one another or with an individual's sense of their own identity. This is illustrated in the recent case of a Spanish athlete who is anatomically female, but in a pre-game genetic test was classified as male. On the basis of that test, she was excluded from the 1985 World University Games. She was then reclassed as female in 1991, when the governing body for track-and-field contests abandoned genetic testing and returned to physical inspection. As the gynecologist for the sports federation noted, "about 1 in 20,000 people has genes that conflict with his or her apparent gender" (Lemonick, 1992).

Nonetheless, just as with race, . . . membership is assigned to one or the other of the sex categories irrespective of inconsistent or ambiguous evidence. Indeed, the conviction that there ought to be consistency between the physical and psychological dimensions of sex propels some people into sex change surgery in an effort to produce a body consistent with their self-identity. Others will pursue psychotherapy seeking an identity consistent with their body. In either case, it makes more sense to us to use surgery and therapy to create consistency than to accept inconsistency: a man who feels like a woman must become a woman rather than just being a man who feels like a woman.

References

Choldin, Harvey. 1994. *Looking For the Last Percent: The Controversy Over Census Undercounts.* New Brunswick, NJ: Rutgers University Press.

De la Garza, Rudolfo, DeSipio, Louis, Garcia, F. Chris, Garcia, John, and Falcon, Angela. 1992. *Latino Voices: Mexican, Puerto Rican, and Cuban Perspectives on American Politics.* Boulder, Colorado: Westview Press.

Espiritu, Yen Le. 1992. *Asian American Panethnicity: Bridging Institutions and Identities.* Philadelphia: Temple University Press.

Henshel, Richard L. and Silverman, Robert. 1975. *Perceptions in Criminology.* New York: Columbia University Press.

Hu-Dehart, Evelyn. 1994. "Asian/Pacific American Issues in American Education. Presented at the 7th Annual National Conference on Race and Ethnicity in American Higher Education, Atlanta. Sponsored by The Southwest Center for Human Relations Studies, University of Oklahoma, College of Continuing Education.

Kessler, Suzanne and McKenna, Wendy. 1978. *Gender: An Ethnomethodological Approach.* New York: Wiley and Sons.

Lemonick, Michael. 1992. "Genetic Tests Under Fire." *Time,* February 24, 65.

Lowry, Ira. 1982. "The Science and Politics of Ethnic Enumeration." Ethnicity and Public Policy. Winston Van Horne (ed.) 42–61. Madison: University of Wisconsin Press.

Marshall, Gloria. 1994. "Racial Classification: Popular and Scientific." The Racial Economy of Science: Toward a Democratic Future. Sandra Harding (ed), 116–127. Bloomington: Indiana University Press.

Mohawk, John. 1992. "Looking For Columbus: Thoughts on the Past, Present and Future of Humanity." *The State of Native America: Genocide, Colonization, and Resistance.* M. Annette Jaimes (ed.) 439–444. Boston: South End Press.

Morrison, Toni. 1992. *Playing in the Dark.* New York: Vintage.

Omi, Michael and Winant, Howard 1994. *Racial Formation in the United States.* New York: Routledge.

Overbey, Mary Margaret. 1994. "Notes From Washington." *Anthropology Newsletter,* December, 31. Washington, D.C. American Anthropological Association.

Pfuhl, Erdwin. 1986. *The Deviance Process.* 2nd ed. Belmont, California: Wadsworth.

Richardson, Laurel. 1988. The Dynamics of Sex and Gender: A Sociological Perspective. 3rd ed. New York: Harper and Row.

Roediger, David. 1994. *Towards The Abolition of Whiteness.* London: Verso.

Shorris, Earl. 1992. Latinos: *A Biography of the People.* New York: W.W. Norton.

Smedley, Audrey. 1993. Race in North America: Origins and Evolution of a Worldview. Boulder: Westview Press.

Smith, Tom. 1992. "Changing Racial Labels: From 'Colored' to 'Negro' to 'Black' to 'African American.'" *American Opinion Quarterly.* 56:496–514.

Spelman, Elizabeth. 1988. *Inessential Woman.* Boston: Beacon Press.

Steinberg, Stephen. 1989. *The Ethnic Myth: Race, Ethnicity, and Class in America.* Boston: Beacon Press.

Takaki, Ronald. 1993. *A Different Mirror.* Boston: Little Brown.

United States Bureau of the Census. 1990. *Definitions of Subject Characteristics.* 1990 Census of Population and Housing. Washington, D.C.: U.S. Government Printing Office.

DISCUSSION QUESTIONS

1. Explain the difference between the "essentialist" and "constructionist" perspectives. Try to develop an example of the difference that parallels the baseball umpire metaphor presented in the reading. Cite examples of each approach to gender and race from your own experiences.

2. Why do group names and definitions matter? What exactly is at stake when the census is conducted? Explain some of the recent changes that have occurred in naming groups. Why did these changes occur? Who initiated the change? Why?

3. How does labeling " . . . serve to both aggregate and disaggregate categories of people"? How and why does aggregation lead to dichotomization? How and why has the concept of race changed over time? How are sex and race similar as social constructions? How are they different?

CURRENT DEBATES

RACE AND SPORTS

How real is race? Is it a matter of biology and genes and evolution or purely a social fiction arising from specific historical circumstances, such as American slavery? Does knowing people's race tell us anything important about them? Does it give any useful information about their character, their medical profiles, their trustworthiness, their willingness to work hard, or their intelligence? Does race play a role in shaping a person's character or his or her potential for success in school or on the job?

This debate about the significance of race and the broader question of "nature versus nurture" has been going on in one form or another for a very long time. One version of the debate has centered on the relationship between intelligence and race. One side of the debate argues that biological or genetic differences make some races more capable than other races. Today, the huge majority of scientists reject this argument and maintain that there is no meaningful connection between race and mental aptitude.[1]

1. For the latest round of arguments in this debate, see Herrnstein, R., & Murray, C. (1994). *The bell curve.* New York: Free Press; and Jacoby, R., & Glauberman, N. (1995). *The bell curve debate.* New York: Random House.

Another manifestation of this debate centers on the relationship between race and sport. The fact is that—contrary to their general status as a minority group—African Americans dominate several different sports in the United States today. For example, African Americans are heavily overrepresented at the highest levels of achievement in basketball, football, track and field, and, to a lesser extent, baseball and soccer. While blacks are only about 13% of the population, they comprise the vast majority of professional basketball and football players and are overrepresented in other sports as well. With Tiger Woods dominating professional golf, only the National Hockey League remains "white" among North American professional team sports. Black Americans are more prominent among professional athletes—and especially among the very elite—than in virtually any other sphere of American life. Furthermore, the phenomenon is worldwide: in international track, athletes of African descent dominate both sprinting and long-distance running.

Why is this so? Has race played a role in establishing this pattern? Are people of African descent "naturally" better athletes? Or are there social, cultural, and environmental forces at work here that produce this extraordinary dominance? One thing we do know, after so many decades of debate on this topic, is that there is no easy choice between nature and nurture; virtually every scholar agrees that explanations must include both genetic heritage and experience.

Journalist Jon Entine has recently argued the view that the dominance of black athletes in some sports is more biological: "Elite athletes who trace most or all of their ancestry to Africa are by and large better than the competition" (Entine, 2000, p. 4). While Entine agrees that the racial performance gap in sports is partly due to cultural and environmental conditions (nurture), he argues that blacks are better athletes mainly because of a superior genetic heritage. The genetic differences are slight, but they are "crucial in competitions in which a fraction of a second separates the gold medalist from the also-ran" (Entine, 2000, p. 4). Specifically, blacks of West African heritage (which would include African Americans, whose ancestors were taken as slaves from this area) have a number of physiological traits that give them a decisive advantage in sprinting, leaping, and quick, explosive movements. These traits, in Entine's view, explain the dominance of blacks in certain sports (sprinting, basketball) and in certain positions (wide receiver in football) that capitalize on these abilities. Athletes of East African descent, on the other hand, inherit a set of abilities that give them greater endurance and lung capacity, traits that, according to Entine, explain the dominance of East Africans (Kenyans, for example) in long-distance races on the international and Olympic levels. In the excerpt below, Entine summarizes the biological advantage of black athletes.

Writer Kenan Malik argues that Entine's argument is based on an arbitrary and uncritical view of race. He raises several questions and probes the weaknesses of some widespread assumptions about race.

The Dominance of Black Athletes Is Genetic

Jon Entine

Since the first known studies of differences between black and white athletes in 1928, the data have been remarkably consistent: In most sports, African-descended athletes have the capacity to do better with their raw skills than whites. Let's summarize the physical and physiological differences known to date. Blacks with West African ancestry generally have relatively less subcutaneous fat on arms and legs and proportionally more lean body and muscle mass . . . bigger, more developed musculature in general, a longer arm span, faster patellar tendon reflex, greater body density, a higher percentage of fast-twitch muscles and more anaerobic enzymes, which can translate into more explosive energy. Relative advantages in these physiological and biomechanical characteristics are a gold mine for athletes who compete in . . . football, basketball, and sprinting . . .

East Africa produces some of the world's best aerobic athletes because of a variety of bio-physiological attributes. Blacks from this region . . . have more energy-producing enzymes in the muscles and an apparent ability to process oxygen more efficiently, resulting in less susceptibility to fatigue; they have a slighter body profile and a larger lung capacity than whites or West Africans, which translates into greater endurance.

White athletes appear to have a physique between . . . West Africans and East Africans. They have more endurance but less explosive running and jumping ability than West Africans; they tend to be quicker than East Africans but have less endurance.

SOURCE: From *Taboo: Why Black Athletes Dominate Sports and Why We're Afraid to Talk About It* by Jon Entine. Copyright © 1999 by Jon Entine. Reprinted by permission of PublicAffairs. A member of Perseus Books, L.L.C.

THE ARGUMENT FOR GENETIC DIFFERENCES IS DEEPLY FLAWED

Kenan Malik

What lies behind black domination of sport? The traditional liberal answer points the finger at social factors. Black people, so the argument goes, have been driven into sport because racism has excluded them from most areas of employment. Racism also makes blacks hungrier than whites for success. . . . Journalist Jon Entine dismisses [this] environmentalist theory of black athletic prowess as "political correctness." . . .

The liberal consensus, Entine argues, has served only to disguise the truth about the black domination of sport—which is that black people are built to run and jump. . . . [Entine and others argue] that it's time we put away our fears of talking about racial differences and face up to the facts of genetic diversity.

The view that black sportsmen and women have a natural superiority rests on the evidence of physiological research, largely into two groups of athletes: East African long-distance runners and West African sprinters.

East Africa, and Kenya in particular, is the powerhouse of middle- and long-distance running. . . . [R]esearch suggests that the secret of such spectacular success lies in superior biology. Athletes of West African descent—and that includes most African Americans . . .—have, on the other hand, a physique that is suited to . . . sprinting and jumping.

For Entine, such . . . differences demonstrate the natural superiority of black athletes. For Entine's critics, . . . the very search for such differences betrays a racist outlook. . . . The . . . problem with the "blacks are born to run" thesis is . . . that it is factually incorrect . . . It is certainly possible to divide humanity into a number of races . . . according to skin colour and body form. However, it is also possible to do it many other ways—using, for instance, blood group, lactose tolerance, sickle cell, or any other genetic trait. Genetically, each would be as valid a criterion as skin colour. The distribution of one physical or genetic characteristic is not necessarily the same as that of another. . . . The current division of the world into black, white, [and] Asian races is, in other words, as rooted in social convention as in genetics.

Entine rejects such criticisms as mere "semantics," but his own argument shows why it is not so. According to Entine, East Africans are naturally superior at endurance sports, West Africans at sprinting and jumping, and "whites fall somewhere in the middle." But if East and West Africans are at either end of a genetic spectrum of athletic ability, why consider them to be part of a single race, and one that is distinct from whites? Only because, conventionally, we use skin colour as the criterion of racial difference. . . .

Not only are genetic notions of population differences distinct from political concepts of race, but the physiology of human differences is not easy to interpret in sporting terms. Jon Entine suggests that West Africans have relatively slender calves compared to whites, and that this helps their sprinting ability. It is difficult to see how, because muscle power increases with cross-sectional area; smaller calves should make it harder, not easier, to excel in explosive sprinting events. . . .

It is true that athletes of West African descent living in North America, Western Europe and the Caribbean dominate many sports. But contemporary West Africans do not. This is the opposite of what one should expect if athletic ability were predominantly determined by genetics. In the United States, considerable intermixing between black and white has meant that the African American population embodies, on average, roughly 30 per cent of genes from populations of European descent. Hence, African Americans should be poorer athletes than West Africans. The reverse is true.

What all this suggests is that the relationship between sport, culture and genetics is much more complex than either liberal anti-racists or conservatives such as Entine . . . will allow. Athletic talent is at least in part inherited, and there are undoubted genetic differences between regional populations. . . . There is no reason to assume that all populations have physical characteristics equally suited to every athletic activity. But are blacks naturally better athletes than whites? Not necessarily. After all, how many African Pygmies have you ever seen climbing on to the winners' rostrum?

SOURCE: Originally titled "Yes, Nature Does Help to Explain African Sporting Success: If You Think That's Racist, Your Idea of Race is Wrong" from *New Statesman*, *129*: 13-18, September 18, 2000. Copyright © New Statesman. All rights reserved. Reprinted with permission.

DEBATE QUESTIONS TO CONSIDER

1. Is Entine using the social or biological definition of race? Is it racist to argue that blacks are "naturally" gifted? Is it appropriate for scientists to pursue the issue raised by Entine?

2. How strong are Malik's arguments? What does he mean when he questions the practice of grouping East and West Africans into the same race? What larger point is he making when he notes the absence of West Africans and Pygmies from the highest levels of sports competition?

3. If Entine is wrong, what social and environmental arguments might explain black dominance of sport? What is Malik implying when he says that these relationships are "more complex" than is commonly recognized? What personal or psychological factors might be relevant? Could it be that blacks are more determined to succeed ("hungrier" in Malik's words) in sports than whites? If so, why?

2

Assimilation and Pluralism

The United States is growing increasingly diverse in terms of ethnicity, race, language, and culture. How should we respond to the challenges created by this increasing diversity? Should we celebrate our pluralism and preserve our differences? Should we stress the traits we have in common and encourage everyone to "Americanize" or assimilate? How much diversity can we tolerate before societal unity is threatened? These are some of the questions raised in this chapter and debated, in one form or another, in U.S. society every day.

One approach to these issues is provided by what we can call "traditional" assimilation theory. This approach is based on decades of sociological research on the experiences of the great wave of immigrants—and their descendants—who came from Europe between the 1820s and the 1920s. It stresses the process of adjustment of the immigrants and their children and grandchildren, as they moved through a series of stages from disparaged outsiders to middle-class respectability. Many versions of this approach assume that assimilation is desirable, a necessity for national unity and stability, and that all groups and people who put forth the effort will eventually find themselves accepted into the "in-group."

This "traditional" approach to assimilation has produced a body of knowledge that is complex, sophisticated, and valuable. However, it has some significant limitations. Most important, perhaps, is that traditional assimilation theory was developed from the experiences of specific groups during a specific historical era. Do these insights apply to the contemporary wave of immigrants, those who have entered the United States over the past four decades? Contemporary immigrants come not just from Europe but from every corner of the globe, and they are much more diverse than previous groups. Some are highly educated and skilled professionals; others bring nothing more than the clothes on their backs and a willingness to take any job, no matter how poorly paid or menial. Will all of these groups assimilate? Will they (or, more likely, their descendants) eventually find a place in middle-class suburban America?

This chapter presents a variety of perspectives on assimilation and pluralism in the United States. Some support the traditional view, while others are highly critical of that approach. The two narrative portraits illustrate the dichotomy. Mario Puzo, the son of Italian immigrants, writes about his faith that he would find a way to succeed in America and realize his dreams. Luis Rodriguez, also the son of immigrants, writes about a very different American reality in which his chances for success are severely limited.

The readings continue to explore diversity and unity in the United States. Fernández-Kelly and Schauffler are critical of traditional assimilation theory and argue that it is inadequate for explaining the realities faced by the contemporary immigrants they study. DePalma follows up on this idea by contrasting the hard-won success of an immigrant from Greece, who arrived in the 1950s, with the struggles of an illegal Mexican immigrant. While the success of the Greek immigrant reinforces the view that American society is open to all who are willing to work, the obstacles faced by the Mexican immigrant seem overwhelming. Does Juan Peralta have the same chances for success as John Zannikos? What changes in the larger society over the past 50 years affect their relative chances for success?

The reading by Kaw takes a different and seldom explored approach to the issues of assimilation and pluralism, stressing the power of Anglo ideals of beauty and, by implication, the powerful attractions of Americanization—even to the point of altering body shape—for immigrant groups. What price do Kaw's subjects pay (beyond money) for their pursuit of a more Anglo appearance? And what role does gender play in the assimilation process?

The Current Debates section presents two views on a continuing controversy related to assimilation: Should the United States have an "English Only" policy? The argument presented by Mujica is consistent with the traditional view of assimilation and stresses the need for social unity and the advantages of language conformity. Hurtado and Vega, in contrast, stress the advantages of bilingualism and argue that language diversity is beneficial and should be encouraged.

Please visit the accompanying website to Race, Ethnicity, and Gender, second edition for the *Public Sociology Assignments* at http://www.pineforge.com/das2.

QUESTIONS TO CONSIDER IN THIS CHAPTER

1. Consider the experiences of Mario Puzo and Luis Rodriguez (Narrative Portraits) and John Zannikos and Juan Peralta (Reading by DePalma). What factors separate the experiences? Is it individual or generational, or has something about U.S. society changed that can explain the differences? If so, what?

2. How important is it for the United States to stress assimilation? How much of their culture should immigrant groups be allowed to retain? Is linguistic diversity a threat to the societal unity? Is it reasonable to insist on "English only"?

3. What holds American society together? Is it a common language? A common core of values and beliefs? A commitment to protect civil, political, and religious rights? Are these sources of unity threatened by the high levels of immigration we are currently experiencing? How? What exactly is at stake here?

NARRATIVE PORTRAITS

ASSIMILATION, THEN AND NOW

Mario Puzo and Luis Rodriguez are both sons of immigrants, but they grew up in two very different Americas. Puzo, best known as the author of *The Godfather*, grew up in the Italian

American community, and his memoir of life in New York City in the 1930s illustrates some of the patterns that are at the root of Gordon's theory of assimilation. Writing in the 1970s, Puzo remembers the days of his boyhood and his certainty that he would escape the poverty that surrounded him. Note also his view of (and gratitude for) an America that gave people (or at least white people) the opportunity to rise above the circumstances of their birth.

Rodriguez paints a rather different picture of U.S society. He grew up in the Los Angeles area in the 1950s and 1960s and was a veteran of gang warfare by the time he reached high school. His memoir, *Always Running: la Vida Loca* (1993), illustrates the realities of segmented assimilation for contemporary immigrants. In this extract, he describes how his high school prepared Mexican American students for life. Contrast his despair with Puzo's gratitude. Which sector of American society is Rodriguez being prepared to enter? In Rodriguez's experience, is assimilation segmented?

Choosing a Dream: Italians in Hell's Kitchen

Mario Puzo

In the summertime, I was one of the great Tenth Avenue athletes, but in the wintertime I became a sissy. I read books. At a very early age I discovered libraries. . . . My mother always looked at all this reading with a fishy Latin eye. She saw no profit in it, but since all her children were great readers, she was a good enough general to know she could not fight so pervasive an insubordination. And there may have been some envy. If she had been able to, she would have been the greatest reader of all.

My direct ancestors for a thousand years have most probably been illiterate. Italy, the golden land, . . . so majestic in its language and cultural treasures . . . has never cared for its poor people. My father and mother were both illiterates. Both grew up on rocky, hilly farms in the countryside adjoining Naples. . . . My mother was told that the family could not afford the traditional family gift of linens when she married, and it was this that decided her to emigrate to America. . . . My mother never heard of Michelangelo; the great deeds of the Caesars had not reached her ears. She never

heard the great music of her native land. She could not sign her name.

And so it was hard for my mother to believe that her son could become an artist. After all, her one dream in coming to America had been to earn her daily bread, a wild dream in itself. And looking back, she was dead right. Her son an artist? To this day she shakes her head. I shake mine with her.

America may be a Fascistic, warmongering, racially prejudiced country today. It may deserve the hatred of its revolutionary young. But what a miracle it once was! What has happened here has never happened in any other country in any other time. The poor, who have been poor for centuries . . . whose children had inherited their poverty, their illiteracy, their hopelessness, achieved some economic dignity and freedom. You didn't get it for nothing, you had to pay a price in tears, in suffering, but why not? And some even became artists.

SOURCE: From *Visions of America* edited by W. Brown and A. Ling, pp. 56-57. Copyright © 1993 by Mario Puzo. Reprinted by permission of Donadio & Olson, Inc.

Always Running: La Vida Loca

Luis Rodriguez

Mark Keppel High School was a Depression-era structure with a brick and art deco facade and small, army-type bungalows in the back. Friction filled its hallways. The Anglo and Asian upper-class students from Monterey Park and Alhambra attended the school. They were tracked into the "A" classes; they were in the school clubs; they were the varsity team members, and lettermen. They were the pep squad and cheerleaders.

But the school also took in the people from the Hills and surrounding community who somehow made it past junior high. They were mostly Mexican, in the "C" track (what were called the "stupid" classes). Only a few of these students participated in school government, in sports, or in the various clubs.

The school had two principal languages. Two skin tones and two cultures. It revolved around class differences. The white and Asian kids . . . were from professional, two-car households with watered lawns and trimmed trees. The laboring class, the sons and daughters of service workers, janitors and factory hands, lived in and around the Hills (or a section of Monterey Park called "Poor Side").

The school separated these two groups by levels of education: The professional-class kids were provided with college-preparatory classes; the blue-collar students were pushed into "industrial arts." . . .

If you came from the Hills, you were labeled from the start. I'd walk into the counselor's office and looks of disdain greeted me—one meant for a criminal, alien, to be feared. Already a thug. It was harder to defy this expectation than just accept it and fall into the trappings. It was a jacket I could try to take off, but they kept putting it back on. The first hint of trouble and the preconceptions proved true. So why not be an outlaw? Why not make it our own?

SOURCE: From *Always Running – La Vida Loca, Gang Days in L.A.* by Luis J. Rodriguez. (Curbstone Press, 1993). Reprinted with permission of Curbstone Press. Distributed by Consortium.

READINGS

In both sociology and U.S. mainstream culture, there are different approaches to thinking about how diverse racial and ethnic groups can live together in one society. We can group these approaches into two main categories: *assimilation* and *pluralism*. Assimilation refers to traditional ideas such as the "melting pot," whereby ethnic differences eventually disappear as groups adapt to the dominant culture over a series of generations. In contrast, pluralism is similar to the concept of "multiculturalism": Different groups coexisting in the same society while maintaining their traditions and some degree of autonomy, ideally in a situation where no one culture is dominant and differences are valued equally. While the assimilation approach most closely fits the experiences of older white immigrant groups, neither approach works as an ideal type that describes the United States fully. However, the nation continues to draw on both of these polar ideals as it struggles to make sense of its increasing diversity today.

Because of its limited explanatory potential, traditional assimilation theory is considered outdated by many sociologists, including the authors of our first reading, Fernández-Kelly and

Schauffler. They make the point, for example, that the notion that assimilation of all immigrant groups will go through a similar stage-like process neglects the social class backgrounds that groups bring with them, the degree of their concentration in certain locations, and their mode of incorporation into the labor market, among other things. The selection by DePalma follows up on the contrast between immigrants "then" and immigrants "now" by comparing and contrasting the situations of two men living in New York City. One immigrated from Greece five decades ago and, after an early period of struggle, enjoys a high level of economic success. The other is an illegal immigrant from Mexico who moves from one dead-end job to another, unable to find a way out of poverty and economic marginalization. Can traditional assimilation theory possibly explain the situations of both men?

The third selection takes a very different approach to assimilation and pluralism. Eugenia Kaw uses in-depth interviews with Asian American women to explore the ways in which the pressure of Americanization is manifested in decisions about cosmetic surgery. Although they see themselves as making individualistic choices about their personal appearance, the decision to "open" their faces is deeply shaped by their status as women and as racial minorities in a white, paternalistic society. Clearly, these women are assimilating at a deeper, more basic (physical) level than did European and immigrants of years past.

Divided Fates: Immigrant Children in a Restructured U.S. Economy

M. Patricia Fernández-Kelly and Richard Schauffler

. . .

Assimilation, perhaps the most enduring theme in the immigration literature, unfolds into descriptive and normative facets. From an empirical standpoint, the concept designates a range of adjustments to receiving environments and points to the manner in which immigrants blend into larger societies. In a normative sense, assimilation is linked to an expectation that foreigners will shed, or at least contain, their native cultures while embracing the mores and language of the host country. Put succinctly, assimilation has always been more than a convenient word to enumerate the ways in which immigrants survive; it has also been a term disclosing hopes about how immigrants "should" behave.

In this article we revisit the descriptive and normative aspects of assimilation from the perspective of political economy and informed by insights from the field of economic sociology.

The first section includes a review of approaches and a discussion of segmented assimilation, a term coined by Portes and Zhou (1993) to denote varying modalities of immigrant incorporation into distinct sectors of American society. The notion is serviceable in that it refines generalizations of the past by pointing to factors that can turn assimilation into an uplifting or a leveling force. At the heart of the discussion is the realization that becoming American encompasses various and sometimes conflicting meanings.

Optimistic accounts of assimilation—captured in the image of the melting pot—coexisted with the early stages of American capitalism when immigrants were the purveyors of labor for an expanding economy. Tales of weary but resolute arrivals at the shores of opportunity became part of collective self-definitions. Assimilation, conceived as the ideal path towards success, also emerged as the wellspring of national identity. Over the last two decades, economic internationalization has transformed the context in which assimilation takes place. In the Fordist era, workers could envision entry-level jobs as the first step in a journey towards prosperity. At present, when firms often subcontract services and even product assembly, many of the paths toward socioeconomic improvement have been blocked. Will the new immigrants—mostly from Asia and Latin America—replicate earlier patterns of success or face conditions of arrested progress?

Sketched in the second section is a theoretical framework that assigns priority to interpersonal networks and social capital, a process by virtue of which individuals use their membership in a particular group to gain access to valuable resources, including information and jobs. We maintain that, all the more so in a restructured economy, the outcomes of assimilation depend on a series of toponomical—that is, socially and physically situated—factors. Immigrants able to draw upon the knowledge of preexisting groups that control desirable economic assets will share an experience much different from those lacking a social nexus to opportunity and resources of high quality.

Collective identity is itself a significant resource in the process of assimilation. Although the fate of immigrants depends upon macrostructural changes like industrial restructuring, it also varies in congruence with the recasting of collective self-definitions. The immigrant condition forces individuals to observe themselves even as they are being observed by others. As a consequence, immigrants repeatedly engage in purposeful acts to signify their intended character and the way that character differs from, or converges with, that of other groups. A stigmatized identity can turn assimilation into an injurious transition unless immigrants resort to shared repertoires based on national origin, immigrant status or religious conviction. Some identities protect immigrants; others weaken them by transforming them into disadvantaged ethnic minorities.

There is an ongoing relationship between migration and ethnicity: today's ethnics are the immigrants of the past and vice versa; present immigrants are already forging tomorrow's ethnic identities. New arrivals interact empirically and symbolically with their predecessors. At that juncture the African-American experience has strategic importance for the study of downward assimilation, a process defined by the incorporation of immigrants into impoverished, generally nonwhite, urban groups whose members display adversarial stances toward mainstream behaviors, including the devaluation of education and diminished expectations.

In defining themselves, immigrants of all nationalities hold the image of the urban underclass as a pivotal referent to delineate their own place in the larger society. Most African Americans were never international migrants in the conventional sense of the word. However, as migrants from the rural South during the first half of the twentieth century, they shared commonalities in profile and expectations with migrants from lands afar. In points of destination, blacks faced barriers that resulted in their arrested socioeconomic advancement. Ironically, current analyses focus not primarily on the migrant past of African Americans, but on the distressing behavioral complex surrounding concentrated poverty in the urban ghetto. Yet one way to reframe that phenomenon is as a product of migration under conditions of extreme hostility over extended periods of time.

In the third section, we pursue the argument through a comparison of five immigrant groups, Mexicans and Vietnamese in southern California and Nicaraguans, Cubans and Haitians in southern Florida. The data to sustain the comparison is drawn from two complementary sources: a national survey of children of immigrants between the ages of twelve and seventeen conducted in 1992 and a series of ethnographic case studies carried out in the latter part of 1993 and early 1994 with a small subset formed by 120 families of immigrant children in the original sample. By combining the strengths of quantitative and qualitative analyses, we draw a profile of diverging adaptations, emerging identities and segmented assimilation.

The concluding section summarizes findings and reconsiders the central questions in the light of those findings.

Assimilation: Old and New

By the time the sociologists of the Chicago School turned their attention to immigration in the 1920s, observers of the American experience had been debating its two presumed outcomes—assimilation and pluralism—for almost 150 years.... Throughout that period, the chronicle of immigration excluded any mention of blacks and indigenous people, focusing primarily on Europeans.

The beginning of the twentieth century witnessed a new phenomenon. For the first time Americans of British origin represented less than half of the country's total population....

Early theories of assimilation were forged against a distinct socioeconomic background. In the early decades of the twentieth century, the Fordist economy generated millions of jobs, almost a third of which were in manufacturing and most of which required little or no previous skill. The economic expansion which promoted rising wages and mass consumption invested with plausibility the story of the widening mainstream. The expectation was that those still struggling on the river banks would soon be engulfed by the broadening waters of economic progress.

There was a major deviation from that optimistic forecast. As foreigners continued to arrive in the United States, the industrial growth of the North fueled a demand for labor which, at the time of World War I, began to be filled by black migrants from the rural South where cotton agriculture was declining. African Americans appeared in cities like Chicago, New York, Boston and Philadelphia under conditions which Robert Park (1950) regarded as optimum for assimilation. Yet the process did not bring about the anticipated effects. The experience of black Americans presented a compelling argument against the certain identification of assimilation with economic success. Although Park himself grew increasingly skeptical about assimilation as a beneficial prospect for all racial and ethnic groups, the concept became paradigmatic in the understanding of immigrant adaptation.

Despite efforts by Frazier (1957) and Gordon (1964), the notion of assimilation remained problematic in subsequent years for several reasons. First, it implied that immigrant and American cultures were mutually exclusive and bounded categories. Retaining one's native culture and becoming American were conceived as a zero-sum game; only by giving up ethnic identity could immigrants fully participate in American life.

Second, the question of agency in the process of assimilation remained ambiguous. Was it American society or the immigrant that was doing the absorbing, appropriating and amalgamating? For the most part, Park and his associates had suggested that the immigrant was the passive object of the host environment. In so doing, society appeared as an unchanging force and the immigrant as the pliant clay of a teleological—and quasi-evolutionary—process that transcended human agency.

Third, what was American took the form of an assumption not a subject for investigation. Since, for the most part, assimilation was not viewed as a reciprocal process, the American condition remained unchanged, stultified. Contestations of the dominant ideology were excluded from discussions about American identity, as were other aspects of the social structure—social class and labor markets in particular.

Finally, the relationship between individual and collective processes was often confused. Park's general description of assimilation and his concept of the marginal man spoke to the plight of the individual. Yet a role was also reserved for communities as mechanisms necessary for individual transitions. This implied relatively autonomous group processes. The paradox entailed in that formulation—how would the last immigrant in a particular group assimilate when the community necessary to facilitate that transition had already disappeared—was not addressed.

In the 1960s and 1970s, the Civil Rights Movement focused attention on the persistent exclusion of African Americans, and new waves of immigrants from Asia, Latin America and the Caribbean provoked a renewed public debate. Pluralism and assimilation were now challenged by a variety of structural approaches of a neo-Marxist inspiration. Research on immigrant enclaves and middleman minorities turned the original conception of assimilation on its head by describing alternative, and often more effective, modes of incorporation. Self-employment, business formation, and the maintenance of shared cultural understanding outside the American mainstream were shown to enhance and accelerate economic mobility. Those views portrayed assimilation as a deflating pressure threatening immigrants' chances for success in counterposition to earlier, more optimistic, interpretations.

Structural perspectives, as well, acknowledged the importance of personal endowments and shared cultural assets, but they assigned equal priority to patterned arrangements that facilitate or impede economic advancement. Works by Blauner (1972) on internal colonialism, Portes and Bach (1986) on ethnic enclaves, and Bonacich (1980) on middleman minorities, privileged labor market inclusion and exclusion patterns, as well as their effect on social mobility. Persistent inequalities were viewed in close relationship to the location of immigrant groups and racial and ethnic minorities within the larger society.

In that context, consensus emerged that the outcome of migration depends on the interaction of three factors: 1) the internal composition of the groups to which immigrants belong, particularly in terms of social class; 2) their degree of concentration in specific locations; and 3) their mode of reception and incorporation into specific labor market strata. The distinction between labor migration, as represented by Mexicans and African Americans, and the immigrant enclave, as illustrated by Cubans, proved to be especially instructive. Cuban success in business formation was partly due to favorable government policies aiding settlement, the presence of a critical mass of entrepreneurs among Cuban exiles, and high levels of concentration in southern Florida. By contrast, the Mexican and African-American migrations were characterized by low levels of internal differentiation, weak or nonexistent resources in the process of adjustment, and high levels of concentration in impoverished neighborhoods. Those differences led, in turn, to varying social profiles and a dissimilar capacity for socioeconomic attainment.

Immigrants have always faced a modicum of discrimination, but their potential for collective progress has depended on a minimal threshold of gradual acceptance. The movement away from the immigrant slum entailed becoming American; almost always, that also meant becoming white. For African Americans the portal leading to economic improvement was exceedingly narrow. Yet increasing opportunities, especially in manufacturing, enabled even those vulnerable groups to make strides during the first half of the twentieth century. Recent changes operating at the global level raise new questions about the nature of immigrant absorption.

As the economic base shifted from manufacturing to services and information processing, cities suffered a process of deterioration but, paradoxically, they also attracted professionals linked to lucrative sectors of the new economy—international banking and finance, communications, and software design, for example. The presence of a new technocratic class in urban centers invigorated the demand for labor-intensive products and services— ranging from domestic help to restaurants and customized furniture and apparel—creating interstices for the employment of new waves of immigrants, now from Asia, Latin America and the Caribbean, many of whom were undocumented. As a result, the global city emerged upon the ruins of the old industrial metropolis as a strategic location for the centralization of coordinating functions vis-à-vis the international economy (Sassen, 1992).

Largely on account of major changes operating at the international level and partly because of regional variations, the options of new immigrants will divide depending on their spatial location, their contact with specific social networks, and their differentiated access to economic and political resources. Those subdivisions are what the notion of segmented assimilation seeks to make comprehensible. The concept builds on structural approaches and applies their insights beyond what has been essentially a discussion of labor market incorporation. The assumption is that amalgamation does take place, but the question is restated to make problematic both the host society and the immigrant population: Assimilation to what? Assimilation by whom? The modifier segmented further underscores that it is not a single mainstream group which serves as the unique reference point for all immigrants. Before exploring these issues in further detail, we sketch a theoretical framework that assigns priority to social networks.

SOCIAL CAPITAL AND IMMIGRANT NETWORKS

Network analysis became popular in the 1960s and 1970s partly in reaction to the determinism of structural functionalism and the methodological individualism fostered by multivariate statistical inquiries. . . .

Here, we take a different approach by grounding our analysis of social networks in the new economic sociology. A central objective of that field is to elucidate the social underpinnings of economic action. The point bears significantly upon immigration research because, as indicated in the previous section, the character of immigrant assimilation depends largely upon social forces leading to differentiated economic outcomes. Indeed, one way to conceptualize immigration is as a phenomenon of labor mobility sustained by interpersonal networks bridging points of origin and points of destination.

. . .

The importance of social networks is exemplified by the functioning of the immigrant enclave. In assembling a remarkable business conglomerate in Miami, Cubans relied on social contacts within and outside their own group. They avoided discrimination from mainstream financial institutions by obtaining loans to capitalize their firms from banks whose owners and personnel were Latin American and, therefore, Spanish speaking. Beyond their strong feeling of membership in the same community, Cubans benefited from their inclusion in a network characterized by high levels of class heterogeneity; that, in turn, enabled its members to establish multiple connections. The opposite is true about Mexicans and African Americans whose social networks are characterized by low degrees of internal differentiation in terms of class.

Those cases, as well, underscore the importance of social capital and its relationship to quality of resources. Several major writings lead to an understanding of social capital as an incorporeal but vital good accruing to individuals by virtue of their membership in particular communities (Coleman, 1988). Social capital is distinct from human capital in that it does not presuppose formal education or skills acquired through organized instruction. Instead, it originates from shared feelings of social belonging, trust and reciprocity. The concentration of immigrants of various nationalities in particular niches of the labor market occurs as a result of word-of-mouth recommendations. Those, in turn, are made possible by immigrants' membership in social networks whose members vouch for one another.

A dramatic illustration of the workings of social capital is Kasinitz and Rosenberg's (1994) study of business activity in an empowerment zone located in the notoriously destitute ghetto of Red Hook, Brooklyn. Although many businesses in the zone employ multiethnic workforces, including crews of West Indian security guards, they refuse to hire local blacks. Prejudice plays a role in this curious subdivision, but the causes of exclusion and inclusion are more complex. West Indians are joined to the employment structure through personal contacts and endorsements. Native blacks share the same physical spaces with the businesses in question, but they are socially disconnected and, therefore, bereft of the necessary links to obtain jobs. In that case, the primary reason for ghetto unemployment is not the lack of nearby opportunities but the absence of social networks that provide entry into the labor market.

As important as social capital is the quality of the resources that can be tapped through its deployment. Interpersonal networks are distinguished as much by their ability to generate a sense of cohesion as by the extent to which they can parlay group membership and mutual assistance into worthwhile jobs and knowledge. What distinguishes impoverished from wealthy groups is not their different capacity to deploy social capital—survival of the poor also depends on cooperation—but their varying access to resources of high quality. Those resources are often embedded in physical locations not available to the impoverished. . . .

To summarize, social networks are complex formations that channel and filter information, confer a sense of identity, allocate resources, and shape behavior. Individual choices depend not only on the availability of material and intangible assets in the society at large, but also on the way in which the members of interpersonal networks interpret information and relate to structures of opportunity. . . .

THE VARIOUS MEANINGS OF BECOMING AMERICAN

The data for this analysis are drawn from a 1992 survey of 5,263 children of immigrants and from in-depth interviews conducted with a subsample formed by 120 of those children and their parents. For the original survey, eighth and ninth grade students in Dade County (Miami), Broward County (Fort Lauderdale), and San Diego schools were randomly selected who met the following definition of second generation: those born in the United States with at least one foreign-born parent or born abroad but having resided in this country for at least five years. Questionnaires were administered to these students in schools selected to include both inner-city and suburban settings and student populations with varying proportions of whites, minorities and immigrants. In the Miami sample, two predominantly Cuban private schools were also included. The sample is evenly divided between boys and girls; the average age of the youngsters was about fourteen.

The follow-up interviews were conducted with a subset of those originally surveyed. The national-origin groups were stratified on the basis of sex, nativity (U.S. born or foreign born), socioeconomic status based on father's occupation, and family structure (two-parent families consisting of the biological parents of the child or other equivalent care-providers). In Miami, the Cuban group was also divided between public and private school students. Names, within the cells thus created, were picked randomly by country of origin for the largest groups in the original sample—Cubans, Nicaraguans, Haitians and West Indians (mostly Jamaicans and Trinidadians) in Dade and Broward Counties; and Vietnamese, Mexicans, Filipinos, Cambodians and Laotians in San Diego. Our analysis begins with cursory descriptions of five illustrative cases.

An Ethnographic Sampler

Haitian Strivers

Being admitted into the home of Aristide Maillol in Sweetwater, Miami, transports the visitor into a transfixed space. The location is American but the essence is that of rural Haiti. Aristide's mother does not speak English. Her eyes drift to the floor when explaining in Creole that her husband is hospitalized and she had to leave her job as a janitor in a local motel to attend to his needs. There is consternation and reserve in her demeanor. (The names in these narratives are pseudonyms.)

In the tiny sitting area adjoining the front door, a large bookcase displays the symbols of family identity in an arrangement suitable for a shrine. Framed by paper flowers at the top is the painted portrait of Mrs. Maillol and her husband. Crude forms and radiant colors capture the couple's dignity. Below, in three separate shelves, several photographs show Aristide's brother and three sisters. The boy

smiles confidently in the cap and gown of a high school graduate. The girls are displayed individually and in clusters, their eyes beaming, their hair pulled back, their attires fitting for a celebration. Interspersed with the photographs are the familiar trinkets that adorn most Haitian homes. Striking, however, is the inclusion of several trophies earned by the Maillol children in academic competitions. At seventeen, Aristide's brother has already been recruited by Yale University. Young Aristide, who is fifteen and wants to be a lawyer, speaks eloquently about the future:

> We are immigrants and immigrants must work hard to overcome hardship. You can't let anything stop you. I know there is discrimination, racism . . . but you can't let that bother you. Everyone has problems, things that hold them back, but if you study . . . [and] do what your mother, what your father, tell you, things will get better. . . . God has brought us here and God will lead us farther.

In silence, Mrs. Maillol nods in agreement.

Nicaraguan Sliders

That evening, in little Havana, the Angulo family prepares for dinner in their shabby apartment. Originally from Managua, Nicaragua, Mr. Angulo holds a degree in chemistry and for a time was the manager of a sizable firm in his home country. His wife belongs to a family with connections to the military. They arrived in Miami in 1985 when their son, Ariel, was eight and their daughter, Cristina, was only two years old. Both think of themselves as exiles but are not recognized as such by the authorities. In earnest, Mr. Angulo explains:

> We came with high hopes, escaping the Sandinistas, thinking this was the land of opportunity . . . ready to work and make progress, but we were stopped in our tracks. We haven't been able to legalize our situation. Every

so often, we get these notices saying we'll be thrown out of the country; it is nerve-wracking. As a result, we haven't been able to move ahead. Look around; this is the only place we've been able to rent since we came [to Miami]. . . . I work for an hourly wage without benefits, although I perform the duties of a professional for a pharmaceutical company. They know they can abuse my condition because I can't go anywhere; no one will hire me!

Mrs. Angulo, who works as a clerk for a Cuban-owned clinic, worries that Ariel, who is approaching college age, will not be eligible for financial assistance. She does not expect him to go beyond high school, although she and her husband place a premium on education and have typical middle class aspirations. As it is, Ariel cannot even apply for a legal summer job given his undocumented status. He attends a troubled school, where he mingles primarily with other Central Americans and African Americans. Conflict is rampant and academic standards are low. He complains that other students ridicule Nicaraguans. Ariel feels that his parents are too demanding; they do not understand the pressures at school or give him credit for his effort. Even more distressing is the fact that he cannot speak either English or Spanish fluently. Almost seventeen, he shares with his mother a dim view of the future.

Cuban Gainers

Ariel's experience is in stark contrast with that of fifteen-year-old Fernando Gómez, whose family migrated to Miami in 1980 as part of the Mariel boatlift. Originally from Oriente (Manzanillo), Cuba, Mr. Gómez was employed as a heavy equipment operator and then as a clerk for the same metallurgical firm prior to his migration to the United States. Since his arrival, he has worked as a mechanic for Dade County. His wife, who used to be a teacher in Cuba, now works providing care for the elderly. Although they hold working-class jobs, the couple's tastes

evince an upwardly bound thrust. Their home is part of a Cuban-owned residential development that combines pathways bordered by russet tile and luscious vegetation with pale exteriors, wrought-iron gates, and roofs of an Iberian derivation. The family's living room is embellished with new furnishings.

Proudly, Mr. Gómez states that he has never experienced discrimination; he is not the kind of man who would ever feel inferior to anyone. He expects Fernando, an even better student than his older brother, to go far. There is no doubt that he will finish college, perhaps work toward an advanced degree. Although Fernando wants to become a policeman like his brother, Mr. Gómez dismisses that intent as a passing whim; he would like his son to work with computers because "that is where the future of the world is."

Mexican Toilers

More than 3,000 miles away, in south central San Diego, Carlos Mendoza's home stands next to a boarded-up crack house. Prior to the police raid that shut it down, the Mendoza family had covered their own windows with planks to avoid witnessing what went on across the alley. The neighborhood is an assortment of vacant lots, abandoned buildings and small homes protected by fences and dogs. Fourteen years ago, the family entered the United States illegally in the trunk of a car. Their goal was to earn enough money to buy a house in their hometown in Michoacan, and although they succeeded—and purchased the house in San Diego as well—they laughingly note that somehow they never made it back to Mexico. The family has now achieved legal status under the amnesty program promoted by the 1986 Immigration Reform and Control Act.

For the past ten years, Mr. Mendoza has worked as a busboy in a fancy restaurant that caters to tourists, a position he secured through a Mexican friend. He is a hard-working and modest man who wants his son, Carlos, to study so that he can get a good job: "[I want him] to be better than me, not for my sake but for his sake and that of his own family." Mrs. Mendoza irons clothes at a Chinese-owned laundry, and complains bitterly that her employers are prejudiced toward her and other Mexicans.

Carlos is doing well in school; he was the only boy at Cabrillo Junior High to be elected to the honor society last year. He wants to become an engineer and go back to Mexico. Life in San Diego has been hard on him; the gold chain his parents gave him as a gift was ripped from around his neck by neighborhood toughs; his bicycle remains locked up inside the house, for to ride it would be to lose it to the same local bullies. His younger sister, Amelia, is not doing as well in school and dresses like a *chola* (female gang member), although she insists it is only for the style. Her parents worry but they feel helpless.

Vietnamese Bystanders

Forty blocks to the east, in another working-class neighborhood populated by Mexicans, Vietnamese and blacks, Mrs. Ly and her daughter Hoa sit in their tiny apartment surrounded by several calendars and clocks, a small South Vietnamese flag, two Buddhist shrines, and four academic achievement plaques. Two of Mrs. Ly's daughters have maintained perfect grades for two years in a row. Hoa, her mother explains, is behind; her grade point average is 3.8 rather than 4.0.

Since their arrival in the United States in 1991, neither Mrs. Ly nor her husband have held jobs; they depend on welfare, although Mrs. Ly is unclear about where exactly the money they receive comes from. Back in Vietnam, she and her husband sold American goods on the black market and supplemented their income by sewing clothes. Leaving their country was filled with trauma; they are still a bit in a daze. In San Diego, the family is isolated; people in the area resent the new arrivals. More than anything else, what keeps the Lys and other Vietnamese families apart is the language barrier: "We can't speak English," says Mrs. Ly, "so the girls don't go out much, they stay home. I raise my children here the same as I raised them in Vietnam: to school and back home."

Hoa's only friend is Vietnamese. Her mother would like her to have more American contacts so that she could learn the language and the culture of their new country. Eventually, she would like her daughter to get an office job or a job in retail sales. Hoa disagrees; she would like to be a doctor.

The cases sketched above provide a glimpse into dissimilar experiences, and the variations are not arbitrary; they are representative of the groups to which the families belong. Nicaraguans expected the treatment afforded to Cubans under what they regarded as similar circumstances. For many, those expectations were dashed as a result of the political complexities surrounding the relationship between the United States and Nicaragua. Bereft of supports in the receiving environment, many of these new immigrants are experiencing a rapid process of downward mobility although many have middle-class backgrounds. Those of humbler provenance are unable to advance. Especially disturbing is the predicament of children who, confined to immigrant neighborhoods but having spent most of their lives in the United States, cannot speak English or Spanish easily. Unable to regularize their immigrant status and facing acute economic need, many of those youngsters are choosing low-paying jobs over education. With an increasing number of high school dropouts and out-of-wedlock pregnancies, many Nicaraguan youth appear to be recapitulating aspects of the African-American trajectory (Fernández-Kelly, 1994).

Cubans, by contrast, represent an unusual case of immigrant success partly owed to conditions antithetical to those characterizing Nicaraguan migration. The first large cohorts arrived in Miami during the 1960s, prompting the customary response of more established populations: departure to the suburbs. In the beginning, Cubans, too, were perceived as an undesirable minority. Nevertheless, by contrast to other arrivals, they were a highly stratified mass that included professionals as well as an entrepreneurial elite. As a result, many were able to escape the pressures of the labor market through self-employment and business formation (Portes and Rumbaut, 1990). That, a shared and vehement opposition to the Castro regime, and assistance from the U.S. government allowed Cubans to form a cohesive community. They proceeded to reconstitute the social foundations to which they had been accustomed, including the establishment of a private school system for those who could afford it.

In 1980, the Mariel boatlift jolted Miami with new waves of mostly working-class immigrants, many of whom were of Afro-Caribbean descent. They, too, were received with a modicum of hostility that included the ambivalent feelings of older Cubans. Nevertheless, continued support on the part of the U.S. government and the preexisting ethnic enclave allowed the newcomers to adjust rapidly. To this day, the tribulations of every *balsero* (rafter) arriving in Miami, in flight from Communism, elicit admiration and reignite feelings about a shared historical experience.

Haitians represent a strategic case that contains, alternatively, elements akin to those found in the Cuban experience and others closer to the experience of Nicaraguans. Despite the ordeal of illegal migration and prejudice in the receiving environment, a substantial number of Haitians, like Aristide Maillol and his brother, are doing surprisingly well in the United States. There is evidence that their fledgling success is rooted in deliberate attempts to disassociate themselves from the stigma imposed upon black populations in the United States through an affirmation of their national identity and their religious fervor.

Other Haitians, however, appear to be blending into impoverished black groups living in ghettos such as Miami's Liberty City. A growing number of Haitian youngsters are showing up in alternative schools, detention centers and penal institutions (Stepick and Dutton-Stepick, 1994). Given their poverty-stricken status and recent arrival, Haitian immigrants were pushed into areas where rental properties were abundant and real estate prices were low. As a result, Little Haiti, a teetering concentration of Haitian homes and businesses, emerged in close proximity to inner-city neighborhoods, and it is from its dwellers that many Haitians are learning their place in American society.

As in the cases of Vietnamese and Mexicans, when Haitian children speak of discrimination, they are often thinking of the verbal and physical abuses they experience at the hands of native black Americans in their neighborhoods and schools. But by contrast to the first two groups, who attend schools characterized by higher levels of ethnic diversity, Haitians do not have alternative referents in their familiar environments. In those circumstances, the choices are clearly bifurcated: either conscious attempts at self-distinction or yielding to the norm through conformity. Insular and destitute environments can rapidly translate conformity into socioeconomic stagnation or decline.

Mexicans represent the longest unbroken migration of major proportions to the United States. Partly as a result of their widespread undocumented status and partly because of geographical proximity, many Mexicans do not see moving to the United States as a long-term decision; instead, they see themselves as sojourners, guided by an economic motive, whose real homes are south of the border. Expectations about the duration of their stay in areas of destination diminish Mexicans' involvement in entrepreneurship and business formation (Roberts, 1995). That attitude, as well, has an impact upon children's prospects because, as Portes (1993:27) puts it: "It is difficult to reach for the future when you are constantly confronting your past." With little differentiation in terms of social class, Mexicans do not hold enough power to resist the embattled conditions in the neighborhoods where they live.

The Vietnamese experience is marked by paradox. An early wave of exiles in the 1970s—many of whose members started small businesses in the United States—was followed by larger groups of peasants and unskilled workers who confronted harsher than usual journeys. In areas of destination they faced hostility, but their rapid legalization entitled them to public assistance and other benefits—up to 50 percent of Vietnamese in California are on welfare (Kitano and Daniels, 1988). Lack of English fluency and the absence of a larger and cohesive community to depend on have translated into acute degrees of isolation. However, in this case, isolation added to a widespread faith in education, discipline and family unity is producing children who are high achievers.

The Vietnamese continue to be in, but not of, the United States.

Figure 2.1 summarizes the nonrandom character of the conditions experienced by the immigrant groups studied. Each group has been assigned a label that captures a distinctive experience (Cubans as Gainers; Vietnamese as Bystanders; Haitians as Strivers; Mexicans as Toilers; and Nicaraguans as Sliders). To complete the comparison, we have added a sixth group (native blacks as Survivors). The purpose of the classification is not to create yet another typology of migration, but to decouple the characteristics of segmented assimilation from national and ethnic referents, thus exposing the outcomes of migration as a function of the factors listed in the column on the left: Internal Differentiation by Class; Type of Reception; Quality of Resources; Degree of Spatial Concentration; and Length of Time in Area of Destination. The first four dimensions designate decisive toponomical factors underpinning the aftermath of various kinds of migration.

Although Figure 2.1 condenses the generalized experiences of the various groups, it does not capture their internal diversity, especially in terms of social class. Its sole purpose is to serve

	Gainers	Bystanders	Strivers	Toilers	Sliders	Survivors
Internal Differentiation by Class	+++	+−	+−	−	+−	−
Type of Reception	+++	++	−	−	−	−−−
Quality of Resources	+++	+−	−	−	−	−−
Degree of Spatial Concentration	++	+−	++	++	+−	+++
Length of Time in Area of Destination	+	−−	−−	++	−−	+++
	1960>	1975>	1980>	1930>	1980>	1630>

Figure 2.1

as a heuristic device for understanding the patterns of adaptation under discussion. The positions occupied by the types in the figure should be understood as approximate points along a continuum. Thus, Type of Reception ranges from highly positive—as indicated by three plus signs—to extremely hostile—as indicated by three minus signs.

Gainers, characterized by high levels of class differentiation, experienced a relatively hospitable reception, including prompt legalization, government support, and low levels of discrimination. For those reasons, they were able to tap resources of high quality, such as effective schools and adequate, affordable housing. Their spatial concentration worked advantageously, facilitating the use of social capital to gain access to information and other desirable assets. Their experience of socioeconomic mobility markedly diverges from that of Survivors, for whom spatial concentration in antagonistic environments translated into diminished connections to the larger society, resources of low quality, and diminished ability to parlay social capital into economic advantage. While Gainers thrive, Survivors endure. The other groups occupy intermediary positions within those two extremes.

The length of time in areas of destination bears a direct relationship to the consolidation of positive or negative behavioral outcomes. Over extended periods of time, low levels of class heterogeneity added to hostile modes of reception, resources of low quality, and high degrees of spatial concentration inevitably lead to a hardening of negative traits among the children and the grandchildren of internal and international migrants. In the case of African Americans, the time line extends beyond the period covered by The Great Black Migration from the rural South (1910–1970) to include a longer stretch which is part of that group's historical memory.

SURVEY FINDINGS

Survey materials contribute additional insights to the picture made vividly real by the testimonies of immigrant children and their families. Table 2.1 condenses information about school performance, parental human capital, and children's aspirations. Some differences and similarities are worth noting. Not surprisingly, Cuban children in private schools display high grade point averages and the highest standardized test scores, followed by the Vietnamese whose grades are better but whose scores lag due to lower English proficiency. Cuban students in private schools dramatically exceed the performance of those in public institutions, illustrating the critical effect of social class even within that highly integrated community. Although they are experiencing downward mobility, the scores of Nicaraguan children, many of whom have middle-class backgrounds, are relatively high. Haitians and Mexicans display comparatively low scores, as generally found in predominantly working-class populations.

Even with that in mind, the contrast between Haitians and Mexicans is noteworthy. On the aggregate, the Haitian indicators are consistent with the divided experience sketched earlier, and those of Mexicans confirm their characterization as a highly homogeneous and vulnerable group. Figures on parents' educational achievement, socioeconomic status and occupational aspirations are compatible with those profiles. And yet, regardless of national origin and social class, most immigrant children voice high educational aspirations, with Haitians second only to Cubans in private schools in their ambition to go beyond college. Again, it comes as no surprise that Mexicans constitute the only group a large proportion of whose members expect never to achieve a college education.

Table 2.2 provides information about the friendship networks of the various populations.

Table 2.1   School Performance, Parental Human Capital, and Children's Aspirations[a]

	School Performance				Parental Human Capital					Child's Aspirations		
	GPA[b]	Std Math Test[c]	Std Reading Test[c]	English Index Score[d]	Percent Father College Grad	Percent Mother College Grad	Father Occup SEF[e]	Mother Occup SEF[e]	Occupational Aspirations[f]	Less Than College (%)	College (%)	Graduate School (%)
Cuban—private School (N = 183)	26	80	69	15.3	55	42	50.4	47.3	65.4	3	32	67
Cuban—public school (N = 1044)	22	56	45	15.4	24	18	37.5	36.9	62.9	18	37	46
Nicaraguan (N = 344)	2.3	55	38	14.8	45	31	39.2	30.5	62.7	21	34	45
Haitian (N = 178)	2.3	45	30	15.2	16	15	29.1	29.4	65.6	16	34	50
Mexican (N = 757)	2.2	32	27	13.9	9	5	26.3	24.9	58.3	39	32	29
Vietnamese (N = 371)	3.0	60	38	13.4	24	14	34.2	32.4	61.8	23	40	37

a. All column differences between national origin groups significant at the .001 level.

b. Grade Point Average as reported by school district.

c. Stanford Achievement Test, 8th edition, percentile score.

d. Self-rated proficiency in reading, writing, speaking, and understanding English.

e. Duncan socioeconomic index score, based respectively on father's/mother's current occupation.

f. Treiman occupational prestige index score for child's desired occupation.

Table 2.2   Friendship Networks[a]

	Number of Close Friends From Abroad			Percentage With Friends Who Are[b]				
	None (%)	Some (%)	Many or Most (%)	Cuban (%)	Nicaraguan (%)	Haitian (%)	Mexican (%)	Vietnamese (%)
Cuban—private school (N = 183)	1.1	5.5	93.4	98.9	7.3	0	na	na
Cuban-public school (N = 1044)	2.5	23.2	74.2	93.8	29.0	3.3	na	na
Nicaraguan (N = 344)	5.1	18.8	76.2	78.1	79.4	3.9	na	na
Haitian (N = 178)	9.8	43.9	46.2	26.1	4.2	87.3	na	na
Mexican (N = 757)	6.6	44.6	48.8	na	na	na	82.9	94.5
Vietnamese (N = 371)	6.5	38.6	54.9	na	na	na	*17.2*	83.1

a. All column differences between national-origin groups are significant at the .001 level.

b. Percentage of those who report having close friends from abroad (i.e., excludes those with none). Numbers in **bold** represent the right-to-left axis of conationals. Numbers in *italics* represent the asymmetrical pairs of nationalities on left-to-right axes.

Regardless of national origin, most children associate with members of their own group and a large number of their friends are foreign born. Within that context, nevertheless, Cubans have the highest degree of contact with members of their own group and the lowest proportion of friendships with outsiders. Oddly, Nicaraguans report a higher degree of relations with Cubans than Cubans voice with respect to Nicaraguans. Similar albeit smaller disparities are found in the contrasting testimonies of Haitians with respect to Cubans and of Mexicans with respect to the Vietnamese. Those discrepancies are explained by two tendencies: that of Cubans and Vietnamese to see themselves as enclosed communities and that of Haitians, Mexicans and Nicaraguans to be more permeable to other groups in their environments. In addition, the relationship between Nicaraguans, Haitians and Cubans is marked by status differences; often, the latter are reluctant to admit they know Nicaraguans and Haitians. That tendency is mirrored by Nicaraguans' generalized feelings that Cubans discriminate against them. In other words, Cubans and Vietnamese display the least degree of porousness of the groups studied.

Most revealing is the information contained in Table 2.3 on perceptions of discrimination and self-identification. Cuban youth report the least discrimination, a fact that is understandable; it is hard for anyone to feel rebuffed when, as Table 2.2 indicates, the overwhelming majority of his contacts are with members of his own group. Nevertheless, Cuban children in public schools experience higher levels of discrimination from both blacks and whites than those in

Table 2.3   Perceptions of Discrimination[a]

	Percent Who Experience Discrimination	Percent of Those Discriminated Against Who Attribute It to:			Percent Residing in U.S. 5–9 Years	Percent Born in U.S.
		Whites	Blacks	Cubans		
Cuban—private school (N = 183)	31.7	46.4	28.6	1.8	3.3	91.3
Cuban—public school (N = 1044)	39.1	31.6	28.9	3.7	10.1	67.6
Nicaraguan (N = 344)	50.6	27.8	22.2	25.0	57.8	7.6
Haitian (N = 178)	62.4	35.8	29.4	9.2	28.7	43.3
Mexican (N = 757)	64.3	42.2	34.4	na	28.4	60.2
Vietnamese (N = 371)	66.3	37.9	40.2	na	42.3	15.6

a. All column differences between national-origin groups are significant at the .001 level.

private schools. In contrast to private institutions, public schools expose children to a plurality of ethnic and national groups and are, therefore, less able to shield them from friction. With the exception of the Vietnamese, all other groups report higher levels of discrimination from whites than from blacks.

Only Nicaraguans see Cubans as a significant source of discrimination. That may be related to a panethnic effect in Miami where the Hispanic community is internally diversified in terms of national origin, with the Cubans occupying a preeminent position and, therefore, becoming easily identifiable as a source of discrimination, particularly toward other Hispanics. On the other hand, the case of Mexicans in San Diego invites reflection because, despite the existence of a large co-ethnic community, membership in it does not shield Mexicans from discrimination. That, too,

may be an effect of localized factors—a continued climate of hostility against Mexican immigration in California has been recently exacerbated by a severe economic downturn following a fiscal crisis of the State government and deep cuts in military spending. Mexicans have become convenient scapegoats for heightened rates of joblessness. Finally, the recently arrived Vietnamese report the most discrimination, a reflection of the negative public reception that greeted their arrival. In addition, they tend to live in working-class neighborhoods populated by black Americans but without the benefit of a "Little Saigon" that might insulate them from conflict.

The data in Table 2.4 summarize selected characteristics of the schools attended by immigrant children in our sample. The patterns revealed are consistent with the descriptions offered earlier. Taken as a whole, Cuban families

Table 2.4   Socioeconomic Status of National Origin Groups[a]

	Low SEI[b](%)	Middle SEI(%)	High SEI(%)	% Attend Majority Black School[c]	% Attend Majority Latin School	% Attend Majority White School	% Attend Central City School[d]	%Attend >2/3 Poor School[e]	% Attend 1/3-2/3 Poor School	% Attend <1/3 Poor School
Cuban—private school (N = 183)	7.7	49.2	43.1	0	100	0	0	0	0	100
Cuban—public school (N = 1044)	25.8	60.1	14.1	2.1	84.2	3.9	26.1	31.1	28.8	40.0
Nicaraguan (N = 344)	23.8	65.8	10.4	7.3	79.4	1.5	27.6	39.4	16.3	44.3
Haitian (N = 178)	31.0	61.9	7.1	66.9	3.4	2.8	83.7	66.9	12.9	20.2
Mexican (N = 757)	66.9	30.4	2.7	.4	17.7	.4	57.7	51.3	38.0	10.7
Vietnamese (N = 371)	45.3	46.9	7.7	.3	.8	0	50.3	39.2	18.8	41.9

a. All column differences between national-origin groups are significant at the .001 level.

b. Based on score on composite index using father's and mother's occupations, education, and home ownership. Corresponds to working class (e.g., busboys, janitors, laborers), middle class (small business owners, teachers), and upper middle class (lawyers, architects, executives).

c. Majority in these three columns means greater than 60% of students who attend the school. Note that we cannot distinguish within the Latin group between immigrants and U.S.-born students.

d. Geographically located within the central city area of Miami and San Diego.

e. "Poor" here is measured by the proxy variable of the percentage of the student body eligible for federally funded free or subsidized lunch.

show a higher degree of class heterogeneity—as reflected in the proportions of children receiving free or subsidized lunch, a proxy measure for poverty. Mexican children are located in schools that mirror their position at the lower end of the class hierarchy. Most Haitian children are to be found in predominantly black, inner-city schools given the proximity of Haitian residential settlement in contiguity to ghettos. Table 2.4 underscores the extent to which schools function as segregative forces sorting out children in terms of social class and location.

ETHNIC IDENTITIES

Ethnographic chronicles underscore the vital role of collective identities in the process of assimilation. Even under auspicious conditions, migration is a jarring experience that pushes individuals and groups to acquire new knowledge as they negotiate survival and adjustment. Immigrants learn how they fit in the larger society through the contacts they establish in familiar environments. Whether youngsters sink or soar frequently depends on how they see themselves, their families and their communities. For that reason, the immigrant life is preeminently an examined life. Iterative processes of symbolic and factual association and detachment shape immigrants' self-definitions. Schools play a major role in that respect (Matute-Bianchi, 1986).

At school, children mingle with groups differentiated by their own self-perceptions and the perceptions of external observers. Especially when they equate success with localized power attained through conflict and physical force—as in the case of youth gangs—those groups can exert a strong downward pull upon immigrant children. The paths that lead youngsters toward specific clusters is complex. However, one of the most effective antidotes against downward mobility is a sense of membership in a group

with an undamaged collective identity. The Méndez children illustrate that proposition.

But for the fact that they are illegal aliens from Nicaragua, sixteen-year-old Omar Méndez and his younger sister Fátima could not be closer to the American Dream. They have grown up in Miami since they were five and three years old, respectively. They are superb students full of spirit and ambition. They attend a school where discipline is strict and where teachers are able to communicate with parents in Spanish. Most decisively, they see themselves as immigrants and that identity protects them from negative stereotypes and incorporation into more popular but less motivated groups in school. In Fátima's words: "We're immigrants! We can't afford to just sit around and blow it like others who've been in this country longer and take everything for granted." To maintain her independence, she withdraws from her peers and endures being called a "nerd." She does not mind because her center of gravitation lies within her family.

Maria Ceballos, a Cuban mother, agrees with Fátima. She despairs about her daughter's interest in material trinkets and her low levels of academic motivation. "At Melanie's age," she states, "I was very determined; maybe because I was born in a different country, I wanted to prove that I was as good as real Americans. My daughter was born here and [therefore] she doesn't have the same push."

Among vulnerable groups, the ability to shift ethnic identity often provides a defense from stigma and an incentive to defy leveling pressures. How they define themselves depends on the context. Miguel Hernández, an illegal Mexican alien in San Diego since 1980, explains that he and his wife define themselves "[depending on] who we are talking to. If we are talking to American people and they don't know the difference, we say 'Latinos'; that's easier for them and we avoid hassles." Miguel consciously avoids being labeled a Chicano because "It's a slang word for lower class types who don't know who they are. They don't want to be Mexicans, but they don't want to just be Americans; they don't even speak English but they don't know Spanish either [and they] fight for and about everything."

In answering questions about who they are, immigrants resort to antinomies, defining other groups in terms opposed to the ones they use to define themselves. Others are generally symbolized by the casualties of earlier migrations, especially inner-city blacks. Typically, immigrants see blacks as the victims of their own individual and collective liabilities. Martin López, a Mexican father, explains:

> Blacks in this country . . . don't want to work; [they] feel very American. They know government has to support every child they breed. [As immigrants] we can't afford to slacken the pace; we have to work hard.

Given phenotypical commonalities with black Americans and disadvantages derived from the locations where they live, the issue of identity is paramount among Haitians. Madeleine Serphy, an ambitious girl at fifteen, has strong feelings about African Americans:

> It may be true that whites discriminate, but I have no complaints [about them] because I don't know many [whites] . . . but blacks, they're trouble; they make fun of the way we [Haitians] speak. . . . They call us stupid and backwards and try to beat us up. I was always scared, so I [tried] to do well in school and that's how I ended [in a magnet school]. There, I don't stand out as much and I can feel good about being Haitian. . . . Haitian is what I am; I don't think about color.

For working-class Cubans, the problem of identity is equally complex, but for different reasons. As members of a successful group, many resent being melded into the broader classification of Hispanic. Such is the case with Doris Delsol, an assertive divorcee who lives on welfare because of a disabling affliction. Although her daughter, Elizabeth, experienced some early setbacks in grade school, Mrs. Delsol doggedly sought paths to uplift her. "We Cubans are not used to failure," she explained. She does not like being called Hispanic because:

> We all speak [Spanish] but there are differences. [Cubans] always had self-respect, a sense of cleanliness and duty towards children, a work ethic. Miami used to be a clean city until the Nicaraguans came and covered everything with graffiti.

About American blacks, Mrs. Delsol thinks they are adversarial to all kinds of people, disruptive, prone to ruin their homes, and lazy. In her view, both Nicaraguans and blacks evince attitudes opposite to those of Cubans.

Ironically, many Nicaraguans think of themselves as Hispanics precisely because they hold perceptions similar to those voiced by Mrs. Delsol. They experience a strong dissociational push away from their own national group. Sixteen-year-old Elsie Rivas avoids discrimination by shifting between a Hispanic and a Nicaraguan self-definition at school and at the supermarket where she works. She doesn't like the way Nicaraguans speak:

> They are vulgar, ignorant. . . . When I am with my Cuban friends I can speak to them normally, but some Nicaraguans make me feel ashamed and I am tempted to deny my nationality; they make all of us look bad because of the way they express themselves, with all the bad words and the cussing.

As the majority of immigrant children, Elsie's younger sister, Alicia, does not care for those distinctions. She feels "Nicaraguan-American because my parents came from Nicaragua and I like the food, but I am really American, more American than those born in this country; here is where I grew up and here is where I am going to stay."

The perceptions of immigrants and their children about themselves and other groups are not always accurate. However, what matters is that, as social constructions, those perceptions are an integral part of a process of segmented assimilation that will eventually yield what Bellah (1985) calls "communities of memory." In their journey, the immigrant children of today are already forging tomorrow's ethnic identities. Contact, friction, negotiation and their eventual incorporation into distinct sectors of the larger society will depend, in the final analysis, upon the insertion of immigrant children into various niches of the restructured economy. Collective self-definitions will improve or worsen depending upon the structure of opportunity.

CONCLUSIONS

Our purpose in this study has been to unfold the various meanings of assimilation for immigrants arriving into locations distinguished by an assortment of physical, social and economic characteristics. We have argued that a limited number of toponomical—that is, socially and physically situated—features determines the outcomes of migration. Our analysis was based on survey and ethnographic data about a small number of groups. However, we have noted that each group represents an experience associated not so much with cultural or national features, but with the attributes of its reception in areas of destination, the character of resources available to it, its degree of internal differentiation in terms of class, its degree of spatial concentration, and the length of time the group's coethnics have resided in the United States.

There is no mystery to tales of immigrant success or failure. The fates of immigrant children divide in consonance with the kind and quantity of economic opportunity. Economic globalization has fostered major transformations, including increasing demand for immigrant labor and the formation of transnational markets unlikely to disappear through purely legislative initiatives. The alternative for policy cannot be solely the regulation of immigrant streams to the exclusion of a more important aspect: the implementation of measures that facilitate the adjustment of new arrivals and increase their connection to the institutions of the larger society. The experience of Gainers shows that a welcoming reception in areas of destination—including government initiatives to facilitate immigrant adaptation—can have long-term benefits. The opposite is also true. Over extended periods of time, hostile receptions have had predictable results: isolation, social dismemberment and the concentration of behavioral pathologies. For policymakers the lesson is clear—the nightmare of an urban underclass need not be repeated among the protagonists of the new migration if we give attention to the lessons of the past.

Once established, immigrant networks acquire a degree of relative autonomy from market forces reducing the costs and risks of migration and promoting the flow of information. When they are internally stratified in terms of class, the spatial concentration of immigrants can yield advantages for the group to which they belong and for the larger society. This, too, has importance for immigration policy. In the 1960s, when the Cuban exile first began, millions of dollars were spent needlessly to scatter the banished around the United States in the belief that this best contributed to their social incorporation. Instead, Cubans gravitated back to Miami where the strength of numbers, connections and entrepreneurial know-how quickly translated into economic prosperity. Atomization and geographical dispersion could have had very different results.

Finally, we have begun a discussion of the ways in which immigrants shape identities through repeated interaction in empirical and symbolic fields with other ethnic groups. Our point has been to underscore the salience of collective self-definitions in the process of segmented assimilation. There is an interactive relationship between the opportunity structure and the way individuals and groups perceive themselves and others. The self-image of the immigrant is, ironically, a hopeful image often bolstered by negative definitions of other groups that have experienced arrested mobility. Whether those hopeful images survive will depend on whether immigrant children succeed or fail in the new economy.

REFERENCES

Baker, R. and W. Dodd, eds. 1926. *Public Papers of Woodrow Wilson.* New York: Harper.

Bellah, R. N. et al. 1985. *Habits of the Heart: Individualism and Commitment in American Life.* Berkeley: University of California Press.

Blauner, R. 1972. *Racial Oppression in America.* New York: Harper & Row.

Bonacich, E. 1980. "Class Approaches to Ethnicity and Race," *Insurgent Sociologist*, 10.

Bourne, R. 1916. *The Radical Will: Selected Writings.* New York: Urizen Books.

Coleman, J. 1988. "Social Capital in the Creation of Human Capital," *American Journal of Sociology (Supplement)*, S95–121.

Fernández-Kelly, M. P. 1994. "Towanda's Triumph: Social and Cultural Capital in the Transition to Adulthood in the Urban Ghetto," *International Journal of Urban and Regional Research*, 18(1): 89–111.

Frazier, E. F. 1957. *Race and Culture Contacts in the Modern World.* New York: Knopf.

Gordon, M. 1964. *Assimilation in American Life: The Role of Race, Religion, and National Origins.* New York: Oxford University Press.

Kasinitz, P. and J. Rosenberg. 1994. "Missing the Connection: Social Isolation and Employment on the Brooklyn Waterfront." Working Paper, Michael Harrington Center for Democratic Values and Social Change. Queens College of the City University of New York.

Kitano, H. and R. Daniels. 1988. *Asian Americans: Emerging Minorities.* Englewood Cliffs, NJ: Prentice Hall.

Matute-Bianchi, M. G. 1986. "Ethnic Identities and Patterns of School Success and Failure among Mexican-Descent and Japanese-American Students in a California High School," *American Journal of Education*, 95:233–255.

Park, R. 1950. *Race and Culture.* Glencoe, IL: The Free Press.

Portes, A. 1993. "The Longest Migration," *The New Republic*, 26:38–42. April.

Portes, A. and R. Bach. 1986. *Latin Journey: Cuban and Mexican Immigrants in the United States.* Berkeley: University of California Press.

Portes, A. and Rubén Rumbaut. 1990. *Immigrant America: A Portrait.* Berkeley: University of California Press.

Portes, A. and M. Zhou. 1993. "The New Second Generation: Segmented Assimilation and Its Variants," *Annals of the American Academy of Political and Social Science*, 530:74–96.

Roberts, B. 1995. "The Effect of Socially Expected Durations on Mexican Migration." In *The Economic Sociology of Immigration: Essays on Networks, Ethnicity, and Entrepreneurship.* New York: Russell Sage Foundation.

Sassen, S. 1995. "Immigration and Local Labor Markets." In *The Economic Sociology of Immigration: Essays on Networks, Ethnicity, and Entrepreneurship*. New York: Russell Sage Foundation.

Stepick, A. and C. Dutton-Stepick. 1994. "Preliminary Haitian Needs Assessment." Report to the City of Miami. June.

SOURCE: From *International Migration Review, 28,* 4: 662-689. Copyright © 1994. Reprinted by permission of International Migration Review, c/o Blackwell Publishing Ltd.

DISCUSSION QUESTIONS

1. Why do different ethnic groups, according to the authors, have such varied experiences in terms of how well they do economically upon arriving in the United States? Does the traditional assimilation model, which criticizes some groups for not doing well and praises others as "model minorities," take these differences into account?

2. If varying social networks result in unequal opportunities for different ethnic groups, should the government intervene to level the playing field? Why or why not?

3. Why do members of some Hispanic groups prefer the label "Latino" while others identify more with their particular ethnicity (for example, Nicaraguan)? How do negative racial stereotypes affect these identifications?

FIFTEEN YEARS ON THE BOTTOM RUNG

Anthony DePalma

In the dark before dawn, when Madison Avenue was all but deserted and its pricey boutiques were still locked up tight, several Mexicans slipped quietly into 3 Guys, a restaurant that the Zagat guide once called "the most expensive coffee shop in New York." . . . More Mexicans filed in to begin their shifts throughout the morning, and by the time John Zannikos, one of the restaurant's three Greek owners, drove in from the north Jersey suburbs to work the lunch crowd, Madison Avenue was buzzing. So was 3 Guys.

"You got to wait a little bit," Zannikos said to a pride of elegant women who had spent the morning at the Whitney Museum of American Art, across Madison Avenue at 75th Street. For an illiterate immigrant who came to New York years ago with nothing but $100 in his pocket and a willingness to work etched on his heart, could any words have been sweeter to say?

With its wealthy clientele, middle-class owners, and low-income workforce, 3 Guys is a template of the class divisions in America. But it is also the setting for two starkly different tales about breaching those divides. The familiar story is Zannikos's. For him, the restaurant—don't dare call it a diner—with its twenty-dollar salads and elegant décor represents the American promise of upward mobility, one that has been fulfilled countless times for generations of hardworking immigrants. But for Juan Manuel Peralta, a thirty-four-year-old illegal immigrant who worked there for five years until he was fired in May 2004[1], and for many of the other illegal Mexican immigrants in the back, restaurant work today is more like a dead end. They are finding the American dream of moving up far more elusive than it was for Zannikos. Despite his efforts to help them, they risk becoming stuck in a permanent underclass of the poor, the unskilled, and the uneducated.

That is not to suggest that the nearly five million Mexicans who, like Peralta, are living in the United States illegally will never emerge from the shadows. Many have, and undoubtedly many more will. But the sheer size of the influx—over 400,000 a year, with no end in sight—creates a problem all its own. It means there is an ever-growing pool of interchangeable workers, many of them shunting from one low-paying job to another. If one moves on, another one—or maybe two or three—is there to take his place.

Although Peralta arrived in New York almost forty years after Zannikos, the two share a remarkably similar beginning. They came at the same age to the same section of New York City, without legal papers or more than a few words of English. Each dreamed of a better life. But monumental changes in the economy and in attitudes toward immigrants have made it far less likely that Peralta and his children will experience the same upward mobility as Zannikos and his family.

Of course, there is a chance that Peralta may yet take his place among the Mexican-Americans who have succeeded here. He realizes that he will probably not do as well as the few who have risen to high office or who were able to buy the vineyards where their grandfathers once picked grapes. But he still dreams that his children will someday join the millions who have lost their accents, gotten good educations, and firmly achieved the American dream.

Political scientists are divided over whether the twenty-five million people of Mexican ancestry in the United States represent an exception to the classic immigrant success story. Some, like John H. Mollenkopf at the City University of New York, are convinced that Mexicans will eventually do as well as the Greeks, Italians, and other Europeans of the last century who were usually well assimilated after two or three generations. Others, including Mexican-Americans like Rodolfo O. de la Garza, a professor at Columbia, have done studies showing that Mexican-Americans face so many obstacles that even the fourth generation trails other Americans in education, home ownership, and household income.

The situation is even worse for the millions more who have illegally entered the United States since 1990. Spread out in scores of cities far beyond the Southwest, they find jobs plentiful but advancement difficult. President Vicente Fox of Mexico was forced to apologize in the spring of 2005 for declaring publicly what many Mexicans say they feel, that the illegal immigrants "are doing the work that not even blacks want to do in the United States." Resentment and race subtly stand in their way, as does a lingering attachment to Mexico, which is so close that many immigrants do not put down deep roots here. They say they plan to stay only long enough to make some money and then go back home. Few ever do. But the biggest obstacle is their illegal status. With few routes open to become legal, they remain, like Peralta, without rights, without security, and without a clear path to a better future. . . .

Little has changed for Peralta, a cook who has worked at menial jobs in the United States for fifteen years. Though he makes more than he ever dreamed of in Mexico, his life is anything but middle class and setbacks are routine. Still, he has not given up hope. "*Querer es poder,*" he sometimes says—want something badly enough and you will get it.

But desire may not be enough anymore. That is what concerns Arturo Sarukhan, Mexico's consul general in New York. In early 2005, Sarukhan took an urgent call from New York's police commissioner about an increase in gang activity among young Mexican men, a sign that they were moving into the underside of American life. Of all immigrants in New York City, officials say, Mexicans are the poorest, least educated, and least likely to speak English. The failure or success of this generation of Mexicans in the United States will determine the place that Mexicans will hold here in years to come, Sarukhan said, and the outlook is not encouraging. "They will be better off than they could ever have been in Mexico," he said, "but I don't think that's going to be enough to prevent them from becoming an underclass in New York."

DIFFERENT RESULTS

. . . "My life story is a good story, a lot of success," Zannikos said, his accent still heavy. He was just a teenager when he left the Greek island of Chios, a few miles off the coast of Turkey. World War II had just ended, and Greece was in ruins. "There was only rich and poor, that's it," Zannikos said. "There was no middle class like you have here." He is seventy now, with short gray hair and soft eyes that can water at a mention of the past.

Because of the war, he said, he never got past the second grade, never learned to read or write. He signed on as a merchant seaman, and in 1953, when he was nineteen, his ship docked at Norfolk, Virginia. He went ashore one Saturday with no intention of ever returning to Greece. He left behind everything, including his travel documents. All he had in his pockets was $100 and the address of his mother's cousin in the Jackson Heights–Corona section of Queens.

Almost four decades later, Juan Manuel Peralta underwent a similar rite of passage out of Mexico. He had finished the eighth grade in the poor southern state of Guerrero and saw nothing in his future there but fixing flat tires. His father, Inocencio, had once dreamed of going to the United States, but never had the money. In 1990, he borrowed enough to give his firstborn son a chance.

Peralta was nineteen when he boarded a smoky bus that carried him through the deserted hills of Guerrero and kept going until it reached the edge of Mexico. With eight other Mexicans he did not know, he crawled through a sewer tunnel that started in Tijuana and ended on the other side of the border, in what Mexicans call El Norte.

He had carried no documents, no photographs, and no money except what his father gave him to pay his shifty guide and to buy an airline ticket to New York. Deep in a pocket was the address of an uncle in the same section of Queens where John Zannikos had gotten his start. By 1990, the area had gone from largely Greek to mostly Latino.

Starting over in the same working-class neighborhood, Peralta and Zannikos quickly learned that New York was full of opportunities and obstacles, often in equal measure. On his first day there, Zannikos, scared and feeling lost, found the building he was looking for, but his mother's cousin had moved. He had no idea what to do until a Greek man passed by. Walk five blocks to the Deluxe Diner, the man said. He did.

The diner was full of Greek housepainters, including one who knew Zannikos's father. On the spot, they offered him a job painting closets, where his mistakes would be hidden. He painted until the weather turned cold. Another Greek hired him as a dishwasher at his coffee shop in the Bronx.

It was not easy, but Zannikos worked his way up to short-order cook, learning English as he went along. In 1956, immigration officials raided the coffee shop. He was deported, but after a short while he managed to sneak back into the country. Three years later he married a Puerto Rican from the Bronx. The marriage lasted only a year, but it put him on the road to becoming a citizen. Now he could buy his own restaurant, a greasy spoon in the South Bronx that catered to a late-night clientele of prostitutes and undercover police officers.

Since, then, he has bought and sold more than a dozen New York diners, but none have been more successful than the original 3 Guys, which opened in 1978. He and his partners own two other restaurants with the same name farther up Madison Avenue, but they have never replicated the high-end appeal of the original.

"When employees come in, I teach them, 'Hey, this is a different neighborhood,'" Zannikos said. What may be standard in some other diners is not tolerated here. There are no Greek flags or tourism posters. There is no television or twirling tower of cakes with cream pompadours. Waiters are forbidden to chew gum. No customer is ever called "Honey." "They know their place and I know my place," Zannikos said of his customers. "It's as simple as that."

His place in society now is a far cry from his days in the Bronx. He and his second wife, June, live in Wyckoff, a New Jersey suburb where he pampers fig trees and dutifully looks after a bird feeder shaped like the Parthenon. They own a condominium in Florida. His three children all went far beyond his second-grade education, finishing high school or attending college.

They have all done well, as has Zannikos, who says he makes about $130,000 a year. He says he is not sensitive to class distinctions, but he admits he was bothered when some people mistook him for the caterer at fund-raising dinners for the local Greek church he helped build.

All in all, he thinks immigrants today have a better chance of moving up the class ladder than he did fifty years ago. "At that time, no bank would give us any money, but today they give you credit cards in the mail," he said. "New York still gives you more opportunity than any other place. If you want to do things, you will." . . .

A Divisive Issue

Juan Manuel Peralta cannot guess what class John Zannikos belongs to. But he is certain that it is much tougher for an immigrant to get ahead today than fifty years ago. And he has no doubt about his own class. "*La pobreza,*" he says. "Poverty."

It was not what he expected when he boarded the bus to the border, but it did not take long for him to realize that success in the United States required more than hard work. "A lot of it has to do with luck," he said during a lunch break on a stoop around the corner from the Queens diner where he went to work after 3 Guys. "People come here, and in no more than a year or two they can buy their town house and have a car," Peralta said. "Me, I've been here fifteen years, and if I die tomorrow, there wouldn't even be enough money to bury me."

In 1990, Peralta was in the vanguard of Mexican immigrants who bypassed the traditional barrios in border states to work in far-flung cities like Denver and New York. The 2000 census counted 186,872 Mexicans in New York, triple the 1990 figure, and there are undoubtedly many more today. The Mexican consulate, which serves the metropolitan region, has issued more than 500,000 ID cards just since 2001. Fifty years ago, illegal immigration was a minor problem. Now it is a divisive national issue, pitting those who welcome cheap labor against those with concerns about border security and the cost of providing social services. Though newly arrived Mexicans often work in industries that rely on cheap labor, like restaurants and construction, they rarely organize. Most are desperate to stay out of sight.

Peralta hooked up with his uncle the morning he arrived in New York. He did not work for weeks until the bakery where the uncle worked had an opening, a part-time job making muffins. He took it, though he didn't know muffins from crumb cake. When he saw that he would not make enough to repay his father, he took a second job making night deliveries for a Manhattan diner. By the end of his first day he was so lost he had to spend all his tip money on a cab ride home.

He quit the diner, but working there even briefly opened his eyes to how easy it could be to make money in New York. Diners were everywhere, and so were jobs making deliveries, washing dishes, or busing tables. In six months, Peralta had paid back the money his father gave him. He bounced from job to job and in 1995, eager to show off his newfound success, went back to Mexico with his pockets full of money, and married. He was twenty-five then, the same age at which Zannikos married. But the similarities end there.

When Zannikos jumped ship, he left Greece behind for good. Though he himself had no documents, the compatriots he encountered on his first days were here legally, like most other Greek immigrants, and could help him. Greeks had never come to the United States in large numbers—the 2000 census counted only 28,805 New Yorkers born in Greece—but they tended to settle in just a few areas, like the Astoria section of Queens, which became cohesive communities ready to help new arrivals.

Peralta, like many other Mexicans, is trying to make it on his own and has never severed his emotional or financial ties to home. After five years in New York's Latino community, he spoke little English and owned little more than the clothes on his back. He decided to return to Huamuxtitlán, the dusty village beneath a flat-topped mountain where he was born.

"People thought that since I was coming back from El Norte, I would be so rich that I could spread money around," he said. Still, he felt privileged: his New York wages dwarfed the $1,000 a year he might have made in Mexico. He met a shy, pretty girl named Matilde in Huamuxtitlán, married her, and returned with her to New York, again illegally, all in a matter of weeks. Their first child was born in 1996. Peralta soon found that supporting a family made it harder to save money. Then, in 1999, he got the job at 3 Guys.

"Barba Yanni helped me learn how to prepare things the way customers like them," Peralta said, referring to Zannikos with a Greek title of respect that means Uncle John. The restaurant became his school. He learned how to sauté a fish so that it looked like a work of art. The three partners lent him money and said they would help him get immigration documents. The pay was good. But there were tensions with the other workers. Instead of hanging their orders on a rack, the waiters shouted them out, in Greek, Spanish, and a kind of fractured English. Sometimes Peralta did not understand, and they argued. Soon he was known as a hothead.

Still, he worked hard, and every night he returned to his growing family. Matilde, now twenty-seven, cleaned houses until their second child, Heidi, was born in 2002. Now Matilde tries to sell Mary Kay products to other mothers at Public School 12, which their son Antony, who is eight, attends.

Most weeks, Peralta could make as much as $600. Over the course of a year that could come to over $30,000, enough to approach the lower middle class. But the life he leads is far from that and uncertainty hovers over everything about his life, starting with his paycheck.

To earn $600, he has to work at least ten hours a day, six days a week, and that does not happen every week. Sometimes he is paid overtime for the extra hours, sometimes not. And, as he found out, he can be fired at any time and bring in nothing, not even unemployment, until he lands another job. In 2004, he made about $24,000.

Because he is here illegally, Peralta can easily be exploited. He cannot file a complaint against his landlord for charging him $500 a month for a nine- by nine-foot room in a Queens apartment that he shares with nine other Mexicans in three families who pay the remainder of the $2,000-a month rent. All thirteen share one bathroom, and the established pecking order means the Peraltas rarely get to use the kitchen. Eating out can be expensive.

Because they were born in New York, Peralta's children are United States citizens, and their health care is generally covered by Medicaid. But he has to pay out of his pocket whenever he or his wife sees a doctor. And forget about going to the dentist.

As many other Mexicans do, he wires money home, and it costs him $7 for every $100 he sends. When his uncle, his nephew, and his sister asked him for money, he was expected to lend it. No one has paid him back. . . .

PROGRESS, BUT NOT SUCCESS

. . . The swirl of immigrants in Peralta's neighborhood is part of the fabric of New York, just as it was in 1953, when John Zannikos arrived. But most immigrants then were Europeans, and though they spoke different languages, their Caucasian features helped them blend into New York's middle class. Experts remain divided over whether Mexicans can follow the same route. Samuel P. Huntington, a Harvard professor of government, takes the extreme view that Mexicans will not assimilate and that the separate culture they are developing threatens the United States.

Most others believe that recent Mexican immigrants will eventually take their place in society, and perhaps someday muster political clout commensurate with their numbers, though significant impediments are slowing their progress. Francisco Rivera-Batiz, a Columbia University economics professor, says that prejudice remains a problem, that factory jobs have all but disappeared, and that there is a growing gap between the educational demands of the economy and the limited schooling that the newest Mexicans have when they arrive.

But the biggest obstacle by far, and the one that separates newly arrived Mexicans from Greeks, Italians, and most other immigrants— including earlier generations of Mexicans—is their illegal status. Rivera-Batiz studied what happened to illegal Mexican immigrants who became legal after the last national amnesty in 1986. Within a few years, there incomes rose 20 percent and their English improved greatly. "Legalization," he said, "helped them tremendously." Although the Bush administration talks about legalizing some Mexicans with a guest workers program, there is opposition to another amnesty, and the number of Mexicans illegally living in the United States continues to soar. Desperate to get their papers any way they can, many turn to shady storefront legal offices. Like Peralta, they sign on to illusory schemes that cost hundreds of dollars but almost never produce the promised green cards.

Until the 1980s, Mexican immigration was largely seasonal and mostly limited to agricultural workers. But then economic chaos in Mexico sent a flood of immigrants northward, many of them poorly educated farmers from the impoverished countryside. Tighter security on the border made it harder for Mexicans to move back and forth in the traditional way, so they tended to stay here, searching for low-paying unskilled jobs and concentrating in barrios where Spanish, constantly replenished, never loses its immediacy. . . . Even now, after fifteen years in New York, Peralta speaks little English. He tried English classes once, but could not get his mind to accept the new sounds. So he dropped it, and has stuck with Spanish, which he concedes is "the language of busboys" in New York. But as long as he stays in his neighborhood, it is all he needs. . . .

Peralta's . . . run-down house, the overheated room, the stacked mattress, and the hoarded toilet paper—all remind him how far he would have to go to achieve a success like John Zannikos's. . . . Still, he says, he has done far better than he could ever have done in Mexico. He realizes that the money he sends to his family there is not enough to satisfy his father. . . . He said his father's images of America came from another era. The older man does not know how tough it is to be a Mexican immigrant in the United States now, tougher than any young man who ever left Huamuxtitlán would admit. Everything built up over fifteen years here can fall apart as easily as an adobe house in an earthquake. And then it is time to start over, again.

NOTE

1. Peralta was fired shortly after joining with an immigrant labor rights center to protest his treatment and lack of opportunities there.

SOURCE: From *Class Matters* by correspondents of the New York Times. Copyright © 2005 The New York Times Co. Reprinted with permission.

DISCUSSION QUESTIONS

1. What are some of the differences between the "old" immigrants like Zannikos and the "new" immigrants like Peralta in terms of cultural, geographic, economic, political, and other structural factors? How do simplistic explanations like "hard work" as a route to immigrant success measure up to these other factors?

2. Why is speaking English such an important part of the public debate about immigration? If Peralta and his family learned how to speak better English, could their class status eventually approximate that of the Zannikos family? If not, what else would need to change?

3. How might immigration policy change in the future to give the Peraltas out there the same chances for economic success that the Zannikoses had? Could there be other public policies might equalize their chances?

4. How has maintaining economic relationships with family members in one's home country affected the immigrant experience? Do you think Mexican immigrants are alone in maintaining such ties? How would global economic policy need to shift in order to change these symbiotic relationships that stunt the economic stability of these "new Americans"?

"OPENING" FACES: THE POLITICS OF COSMETIC SURGERY AND ASIAN AMERICAN WOMEN

Eugenia Kaw

Ellen, a Chinese American in her forties, informed me she had had her upper eyelids surgically cut and sewed by a plastic surgeon twenty years ago in order to get rid of "the sleepy look," which her naturally "puffy" eyes gave her. She pointed out that the sutures, when they healed, became a crease above the eye which gave the eyes a more "open appearance." She was quick to tell me that her decision to undergo "double-eyelid" surgery was not so much because she was vain or had low self-esteem, but rather because the "undesirability" of her looks before the surgery was an undeniable fact.

During my second interview with Ellen, she showed me photos of herself from before and after her surgery in order to prove her point. When Stacy, her twelve-year-old daughter, arrived home from school, Ellen told me she wanted Stacy to undergo similar surgery in the near future because Stacy has only single eyelids and would look prettier and be more successful in life if she had a fold above each eye. Ellen brought the young girl to where I was sitting and said, "You see, if you look at her you will know what I mean when I say that I had to have surgery done on my eyelids. Look at her eyes. She looks just like me before the surgery." Stacy seemed very shy to show me her face. But I told the girl truthfully that she looked fine and beautiful the way she was. Immediately she grinned at her mother in a mocking, defiant manner, as if I had given her courage, and put her arm up in the manner that bodybuilders do when they display their bulging biceps.

As empowered as Stacy seemed to feel at the moment, I could not help but wonder how many times Ellen had shown her "before" and "after" photos to her young daughter with the remark that "Mommy looks better after the surgery." I also wondered how many times Stacy had been asked by Ellen to consider surgically "opening" her eyes like "Mommy did." And I wondered about the images we see on television and in magazines and their often negative, stereotypical portrayal of "squinty-eyed" Asians (when Asians are featured at all). I could not help but wonder how normal it is to feel that an eye without a crease is undesirable and how much of that feeling is imposed. And I shuddered to think how soon it might be before twelve-year-old Stacy's defenses gave away and she allowed her eyes to be cut.

The permanent alteration of bodies through surgery for aesthetic purposes is not a new phenomenon in the United States. As early as World War I, when reconstructive surgery was performed on disfigured soldiers, plastic surgery methods began to be refined for purely cosmetic purposes (that is, not so much for repairing and restoring but for transforming natural features a person is unhappy with). Within the last decade, however, an increasing number of people have opted for a wide array of cosmetic surgery procedures, from tummy tucks, facelifts, and liposuction to enlargement of chests and calves. By 1988, two million Americans had undergone cosmetic surgery (Wolf, 1991:218), and a 69 percent increase had occurred in the number of cosmetic surgery procedures between 1981 and 1990, according to the ASPRS, or American Society of Plastic and Reconstructive Surgeons (n.d.).

Included in these numbers are an increasing number of cosmetic surgeries undergone by people like Stacy who are persons of color (American Academy of Cosmetic Surgery press release, 1991). In fact, Asian Americans are more likely than any other ethnic group (white or nonwhite) to pursue cosmetic surgery. ASPRS reports that over thirty-nine thousand of the aesthetic procedures performed by its members in 1990 (or more than 6 percent of all procedures performed that year) were performed on Asian Americans, who make up 3 percent of the U.S. population (Chen, 1993:15). Because Asian Americans seek cosmetic surgery from doctors in Asia and from doctors who specialize in fields other than surgery (e.g., ear, nose, and throat specialists and ophthalmologists), the total number of Asian American patients is undoubtedly higher (Chen 1993:16).

The specific procedures requested by different ethnic groups in the United States are missing from the national data, but newspaper reports and medical texts indicate that Caucasians and nonwhites, on the average, seek significantly different types of operations (Chen, 1993; Harahap, 1982; Kaw, 1993; LeFlore, 1982; McCurdy, 1980; Nakao, 1993; Rosenthal, 1991). While Caucasians primarily seek to augment breasts and to remove wrinkles and fat through such procedures as facelifts, liposuction, and collagen injection, African Americans more often opt for lip and nasal reduction operations; Asian Americans more often choose to insert an implant on their nasal dorsum for a more prominent nose or undergo double-eyelid surgery whereby parts of their upper eyelids are excised to create a fold above each eye, which makes the eye appear wider.

Though the American media, the medical establishment, and the general public have debated whether such cosmetic changes by nonwhite persons reflect a racist milieu in which racial minorities must deny their racial identity and attempt to look more Caucasian, a resounding no appears to be the overwhelming opinion of people in the United States. . . . Much of the media and public opinion also suggests that there is no political significance inherent in the cosmetic changes made by people of color which alter certain conventionally known, phenotypic markers of racial identity. On a recent Phil Donahue show where the racially derogatory nature of blue contact lenses for African American women was contested, both white and nonwhite audience members were almost unanimous that African American women's use of these lenses merely reflected their freedom to choose in the same way that Bo Derek chose to wear corn rows and white people decided to get tans (Bordo, 1990). . . . When critics speculate on the possibility that a person of color is attempting to look white, they often focus their attack on the person and his or her apparent lack of ethnic pride and self esteem. For instance, a *Newsweek* article, referring to Michael Jackson's recent television interview with Oprah Winfrey, questioned Jackson's emphatic claim that he is proud to be a black American (Fleming & Talbot, 1993:57). Such criticisms, sadly, center around Michael Jackson the person instead of delving into his possible feelings of oppression or examining society as a potential source of his motivation to alter his natural features so radically.

. . . Based on structured, open-ended interviews with Asian American women like Ellen who have or are thinking about undergoing cosmetic surgery for wider eyes and more heightened noses, I attempt to convey more emphatically the lived social experiences of people of color who seek what appears to be conventionally recognized Caucasian features. Rather than mock their decision to alter their features or treat it lightly as an expression of their freedom to choose an idiosyncratic look, I examine everyday cultural images and social relationships which influence Asian American women to seek cosmetic surgery in the first place. Instead of focusing, as some doctors do (Kaw, 1993), on the size and width of the eyelid folds the women request as indicators of the women's desire to look Caucasian, I examine the cultural, social, and historical sources that allow the women in my study to view their eyes in a negative fashion—as "small" and "slanted"

eyes reflecting a "dull," "passive" personality, a "closed" mind, and a "lack of spirit" in the person. I explore the reasons these women reject the natural shape of their eyes so radically that they willingly expose themselves to a surgery that is at least an hour long, costs one thousand to three thousand dollars, entails administering local anesthesia and sedation, and carries the following risks: "bleeding and hematoma," "hemorrhage," formation of a "gaping wound," "discoloration," scarring, and "asymmetric lid folds" (Sayoc, 1974:162–166).

In our feminist analyses of femininity and beauty we may sometimes find it difficult to account for cosmetic surgery without undermining the thoughts and decisions of women who opt for it (Davis, 1991). However, I attempt to show that the decision of the women in my study to undergo cosmetic surgery is often carefully thought out. Such a decision is usually made only after a long period of weighing the psychological pain of feeling inadequate prior to surgery against the possible social advantages a new set of features may bring. Several of the women were aware of complex power structures that construct their bodies as inferior and in need of change, even while they simultaneously reproduced these structures by deciding to undergo surgery (Davis, 1991:33).

I argue that as women and as racial minorities, the psychological burden of having to measure up to ideals of beauty in American society falls especially heavy on these Asian-American women. As women, they are constantly bombarded with the notion that beauty should be their primary goal (Lakoff & Scherr, 1984; Wolf, 1991). As racial minorities, they are made to feel inadequate by an Anglo American dominated cultural milieu that has historically both excluded them and distorted images of them in such a way that they themselves have come to associate those features stereotypically identified with their race (i.e., small, slanty eyes, and a flat nose) with negative personality and mental characteristics.

In a consumption-oriented society such as the United States, it is often tempting to believe that human beings have an infinite variety of needs which technology can endlessly fulfill, and that these needs, emerging spontaneously in time and space, lack any coherent patterns, cultural meanings, or political significance (Bordo, 1991; Goldstein, 1993; O'Neill, 1985:98). However, one cannot regard needs as spontaneous, infinite, harmless, and amorphous without first considering what certain groups feel they lack and without first critically examining the lens with which the larger society has historically viewed this lack . . .

Method and Description of Subjects

In this article, I present the findings of an ethnographic research project completed in the San Francisco Bay Area. I draw on data from structured interviews with doctors and patients, basic medical statistics, and relevant newspaper and magazine articles. The sampling of informants for this research was not random in the strictly statistical sense since informants were difficult to find. Both medical practitioners and patients treat cases of cosmetic surgery as highly confidential. To find a larger, more random sampling of Asian American informants, I posted fliers and placed advertisements in various local newspapers. Ultimately, I was able to conduct structured, open-ended interviews with eleven Asian American women, four of whom were referred to me by the doctors in my study and six by mutual acquaintances; I found one through an advertisement. Nine had had cosmetic surgery of the eye or the nose; one recently considered a double-eyelid operation; one is considering undergoing a double-eyelid operation in the

next few years. . . . The ages of the Asian American women in my study range from eighteen to seventy-one; one woman was only fifteen at the time of her operation. Their class backgrounds are similar in that they were all engaged in middle-class, white-collar occupations.

Although I have not interviewed Asian American men who have or are thinking of undergoing cosmetic surgery, I realize that they too undergo double-eyelid and nose bridge operations. Their motivations are, to a large extent, similar to those of the women in my study (Iwata, 1991). Often their decision to undergo surgery also follows a long and painful process of feeling marginal in society (Iwata, 1991). I did not purposely exclude Asian American male patients from my study; rather, none responded to my requests for interviews. To understand how plastic surgeons view the cosmetic procedures performed on Asian Americans, five structured, open-ended interviews were conducted with five plastic surgeons, all of whom practice in the Bay Area. I also examined several medical books and plastic surgery journals which date from the 1950s to 1990. And I referenced several news releases and informational packets distributed by such national organizations as the American Society of Plastic and Reconstructive Surgeons, an organization which represents 97 percent of all physicians certified by the American Board of Plastic Surgery.

To examine popular notions of cosmetic surgery, in particular how the phenomenon of Asian American women receiving double-eyelid and nose bridge operations is viewed by the public and the media, I have referenced relevant newspaper and magazine articles.

I obtained national data on cosmetic surgery from various societies for cosmetic surgeons, including the American Society of Plastic and Reconstructive Surgeons. Data on the specific types of surgery sought by different ethnic groups in the United States, including Asian Americans, were missing from the national statistics. At least one public relations coordinator told me that such data are unimportant to plastic surgeons. To compensate for this lack of data, I asked the doctors in my study to provide me with figures from their respective clinics. Most told me they had little data on their cosmetic patients readily available.

Colonization of Asian American Women's Souls: Internalization of Gender and Racial Stereotypes

Upon first talking with my Asian American women informants, one might conclude that the women were merely seeking to enhance their features for aesthetic reasons and that there is no cultural meaning or political significance in their decision to surgically enlarge their eyes and heighten their noses. As Elena, a twenty-one-year-old Chinese American who underwent double-eyelid surgery three years ago from a doctor in my study, stated: "I underwent my surgery for personal reasons. It's not different from wanting to put makeup on. . . . I don't intend to look Anglo-Saxon. I told my doctor, 'I would like my eyes done with definite creases on my eyes, but I don't want a drastic change.'" Almost all the other women similarly stated that their unhappiness with their eyes and nose was individually motivated and that they really did not desire Caucasian features. In fact, one Korean American woman, Nina, age thirty-four, stated she was not satisfied with the results of her surgery from three years ago because her doctor made her eyes " too round" like that of Caucasians. One might deduce from such statements that the women's decision to undergo cosmetic surgery of the eye and nose is harmless and may be even empowering to

them, for their surgery provides them with a more permanent solution than makeup for "personal" dissatisfactions they have about their features.

However, an examination of their descriptions of the natural shape of their eyes and nose suggests that their "personal" feelings about their features reflect the larger society's negative valuation and stereotyping of Asian features in general. They all said that "small, slanty" eyes and a "flat" nose suggest, in the Asian person, a personality that is "dull," "unenergetic," "passive," and "unsociable," and a mind that is narrow and "closed." For instance, Elena said, "When I look at other Asians who have no folds and their eyes are slanted and closed, I think of how they would look better more awake." Nellee, a twenty-one-year-old Chinese American, said that she seriously considered surgery for double eyelids in high school so that she could "avoid the stereotype of the 'oriental bookworm'" who is "dull and doesn't know how to have fun." Carol, a thirty-seven-year-old Chinese American who received double eyelids seven years ago, said: "The eyes are the window of your soul . . . [yet] lots of oriental people have the outer corners of their eyes a little down, making them look tired. [The double eyelids] don't make a big difference in the size of our eyes but they give your eyes more spirit." Pam, a Chinese American, age forty-four, who received double-eyelid surgery from another doctor in my study, stated, "Yes. Of course. Bigger eyes look prettier. . . . Lots of Asians' eyes are so small they become little lines when the person laughs, making the person look sleepy." Likewise, Annie, an eighteen-year-old Korean American woman who had an implant placed on her nasal dorsum to build up her nose bridge at age fifteen, said: "I guess I always wanted that sharp look—a look like you are smart. If you have a roundish kind of nose it's like you don't know what's going on. If you have that sharp look, you know, with black eyebrows, a pointy nose, you look more alert. I always thought that was cool." The women were influenced by the larger society's negative valuation of stereotyped Asian features in such a way that they evaluated themselves and Asian women in general with a critical eye. Their judgments were based on a set of standards, stemming from the eighteenth- and nineteenth-century European aesthetic ideal of the proportions in Greek sculpture, which are presumed by a large amount of Americans to be within the grasp of every woman (Goldstein, 1993:150, 160).

Unlike many white women who may also seek cosmetic surgery to reduce or make easier the daily task of applying makeup, the Asian American women in my study hoped more specifically to ease the task of creating with makeup the illusion of features they do not have as women who are Asian. . . . Jo, a twenty-eight-year-old Japanese American who already has natural folds above each eye but wishes to enlarge them through double-eyelid surgery, explained:

> I guess I just want to make a bigger eyelid [fold] so that they look bigger and not slanted. I think in Asian eyes it's the inside corner of the fold [she was drawing on my notebook] that goes down too much. . . . Right now I am still self-conscious about leaving the house without any makeup on, because I feel just really ugly without it. I try to curl my eyelashes and put on mascara. I think it makes my eyes look more open. But surgery can permanently change the shape of my eyes. I don't think that a bigger eyelid fold will actually change the slant but I think it will give the perception of having less of it, less of an Asian eye.

For the women in my study, their oppression is a double encounter: one under patriarchal definitions of femininity (i.e., that a woman should care about the superficial details of her look), and the other under Caucasian standards of beauty. The constant self-monitoring of their anatomy and their continuous focus on detail exemplify the extent to which they feel they must measure up to society's ideals.

In the United States, where a capitalist work ethic values "freshness," "a quick wit," and assertiveness, many Asian American women are already disadvantaged at birth by virtue of their inherited physical features which society associates with dullness and passivity. In this way, their desire to look more spirited and energetic through the surgical creation of folds above each eye is of a different quality from the motivation of many Anglo Americans seeking facelifts and liposuction for a fresher, more youthful appearance. Signs of aging are not the main reason Asian American cosmetic patients ultimately seek surgery of the eyes and the nose; often they are younger (usually between eighteen and thirty years of age) than the average Caucasian patient (Kaw, 1993). Several of the Asian American women in my study who were over thirty years of age at the time of their eyelid operation sought surgery to get rid of extra folds of skin that had developed over their eyes due to age; however, even these women decided to receive double eyelids in the process. When Caucasian patients undergo eyelid surgery, on the other hand, the procedure is almost never to create a double eyelid (for they already possess one); in most cases, it is to remove sagging skin that results from aging. Clearly, Asian American women's negative image of their eyes and nose is not so much a result of their falling short of the youthful, energetic beauty ideal that influences every American as it is a direct product of society's racial stereotyping.

The women in my study described their own features with metaphors of dullness and passivity in keeping with many Western stereotypes of Asians. Stereotypes, by definition, are expedient caricatures of the "other," which serve to set them apart from the "we"; they serve to exclude instead of include, to judge instead of accept (Gilman, 1985:15). Asians are rarely portrayed in the American print and electronic media. For instance, Asians (who constitute 3 percent of the U.S. population) account for less than 1 percent of the faces represented in magazine ads, according to a 1991 study titled "Invisible People" conducted by New York City's Department of Consumer Affairs (cited in Chen, 1993:26). When portrayed, they are seen in one of two forms, which are not representative of Asians in general: as Eurasian-looking fashion models and movie stars (e.g., Nancy Kwan who played Suzie Wong) who already have double eyelids and pointy noses; and as stereotypically Asian characters such as Charlie Chan, depicted with personalities that are dull, passive, and nonsociable (Dower, 1986; Kim, 1986; Ramsdell, 1983; Tajima, 1989). The first group often serves as an ideal toward which Asian American women strive, even when they say they do not want to look Caucasian. The second serves as an image from which they try to escape.

Asian stereotypes, like all kinds of stereotypes, are multiple and have changed throughout the years; nevertheless they have maintained some distinct characteristics. Asians have been portrayed as exotic and erotic (as epitomized by Suzie Wong, or the Japanese temptress in the film *The Berlin Affair),* and especially during the U.S. war in the Pacific during World War II, they were seen as dangerous spies and mad geniuses who were treacherous and stealthy (Dower, 1986; Hurh & Kim, 1989). However, what remains consistent in the American popular image of Asians is their childishness, narrow-mindedness, and lack of leadership skills. Moreover, these qualities have long been associated with the relatively roundish form of Asian faces, and in particular with the "puffy" smallness of their eyes. Prior to the Japanese attack on

Pearl Harbor, for instance, the Japanese were considered incapable of planning successful dive bombing attacks due to their "myopic," "squinty" eyes. During the war in the Pacific, their soldiers were caricatured as having thick horn-rimmed glasses through which they must squint to see their targets (Dower, 1986). Today, the myopic squinty-eyed image of thc narrow-minded Asian persists in the most recent stereotype of Asians as "model minorities" (as epitomized in the Asian exchange student character in the film *Sixteen Candles).* The term *model minority* was first coined in the 1960s when a more open-door U.S. immigration policy began allowing an unprecedented number of Asian immigrants into the United States, many of whom were the most elite and educated of their own countries (Takaki, 1989). Despite its seemingly complimentary nature, *model minority* refers to a person who is hardworking and technically skilled but desperately lacking in creativity, worldliness, and the ability to assimilate into mainstream culture (Hurh & Kim, 1989; Takaki, 1989). Representations in the media, no matter how subtle, of various social situations can distort and reinforce one's impressions of one's own nature (Goffman, 1979).

Witnessing society's association of Asian features with negative personality traits and mental characteristics, many Asian Americans become attracted to the image of Caucasian, or at least Eurasian, features. Several of the women in my study stated that they are influenced by images of fashion models with Western facial types. As Nellee explained: "I used to read a lot of fashion magazines which showed Occidental persons how to put makeup on. So I used to think a crease made one's eyes prettier. It exposes your eyelashes more. Right now they all go under the hood of my eyes." Likewise, Jo said she thought half of her discontent regarding her eyes is a self-esteem problem, but she blames the other half on society: "When you look at all the stuff that they portray on TV and in the movies and in Miss America Pageants, the epitome of who is beautiful is that all-American look. It can even include African Americans now but not Asians." According to Jo, she is influenced not only by representations of Asians as passive, dull, and narrow-minded, but also by a lack of representation of Asians in general because society considers them un-American, unassimilable, foreign, and to be excluded.

Similar images of Asians also exist in East and Southeast Asia, and since many Asian Americans are immigrants from Asia, they are likely influenced by these images as well. . . .

Jane, a twenty-year-old Korean American who underwent double-eyelid surgery at age sixteen and nasal bridge surgery at age eighteen, thumbed through Korean fashion magazines which she stored in her living room to show me photos of the Western and Korean models who she thought looked Caucasian, Eurasian, or had had double-eyelid and nasal bridge surgeries. She said these women had eyes that were too wide and noses that were too tall and straight to be on Asians. Though she was born and raised in the United States, she visits her relatives in Korea often. She explained that the influences the media had on her life in Korea and in the United States were, in some sense, similar: "When you turn on the TV [in Korea] you see people like Madonna and you see MTV and American movies and magazines. In any fashion magazine you don't really see a Korean-type woman; you see Cindy Crawford. My mother was telling me that when she was a kid, the ideal beauty was someone with a totally round, flat face. Kind of small and five feet tall. I guess things began to change in the 1950s when Koreans started to have a lot of contact with the West." The environment within which Asian women develop a perspective on the value and meaning of their facial features is

most likely not identical in Asia and the United States, where Asian women are a minority, but in Asia one can still be influenced by Western perceptions of Asians. . . .

In the present global economy, where the movement of people and cultural products is increasingly rapid and frequent and the knowledge of faraway places and trends is expanding, it is possible to imagine that cultural exchange happens in a multiplicity of directions, that often people construct images and practices that appear unconnected to any particular locality or culture (Appadurai, 1990). One might perceive Asian American women in my study as constructing aesthetic images of themselves based on neither a Caucasian ideal nor a stereotypical Asian face. The difficulty with such constructions, however, is that they do not help Asian Americans to escape at least one stereotypical notion of Asians in the United States—that they are "foreign" and "exotic." Even when Asians are considered sexy, and attractive in the larger American society, they are usually seen as exotically sexy and attractive (Yang & Ragaz, 1993:21). Since their beauty is almost always equated with the exotic and foreign, they are seen as members of an undifferentiated mass of people. Even though the women in my study are attempting to be seen as individuals, they are seen, in some sense, as less distinguishable from each other than white women are. As Lumi, a Japanese former model recently told *A. Magazine: The Asian American Quarterly,* "I've had bookers tell me I'm beautiful, but that they can't use me because I'm 'type.' All the agencies have their one Asian girl, and any more would be redundant" (Chen, 1993:21).

The constraints many Asian Americans feel with regard to the shape of their eyes and nose are clearly of a different quality from almost every American's discontent with weight or signs of aging; it is also different from the dissatisfaction many women, white and nonwhite alike, feel about the smallness or largeness of their breasts. Because the features (eyes and nose) Asian Americans are most concerned about are conventional markers of their racial identity, a rejection of these markers entails, in some sense, a devaluation of not only oneself but also other Asian Americans. It requires having to imitate, if not admire, the characteristics of another group more culturally dominant than one's own (i.e., Anglo Americans) in order that one can at least try to distinguish oneself from one's own group. Jane, for instance, explains that looking like a Caucasian is almost essential for socioeconomic success: "Especially if you go into business, or whatever, you kind of have to have a Western facial type and you have to have like their features and stature—you know, be tall and stuff. So you can see that [the surgery] is an investment in your future."

Unlike those who may want to look younger or thinner in order to find a better job or a happier social life, the women in my study must take into consideration not only their own socioeconomic future, but also more immediately that of their offspring, who by virtue of heredity, inevitably share their features. Ellen, for instance, said that "looks are not everything. I want my daughter, Stacy, to know that what's inside is important too. Sometimes you can look beautiful because your nice personality and wisdom inside radiate outward, such as in the way you talk and behave." Still, she has been encouraging twelve-year-old Stacy to have double eyelid surgery because she thinks "having less sleepy looking eyes would make a better impression on people and help her in the future with getting jobs." Ellen had undergone cosmetic surgery at the age of twenty on the advice of her mother and older sister and feels she has benefited. Indeed, all three women in the study under thirty who have actually undergone cosmetic surgery did so on the advice of their mother and in their mother's presence at the clinic. Elena, in

fact, received her double-eyelid surgery as a high school graduation present from her mother, who was concerned for her socioeconomic future. The mothers, in turn, are influenced not so much by a personal flaw of their own which drives them to mold and perfect their daughters as by a society that values the superficial characteristics of one race over another.

A few of the women's dating and courtship patterns were also affected by their negative feelings toward stereotypical Asian features. Jo, for example, who is married to a Caucasian man, said she has rarely dated Asian men and is not usually attracted to them, partly because they look too much like her: "I really am sorry to say that I am not attracted to Asian men. And it's not to say that I don't find them attractive on the whole. But I did date a Japanese guy once and I felt like I was holding my brother's hand [she laughs nervously]." . . .

CONCLUSION: PROBLEM OF RESISTANCE IN A CULTURE BASED ON ENDLESS SELF-FASHIONING

My research has shown that Asian American women's decision to undergo cosmetic surgery for wider eyes and more prominent noses is very much influenced by society's racial stereotyping of Asian features. Many of the women in my study are aware of the racial stereotypes from which they suffer. However, all have internalized these negative images of themselves and of other Asians, and they judge the Asian body, including their own, with the critical eye of the oppressor. Moreover, almost all share the attitude of certain sectors of the media and medicine in regard to whether undergoing a surgical operation is, in the end, harmful or helpful to themselves and other Asian Americans; they say it is yet another exercise of their freedom of choice. . . .

The constraints Asian American women in my study feel every day with regard to their natural features are a direct result of unequal race relationships in the United States. These women's apparent lack of concern for their racial oppression is symptomatic of a certain postmodern culture arising in the United States which has the effect of hiding structural inequalities from public view (Bordo, 1990). In its attempt to celebrate differences and to shun overgeneralizations and totalizing discourses that apparently efface diversity among people in modern life, this postmodern culture actually obscures differences; that is, by viewing differences as all equally arbitrary, it effaces from public consciousness historically determined differences in power between groups of people. Thus, blue contact lenses for African American women, and double eyelids and nose bridges for Asian women are both seen as forms of empowerment and indistinguishable in form and function from perms for white women, corn rows on Bo Derek, and tans on Caucasians. All cosmetic changes are seen in the same way—as having no cultural meaning and no political significance. . . .

Thus, instead of becoming a battleground for social and cultural resistance, the body has become a playground (Bordo, 1990:667). Like Michael Jackson's lyrics in the song "Man in the Mirror" ("If you want to make the world a better place, then take a look at yourself and make a change"; Jackson, 1987), it is ambiguous whether political change and social improvement are best orchestrated through changing society or through an "act of creative interpretation" (Bordo, 1990) of the superficial details of one's appearance. The problem and dilemma of resistance in U.S. society are best epitomized in this excerpt of my interview with Jo, the twenty-eight-year-old law student who is thinking of having double-eyelid surgery:

Jo: In my undergraduate college, every Pearl Harbor Day I got these phone calls and people would say, "Happy Pearl Harbor Day," and they made noises like bombs and I'd find little toy soldiers at my dorm door. Back then, I kind of took it as a joke. But now, I think it was more malicious. . . . [So] I think the surgery is a lot more superficial. Affecting how society feels about a certain race is a lot more beneficial. And it goes a lot deeper and lasts a lot longer. . . .

Jo recognizes that undergoing double-eyelid surgery, that is, confirming the undesirability of Asian eyes, is in contradiction to the work she would like to do as a teacher and legal practitioner. However, she said she cannot easily destroy the negative feelings she already possesses about the natural shape of her eyes.

IMPLICATIONS: ASIAN AMERICANS AND THE AMERICAN DREAM

The psychological burden of having constantly to measure up has been often overlooked in the image of Asian Americans as model minorities, as people who have achieved the American dream. The model minority myth assumes not only that all Asian Americans are financially well-to-do, but also that those Asian Americans who are from relatively well-to-do, non-working-class backgrounds (like many of the women in my study) are free from the everyday constraints of painful racial stereotypes (see Takaki, 1989; Hurh & Kim, 1989). As my research has shown, the cutting up of Asian Americans' faces through plastic surgery is a concrete example of how, in modern life, Asian Americans, like other people of color, can be influenced by the dominant culture to loathe themselves in such a manner as to begin mutilating and revising parts of their body.

REFERENCES

American Society of Plastic and Reconstructive Surgeons (ASPRS). N.d. "Estimated Number of Cosmetic Surgery Procedures Performed by ASPRS Members in 1990." Pamphlet.

Appadurai, Arjun. 1990. "Disjuncture and Difference in the Global Cultural Economy." *Public Culture* 2(2):I-24.

Blacking, John. 1977. *The Anthropology of the Body.* London: Academic Press.

Bordo, Susan. 1990. "Material Girl: The Effacements of Postmodern Culture." *Michigan Quarterly Review 29*:635–676.

Brain, Robert. 1979. *The Decorated Body.* New York: Harper and Row.

Chen, Joanne. 1993. "Before and After: For Asian Americans, the Issues Underlying Cosmetic Surgery Are Not Just Skin Deep." *A. Magazine: The Asian American Quarterly* 2(1):15–18, 26–27.

Daly, Mary. 1978. *Gyn/ecology: The Metaethics of Radical Feminism.* Boston: Beacon Press.

Davis, Kathy. 1991. "Remaking the She-Devil: A Critical Look at Feminist Approaches to Beauty." *Hypatia* 6(2):21–43.

Dower, John. 1986. *War without Mercy: Race and Power in the Pacific War.* New York: Pantheon.

Fleming, Charles, and Mary Talbot. 1993. "The Two Faces of Michael Jackson." *Newsweek,* February 22, P. 57.

Gilman, Sander L. 1985. *Difference and Pathology. Stereotypes of Sexuality, Race and Madness.* Ithaca, NY. Cornell University Press.

Goffman, Erving. 1979. *Gender Advertisement.* Cambridge: Harvard University Press.

Goldstein, Judith. 1993. "The Female Aesthetic Community." *Poetics Today* 14 (1):143–163.

Harahap, Marwali. 1982. "Oriental Cosmetic Blepharoplasty." In *Cosmetic Surgery for Nonwhite Patients,* ed. Harold Pierce, pp. 79–97. New York: Grune & Stratton.

Hurh, Won Moo, and Kwang Chung Kim. 1989. "The 'Success' Image of Asian Americans: Validity, and Its Practical and Theoretical Implications." *Ethnic and Racial Studies* 12(4):512–537.

Iwata, Edward. 1991. "Race without Face. *San Francisco Image Magazine,* May, pp. 51–55.

Jackson, Michael. 1987. "Man in the Mirror." On *Bad.* Epic Records, New York.

Kaw, Eugenia. 1993. "Medicalization of Racial Features: Asian American Women and Cosmetic Surgery." *Medical Anthropology Quarterly 7* (1):74–89.

Kim, Elaine. 1986. "Asian-Americans and American Popular Culture" In *Dictionary of Asian-American History,* ed. Hyung-Chan Kim. New York: Greenwood Press.

Lakoff, Robin T., and Raquel L. Scherr. 1984. *Face Value: The Politics of Beauty.* Boston: Routledge & Kegan Paul.

LeFlore, Ivens C. 1982. "Face Lift, Chin Augmentation and Cosmetic Rhinoplasty in Blacks. *In Cosmetic Surgery in Non-White Patients,* ed. Harold Pierce. New York: Grune & Stratton.

Lock, Margaret, and Nancy Scheper-Hughes. 1990. "A Critical-Interpretive Approach in Medical Anthropology: Rituals and Routines of Discipline and Dissent." In *Medical Anthropology: Contemporary Theory and Method,* ed., Thomas Johnson and Carolyn Sargent, pp. 47–72. New York: Praeger.

McCurdy, John A. 1990. *Cosmetic Surgery of the Asian Face.* New York: Thieme Medical Publishers.

MacGregor, Frances C. 1967. "Social and Cultural Components in the Motivations of Persons Seeking Plastic Surgery of the Nose." *Journal of Health and Social Behavior* 8(2):125–135.

Merrell, Kathy H. 1994. "Saving Faces." *Allure,* January, pp. 66–68.

Nakao, Annie. 1993. "Faces of Beauty: Light Is Still Right." *San Francisco Examiner and Chronicle,* April 11, p. D4.

O'Neill, John. 1985. *Five Bodies.* Ithaca, NY: Cornell University Press.

Ong, Aihwa. 1987. *Spirits of Resistance and Capitalist Discipline: Factory Women in Malaysia.* Albany: State University of New York Press.

Ramsdell, Daniel. 1983. "Asia Askew: U.S. Bestsellers on Asia. 1931–1980." *Bulletin of Concerned Asian Scholars* 15(4):2–25.

Rosenthal, Elisabeth. 1991. "Ethnic Ideals: Rethinking Plastic Surgery." *New York Times,* September 25, p. B7.

Sayoc, B. T. 1974. "Surgery of the Oriental Eyelid." *Clinics in Plastic Surgery* 1(1):157–171.

Sheets-Johnstone, Maxine, ed. 1992. *Giving the Body Its Due.* Albany: State University of New York Press.

Tajima, Renee E. 1989. "Lotus Blossoms Don't Bleed: Images of Asian Women." In *Making Waves: An Anthology of Writings by and about Asian American Women,* ed. Diane Yeh-Mei Wong, pp. 308–317. Boston: Beacon Press.

Takaki, Ronald. 1989. *Strangers from a Different Shore.* Boston: Little, Brown.

Turner, Terence. 1980. "The Social Skin." In *Not Work Alone,* ed. J. Cherfas and R. Lewin, pp. 112–114. London: Temple Smith.

Wolf, Naomi. 1991. *The Beauty Myth: How Images of Beauty Are Used Against Women.* New York: Morrow.

Yang, Jeff, and Angelo Ragaz. 1993. "The Beauty Machine." *A. Magazine. The Asian American Quarterly* 2(1):20–21.

DISCUSSION QUESTIONS

1. Kaw entertains two main types of reasoning to explain why Asian Americans undergo eye fold cosmetic surgery—one that they are living the American dream by exercising freedom of choice and expression, and the other that they are altering themselves to conform to an ideal image of beauty that devalues stereotypically Asian physical features (a reaction to racism). The first argument is a color-blind one that largely ignores the significance of race, and Kaw discounts this position with her data. Do you agree with her that these surgeries are an unfortunate consequence of racism, or do they simply represent the beauty of the American way?

2. Kaw's respondents emphasize the importance of their surgeries as paving the way for heightened socioeconomic success. How important is physical appearance to the attainment of prestige in the United States, and how does racism shape these opportunities?

3. Why do you think Kaw was unable to find any Asian American men to participate in her study? What are the gendered dynamics of this type of assimilation? In general, do you think it is easier for women or men of immigrant groups to assimilate? Why? Does it depend upon the particular group in question? Can you generate any specific examples to support your answers?

4. Does the availability of cosmetic surgery as a cultural phenomenon change the dynamics of assimilation as we know it in modern society? Is it simply physical features that define "race"? Can you think of any other recent technological advances that could change how racial-ethnic assimilation operates in today's society?

CURRENT DEBATES

ENGLISH ONLY?

What role should learning English take in the process of adjusting to the United States? Should English-language proficiency be a prerequisite for full inclusion in the society? Should English be made the official language of the nation? Does the present multiplicity of languages represent a danger for social cohesion and unity? Following are two reactions to these questions.

The first excerpt is from Mr. Mauro Mujica, the chairman of U.S. English, Inc. (www.us-english.org/inc/), an immigrant himself, and a passionate advocate for the unifying power of a single national language. His organization opposes efforts to recognize Spanish as an official second language (in part because of the expense and confusion that would ensue if all government documents, election ballots, street signs, etc., were published in both English and Spanish) and most forms of bilingual education. He is particularly concerned with stressing that the primary beneficiaries of learning English will be the immigrants.

An opposing point of view is presented by Hurtado and Vega, both professors of psychology. They argue that "English only" is a thinly disguised attack on Latinos and that there are multiple benefits, on a number of levels, from encouraging bilingualism.

ENGLISH ONLY WILL SPEED THE ASSIMILATION OF IMMIGRANTS

Mauro Mujica

[During my 11 years as chairman] of U.S. ENGLISH . . . I have encountered many myths about official English legislation. . . . A few of these myths were recently repeated in an opinion piece in the *Contra Costa Times*. [The author] . . . writes, ". . . the anti-bilingual education movement and the English-only movement could easily be labeled an anti-Spanish movement."

In that one sentence, [the author] repeats two of the most ridiculous myths about official English. There are other distortions as well. These will likely come up as Congress debates HR 997, the English Language Unity Act of 2003, which would make English the official language of the United States. (NOTE: This bill has been passed by the U.S. Senate . . .).

Here are five of the most common myths about official English and the realities behind them.

Myth No. 1: Official English Is Anti-Immigrant. Declaring English the official language benefits all Americans, but it benefits immigrants most of all. Immigrants who speak English earn more money, do better in school and have more career options than those who do not.

As an immigrant from Chile, I can testify that English proficiency is the most important gift we can give to newcomers. In fact, polls show that 70% of Hispanics and 85% of all immigrants support making English the official language of the United States. Learning English is the key to assimilating into the mainstream of American society. That is why our organization, U.S. ENGLISH, Inc., advocates for English immersion classes for immigrant students and adults.

Myth No. 2: Official English Is "English Only." Many far-left opponents of official English, such as the ACLU, refer to our legislation as "English Only." Official English simply requires that government conduct its business in English. It does not dictate what language must be spoken in the home, during conversation, cultural celebrations or religious ceremonies. It does not prohibit the teaching of foreign languages. It does not affect private businesses or the services offered by them. In addition, HR 997 makes exceptions for emergency situations.

Myth No. 3: Today's Immigrants Are Learning English Just Like the Immigrants of Old. The

United States has a rapidly growing population of people—often native born—who are not proficient in English. The 2000 Census found that 21.3 million Americans (8% of the population) are classified as "limited English proficient," a 52% increase from 1990, and more than double the 1980 total. More than 5.6 million of these people were born in the United States. In states like California, 20% of the population is not proficient in English.

The Census also reports that 4.5 million American households are linguistically isolated, meaning that no one in the household older than age 14 can speak English. These numbers indicate that the American assimilation process is broken. If not fixed, we will see our own "American Quebec" in the Southwestern United States and perhaps other areas of the country.

Myth No. 4: The Founding Fathers Rejected Making English the Official Language. English has been the language of our nation from its earliest days. In 1789, 90% of our nation's non-slave inhabitants were of English descent. Any notion that they would have chosen another language or used precious resources on printing documents in multiple languages lacks common sense.

The issue of an official language was never discussed at the Constitutional Convention as the topic was not controversial enough to be debated. Even the Dutch colonies had been under English rule for more than a century. Contrary to popular belief, Congress never voted on a proposal to make German the official language. This myth is probably based on a 1794 bill to translate some documents into German (it was defeated).

Myth No. 5: In a Global Culture, an Official Language Is Anachronistic. Ninety-two percent of the world's countries (178 of 193) have at least one official language. English is the sole official language in 31 nations and has an official status in 20 other nations, including India, Singapore, the Philippines, Samoa and Nigeria.

There has never been a language so widely spread in so short a time as English. It is the lingua franca of the modern world as much as Latin was the common tongue of the Roman Empire. Roughly one quarter of the world's population is already fluent or competent in English and this number grows by the day.

English is the global language of business, communications, higher education, diplomacy, aviation, the Internet, science, popular music, entertainment and international travel. Immigrants who don't know English not only lose out in the American economy, but also in the global economy.

These are just some of the myths that must be corrected if we are to have a debate on a coherent language policy. This policy should be built on fact, not myth. Multilingual government is a disaster for American unity and results in billions of dollars in unnecessary government spending. We need only to look at Canada to see the problems that multilingualism can bring. HR 997 could be our last best chance to stop this process and we cannot let distortions about official English sidetrack this legislation.

SOURCE: Originally titled "Official English Legislation: Myths and Realities" from *Human Events, 59,* July 28, 2003. Copyright © 2003 Human Events Inc. Reprinted with permission.

BILINGUALISM SHOULD BE ENCOURAGED[1]

Aida Hurtado and Luis A. Vega

Brown vs. the Board of Education of Topeka Kansas (1954) was the beginning of dismantling inequalities in education. As progress was made, . . . other indicators of group membership were examined to uncover their use in justifying blocked educational opportunity. Ethnicity, culture, language, and gender all began to be conceptualized as part of the social constellation used to justify certain groups not having the same educational access as others. For Latinos, . . . the Spanish language is a salient marker of their ethnic group membership. The use of Spanish, especially in an educational system that privileges the use of English . . . has been consistently used to justify repressive practices against its use, to assign Spanish-speaking children to special education regardless of intellectual abilities, and as an explanation for Latinos' lack of educational achievement and attainment.

The use of Spanish by Latinos in the United States has been identified as a social problem leading to increased economic and social isolation. Recent social policies, therefore, have focused on . . . limiting bilingual programs . . . , efforts to make English the official language of the United States, and English-only local laws. Efforts to limit the use of Spanish in public life have impacted public translation services in courts and in voting ballots, further stigmatizing entire communities for the use of their ethnic groups' language. At the same time, multicultural diversity has increased in this country and economic and social globalization demands an increase in bilingual and multilingual citizens who can lead, work with, and manage a diverse workforce. . . . The Latino population is now the largest minority group . . . [and their] educational achievement continues to lag behind all other ethnic and racial groups. . . . The use of Spanish and transition into English become an important topic to achieve the goal of educational equity.

STUDIES ON SPANISH TO ENGLISH SHIFT

Spanish to English shift refers to the transition from Spanish monolingualism, to English monolingualism, with bilingualism defining this continuum. . . . Several researchers posit that situational pressures have the most important influence on the pace at which language shift occurs. For example, . . . a survey about language use among high school students of Mexican descent . . . found an equal level of Spanish proficiency in first generation (immigrant) and second-generation (children born in the United States of Mexican parents) students. These findings are surprising considering that a rapid language shift occurs from Spanish to English in both first and second generations.

However, [an important reason for this is that] . . . Spanish serves an important social function for Spanish speakers—while English facilitates communication in most public settings, Spanish facilitates it in the intimate settings of home and community. Consequently, situational pressures come into play when most Latinos find occasions when Spanish is the preferred language . . .

[A]n analysis of language maintenance [shows that], . . . as shift in language happens from Spanish to English and from one generation to the next, different levels of language use occur within the home, allowing exposure of Spanish to children, and exposure of English to parents. . . . These different levels or degrees of language use we have labeled "linguistic bands" . . .

It is the presence of linguistic bands that facilitate communication across different sociolinguistic domains. For example, parents . . . who speak predominantly Spanish represent one linguistic band within the family . . . , their children who speak mostly English represent another. [The] different linguistic bands in the home environment . . . allow for learning to take place across bands, resulting in . . . varying degrees of English/Spanish bilingualism by all members of the household. . . . Bilingualism occurs when predominantly Spanish-speaking parents understand English, and when predominantly

English-speaking children understand Spanish. [This will allow] Spanish to flourish in the future given an appropriate context . . .

Shift happens, shift is inevitable. This study shows that language transition from Spanish to English among Mexican descendants is most pronounced inter-generationally. That is, succeeding generations of Mexicans continue the shift to English monolingualism, and while it might be expected that Spanish language loss is the price to pay, such is not the case, for the knowledge of the Spanish language remains viable through different degrees of bilingualism. This is made possible through linguistic bands, which allow for exposure of Spanish and English to speakers of only one language. . . . the use of Spanish or English at no time becomes mutually exclusive . . . Our findings suggest that Spanish will not disappear but instead, it will [survive] through different degrees of bilingualism. . . . Hence, given the appropriate contexts, Spanish will flourish and remain a viable language . . .

Policy Recommendations

Cultural and linguistic assimilation consistently has been recommended . . . as the solution to Latinos' lack of full educational and economic integration. However, recent demographic changes and the globalization of the U. S. economy require that all citizens become adept at functioning in multiple cultural settings. Our results indicate that many Latinos begin life with an invaluable language resource that could be cultivated, rather than repressed or neglected, and that could blossom into full-scale bilingualism. In fact, . . . youth [from various groups] who are bilingual are less likely to drop out of school than those in English-dominant or English-limited households. . . . [Various studies suggest that] it is not the most acculturated but rather those who have not abandoned their ethnic cultures that experience the greatest educational success. It is bicultural youths who can draw on resources from both the immigrant community and mainstream society who are best situated to enjoy educational success. Similarly, . . . second generation students who became fluent bilinguals report better relations with their families, greater self-esteem, and higher educational aspirations than those who became English monolinguals. . . .

Many states have dismantled long-term bilingual education and have opted for transitioning Limited Proficiency Students (LEP) as quickly as possible into English by disregarding the cultivation of their ethnic language. A more sensible strategy would be . . . to cultivate the children's [bilingual] skills. . . . There is beginning to be evidence that this approach may facilitate the initial goals set forth by Brown vs. the Board of Education of Topeka Kansas (1954), insuring the full educational and economic integration of all children regardless of race, ethnicity, language, and gender.

Note

1. To conserve space, references and footnotes have been omitted.

SOURCE: Originally titled "Shift Happens: Spanish and English Transmission Between Parents and Their Children" from *Journal of Social Issues, 60* (1): 137-155. Copyright © 2004. Reprinted with permission of Blackwell Publishing Ltd.

DEBATE QUESTIONS TO CONSIDER

1. What assumptions are these authors making about the role of language in the process of assimilation? Can a group adjust successfully to U.S. society without learning English?

2. What reaction would other groups (recent immigrants, African Americans, Native Americans, white ethnics) have to making Spanish an official second language? What stake would they have in this policy issue?

3. As you think about the issue of bilingualism and multilingualism, see if you can identify some social class aspects. Which economic classes would benefit from an English-only policy? Which economic classes are hurt? How? Why?

4. Mujica argues that English is a global language and that non-English speakers are handicapped not only in the U.S. but in the global economy. Hurtado and Vega argue that bilingualism and biculturalism are important resources for success in the world and that the U.S. would greatly benefit from having more people that can truly function in multicultural settings. Who's right? Does the emerging global economy demand fluent English or fluency in multiple languages?

5. Should Spanish be made an official second language? Would this threaten societal unity (as Mujica argues) or would it empower currently excluded Spanish speakers (as Hurtado and Vega argue)?

Part II

THE EVOLUTION OF DOMINANT-MINORITY
RELATIONS IN THE UNITED STATES

3

THE DEVELOPMENT OF DOMINANT-MINORITY RELATIONS IN PRE-INDUSTRIAL AMERICA

The Origins of Slavery

What was it like to be a slave? Why did colonial America create the institution of slavery? What impact did slavery have on the development of African American culture? What role did gender play in Southern society? What did black and white females have in common? How did they differ? How did slavery shape American social institutions? What echoes of slavery can be heard in present-day race relations?

These are some of the issues raised in this chapter. We begin with the memoirs of two of the victims of slavery: a male and female slave. Both managed to escape to the North, where they devoted their lives to the abolition of the system that had imprisoned them and their families. These memoirs give us insight not only into the everyday lives of slaves but also into the gender issues that differentiated the lives of slaves.

The two readings discuss the origin of slavery and its implications for the South and for society as a whole. Joe R. Feagin argues that slavery, racial inequality, and racism lie at the very heart of the American experience, along with our ideas about democracy, freedom, and equality. He explores the rationales for the system of bondage and compares it to other slave systems and argues that the American slave system was especially cruel. Deborah Gray White examines race and gender in the old South. She focuses on slave women but also compares their situation with that of white women and white and black men.

The selections in the Current Debates section explore the effects of slavery on the growth of African American culture. Stanley Elkins argues that slavery severed all ties with African cultures and that African American culture was formed in reaction to the oppressive system of slavery. William Piersen takes an opposing position and argues that the connections with Africa were not completely severed and had a significant impact on the development of African American culture.

Please visit the accompanying website to Race, Ethnicity, and Gender, second edition for the *Public Sociology Assignments* at http://www.pineforge.com/das2.

QUESTIONS TO CONSIDER IN THIS CHAPTER

1. Why is it important to consider the questions raised in this chapter? What relevance can slavery have for today? What difference does it make if African Americans remained connected to African traditions as they shaped their culture in colonial times?

2. How important is the concept of gender in shaping the early experiences of African Americans? How did the experiences of black women vary from those of white women? Do these differences have any consequences in the present?

3. Systems of slavery have existed throughout history and across the world (and continue to exist today). How did the American slavery system differ from other systems? Was it especially cruel and oppressive? How? What implications do these characteristics have for the situation of African Americans today?

NARRATIVE PORTRAITS

A SLAVE'S LIFE

This section presents a vivid portrait of American slavery as experienced by two of its victims. Harriet Jacobs grew up as a slave in Edenton, North Carolina, and, in this excerpt, she recounts some of her experiences, especially the sexual harassment she suffered at the hand of her master. Her narrative illustrates the dynamics of power and sex in the "peculiar institution" and the very limited options she had for defending herself from the advances of her master. She eventually escaped from slavery by hiding in her grandmother's house for nearly seventeen years and then making her way to the North.

The second memoir was written by Henry Bibb, who was also able to flee from the South. Bibb was married and had a child when he escaped to the North, where he spent the rest of his life working for the abolition of slavery. The passage gives an overview of his early life and expresses his commitment to freedom and his family. He also describes some of the abuses he and his family suffered under the reign of a particularly cruel master. Bibb was unable to rescue his daughter from slavery and agonizes over leaving her in bondage.

LIFE AS A SLAVE GIRL

Harriet Jacobs (edited by Jean F. Yellin)

During the first years of my service in Dr. Flint's family, I was accustomed to share some indulgences with the children of my mistress. Though this seemed to me no more than right, I was grateful for it, and tried to merit the kindness by the faithful discharge of my duties. But I now entered on my fifteenth year—a sad epoch in the life of a slave girl. My master began to whisper foul words in my ear. Young as I was, I could not remain ignorant of their import. I tried to treat them with indifference or contempt. The master's age, my extreme youth, and the fear that misconduct would be reported to my grandmother made him bear this treatment for many months.

He was a crafty man, and resorted to many means to accomplish his purposes. Sometimes he had stormy, terrific ways, that made his victims tremble; sometimes he assumed a gentleness that he thought must surely subdue. Of the two, I preferred his stormy moods, although they left me trembling. He tried his utmost to corrupt the pure principles my grandmother had instilled. He peopled my young mind with unclean images, such as only a vile monster could think of. I turned from him with disgust and hatred. But he was my master. I was compelled to live under the same roof with him, where I saw a man forty years my senior daily violating the most sacred commandments of nature. He told me I was his property; that I must be subject to his will in all things. My soul revolted against the mean tyranny. But where could I turn for protection? No matter whether the slave girl be as black as ebony or as fair as her mistress. In either case, there is no shadow of law to protect her from insult, from violence, or even from death; all these are inflicted by fiends who bear the shape of men. The mistress, who ought to protect the helpless victim, has no other feelings towards her but those of jealousy and rage. The degradation, the wrongs, the vices that grow out of slavery, are more than I can describe. They are greater than you would willingly believe. Surely, if you credited only half the truths that are told you concerning the helpless millions suffering in this cruel bondage, you at the north would not help tighten the yoke. You surely would refuse to do for the master, on your own soil, the mean and cruel work which trained bloodhounds and the lowest class of whites do for him at the south.

SOURCE: Reprinted by permission of the publisher from *Incidents in the Life of a Slave Girl, Written by Herself* by Harriet A. Jacobs, edited and with an introduction by Jean Fagen Yellin, pp. 27-30, Cambridge, MA: Harvard University Press. Copyright © 1987, 2000 by the President and Fellows of Harvard College.

NARRATIVE OF THE LIFE AND ADVENTURES OF HENRY BIBB

Henry Bibb (edited by Gilbert Osofsky)

I was born May 1815, of a slave mother, in Shelby County, Kentucky, and was claimed as the property of David White. I was brought up . . . or, more correctly speaking, I was *flogged up;* for where I should have received moral, mental, and religious instruction, I received stripes without number, the object of which was to degrade and keep me in subordination. . . . The first time I was separated from my mother, I was young and small . . . I was . . . hired out to labor for various persons and all my wages were expended for the education of [my master's daughter]. It was then I first commenced seeing and feeling that I was a wretched slave, compelled to work under the lash without wages, and often without clothes to hide my nakedness. . . .

All that I heard about liberty and freedom . . . I never forgot. Among other good trades I learned the art of running away to perfection. I made a regular business of it, and never gave it up, until I had broken the bands of slavery, and landed myself safely in Canada, where I was regarded as a man, and not a thing.

[Bibb describes his childhood and adolescence, his early attempts to escape to the North, and his marriage to Malinda.] Not many months [later] Malinda made me a father. The dear little daughter was called Mary Frances. She was nurtured and caressed by her mother and father. . . . Malinda's business was to labor out in the field the greater part of her time, and there was no one to take care of poor little Frances. . . . She was left at the house to creep under the feet of an unmerciful old mistress, Mrs. Gatewood (the owner's wife). I recollect that [we] came in from the field one day and poor little Frances came creeping to her mother smiling, but with large tear drops standing in her dear little eyes. . . . Her little face was bruised black with the whole print of Mrs. Gatewood's hand. . . . Who can imagine the feelings of a mother and father, when looking upon their infant child whipped and tortured with impunity, and they placed in a situation where they could afford it no protection? But we were all claimed and held as property; the father and mother were slaves!

On this same plantation, I was compelled to stand and see my wife shamefully scourged and abused by her master; and the manner in which this was done was so violent and inhuman that I despair in finding decent language to describe the bloody act of cruelty. My happiness or pleasure was all blasted; for it was sometimes a pleasure to be with my little family even in slavery.

I loved them as my wife and child. Little Frances was a pretty child; she was quiet, playful, bright, and interesting. . . . But I could never look upon the dear child without being filled with sorrow and fearful apprehensions, of being separated by slaveholders, because she was a slave, regarded as property. . . . But Oh! when I remember that my daughter, my only child, is still there, . . . it is too much to bear. If ever there was any one act of my life as a slave, that I have to lament over, it is that of being a father and a husband to slaves. I have the satisfaction of knowing that I am the father of only one slave. She is bone of my bone, and flesh of my flesh; poor unfortunate child. She was the first and shall be the last slave that ever I will father, for chains and slavery on this earth.

SOURCE: From *Puttin' on Ole Massa: The Slave Narratives of Henry Bibb, William Wells Brown, and Solomon Northup.* Copyright © 1969. Harper and Row. Reprinted with permission of Marcia Osofsky, Ph.D.

READINGS

Although chattel slavery officially ended in 1865, social scientists are still exploring many aspects of this "peculiar institution" and adding depth to our understanding of the system that held African Americans in bondage for two centuries. It is perhaps the brutality and inhumanity of slavery that makes it possible only now for such information to be heard and accepted. The two readings that follow explore gender and race relations during the time of slavery and challenge many myths surrounding the subject matter. The first reading, by Joe Feagin, examines slavery not as a slight temporary deviation from democratic ideals, but as the "bloody foundation" of the United States, forming the very basis for the new nation. Many signers of the Declaration of Independence, presidents, speakers of the house, and senators were slaveholders themselves, and saw to it that the legal structure preserved slavery. But even those who were not of the wealthy slaveholding class received "ill-gotten gains" from the system of slavery, since all those who bought and sold plantation-made products benefited from their labor. Feagin also points out that the form of chattel slavery that existed in the United States was particularly brutal and dehumanizing, more so than any other slave or servant system existing elsewhere. Slave status existed for the entire duration of a person's life, and she or he was denied most all of the basic human rights, such as voting, reading, writing, and getting an education. Although African nations may have willingly given over some of their citizens to the United States, they had no idea of the fate that would befall them. Feagin touches upon only some of the many cruelties that slave masters perpetrated against their slaves, including the forcible rapes that were regularly committed against black women.

The second reading, by Deborah Gray White, continues this focus on women by exploring the images of black women that developed in the antebellum South. White explores the social, political, and cultural dynamics that led black women to be characterized as both sensuous seductresses and nurturing maternal figures. She also notes that, in spite of their shared victimization by a paternalistic society, black and white women shared little in common and had scant grounds for common action. Southern white women sometimes celebrated the paternalistic culture that placed them on a pedestal as chaste guardian of the domestic realm, a position that race and class barriers prevented black women (and lower-class white women) from reaching.

Paternalism, in which white men "protected" those who were seen as incapable of protecting themselves, was indeed the very foundation of Southern culture. White's argument also refutes any assertion that black women experienced some sort of strength or equality through slavery. Just because black men could not access the full force of patriarchy does not mean by default that black women were somehow "liberated." The lives of all Southerners—male or female, black or white—were shaped by the institution of slavery, the economic and social foundation of the plantation economy. A complete understanding of this era (and its consequences for today) requires that we take into account the interactions of race, class, and gender as central dictators of the Southerner's experiences.

Slavery Unwilling to Die: The Historical Development of Systematic Racism

Joe R. Feagin

A Bloody Foundation: Genocide and Slavery

This nation was born in blood and violence against the racialized "others." This grim historical reality must be understood well if we are to comprehend contemporary racism and interracial relations. As the European colonists established permanent settlements in North America, they intentionally drove off or killed the indigenous inhabitants and took their land. These colonists enriched themselves in a process of genocide against the indigenous peoples.

Attacking Native Americans

Article 11 of the United Nations Convention on the Prevention and Punishment of Genocide defines genocide as "acts committed with intent to destroy, in whole or in part, a national, ethnical, racial, or religious group." These acts specifically include "causing serious bodily or mental harm" and "deliberately inflicting on the group conditions of life calculated to bring about its physical destruction in whole or in part."[1] From the late 1400s to the first decades of the 1900s, the European colonizers and their descendants periodically and deliberately inflicted conditions of life that brought about the physical devastation, in whole or in part, of numerous indigenous societies across the Caribbean islands and North and South America. Indeed, the intentional attacks on indigenous peoples—and the effects of European diseases—are estimated to have cost as many as ninety to one hundred million casualties—the largest example of human destruction in recorded history.[2] The brutal and exploitative practices of whites were not aberrations; they were common practice in European colonialism.

The English colonists on the Atlantic coast relied on indigenous peoples to survive the first difficult years. Soon, however, these Europeans turned on the indigenous inhabitants. As early as 1637, a war with the Pequots in New England ended when whites massacred several hundred inhabitants of a village and sent the rest into slavery. The 1675–1676 King Philip's War with the Wampanoag society and its allies, precipitated by the actions of the colonists, resulted in substantial losses on both sides. The Native American leader, Metacom (known by the English as King Philip), was "captured, drawn, and quartered: his skull remained on view on a pole in Plymouth as late as 1700."[3] Again, the survivors were sold as slaves by European colonists who, ironically, saw themselves as a "civilized" people dealing with "savage" peoples. It is not well known that European colonists enslaved some Native Americans as part of their initial attempts to find exploitable labor. In the mid-eighteenth century about 5 percent of those enslaved in several of the North American colonies were Native American.

Recall James Madison's comment that the stereotyped "red race" was second only to the "black race" in the openly racist concerns of whites.[4] What should be done with these people who stood in the way of European lust for the land and riches of the Americas? Few European colonizers made an effort to understand the attempts of indigenous peoples to protect themselves from European invaders. While some leaders like Benjamin Franklin and Thomas Jefferson expressed admiration for Indian societies (even viewing them as "the white men of America"), most whites more than balanced their admiration with hostility and negative imagery.[5]

Until the middle decades of the nineteenth century the majority of Native American societies maintained a substantial degree of political and cultural autonomy. Europeans were frequently forced by the strength of Native American societies to negotiate with them for land and other resources. A process of gradual encroachment became the rule. Europeans would move into Native American lands (often violating treaties), Native Americans would respond with defensive violence, U.S. troops would put the rebellion down, and a new treaty securing much or all of the stolen land for whites would be made. There was at least a pretense of negotiation and legal treatymaking. However, by the 1830s—with President Andrew Jackson's decision to expel Cherokees and other Native American groups from the eastern states by force (the infamous "trail of tears" that cost at least 4,000 lives)—Native American societies increasingly faced a policy of overt displacement from white areas to western reservations or renewed attacks designed to eliminate whole societies. Even the pretense of legality was gradually disappearing.

Indeed, by 1831 the Supreme Court was moving to redefine indigenous societies as "domestic dependent nations."[6]

THE LOSING STRUGGLE FOR SOCIAL INDEPENDENCE

In the 1857 Dred Scott decision the U.S. Supreme Court showed that leading whites viewed the situations of Native Americans and African Americans as quite different. Indians, Chief Justice Roger B. Taney asserted, had "formed no part of the colonial communities, and never amalgamated with them in social connections or in government. But although they were uncivilized, they were yet a free and independent people, associated together in nations or tribes, and governed by their own laws. . . . But they may, without doubt, like the subjects of any other foreign Government, be naturalized by the authority of Congress, and become citizens of a State, and of the United States; and if an individual should leave his nation or tribe, and take up his abode among the white population, he would be entitled to all the rights and privileges which would belong to an emigrant from any other foreign people."[7] Whites, the judge asserted, had long viewed Native American groups as autonomous nations, though less civilized than whites. In contrast, in this decision about the status of an enslaved black American, the white judges viewed black Americans not as a nation to be negotiated with, but rather as "beings of an inferior order, and altogether unfit to associate with the white race, either in social or political relations; and so far inferior, that they had no rights which the white man was bound to respect."[8] Whites' racist views of indigenous societies often allowed for more independence, albeit as groups only beyond white borders and as individuals only if assimilated. Moreover, over the centuries each Native American society has confronted whites on its own turf, with much strength arising from the indigenous cultural and geographical resources. In contrast, those peoples taken from the diverse societies of Africa had to face their white oppressors on white turf, completely severed from their families and home societies.

Native Americans lost their ability to make treaties in 1871. Over the next several decades, federal government policies forced many of the remaining Native Americans onto federally supervised and segregated reservations. With some oscillation, federal policies allowed whites to take more Native American land and pressured Native Americans to assimilate to white ways. By 1890, with most forced onto reservations, the number of Native Americans in North America had decreased to only about 250,000, sharply down from an estimated fifteen million people when the Europeans arrived in the late 1400s. The brutal and bloody consequences of the European conquests do indeed fit the United Nations definition of genocide.

SLAVERY AND MODERN CAPITALISM

In the Spanish colonies in Mexico and South America, Native Americans were the major source of labor, and thus they were central to the internal development of these colonial societies. This was not true for the English colonies. . . .

". . . The Indian played virtually no significant role in the internal functioning of the colonial society, but [did play] a crucial role in defining its frontier."[9] It was Africans who would play a central role in the functioning of colonial society. By the early 1700s people of African descent had become a major source of labor for the colonies, and the economic foundation for several centuries of undeserved enrichment for whites was firmly set in place.

The North American colonies developed two major modes of economic production. One type of production was the subsistence economy of small-scale farmers, who were either European immigrants or their descendants. Early on, the North American colonies became places to dump surplus peasants and workers displaced by the reorganization of agricultural economies in European societies. Alongside this subsistence farming economy was a profit-making commercial economy, much of which was rooted in the slave trade, slave plantations, and the commercial businesses essential to the burgeoning slavery economy. Slavery in the Americas was generally a commercial and market-centered operation, which distinguished it from slavery in the ancient world.[10]

With much farm land available for the new European immigrants coming into the colonies, it was frequently difficult for colonial entrepreneurs and development companies to secure enough white laborers, particularly for large-scale agriculture. At first, the larger landowners made use of white indentured servants, but it became clear that these laborers could be difficult to control. By the late seventeenth century the white elites were worried about periodic revolts from white laborers and small farmers. White indentured servants also worked off their terms of servitude and went into farming for themselves. The enslavement of African women, men, and children not only stemmed from a desire for profit but also from a concern with developing a scheme of social control that maintained bond-labor against the resistance of those enslaved. The color and cultural differences of Africans made them easier for whites to identity for purposes of enslavement and control.

The Legal Establishment of Slavery

The first Africans brought into the English colonies were bought by the Jamestown colonists from a Dutch ship in 1619. Laws firmly institutionalizing slavery were not put in place in the English colonies until the mid-seventeenth century. In the decades prior to that time some imported Africans were treated more like indentured servants than slaves. Some were able to work out from under their servitude. However, even in this early period those of African descent were by no means the social or legal equals of the

Europeans. During the earliest decade, the 1620s, the Africans for whom we have records were often treated differently from the English colonists. For one thing, all African laborers and servants were brought in involuntarily, even if they were in some cases allowed to work out their servitude. Moreover, getting out of servitude usually meant converting to Christianity. As early as 1624, one court case made it clear that a "negro"—note the early naming of Africans and the lowercase spelling—could testify in court only because he was a convert to Christianity. A "negro" status was already socially and legally inferior to a European colonist's status.[11] Forrest Wood has argued that Christianity in this colonial period, as later in U.S. history, was highly dogmatic, Eurocentric, and antiblack "in its ideology, organization, and practice."[12] As we see in this 1624 example, central to the Eurocentric viewpoint was the idea that every person must become a Christian in order to have any legal rights. Indeed, many apologists for the enslavement of African Americans, from the seventeenth century to the present day, have argued that one of the virtues of slavery was its bringing Christianity to those enslaved.

By the 1670s the lives of most people of African descent were severely restricted by the new laws legitimating and protecting slavery. The degradation of this slavery was clear. In one 1671 declaration Virginia's General Assembly put "sheep, horses, and cattle" in the same category as "negroes." Colonial laws early attempted to prevent black men and women from running away; there were barbaric laws encompassing the whipping, castration, or killing of rebellious slaves.[13] Slavery was much more than a system of coerced labor. Enslaved blacks were legally subjugated in or excluded from all societal institutions including the economic, legal, and political institutions. Slavery was a totalitarian system in which whites controlled the lives of black men, women, and children—a total racist society protecting white interests.

. . . In the 1770s and 1780s the white group interest in the slavery system was recognized in the defining political documents of the new nation. The Declaration of Independence, prepared mostly by the slaveholder Thomas Jefferson, originally contained language accusing the British king of pursuing slavery, of waging "cruel war against human nature itself, violating its most sacred rights of life and liberty in the persons of a distant people who never offended him, captivating them and carrying them into slavery in another hemisphere, or to incur miserable death in the transportation thither."[14] Such accusations against the king were hypocritical, since at least half the signatories to the Declaration, including Jefferson, were important slaveholders or involved in the slave trade. Moreover, because of pressure from slaveholding interests in the South and slave-trading interests in the North, this critique of slavery was omitted from the final version of the Declaration. Recall too that in 1787 the U.S. Constitution was made by elite white men, many of whom had strong ties to the entrenched system of black enslavement. . . .

VARIATIONS IN PLANTATION CAPITALISM

. . . For most slaveholders in the South there was more to slavery than just profit making. As Jefferson and other leading slaveholders emphasized, an agricultural society was to be preferred to an urban society. In their view the gentleman's life necessitated owning black men, women, and children for social status as well as for profit.[15] One of the great ironies of the slavery system is the accent that these "gentlemen" and their "ladies" put on values such as chivalry and honor, even as they practiced barbarism.[16] The political economy of slavery was a blending of capitalism with persisting elements of feudalism.

In the decade preceding the Civil War, a quarter of the white families in southern and border states owned nearly four million black men, women, and children. Thus, a large number of white families were directly involved in slavery. It was these families, especially those who held the largest number of slaves on big farms and plantations, who were the most influential in controlling the regional economy and politics. An array of ordinary whites provided the infrastructure of the slavery system—providing transport, growing foodstuffs, policing slaves, running local government, and providing many of the skilled trades. The slaveholding oligarchy—all white men—maintained its hegemony over the nonslaveholding white majority not only by these critical economic ties but also by propagating an ideology of white supremacy and providing certain types of white privilege. Most whites accepted the reality of slavery because "it provided not only an escalator by which they might one day rise, but also a floor beneath which they could not fall." As long as this was the case, "a Southern white consensus in defense of the peculiar institution was more or less assured."[17]

What was the position of white women in this system? Whatever their class level, they were generally under the control of husbands and fathers. They clearly had far fewer rights than white men, and all suffered significantly from patriarchal oppression. Working-class women, the majority of southern white women, provided most of the household labor that supported male workers and farmers. Women in the affluent slaveholding families sometimes inherited slaves or controlled some of their husband's slaves. They played a direct role in maintaining the racist system. One prominent analysis notes that white "mistresses, even the kindest, commonly resorted to the whip to maintain order among people who were always supposed to be on call; among people who inevitably disappointed expectations; among people whose constant presence not merely as servants but as individuals with wills and passions of their own provided constant irritation along with constant, if indifferent, service."[18] There was some recorded discontent from these slaveholding women about their lives, but rarely did they oppose the slavery system that gave them their own version of white privilege.

Among social scientists there is some debate as to whether the southern system was capitalistic or just a unique enclave economy imbedded in a capitalistic market system.[19] However, both groups of scholars generally agree on two points that are important for our analysis: (1) the larger slaveholders were oriented to making profits off their enslaved laborers; and (2) these slaveholders oriented themselves to trading within a capitalistic world-market system. Whatever other social values they may have held, the larger plantation owners were also early capitalists. Slavery capitalism was a system of worker control no other capitalist system could match. Enslaved men and women had a larger share of the worth of their work taken from them than did wage workers because they were chattel property and at the mercy of their owners at all hours of the day.

THE STRUCTURE OF SLAVERY IN THE NORTH

Many northern merchants and manufacturers were active in the slave trade or had economic ties to the slave plantations. At the time of the American Revolution, the slave trade was, in Lorenzo Greene's detailed analysis, the "very basis of the economic life of New England; about it revolved, and on it depended, most of [the region's] other industries."[20] Greene lists more than 160 prominent slaveholding families in the area. Slavery-linked businesses included those dealing in sugar, molasses, and rum, as well as those dealing with shipbuilding and shipping. Leading textile manufacturers were "active participants in the slave trade or active in commercial and industrial endeavors that were closely

intertwined with the slave(ry) trade."[21] Indeed, some northern industrialists were strong supporters of southern slaveholders, and most others colluded in the slavery structure that buttressed their industries. In addition, northern manufactures, farmers, and professionals sometimes bought black laborers or servants for their families. Even some antislavery advocates, such as the respected Benjamin Franklin, had owned slaves at some point in their lives.

Significant numbers of black Americans were enslaved in some northern areas well into the 1800s. The colony of Massachusetts Bay had been the first to legalize slavery, and by the mid-1600s there were strict slavery laws throughout the northern colonies. By the 1720s more than a fifth of New York City's population was black, and most of these New Yorkers were enslaved. Indeed, New York City's famous Wall Street area was one of the first large colonial markets where whites bought and sold slaves. This savage business lasted in New York City until 1862, even after the Civil War had begun.[22]

White northerners sometimes responded to black attempts to break the bonds of slavery in the same way as white Southerners—with barbaric brutality. In New York there was great fear of slave revolts. In 1712 there was a major slave revolt in New York City; in retaliation whites hung, starved, or roasted to death fifteen African Americans. In New York state, where slaves made up 7 percent of the population in 1786, even a partial emancipation statute was not passed until 1799—and that statute only freed enslaved children born after July 4, 1799 and then only when they reached their mid-twenties. All enslaved black Americans there did not become free until the 1850s. In Massachusetts, famous for its antislavery abolitionists, one attempt to abolish slavery failed in the state House of Representatives in 1767. Not until the 1780s did pressures from the white populace force the abolition of slavery in New England. Even then, it was not a recognition of black civil rights but pressure from white workers, who objected to competing with enslaved laborers, that played the major role in forcing slavery's abolition.[23] Moreover, in northern states where black workers and their families were emancipated, they faced Jim Crow segregation and regular discrimination in jobs, housing, and public accommodations. They also faced much racist mocking in newspapers and in public entertainments such as blackface minstrelsy. The early enslavement of black Americans in the North was indeed a "deeply engrained coding" that facilitated later patterns of segregation and other institutional racism.[24]

Most white northerners, including most religious leaders, did not support the immediate emancipation of enslaved African Americans in the South until the first battles of the Civil War made this expedient.[25] Prior to the Civil War many whites in all regions felt that slavery could not be abolished because of its economic importance. Indeed, into the 1850s much of the merchant class of the North was allied politically with the southern planter class. Not only did northern merchants and traders buy products from southern plantations, they also made up a substantial part of the Democratic party in the North, while southern elites dominated that party in the South.

Unjust Immiseration: The Terrible Costs for Africans and African Americans

The Barbarity of Slavery

Unjust enrichment for whites brought great immiseration for blacks. Considering the number of people killed or maimed in the process, and the scale and time involved, the enslavement of Africans is one of the most savage and barbaric aspects of European and American history. According to those enslaved, the slavery system was hellish and deadly beyond description and

comprehension. Once captured, enslaved Africans were often taken to slave corrals or castles in Africa where they were chained, branded, and held for shipping abroad. Many died there in barbaric conditions. On the Atlantic voyage those enslaved were chained together in close quarters, again in death-dealing conditions. The horror of the Atlantic trade was summed up by one young African, who in his autobiography explained, "I was soon put down under the decks, and there I received such a salutation in my nostrils as I had never experienced in my life: so that with the loathsomeness of the stench, and crying together, I became so sick and low that I was not able to eat, nor had I the least desire to taste any thing. . . . On my refusing to eat, one of them held me fast by the hands, and laid me across, I think the windlass, and tied my feet, while the other flogged me severely. . . . One day, when we had a smooth sea and moderate wind, two of my wearied countrymen who were chained together (I was near them at the time), preferring death to such a life of misery, somehow made through the nettings and jumped into the sea."[26]

The conditions of those enslaved at the points of destination were also brutal and oppressive. William Wells Brown, the son of a white slaveowner and an enslaved black woman, reported on what happened to an assertive man named Randall. One day a white overseer, named Grove Cook, got three white friends to help him subdue Randall. As Brown explains, "He refused to go; whereupon he was attacked by the overseer and his companions, when he turned upon them, and laid them, one after another, prostrated on the ground. [One man] drew out his pistol, and fired at him, and brought him to the ground by a pistol ball. The others rushed upon him with their clubs, and beat him over the head and face, until they succeeded in tying him. He was taken to the barn, and tied to a beam. Cook gave him over one hundred lashes with a heavy cowhide, had him washed with salt and water, and left him tied during the day. The next day he was untied, and taken to a blacksmith's shop, and had a ball and chain attached to his leg."[27]

Brown recounts that this brave man was forced to work hard in the fields with the chain on him and that the slaveowner was pleased with the sadistic cruelty of his overseer. Brown observed numerous beatings and killings of black men and women by whites during years of enslavement. The extant narratives of those enslaved are replete with accounts of chains, mutilation, stocks, whippings, starvation, and imprisonment.[28]

THE RAPE OF ENSLAVED WOMEN

Once fully instituted, the arrangements of slavery became much more than a machine for generating economic wealth. They constituted a well-developed system for the social and sexual control of black men and women.[29] During slavery, and later under legal segregation, many African and African American women were raped by white men, including sailors, slave-masters, overseers, and employers. Under the American system of racism the children resulting from the coerced sexual relations were automatically classified as black, even though they had substantial European ancestry. Indeed, it is estimated today that at least three-quarters of "black" Americans have at least one white ancestor. No other racial or ethnic group's physical makeup has been so substantially determined by the sexual depredations of white men. Recently, Patricia Williams, a black law professor, has described the case of Austin Miller, the thirty-five-year-old white lawyer who bought her eleven-year-old great-great-grandmother, Sophie. By the time Sophie was twelve, Miller had made her pregnant with the child who was Williams's great-grandmother Mary. Sophie's child was taken from her and became a house servant to Miller's white children. Williams's great-great-grandfather was thus one of a large number of white men who were rapists of black women or molesters of black children.[30]

Most of the surviving narratives of enslaved black women have accounts—sometimes quite numerous—of sexual exploitation by white men. Take the case of an enslaved black woman named Celia. In 1850 a prosperous Missouri farmer, Robert Newsom, bought Celia, then a fourteen-year-old, and soon thereafter raped her. Over the next five years, Newsom sexually attacked her numerous times, fathering two children by her. In the summer of 1855 Newsom came to Celia's cabin one last time to rape her, she hit him with a stick, and he died from the blows. In a travesty of justice, Celia was convicted in a Missouri court of the "crime" and hung in late December 1855.[31] Black women were doubly oppressed by the institution of slavery; they had no redress for the brutal crimes committed against them.

Like Miller and Newsom, many of these oppressors were respectable men in their communities. One of the most famous was Thomas Jefferson. In his forties he coerced the enslaved teenager Sally Hemings into his bed. That he fathered at least one child with her has now been confirmed by DNA testing, and it is presumed that he fathered several other children by her. Yet in his lifetime Jefferson never admitted to this coercive relationship.[32] Until the DNA evidence showed the reality of the relationship, most white historians and commentators denied that Jefferson could have had children with an enslaved woman. The reason for this denial doubtless lies in the fact that Jefferson is an American icon. As the first professional biographer of Jefferson, James Parton, put it in 1874, "If Jefferson was wrong, America is wrong. If America is right, Jefferson was right."[33]

One of the most oppressive aspects of American racism lies in this sexual thread, which weaves itself through various manifestations of racism to the present. White men have often raped African American women with impunity, especially during the nation's first three centuries. Many white men developed a contradictory set of attitudes that saw black women as human enough to be exotic objects of sexual desire, yet as less than human in their rights to protection from sexual attack. Given that most such men proclaimed themselves to be virtuous and religious, such sexual attitudes and actions contradicted their expressed morality. The tensions between this image of themselves as virtuous and their sexualized feelings and actions toward black women—often coupled with a denial at the conscious level of these feelings—seem to have led to a projection of many white men's sexual desires onto black men. As the historian Winthrop Jordan has argued, white men's passion for black women was "not fully acceptable to the society or the self and hence not readily admissible. Sexual desires could be effectively denied and the accompanying anxiety and guilt in some measure assuaged, however, by imputing them to others."[34]

Given this projection of white males' desires into black men, one can better understand certain aspects of U.S. racism—the obsession of many white men (and women) with the black man as a rapist . . . and the extraordinarily brutal and often sexualized attacks on black men in thousands of lynchings and other violent attacks. . .

African Immiseration

Numerous African societies paid a heavy, often catastrophic, price for the Atlantic slave trade. For several centuries many of the African continent's young people were ripped from its shores, thereby damaging the future development of the continent. Millions of Africans were lost in the slave trade, so many that the use of the term *the black holocaust* seems appropriate for this savage process. An estimated ten million Africans survived the Atlantic crossings to the Americas, with many millions more killed or lost to deprivation and disease on the way, or back in Africa before embarkation. Estimates for the total number enslaved or killed in the attempt to enslave at all points in Africa and the Atlantic trade suggest a figure of at least twenty-eight million from the 1400s to slavery's abolition in most areas by the late 1800s.[35]

Over time, this Atlantic trade in human beings had serious negative effects on social institutions in parts of Africa, a destruction that greatly facilitated later European exploitation of that continent. Recall W. E. B. Du Bois's argument that African colonization is usually omitted or downplayed in mainstream histories of European development, wealth, and affluence. Yet any serious understanding of the development of European wealth must center on early and late African colonialism, for the labor and mineral resources of Africans were taken to help create that European prosperity. Similarly, much African immiseration is linked to the creation of white prosperity over the course of North American history.

A number of scholars and popular writers have accented the role of Africans in this Atlantic slave trade, sometimes in order to play down the European role.[36] Yet one must put the African participation in perspective. Europeans were not enslaved by Africans. And virtually all Africans enslaved in the Americas were taken from their continent by European traders or merchants and sold to Europeans in the Americas. This Atlantic trade in human beings began when European ships arrived seeking commerce with African societies whose economies were not centered in profit making from enslavement. As Europeans grew in power along the coast, African nations were played off against each other, just as European colonizers in the Americas played off one indigenous nation there against another. Significantly, the European intruders had some six hundred slave ports built for their bloody trade, and they themselves recorded at least three hundred battles with Africans as part of the enslavement process. Africans did not seek out this system. In some cases Africans were kidnapped directly by European slavers. In numerous other cases African political leaders, who had often at first traded certain African goods for European goods, ran out of these items and, pressed by the European slavers, turned to trading people held in servitude.[37]

Certainly, some leaders at the top of the hierarchies of African societies worked with the European slavers to provide the human cargo the latter sought. Indeed, trading in slaves became addictive for some African leaders without other goods to trade to Europeans. Those who were traded as slaves often included temporary wards, such as children of the poor or widows (who were then in the care of African leaders), as well as those captured in battles with other societies. Apparently, most African leaders did not realize that those traded would become permanently enslaved as property without *any* human rights and would often be worked to death in just a few years. In numerous West African societies many of those held in involuntary servitude were treated more like wards or indentured servants than like the rights-less chattel property they became in the Americas. They were often part of a family unit, had some legal rights, and could marry, own property, and sometimes inherit from their masters.[38] It is also important to note that many Africans saw the Atlantic slave trade as a serious threat, even as a sickness, and local healing societies developed to fight it. There was also substantial violent resistance to the Atlantic slave trade by Africans.

A DISTINCTIVE FORM OF SLAVERY

The enslavement of Africans in the Americas was not only more extreme than slavery in most African societies but also more oppressive than slavery in ancient societies such as the Roman Empire. Unlike Roman slaves, American slaves were generally forbidden by law to read or write. In the Americas the Europeans applied slavery, as Du Bois reminds us, "on a scale and with an elaborateness of detail of which no former world ever dreamed. The imperial width of the thing—the heaven-defying audacity—makes its modern newness."[39] An essential feature of North American slavery was the denial of most human liberties. Slaves "could own nothing; they could make no contracts; they could hold no property; nor traffic in property; they could not hire out; they could not legally marry . . . they could not appeal from their master; they could be punished at will."[40] In North America human beings were reduced to the status of things to be bought and sold.

Even the English language was "made an instrument of domination and silencing; it was used to regulate and police access to authority and knowledge among colonized peoples."[41] Enslaved Africans were from many different societies, and they were forced to learn the language of their oppressors. This was probably the most forced of all adaptations to the English language. Voluntary immigrants to the United States have been allowed to retain much more of their home languages and have probably kept more of the home culture associated with those languages. In the destruction of African languages and their more or less complete replacement by a new language we see how extensive the system of antiblack racism is. Enforced adaptation to the English language not only marked the movement of early English colonizers across the lands of conquest, but also marks today—in attacks on black English and on Spanish—similar attempts to maintain white cultural dominance over those long subordinated.

ILL-GOTTEN GAINS: WEALTH AND PROSPERITY FROM SLAVERY

The enslavement of Africans was not just the work of slave traders and adventurers. Nor was it something marginal to the economic interests of the elites on both sides of the Atlantic. Instead, slavery was a system created, supported, and financed by a very large number of the leading political, business, and intellectual figures of the day. We can, as an example, take just one major enterprise of the early eighteenth century, the famous British South Sea Company. This was an official company set up to transport enslaved Africans overseas. Stockholders in this company included the leading physical scientist Sir Isaac Newton, major authors like Jonathan Swift and Daniel Defoe, and the founder of the Bank of England, the Earl of Halifax. They also included most members of the House of Lords and of the House of Commons. Many aristocrats also held stock in the company.[42] Clearly, the leading men of Britain were directly and financially involved in the slave trade. Similarly, many leading Americans, including George Washington, Thomas Jefferson, Patrick Henry, George Mason, and James Madison, profited greatly from slavery or the slave trade. These men saw slavery as an honorable business activity.

BUILDING THE WEALTH OF BRITAIN AND CONTINENTAL EUROPE

The British merchants of the eighteenth century recognized the centrality of slavery in building the wealth of their nation. For example, in the 1740s one business pamphleteer wrote about Britain's wealth this way:

> The most approved judges of the Commercial Interests of these Kingdoms have ever been of the opinion that our West-India and African Trades are the most nationally beneficial of any we carry on. It is also allowed on all hands, that the trade to Africa is the Branch which renders our American Colonies and Plantations so advantageous to Great Britain: that Traffic only affording our Planters a constant supply of Negro Servants for the Culture, of their Lands in the Produce of Sugars, Tobacco, Rice, Rum, Cotton, Fustick, Pimento, and all other our Plantation Produce: so that the extensive Employment of our Shipping in, to, and from America, the great Brood of Seamen consequent thereupon, and the daily Bread of the most considerable Part of our British Manufactures, are owing primarily to the Labour of Negroes; who, as they were the first happy instruments of raising our Plantations: so their Labour only can support and preserve them, and render them still more and more profitable to their Mother-Kingdom. The Negro-Trade therefore, and the natural consequences resulting from it, may be justly esteemed an inexhaustible Fund of Wealth and Naval Power to this Nation.[43]

This remarkable business summary accents the primary role of the "labour of Negroes" to British shipping and manufacturing, and thus to "inexhaustible fund of wealth" for that nation.

The economic trade generated by British and French plantations in the Americas was the source of much of the capital for the commercial and industrial revolutions of the two nations. British and French industry, shipping, naval and merchant marine development, banking, and insurance were significantly stimulated by or grounded in the labor of enslaved Africans in their respective colonies.[44] From the early 1700s to the mid-1800s a large proportion of the major agricultural exports in world trade were produced by enslaved Africans. British port cities became prosperous as centers for the trade in Africans and British industrial cities became prosperous because of the manufacturing of goods with cotton from slave plantations. Textiles manufacturing was the core industry of the Industrial Revolution, and most of the raw cotton was grown by enslaved laborers. Liverpool slave traders, Caribbean sugar planters, and Manchester manufacturers were major sources of circulating capital in the eighteenth and early nineteenth centuries. Circulating through banking and lending enterprises, the profits from international trade—much of it directly or indirectly related to the slave trade and the trade in slave-produced products—provided a substantial part of the large-scale investments in British industry in this period, growth that in turn led to many new technologies and products of the Industrial Revolution. These investments also spurred a rapid buildup of the financial and insurance industries.[45] Some of these powerful institutions have persisted to the present day. Barclay's Bank was founded with profits from the slave trade, and Lloyds of London prospered early on by insuring slave ships and their cargos.[46]

The most famous technological development of the period, James Watt's much-improved version of the steam engine developed during the 1760s, accelerated the industrial development of Europe and its far-flung colonies. Capital accumulated from the West Indies trade in slaves and slave-produced products directly bankrolled Watt's reworking of the steam engine. Numerous industries, such as the metallurgical industries—which made possible the manufacturing of chains for slaves as well as new machinery, bridges, and rails— and the important railroad industry, were significantly spurred by the profits generated from the trade in slaves, products of plantations, and food and manufacturing exports flowing from Britain back to the American plantations and

to Africa. In turn, much additional economic activity was generated as these profits flowed into all forms of European and colonial consumption. Economic activity was stimulated even if the recipients of the income from the slave trade and plantations put it into land, coaches, or banks.[47]

Slaveholders were not the only beneficiaries of the slavery system; those who bought and sold products of plantations were also major beneficiaries. This latter group included merchants and consumers in many nations. In addition, many white workers in Britain and other parts of Europe owed their livelihoods directly or indirectly to the trade in slaves and plantation products.[48] It seems unlikely that British and other European economic development would have occurred when it did without the very substantial capital generated by the slavery system.

We should note some important political and cultural linkages to this burgeoning economic system. In the eighteenth and early nineteenth centuries the British parliament was dominated on many issues by those with economic interests in the slave trade, slave plantations, or commercial trade with the plantations.[49] In addition, in Britain and North America the revival of the arts—music, painting, sculpture, and essay writing—in this period was spurred in part by substantial funding from patrons made prosperous by various slavery enterprises. For example, some of George Frideric Handel's oratorios and anthems were commissioned by an investor in slave plantations (the Duke of Chandos), and major libraries and art galleries were built by similar patrons.[50]

SLAVERY AND ECONOMIC
DEVELOPMENT IN THE AMERICAS

Coerced black laborers constituted the "founding stone of a new economic system . . . for the modem world."[51] It is unlikely that the American colonies and, later, the United States would have seen dramatic agricultural and industrial development in the eighteenth and nineteenth centuries without the blood and sweat of those enslaved. Much of the wealth generated between the early 1700s and the 1860s came from the slave trade and the labor of enslaved men, women, and children on plantations and in other profit-making enterprises. In the seventeenth century the famous triangular trade emerged between Europe, Africa, and the American colonies. Europe and America provided ships and some agricultural exports, while Africa provided the enslaved laborers. As Eric Williams has noted, sugar plantations in the West Indies "became the hub of the British Empire, of immense importance to the grandeur and prosperity of England," and it was the African laborers who made the West Indies the "most precious colonies ever recorded in the whole annals of imperialism."[52] Recent reviews of the evidence have concluded that the main economic bridge between Europe and the overseas colonies in this period was the slave-sugar complex.[53] The Caribbean plantations also spurred mainland development. Much of the oats, corn, flour, fish, lumber, soap, candles, and livestock exported by the continental colonies went to the West Indies plantations. In 1770 no less than *three-quarters* of all New England exports of food-stuffs went to the West Indian plantations or to Africa.[54] A substantial proportion of the wealth of the New England and Middle Atlantic colonies came from the nefarious trade with slave plantations in the southern colonies and the Caribbean.

From the early 1700s to the mid-1800s much of the surplus capital and wealth of North America came directly, or by means of economic multiplier effects, from the slave trade and slave plantations.[55] With the growing demand for textiles, U.S. cotton production expanded greatly between the 1790s and the beginning of the Civil War. Cotton was shipped to British and New England textile mills, greatly spurring the wheels of British, U.S., and international commerce. By the mid-nineteenth century New England cotton mills were the industrial leaders in value added, and second in number of employees, in the United States. Without slave labor it seems likely that there would have been no successful textile industry, and without the cotton textile industry—the first major U.S. industry—it is unclear how or when the United States would have become a major industrial power.[56] In the first half of the nineteenth century many northern merchants, bankers, and shipping companies became, as Douglass North has noted, "closely tied to cotton. New York became both the center of the import trade and the financial center for the cotton trade."[57] Slave-grown cotton became ever more central to the U.S. economy and accounted for about half of all exports, and thus for a large share of the profits generated by exports.

In the North the profits from the cotton economy and from the sale of products to slave plantations stimulated the growth of investment in financial and insurance enterprises, other service industries, and various types of manufacturing concerns, as well as, by means of taxes, of investment in government infrastructure projects. Cotton-related activities were perhaps the most important source of economic expansion in the United States before the Civil War, and most of the cotton was grown by enslaved black Americans.[58] Their agricultural production undergirded national economic development. As Ronald Takaki has noted, "The income derived from the export of cotton set in motion the process of accelerated market and industrial development—the Market Revolution."[59]

Before the American revolution, trading in slaves was an honorable profession in northern ports, and after the revolution it was equally honorable to trade in products made by slaves or in manufactured products traded to plantations. One biographer of the leading merchant, T. H.

Perkins, concluded that there was not a New England "merchant of any prominence who was not then directly or indirectly involved in this trade."[60] As the nineteenth century progressed, the sons and grandsons of the earlier traders in slaves and slave-related products often became the captains of the textile and other major industries in the North. The business profits made off enslavement were thereby transmitted across generations.[61]

British and New England manufacturers' demand for cotton fueled the demand for more enslaved workers and for more Native American land. The leading cotton states—Mississippi, Alabama, and South Carolina—were carved out of Native American lands, and as the cotton system expanded westward, the lands of more indigenous societies were taken. Land was usually taken by force or threat of force.[62] By 1850 most of the nation's enslaved population was involved in cotton production. Labor was perhaps the most critical factor in American economic production in the eighteenth and nineteenth centuries, so any scarcity in workers slowed development. "Slave labor not only removed this scarcity, but also made possible the development of the industry that spurred economic growth."[63] In the decade before the Civil War the dollar value of those enslaved was estimated by one leading planter to be $2 billion—a figure then exceeding the total value of *all* northern factories.[64]

Not only did the southern agricultural system provide fiber for the textile mills of the North, but profits from the cotton trade also generated demand for western foodstuffs and northern manufactured products. And the coerced labor of black men, women, and children in southern agriculture built up profits that were used by many white slaveowners for luxurious living, for further investments in plantations and related enterprises, for deposits in banks, or for paying off bank loans. Such capital—and the related capital generated in

the international trade in southern products—could be used or borrowed by merchants, shippers, railroad executives, and other industrialists in the North or South.[65]

The economic prosperity and industrial development of Western nations, including the United States, were grounded to a substantial degree in the slavery system. Ali Mazrui summarizes the point, saying that "one of the forces that fed into the industrial revolution was slave labor. Western production levels were transformed. But so were Western living standards, life expectancy, population growth, and the globalization of capitalism."[66] Indeed, even the educational system of the new nation was sometimes funded from profits off slavery or the slave trade. For example, the founders of Brown University in Rhode Island made some of their fortunes by building slave ships and investing in the slave trade.[67]

THE WEALTH OF POWERFUL SLAVEHOLDERS

In the century prior to the Civil War the slaveholding oligarchy of the southern and border states controlled a huge share of the resources and riches of the nation. By the early nineteenth century the slaveholders owned much of the nation's most productive land and much of the agricultural produce for export. They owned a large proportion of the nation's livestock, warehouses, plantation buildings, and processing mills, as well as large numbers of enslaved workers. As a result, the South was the most economically prosperous and politically powerful region from the mid-1700s to the 1850s.[68]

The theft of land and the enslavement of Africans became the foundation of prosperity for many white families. George Washington, the leading general, chair of the Constitutional Convention, and first president, was one of the wealthiest Americans. Owner of more than 36,000 acres in Virginia and Maryland, he held substantial securities in banks and land companies. By 1783 his own accounting showed 216 enslaved black Americans under his control, including those he held and those of his wife's estate; in their lifetimes he and his wife had enslaved many more. Reading Washington's careful records, one can see that Washington viewed black men, women, and children as "little more than economic units," like farm animals whose purpose was to bring him monetary profit.[69] Enslaved blacks made possible his luxurious lifestyle. As Fritz Hirchfeld has documented, "Slaves washed his linens, sewed his shirts, polished his boots, saddled his horse, chopped the wood for his fireplaces, powdered his wig, drove his carriage, cooked his meals, served his table, poured his wine, posted his letters, lit the lamps, swept the porch, looked after the guests, planted the flowers in his gardens, trimmed the hedges, dusted the furniture, cleaned the windows, made the beds, and performed the myriad domestic chores. . . ."[70] Though Washington said he was opposed to violent brutality against those enslaved, his actions contradicted his stated view. His overseers were allowed to use flogging, and he vigorously pursued runaways. He could be severe in his punishment, as in the case of one black man sold to the West Indies plantations—unusually savage places known for enslaved laborers being worked to an early death. Exhibiting his inhumanity, Washington wrote to his broker that this black man, was a "rogue and a runaway" and should be kept handcuffed.[71]

Similarly, the principal author of the Declaration of Independence, Thomas Jefferson, was considered very wealthy because he owned 10,000 acres of land and because, by the early 1800s, he held 185 African Americans in bondage. He owned several hundred black Americans over his lifetime. His often extravagant lifestyle was made possible by those he enslaved. While Jefferson was sometimes critical of slavery, he rarely freed any slaves. The man seen as a principal progenitor of American liberty, who penned the phrase "all men are created equal," was an unrepentant Virginia slaveholder. He fathered at least one child whom he kept as a slave, and he chased down his fugitive slaves and had them severely whipped.[72] Like many wealthy men in the South and the North, Washington and Jefferson gained their prosperity on the bloody backs of those black men, women, and children they enslaved.

SLAVEHOLDERS AND THE AMERICAN GOVERNMENT

Another Irony of the American Revolution

Without the capital and wealth generated by enslaved black Americans it is possible that there would not have been an American Revolution and, thus, a United States. One of history's great ironies is the fact that the Declaration of Independence's "all men are created equal" did not apply to African Americans, yet the American victory in the struggle against Great Britain was possible substantially because the wealth generated by the slavery system and its economic spinoffs was available to help finance and support the American Revolution. A significant proportion of the money amassed or borrowed to fight that revolution came, directly or indirectly, from capital generated by the plantations and the trade in slaves and slave-produced products.[73] Money borrowed from northern sources often had its ultimate origin in the slavery constellation, as did some of the money borrowed from overseas. France's involvement in the American Revolution was essential to its successful outcome, and, as Edmund Morgan has shown, the "single most valuable product with which to purchase assistance was tobacco, produced mainly by slave labor. . . . To a large degree it may be said that Americans bought their independence with slave labor."[74]

The political structure established after the revolution continued to reflect the elite interest in slavery and in controlling African Americans, whether enslaved or free. The mainstream view of the U.S. government sees it and its actions as set, from its first decades, in the context of democracy—as the result of competing group interests jockeying for position through democratic political mechanisms. From this viewpoint, there is often a denial of the highly elitist and racialized character of the U.S. government.

A contrasting view sees the early U.S. state as very undemocratic and as central to the creation of systemic racism and to the formation of racial groups.[75] Historically, white male elites have worked through local and federal governments to create social institutions serving their interests. In the early development of the U.S. state, white women, African Americans, and Native Americans had no representation. The white male ruling class created a racialized state, which played a central role in defining who was "black" and "white" and what the benefits of being in each racial class were. For African Americans—and Native Americans forced onto reservations—this took the form of a police state. The standard dictionary definition of *police state* is "a political unit characterized by repressive governmental control of political, economic, and social life usually by an arbitrary exercise of power by police."[76] While the usual example of this is a totalitarian exercise of European government such as that of Nazi Germany, for most blacks police-state repression of their lives lasted, under slavery and later segregation, until the 1960s. Indeed, certain elements of this police state can still be seen in contemporary policing practices that unjustly target black men and women.

Slavery dominated U.S. politics in many ways between the making of the Constitution and the beginning of Civil War. The first U.S. president was a leading slaveholder, as were the third and fourth presidents. For fifty of the first sixty-four years of the new nation the president of the United States was a slave owner. The Speaker of the House was a slave owner for twenty-eight of the first thirty-five years of the nation's history, and before the Civil War the president pro tem of the Senate was usually a slaveholder.[77] The Chief Justices of the Supreme Court for most of the period up to the Civil War, John Marshall and Roger B. Taney, were slaveholders, as were numerous other members of that high court.

In the decades after the U.S. Constitution was put into place, the slavery system continued to shape legal and political decision making in fundamental ways, including the building of constitutional law in a series of federal court decisions such as *Dred Scott*. . . . For decades few major decisions made by the federal legislative and judicial branches went against the interests of the nation's slaveholding oligarchy, and foreign and domestic policies generally did not conflict with the interests of those centrally involved with the slavery system. George Washington's presidential administration even lent money to French planters in Haiti to put down a major slave uprising there. John Adams, his successor and not a slaveholder, took action to support the rebels, with an eye to U.S. influence in the area. Thomas Jefferson, another slaveholder and the third president, reversed Adams's policy and moved to support France's attempt to reconquer Haiti. Moreover, in the first half of the nineteenth century much U.S. territorial expansion, such as into areas of Mexico, was undergirded by the slaveholders' interest in additional land for yet more slave plantations.[78]

The slaveholding oligarchy was not seriously challenged until the middle of the nineteenth century. By the decade of the 1850s a major schism in the ruling class, that between southern planters and northern industrialists who had little economic interest in slavery, was becoming clear in battles over such issues as the expansion of slavery into western lands and over tariffs. Southern planters opposed tariffs on imports and pressed for expansion of the slave-holding system into new western areas, while northern immigrant farmers and allied railroad interests increasingly pressed to keep those lands available for immigrant farmers. Fearful of its economic and political future, the South's slaveholding oligarchy eventually moved to secede. The victory of the North in the subsequent Civil War marked the arrival of northern industrialists and merchants as a dominant force in the U.S. economy and government.[79]

The grip of slavery on the nation could be seen even as the southern states were seceding and the nation was moving to war. Recall that President Abraham Lincoln was willing to make major concessions to slaveholding interests to preserve the union. Certain members of the Republican Party talked with representatives of the southern planters and proposed a thirteenth amendment to the Constitution that would guarantee slavery in the South. Lincoln was willing to accept this amendment, even though it perpetuated enslavement. Yet the southern oligarchy rejected this compromise proposal, apparently because they thought they could win a war.[80]

. . .

NOTES

1. United Nations, "Convention on the Prevention and Punishment of Genocide," *The United Nations and Human Rights: 1945–1995* (New York: United Nations Department of Public Information, 1995), p. 151.

2. Charles W. Mills, *The Racial Contract* (Ithaca, NY: Cornell University Press, 1997), pp. 98, 155; David E. Stannard, *The American Holocaust: Columbus and the Conquest of the New World* (New York: Oxford University Press, 1992).

3. William T. Hagan, *American Indians* (Chicago: University of Chicago Press, 1961), p. 14. The discussion of these wars is taken from pp. 12–15. An earlier, much less developed version of this discussion, as well as that in a few later paragraphs of this chapter, appears in Joe R. Feagin and Clairece B. Feagin, *Racial and Ethnic Relations*, 6th ed. (Upper Saddle River, NJ: Prentice Hall, 1999), chapters 7 and 8.

4. Michael P. Rogin, *Fathers and Children: Andrew Jackson and the Subjugation of the American Indian* (New York: Knopf, 1975), p. 319.

5. Winthrop D. Jordan, *White over Black: American Attitudes toward the Negro, 1550–1812* (Chapel Hill: University of North Carolina Press, 1968), pp. 239–41.

6. Benjamin B. Ringer, *"We the People" and Others* (New York: Tavistock, 1983), pp. 134–38.

7. *Dred Scott v. John F. A. Sandford*, 60 U.S. 393, 403–404 (1857).

8. Ibid., 408.

9. Ringer, *"We the People" and Others*, p. 36.

10. Robin Blackburn, *The Making of New World Slavery: From the Baroque to the Modern, 1492–1800* (London: Verso, 1997), p. 10.

11. A. Leon Higginbotham, Jr., *Shades of Freedom: Racial Politics and the Presumptions of the American Legal Process* (New York: Oxford University Press, 1996), pp. 14–51.

12. Forrest G. Wood, *The Arrogance of Faith: Christianity and Race in America from the Colonial Era to the Twentieth Century* (New York: Knopf, 1990), p. xviii.

13. Higginbotham, *Shades of Freedom*, p. xxiii; Lawrence M. Friedman, *A History of American Law* (New York: Simon and Schuster, 1973), pp. 72–76, 192–200; Herbert Aptheker, *American Negro Slave Revolts* (New York: International Publishers, 1943), pp. 53–78.

14. Thomas Jefferson, quoted in Peter M. Bergman, *The Chronological History of the Negro in America* (New York: Harper & Row, 1969), p. 52.

15. Ronald Segal, *The Black Diaspora* (New York: Farrar, Straus and Giroux, 1995), pp. 58–59.

16. Kenneth S. Greenberg, *Honor and Slavery* (Princeton, NJ: Princeton University Press, 1996).

17. Peter J. Parish, *Slavery: History and Historians* (New York: Harper and Row, 1989), p. 129; see also pp. 126–32.

18. Elizabeth Fox-Genovese, *Within the Plantation Household: Black and White Women of the Old South* (Chapel Hill: University of North Carolina Press, 1988), p. 24.

19. See Kenneth Stampp, *The Peculiar Institution: Slavery in the Ante-Bellum South* (New York: Vintage Books, 1956); and Robert W. Roel and Stanley Engerman, *Time on the Cross: The Economics of American Negro Slavery* (Boston: Little, Brown, 1974). For a summary of the scholars and their views, see Fox-Genovese, *Within the Plantation Household*, pp. 56–86.

20. Lorenzo J. Greene, *The Negro in Colonial New England* (New York: Atheneum, 1969), pp. 56–69. This quote is on pp. 68–69.

21. Ronald Bailey, "The Other Side of Slavery," *Agricultural History* 68 (Spring 1994): 36.

22. James W. Loewen, *Lies My Teacher Told Me: Everything Your American History Textbook Got Wrong* (New York: The New Press, 1995), p. 135.

23. A. Leon Higginbotham, Jr., *In the Matter of Color* (New York: Oxford University Press, 1978), pp. 63–70, 144–49. An earlier discussion of some data in this section appeared in Joe R. Feagin, "Slavery Unwilling to Die: The Background of Black Oppression in the 1980s," *Journal of Black Studies* 17 (December 1986): 173–200.

24. Ringer, *"We the People" and Others*, p. 533.

25. John R. McKivigan, "The Northern Churches and the Moral Problem of Slavery," in *The Meaning of Slavery in the North*, eds. David Roediger and Martin H. Blatt (New York: Garland, 1998), pp. 77–94.

26. Olaudah Equiano, "The Interesting Narrative of the Life of Olaudah Equiano," in *Afro-American History*, ed. Thomas R. Frazier (New York: Harcourt, Brace & World, 1970), pp. 18–20.

27. William Wells Brown, *From Fugitive Slave to Free Man*, ed. William L. Andrews (New York: Mentor Books, 1993), p. 30.

28. See T. Lindsay Baker and Julie P. Baker, eds., *The WPA Oklahoma Slave Narratives* (Norman: University of Oklahoma Press, 1996).

29. See Patricia Morton, introduction to *Discovering the Women in Slavery*, ed. Patricia Morton (Athens: University of Georgia Press, 1996).

30. Patricia J. Williams, *The Alchemy of Race and Rights* (Cambridge, MA: Harvard University Press, 1991), pp. 154–56.

31. Melton A. McLaurin, *Celia: A Slave* (Athens: University of Georgia Press, 1991); see also Harriet A. Jacobs, *Incidents in the Life of a Slave Girl*, ed. Jean Fagan Yellin (Cambridge, MA: Harvard University Press, 1987).

32. The three-quarters-white Hemings was the half-sister of Jefferson's deceased wife. Jerry Fresia, *Toward an American Revolution: Exposing the Constitution and Other Illusions* (Boston: South End, 1988), pp. 1–2; Dinitia Smith and Nicholas Wade, "DNA Evidence Links Thomas Jefferson to Slave's Offspring," *Gainesville Sun*, November 1, 1998, 4A.

33. James Parton, quoted in Paul Finkelman, *Slavery and the Founders: Race and Liberty in the Age of Jefferson* (Armonk, NY: M. E. Sharpe, 1996), p. 143.

34. Jordan, *White over Black*, p. 153

35. The lower estimates come from Philip D. Curtin, *The African Slave Trade: A Census* (University of Wisconsin Press, 1968). The higher and probably more accurate figures are calculated in Joseph E. Inikori, ed., *Forced Migration* (New York: Africana Publishing, 1982), pp. 19–33; and S. E. Anderson, *The Black Holocaust* (New York: Writers and Readers Press, 1995), pp. 156–58.

36. See Dinesh D'Souza, *The End of Racism: Principles for a Multiracial Society* (New York: Free Press, 1995), pp. 70–87.

37. I am partially indebted here to an interpretation of the literature suggested to me by Holly Hanson. See also John Thornton, *Africa and Africans in the Making of the Atlantic World, 1400–1680* (New York: Cambridge University Press, 1992), pp. 5–9; and Molefi Kete Asante, "The Wonders of Africa," post to Discussion List for African American Studies (H-Afro-Am), November, 1999.

38. Stanley M. Elkins, *A Problem in American Institutional and Intellectual Life* (New York: Grosset and Dunlap, 1963), pp. 96–97. This was true as well of the slave trade between sub-Saharan Africa and certain Islamic countries.

39. W. E. B. Du Bois, *Darkwater* (1920), as reprinted in *The Oxford W. E. B. Du Bois Reader*, ed. Eric J. Sundquist (New York: Oxford, 1996), p. 504.

40. W. E. B. Du Bois, *Black Reconstruction in America 1860–1880* (New York: Atheneum, 1992 [1935]), p. 10.

41. John Willinsky, *Learning to Divide the World: Education at Empire's End* (Minneapolis: University of Minnesota Press, 1998), p. 191.

42. Rafael Tammariello, "The Slave Trade," *Las Vegas Review-Journal*, February 8, 1998, 1E.

43. J. H. Parry and P. M. Sherlock, *A Short History of the West Indies*, 3rd ed. (New York: St. Martin's Press, 1971), p. 110–11. I am influenced here by William M. Wiecek, *The Sources of Antislavery Constitutionalism in America, 1760–1848* (Ithaca, NY: Cornell University Press, 1977), pp. 15–16.

44. William M. Wiecek, "The Origins of the Law of Slavery in British North America," *Cardozo Law Review* 17 (May, 1996): 1739.

45. Williams, *Capitalism and Slavery*, pp. 98–107; Douglass C. North, *The Economic Growth of the United States, 1790–1860* (Englewood Cliffs, NJ: Prentice Hall, 1961), pp. 38–45; Bailey, "The Other Side of Slavery," p. 40; Blackburn, *The Making of New World Slavery*, chapter 12.

46. Anderson, *The Black Holocaust*, p. 19.

47. Barbara L. Solow and Stanley L. Engerman, "British Capitalism and Caribbean Slavery: The Legacy of Eric Williams: An Introduction," in *British Capitalism and Caribbean Slavery: The Legacy of Eric Williams* (Cambridge: Cambridge University Press, 1987), pp. 8–9.

48. Wilson E. Williams, *Africa and the Rise of Capitalism* (New York: AMS Press, 1975 [1938]), pp. 23–25.

49. Williams, *Capitalism and Slavery*, pp. 93–95, 102–107.

50. See the documentary *The Art of Darkness*, written by David Dabydeen and directed by David Maloney, Central Production, 1986. I am indebted to Joseph Rahme for suggesting this point.

51. Du Bois, *Black Reconstruction*, p. 15.

52. Williams, *Capitalism and Slavery*, p. 52.

53. Solow and Engerman, "British Capitalism and Caribbean Slavery," p. 4.

54. Ibid., pp. 5–7; Ronald Bailey, "'Those Valuable People, the Africans,'" in *The Meaning of Slavery in the North*, eds. Roediger and Blatt, p. 11.

55. See Fred Bateman and Thomas Weiss, *A Deplorable Scarcity: The Failure of Industrialization in the Slave Economy* (Chapel Hill: University of North Carolina Press, 1981); and Stanley Lebergott, *The Americans: An Economic Record* (New York: Norton, 1984).

56. Robert S. Browne, "Achieving Parity through Reparations," in *The Wealth of Races: The Present Value of Benefits from Past Injustices*, ed. Richard F. America (New York: Greenwood Press, 1990), pp. 201–202.

57. North, *The Economic Growth of the United States, 1790–1860*, p. 63.

58. Ibid., p. 68.

59. Ronald T. Takaki, *Iron Cages: Race and Culture in 19th-Century America* (New York: Oxford University Press, 1990), p. 78.

60. Bailey, "'Those Valuable People, the Africans,'" in *The Meaning of Slavery in the North*, eds. Roediger and Blatt, p. 14.

61. Ibid., p. 19.

62. North, *The Economic Growth of the United States, 1790–1860*, p. 41; Takaki, *Iron Cages*, p. 77.

63. Browne, "Achieving Parity through Reparations," p. 201.

64. Segal, *The Black Diaspora*, pp. 56–58.

65. North, *The Economic Growth of the United States, 1790–1860*, p. 122.

66. Ali A. Mazrui, "Who Should Pay for Slave Reparations to Africa," *World Press Review* (August 1993): 22.

67. Anderson, *The Black Holocaust*, p. 20.

68. Herbert Aptheker, *The Unfolding Drama: Studies in U.S. History*, ed. Bettina Aptheker (New York: International Publishers, 1978-84). Slavery was profitable for most slaveholders and the cost of maintaining slave labor was low. See Segal, *The Black Diaspora*.

69. Fritz Hirschfeld, *George Washington and Slavery: A Documentary Portrayal* (Columbia: University of Missouri Press, 1997), p. 49. See pp. 16, 37.

70. Hirschfeld, *George Washington and Slavery*, 236.

71. Ibid., pp. 68–69.

72. Takaki, *Iron Cages*, pp. 43–54.

73. Derrick Bell, "White Supremacy in America: Its Legal Legacy, Its Economic Costs," in *Critical White Studies: Looking Behind the Mirror*, eds. Richard Delgado and Jean Stefancic (Philadelphia: Temple University Press, 1999), p. 596.

74. Edmund S. Morgan, *American Slavery, American Freedom: The Ordeal of Virginia* (New York: Norton, 1975), p. 5.

75. Jack Niemonen, "The Role of the State in the Sociology of Racial and Ethnic Relations: Some Theoretical Considerations," *Free Inquiry in Creative Sociology* 23 (May 1995).

76. *Merriam-Webster's Collegiate Dictionary*, 10th ed. (Springfield, MA: Merriam-Webster, 1999), p. 901.

77. William Lee Miller, *Arguing about Slavery: The Great Battle in the United States Congress* (New York: Knopf, 1996), p. 13.

78. Loewen, *Lies My Teacher Told Me*, p. 143–144.

79. Aptheker, *The Unfolding Drama*, p. 83.

80. Herbert Aptheker, unpublished lectures on American History, Minneapolis, University of Minnesota, 1984. I draw here on tapes of the lectures.

Discussion Questions

1. How was slavery in the United States different from slavery anywhere else? What sorts of human rights were limited for African Americans under slavery? What were some of the types of barbarities committed by slave masters? Did they vary by gender (of whites and of blacks)?

2. What were some facts you learned about America's forefathers and slavery that you never knew before reading this essay? Why do you think such history is not taught in schools? Should it be? Why or why not?

3. Typically we think of only the South being involved in slavery. What are the ways Feagin outlines that white Northerners, as well as other non-slave-holding whites, benefited from the institution of slavery? Was there any slavery in the North? Why does history teach us a more "spotless" version of the North and its leaders than the one that Feagin presents?

Jezebel and Mammy: The Mythology of Female Slavery

Deborah Gray White

From the intricate web of mythology which surrounds the black woman, a fundamental image emerges. It is of a woman of inordinate strength, with an ability for tolerating an unusual amount of misery and heavy, distasteful work. This woman does not have the same fears, weaknesses, and insecurities as other women, but believes herself to be and is, in fact, stronger emotionally than most men. Less of a woman in that she is less "feminine" and helpless, she is really more of a woman in that she is the embodiment of Mother Earth, the quintessential mother with infinite sexual, life-giving, and nurturing reserves. In other words, she is a superwoman.

The uniqueness of the African-American female's situation is that she stands at the crossroads of two of the most well-developed ideologies in America, that regarding women and that regarding the Negro. Although much of the race and sex ideology that abounds in America has its roots in history that is older than the nation, it was during the slavery era that the ideas were molded into a peculiarly American mythology. As if by design, white males have been the primary beneficiaries of both sets of myths which, not surprisingly, contain common elements in that both blacks and women are characterized as infantile, irresponsible, submissive, and promiscuous. Both blacks and women have generally been dependent politically and economically upon white men. Both groups are consigned to roles that are subservient, both groups have shared a relationship of powerlessness vis-à-vis white males, and both groups, as a matter of automatic response, have been treated as outsiders and inferiors.

The black woman's position at the nexus of America's sex and race mythology has made it most difficult for her to escape the mythology. Black men can be rescued from the myth of the Negro. . . . They can be identified with things masculine, with things aggressive, with things dominant. White women, as part of the dominant racial group, have to defy the myth of woman, a difficult, though not impossible task. The impossible task confronts the black woman. If she is rescued from the myth of the Negro, the myth of woman traps her. If she escapes the myth of woman, the myth of the Negro still ensnares her. Since the myth of woman and the myth of the Negro are so similar, to extract her from one gives the appearance of freeing her from both. She thus gains none of the deference and approbation that accrue from being perceived as weak and submissive, and she gains none of the advantages that come with being a white male. To be so "free," in fact, has at times made her appear to be a superwoman, and she has attracted the envy of black males and white females. Being thus exposed to their envy she has often become their victim.

When antebellum Southerners thought about black women they did not conjure up images of an indolent Sambo, a rabid rapist, or an affable helpmeet. The first two explained black men, the latter, Southern white women. Black women had something in common with both black men and white women and the characterization of them, while unique, was an odd blend of the ideas formed about these two groups. In antebellum America, the female slave's chattel status, sex, and race combined to create a complicated set of myths about black womanhood.

One of the most prevalent images of black women in ante-bellum America was of a person governed almost entirely by her libido, a Jezebel character. In every way Jezebel was the counter-image of the mid-nineteenth-century ideal of the Victorian lady. She did not lead men and children to God; piety was foreign to her. She saw no advantage in prudery, indeed domesticity paled in importance before matters of the flesh. How white Americans, and Southerners in particular, came to think of black women as sensual beings has to do with the impressions formed during their initial contact with Africans, with the way black women were forced to live under chattel slavery, and with the ideas that Southern white men had about women in general.

The idea that black women were exceptionally sensual first gained credence when Englishmen went to Africa to buy slaves. Unaccustomed to the requirements of a tropical climate, Europeans mistook semi-nudity for lewdness. Similarly, they misinterpreted African cultural traditions, so that polygamy was attributed to the Africans' uncontrolled lust, tribal dances were reduced to the level of orgy, and African religions lost the sacredness that had sustained generations of ancestral worshippers. . . .

[The Jezebel image was reinforced by the conditions under which many slave women worked and the] sight of semi-clad black women nurtured white male notions of their promiscuity. Even the usually objective Frederick Law Olmsted, the famous Northern architect, had trouble avoiding the association. He stood for a long time watching slave women repair a road on a South Carolina plantation. The women had their coarse gray skirts "reefed up" around their waist and did no more than complete their assigned tasks. Nevertheless, Olmsted's impressions of them were distinctly negative. He described them as "clumsy," "gross," and "elephantine," yet added that in their demeanor the women were "sly," "sensual," and "shameless."[1] In the South, where it was not unusual for female slaves to work bent over with their skirts up, it was easy to come to such conclusions.

The exposure of women's bodies during whippings had similar consequences. Christopher Nichols, an escaped slave living in Canada, remembered how his master laid a woman on a bench, threw her clothes over her head, and whipped her. Another refugee remembered that when his mother was whipped, she was stripped completely naked: "Dey didn't care nothing 'bout it. Let everybody look on at it."[2] . . . Without doubt, some whippings of female slaves were sexually suggestive.

Whether or not slave women desired relationships with white men was immaterial, the conventional wisdom was that black women were naturally promiscuous, and thus desired such connections. If, in order to ease the burdens of slavery, they made themselves available, they only fulfilled the prophecy of their lustfulness, which in turn made it more difficult for other black women to reject the overtures made by white men. While slave women became the easy prey of profligates, justification for their exploitation came from the lips of some of the South's leading statesmen. This was particularly true after Northern abolitionists questioned the moral health of Southern society, a society that degraded and exploited a class of its women and ignored the involvement of its male youth with women alleged by Southerners themselves to be immoral. Rather than fault themselves, some Southern spokesmen blamed black women.

Those who used this rationalization found morality wanting in black society as a whole. Black men and women were thought to have such insatiable sexual appetites that they had to go beyond the boundaries of their race to get satisfaction. It was black women who, many claimed, tempted men of the superior caste. White men, it was argued, never had to use authority or violence to obtain compliance from bonded women because the latter's morals were so relaxed. Proponents of this line of reasoning actually celebrated the societal stratification that made black women available but put white women out of reach. Northerners, they argued, debased the civilized; they defamed the white prostitute, cut her off from the hope of useful and profitable employment, immured her in a state of depravity. By contrast, Southern white women were kept free and pure from the taint of immorality because black women acted as a buffer against their degradation. . . .

To successfully rebut abolitionist charges of Southern degeneracy, Southerners had to come up with alternative justifications of slavery and a more positive image of black women. Their society and their labor system had to be exalted on the basis that everyone benefited, both black and white. Slavery had to be explained in a context that was in keeping with the idea of white moral supremacy. Since in her role as mother and wife it was woman's responsibility to be the guardian of morality, much of the South's defense hinged on how virtuous it could show its women, both black and white, to be.

To this end, Southern men claimed that slavery uplifted white women. It was argued that only those women at the very lowest rung of society debased themselves by having illicit sex. For those in the middle and upper strata of society, slavery had an ameliorative effect. William Drayton argued that one of the first fruits of slavery was to rescue women from "their undeserved and wretched fate" and afford them leisure time to improve themselves. The Southern white woman gained from slavery in several ways: "Her faculties are developed; her gentle and softening influence is seen and felt; she assumes the high station for which nature designed her; and happy in the hallowed affections of her own bosom, unwearily exerts those powers so well adapted to the task of humanizing and blessing others."[3] George Fitzhugh argued that women in the slave South had not been robbed of the softness of their own sex, as was the case in the North where women had been thrown into the arena of industrial war. Women in the North, he argued, were in a false position. In contrast, "be she white, or be she black, she is treated with kindness and humanity in the slaveholding South."[4]

As suggested by Fitzhugh, black women also benefited from slavery. [Many southerners] . . . argued that slavery was at the root of the black woman's reformation. Fitzhugh maintained that "the intercourse of the house-servants with the white family assimilated . . . their moral conduct to that of the whites."[5] George S. Sawyer, an antebellum Louisiana lawyer, thought that slavery afforded the female slave "encouragement to lead a virtuous life." If she chose to avail herself of the opportunity, the institution of slavery would throw a "shield of protection" around her.[6] In some proslavery rhetoric, therefore, Jezebel was made chaste, and the idea of chaste slave women was soothing to many Southern whites.

To those who rebutted the abolitionist charge that the South was a land of immorality, the regenerative power of slavery was an extremely convenient concept. Once they embraced it they argued that slaveholders never came in contact with the most debased slave women because none but the most righteous were allowed to serve in Southern households. . . .

Those so trained became trusted servants who, according to this proslavery argument, were well cared for, even through old age. Thomas Cobb thought this one of the most beneficent aspects of slavery. Once a slave became part of the "white family," that slave was cared for through the aged and infirm years. While abolitionists criticized those conditions that made sexual liaisons between adolescent white boys and female slaves a probability, Southerners . . . were more apt to emphasize the innocent quality of the relationship between white children and slave women. So strong were the ties, said Cobb, that "even the young spendthrift experiences a pang in sundering a relation he has recognized from his infancy."[7]

Southerners, therefore, were hardly of one mind concerning African-American women. Jezebel was an image as troubling as it was convenient and utilitarian. When forced to defend it, many Southerners quickly retreated and revised their thinking. They did not necessarily abandon Jezebel nor their rationalizations of her. Rather many Southerners were able to embrace both images of black women simultaneously and to switch from one to the other depending on the context of their thought. On the one hand there was the woman obsessed with matters of the flesh, on the other was the asexual woman. One was carnal, the other maternal. One was at heart a slut, the other was deeply religious. One was a Jezebel, the other a Mammy.

* * *

Who was the black Mammy? What did she do and how did she do it? Most of what we know about Mammy comes from memoirs written after the Civil War. The descriptions are written with a certainty and definitiveness that seem to defy question. According to these accounts, Mammy was the woman who could do anything, and do it better than anyone else. Because of her expertise in all domestic matters, she was the premier house servant and all others were her subordinates. Thus, Susan Bradford Eppes grew up on a Florida plantation where Mammy was selected for "her worth and reliability." Her authority extended to all the "sub-nurses" and she ruled them with a "rod of iron."[8] Louisa Campbell Sheppard described Mary, the Mammy on her father's Missouri plantation, as a cook who not only ruled supreme in the kitchen, but who was the general superintendent of the younger servants as well[9] . . .

In these and similar sources, Mammy is especially remembered for her love of her young white charges. . . . On the White Hill plantation in Virginia, Mammy seemed to be always around to humor and protect. "No cry from the school room escaped her ears," for Mammy was always there to defend "her children."[10] A Louisiana black woman's recollections ... made Mammy seem almost majestic: "All the niggers have to stoop to Aunt Rachel just like they curtsy to Missy."[11]

This, therefore, is the broad outline of Mammy. She was a woman completely dedicated to the white family, especially to the children of that family. She was the house servant who was given complete charge of domestic management. She served also as friend and advisor. She was, in short, surrogate mistress and mother.

The Mammy image is fully as misleading as that of Jezebel. Both images have just enough grounding in reality to lend credibility to stereotypes that would profoundly affect black women. For instance, most house servants were, indeed, female. Black women served in all capacities, from cook to waiting maid, from wet nurse to mantua maker, or seamstress. In very wealthy Southern households there were many female servants. While the Mammy tradition is usually associated with upper-class whites, black women also served in less wealthy households, though they were not as numerous, and they sometimes doubled as field workers. Children in these homes could become just as attached to female servants as children of wealthier families, and in their adult years when they laid claim to the status that went along with having had a black Mammy they could do so with some credibility.

If the Mammy myth is grounded in the reality of black female house service, the idyllic aspect of the myth also gains support from the fact that house service was less physically demanding than field work, and very often translated into better care for the housemaids involved. Hard as cleaning, cooking, sewing, dairy work, and child care were, they were not as physically taxing as a sun up to sun down day in the crop—be it sugar, rice, or cotton. On the whole, house women could expect to eat better, dress better, and get better medical care than field women, if only because they were more familiar to the master and mistress, not to

mention nearer to the kitchen and potential hand-me-downs. Some women were given relatively exceptional wedding services, others were allowed an opportunity, rare for slave women, to leave the plantation as waiting maid for their traveling mistresses. Still others were taught to read and write by members of the white family. Furthermore, genuine affection sometimes developed between the white children and house servants on Southern plantations and farms. There was, therefore, much in the reality of house service on which to base a romantic view of female household help.

Such a view required that some of the uglier and perverse aspects be overlooked. If, as Eliza Riply claimed, Mammy Charlotte was never beyond a summons day or night, then Mammy Charlotte was a very tired woman. Indeed, house servants were on call at all hours. They probably had less private time than field workers. They were always under the scrutiny of the white family and far more subject to their mood swings, particularly to those of the mistress, than other slaves. House servants had to be on guard constantly lest a master or mistress, angry at who knows what, swung an open palm or closed fist in their direction. Obsequious behavior was, therefore, more of a must for them, and the pretty, even the comely, could never rest easy once the master's sons reached puberty, or the master himself developed a roving eye. That roving eye, of course, presented a problem that is ignored in romantic views of female house service.

Probably there was too much work in Southern households for *any* one woman, black or white. Everyday chores like cooking, cleaning, washing, ironing, and milking were not aided by many time- or labor-saving devices.[12] Childcare duties were performed in addition to everything else and, contrary to legend, not all Southern wealthy white women handed over the care of children to a black Mammy. Mrs. Isaac Hilliard, for instance, had several house slaves, but would not allow her son Henry to be cared for by anyone but herself. "I cannot conceive," she wrote, "how a mother can rest satisfied, to put her tender and helpless babes out to nurse. Who but a mother, would patiently undergo the fatigue and sleepless nights."[13]

The portrait slaves paint of Southern mistresses is very similar to the one painted by Southern women themselves, if not more revealing. Southern white mistresses were anything but idle. Along with house slaves they often spun thread, wove cloth, and sewed garments. Polly Colbert observed that while slave women did the spinning and weaving "Miss Betsey cut out all de clothes and helped wid de sewing. . . . She learnt all her women to sew. . . . She done all the sewing for de children."[14] . . .

The mythology of Mammy has her well cared for in old age, but in reality many old female house servants were mistreated and many were abandoned. Frederick Douglass' grandmother suffered such a fate. She had been a faithful nurse and housekeeper all of her life, yet she lived to see her children, her grandchildren, and her great-grandchildren divided like so many sheep and sold away. In her final years she was of little value to her owners, and despite her frail condition they took her to the woods, built her a little hut with a mud chimney, and left her there to support and care for herself. As Douglass put it, they turned her out to die.[15] Other forms of abuse were not unknown to Mammies. Former slave Jacob Stroyer told a particularly harrowing story of a woman named Aunt Betty. She had nursed her master through infancy, lived to see him become a drunk, and then became his victim when, during one of his drunken rampages, he took his shotgun and killed her.[16]

In reality there were no certainties for Mammy, but she could hope that the odds would come up in her favor. One may well assume that self-preservation motivated Mammy as much, if not more, than any particular loyalty she had to her owners. This is Genovese's view. He noted that Mammy was probably not nearly as

"white-washed" as the legend has it. Genovese cautioned against simplistic analyses of Mammy and reminded us of Mammy's many positive traits. He noted, for instance, that Mammy carried herself with "courage, compassion, dignity and self-respect." She served her white folks well, but she was ever-mindful of the well-being of her own family. Mammy knew that by becoming a friend, confidante, and indispensable servant to the whites, she and her family might gain some immunity against sale and abuse. According to Genovese, Mammy did not always denigrate black people. She knew what was fair and proper, and often even defended black dignity, or championed the cause of an abused slave. "Her tragedy lay, not in her abandonment of her own people," said Genovese, "but in her inability to offer her individual power and beauty to black people on terms they could accept without themselves sliding further into a system of paternalistic dependency."[17]

Genovese did much to reshape the image of Mammy but there is still something about Mammy that is enigmatic. If the reality of Mammy and female household service does not square with the Mammy legend, why was the image of this domestic necessary at all and why did the image take the form it did? In order to answer the latter question one has to consider the period in American history when the first comprehensive descriptions of Mammy appear, namely during the thirty or so years prior to the Civil War. As advisor and confidante, surrogate mistress and mother, as one who was tough, diplomatic, efficient, and resourceful, Mammy was not merely a female slave housekeeper who identified more with her master than her fellow slaves. The image of Mammy taking care of the children, performing and supervising household chores, lending an ear and offering advice to master, mistress, and white children, was in keeping with the maternal or Victorian ideal of womanhood prevalent in nineteenth-century America.

The maternal ideal achieved its quintessential expression in the writings of the mid-nineteenth century. Women, according to the prevailing Victorian image, were supremely virtuous, pious, tender, and understanding. Although women were also idealized as virgins, wives, and Christians, it was above all as mothers that women were credited with social influence as the chief transmitters of religious and moral values. Other female roles—wife, charity worker, teacher, sentimental writer—were in large part culturally defined as extensions of motherhood, all similarly regarded as nurturing, empathetic, and morally directive.[18]

In the antebellum South this ideal found expression in writings that delineated the virtues of the farm wife. This genre cautioned women against too much fashion and too many leisure pastimes and ornamental attainments. The proper woman was one who made the home her primary sphere, who was a helpmate to her husband, who raised her children according to Christian principles, who knew how to cook, sew, and garden.[19] . . .

Not surprisingly, much of the Southern literature which espoused the "cultural uplift" theory of slavery also preached the gospel of domesticity. John Pendleton Kennedy's *Swallow Barn* was the first in a long string of novels that did both. Of the blacks on the Swallow Barn plantation he wrote that "no tribe of people have ever passed from barbarism to civilization whose middle stage of progress has been more secure from harm, more genial to their character, or better supplied with mild and beneficent guardianship." The mistress of Swallow Barn, Lucretia, is typical of all his white female characters. She takes care of the household affairs "as one who had a reputation to stake upon her administration." Lucretia raises housekeeping to a science. Mornings were the best time to watch her operate as she "rather tyrannically enforced her regimen against the youngsters of her numerous family, both white and black."

Reminiscent of Mammy's supposed magic in the kitchen, Kennedy's Lucretia made such fantastic breakfasts that "a small regiment might march in upon her without disappointment."[20]

Beverly Tucker similarly described blacks and women. In *George Balcombe* the blacks are servile, loyal, and affectionate, the women are all models of domesticity. In one of his many soliloquies Balcombe reasons that only effeminate men marry educated women. Most men, he claims, "prefer the plain housewifely girl, who reads her Bible. . . darns her stockings, and boils her bacon and greens together." . . .

In the antebellum South, therefore, ideas about women went hand in hand with ideas about race. Women and blacks were the foundation on which Southern white males built their patriarchal regime. If, as seemed to be happening in the North during the 1830s, blacks and women conspired to be other than what white males wanted them to be, the regime would topple. . . .

Mammy was . . . the perfect image for antebellum Southerners. As the personification of the ideal slave, and the ideal woman, Mammy was an ideal symbol of the patriarchal tradition. She was not just a product of the "cultural uplift" theory, she was *also* a product of the forces that in the South raised motherhood to sainthood. As part of the benign slave tradition, and as part of the cult of domesticity, Mammy was the centerpiece in the antebellum Southerner's perception of the perfectly organized society. . . .

If Mammy stands apart from the moral mother tradition she does so on at least two points. The children and household upon which she lavished her attentions were, of course, not her own. There was room for black women in the Victorian tradition only to the extent that Mammy's energies were expended on whites. The other distinct feature about Mammy was her advanced age. . . . Mammy's age might . . . be a metaphor for the asexuality attributed to her. Among Anglo-American Protestant middle and upper classes, the Victorian maternal ideal was understood in terms of asexuality. Very likely the Jezebel image of black females got in the way of a perception of young or middle-aged black women as maternal domestics. Old age, thus, put Mammy beyond the pale of the carnal, above the taint of Jezebel.

In sum, the forces that made the Mammy image were many. It cannot be fully understood independent of the Jezebel conceptualization because they are inverse images that existed simultaneously in the Southern mind. They are black images but, being almost as old as the images of Eve and the Virgin Mary, they are also universal female archetypes. When, beginning in the 1830s, Southerners were forced to justify slavery and race relations, they adjusted their thinking to make slavery a positive good. At the same time that the "positive good" proslavery argument was presented, the maternal domestic ideal was being perfected. It was a small matter, but a major necessity, to incorporate this ideal into the "cultural uplift" theory that was being applied to female slaves. The image of Jezebel excused miscegenation, the sexual exploitation of black women, and the mulatto population. It could not, however, calm Southern fears of moral slippage and "mongrelization," or man's fear of woman's emasculating sexual powers. But the Mammy image could. Mammy helped endorse the service of black women in Southern households, as well as the close contact between whites and blacks that such service demanded. Together Jezebel and Mammy did a lot of explaining and soothed many a troubled conscience.

In the long run Mammy was of special importance to Southern perceptions, for she reflected two traditions perceived as positive by Southerners—that of the idealized slave and that of the idealized woman. For proslavery advocates, Southern apologists, antifeminist propagandists, and for those who genuinely loved their black nurses, Mammy was a Godsend. The last group took particular comfort in the belief that their black guardians were

regarded by some as highly as Southern white women. For the others, Mammy symbolized race and sex relations at their best. She was at once black and female. In reality, as well as in mythology, both blacks and women were ultimately subservient to white males. Thus in 1897, Thomas Nelson Page, a Virginia romanticist, could describe both groups as slaves.[21]

Notes

1. Olmstead, Frederick L. 1971. *The Cotton Kingdom.* Hawke, D. F. (ed.) New York: Bobbs-Merrill. p. 163.

2. Drew, Benjamin. 1969. "The Refugee: A North-Side View of Slavery." In *Four Fugitive Slave Narratives.* Reading Mass.: Addison-Wesley. pp. 48-49, 92.

3. William Drayton, *The South Vindicated from the Treason and Fanaticism of Northern Abolitionists* (Philadelphia: H. Manley, 1836), p. 104.

4. George Fitzhugh, *Sociology for the South; or The Failure of Free Society.* (Richmond, Va.: A. Morris, 1854), p. 213.

5. George Fitzhugh, *Cannibals All! or Slaves Without Masters* (Cambridge: The Belknap Press of Harvard University Press, 1960 [1857]), p. 29.

6. George S. Sawyer, *Southern Institutes or, An Inquiry into the Origin and Early Prevalence of Slavery and the Slave Trade* (Philadelphia: J. B. Lippincott, 1858), p. 221.

7. Thomas R. R. Cobb, *An inquiry into the Law of Negro Slavery in the United States of America to which is prefixed An Historical Sketch of Slavery* (New York: Negro University Press, 1968 [1858]), p. ccxvii. See also Edward Pollard, *Black Diamonds Gathered in the Darky Homes of the South* (Washington, DC: Pudney and Rusell, 1859), p. 95.

8. Mrs. Nicholas Ware Eppes, *The Negro of the Old South* (Chicago: Joseph G. Branch, 1925), p. 74.

9. Louisa Campbell Sheppard, "Recollections" (typescript, 1892), SHC., p. 7.

10. *Recollections of the Daughter of Charles Friend,* White Hill Plantation Books, SHC p. 5, 41.

11. Botkin, B. A. (ed.) 1945. *Lay My Burden Down.* Chicago: University of Chicago Press p. 125.

12. Strasser, Susan. 1982. *Never Done. A History of American Housework* (New York: Pantheon Books), pp. 1-125.

13. Hilliard, Mrs. Isaac "Diary, 1849-1850" Department of Archives, Louisiana State University, in *Southern Historical Manuscripts* (Westport, Conn.: Greenwood Press), p. 58.

14. Okla., 7:36; See also Miss., 7:140,158-159.

15. Douglass, Frederick, 1855. *My Bondage and My Freedom* (New York: Mulligan, New York and Auburn), p. 180.

16. Stroyer, Jacob, 1898. *My Life in the South* (Salem, Mass.: New Comb and Gavs), pp. 78-80.

17. Genovese, Eugene. 1974. *Roll, Jordan, Roll: The World the Slaves Made* (New York: Random House), pp. 360-361.

18. Bloch, Ruth H. 1978. "American Feminine Ideals in Transition: The Rise of the Moral Mother, 1785-1815," in *Feminist Studies* (June), 4(2): 101.

19. Hagler, D. Harland. 1980. "The Ideal Woman in the Antebellum South: Lady or Farmwife" *The Journal of Southern History* (August) 46(3):410.

20. Kennedy, John Pendleton, *Swallow Barn* or *Sojourn in the Old Dominion* (New York: Harcourt, Brace, 1929 [1832]), pp. 31-33, 192-193. See also Francis Pendleton Gaines, *The Southern Plantation, a Study of the Development and the Accuracy of a Tradition* (Gloucester, Mass.: Peter Smith, 1962), pp. 1822.

21. Page, Thomas Nelson, 1897. *Social Life in Old Virginia Before the War* (New York: C. Scribner's Sons), pp. 57-58.

DISCUSSION QUESTIONS

1. How exactly were black men and black and white women dependent on white men? How did these relationships vary by group? Were black women also subservient to black men?

2. How were the "myths" of black women sustained by everyday life in the South? How and why did these stereotypical views vary from the view of white women and black men?

3. What do these images say about the distribution of power and status under slavery? Do the Jezebel and Mammy myths persist today? In what form? Why?

CURRENT DEBATES

HOW DID SLAVERY AFFECT THE ORIGINS OF AFRICAN AMERICAN CULTURE?

A debate over the impact of slavery on African American culture began in the 1960s and continues to the present day. Stanley Elkins, in his 1959 book, *Slavery: A Problem in American Institutional and Intellectual Life*, laid down the terms of the debate. Elkins concluded that black culture in America was created in response to the repressive plantation system and in the context of brutalization, total control of the slaves by their owners, and dehumanization. He argued that black culture was "made in America," but in an abnormal, even pathological social setting. The plantation was a sick society that dominated and infantilized black slaves. The dominant reality for slaves—and the only significant other person in their lives—was the master. Elkins described the system as a "perverted patriarchy" that psychologically forced the slaves to identify with their oppressors and to absorb the racist values at the core of the structure.

Elkins's book has been called "a work of great intellectual audacity, based on a methodology which has little connection with conventional historical research and arriving at conclusions which were challenging or outrageous, according to one's point of view."[1] The book stimulated an enormous amount of controversy and research on the impact of slavery and the origins of African American culture. This body of research developed new sources of evidence and new perspectives and generally concluded that African American culture is a combination of elements, some from the traditional cultures of Africa and others fabricated on the plantation. The selection from the work of historian William Piersen illustrates this argument while focusing on West African and Africa American family customs.

---

1. Parish, P. (1989). *Slavery: History and historians.* New York: Harper & Row, p. 7.

Slavery Created African American Culture

Stanley Elkins

Both [the Nazi concentration camps and the American slave plantations] were closed systems from which all standards based on prior connections had been effectively detached. A working adjustment to either system required a childlike conformity, a limited choice of "significant other." Cruelty per se cannot be considered the primary key to this; of far greater importance was the simple "closedness" of the system, in which all lines of authority descended from the master and in which alternative social bases that might have supported alternative standards were systematically suppressed. The individual, consequently, for his very psychic security, had to picture his master in some way as the "good father," even when, as in the concentration camp, it made no sense at all.

For the Negro child, in particular, the plantation offered no really satisfactory father image other than the master. The "real" father was virtually without authority over his child, since discipline, parental responsibility, and control of rewards and punishments all rested in other hands; the slave father could not even protect the mother of his children.

From the master's viewpoint, slaves had been defined in law as property, and the master's power over his property must be absolute. . . . Absolute power for him meant absolute dependency for the slave—the dependency not of the developing child but of the perpetual child. For the master, the role most aptly fitting such a relationship would naturally be that of father.

SOURCE: From *Slavery: A Problem in American Institutional and Intellectual Life* by Stanley Elkins. Copyright ©1959, 1968, 1976 by University of Chicago Press. Reprinted by permission of The University of Chicago Press and the author.

African American Culture Was Created by an Interplay of Elements From Africa and America

William D. Piersen

In the colonial environment . . . , [African and European] traditions were fused . . . The result was an unprecedented and unintended new multicultural American way of life. . . .

[Africans] had little choice [but this] adjustment was not as difficult . . . as we might suppose: the cultures of Africa and Europe were both dominated by the rhythms and sensibilities of a premodern, agricultural way of life shaped more by folk religion than by science, and domestic responsibilities were relatively similar on both continents. . . .

One of the greatest sacrifices that faced the new African Americans was the loss of the extended families that had structured most social relationships in Africa. . . . [African marriage customs were usually polygynous (permitting more than one wife) and patrilineal (tracing ancestry through the male side)]. With marriage, most African Americans seem . . . to have settled quickly into Euro-American-style monogamous nuclear families that trace inheritance bilaterally through the lines of both parents. Nonetheless, colonial naming choices show the continuing importance of African ideas of kinship among African Americans, for black children were more commonly . . . named after recently deceased relatives, a practice rooted in the African belief of rebirth across generations. . . .

African Americans . . . tried to rebuild as best they could the social cohesion once provided by the now missing extended families of Africa. [They] tried to duplicate some of the kinship . . . functions . . . by forging close relationships with their countrymen and shipmates from the Middle Passage. . . . [Many] treated both the blacks and whites that lived with them . . . as a kind of artificial kin . . .

In North America many white colonials soon gave up traditional European village residence patterns to move out individually on the land, but African Americans, when they had the choice, generally preferred to stay together . . . Such communalism [was] a reflection of the value that Africans and African Americans put on collective living.

In West Africa kin groups gathered in their housing together in large compounds that featured centralized open spaces devoted to social functions and collective recreation. Husbands and wives within the compounds usually had their own separate family quarters . . . In colonial African American housing the old ways were maintained. . . . [In early 18th century Virginia] most slaves lived in clusterings of more than 10 people. In these quarters, black social life was centered not on the interior of the small dark sleeping structures but outside on the common space devoted to social functions.

SOURCE: From *From Africa to America: African American History from the Colonial Era to the Early Republic, 1526-1790* by William D. Piersen. New York: Twayne, 1996.

DEBATE QUESTIONS TO CONSIDER

1. Why is the origin of African American culture an important issue? What difference does it make today? If you believe Elkins is correct, what are the implications for dealing with racial inequality in the present? Could a culture that was created under a pathological system and a sick society be an adequate basis for the pursuit of equality and justice today? Is Elkins's thesis a form of blaming the victim? Is it a way of blaming the present inequality of the black community on an "inadequate" culture, thus absolving the rest of society from blame?

2. If you agree with Piersen's viewpoint, what are the implications for how African Americans think about their history and about themselves? What difference does it make if your roots are in Africa or in colonial Virginia or, as Piersen argues, in both?

3. What gender issues can you identify in this debate? Are Elkins and Piersen talking about all slaves or just male slaves? Using the other readings in this chapter as a basis, what important gender differences existed in American slavery? What consequences might those differences have for black Americans today?

4

Industrialization and Dominant-Minority Relations

From Slavery to Segregation and the Coming of Post-Industrial Society

American race relations entered a new era with the emancipation of the slaves at the end of the Civil War. After Reconstruction, a brief respite from racial oppression, whites in the South built a system of racial segregation under which blacks were consigned to an inferior status by force of law. By the dawn of the 20th century, de jure segregation was in full force. There were separate and unequal black school systems, job markets, and neighborhoods, and racial inequality was institutionalized in virtually every aspect of Southern society, including public transportation, parks and playgrounds, and restrooms and water fountains. Black Southerners were disenfranchised and left politically powerless and without basic civil and political rights. Millions of black Southerners reacted to Southern segregation by seeking new lives in the urban, industrializing North and Midwest. Of course, life outside the South was hardly a racial utopia, and black migrants were forced to deal with new forms of discrimination and racism. The Narrative Portrait in this chapter is a selection from Richard Wright that eloquently expresses the agonies and hopes of the black migrants from the South. The first reading, by Angela Davis, examines the situation of black women following emancipation and argues strongly that de jure segregation simply continued (and sometimes worsened) the exclusion and oppression of slavery.

As racial segregation evolved in the South, other minority groups were being victimized by systems of oppression and exploitation. Mexican Americans in the Southwest were used as a cheap labor force in agriculture, mining, railroad construction, and other areas of the economy. Native Americans were herded onto reservations where they were either forced to Americanize or were ignored and left to starve. Immigrants from Europe became a seemingly inexhaustible source of labor power for the industrializing east coast, while immigrants from Asia helped to build railroads, dig mines, and do menial farm work on the west coast.

Underlying the various dominant-minority relations was the powerful hand of industrialization, urbanization, and modernization. As the United States switched from the labor-intensive economies of an agricultural nation to the machine-dependent technologies of the industrial era, new minority groups were created and the situations of other minority groups were transformed.

Throughout the 20th century, dominant-minority relations continued to change as U.S. society continued to evolve. As some issues were resolved, others rose in their place, and discussion and debate, conflict and change continued to animate group relations. For example, the Civil Rights movement of the 1950s and 1960s, largely a Southern black phenomenon, pushed the nation to commit itself as never before to the ideals of racial equality, freedom, and justice. As this national consensus solidified on these issues, new questions arose: How exactly do we create true racial equality? Now that there is agreement on the principle of equal opportunity, how do we actually implement this ideal?

The structures that perpetuated racial inequality in the past—slavery and de jure segregation—have been dismantled, but large, persistent gaps remain between virtually every minority group and the dominant group in income, education, occupational prestige, health care, and other measures of equality, life chances, and quality of life. These gaps are partly the legacy of the inequalities of the past and partly the result of continuing (but more subtle) discrimination in the present. Similar gaps and similar issues characterize gender relations in modern America. In both cases, these gaps remain and persist due in part to lingering beliefs about biologically based and/or culturally based inferiority that has led to unequal access to resources and opportunities.

One proposal for addressing these persistent gaps is affirmative action, a term that refers to a number of different strategies for addressing issues of racial and gender inequality and moving the United States closer to the ideal of a truly equal society. In the second reading, Fred Pincus identifies and summarizes seven types of affirmative action policies and dispels many of the myths and misunderstandings that surround this program, especially the idea that many American institutions and organizations are required to adhere to "quotas" or strict percentages of minority group representation. Our treatment of affirmative action continues in the Current Debates section. Thomas Sowell presents arguments against affirmative action, and Orlando Patterson counters with arguments in support.

As society industrialized and struggled with different racial, ethnic, and gender groups coming into contact with each other in the workplace, these deep divisions (especially of class) began to take new form during the process of suburbanization. The suburbs, sheltered from the harsher economic conditions of center cities, developed their own cultures and, with them, some unique sets of problems as well. The final reading addresses one such problem: school shootings, the seemingly random attacks by schoolchildren on their classmates and teachers. Kimmel and Mahler explore issues of masculinity and homophobia, race and class, and local cultural characteristics and argue that issues of gender and adolescent masculinity have been largely unexplored as underlying causes of these horrific acts of violence.

Please visit the accompanying website to Race, Ethnicity, and Gender, second edition for the *Public Sociology Assignments* at http://www.pineforge.com/das2.

QUESTIONS TO CONSIDER IN THIS CHAPTER

1. How are relations between groups affected by changes in the larger society? For example, if slavery had not ended in 1865, could it have persisted as the U.S. industrialized? How does the present post-industrial economy, which de-emphasizes manual labor and rewards high levels of education and technical skills, shape group relations?

2. There is a great deal of disagreement and controversy over programs of affirmative action. As you read the selections in this chapter, what strong and weak points can you identify in the arguments? If affirmative action is being phased out, what other programs for achieving equality might replace it? Would programs based on social class rather than race, ethnicity, or gender be effective?

3. Historically, U.S. culture has been dominated by the ideologies of racism and sexism and has privileged whites, men, and heterosexuals. What commonalities and differences can you identify in these patterns? How are gender and race manifested in the phenomena explored in this chapter, including such seemingly disparate realities as employment discrimination and school violence?

NARRATIVE PORTRAIT

THE KITCHENETTE

Richard Wright (1908–1960), one of the most powerful writers of the 20th century, lived through and wrote about many of the social changes that affected African Americans since the end of slavery. He grew up in the South during the height of the Jim Crow system, and his passionate hatred for segregation and bigotry is expressed in his major works *Native Son* (1940) and the autobiographical *Black Boy* (1945). In 1941, Wright also helped to produce *12 Million Black Voices*, a folk history of African Americans. A combination of photos and brief essays, the work is a powerful commentary on three centuries of oppression.

The following selection is adapted from "Death on the City Pavement," which expresses Wright's view of the black migration out of the South, a journey he himself experienced. This bittersweet migration often traded the harsh, rural repression of the South for the overcrowded, anonymous ghettos of the North. Housing discrimination, both overt and covert, confined black migrants to the least desirable, most overcrowded areas of the city—in many cases, the neighborhoods that had first housed immigrants from Europe. Unscrupulous landlords subdivided buildings into the tiniest possible apartments ("kitchenettes"), and as impoverished newcomers who could afford no better, black migrants were forced to cope with overpriced, substandard housing as best they could. Much of the passage, incidentally, could have been written about any 20th century minority group.

DEATH ON THE CITY PAVEMENT

Richard Wright

A war sets up in our emotions: one part of our feelings tells us it is good to be in the city, that we have a chance at life here, that we need but turn a corner to become a stranger, that we need no longer bow and dodge at the sight of the Lords of the Land. Another part of our feelings tells us that, in terms of worry and strain, the cost of living in the kitchenettes is too high, that the city heaps too much responsibility on us and gives too little security in return. . . .

The kitchenette, with its filth and foul air, with its one toilet for thirty or more tenants, kills our black babies so fast that in many cities twice as many of them die as white babies. . . .

The kitchenette scatters death so widely among us that our death rate exceeds our birth rate, and if it were not for the trains and autos bringing us daily into the city from the plantations, we black folk who dwell in northern cities would die out entirely over the course of a few years. . . .

The kitchenette throws desperate and unhappy people into an unbearable closeness of association, thereby increasing latent friction, giving birth to never-ending quarrels of recrimination, accusation, and vindictiveness, producing warped personalities.

The kitchenette injects pressure and tension into our individual personalities, making many of us give up the struggle, walk off and leave wives, husbands, and even children behind to shift for themselves....

The kitchenette reaches out with fingers of golden bribes to the officials of the city, persuading them to allow old firetraps to remain standing and occupied long after they should have been torn down.

The kitchenette is the funnel through which our pulverized lives flow to ruin and death on the city pavement, at a profit. . . .

SOURCE: From *12 Million Black Voices* by Richard Wright. New York: Thunder's Mouth Press, 1988.

READINGS

In this section, we explore the impact of industrial and post-industrial economies on dominant-minority relations in the United States and a variety of issues including slavery, affirmative action, and the gender and racial dynamics of school shootings. These diverse topics are linked by the overarching notion that group relations are shaped by the level of development of the larger society and change as the level of development changes. American slavery was created to supply a highly controlled labor force in a labor-intensive, agricultural economy. As America industrialized in the 19th and 20th centuries, work shifted from fields and farms to cities and factories and the dynamics of intergroup relations changed accordingly. At our present, 21st-century post-industrial stage of development, we are faced with a broad range of issues of inclusion and fairness in the job structure. One attempt to move the society closer to the ideal of equality in this atmosphere is affirmative action, a set of programs that are widely misunderstood and controversial.

It is evident that the job opportunity structure at any given time has clear implications for minority group members, who often occupy the lowest-rung positions on the stratification ladder. The first reading by Angela Davis, "The Meaning of Emancipation According to Black Women," is perhaps the most striking example of this reality, since black women occupy the lowest rung on both race and gender dimensions of inequality. Davis makes a crucial point not often acknowledged in modern discussions of African Americans—that the deplorable, government-sanctioned mistreatment of blacks in the United States did not end with the cessation of slavery. In fact, the post-slavery jobs available to African Americans—in sharecropping, the convict lease system, and domestic work—were in some ways worse than their fate under slavery. We see that de jure segregation, or segregation by law, often referred to as Jim Crow, greatly curtailed any prospects of freedom for African Americans for another hundred years following the Emancipation Proclamation. Not unlike under slavery, black women who worked as domestics additionally faced the threat of sexual abuse at the hands of white men, who faced no repercussions for their actions.

We turn our attention to the post-industrial economy, where racism is expressed in more subtle but still devastating forms of institutional discrimination. Today, the most blatant forms of discrimination—such as "whites only" elections and businesses that refuse to serve non-whites—are no longer practiced. However, the system of racial advantage continues to be perpetuated by more indirect and hidden mechanisms. For example, consider "past-in-present" discrimination, which involves practices in the present that have discriminatory consequences because of some pattern of discrimination or exclusion in the past (Feagin & Feagin, 1986, p. 32). One form of this discrimination is found in systems of seniority commonly found in American workforces. In these systems, workers who have been on the job longer have higher incomes and privileges, such as longer vacations. More senior workers have greater job security and are designated in official policy as the last to be fired or laid off in the event of hard times. This personnel policy may seem perfectly reasonable and fair. However, seniority can have discriminatory results in the present because in the past, members of minority groups and women were excluded from specific occupations by racist or sexist labor unions, discriminatory employers, or both. As a result, minority group workers and women may have fewer years of experience than dominant group workers and may be the first to go when layoffs are necessary. The adage "last hired, first fired" describes the situation of minority group and female employees who are more vulnerable not because of some overtly racist or sexist policy, but because of the routine operation of the seemingly neutral principle of seniority.

It is much more difficult to identify, measure, and eliminate this more subtle form of institutional discrimination, and some of the most heated disputes in recent group relations have concerned public policy and law in this area. Among the most controversial issues are affirmative action programs that attempt to ameliorate the legacy of past discrimination or increase diversity in the workplace or in schools. The selection by Fred Pincus begins our coverage of this issue. There is a great deal of misinformation and misunderstanding, and Pincus attempts to clear the air by listing and describing the types of affirmative action programs. Note, in particular, that affirmative action policy requires much less than people commonly believe and that specific quotas are used only in very limited cases (which are becoming increasingly unusual as we move further away in time from the era of blatant discrimination).

Affirmative action efforts are based in part on the notion that workplaces are gendered and raced, and these lenses shape who is hired, fired, and promoted whether we realize it or not. The same can be said of educational cultures—schools are gendered and raced, whether we would like them to be or not. The selection by Kimmel and Mahler draws our attention to some neglected areas of inquiry and analysis with regard to school shootings. The authors argue that school violence is more understandable if seen as a manifestation of local cultural traits and homophobic response to merciless teasing and bullying, as a form of over-conformity to adolescent views of what it means to be masculine. The boys who commit these violent attacks have been marginalized in their school cultures, accused of being insufficiently masculine, and are "getting even" for the bullying, gay-baiting, and exclusion that make their life at school an ongoing misery. For them, violence is an assertion of maleness in a culture that continues to maintain strong traditions of racism, paternalism, and homophobia. Why has this violent "boy culture" developed in the United States? How and why does it persist?

THE MEANING OF EMANCIPATION ACCORDING TO BLACK WOMEN

Angela Davis

After a quarter of a century of "freedom," vast numbers of Black women were still working in the fields. Those who had made it into the "big house" found the door toward new opportunities sealed shut—unless they preferred, for example, to wash clothes at home for a medley of white families as opposed to performing a medley of household jobs for a single white family. Only an infinitesimal number of Black women had managed to escape from the fields, from the kitchen or from the washroom. According to the 1890 census, there were 2.7 million Black girls and women over the age of ten. More than a million of them worked for wages: 38.7 percent in agriculture; 30.8 percent in household domestic service; 15.6 percent in laundry work; and a negligible 2.8 percent in manufacturing.[1] The few who found jobs in industry usually performed the dirtiest and lowest-paid work. And they had not really made a significant breakthrough, for their slave mothers had also worked in the Southern cotton mills, in the sugar refineries and even in the mines. For Black women in 1890, freedom must have appeared to be even more remote in the future than it had been at the end of the Civil War.

As during slavery, Black women who worked in agriculture—as sharecroppers, tenant farmers or farmworkers—were no less oppressed than the men alongside whom they labored the day long. They were often compelled to sign "contracts" with landowners who wanted to reduplicate the antebellum conditions. The contract's expiration date was frequently a mere formality, since landlords could claim that workers owed them more than the equivalent of the prescribed labor period. In the aftermath of emancipation the masses of Black people— men and women alike—found themselves in an indefinite state of peonage. Sharecroppers, who ostensibly owned the products of their labor, were no better off than the outright peons. Those who "rented" land immediately after emancipation rarely possessed money to meet the rent payments, or to purchase other necessities before they harvested their first crop. Demanding as much as 30 percent in interest, landowners and merchants alike held mortgages on the crops.

> Of course the farmers could pay no such interest and the end of the first year found them in debt—the second year they tried again, but there was the old debt and the new interest to pay, and in this way, the "mortgage system" has gotten a hold on everything that it seems impossible to shake off.[2]

Through the convict lease system, Black people were forced to play the same old roles carved out for them by slavery. Men and women alike were arrested and imprisoned at the slightest pretext—in order to be leased out by the authorities as convict laborers. Whereas the slaveholders had recognized limits to the cruelty with which they exploited their "valuable" human property, no such cautions were necessary for the postwar planters who rented Black convicts for relatively short terms. "In many cases sick convicts are made to toil until they drop dead in their tracks."[3]

Using slavery as its model, the convict lease system did not discriminate between male and female labor. Men and women were frequently housed together in the same stockade and were yoked together during the workday. In a resolution passed by the 1883 Texas State Convention of Negroes, "the practice of yoking or chaining male and female convicts together" was "strongly condemned."[4] Likewise, at the Founding Convention of the Afro-American League in 1890, one of the seven reasons motivating the creation of this organization was "(t)he odious and demoralizing penitentiary system of the South, its chain gangs, convict leases and indiscriminate mixing of males and females."[5]

As W.E.B. DuBois observed, the profit potential of the convict lease system persuaded many Southern planters to rely exclusively on convict labor—some employing a labor force of hundreds of Black prisoners.[6] As a result, both employers and state authorities acquired a compelling economic interest in increasing the prison population. "Since 1876," DuBois points out, "Negroes have been arrested on the slightest provocation and given long sentences or fines which they were compelled to work out."[7]

This perversion of the criminal justice system was oppressive to the ex-slave population as a whole. But the women were especially susceptible to the brutal assaults of the judicial system. The sexual abuse they had routinely suffered during the era of slavery was not arrested by the advent of emancipation. As a matter of fact, it was still true that "colored women were looked upon as the legitimate prey of white men . . ."[8]—and if they resisted white men's sexual attacks, they were frequently thrown into prison to be further victimized by a system which was a "return to another form of slavery."[9]

During the post-slavery period, most Black women workers who did not toil in the fields were compelled to become domestic servants. Their predicament, no less than that of their sisters who were sharecroppers or convict laborers, bore the familiar stamp of slavery. Indeed, slavery itself had been euphemistically called the "domestic institution" and slaves had been designated as innocuous "domestic servants." In the eyes of the former slaveholders, "domestic service" must have been a courteous term for a contemptible occupation not a half-step away from slavery. While Black women worked as cooks, nursemaids, chambermaids and all purpose domestics, white women in the South unanimously rejected this line of work. Outside the South, white women who worked as domestics were generally European immigrants who, like their ex-slave sisters, were compelled to take whatever employment they could find.

The occupational equation of Black women with domestic service was not, however, a simple vestige of slavery destined to disappear with the passage of time. For almost a century they would be unable to escape domestic work in any significant numbers. A Georgia domestic worker's story, recorded by a New York journalist in 1912,[10] reflected Black women's economic predicament of previous decades as well as for many years to come. More than two thirds of the Black women in her town were forced to hire themselves out as cooks, nursemaids, washerwomen, chambermaids, hucksters and janitresses, and were caught up in conditions ". . . just as bad as, if not worse than, it was during slavery."[11]

For more than thirty years this Black woman had involuntarily lived in all the households where she was employed. Working as many as fourteen hours a day, she was generally allowed an afternoon visit with her own family only once every two weeks. She was, in her own words, "the slave, body and soul"[12] of her white employers. She was always called by her first name—never Mrs. . . .—and was not infrequently referred to as their "nigger," in other words, their slave.[13]

One of the most humiliating aspects of domestic service in the South—another affirmation of its affinity with slavery—was the temporary revocation of Jim Crow laws as long as the Black servant was in the presence of a white person.

> . . . I have gone on the streetcars or the railroad trains with the white children, and . . . I could sit anywhere I desired, front or back. If a white man happened to ask some other white man, "What is that nigger doing in here?" and was told, "Oh, she's the nurse of those white children in front of her" immediately there was the hush of peace. Everything was all right, as long as I was in the white man's part of the streetcar or in the white man's coach as a servant—a slave—but as soon as I did not present myself as a menial . . . by my not having the white children with me, I would be forthwith assigned to the "nigger" seats or the "colored people's coach."[14]

From Reconstruction to the present, Black women household workers have considered sexual abuse perpetrated by the "man of the house" as one of their major occupational hazards. Time after time they have been victims of extortion on the job, compelled to choose between sexual submission and absolute poverty for themselves and their families. The Georgia woman lost one of her live-in jobs because "I refused to let the madam's husband kiss me."[15]

. . . (S)oon after I was installed as cook, he walked up to me, threw his arms around me, and was in the act of kissing me, when I demanded to know what he meant, and shoved him away. I was young then, and newly married, and didn't know then what has been a burden to my mind and heart ever since: that a colored woman's virtue in this part of the country has no protection.[16]

As during slavery times, the Black man who protested such treatment of his sister, daughter or wife could always expect to be punished for his efforts.

When my husband went to the man who had insulted me, the man cursed him, and slapped him, and—had him arrested! The police fined my husband $25.[17]

After she testified under oath in court, "(t)he old judge looked up and said: 'This court will never take the word of a nigger against the word of a white man.'"[18]

In 1919, when the Southern leaders of the National Association of Colored Women drew up their grievances, the conditions of domestic service were first on their list. It was with good reason that they protested what they politely termed, "exposure to moral temptations"[19] on the job. Undoubtedly, the domestic worker from Georgia would have expressed unqualified agreement with the Association's protests. In her words,

I believe nearly all white men take, and expect to take, undue liberties with their colored female servants—not only the fathers, but in many cases the sons also. Those servants who rebel against such familiarity must either leave or expect a mighty hard time, if they stay.[20]

Since slavery, the vulnerable condition of the household worker has continued to nourish many of the lingering myths about the "immorality" of Black women. In this classic "catch-22" situation, household work is considered degrading because it has been disproportionately performed by Black women, who in turn are viewed as "inept" and "promiscuous." But their ostensible ineptness and promiscuity are myths which are repeatedly confirmed by the degrading work they are compelled to do. As W.E.B. DuBois said, any white man of "decency" would certainly cut his daughter's throat before he permitted her to accept domestic employment.[21]

When Black people began to migrate northward, men and women alike discovered that their white employers outside the South were not fundamentally different from their former owners in their attitudes about the occupational potentials of the newly freed slaves. They also believed, it seemed, that *"Negroes are servants, servants are Negroes."*[22] According to the 1890 census, Delaware was the only state outside the South where the majority of Black people were farmworkers and sharecroppers as opposed to domestic servants.[23] In thirty-two out of forty-eight states, domestic service was the dominant occupation for men and women alike. In seven out of ten of these states, there were more Black people working as domestics than in all the other occupations combined.[24] The census report was proof that *Negroes are servants, servants are Negroes.*

Isabel Eaton's companion essay on domestic service, published in DuBois' 1899 study *The Philadelphia Negro,* reveals that 60 percent of all Black workers in the state of Pennsylvania were engaged in some form of domestic work.[25] The predicament of women was even worse, for all but nine percent—14,297 out of 15,704—of Black women workers were employed as domestics.[26] When they had traveled North seeking to escape the old slavery, they had discovered that there were simply no other occupations open to them. In researching her study, Eaton interviewed several women who had previously taught school, but had been fired because of "prejudice."[27] Expelled from the classroom, they were compelled to work in the washroom and the kitchen.

Of the fifty-five employers interviewed by Eaton, only one preferred white servants over Black ones.[28] In the words of one woman,

> I think the colored people are much maligned in regard to honesty, cleanliness and trustworthiness; my experience of them is that they are immaculate in every way, and they are perfectly honest; indeed I can't say enough about them.[29]

Racism works in convoluted ways. The employers who thought they were complimenting Black people by stating their preference for them over whites were arguing, in reality, that menial servants—slaves, to be frank—were what Black people were destined to be. Another employer described her cook as "... very industrious and careful—painstaking. She is good, faithful creature, and very grateful."[30] Of course, the "good" servant is always faithful, trustworthy and grateful. U.S. literature and the popular media in this country furnish numerous stereotypes of the Black woman as faithful, enduring servant. The Dilseys (à la Faulkner), the Berenices (of *Member of the Wedding*) and the Aunt Jemimas of commercial fame have become stock characters of U.S. culture. Thus the one woman interviewed by Eaton who did prefer white servants confessed that she actually employed Black help "... because they look more like servants."[31] The tautological definition of Black people as servants is indeed one of the essential props of racist ideology.

Racism and sexism frequently converge—and the condition of white women workers is often tied to the oppressive predicament of women of color. Thus the wages received by white women domestics have always been fixed by the racist criteria used to calculate the wages of Black women servants. Immigrant women compelled to accept household employment earned little more than their Black counterparts. As far as their wage-earning potential was concerned, they were closer, by far, to their Black sisters than to their white brothers who worked for a living.[32]

If white women never resorted to domestic work unless they were certain of finding nothing better, Black women were trapped in these occupations until the advent of World War II. Even in the 1940s, there were street-corner markets in New York and other large cities—modern versions of slavery's auction block—inviting white women to take their pick from the crowds of Black women seeking work.

> Every morning, rain or shine, groups of women with brown paper bags or cheap suitcases stand on streetcorners in the Bronx and Brooklyn waiting for a chance to get some work. . . . Once hired on the "slave market," the women often find after a day's back-breaking toil, that they worked longer than was arranged, got less than was promised, were forced to accept clothing instead of cash and were exploited beyond human endurance. Only the urgent need for money makes them submit to this routine daily.[33]

New York could claim about two hundred of these "slave markets," many of them located in the Bronx, where "almost any corner above 167th Street" was a gathering point for Black women seeking work.[34] In a 1938 article published in *The Nation*, "Our Feudal Housewives," as the piece was entitled, were said to work some seventy-two hours a week, receiving the lowest wages of all occupations.[35]

The least fulfilling of all employment, domestic work has also been the most difficult to unionize. As early as 1881, domestic workers were among the women who joined the locals of the Knights of Labor when it rescinded its ban on female membership.[36] But many decades later, union organizers seeking to unite domestic workers confronted the very same obstacles as their predecessors. Dora Jones founded and led the New York Domestic Workers Union during the 1930s.[37] By 1939—five years after the union was founded—only 350 out of 100,000 domestics in the state had been recruited. Given the enormous difficulties of organizing domestics, however, this was hardly a small accomplishment.

White women—feminists included—have revealed a historical reluctance to acknowledge the struggles of household workers. They have rarely been involved in the Sisyphean task of ameliorating the conditions of domestic service. The convenient omission of household workers' problems from the programs of "middle-class" feminists past and present has often turned out to be a veiled justification—at least on the part of the affluent women—of their own exploitative treatment of their maids. In 1902 the author of an article entitled "A Nine-Hour Day for Domestic Servants" described a conversation with a feminist friend who had asked her to sign a petition urging employers to furnish seats for women clerks.

> "The girls," she said, "have to stand on their feet ten hours a day and it makes my heart ache to see their tired faces."
>
> "Mrs. Jones," said I, "how many hours a day does your maid stand upon her feet?"
>
> "Why, I don't know," she gasped, "five or six I suppose."
>
> "At what time does she rise?"
>
> "At six."
>
> "And at what hour does she finish at night?"
>
> "Oh, about eight, I think, generally."
>
> "That makes fourteen hours. . . ."
>
> ". . . (S)he can often sit down at her work."
>
> "At what work? Washing? Ironing? Sweeping? Making beds? Cooking? Washing dishes? . . .

> Perhaps she sits for two hours at her meals and preparing vegetables, and four days in the week she has an hour in the afternoon. According to that, your maid is on her feet at least eleven hours a day with a score of stair-climbings included. It seems to me that her case is more pitiable than that of the store clerk."
>
> My caller rose with red cheeks and flashing eyes. "My maid always has Sunday after dinner," she said.
>
> "Yes, but the clerk has all day Sunday. Please don't go until I have signed that petition. No one would be more thankful than I to see the clerks have a chance to sit. . . ."[38]

This feminist activist was perpetrating the very oppression she protested. Yet her contradictory behavior and her inordinate insensitivity are not without explanation, for people who work as servants are generally viewed as less than human beings. Inherent in the dynamic of the master-servant (or mistress-maid) relationship, said the philosopher Hegel, is the constant striving to annihilate the consciousness of the servant. The clerk referred to in the conversation was a wage laborer—a human being possessing at least a modicum of independence from her employer and her work. The servant, on the other hand, labored solely for the purpose of satisfying her mistress' needs. Probably viewing her servant as a mere extension of herself, the feminist could hardly be conscious of her own active role as an oppressor.

As Angelina Grimke had declared in her *Appeal to the Christian Women of the South,* white women who did not challenge the institution of slavery bore a heavy responsibility for its inhumanity. In the same vein, the Domestic Workers Union exposed the role of middle-class housewives in the oppression of Black domestic workers.

> The housewife stands condemned as the worst employer in the country. . . .

The housewives of the United States make their million and a half employees work an average of seventy-two hours a week and pay them . . . whatever they can squeeze out of their budget after the grocer, the butcher . . . (etc.) have been paid.[39]

Black women's desperate economic situation—they perform the worst of all jobs and are ignored to boot—did not show signs of change until the outbreak of World War II. On the eve of the war, according to the 1940 census, 59.5 percent of employed Black women were domestic workers and another 10.4 percent worked in non-domestic service occupations.[40] Since approximately 16 percent still worked in the fields, scarcely one out of ten Black women workers had really begun to escape the old grip of slavery. Even those who managed to enter industry and professional work had little to boast about, for they were consigned, as a rule, to the worst-paid jobs in these occupations. When the United States stepped into World War II and female labor kept the war economy rolling, more than four hundred thousand Black women said goodbye to their domestic jobs. At the war's peak, they had more than doubled their numbers in industry. But even so—and this qualification is inevitable—as late as 1960 at least one-third of Black women workers remained chained to the same old household jobs and an additional one-fifth were nondomestic service workers.[41]

In a fiercely critical essay entitled "The Servant in the House," W. E. B. DuBois argued that as long as domestic service was the rule for Black people, emancipation would always remain a conceptual abstraction. ". . . (T)he Negro," DuBois insisted, "will not approach freedom until this hateful badge of slavery and medievalism has been reduced to less than ten percent."[42] The changes prompted by the Second World War provided only a hint of progress. After eight long decades of "emancipation," the signs of freedom were shadows so vague and so distant that one strained and squinted to get a glimpse of them.

NOTES

1. Wertheimer, *op. cit.*, p. 228.
2. Aptheker, *A Documentary History*, Vol. 2, p. 747. "Tenant Farming in Alabama, 1889" from *The Journal of Negro Education* XVII (1948), pp. 46ff.
3. Aptheker, *A Documentary History*, Vol. 2, p. 689. Texas State Convention of Negroes, 1883.
4. *Ibid.*, p. 690.
5. Aptheker, *A Documentary History*, Vol. 2, p. 704. Founding Convention of Afro-American League, 1890.
6. DuBois, *Black Reconstruction in America*, p. 698.
7. *Ibid.*
8. *Ibid.*, p. 699.
9. *Ibid.*, p. 698.
10. Aptheker, *A Documentary History of the Negro People in the United States*, Vol. 1 (Secaucus, N.J.: The Citadel Press, 1973), p. 46. "A Southern Domestic Worker Speaks," *The Independent*, Vol. LXXII (January 25, 1912).
11. *Ibid.*, p. 46.
12. *Ibid.*, p. 47.
13. *Ibid.*, p. 50.
14. *Ibid.*
15. *Ibid.*, p. 49.
16. *Ibid.*
17. *Ibid.*
18. *Ibid.*
19. Lerner, *Black Women in White America*, p. 462. "The Colored Women's Statement to the Women's Missionary Council, American Missionary Association."
20. Aptheker, *A Documentary History*, Vol. 1, p. 49.
21. DuBois, *Darkwater*, p. 116.
22. *Ibid.*, p. 115.
23. Isabel Eaton, "Special Report on Negro Domestic Service" in W.E.B. DuBois, *The Philadelphia Negro* (New York: Schocken Books, 1967. First edition: 1899), p. 427.
24. *Ibid.*
25. *Ibid.*, p. 428.
26. *Ibid.*
27. *Ibid.*, p. 465.
28. *Ibid.*, p. 484.
29. *Ibid.*, p. 485.

30. *Ibid.*

31. *Ibid.*, p. 484.

32. *Ibid.*, p. 449. Eaton presents evidence which ". . . points to the probability that among women in domestic service at least, there is no difference between 'white pay and black pay,' . . ."

33. Lerner, *Black Women in White America*, pp. 229–231. Louise Mitchell, "Slave Markets Typify Exploitation of Domestics," *The Daily Worker*, May 5, 1940.

34. Gerda Lerner, *The Female Experience: An American Documentary* (Indianapolis: Bobbs-Merrill, 1977), p. 269.

35. *Ibid.*, p. 268.

36. Wertheimer, *op. cit.*, pp. 182–183.

37. Lerner, *Black Women in White America*, p. 232.

38. Inez Goodman, "A Nine-Hour Day for Domestic Servants," *The Independent*, Vol. LIX (February 13, 1902). Quoted in Baxandall *et al., op. cit.*, pp. 213–214.

39. Lerner, *The Female Experience*, p. 268.

40. Jacquelyne Johnson Jackson, "Black Women in a Racist Society," in Charles Willie et al., editors, *Racism and Mental Health* (Pittsburgh: University of Pittsburgh Press, 1973), p. 236.

41. *Ibid.*

42. DuBois, *Darkwater*, p. 115.

SOURCE: From *Women, Race, and Class* by Angela Davis. Copyright © 1981 Angela Davis. Used by permission of Random House, Inc.

DISCUSSION QUESTIONS

1. Why does Davis link both the convict lease system and domestic service to slavery? What aspects of work resemble slavery and why? Do you agree with her characterization? Why or why not?

2. After the end of slavery, were conditions for blacks any better in the North? What problems and difficulties existed in the North in terms of black employment?

3. What does Davis mean when she says that white feminists perpetuate "the very oppression she protested"? Why was the liberation of women narrowly defined so as not to include the liberation of black women from domestic servitude? Today, is feminism in general defined in such a way that it has limited appeal for women of color? Why or why not?

WHAT IS AFFIRMATIVE ACTION?[1]

Fred L. Pincus

. . . Because there is a high level of ignorance about affirmative action, this reading will describe seven different types of affirmative action policies. Some of the policies do not involve quotas and preferences. Those that do must meet strict legal guidelines.

OFFICE OF FEDERAL CONTRACT COMPLIANCE PROGRAMS AFFIRMATIVE ACTION GUIDELINES

The largest federal affirmative action program is based on Executive Order 11246 issued by President Lyndon B. Johnson in 1965. Guidelines to implement this program were first issued in 1968 and revised in 1971.[2] Federal contractors and subcontractors, excluding those in construction, who have 50 or more employees and a federal contract for more than $50,000 are required to develop an affirmative action plan within 120 days of receiving a contract. Failure to develop and implement an affirmative action plan could result in a firm losing the current contract and being declared ineligible to receive additional contracts. This is called being *debarred*.

Contractors must first conduct a *utilization study* of their employees. Basically, they must count the number of women and minority employees in each department and in each occupational category and be able to say that "X% of skilled blue-collar workers in the maintenance department are black" or "Y% of the managers in the sales department are Hispanic."

The employer must also determine the percentage of minority and female employees who are in the "availability pool," those who are qualified and potentially available for the job. This is a complex issue and requires some explanation.

For most of the less-skilled clerical, sales, blue-collar, and service jobs, the availability pool is the labor force in the immediate geographical area of the employer. Availability is calculated as the percentage of minorities or women in the surrounding labor force. If the labor force is 5% Hispanic, for example, the availability of Hispanic clerical workers would be 5%. In more-skilled jobs like carpenters, on the other hand, the availability would be the percentage of minority or women workers employed in that job. The surrounding labor force might be 40% female, but the availability of women carpenters might only be 5%.

For professional and managerial jobs, however, the availability may well be statewide or even national. For nurses, for example, the black availability might be defined as the percentage of blacks getting nursing degrees in the entire state in the last five years. For college faculty, on the other hand, the availability of female psychologists might be the percentage of doctorates in psychology granted to women in the past five years in the entire country.

There are pages of regulations specifying how these figures are calculated. In the construction industry, the national goal for women is only 6.9% (OFCCP, 2002). The important point here is that the availability pool is an estimate of the percentage of qualified minority and female workers in a particular job category.

It is then necessary for employers to compare the actual distribution of minority or female employees in a specific job category in a specific department to the minority and female distribution in the availability pool. If the actual employment is equal to or greater than the availability (e.g., the availability of women sales managers is 15% and 15% of the sales managers actually employed are female), then the employer is "in compliance." If, on the other hand, the actual employment distribution is below the availability figure (e.g., only 5% of the sales managers are female), then the employer is "underutilized." The employer must follow this same procedure for each job category in each department.

If a contractor is underutilized, a set of goals and timetables must be included in the affirmative action plan. An appropriate goal would be to hire enough qualified female or minority employees to reach the percentage distribution stated in the availability pool. In the above example, the contractor tries to hire enough female sales managers so that 15% of its sales managers are female.

The timetable must be based on the conditions facing that specific contractor. Employers with big job turnover might be able to reach the goal in a few months, whereas one with little turnover might take a few years. Contractors in expanding industries have shorter timetables than those in stagnant or contracting industries.

Next, the contractor must specify procedures to achieve the goal. This means trying to "cast a broad net" to encourage diversity among those who apply for the position. Employers should publicly advertise jobs rather than relying on informal networking. Advertisements should contain a statement like "Equal Opportunity Employer; Women and Minorities Encouraged to Apply." Some advertisements should be placed in publications targeted at qualified women and minorities. Employers should send letters to well-known women and minorities in the field asking for referrals, send letters to schools who train large numbers of qualified women and minorities, and make recruiting trips to conferences that might be attended by qualified women and minorities. In other words, employers must go out of their way to increase the hiring pool of potential women and minority candidates.

After the contractor designates an employee as the affirmative action representative who oversees this process, the affirmative action plan is then complete. It is important to realize that the contractor is *not* required to submit the plan to the Office of Federal Contract Compliance Programs (OFCCP) for approval; the plan must simply be kept on file in the contractor's office. However, the contractor is expected to make a "good-faith effort" to implement the plan.

What happens if the contractor fails to meet the goal specified in the plan? Does the contractor face the loss of the federal contract because a white male was hired rather than a black female? Probably not. In fact, no one but the employer is likely to know that the goal was not met. The OFCCP does not review the hiring process of each employer for each year. More importantly, the contractor is only required to make a good-faith effort to achieve the goal, not to succeed. In the unlikely event that the contractor was ever investigated by the OFCCP, all it would have to do is show that it followed the procedures to encourage women and minorities to apply for the job in question. If the contractor can demonstrate that the white male who applied for the administrative position was more qualified than the black and female applicants, there is no problem. Affirmative action guidelines *require* meritocratic

hiring. Preferential treatment or quotas are *illegal* under these guidelines.

Although these affirmative action regulations involve a certain amount of effort and cost on the part of federal contractors, they do not force contractors to hire unqualified people, nor do they permit reverse discrimination. All contractors have to do is offer reasonable explanations as to why their employment levels are below the percentages in the availability pool. Some contractors, however, may pressure personnel officers to illegally hire unqualified, underutilized minorities to avoid problems with OFCCP officials. It is difficult to determine how extensive this practice is.

Construction contractors are also required to establish goals and timetables. However, they are not required to have full affirmative action plans on file because they do not have the same kind of stable labor force that a manufacturer might have. Many construction contractors hire different people from one job to the next.

The OFCCP does conduct "compliance reviews" of certain contractors who are suspected of not fully complying with guidelines. A compliance officer spends an average of three weeks conducting one of these reviews.[3] In 2000, the OFCCP conducted 4,162 compliance reviews, a 33% decline from the 6,232 reviews conducted in 1989. The decline in the number of reviews is due to a 17% decline in OFCCP staff between 1992 and 1997, although both staffing and number of compliance reviews have both increased between 1997 and 2000. In two-thirds of these reviews, the contractor agreed to change some aspect of the affirmative action plan to bring it into compliance (OFCCP, 2002; OFCCP, n.d.; U.S. Department of Labor, 1997; Pincus, 1993).

Although 4,162 may seem like a large number of reviews, it is important to remember that there were over 192,000 contractors and even a larger number of subcontractors that fell under the OFCCP guidelines in 2000. At the rate of 4,162 reviews each year, it would take the OFCCP over 46 years to review all contractors even once. Consequently, contractors do not have to worry very much about being reviewed.

If the compliance officer and the contractor cannot reach an agreement, there are several levels of appeal available to the contractor. Recalcitrant contractors can ultimately be debarred; however, this is extremely rare. According to the OFCCP, only 43 contractors have been debarred in the 37-year history of the agency, which averages out to about 1.2 debarments per year.[4] These 43 companies account for a tiny fraction of the more than 500,000 that have been government contractors since 1972. Twenty-five of the companies were declared ineligible during the 1972–1980 period, which included the Richard Nixon, Gerald Ford, and Jimmy Carter administrations. Four were declared ineligible under Ronald Reagan (1981–1988), three under George H. W. Bush (1989–1992), eight under Bill Clinton (1993–2000), and one during the first two years of the George W. Bush presidency.

What does a government contractor have to do to be debarred? The official list provides this information on 40 of the 43 companies. Half of the companies flagrantly violated the OFCCP regulations by refusing to develop an affirmative action plan or refusing to submit required statistical information. The other half refused to make good-faith efforts to implement goals and timetables or did not abide by some other part of the conciliation agreement.

The reality is that the federal affirmative action regulations that are administered by the OFCCP do not put a great deal of pressure on federal contractors to increase their hiring of women and minority workers. If a contractor is willing to be even the least bit flexible, the chances are good that the OFCCP will sign off on its affirmative action plans. Even after being debarred, companies can be reinstated if they make the necessary changes. Sixty percent of the debarred companies were eventually reinstated. In fact, the median period of debarment for the 26 reinstated contractors was only 9.5 months.

I have gone into so much detail about the OFCCP guidelines for several reasons. First, they are the least known of all affirmative action policies. Second, affirmative action critics usually do not discuss them. Third, they are the least controversial because the final hiring decisions are supposed to be meritocratic and companies are only required to *try* to meet OFCCP goals. Employers are only required to show that they have cast a broad net to find qualified candidates. Finally, they affect more employees than other affirmative action policies do.

GOVERNMENT AGENCIES

Ever since the John F. Kennedy administration in the early 1960s, executive orders have required federal agencies to pursue vigorous antidiscrimination policies. This requirement was further institutionalized by the 1972 Equal Employment Opportunities Act (EEOA). While not using the term "affirmative action," the EEOA specified numerous affirmative action-like procedures that should be followed, including:

Developing equal employment opportunity (EEO) goals and plans to achieve them; identifying underutilized talent; using recruitment methods that reach the whole pool of job candidates; developing and fully utilizing employees' skills; cooperating with community groups, schools, and other employers to improve community conditions that affect employability; identifying target positions for which lower level employees might be eligible; training lower-level employees to enhance their promotion opportunities; monitoring sex and race differences in time in grade; increasing the representation of women and minorities through recruitment at specific grade levels and in specific job ladders; and undertaking self-evaluation. (Reskin, 1998: 12–13)

All of these procedures are intended to increase the pool of qualified minority workers and none require hiring and promotion quotas. Three million federal workers were covered by these affirmative action regulations.

Reskin also states that in the middle and late 1980s, 35 states and the District of Columbia had some kind of affirmative action policies passed by their own legislatures, as did 80% of the major cities and counties with populations of more than 100,000. Because the nature of these policies varied from state to state, it is difficult to characterize them.

Hiring and Promotion Quotas

The most controversial of all affirmative action policies are "quotas," programs that reserve certain positions for qualified minority or female candidates. These quotas specify a hiring or promotion *floor,* the minimum number of women or minorities that must be hired or promoted. These are different from the historic use of anti-Semitic quotas as a *ceiling,* a requirement that no more than a certain number of Jews may be hired.

Although the concept of quotas is controversial, one thing is clear: quotas and goals are not the same. First, especially in court-imposed quotas, the employer or school in question must hire or promote a minority or female for that position, under penalty of law. If no qualified minority or woman is found, either the position must remain empty or the employer must seek special permission to hire

or promote a white male. In the case of goals, however, the employer must merely make a good-faith effort to hire or promote a qualified minority or woman; if none is found, there are no legal consequences and a white or male may be hired or promoted.

Second, in a consent decree with quotas, a white male with superior work experience or credentials could be passed over in favor of a *qualified,* but less-experienced minority or female applicant. When goals are being used, a more-qualified white male must be hired or promoted over a less-qualified minority or female applicant because the final hiring must be meritocratic. Affirmative action critics who say that goals and quotas are the same are either ignorant or intellectually dishonest.

The 1972 Equal Employment Opportunities Act made it legal for courts to impose hiring and promotion quotas on employers that were found guilty of discrimination. Quotas could also be used as a remedy as part of consent decrees, or out-of-court settlements in discrimination lawsuits. Before a quota can be imposed by a court, a group of minority or female employees generally sues an employer for race or sex discrimination. One possible outcome of these lawsuits is that the government and plaintiffs enter into a consent decree with the employer that contains a quota system of hiring and/or promotion. The quotas might require the hiring of one black for every five whites until the percentage of black employees reaches the level of blacks in the availability pool.

Even under quotas, employers are not forced to hire unqualified people. Generally, the employer has some criteria by which a prospective employee can be considered "qualified," such as an educational credential, a minimum score on a test, or a minimum level of experience. Employees who do not meet these criteria cannot be considered for the position. All those who do meet the criteria are seen as eligible to carry out the duties of the position.

Next, the qualified whites (or males) are ranked from "most qualified" to "least qualified" in terms of the criteria. The same is done for the qualified minorities (or women). If only ten people can be hired or promoted and there is a 50–50 quota, the top five whites and the top five minorities are chosen. Even though all of the selected minorities (or women) are qualified, it is possible that some of them may be less qualified (for example, earning lower test scores) than some of the whites (or men) that were not chosen. For example, a woman who scored 85 out of 100 might be promoted while a man who scored 86 would not. Although such a decision has a great impact on that particular man, such small differences in scores would not warrant the conclusion that the man would have done a better job than the woman.

There is a widespread belief, especially among whites, that quotas are common nationwide. However it is getting more and more difficult for hiring and promotion quotas to meet the test of constitutionality. A variety of court decisions has resulted in a set of "strict scrutiny" criteria that must be met. First, there must be a "compelling state interest" to justify a quota. This is usually interpreted as combating intentional race or gender discrimination when no other policy is likely to work. Second, the quota system must be "narrowly tailored," which is generally interpreted as not "unduly trammeling" on the rights of white males. The consent decree cannot require that 100% of new hires be minorities or women because this would make it impossible for white males. In fact, the quota proportions must have some connection to the availability pool. In addition, the quota system cannot be in effect indefinitely; for instance, it may be in effect until the percentage of minority or female employees reaches a percentage equivalent to the availability pool.

In fact, court-imposed quotas are few and far between. Reskin (1998) says that there were only 51 court-approved quotas in effect in the early 1980s. It is generally illegal for an employer to voluntarily adopt a quota hiring system without obtaining court approval. Courts impose quotas only in cases where there is a long history of explicit discrimination and the employer fails to take corrective action; in general, such quotas are generally seen as policies of last resort. The conservative U.S. Supreme Court has issued numerous anti-affirmative action rulings in recent years, which have restricted the scope of quota systems. For example, it is unconstitutional to use race or sex as part of the criteria in the decision to lay off workers. Affirmative action supporters fear that the Supreme Court will continue on this anti-affirmative action trend.

RACE/GENDER-PLUS POLICIES

Occupying a space somewhere between the goals/timetables approach and the quota approach is using race or gender as one of many factors. The goals/timetables approach requires strong outreach procedures but also that the final hiring or promotion decision be meritocratic. Quotas, on the other hand, require race or gender to be a major factor in the final hiring/promotion decision.

Race/gender-plus policies permit race or gender to be considered as one of many factors in the final decision as long as it is not the *major* factor. Employers can use the race/gender-plus policy on a voluntary basis only to rectify severe employment segregation. The race-plus policy has been used much more extensively in higher education.

The underrepresentation of blacks, Hispanics, and Native Americans in higher education has been a major national issue for four decades. Since the late 1970s, colleges and universities around the country have used the "race-plus" principle articulated in the 1978 Bakke decision to help diversify their campuses (*Regents of the University of California v Bakke,* 1978). Alan Bakke, a white student, was not admitted to the University of California at Davis medical school and sued, claiming that he was discriminated against because of his race. UC-Davis had set aside 18 seats for people of color, and Bakke claimed that less qualified minorities were admitted over him. The Supreme Court found in favor of Bakke in a divided and complex decision. The quota system was ruled unconstitutional because there was no previous discrimination that needed a remedy; UC-Davis was a new medical school.

There were several important principles that resulted from this decision. First, the court ruled that although race cannot be considered as the *only* factor, it can be considered along with other factors, such as economic disadvantage, athletic and music skills, parents' alumni status, and so forth. In this case, race might count for only 5% of the admissions score, not 50%. The court specifically cited Harvard University's undergraduate admissions policy as an example. As a result of the Bakke decision, this race-plus policy was used in admissions to undergraduate, graduate, and professional schools around the country. However, the race-plus policy was not justified on the basis that having a diverse student body was the right or fair thing to do. Justice Lewis Powell said that a diverse student body contributes to a better educational experience for students through a more robust interchange of ideas. This, he argued, is part of the central mission of the university.

Several developments during the mid-1990s led to restrictions on the use of the race-plus principle. In 1995, the Regents of the University of California voted to ban the use of race in admissions and hiring. The following year, California voters approved Proposition 209, which banned the use of race as a factor in admissions, hiring, and promotions in all public institutions throughout the state. The

U.S. Supreme Court declined to rule on a legal challenge to Proposition 209. The state of Washington has a similar policy.

Also in 1996, the Federal Appeals Court for the Fifth Circuit issued the *Hopwood v Texas* (1996) decision, which involved the University of Texas law school. Four white students sued the university on the basis of reverse discrimination, alleging that they were passed over for admission while blacks and Hispanics with lower scores were admitted. The court held that the "race-plus" principle was unconstitutional. Because the U.S. Supreme Court refused to rule on the case, none of the educational institutions in the Fifth Circuit (Texas, Mississippi, and Louisiana) can use the Bakke principle, while the rest of the country can.

The race-plus policies at the University of Michigan are also under legal scrutiny, at the time of this writing, after several white students sued on the basis of reverse discrimination. One suit involves undergraduate admissions (*Gratz v Bollinger*), while the other involves the law school (*Grutter v Bollinger*). [*Editor's note:* The U.S. Supreme Court ruled in both of these cases in the Spring of 2003. The Court ruled in favor of the Law School program, an indication that it is constitutional to use race as one criterion in making admissions decisions. The Court ruled against the undergraduate admissions program, which awarded points automatically to minority candidates. These split rulings were interpreted as, at best, a weak endorsement of very limited affirmative action programs.] One of the major legal issues of these cases revolves around Justice Powell's statement that a diverse student body results in a more meaningful educational experience for students. Powell offered no evidence for this assertion, and affirmative action critics have challenged its validity. Social scientists at the University of Michigan, under the leadership of psychologist Patricia Gurin (n.d.), have conducted literature reviews and empirical studies that support the assertion that diversity is good for education (also see Orfield, 2001). . . .

In 1978, many affirmative action supporters viewed the Bakke decision as a defeat for affirmative action because the court limited the use of voluntary quotas. There were numerous large demonstrations across the country criticizing the court. It is ironic that some 25 years later, even the Bakke decision is under legal attack and affirmative action supporters are mounting a vigorous campaign to defend what they once criticized.

RACE-BASED SCHOLARSHIPS

Another policy intended to increase minority enrollment in higher education has also come under fire. Some states and many individual colleges, both public and private, have established special scholarships for minority students; whites could not even apply for these awards. Although the scholarships were a source of great controversy, they were relatively small in number. According to the American Council on Education, less than 3% of minority students received scholarships specially designated for minorities. This accounted for 2% of all aid to college students (DeWitt, 1991).

In 1994, however, the U.S. Appeals Court for the Fourth Circuit ruled that these scholarships were unconstitutional (*Podberesky v Maryland,* 1994). A white student who claimed some Hispanic background sued the University of Maryland College Park because he could not qualify for the all-black Banneker Scholarship. In spite of the fact that the university was formally segregated until 1954 and that blacks have been underrepresented on campus ever since, the court struck down the scholarship. The U.S. Supreme Court declined to rule on the case. Many schools in Maryland and Virginia have since opened such scholarships to non-minority students, and many others are reconsidering their policies (Lederman, 1996).

Race-based scholarships are still legal outside the Fourth Circuit states.

GOVERNMENT CONTRACT SET-ASIDES

During the late 1960s, after several summers of urban riots, the federal, state, and local governments began to develop programs that mandated a small percentage of government contracts to be set aside for minority contractors. In part, this was a reaction to demands for equal opportunity from the minority business community. In addition, conservative politicians saw such programs as a way to strengthen minority business people who, presumably, would be more respectable (and conservative) role models than the militant civil rights activists. Many observers argue that these set-aside programs were a major reason for the expansion of minority-owned businesses in the 1970s and 1980s (Bates, 1993; LaNoue, 1992).

In spite of the set-aside programs, minority businesses remain underrepresented among government contractors. In 2000, for example, the Small Business Administration estimates that only 6.2% of all federal contracts went to minority-owned businesses (Office of Advocacy, 2001a; also see Stout and Rodriguez, 1997). Nevertheless, white business people began to bring a variety of lawsuits alleging racial discrimination. In the *City of Richmond v Croson* (1989) decision the U.S. Supreme Court severely restricted the ability of state and local governments to provide set-aside programs by saying that the strict scrutiny must be applied. Specifically, state and local governments would have to prove that there was a history of discrimination for which the set-aside program was the only possible remedy. In addition to the methodological difficulties in proving discrimination, state and local governments were put in the awkward position of condemning themselves in order to justify the set aside program.

The Croson decision specifically said that federal programs had more leeway and did not have to meet strict scrutiny criteria. In *Adarand v Pena* (1995), however, the U.S. Supreme Court also applied the strict scrutiny standard to federal set-aside programs. Despite the fact that minority contractors are underrepresented at all levels of government, the courts have put strict limits on set-aside programs that could help remedy this situation. This is another example of how a more conservative Supreme Court is restricting affirmative action.

VOLUNTARY AFFIRMATIVE ACTION

Reskin (1998) estimates that as many as one-fifth of private employers have voluntarily adopted some form of affirmative action policy, which tends to involve outreach and training, the less controversial aspects of affirmative action. Without a court's approval, private companies can use race/gender-plus principles only to overcome substantial segregation within their organizations; they cannot use quotas.

CONCLUSION

This brief review demonstrates how wide-ranging affirmative action policies are and how they are supposed to work. When I discuss these issues in class, my students are often shocked to see that so much of affirmative action has nothing to do with quotas or preferences. They are amazed that the OFCCP guidelines are so modest and that the legal justifications of quotas are so stringent. They are also surprised at the difference between goals and quotas and were unaware of the small size of race-based financial aid for college students.

Good people can differ over their views toward affirmative action. However, support of or opposition to affirmative action should be based on accurate information, not on disinformation and mythology. . . .

NOTES

1. This chapter is an expanded and updated version of Pincus (1999c).

2. The following discussion is based on a review of federal affirmative action guidelines and on discussion with several OFCCP officials.

3. Orlans (1992) describes an unusual compliance review of a bank in 1979 that lasted two years.

4. The following discussion of affirmative action violators is based on "Companies Ineligible for Federal Contracts Under the Regulations of the Office of Federal Contract Compliance Programs" (n.d.). The keeper of the list is David Hess, who has kindly sent me various updates since 1993. I received the most recent edition in December 2002.

REFERENCES

Bates, Timothy. 1993. Banking on Black Enterprise: The Potential of Emerging Firms For Revitalizing Urban Economies. Washington, DC: Joint Center for Political and Economic Studies.

DeWitt, Karen. 1991. "Limits Proposed for Race-Based Scholarships." New York Times, December 5:A26.

Gurin, Patricia. n.d. "The Expert Eyewitness Report of Patricia Y. Gurin." Available at www.umich.edu.

LaNoue, George R. 1992. "Split Visions: Minority Business Set Asides." Annals of the AAPSS (523): 104–116.

Lederman, Douglas. 1996. "The Impact of a Court Ruling Against Minority Scholarships, Two Years Later." *Chronicle of Higher Education,* October 25: A38.

Office of Advocacy. 2001. *Minorities in Business, 2001.* Small Business Administration. Available at www.sba.gov/advo/press/02–02.html.

OFCCP (Office of Federal Contract Compliance Programs). 2002. "Facts on Executive Order 11246 Affirmative Action." Available at www.dol.gov/esa/regs/compliance/ofccp/aa.htm.

Orfield, Gary (ed.). 2001. *Diversity Challenged: Evidence on the Impact of Affirmative Action.* Cambridge: The Civil Rights Project: Harvard Publishing Group.

Orlans, Harold. 1992. "National Bank of Greenwood." *Annals of the AAPSS* (523): 186–195.

Reskin, Barbara. 1998. *The Realities of Affirmative Action in Employment.* Washington, DC: American Sociological Association

Stout, Hilary and Rodriguez, Eva. 1997. "Government Contracts to Minority Firms Increase Despite Court's 1995 Curb on Affirmative Action." *Wall Street Journal,* May 7: A20.

DISCUSSION QUESTIONS

1. What are "quotas"? What are the rare cases in which they may legally be applied? How does this information contrast with the popular image of affirmative action as quotas? How are antidiscrimination laws typically enforced? What is the likelihood that a firm who does not hire a qualified minority candidate will be penalized, based on statistics presented by Pincus? How does this contrast with the image that companies are being "forced" to hire women and minorities?

2. How are "race/gender-plus" affirmative action plans implemented? How does this contrast with the "unqualified minority" myths about affirmative action?

3. As prototypical examples of the two above-discussed types of affirmative action, compare and contrast the Bakke case with the University of Michigan cases, reflecting upon how things have changed historically between these two times. Research the consequences these rulings (especially the Michigan cases) have had on diversity in higher education.

4. Were you aware that there were so many different types of affirmative action programs? Do you believe the general public is aware of them and how they actually function and are monitored? Would more awareness change the state of public opinion surrounding these programs? Are there other types of affirmative action programs you could suggest, or ways the ones outlined here could be changed or improved?

ADOLESCENT MASCULINITY, HOMOPHOBIA, AND VIOLENCE: RANDOM SCHOOL SHOOTINGS, 1982–2001

Michael S. Kimmel and Matthew Mahler

Violence is one of the most urgent issues facing our nation's schools. All over the country, Americans are asking why some young people open fire, apparently randomly, killing or wounding other students and their teachers. Are these teenagers emotionally disturbed? Are they held in the thrall of media-generated violence—in video games, the Internet, rock or rap music? Are their parents to blame?

In our analysis of the commentary and literature on school violence, we find that they all ignore the one factor that cuts across all cases of random school shootings—masculinity. Thus, we argue that any approach to understanding school shootings must take gender seriously—specifically the constellation of adolescent masculinity, homophobia, and violence. We go on to argue that all or most of the shooters had tales of being harassed—specifically, gay-baited—for inadequate gender performance; their tales are the tales of boys who did not measure up to the norms of hegemonic masculinity. Thus, in our view, these boys are not psychopathological deviants but rather overconformists to a particular normative construction of masculinity, a construction that defines violence as a legitimate response to a perceived humiliation.

MISSING THE MARK

Some have argued that Goth music, Marilyn Manson, and violent video games are the causes of school shootings. For others, the staggering statistics linking youth violence and the availability of guns point to a possible cause. These accounts, however, that blame a media purportedly overly saturated by violence and a society infatuated with guns are undercut by two important facts, which are often conveniently forgotten amid the fracas. The first is that whereas the amount of violent media content has ostensibly been increasing, both youth violence, in general, and school violence, in particular, have actually been decreasing since 1980. And second, juvenile violence involving guns has been in decline since 1994 (largely as a result of the decline of the crack epidemic).[1]

Finally, some have proposed psychological variables, including a history of childhood abuse, absent fathers, dominant mothers, violence in childhood, unstable family environment, or the mothers' fear of their children, as possible explanations (see, e.g., Elliot, Hamburg, & Williams, 1998; Garbarino, 1998). Although these explanations are all theoretically possible, empirically, it appears as though none of them holds up. Almost all the shooters came from intact and relatively stable families, with no history of child abuse.

This search for causal variables is also misguided because it ignores a crucial component

of all the shootings. These childhood variables would apply equally to boys and to girls.[2] Thus, they offer little purchase with which to answer the question of why it is that only boys open fire on their classmates. None examine local cultures, local school cultures, or gender as an antecedent or risk factor. They use such broad terminology as "teen violence," "youth violence," "gang violence," "suburban violence," and "violence in the schools" as though girls are equal participants in this violence. They pay little or no attention to the obvious fact that *all the school shootings were committed by boys*—masculinity is the single greatest risk factor in school violence. This uniformity cuts across all other differences among the shooters: Some came from intact families, others from single-parent homes; some boys had acted violently in the past, others were quiet and unsuspecting; and some boys also expressed rage at their parents (two killed their parents the same morning), whereas others seemed to live in happy families. And yet, if the killers in the schools in Littleton, Pearl, Paducah, Springfield, and Jonesboro had all been girls, gender would undoubtedly be the only story (Kimmel, 2001; see also Klein & Chancer, 2000). Someone might even blame feminism for causing girls to become violent in vain imitation of boys.

But the analytic blindness of these studies runs deeper than gender. We can identify two different waves of school violence since 1980. In the first, from 1982 to 1991, the majority of all the school shootings were nonrandom (i.e., the victims were specifically targeted by the perpetrators). Most were in urban, inner-city schools and involved students of color. Virtually all involved handguns, all were sparked by disputes over girlfriends or drugs, and all were committed by boys.

These cases have not entirely disappeared, but they have declined dramatically. Since 1992, only 1 of the random school shootings occurred in inner-city schools (it was committed by a

Black student), whereas the remaining 22 have been committed by White students in sub-urban schools. Virtually all involved rifles, not handguns—a symbolic shift from urban to rural weaponry. However, once again, all shoot-ings were committed by boys.

As the race and class of the perpetrators have shifted, so too has the public perception of school violence. No longer do we hear claims about the "inherent" violence of the inner city or, what is even more pernicious, the "inherently" violent tendencies of certain racial or ethnic groups. As the shooters have become White and suburban middle-class boys, the public has shifted the blame away from group characteris-tics to individual psychological problems, assuming that these boys were deviants who broke away from an otherwise genteel suburban culture—that their aberrant behavior was explainable by some psychopathological factor. Although it is no doubt true that many of the boys who committed these terrible acts did have serious psychological problems, such a framing

masks the significant role that race and class, in addition to gender, play in school violence.

WHO SHOOTS AND WHY?

Still, most students—White or non-White, male or female—are not violent, schools are predominantly safe, and school shootings are aberrations. As a public, we seem concerned with school shootings because its story is not "when children kill" but specifically when sub-urban White boys kill. To illustrate the distribu-tion of shootings across the country, we have mapped all cases of random school shootings since 1982 (see Figure 1). There were five cases documented between 1982 and 1991; there have been 23 cases since 1992 (see the appendix for a list of the shootings).

Figure 4.1 reveals that school shootings do not occur uniformly or evenly in the United States . . . School shootings are decidedly *not* a national trend. Of 28 school shootings between 1982 and

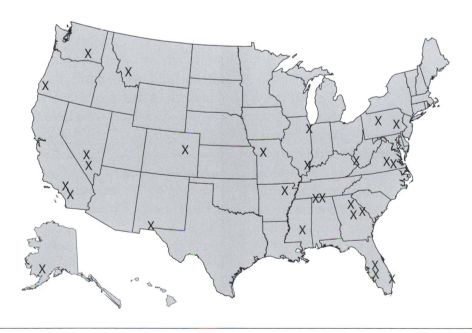

Figure 4.1   Map of the United States, Showing All Cases of Random School Shootings, 1982-2001

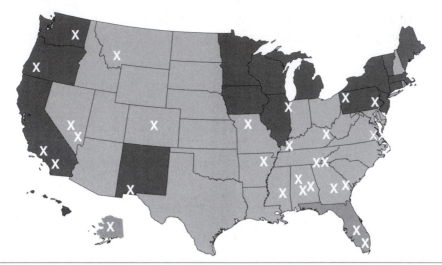

Figure 4.2   Map of the United States, Showing All Cases of Random School Shootings, 1982-2001, Superimposed on Map of State-by-State Voting for President, 2000

2001, all but 1 were in rural or suburban schools (1 in Chicago). All but 2 (Chicago again and Virginia Beach) were committed by a White boy or boys.

School shootings can be divided even further, along the lines of a deep and familiar division in American society (see Figure 4.2).

Contrary to Alan Wolfe's assertion that we are "one nation, after all," it appears that we are actually two nations: "red states" (states that voted for George W. Bush in the 2000 presidential election) and "blue states" (states that voted for Al Gore in the 2000 election). Of the 28 school shootings, 20 took place in red states (marked with light gray in Figure 2). Of those in the blue states (marked with dark gray in Figure 2), all but one (in Chicago) were in rural or suburban areas. Of those 8 from blue states, half of the counties in those blue states (Santee, CA; Red Hill, PA; Moses Lake, WA; and Deming, NM) voted Republican in the last election.

What this suggests is that school violence is unevenly distributed. We need to focus less on the form of school violence—documenting its prevalence and presenting a demographic profile of the shooters—and more on the *content* of

the shootings; instead of asking psychological questions about family dynamics and composition, psychological problems, and pathologies, we need to focus our attention on local school cultures and hierarchies, peer interactions, normative gender ideologies, and the interactions among academics, adolescence, and gender identity.

With this as our guiding theoretical framework, we undertook an analysis of secondary media reports on random school shootings from 1982 to 2001. Using the shooters' names as our search terms, we gathered articles from six major media sources—the three major weekly news magazines: *Time, Newsweek,* and *U.S. News and World Report* (in order from greatest circulation to least); and three major daily newspapers: *USA Today, New York Times,* and the *Los Angeles Times.*[3] In conducting our analysis, we found a striking pattern from the stories about the boys who committed the violence: Nearly all had stories of being constantly bullied, beat up, and, most significantly for this analysis, "gay-baited." Nearly all had stories of being mercilessly and constantly teased, picked on, and threatened. And most strikingly, it was *not* because they were gay (at least there is no evidence to suggest that any of them were gay) but because they were *different* from the other boys—shy, bookish, honor students, artistic, musical, theatrical, nonathletic, "geekish," or weird. Theirs are stories of "cultural marginalization" based on criteria for adequate gender performance, specifically the enactment of codes of masculinity.

In a recent interview, eminent gender theorist Eminem poignantly illustrated the role of "gay-baiting" in peer interactions. In his view, calling someone a "faggot" is not a slur on his sexuality but on his gender. He says,

> The lowest degrading thing that you can say to a man . . . is to call him a faggot and try to take away his manhood. Call him a sissy. Call him a punk. "Faggot" to me doesn't necessarily mean gay people. "Faggot" to me just means taking away your manhood. (Kim, 2001, p. 5)

In this rationalization, Eminem, perhaps unwittingly, speaks to the central connection between gender and sexuality and particularly to the association of gender nonconformity with homosexuality. Here, homophobia is far less about the irrational fears of gay people, or the fears that one might actually be gay or have gay tendencies, and more the fears that *heterosexuals* have that others might *(mis)perceive them as gay* (Kimmel, 1994). Research has indicated that homophobia is one of the organizing principles of heterosexual masculinity, a constitutive element in its construction (see, e.g., Epstein, 1995, 1998; Herek, 1998, 2000; Herek & Capitano, 1999). And as an organizing principle of masculinity, homophobia—the terror that others will see one as gay, as a failed man—underlies a significant amount of men's behavior, including their relationships with other men, women, and violence. One could say that homophobia is the hate that makes men straight. There is much at stake for boys and, as

a result, they engage in a variety of evasive strategies to make sure that no one gets the wrong idea about them (and their manhood) . . . .The impact of homophobia is felt not only by gay and lesbian students but also by heterosexuals who are targeted by their peers for constant harassment, bullying, and gay-baiting. In many cases, gay-baiting is "misdirected" at heterosexual youth who may be somewhat gender nonconforming. This fact is clearly evidenced in many of the accounts we have gathered of the shootings.

For example, young Andy Williams, recently sentenced to 50 years to life in prison for shooting and killing two classmates in Santee, California, and wounding several others was described as "shy" and was "constantly picked on" by others in school. Like many of the others, bullies stole his clothes, his money, and his food, beat him up regularly, and locked him in his locker, among other daily taunts and humiliations (Green & Lieberman, 2001). One boy's father baited him and called him a "queer" because he was overweight. Classmates described Gary Scott Pennington, who killed his teacher and a custodian in Grayson, Kentucky, in 1993 as a "nerd" and a "loner" who was constantly teased for being smart and wearing glasses (Buckley, 1993). Barry Loukaitas, who killed his algebra teacher and two other students in Moses Lake, Washington, in 1996 was an honor student who especially loved math; he was also constantly teased and bullied and described as a "shy nerd" ("Did Taunts Lead to Killing?" 1996). And Evan Ramsay, who killed one student and the high school principal in Bethel, Alaska, in 1997 was also an honor student who was teased for wearing glasses and having acne (Fainaru, 1998). Luke Woodham was a bookish and overweight 16-year-old in Pearl, Mississippi. An honor student, he was part of a little group that studied Latin and read Nietzsche. Students teased him constantly for being overweight and nerdy and taunted him as "gay" or "fag." Even his mother called him fat, stupid, and lazy. Other boys bullied him routinely and, according to one fellow student, he "never fought back when other boys called him names" (Holland, 1997, p. 1). On October 1, 1997, Woodham stabbed his mother to death in her bed before he left for school. He then drove her car to school, carrying a rifle under his coat. He opened fire in the school's common area, killing two students and wounding seven others. After being subdued, he told the assistant principal, "The world has wronged me" (Lacayo, 1998, p. 38). Later, in a psychiatric interview, he said,

> I am not insane. I am angry. . . . I am not spoiled or lazy; for murder is not weak and slow-witted; murder is gutsy and daring. I killed because people like me are mistreated every day. I am malicious because I am miserable. (Chua-Eoan, 1997, p. 54)

Fourteen-year-old Michael Carneal was a shy and frail freshman at Heath High School in Paducah, Kentucky, barely 5 feet tall, weighing 110 pounds. He wore thick glasses and played in the high school band. He felt alienated, pushed around, and picked on. Boys stole his lunch and constantly teased him. In middle school, someone pulled down his pants in front of his classmates (Adams & Malone, 1999). He was so hypersensitive and afraid that others would see him naked that he covered the air vents in the bathroom. He was devastated when students called him a "faggot" and almost cried when the school gossip sheet labeled him "gay." On Thanksgiving, 1997, he stole two shotguns, two semiautomatic rifles, a pistol, and 700 rounds of ammunition and after a weekend of showing them off to his classmates, brought them to school hoping that they would bring him some instant recognition. "I just wanted the guys to think I was cool," he said. When the cool guys ignored him, he opened fire on a morning prayer

circle, killing three classmates and wounding five others. Now serving a life sentence in prison, Carneal told psychiatrists weighing his sanity, "People respect me now" (Blank, 1998, p. 94).

At Columbine High School, the site of the nation's most infamous school shooting, this connection was not lost on Evan Todd, a 255-pound defensive lineman on the Columbine football team, an exemplar of the jock culture that Dylan Klebold and Eric Harris found to be such an interminable torment. "Columbine is a clean, good place, except for those rejects," Todd said.

> Sure we teased them. But what do you expect with kids who come to school with weird hairdos and horns on their hats? It's not just jocks; the whole school's disgusted with them. They're a bunch of homos. . . . If you want to get rid of someone, usually you tease 'em. So the whole school would call them homos. (Gibbs & Roche, 1999, p. 48)

Ben Oakley, a soccer player, agreed. "Nobody liked them," he said. "The majority of them were gay. So everyone would make fun of them" (Cullen, 1999). Athletes taunted them: "Nice dress," they'd say. They would throw rocks and bottles at them from moving cars. The school newspaper had recently published a rumor that Harris and Klebold were lovers.

Both were reasonably well-adjusted kids. Harris's parents were a retired Army officer and a caterer—decent, well-intentioned people. Klebold's father was a geophysicist who had recently moved into the mortgage services business and his mother worked in job placement for the disabled. Harris had been rejected by several colleges; Klebold was due to enroll at Arizona in the fall. But the jock culture was relentless. Said one friend,

> Every time someone slammed them against a locker and threw a bottle at them, I think they'd

go back to Eric or Dylan's house and plot a little more—at first as a goof, but more and more seriously over time. (Pooley, 1999, p. 30)

The rest is all too familiar. Harris and Klebold brought a variety of weapons to their high school and proceeded to walk through the school, shooting whomever they could find. Students were terrified and tried to hide. Many students who could not hide begged for their lives. The entire school was held under siege until the police secured the building. In all, 23 students and faculty were injured and 15 died, including one teacher and the perpetrators.

In the videotape made the night before the shootings, Harris says, "People constantly make fun of my face, my hair, my shirts." Klebold adds, "I'm going to kill you all. You've been giving us shit for years." What Klebold said he had been receiving for years apparently included constant gay-baiting, being called "queer," "faggot," "homo," being pushed into lockers, grabbed in hallways, and mimicked and ridiculed with homophobic slurs. For some boys, high school is a constant homophobic gauntlet and they may respond by becoming withdrawn and sullen, using drugs or alcohol, becoming depressed or suicidal, or acting out in a blaze of overcompensating violent "glory" (see Egan, 1998).

Before we continue, let us be completely clear: Our hypotheses are decidedly not that gay and lesbian youth are more likely to open fire on their fellow students. In fact, from all available evidence, *none* of the school shooters was gay. But that is our organizing hypothesis: Homophobia—being constantly threatened and bullied *as if you are gay* as well as the homophobic desire to make sure that others know that you are a "real man"—plays a pivotal and understudied role in these school shootings. But more than just taking gender performance and its connections to homosexuality seriously, we argue that we must also carefully investigate the dynamics of gender within these

local cultures, especially local school cultures and the typically hegemonic position of jock culture and its influence on normative assumptions of masculinity, to begin to understand what pushes some boys toward such horrific events, what sorts of pressures keep most boys cowed in silence, and what resources enable some boys to resist. To understand the specificity of these events and the continuing power of gender as an analytic category through which to view them and the dynamics they represent, we conclude here with three important questions and suggest some tentative answers.

WHY BOYS AND NOT GIRLS?

Despite the remarkable similarities between the sexes on most statistical measures, the single most obdurate and intractable gender difference remains violence, both the willingness to see it as a legitimate way to resolve conflict and its actual use. Four times more teenage boys than teenage girls think fighting is appropriate when someone cuts to the front of a line. Half of all teenage boys get into a physical fight each year (Kimmel, 2000). Undoubtedly, violence is normative for most boys (see also Lefkowitz, 1997).

Historically, no industrial society other than the United States has developed such a violent "boy culture," as historian E. Anthony Rotundo (1993) calls it in his book *American Manhood*. It is here where young boys, as late as the 1940s, actually carried little chips of wood on their shoulders daring others to knock it off so that they might have a fight. It is astonishing to think that "carrying a chip on your shoulder" is literally true—a test of manhood for adolescent boys. And it is here in the United States where experts actually *prescribed* fighting for young boys' healthy masculine development.

It is interesting to note that in a recently thwarted school shooting in New Bedford,

Massachusetts, it was a young woman, Amylee Bowman, 17, who could not go through with the plot and decided to reveal the details to the authorities. Eric McKeehan, 17, one of the coconspirators, was described in media accounts as constantly angry, especially at being slighted by other students. The mother of a second boy accused in the plot said, "Eric has a temper. He says what's on his mind. He's been known to hit walls and lockers, but what teenage boy hasn't?" (Heslam & Richardson, 2001, p. 6).

Indeed, what teenage boy hasn't? Eminem had that part right. Calling someone a "faggot" means questioning his manhood. And in this culture, when someone questions your manhood, we do not just get mad, we get even.

WHY WHITE BOYS?

There may be a single "boy code" but there are also a variety of ways in which different boys and men relate to it, embrace it, and enact it—in short, there are a variety of young masculinities. Making gender visible ought not to make other elements of identity—age, sexuality, race, ethnicity, class—invisible. What it means to be a 71-year-old Black, gay man in Cleveland is probably radically different from what it means to be a 19-year-old White, heterosexual, farm boy in Iowa.

At the same time, we must also remember that all masculinities are not created equal. All American men also contend with a singular hegemonic vision of masculinity, a particular definition that is held up as the model against which we all measure ourselves. We thus come to know what it means to be a man in our culture by setting our definitions in opposition to a set of subordinated "others"—racial minorities, sexual minorities, and above all, women. As the sociologist Erving Goffman (1963) once wrote,

In an important sense there is only one complete unblushing male in America: a young, married, white, urban, northern, heterosexual, Protestant, father, of college education, fully employed, of good complexion, weight, and height, and a recent record in sports. . . . Any male who fails to quality in any one of these ways is likely to view himself—during moments at least—as unworthy, incomplete, and inferior. (p. 128)

It is crucial to listen to those last few words. When we feel that we do not measure up we are likely to feel unworthy, incomplete, and inferior. It is here, from this place of unworthiness, incompleteness, and inferiority, that boys begin their efforts to prove themselves as men.

By pluralizing the term masculinity, we also make it possible to see places where gender *appears* to be the salient variable but may, in fact, be what sociologist Cynthia Fuchs Epstein calls a "deceptive distinction," something that looks like gender difference but is in fact a difference based on some other criterion. Thus, for example, we read of how male cadets at Virginia Military Institute (VMI) or the Citadel would be distressed by and uncomfortable with women's presence on campus. Of course, in reality, there were plenty of women on campus—they cleaned the rooms, made and served the food, taught the classes, and were readily available as counselors and medical personnel. What bothered the men was not gender but class, that is, women's institutional equality.

Most important for our current discussion, though, is the fact that failure to see race while looking at gender will cause us to miss the real story. We know that African American boys face a multitude of challenges in schools—racial stereotypes, formal and informal tracking systems, low expectations, and underachievement. But the one thing they do not do is plan and execute random and arbitrary mass shootings. And this is particularly interesting because the dynamics of the classroom and academic achievement have different valences for African American girls and African American boys. In their fascinating ethnographies of two inner-city public high schools, both Signithia Fordham (1996) and Ann Ferguson (2000) discuss these differences. When African American girls do well in school, their friends accuse them of "acting White." But when African American boys do well in school, their friends accuse them of "acting like girls."

We might posit that cultural marginalization works itself out differently for subordinates and superordinates. Even if they are silenced or lose their voice, subordinates—women, gays and lesbians, and students of color—can tap into a collective narrative repertoire of resistance. They can collectivize their anguish so that the personally painful may be subsumed into readily available political rhetorics. White boys who are bullied are supposed to be real men, supposed to be able to embody independence, invulnerability, and manly stoicism. In fact, the very search for such collective rhetorics can be seen as an indication of weakness. Thus, we might hypothesize that the cultural marginalization of the boys who did commit school shootings extended to feelings that they had no other resource: they had no access to other methods of self-affirmation.

WHY THESE PARTICULAR BOYS AND NOT OTHERS WHO HAVE HAD SIMILAR EXPERIENCES?

Walk down any hallway in any middle school or high school in America and the single most common put-down that is heard is "That's so gay." It is deployed constantly, casually, unconsciously. Boys hear it if they try out for the school band or orchestra, if they are shy or small, physically weak and unathletic, if they are smart, wear glasses, or work hard in school. They hear it if they are seen to like girls too much or if they are too much "like" girls. They hear it if their body language, their clothing, or their musical preferences do not conform to the norms of their peers. And they hear it not as an assessment of their present or future sexual orientation but as a commentary on their masculinity.

But not all boys who are targeted like that open fire on their classmates and teachers. In fact, very few do. So how is it that some boys—many boys, in fact—resist? Perhaps there is what Robert Brooks, of Harvard Medical School, calls the "charismatic adult" who makes a substantial difference in the life of the child. Most often this is one or the other parent, but it can also be a teacher or some other influential figure in the life of the boy. Perhaps the boy develops an alternative substantive pole around which to organize competence. Gay-baiting suggests that he is a failure at the one thing he knows he wants to be and is expected to be—a man. If there is something else that he does well—a private passion, music, art—someplace where he feels valued—he can develop a pocket of resistance.

Similarly, the structures of his interactions also can make a decisive difference. A male friend, particularly one who is not also a target but one who seems to be successful at masculinity, can validate the boy's sense of himself as a man. But equally important may be the role of a female friend, a potential if not actual "girlfriend." Five of the school shooters had what they felt was serious girl trouble, especially rejection. Luke Woodham was crushed when his girlfriend broke up with him. "I didn't eat, I didn't sleep. It destroyed me," he testified at trial. She was apparently his primary target and was killed. Michael Carneal may have had a crush on one of his victims. Mitchell Johnson was upset that his girlfriend had broken up with him.

Although all the shooters have been boys, that does not mean that girls are inconsequential in boys' cognitive mapping of their social worlds. It may be that the boys who are able to best resist the torments of incessant gay-baiting and bullying are those who have some girls among their friends, and perhaps even a girl-friend, that is, girls who can also validate their sense of masculinity (which other boys do as well) as well as their heterosexuality (which boys alone cannot do). If masculinity is largely a homosocial performance, then at least one male peer, who is himself successful, must approve of the performance. The successful demonstration of *heterosexual* masculinity,

which is the foundation, after all, of gay-baiting, requires not only the successful performance for other men but also some forms of "sexual" success with women.[4]

These sorts of questions—the dynamics of local culture, the responsiveness of adults and institutions, and the dynamics of same-sex and cross-sex friendships—will enable us to both understand what led some boys to commit these terrible acts and what enable other boys to develop the resources of resistance to daily homophobic bullying.

APPENDIX

All Cases of Random School Shootings, 1982–2001

March 19, 1982, Las Vegas, Nevada. Patrick Lizotte, age 18.

March 2, 1987, DeKalb County, Missouri. Nathan Faris, age 12.

February 11, 1988, Pinellas Park, Florida. Jason Harles, age 16.

December 16, 1988, Virginia Beach, Virginia. Nicholas Elliott, age 15.

September 27, 1990, Las Vegas, Nevada. Curtis Collins, age 15.

November 20, 1992, Edward Tilden High School, Chicago, Illinois. Joseph White, age 15.

January 18, 1993, East Carter High School, Grayson, Kentucky. Gary Scott Pennington, age 17.

February 22, 1993, Reseda High School, Reseda, California. Robert Heard, age 15.

March 18, 1993, Harlem High School, Harlem, Georgia. Edward Gillom.

May 24, 1993, Upper Perkiomen High School, Red Hill, Pennsylvania. Jason Michael Smith, age 15.

November 1, 1993, Sullivan High School, Chicago, Illinois. Troy Jones, age 15.

April 12, 1994, Margaret Leary Elementary School, Butte, Montana. James Osmanson, age 10.

September 30, 1995, Tavares Middle School, Taveras, Florida. Keith Johnson, age 14.

November 15, 1995, Richland High School, Lynnville, Tennessee. Jamie Rouse, age 18.

February 2, 1996, Frontier High School, Moses Lake, Washington. Barry Loukaitas, age 14.

September 25, 1996, DeKalb Alternative School, Stone Mountain, Georgia. David Debose Jr., age 16.

January 27, 1997, Conniston Middle School, West Palm Beach, Florida. Tonneal Mangum, age 14.

February 19, 1997, Bethel Regional High School, Bethel, Alaska. Evan Ramsey, age 16.

October 1, 1997, Pearl High School, Pearl, Mississippi. Luke Woodham, age 16.

December 1, 1997, Heath High School, West Paducah, Kentucky. Michael Carneal, age 14.

March 24, 1998, Westside Middle School, Jonesboro, Arkansas. Andrew Golden, age 11, and Mitchell Johnson, age 13.

April 24, 1998, Parker Middle School, Edinboro, Pennsylvania. Andrew Wurst, age 14.

May 19, 1998, Lincoln County High School, Fayetteville, Tennessee. Jacob Davis, age 18.

May 21, 1998, Thurston High School, Springfield, Oregon. Kipland Philip Kinkel, age 15.

June 15, 1988, Armstrong High School, Richmond, Virginia. Quinshawn Booker, age 14.

April 20, 1999, Columbine High School, Littleton, Colorado. Eric Harris, age 18, and Dylan Klebold, age 17.

May 20, 1999, Heritage High School, Conyers, Georgia. Anthony Solomon, age 15.

November 19, 1999, Deming Middle School, Deming, New Mexico. Victor Cordova, age 12.

March 5, 2001, Santana High School, Santee, California. Charles Andrew Williams, age 15.

NOTES

1. This is not to entirely dismiss the potential links between school shootings and the availability of guns. Although many boys are frustrated, harassed, and saturated with media violence, not all of them have equal access to guns.

2. This same critique also could be directed at the aforementioned arguments blaming the media and/or the prevalence of guns.

3. These articles were selected because they comprise three of the top four daily newspapers in circulation. The Wall Street Journal, which has the highest circulation of any daily newspaper in the United States, was not included in our analysis because its substantive focus is on business-related issues. To extend our analysis to local media outlets, we also selectively sampled from smaller regional newspapers. We recognize that using secondary media reports as indicators of "what really happened" leading up to and during these shootings is a questionable tactic. To further tease out the causes of these shootings, one would have to conduct firsthand interviews with those directly involved in the shootings— the shooters themselves, classmates, teachers, administrators, parents, and so forth. However, we feel that an analysis of media reports is nevertheless a valuable approach in this instance because one of our major points is that although virtually all of these accounts contained some evidence indicating the connections between masculinity, homophobia, and violence, they all somehow overlooked this fact.

4. The word sexual is in quotations because this does not necessarily mean actual sexual contact but rather a sexualized affirmation of one's masculinity by girls and women.

REFERENCES

Adams, J., & Malone, J. (1999, March 18). Outsider's destructive behavior spiraled into violence. *Louisville Courier Journal.*

Anderson, M., Kaufman, J., Simon, T., Barrios, L., Paulozzi, L., Ryan, R., et al. (2001). School associated violent deaths in the United States, 1994–1999. *Journal of the American Medical Association, 286,* 2695–2702.

Blank, J. (1998, December). The kid no one noticed. *U.S. News and World Reports,* p. 27.

Bok, S. (1999). *Mayhem: Violence as public entertainment.* Cambridge, MA: Perseus.

Bronski, M. (1999, July). Littleton, movies and gay kids. *Z Magazine.*

Buckley, J. (1993, November 8). The tragedy in room 108. *U.S. News and World Report,* p. 41.

Carlson, D., & Simmons, W. (2001). Majority of parents think a school shooting could occur in their community. *Gallup Poll Release.* Retrieved March 6 from http://www.gallup.com/poll/releases/pr010306.asp.

Centers for Disease Control and Prevention. (2001). Web-based injury statistics query and reporting system (WISQARS). National Center for Injury Prevention and Control, Centers for Disease Control and Prevention. Retrieved February 2, 2002, from www.cdc.gov/ncipc/wisqars

Chu, J. (2000). *Learning what boys know: An observational and interview study with six four-year-old boys.* Unpublished doctoral dissertation, Graduate School of Education, Harvard University. Cambridge, MA.

Chua-Eoan, H. (1997, October 20). Mississippi: In a dramatic turn, an alleged one-man rampage may have become a seven-pointed conspiracy. *Time,* p. 54.

Cloud, J. (2001, March 19). The legacy of Columbine. *Time,* p. 32.

Cullen, D. (1999). The rumor that won't go away. *Salon.* Retrieved February 2, 2002, from www.salon.com/news/feature/1999/04/24/rumors/index.html

Did taunts lead to killing? (1996, February 4). *Minneapolis Star Tribune,* p. 14.

Egan, T. (1998, June 15). Patterns emerging in attacks at schools. *New York Times,* p. A1.

Elliott, D.S., Hamburg, B. A., & Williams, K. R. (1998). *Violence in American schools.* New York: Cambridge University Press.

Epstein, D. (1995). Keeping them in their place: Hetero/sexist harassment, gender and the enforcement of heterosexuality. In J. Holland & Adkins (Eds.), *Sex, sensibility and the gendered body.* London: Macmillan.

Epstein, D. (Ed.). (1998). Real boys don't work: Underachievement, masculinity and the harassment of sissies. In *Failing boys? Issues in gender and achievement.* London: Open University Press.

Fainaru, S. (1998, December 4). Alaska teen's path to murder. *Dallas Morning News,* p. 48A. Fear of classmates. (1999, April 22). *USA Today,* p. A1.

Ferguson, A. (2000). *Bad boys: Public schools in the making of Black masculinity.* Ann Arbor: University of Michigan Press.

Fordham, S. (1996). *Blacked out: Dilemmas of race, identity, and success at Capital High.* Chicago: University of Chicago Press.

Garbarino, J. (1998). *Lost boys.* New York: Free Press.

Gaughan, E., Cerio, J., & Myers, R. (2001). *Lethal violence in schools: A national survey. Final report.* Alfred, NY: Alfred University.

Gibbs, N., & Roche, T. (1999, December 20). The Columbine tapes: In five secret videos they recorded before the massacre, the killers reveal their hatreds—and their lust for fame. *Time,* p. 40.

Gilligan, J. (1996). *Violence.* New York: Vintage.

Glassner, B. (1999a). *The culture of fear.* New York: Basic Books.

Glassner, B. (1999b, August 13). School violence: The fears, the facts. *New York Times,* p. A27.

Goffman, E. (1961). *Asylums.* New York: Vintage.

Goffman, E. (1963). *Stigma: Notes on the management of spoiled identity.* Englewood Cliffs, NJ: Prentice Hall.

Green, K., & Lieberman, B. (2001, March 10). Bullying, ridicule of Williams were routine, friends say. *San Diego Union-Tribune,* p. A1.

Half of teens have heard of a gun threat at school. (2001, November 27). *USA Today,* p. 6D.

Herek, G. (Ed.). (1998). *Stigma and sexual orientation: Understanding prejudice against lesbians, gay men and bisexuals.* Newbury Park, CA: Sage.

Herek, G. (2000). The psychology of sexual prejudice. *Current Perspectives in Psychological Science, 9*(1), 19–22.

Herek, G., & Capitano, J. (1999). Sex differences in how heterosexuals think about lesbians and gay men: Evidence from survey context effects. *Journal of Sex Research, 36*(4), 348–360.

Heslam, J., & Richardson, F. (2001, November 26). Suspect labeled outcast, estranged from family. *Boston Herald,* p. 6.

Holland, G. (1997, October 3). "I am not insane, I am angry": Suspect in Pearl handed classmate a chilling note. *Biloxi Sun Herald,* p. 1.

Human Rights Watch. (2001). *Hatred in the hallways: Violence and discrimination against lesbian, gay, bisexual, and transgender students in the U.S.* New York: Author.

Kelleher, M. (1998). *When good kids kill.* New York: Dell.

Kim, R. (2001, March 5). Eminem—Bad rap? *The Nation,* p. 4.

Kimmel, M. (1994). Masculinity as homophobia: Fear, shame and silence in the construction of gender identity. In H. Brod & M. Kaufman (Eds.), *Theorizing masculinities* (pp. 119–141). Newbury Park, CA: Sage.

Kimmel, M. (1996). *Manhood in America: A cultural history.* New York: Free Press.

Kimmel, M. (2000). *The gendered society.* New York: Oxford University Press.

Kimmel, M. (2001, March 9). Snips and snails . . . and violent urges. *Newsday, Minneapolis Star-Tribune, San Francisco Examiner,* p. A41.

Klein, J., & Chancer, L. S. (2000). Masculinity matters: The omission of gender from high-profile school violence cases. In S. U. Spina (Ed.), *Smoke and mirrors: The hidden content of violence in schools and society.* Lanham, MD: Rowman & Littlefield.

Lacayo, R. (1998, April 6). Toward the root of the evil. *Time,* pp. 38–39.

Lefkowitz, B. (1997). *Our guys: The Glenn Ridge rape and the secret life of the perfect suburb.* Berkeley: University of California Press.

Ma, X. (2001). Bullying and being bullied: To what extent are bullies also victims? *American Educational Research Journal, 38,* 351–370.

Nansel, T., Overpeck, M., Pilla, R., Rune, J., Simmons-Morton, B., & Scheidt, P. (2001). Bullying behaviors among U.S. youth: Prevalence and association with psychological adjustment. *Journal of the American Medical Association, 285*(16), 2094–2100.

The news of the week in review. (1999, November 15). *The Nation,* p. 5.

Noguera, P. (2001). The trouble with Black boys. *Harvard Journal of African American Public Policy, 7*(Summer), 23–46.

Olweus, D. (1978). *Aggression in the schools.* Washington, DC: Hemisphere.

Olweus, D. (1991). Victimization among school children. In R. Baenninger (Ed.), *Targets of violence and aggression* (pp. 45–102). Amsterdam: Elsevier.

O'Toole, M. (2000). *The school shooter: A threat assessment perspective.* Quantico, VA: National Center for the Analysis of Violent Crime, FBI Academy.

Pooley, E. (1999, May 10). Portrait of a deadly bond. *Time,* pp. 26–27.

Puffer, J. A. (1912). *The boy and his gang.* Boston: Houghton.

Rotundo, E. A. (1993). *American manhood.* New York: Basic Books.

Salmon, G., James, A., & Smith, D. M. (1998, October). Bullying in schools: Self-reported anxiety, depression and self-esteem in secondary school children, *British Medical Journal, 317,* 924–925.

Smith, P., & Brain, P. (2000). Bullying in schools: Lessons from two decades of research. *Aggressive Behavior, 26*(1), 1–10.

Stearns, P. (1994). *American cool.* New York: New York University Press.

U.S. Department of Justice, Bureau of Justice Statistics. (2000). *Indicators of school crime and safety, 2000.* Washington, DC: Office of Justice Programs.

Youth violence: A report of the Surgeon General. (2001). Washington, DC: Department of Health and Human Services.

Discussion Questions

1. Think back to the Rosenblum and Travis reading we presented in Chapter 1, about how categories are constructed and dichotomized, with one half of this dichotomy stigmatized. How does this crucial point relate to Kimmel and Mahler's argument that if the school shooters had been predominantly female, gender would have been a central focus of the media coverage, but since they are male, gender is relegated to the insignificant? Why is the gender of the shooters so absent from the public conversation about them?

2. Likewise, why is the shooters' race removed from the national conversation? Is it simply because

we are now supposedly a "color-blind" society? What are Kimmel and Mahler's arguments about the race and class of the shooters and how they become important to the gendered dimension of their crimes?

3. Why aren't "us-and-them" dichotomies set up in the media coverage of the school shootings the way they are with, say, coverage of terrorist attacks? How do race, gender, class, age, and nationality converge to direct our conversations toward the "psychological profiles" of school shooting offenders, rather than the other social commonalities they share?

4. What argument is presented in this article about the connection of homophobia to the

gendered experience of the shooters? Is it their sexual orientation that distinguishes them, or something else? Discuss the relationship between gender and sexual orientation.

5. What suggestions, both explicit and implicit, do Kimmel and Mahler make for reducing these "random" school shootings based upon their analyses of the causes? For those interested in going onto careers in educational fields, how would you envision such solutions being implemented at the school level? (Research current anti-bullying educational programs going on in schools now to see if they sufficiently address the gender, race, class, and homophobia dimensions raised by Kimmel and Mahler.)

CURRENT DEBATES

AFFIRMATIVE ACTION

Should members of minority groups be favored in the job market? Should colleges and graduate schools judge minority candidates differently than members of the dominant group? Programs that confer advantages on minorities at work and at school—attempts to take affirmative action in the struggle to achieve racial integration and equality—have been controversial since their inception four decades ago. The arguments in favor of affirmative action usually cite the intractability of institutional discrimination, the pervasiveness of racism, and the continuing importance of race in American life. Without a strong program to force employers to balance their workforces and to require college admissions programs to seek out qualified minority candidates, the racial status quo will be perpetuated indefinitely. Some of these arguments are presented below by Orlando Patterson, a sociologist and an African American.

An opposing point of view is presented by Thomas Sowell, an economist and also an African American. Opponents of affirmative action often argue, as does Sowell, that the program actually hurts the groups it is intended to help and that "reverse discrimination" is simply wrong. If racial discrimination was wrong when used to perpetuate the privileges of whites under slavery and segregation, then it is just as wrong as a technique to combat racial inequality. Discrimination is discrimination, and the United States should strive to be "color-blind," not color-conscious.

The debate over affirmative action is often so intense that other ways of addressing the problems of exclusion and equality are not considered. One such alternative would be the argument that the real barriers to equality are based on class, not race or gender, and that affirmative action programs need to be reformulated on this basis. Affirmative action based on class would attempt to equalize life chances and opportunities for education and jobs by awarding advantages to people who are born poor or disadvantaged. Programs formulated on the basis of class might avoid the controversies that surround charges of reverse discrimination and, since race and class are so highly correlated, simultaneously reach many of the goals of present-day affirmative action program.[1]

---

1. For one presentation of this argument, see Kahlenberg, R. (1997). *The remedy: Class, race, and affirmative action.* New York: Basic Books.

AFFIRMATIVE ACTION CASTS SUSPICIONS ON LEGITIMATE
BLACK ACHIEVEMENT AND DEPICTS AFRICAN AMERICANS AS INCAPABLE

Thomas Sowell

The Hippocratic Oath says: "First, do no harm." By that standard, affirmative action would have been gotten rid of years ago. There are many ways in which it hurts the very people it claims to help, as well as polarizing the society at large.

A couple of years ago, I met with the editorial staff of one of the leading publications in America. Among them was a black man who was by no means stupid—but he said many stupid things at that meeting. . . . Why? He was mismatched, out of his league, among people who were at the pinnacle of their profession. If he played it straight, he would have been nobody in this setting, though there are probably hundreds of other reputable publications on which he would have been a valuable and respected writer. Saying off-the-wall things was his only way of even seeming to be significant among the cream of the crop of his profession. . . . Nor was this man unique. There is a whole class of such people teaching in the leading law schools, many of them promoting a convoluted set of doctrines known as critical race theory. Their counterparts can also be found in literature, among other fields. . . .

Affirmative action also amounts to a virtual moratorium on recognition of black achievement. Consider the case of [Supreme Court] Justice Clarence Thomas. His critics have repeatedly accused him of benefiting from affirmative action, when he went to college or to law school, and then wanting to deny its benefits to other blacks. In all the endless reiterations of this theme, no one has ever found it necessary to demonstrate that it was true. It so happens that affirmative action had not yet begun when Clarence Thomas entered Holy Cross College. Nor has anyone even considered it necessary to try to show that Thomas was admitted under the Yale law school's affirmative action program, rather than by the regular admissions process. . . . Justice Thomas' credentials are questioned precisely because of affirmative action. . . .

In short, blacks fall under a cloud of suspicion of being substandard, even when they match or surpass the performances of their white counterparts. Who gains from creating such awkward situations and the unnecessary problems that flow from them?

Guilty whites gain by salving their guilt through affirmative action. Black hustlers gain by either getting things for themselves or by leading movements which are able to dispense largess that they have talked or pressured guilty whites into providing.

Institutions, such as universities, that receive millions of federal dollars gain by having enough black body count around to avoid having the flow of that money jeopardized by claims of discrimination based on statistics.

Liberals who secretly believe that blacks are innately inferior . . . feel like they have done the best they can do by giving blacks or other minorities something that those minorities would otherwise be incapable of getting.

Do any of the people who claim to want to see blacks advance ever ask: Under what conditions have blacks in fact been most successful? Where have they advanced most? Blacks have done best in situations radically different from those of affirmative action. Blacks are overrepresented in sports and entertainment, especially among the highest-paid performers. In both fields, competition is merciless. You can be the top performer this year and yet they will drop you like a hot potato if your performance slacks off next year.

Nobody has given blacks anything in sports or entertainment. Blacks have had to shape up or ship out. Most shape up. It is where blacks are given double standards and coddled that they end up tarnished in their own eyes or in the eyes of others.

SOURCE: Originally titled "How Affirmative Action Hurts Blacks" from *Forbes*, October 6, 1997. Reprinted by permission of Forbes Magazine. Copyright © 2006 Forbes Inc.

WHY WE STILL NEED AFFIRMATIVE ACTION

Orlando Patterson

The most important way in which affirmative action helps those on the outside is to provide them access to circles and networks that they would otherwise never penetrate.

For Afro-Americans, one of the most egregious effects of past . . . exclusion has been their isolation from cultural capital and personal networks that are essential for success. . . . This important sociological fact is usually simply neglected by those who imagine capitalist America to be a perfectly competitive, meritocratic system in which people rise to their positions based solely on their training and motivation. There is some truth to this but it is at best a half-truth. . . .

Let us assume that there is a firm with one hundred entry level employees, exactly 13 of whom are Afro-Americans, and that all these employees have . . . equal . . . ability, educational attainment, and motivation. Let us assume further an . . . unbiased . . . organization [and staff]. . . . Even under these circumstances . . . it is almost certain that the Afro-American . . . employees will never make it to the top echelons of the organization if there is no account taken of ethnicity in promotion; indeed, they will hardly move beyond their entry-level jobs.

These claims seem counterintuitive because we assume that, in the normal course of events, each equally qualified entry-level Afro-American will have a 13% chance of being promoted, resulting eventually in a similar ratio of Afro-Americans moving up the firm's opportunity ladder. This is what misguided liberal and neo-conservatives have in mind when they speak naively about a "color-blind" system. The problem . . . [is] that when firms promote workers they consider not simply the characteristics of the employees but organizational criteria, among the most important of which is the degree to which a candidate . . . will fit into the upper echelon for which he or she is being considered. And it is precisely here that Afro-Americans lose out because of their small numbers, their ethnic differences, and the tendency of personnel officers to follow one well-established law of microsociology, first formally propounded by the sociologist George Casper Homans.

The very simple principle of human behavior—call it the principle of homo-phyly—is that people who share common attitudes tend to marry each other, . . . play more together, and in general tend to get along better and to form more effective work teams. Thus, a non-racist personnel officer, under no pressure to consider ethnic attributes—indeed, under strong . . . pressure to follow a "color-blind" policy—would always find it organizationally rational to choose a Euro-American . . . in spite of the technical equality of the Afro-American candidates. The Euro-American person's organizational fit—which comes simply from being

Euro-American—will so significantly reduce the cost . . . of incorporation and training that it would be irresponsible of our ethnically unbiased personnel officer, under orders to select in a color-blind manner, ever to promote an Afro-American person.

Of course, when one introduces one well-known real-world feature of American society to this model of "color-blind" organizational behavior, the cards are even more heavily stacked against our thirteen entry-level Afro-American employees: This is the fact that Euro-Americans have a hard time taking orders from Afro-American supervisors. . . . This being so, the cost to our non-racist . . . personnel officer becomes even greater; and it gets worse the more real-world attitudes and behaviors we introduce.

SOURCE: From *The Ordeal of Integration* by Orlando Patterson. Copyright © 1997 by Orlando Patterson. Reprinted by permission of Counterpoint, a member of Perseus Books, L.L.C.

DEBATE QUESTIONS TO CONSIDER

1. What assumptions does Sowell make about the overall fairness of the American workplace? What are the implications of his argument that blacks have been most successful precisely in the areas in which affirmative action has been irrelevant: entertainment and sports? In contrast, what assumptions does Patterson make about the ability of employers to make unbiased decisions about promotions?

2. What are the limitations of the "color-blind" approach advocated by Sowell? Why does Patterson call it "naive"? How strong is his argument compared with Sowell's? Which would you choose? Why? Would class-based approaches to effecting equal opportunity be more successful in addressing discrimination?

3. Which of these positions is most appealing to you? If you agree with Sowell, what other programs might combat institutionalized discrimination effectively? If you agree with Patterson, how would you respond to the charge of "reverse discrimination"? If you prefer class-based remedies, do these programs ignore the realities of racism and prejudice?

Part III

UNDERSTANDING DOMINANT-MINORITY
RELATIONS IN THE UNITED STATES TODAY

5

AFRICAN AMERICANS

The system of de jure segregation that perpetuated the oppression and exploitation of African Americans following slavery came to an end in the 1960s, destroyed by a combination of court rulings, legislation, and the courageous activism of civil rights demonstrators. Since that time, the status of African Americans has improved in many ways. The black middle class has increased in size and affluence, average levels of education have risen, and the income gap between blacks and whites has diminished. At the dawn of the 21st century, African Americans can be found at all levels of society and include some of the wealthiest, most respected and prestigious people in the world.

At the same time, enormous problems of poverty and powerlessness, racism, and exclusion remain. Black Americans are still almost three times more likely to live in poverty as whites and, even more distressing, one third of black children (versus about 14 percent of white children) will be raised in poverty. The black urban underclass continues to grow, and black Americans are the victims of continuing, systematic discrimination in every societal institution, including, in particular, the criminal justice system. Antiblack prejudice and racism persist in American culture and in the minds of many, albeit in a somewhat muted and covert form.

The selections in this chapter address this mixture of racial progress and failure from a number of angles. The Narrative Portraits focuses on the continuing stereotypes of blacks as manifested by the behavior of whites on public streets. Public opinion polls over the past half century demonstrate a marked decline in the willingness of whites to endorse overtly prejudicial statements. The reactions of whites to a black man (journalist Brent Staples) who is just walking down the street show that the levels of antiblack prejudice are deeper and more persistent than many would like to admit. Novelist Danzy Senna also reflects on the more subtle but still intense racism of the present but from the perspective of a person of mixed race heritage.

The Readings examine antiblack racism, discrimination, and exclusion across a broad spectrum of American life. Eduardo Bonilla-Silva and Tyrone Forman document the "modern" or symbolic form that racism has assumed in the United States. The overt, unapologetic prejudice of the past has evolved into a more subtle form that tends to hide just below the surface but continues to view African Americans as unworthy of full equality. Angela Davis explores the dynamics of racism and discrimination in the criminal justice system, an area in which race relations are particularly volatile and sensitive. She documents the racism, discrimination, and sexism that is built into the system, including the racist results of the so-called War on Drugs. She then examines the many ways in which the disproportionate imprisonment of blacks is blamed on the black community, blaming the victims and thereby insulating the institution from charges of racism.

In the third reading, Kathleen Korgen analyzes the ways in which racism affects close, cross-racial friendships. She finds that the members of these intimate relationships develop strategies for avoiding the topic of race and ignoring the "elephant in the living room." Racism remains so pervasive in American society, however, that it affects even close friendships, a fact that suggests how far we remain from the ideal of a truly "color-blind" society.

The Current Debates section focuses on a proposal for narrowing the racial gaps in income and quality of life. The idea of paying reparations to blacks for the kidnapping of their ancestors from Africa, the centuries of slavery, and the continued exploitation under de jure segregation is controversial, to say the least. The black community is not unanimous in its support for reparations, as pointed out by John McWhorter, but there are some compelling reasons to consider the possibility, as argued by Manning Marable. Furthermore, as Joe Feagin and Eileen O'Brien point out, there are precedents for such repayments and the possibility of positive outcomes far exceed the mere transfer of cash.

Please visit the accompanying website to Race, Ethnicity, and Gender, second edition for the *Public Sociology Assignments* at http://www.pineforge.com/das2.

QUESTIONS TO CONSIDER IN THIS CHAPTER

1. Many Americans believe that antiblack prejudice, racism, and discrimination are things of the past. What evidence is presented in this chapter to challenge those views? How persuasive is the evidence? What forms do modern day prejudice and discrimination take?

2. Korgen argues that people in intimate cross-racial friendships ignore the "elephant in the living room" of racism and prejudice. To what extent do *all* Americans ignore the problems and grievance of peoples of color? Why?

3. Besides reparations (and affirmative action, as discussed in Chapter 4), what other approaches might be effective in addressing the patterns of racial inequality that remain on your campus? In your hometown? In the nation?

4. What gender dimensions can you identify in the issues raised in this chapter? How does gender impact (for example) prejudice, the criminal justice system, and cross-racial friendships?

NARRATIVE PORTRAITS

THE PERSISTENCE OF RACISM

This section presents two views of black-white relations in the modern United States. Both selections are written by African Americans, the first by journalist Brent Staples and the second by novelist Danzy Senna. Staples's experiences walking the streets of Chicago and New York challenge the notion that American society has overcome its ancient prejudices and that racial stereotyping is a thing of the past. His experiences underscore the often large differences between what people say (for example, the low levels of overt prejudice measured in public opinion polls) and what they do (for example, their panicky, fearful reactions to sharing the sidewalk with a black male). Which of these—saying or doing—is the more valid indicator of the level of racism in American society? Also note how Staples defuses potentially tense sidewalk situations by whistling themes from classical music: what racial (and gender) stereotypes is he challenging?

Senna is the author of several novels, including *Caucasia* and *Symptomatic*. In this selection, she reflects on changing fashions in race and the rising popularity of mulattos.

She discusses the pressures that caused her to identify as black in spite of the fact that her mother was white and her father black-Mexican and suggests that the enhanced popularity of "hybrids" may be deflecting attention away from the continuing racism of American society.

JUST WALK ON BY: A BLACK MAN PONDERS
HIS POWER TO ALTER PUBLIC SPACE

Brent Staples

My first victim was a woman—white, well dressed, probably in her early twenties. I came upon her late one evening on a deserted street in Hyde Park, a relatively affluent neighborhood in an otherwise mean, impoverished section of Chicago. As I swung onto the avenue behind her, there seemed to be a discreet, uninflammatory distance between us. Not so. She cast back a worried glance. To her, the youngish black man—a broad six feet two inches with a beard and billowing hair, both hands shoved into the pockets of a bulky military jacket—seemed menacingly close. After a few more quick glimpses, she picked up her pace and was soon running in earnest. Within seconds she disappeared into a cross street.

That was more than a decade ago. I was 22 years old, a graduate student newly arrived at the University of Chicago. It was in the echo of that terrified woman's footfalls that I first began to know the unwieldy inheritance I'd come into—the ability to alter public space in ugly ways. It was clear that she thought herself the quarry of a mugger, a rapist, or worse. Suffering a bout of insomnia, however, I was stalking sleep, not defenseless wayfarers. As a softy who is scarcely able to take a knife to a raw chicken—let alone hold it to a person's throat—I was surprised, embarrassed, and dismayed all at once. Her flight made me feel like accomplice in tyranny. It also made it clear that I was indistinguishable from the muggers who occasionally seeped into the area from the surrounding ghetto. That first encounter, and those that followed, signified that

a vast, unnerving gulf lay between nighttime pedestrians—particularly women—and me. And I soon gathered that being perceived as dangerous is a hazard in itself. I only needed to turn a corner into a dicey situation, or crowd some frightened, armed person in a foyer somewhere, or make an errant move after being pulled over by a policeman. Where fear and weapons meet—and they often do in urban America—there is always the possibility of death.

In that first year, my first away from my hometown, I was to become thoroughly familiar with the language of fear. At dark, shadowy intersections in Chicago, I could cross in front of a car stopped at a traffic light and elicit the *thunk, thunk, thunk, thunk* of the driver—black, white, male, female—hammering down the door locks. On less-traveled streets after dark, I grew accustomed to but never comfortable with people who crossed to the other side of the street rather than pass me. Then there were the standard unpleasantries with police, doormen, bouncers, cab drivers, and others whose business it is to screen out troublesome individuals *before* there is any nastiness.

I moved to New York nearly two years ago and I have remained an avid night walker. I often witness [the] "hunch posture," from women after dark on the warrenlike streets of Brooklyn where I live. They seem to set their faces on neutral and, with their purse straps strung across their chests bandolier style, they forge ahead as though bracing themselves against being tackled. I understand, of course, that the danger they perceive is not a hallucination. Women are particularly vulnerable to street violence, and young black males are drastically overrepresented among the perpetrators of that violence. Yet these truths are no solace against the kind of alienation that comes of being ever the suspect, against being set apart, a fearsome entity with whom pedestrians avoid making eye contact.

It is not altogether clear to me how I reached the ripe old age of 22 without being conscious of the lethality nighttime pedestrians attributed to me. Perhaps it was because in Chester, Pennsylvania, the small, angry industrial town where I came of age in the 1960s, I was scarcely noticeable against a backdrop of gang warfare, street knifings, and murders. I grew up one of the good boys, had perhaps a half-dozen fist fights. In retrospect, my shyness of combat has clear sources.

Many things go into the making of a young thug. One of those things is the consummation of the male romance with the power to intimidate. . . . I recall the points at which some of my boyhood friends were finally seduced by the perception of themselves as tough guys. When a mark cowered and surrendered his money without resistance, myth and reality merged—and paid off. It is, after all, only manly to embrace the power to frighten and intimidate. We, as men, are not supposed to give an inch of our lane on the highway; we are to seize the fighter's edge in work and in play and even in love; we are to be valiant in the face of hostile forces.

Unfortunately, poor and powerless young men seem to take all this nonsense literally. As a boy, I saw countless tough guys locked away; I have since buried several, too. They were babies, really—a teenage cousin, a brother of 22, a childhood friend in his mid-twenties—all gone down in episodes of bravado played out in the streets. I came to doubt the virtues of intimidation early on. I chose, perhaps even unconsciously, to remain a shadow—timid, but a survivor. . . . In time, I learned to smother the rage I felt at so often being taken for a criminal. Not to do so would surely have led to madness. . . .

I began to take precautions to make myself less threatening. I move about with care, particularly late in the evening. I give a wide berth to nervous people on the subway platforms during the wee hours, particularly when I have exchanged business clothes for jeans. If I happen to be entering a building behind some people who appear skittish, I may walk by, letting them clear the lobby before I return, so as not to seem to be following them. I have been calm and extremely congenial on those rare occasions when I've been pulled over by the police.

And on late-evening constitutionals along streets traveled by, I employ what has proved to be an excellent tension-reducing measure: I whistle melodies from Beethoven and Vivaldi and the more popular classical composers. Even steely New Yorkers hunching toward nighttime destinations seem to relax, and occasionally they even join in the tune. Virtually everybody seems to sense that a mugger wouldn't be warbling bright, sunny selections from Vivaldi's *Four Seasons*. It is my equivalent of the cowbell that hikers wear when they know they are in bear country.

SOURCE: Reprinted by permission of the author. Brent Staples writes editorials for *New York Times* and is author of the memoir, *Parallel Time: Growing Up in Black and White.*

THE MULATTO MILLENNIUM

Danzy Senna

Strange to wake up and realize you're in style. That's what happened to me the other morning. It was the first day of the new millennium and I woke up to find that mulattos had taken over. They were everywhere. Playing golf, running the airwaves, opening their own restaurants, modeling clothes. . . . The radio played a steady stream of Lenny Kravitz, Sade, and Mariah Carey. I thought I'd died and gone to Berkeley. . . . Pure breeds (at least the black ones) are out and hybridity is in. America loves us in all of our half-caste glory. . . . Major new magazines announce our existence as if we are proof of extraterrestrial life. They claim we're going to bring about the end of race as we know it.

. . .

I guess I should have seen it coming. Way back in the fall of 1993, *Time* magazine put on its cover "The New Face of America," a computer morphed face of fourteen models of different racial backgrounds, creating a woman they called Eve. The managing editor wrote [that the women was created as] "a symbol of the future, multiethnic face of America. . . ." As I read the article, it reminded me of an old saying they used to have down South during Jim Crow: "If a black man wants to sit in the front of the bus, he just puts on a turban." Maybe the same rule applies here: call yourself mixed and you just might find the world smiles a little brighter on you.

Mulattos may not be new. But the mulatto-pride folks are a new generation. They want their own special category or no categories at all. . . .

Before all this radical ambiguity, I was a black girl . . . Not your ordinary black girl, if such a thing exists. But, rather, a black girl with a WASP mother and a black-Mexican father, and a face that harkens to Andalusia, not Africa. . . .

Not only was I black . . . , I was an enemy of the people. The mulatto people, that is. I sneered at those byproducts of miscegenation who chose to identify as mixed, not black. I thought it was wishy-washy, an act of flagrant assimilation, treason, passing even.

It was my parents who made me this way. In Boston in 1975, mixed wasn't really an option. . . . You were either black or white. No checking "Other." . . . Sure, I received some strange reactions from all quarters when I called myself black. But black people usually got over their initial surprise and welcomed me into their ranks.

It was the white folks who grew most uncomfortable with the dissonance between the face they saw and the race they didn't. Upon learning who I was, they grew paralyzed with fear that they might have "slipped up" in my presence, that is, said something racist, not knowing that there was a Negro in their midst. Often, they had. . . .

My parent's decision [to raise us as black] arose out of the rising black power movement, which made identifying as black . . . a conscious choice. *You told us all along that we had to call ourselves black because of this so-called one drop [rule]. Now that we don't have to anymore, we choose to. Because black is beautiful. Because black is not a burden, but a privilege. . . .*

There had been moments in my life when I had not asserted my black identity. I hadn't "passed" in the traditional sense of the word, but in a more subtle way, by simply mumbling that I was mixed. Then the white people in my midst seemed to forget whom they were talking to, and countless times I was silent witness to their candid racism. When I would remind them that my father was black, they would laugh and say, "But you're different." That was somewhere I never wanted to return. There was danger in this muddy middle stance. A danger of disappearing. Of being swallowed whole by the great white whale. I had seen the arctic belly of the beast and didn't plan on returning. . . .

My mulatto experience . . . was difficult not because things were confusing but because they were so painfully clear. Racism, as well as the absurdity of race, were obvious to me in ways that they perhaps weren't to those whose racial classification was a given. Racism . . . is a slippery devil. . . . Today, sans burning crosses and blatant epithets, racism is harder to put one's finger on. . . . In all this mulatto fever, people seem to have forgotten that racism exists with or without miscegenation. Instead of celebrating a "new race," . . . can't we take a look at the new racism?

SOURCE: Copyright © 1998 by Danzy Senna. Reprinted with the permission of The Wylie Agency, Inc.

READINGS

To comprehend fully the situation of African Americans today, it is necessary to understand the dynamics of *modern racism* (also sometimes referred to as *laissez-faire racism, symbolic racism,* or *color-blind racism*). The three readings for this section examine how modern racism manifests itself in the United States in the criminal justice system, in whites' attitudes about African Americans, and even in the more intimate settings of close black-white friendships. The first reading, "I Am Not a Racist But . . . ," reviews some of the literature on symbolic or laissez-faire racism, which shows that on traditional measures of prejudice, whites' abstract attitudes on race have become more egalitarian, yet whites also tend not to support concrete policy measures to ensure that equality. However, having done their own research study combining surveys and in-depth interviews, Eduardo Bonilla-Silva and Tyrone A. Forman demonstrate that even the idea that white prejudice has declined should be suspect, since the same whites who answer in non-prejudiced ways on surveys express more prejudiced views in an in-depth interview setting where they are able to qualify and clarify their opinions. In the interviews, respondents use what the authors call a "new 'racetalk,'" which presents prejudiced views in a more "sanitized" way. For example, in response to a question about whether blacks are lazy, one respondent says, "I don't want to say waiting for a handout, but [to] some extent, that's kind of what I am hinting at." We see that a large majority of the whites interviewed do not believe African Americans face discrimination to any significant extent, and in fact, more than a third of the sample described blacks as whining or lying about discrimination. Thus, rather than attributing the disadvantaged situation of blacks to *structural* sources such as institutionalized discrimination (as do only a few "progressive" interviewees), most of the whites see blacks' situation in the United States as a result of their supposed cultural inferiority (also known as the *culture of poverty* argument). Such misattribution, coupled with the new "racetalk" that seeks to avoid stating prejudice directly, is described as *color-blind racism*—the post-1960s way that racial inequality is maintained and reproduced.

Some of the policy implications of this modern form of racism are explored in the second reading, "Race and Criminalization," about African Americans and the prison industry. Like the authors of the first reading, Angela Davis describes race as being disguised in "encoded language" today, amounting to what she terms "camouflaged racism." An example is the "Three strikes, you're out" laws requiring life sentences for those convicted for a crime three times. Although this law appears race-neutral, it has a major disproportionate impact on African Americans, an effect people tend to blame on the "culture of poverty" of blacks rather than on structural racism embedded in the criminal justice system. Davis points out this is done by Republicans and Democrats alike, citing President Bill Clinton as an example of someone who spoke of racial inequality as a matter of the "heart" (or as traditional prejudice) rather than as institutional. The high statistics of black representation in prisons that have become familiar to many are often taken as evidence of "black criminality" rather than as a problem with the system. Davis also links the expansion of the prison industry to the globalization of capitalism, since corporations are now turning to the cheap labor of prisoners in the same way they exploit unorganized labor in Third World countries. Thus, now capitalist profit depends upon keeping the prisons full, and effectively disenfranchised African Americans serve as easy targets to this end. As the prison population increases dramatically, one of the fastest growing groups of prisoners has been women, and especially black women. Davis explores this gender and race connection as well, bringing our attention to how sexist and racist stereotypes converge upon black female drug users, whose only options become being criminalized as unfit mothers in order to get treatment for their addictions. Even though the majority of U.S. drug users are white, prisons continue to be filled with African American women and men, most of whom are there for drug-related crimes. Again, the apparently race-neutral War on Drugs provides yet another example of modern racism (and sexism) in action.

The third reading provides a final look at how Americans seek to minimize overt references to race even in the context of their close interracial friendships. In her article "The Elephant in the Living Room," Kathleen Korgen reveals that a majority of the 40 black-white close friendship pairs she interviewed did not seriously discuss race at any point during their relationship. The color-blind strategy to ignore or avoid race, or else to relegate it to the nonserious realm of joking, is prevalent with her respondents and further illustrates the color-blind racism discussed in the first reading. Korgen's research also raises the issue of how power shapes the meaning of interactions between dominant and minority group members. Specifically, when two friends joke about each other's race, whether someone has "crossed the line" really depends on who is saying what, because of the different racial histories of the two groups. Also, for the few friends who do discuss seriously issues of race, the teaching process does not become an even trade, since the black friends end up doing far more educating of their white friends than the reverse. Thus, even as the few progressives in Bonilla-Silva and Forman's research are still struggling with their own stereotypes, so too are these few progressive cross-racial friendships dealing with the legacy of racism as they try to break down its barriers. These readings taken together show us just how much work still needs to be done to ensure full social and political equality for African Americans.

"I Am Not a Racist But . . . ": Mapping White College Students' Racial Ideology in the USA

Eduardo Bonilla-Silva and Tyrone A. Forman

Since the civil rights period it has become common for Whites to use phrases such as "I am not a racist, but . . ." as shields to avoid being labeled as "racist" when expressing racial ideas (Van Dijk, 1984: 120). These discursive maneuvers or *semantic moves* are usually followed by negative statements on the general character of minorities (e.g. "they are lazy," "they have too many babies") or on government-sponsored policies and programs that promote racial equality (e.g. "affirmative action is reverse discrimination," "no-one should be forced to integrate").[1] Qualitative work has captured these discursive maneuvers on issues as diverse as crime, welfare, affirmative action, government intervention, neighborhood and school integration (Blauner, 1989; Feagin and Sikes, 1994; Feagin and Vera, 1995; MacLeod,

1995; Rieder, 1985; Rubin, 1994; Terkel, 1993; Weis and Fine, 1996; Wellman, 1977). For example, Margaret Welch, angry about not getting a scholarship in college, told Studs Terkel: "I've never been prejudiced, but why the hell are you doing this to me?" (Terkel, 1993: 70). Doug Craigen, a 32-year-old White truck driver, declared to Lillian Rubin: "I am not a racist, but sometimes they [Asians] give me the creeps" (Rubin, 1994: 188). . . .

These prejudiced expressions clash with research that suggests that racial attitudes have improved dramatically in the USA. Beginning with Hyman and Sheatsley's widely cited paper in *Scientific American* (1964), survey research has documented substantial change in Whites' racial views (e.g. Firebaugh and Davis, 1988; Lipset, 1996; Niemi, Mueller and Smith, 1989; Smith and

Sheatsley, 1984; Schuman et al., 1988; Sniderman and Piazza, 1993). . . .

The conflicting findings regarding the character of Whites' racial views based on interviews and surveys as well as the differing interpretations of survey-based attitudinal research (see Bobo and Hutchings, 1996; Hochschild, 1995; Kinder and Sanders, 1996; Lipset, 1996; Schuman et al., 1988, 1997; Sniderman and Carmines, 1997; Sniderman and Piazza, 1993) have produced a new puzzle: *What is the meaning of contemporary Whites' racial views?* How can *Whites* claim to believe in racial equality and yet oppose programs to reduce racial inequality? Why is it that a large proportion of *Whites,* who claim in surveys that they agree with the principle of integration, do not mind their kids mixing with non-Whites, have no objection to interracial marriages, and do not mind people of color moving into their neighborhoods continue to live in all-White neighborhoods and send their kids to mostly White schools? Finally, why is it that interview-based research consistently reports higher levels of prejudice among Whites?

To explore the meaning of contemporary Whites' views, this article examines White racial attitudes from both a different conceptual perspective and with a different methodology. Conceptually, we situate the racial attitudes of Whites as part of a larger racial ideology that functions to preserve the contemporary racial order.[2] Here we build on the work of others who have argued that the complexity of contemporary White racial attitudes reflects changes occurring in the USA since the late 1940s (Bonilla-Silva and Lewis, 1999; Brooks, 1990; Smith, 1995). Specifically, they claim that the dramatic social, political, economic and demographic changes in the USA since the 1940s combined with the political mobilization of various minority groups in the 1950s and 1960s, forced a change in the US racial structure—the network of social, political, and economic racial

relations that produces and reproduces racial positions. In general terms, White privilege since the 1960s is maintained in a new fashion, in covert, institutional, and apparently nonracial ways (Bobo et al., 1997; Bonilla-Silva and Lewis, 1999; Jackman, 1994, 1996; Kovel, 1984; Smith, 1995; Wellman, 1977).

In consonance with this new structure, various analysts have pointed out that a new racial ideology has emerged that, in contrast to the Jim Crow racism or the ideology of the color line (Johnson, 1943, 1946; Myrdal, 1944), avoids direct racial discourse but effectively safeguards racial privilege (Bobo et al., 1997; Bonilla-Silva and Lewis, 1999; Essed, 1996; Jackman, 1994; Kovel, 1984). That ideology also shapes the very nature and style of contemporary racial discussions. In fact, in the post civil rights era, overt discussions of racial issues have become so taboo that it has become extremely difficult to assess racial attitudes and behavior using conventional research strategies (Myers, 1993; Van Dijk, 1984, 1987, 1997). Although we agree with those who suggest that there has been a normative change in terms of what is appropriate racial discourse and even racial etiquette (Schuman et al., 1988), we disagree with their interpretation of its meaning. Whereas they suggest that there is a "mixture of progress and resistance, certainty and ambivalence, striking movement and mere surface change" (p. 212), we believe (1) that there has been a rearticulation of the dominant racial themes (less *overt* expression of racial resentment about issues anchored in the Jim Crow era such as strict racial segregation in schools, neighborhoods, and social life in general, and more resentment on new issues such as affirmative action, government intervention, and welfare) and (2) that a new way of talking about racial issues in public venues—a new *racetalk*—has emerged. Nonetheless, the new racial ideology continues to help in the reproduction of White supremacy.

. . . Our main concern in this article is tracking White college students' interpretive repertoires on racial matters as expressed during in-depth interviews and comparing them to their views as expressed in responses to survey items. We do this in order to demonstrate that the survey research paradox of contemporary White views on race is not a paradox after all.

RESEARCH DESIGN

The 1997 Social Attitudes of College Students Survey was a sample of undergraduate students at four universities. One school was located in the south, another in the midwest, and two were located in the west. Data collection occurred during the spring of 1997. All students surveyed were enrolled in social science courses. The questionnaire was administered during a class period. Students were informed that participation in the study was voluntary. Fewer than 10 percent declined to participate and a total of 732 students completed the survey. There were no significant differences on demographic characteristics between students who chose to participate and those that did not. All of the analyses reported in this article use only White respondents ($N = 541$). The sample sizes of other racial groups are too small for reliable statistical comparison. . . .

We conducted in-depth interviews with a random sample of the White college students that had completed the survey because prior research has found differences in Whites' racial attitudes depending on mode of data collection (Dovidio and Gaertner, 1986; Dovidio et al., 1989; Groves, Fultz et al., 1992; Krysan, 1998; Sigall and Page, 1971). . . . In order to facilitate our selection of respondents for the in-depth interviews, we asked each respondent surveyed to provide on the first page of the survey their name, telephone, and e-mail address. After the students were chosen the page was discarded.

Over 80 percent of the . . . White college students who completed the survey . . . provided contact information. There were no significant differences between students that provided contact information and the 20 percent who did not on either several racial attitude items or demographic characteristics. We randomly selected 41 White college students (approximately 10%) who had completed the survey and provided contact information. Interviews were conducted during the spring of 1997. In order to minimize race of interviewer effects (see Anderson et al., 1988a, 1988b), the interviews were conducted by three White graduate students and two White advanced undergraduate students. Whenever possible, we also matched respondents by gender (Kane and Macaulay, 1993). The interviews were conducted using an interview guide that addressed several issues explored in the survey instrument. The time of interviews ranged from 1 to 2.5 hours. The present study draws more extensively on the in-depth interview data, addressing White college students' general and specific racial attitudes, social distance preferences, and reported interactions with racial minorities. . . .

TOWARD AN ANALYSIS OF CONTEMPORARY WHITE IDEOLOGY

White College Students' Views: Survey Results

Table 5.1 shows the responses of White students to questions on affirmative action. The table provides results on the total sample . . . as well as on the 41 students selected for the interviews. A number of things are clear from these data. First, the interview sample mirrors the total sample, something that holds for all the tables.[3] If anything, the interview respondents are slightly more likely to support affirmative action measures. Second, Whites seem to openly oppose or have serious reservations about these

Table 5.1   White Students' Views on Affirmative Action Items

Affirmative Action Questions	Survey Sample (%) (N = 410)	Interview Sample (%) (N = 41)
B21. An anti-affirmative action proposition passed by a substantial margin in California in 1996. If a similar proposition was put on the ballot in your locality, would you support it, oppose it, or would you neither oppose nor support it?		
1. Support	25.8	37.5
2. Neither Support Nor Oppose	38.3	25.0
3. Oppose	35.9	37.5
χ^2		n.s.
C18. Sometimes Black job seekers should be given special consideration in hiring.		
1. Agree	13.3	17.9
2. Neither Agree Nor Disagree	21.6	17.9
3. Disagree	65.2	64.1
χ^2		n.s.
G1. Affirmative Action programs for Blacks have reduced Whites' chances for jobs, promotions, and admissions to schools and training programs.		
1. Agree	50.8	36.6
2. Neither Agree Nor Disagree	26.2	17.1
3. Disagree	23.0	46.3
χ^2		**
G2. What do you think are the chances these days that a White person won't get a job or a promotion while an equally or less qualified Black person gets one instead?		
1. Very Likely	11.1	17.9
2. Somewhat Likely	60.3	46.2
3. Not very Likely	28.7	35.9
χ^2		n.s.
G3. What do you think are the chances these days that a White person won't get admitted to a school while an equally or less qualified Black gets admitted instead?		
1. Very Likely	26.3	15.0
2. Somewhat Likely	52.9	60.0
3. Not very Likely	20.8	25.0
χ^2		n.s.
G4. Some people say that because of past discrimination it is sometimes necessary for colleges and universities to reserve openings for Black students. Others oppose quotas because they say quotas discriminate against Whites. What about your opinion: Are you for or against quotas to admit Black students?		
1. For	12.4	22.5
2. Not Sure	36.7	27.5
3. Against	50.9	50.0
χ^2		n.s.

SOURCE: Social Attitudes of College Students Survey, 1997.

$*p < .05, **p < .01$, n.s. = not significant.

programs, regardless of how the question is worded. These findings are quite consistent with previous research on Whites' attitudes toward affirmative action (Kluegel, 1990; Kluegel and Smith, 1986; Lipset, 1996; Schuman and Steeh, 1996; Steeh and Krysan, 1996). . . . Third, most of the respondents fear the effects of affirmative action programs on their life chances. This fear is evident in the large proportion of respondents (70% or higher) who believe that it is "somewhat likely" or "very likely" that they will lose out on a job, promotion, or admission to a college due to affirmative action (see questions G1, G2, and G3). This finding is interesting because it goes against other research on affirmative action that shows that these programs have had little impact on Whites (Badgtee and Hartmann, 1995; Glass Ceiling Commission, 1995; Edley, 1996; Herring and Collins, 1995; Hochschild, 1995; Wicker, 1996). More significantly, the results are intriguing because these college students are from mostly middle-class backgrounds and are not in a vulnerable social position.

In Table 5.2 we show the results on social distance items. Our results in Table 5.2 are consistent with those of previous research. A very high proportion of Whites claim to approve of interracial marriage, friendship with Blacks, and with people of color moving into predominantly White neighborhoods (Firebaugh and Davis, 1988; Niemi et al., 1989; Schuman et al., 1988; Sniderman and Piazza, 1993). However, results based on two non-traditional measures of social distance from Blacks indicate something different. A majority of Whites (68%) state that they do not interact with any Black person on a daily basis and that they have not recently invited a Black person for lunch or dinner. Although suggestive, this finding is somewhat inconclusive since it is possible that Whites have changed their attitudes on social distance but do not have the opportunity to interact meaningfully with Blacks because of residential and school segregation (Massey and Denton, 1993; Orfield and Eaton, 1996; Wilson, 1987).

Finally, in Table 5.3 we display our results on Whites' beliefs about the significance of discrimination for Blacks' life chances. Interestingly, most Whites (87%) believe that discrimination affects the life chances of Blacks and approximately a third (30%) agree with the statement that "Blacks are in the position that they are because of contemporary discrimination" (for similar findings, see Lipset and Schneider, 1978). In contrast, a slight majority of White college students believe that preferences should not be used as a criterion for hiring (53.4% were "against") and 83 per cent of the White respondents also believe that Whites either want to give Blacks a "better break" or at least "don't care one way or the other." Again, these results are somewhat contradictory (Schuman et al., 1988).

Although most White college students believe that Blacks experience discrimination and that this explains in part their contemporary status, at the same time, they believe that most Whites want to give Blacks a "better break" or "don't care one way or another" and that preferences should not play any part in hiring and promotion decisions.

Accordingly, based on these survey results, we could construct a variety of interpretations of White college students' racial attitudes. If we based our analysis on the respondents' answers to traditional questions, we would conclude, as most social scientists do, that Whites are racially tolerant. If we use all of our survey findings, we could conclude, as Schuman and his colleagues do (1988), that Whites have contradictory racial views. Finally, if we give more credence to our respondents' answers to the modern racism questions (B17, C18, E6, G1, G2, G3, and G4) and some of the new questions (A13, A15, B21) than to their answers to traditional items, we could conclude that Whites are significantly more racially prejudiced in their views than previous research has concluded. In the next section we use the 41 in-depth interviews with White students to make sense of our conflicting survey findings.

Table 5.2 White Students' Views on Social Distance Items

Social Distance Questions	Survey Sample (%) (N = 410)	Interview Sample (%) (N = 41)
Traditional Items		
B2. If a Black family with about the same income and education as you moved next door, would you mind it a lot, a little, or not at all?		
1. Not at all	92.1	95.1
χ^2		n.s.
B12. Do you approve or disapprove of marriage between Whites and Blacks?		
1. Approve	79.4	90.2
2. Not Sure	13.7	4.9
3. Disapprove	6.9	4.9
χ^2		n.s.
B7. How strongly would you object if a member of your family had a friendship with a Black person?		
1. No objection	91.9	95.1
χ^2		n.s.
Nontraditional Items		
A13. Think of the five people with whom you interact the most on an almost daily basis. Of these five, how many of them are Black?		
1. None	67.7	68.3
2. One	19.6	24.4
3. Two or more	12.7	7.3
χ^2		n.s.
A15. Have you invited a Black person for lunch or dinner recently?		
1. No	67.8	75.0
2. Yes	32.2	25.0
χ^2		n.s.

SOURCE: Social Attitudes of College Students Survey, 1997.
$*p < .05, **p < .01$, n.s. = not significant.

White College Students' Views—In-Depth Interviews

"If Two People Love Each Other . . .": Whites' Views on Interracial Marriages

Our strategy for interpreting our interview data on intermarriage was as follows. First, we read carefully the respondents' answers to a specific question about whether or not they approved of interracial marriages. Then we examined their romantic history and what kind of friends they had throughout their lives. In some cases, we examined their views on other matters because they contained information relevant to

Table 5.3   White Students' Views on Significance of Discrimination on Blacks' Life Chances

Significance of Discrimination Questions	Survey Sample (%) (N = 410)	Interview Sample (%) (N = 41)
B13. Do you agree or disagree with the following statement? Discrimination against Blacks is no longer a problem in the United States		
1. Agree	8.1	7.3
2. Neither Agree Nor Disagree	4.9	4.9
3. Disagree	87.0	87.8
χ^2		n.s.
B17. On the whole, do you think that most Whites in the USA want to see Blacks get a better break, do they want to keep Blacks down, or don't care one way or the other?		
1. Better Break	20.1	17.5
2. Don't Care One Way or the Other	62.9	65.0
3. Keep Blacks Down	17.0	17.5
χ^2		n.s.
E6. Some people say that because of past discrimination against Blacks, preference in hiring and promotion should be given to Blacks. Others say preferential hiring and promotion of Blacks is wrong because it gives Blacks advantages that they haven't earned. Are you for or against preferences in hiring and promotion to Blacks?		
1. Against	54.1	47.5
2. Not Sure	38.6	47.5
3. For	7.1	5.0
χ^2		n.s.
F5. Blacks are in the position that they are as a group because of contemporary discrimination.		
1. Agree	30.6	48.7
2. Neither Agree Nor Disagree	39.3	20.5
3. Disagree	30.1	30.8
χ^2		*

SOURCE: Social Attitudes of College Students Survey, 1997.
$*p < .05, **p < .01$, n.s. = not significant.

interracial marriage. Based on the composite picture of the respondents that we obtained using this strategy, we classified them into six categories (see Table 5.4).

Five of the respondents (category 1) had lifestyles consistent with their views on intermarriages, 28 had reservations from serious to outright opposition (categories 3–6), and 7 claimed to approve of intermarriage but had lifestyles inconsistent with the interracial perspective that they presumably endorsed (category 2). For presentation purposes, we will

Table 5.4   Views on Interracial Marriage (Total sample, N=40)[1]

	Respondents % (N)
Support Interracial Marriage/Integrated Life	12.5 (5)
Support Interracial Marriage/Segregated Life	17.5 (7)
Reservations toward Interracial Marriage/Integrated Life	10.0 (4)
Reservations toward Interracial Marriage/Segregated Life	52.5 (21)
Oppose Interracial Marriage/Integrated Life	0 (0)
Oppose Interracial Marriage/Segregated Life	7.5 (3)

1. The question was not asked of one of the students in the sample.

provide one example of respondents in category 2 (since this was the hardest group to make sense of) and one of the respondents in categories 4 (the modal category) and 6.

The first case is Ray, a student at a large midwestern university, an example of students in category 2. Ray answered the question about interracial marriage by stating that:

> I think that there's . . . *I think that interracial marriage is totally legitimate. I think if two people love each other* and *they* want to spend the rest of their lives together, I think *they* should definitely get married. And race should in no way be an inhibitive factor. . . . (Interview # 150: 13)

Although Ray supports interracial marriages (despite using some *indirectness*), his life prior to college and during college was racially segregated. He grew up in a large city in the midwest, in an upper middle-class neighborhood that he characterized as "all *White*" (Interview # 150: 2) and described his friends as "what the average suburban kid is like nowadays" (Interview # 150: 3). More significantly, Ray, who was extremely articulate in the interview, stuttered remarkably in the question (asked *before* the one on intermarriage) dealing with whether or not he had ever been attracted to Blacks. His response was as follows:

> . . . Um, so, to answer that question, no. Um, but I would not . . . I mean, *I would not . . . I mean, I would not ever preclude, uh, a Black woman from being my girlfriend on the basis that she was Black.* Ya know, I mean . . . ya know what I mean? If you're looking from the standpoint of attraction, I mean, I think that, ya know . . . I think, ya know, I think, ya know, I think, ya know, all women are, I mean, all women have a sort of different type of beauty if you will. And I think that for Black women it's somewhat different than *White* women. Um, but I don't think it's, ya know, I mean, it's, it's . . . it's nothing that would ever stop me from like, uh . . . I mean, I don't know, I mean, I don't [know] if that's . . . I mean, that's just sort of been my impression. I mean, it's not like I would ever say, "no, I'll never have a Black girlfriend," *but it just seems to me like I'm not as attracted to Black women as I am to White women for whatever reason. It's not about prejudice, it's just sort of like, ya know, whatever. Just sort of the way . . . way . . . like, I see White women as compared to Black women, ya know?* (Interview # 150: 12)

As is evident from Ray's statement, he is not attracted to Black women, something that clashes with his self-proclaimed color-blind approach to love and his support for interracial marriages. More significantly, he seemed aware of how problematic that sounded and used all sorts of rhetorical strategies to save face.

The next case is an example of students who had reservations about interracial marriages who lived a primarily segregated life (category 4), the modal group in our sample. We found regularities (Brown and Yule, 1983) in the structure of their answers similar to the ones we found among those who responded "yes and no" to the affirmative action question. Their answers usually included the rhetorical moves of *apparent agreement* and *apparent admission*—a formal statement of support for interracial marriages followed or preceded by statements qualifying the support in terms of what might happen to the kids, how the relationship might affect the families, or references to how their parents would never approve of such relationships.

The next example is Sally, a student at a large midwestern university. She replied to the interracial marriage question as follows:

> I certainly don't oppose the marriage, not at all. Um . . . *depending on where I am, if I had to have a concern, yes, it would be for the children.* . . . Ya know, it can be nasty and then other kids wouldn't even notice. I think . . . *I could care less what anyone else does with their lives, as long as they are really happy.* And if the parents can set a really strong foundation at home, it can be conquered, *but I'm sure, in some places, it could cause a problem.* (Interview # 221: 5)

Sally's answer included displacement (concerns for the children and the certainty that interracial marriages would be problematic in some places) and indirectness ("I could care less what *anyone else* does . . . as long as *they* are really happy") alongside her initial apparent admission semantic move ("I certainly don't oppose the marriage"). Sally's apprehension on this subject matched the nature of her life and her specific views on Blacks. Sally's life was, in terms of interactions, relationships, and residence, almost entirely racially segregated. When questioned about her romantic life, Sally said that she had never dated a person of color and recognized that "I've never been attracted to a Black person" and that "I never look at what they look like . . . it just hasn't occurred in my life" (Interview # 221: 5).

The final case is Eric, a student at a large midwestern university, an example of the students who openly expressed serious reservations about interracial marriages (category 6). It is significant to point out that even the three students who stated that they would not enter into these relationships claimed that there was nothing wrong with interracial relationships per se. . . .

Eric used the *apparent admission* semantic move ("I would say that I agree with that") in his reply but could not camouflage very well his true feelings ("If I were to ask if I had a daughter or something like that, or even one of my sisters, um . . . were going to get married to a minority or a Black, I . . . I would probably . . . it would probably bother me a little bit"). Interestingly, Eric claimed in the interview that he had been romantically interested in an Asian-Indian woman his first year in college. However, that interest "never turned out to be a real big [deal]" (Interview # 248: 9). Despite Eric's fleeting attraction to a person of color, his life was racially segregated: no minority friends and no meaningful interaction with any Black person.

The results in this section clash with our survey results. Whereas in the survey the students seemed to favor interracial contacts of all kinds with Blacks, the interview data suggest otherwise. Whites' serious reservations if not opposition to interracial marriages are expressed as "concerns" for the welfare of the offspring of those relationships, upsetting the family, or the reaction of the larger community to the marriage. All these statements—a number of the respondents themselves classified these arguments as excuses—seem to be rationalizations to *discursively* avoid stating opposition to interracial marriages. This is quite significant since they could easily *state* that they have no problems with intermarriage. The fact that very few do so in an unequivocal manner gives credence to the argument that Whites' racial aversion for Blacks is deeply ingrained into their unconscious (Fanon, 1967; Hernton, 1988; Jordan, 1977; Kovel, 1984). Finally, the respondents' comments about their romantic lives and friendships clearly indicate that rather than being color-blind, they are very color conscious.

"I KIND OF SUPPORT AND OPPOSE . . .": WHITES' VIEWS ON AFFIRMATIVE ACTION

Intentionally, we did not define affirmative action in our interview protocol. We were particularly interested in how the respondents themselves defined the various programs that have emerged since the 1970s to enhance the chances of minorities getting jobs, promotions, access to institutions of higher learning, etc.[4] Although some of the students hesitated and asked for a definition of the program, to which our interviewers replied "what do you think it is?," most answered based on what they thought affirmative action meant.

Content analysis of the responses of the 41 students interviewed shows that most (85%) oppose affirmative action. This degree of opposition was somewhat higher than the results obtained in the survey. However, unlike in the survey, only a quarter (10 out of 41) came out and opposed affirmative action in a straightforward manner. In part, this may be the result of a general belief that if they express their views too openly on affirmative action, diversity, or any other race-related issue, they are going to be labeled as "racist."[5] Although we were able to detect some of this reticence through discursive analysis, many respondents expressed their concern explicitly. For instance, Bob, a student at a large southern university and who openly opposed affirmative action, said, "I oppose them

[affirmative action programs], mainly because, *I am not a racist but* because I think you should have the best person for the job" (Interview # 6: 13). Mark, a student, at a large midwestern university, who said that he couldn't give a "definite answer" on affirmative action, later mentioned that companies need to diversify because "we need diversity, and if you don't have diversity, *then people call you a racist and you have to deal with all of those accusations*" (Interview # 6: 24).

Since respondents were very sensitive to not appearing "racist," most (26 out of 41) expressed their opposition to affirmative action indirectly. Brian, a student at a large southern university, responded to the affirmative action questions by saying: "Man . . . that's another one where [laughs] . . . *I kind of support and oppose it*" (Interview # 10: 8). If we had based our analysis only on the students' responses to this one question, we would have had to conclude that most Whites are truly torn apart about affirmative action, that they have "non attitudes" (see Converse, 1964, 1970, 1974), or are "ambivalent" (Katz et al., 1986). However, we included several questions in the interview schedule that dealt either directly or indirectly with affirmative action. Therefore we were able to make sense of respondents' vacillations concerning affirmative action.

In many cases, a thorough reading of the complete response to the primary affirmative action question helped us to understand that the "yes and no" responses really meant "no." For example, Brian, the student cited earlier who was seemingly ambivalent about affirmative action, went on to say, "Pretty much the same thing I said before . . . I don't know, *if I come,* I don't know, *somebody underqualified shouldn't get chosen,* you know?" (Interview # 6: 8). After being probed about whether he thought that what he had just described was an example of reverse discrimination, Brian replied, "Um, pretty much, I mean, yeah."

Furthermore, Brian's response to a specific question asking if he supported a program to give minorities unique opportunities in education suggests that his hesitations and his *topic avoidance by claiming ignorance* and *ambivalence* ("I don't know" and "I am not sure") in the earlier quote were just semantic moves that allowed him to voice safely his opposition to affirmative action ("somebody underqualified shouldn't get chosen") (see Van Dijk, 1984: 109, 131–2). Brian's response to a question about providing unique educational opportunities to minorities was the following:

Brian: Um . . . mmm, that's a tough one. *I don't, you mean, unique opportunities, as far as, just because you are, they are that race, like quotas type of thing or . . .*

Int.: Well, why don't you stipulate the kind of program that you would support and where your limits might be for that.

Brian: All right. . . . Um . . . mmm, let's see, uh . . . I, I don't know (laughs), *I am not sure about like, the problem is like, I don't know, like, 'cause I don't think race should come into like the picture at all, like I don't think they should be given unique opportunities. . . .* (Interview # 10: 8)

In Brian's case as well as in many of the other cases where students apparently wavered on affirmative action, we looked at their responses to questions dealing with job-related cases at the fictitious ABZ company.[6] Brian's answers to these questions clearly indicate that he believes that programs that give *any* additional opportunities to minorities to compensate for past and present discrimination amount to reverse discrimination. For instance, Brian's response to the first scenario included the displacement semantic move, "It seems like *the White guy* might be a little upset," although at the end of his statement he resorted to apparent admission by

saying, "I guess I don't have a problem with it." Moments later, when probed about how he would respond to someone who characterized the company's decision as reverse racism, Brian said that "I would say, *yeah, it is*" (Interview # 6: 9). . . .

The student's comments on affirmative action in interviews suggest that there is even more opposition to affirmative action than our survey results indicate. Also, the opposition to affirmative action of our respondents seems to be related to racial prejudice. However, we recognize that many survey analysts doubt this interpretation and suggest that Whites' opposition to these programs is "political," "ideological," or that it expresses "value duality" (Katz et al., 1986; Kluegel and Smith, 1986; Lipset, 1996; Sniderman and Piazza, 1993). Thus, to strengthen our case, we add another piece of information. In the elaboration of their arguments against affirmative action, 27 of the 41 respondents used spontaneously one of two story-lines or argumentation schemata (Van Dijk, 1984, 1987). The fact that so many of the respondents used the same "stories" underscores the fact that Whites seem to have a shared cognition and that these stories have become part of the ideological racial repertoire about how the world is and ought to be. The two stories were "The past is the past" and "Present generations cannot be blamed for the mistakes of past generations" and were mobilized as justification for not doing anything about the effects of past and contemporary discrimination.

We present one example to illustrate how these stories were mobilized. The example is Sally, a student at a large midwestern university, who answered the question about whether or not Blacks should be compensated for the history of oppression that they have endured by saying:

Absolutely no. How long are you gonna rely on it? I had nothing to do with it. . . . I think it's turning into a crutch that they're getting to fall back on their histories. . . . I just think that every individual should do it for themselves and achieve for themselves. (Interview # 221: 10)

Sally's angry tone in this answer saturated all her responses to the affirmative action questions. For instance, she stated in her response to another question that minorities feel like "super-victims" and asked rhetorically, inspired by the arguments from Shelby Steele that she learned in her sociology course, "For how long are you gonna be able to rely on an oppressed history of your ancestors?" (Interview # 221: 11–12).

"I BELIEVE THAT THEY BELIEVE . . .": WHITE BELIEFS ABOUT CONTEMPORARY DISCRIMINATION AGAINST BLACKS

We asked the subjects to define racism for us and then followed up with five related questions.[7] The students that we interviewed defined racism as "prejudice based on race," "a feeling of racial superiority," "very stupid . . . lots of ignorance," "psychological war," "hating people because of their skin color," and "the belief that one race is superior to the other." Only five of the subjects mentioned or implied that racism was societal, institutional, or structural, and of these only two truly believed that racism is part and parcel of American society. More importantly, very few of the subjects described this country as "racist" or suggested that minorities face systemic disadvantages, in this or in any other part of the interviews. Thus, Whites primarily think that racism is a belief that a few individuals hold and which might lead them to discriminate against some people.

Notwithstanding these findings, it is important to explore Whites' beliefs about the prevalence of discrimination against minorities and about how much it affects the life chances of minorities in the USA. Our analysis revealed that most of the subjects (35 out of 41) expressed serious doubts about whether discrimination affects minorities in a significant way. As in the cases of their responses to the affirmation action and intermarriage questions, very few respondents (14%) who expressed doubts about the significance of discrimination did so consistently in all the questions. . . .

The students provided several examples, suggesting that minorities use racism as an excuse, that discrimination works against Whites nowadays, that discrimination is not such an important factor in the USA, and that other factors such as motivation, values, or credentials may account for Blacks' lack of mobility. . . .

If Whites . . . do not understand or appreciate how race matters for minorities in the USA and yet hear them complaining about discrimination, then the obvious next step is to regard minorities' complaints as whining, excuses, or untrue (Hochschild, 1995). This specific charge was made directly by 14 of the respondents. For example, Kara, a student at a large midwestern university, denied explicitly and without discursive reservations that discrimination affects significantly the life chances of minorities, in her answer to the first question on discrimination:

Int.: Some Black people claim that they face a great deal of racism in their daily lives, and a lot of other people claim that that's not the case. What do you think?

Kara: I would think, presently speaking, like people in my generation, I don't think it's . . . as much that there is racism that, *but Black people almost go into their experiences feeling like they should be discriminated against and I think that makes them hypersensitive.* (Interview # 251: 13)

Kara went on to say that she believes that Blacks receive preferential treatment in admissions or, in her words "being Black, if you just look at applying to graduate schools or things, that's a big part." To the question of why she thinks Blacks have worse jobs, income, and housing than Whites she replied:

> . . . part of me wants to say like work ethic, but I don't know if that is being fair. . . . I just don't know, I think that if you look at the inner city, you can definitely see they're just stuck, like those people cannot really get out . . . like in the suburbs . . . I don't know why that would be. I mean, I am sure they are discriminated against but . . . (Interview # 251: 13)

Immediately after, Kara answered the question about whether or not Blacks are lazy by saying that:

> *I think, to some extent, that's true.* Just from like looking at the Black people that I've met in my classes and the few I knew before college that . . . not like they're—*I don't want to say waiting for a handout, but [to] some extent, that's kind of what I am hinting at.* Like almost like they feel like they were discriminated against hundreds of years ago, now what are you gonna give me? Ya know, or maybe even it's just their background, that they've never, like maybe they're first generation to be in college so they feel like, just that is enough for them. (Interview # 251: 14)

Although some Whites acknowledge that minorities experience discrimination or racism, they still complain about reverse racism, affirmative action, and a number of other racially perceived policies. This occurs in part because in their view, racism is a phenomenon that affects few minorities or affects them in minor ways, and thus has little impact on the life chances of minorities, in particular, and American society more generally. For many Whites, racism is a matter of a few rotten apples such as David Duke, Mark Fuhrman, and the policemen who beat Rodney King rather than a "system of social relations in which Whites typically have more access to the means of power, wealth, and esteem than Blacks [and other minorities]" (Hartman and Husband, 1974: 48). Furthermore, Whites either do not understand or do not believe the new institutional, subtle, and apparently non-racial character of the American racial structure (Bonilla-Silva and Lewis, 1999; Carmichael and Hamilton, 1967; Hochschild, 1995; Jackman, 1994; Smith, 1995). These two factors combined may explain why Whites regard the complaints of minorities about discrimination as exaggerations or excuses. If Whites "don't see" discrimination and do not understand the systemic racial character of our society (Kluegel and Smith, 1982, 1986), then they must interpret minorities' claims of discrimination as false (Essed, 1996) and blame minorities for their lower socioeconomic status (Kluegel, 1990).

COLOR-BLIND RACISM: TOWARD AN ANALYSIS OF WHITE COLLEGE STUDENTS' COLLECTIVE REPRESENTATIONS IN THE USA

In the previous sections we demonstrated that White students use a number of rhetorical strategies that allow them to safely voice racial views that might be otherwise interpreted as racist. In this section, we examine whether or not what students were saying through the rhetorical maze of "I don't know," "I am not sure," and "I am not a racist, but" fits the themes of color blind racism, the dominant racial ideology in the post-civil rights era (Bonilla-Silva, 1998). . . .

The Central Themes of Color-Blind Racism

In recent work, Bobo and his coauthors (Bobo and Kluegel, 1997, Bobo et al., 1997) have labeled post civil rights racial ideology as "laissez faire racism." Laissez faire racism, unlike Jim Crow racism, is "an ideology that blames Blacks themselves for their poorer relative economic standing, seeing it as a function of perceived cultural inferiority" (Bobo and Kluegel, 1997: 95). Other social analysts have pointed out that post civil rights racial hostility is "muted" (Jackman, 1994) or is expressed as "resentment" (Kinder and Sanders, 1996). We argue that post civil rights racial ideology should be called *color-blind racism* since the notion of color blindness is the global justification Whites use to defend the racial status quo. Table 5.5 presents the central elements of color-blind racism and of alternative racial ideologies (Bonilla-Silva, 1998; Crenshaw, 1996; Essed, 1996; Jackman, 1994; Kovel, 1984). . . .

Table 5.5 Central Elements of Dominant and Alternative Contemporary Racial Interpretive Repertoires in the USA.

Dominant Framework (Color-Blind Ideology)	*Alternative Frameworks (Cultural Pluralism, Nationalism, & Others)*
1. *Abstract and decontextualized* notions of liberalism (e.g. "Race should not be a factor when judging people")	*Concrete and contextualized* notions of liberalism or more radical egalitarian theories for distributing social goods
2. *Cultural* rationale for explaining the status of racial subjects in society (e.g. "Blacks are lazy" or "Blacks lack the proper work ethic")	*Political* rationale for explaining the status of racial subjects in society (e.g. "Blacks have been left behind by the system")
3. Avoidance of racist language and direct racial references in explaining racially based or racially perceived issues such as affirmative action, school busing, or interracial dating (Note: Color-blinders utilize indirect subtle and racially coded words to talk about racial matters)	
4. *Naturalization* of matters that reflect the effects arguments (e.g. explaining segregation or limited interracial marriage as a natural outcome)	Explanation of race-related issues with race-related white supremacy (e.g. segregation as the product of the racialized actions of the state, realtors, and individual Whites)
5. Denial of *structural* character of "racism" and discrimination viewed as limited, sporadic, and declining in significance	Understanding racism as "societal" and recognition of new forms of discrimination
6. Invoke the *free-market* or *laissez faire* ideology thus to justify contemporary racial inequality (e.g. "Kids should be exposed to all kinds of cultures but it cannot be imposed on them through busing")	Recognition that "market" outcomes have a racial bent and support of special programs to ameliorate racial inequities

"They Are" and "We Are": Otherizing Talk Among Students

If the USA had truly achieved the color blind dream of Martin Luther King, Whites would not see Blackness as otherness, as difference that entails inferiority. However, in interview after interview, White students constructed a "we-they" dichotomy of Blacks and Whites.

For instance, Bob, a student at a southern university from a working-class background, argued that Blacks have a different culture than Whites. He states:

I think it's true. Um, I think that Blacks have a lot stronger sense of family. Well at least from my own um I always hear about my friends going to family picnics and going to the park and stuff and church, um. My parents, um, I know I have over thirty cousins, and I know like three of them. So I, I think, I think it has to do with family values. (Interview # 6: 8)

Although Bob seems to have positive valuation of Blacks' culture, his next comment suggests otherwise. Bob's answer to the questions, "Do you think the origins of these differences, are they natural, cultural, environmental?" was the following:

I think it's cultural, they way they were raised, the way their parents were raised. My parents worked, my grandparents worked, so they didn't have a lot of strong family outings and gatherings, like Easter, stuff like that, that's about it, um . . . that's what I think. (Interview # 6: 8)

As evident from this statement, Bob's apparently positive evaluation of the family life of Blacks is tied to his belief that Blacks do not work. Hence, he believes that, unlike Whites, Blacks have time to concentrate on family matters. This interpretation of Bob's views was confirmed by Bob himself later on in the interview in his response to a question dealing with why Blacks have worse jobs, income, and housing than Whites. After pointing out that discrimination "may play a factor," Bob added that there were other factors. We cite him at length because his answer clearly illustrates his negative views on Blacks' culture.

Like . . . motivation, uh, family values. . . . Here I, I know I argued a minute ago that they have stronger family values but I know a lot of my [minority] friends didn't have fathers, and they don't have . . . Their mothers were gone all the time, so they'd stay out and play all day. If they wanted something, they'd go out and steal it. Um,

they don't have the money to have a lawn mower, so they can't mow yards like I did. And granted, I didn't even have to do that. I mean, my parents wouldn't give me things I asked, but if I really needed something, I'd get it. Um, if I, they'd let me work it off but these kids, they couldn't do that, so they'd get stuck in a rut, they'd start making minimum wage, they get a girlfriend, get her pregnant and they get stuck in a big ongoing cycle, a big circle, and their kids, and their kids, like that. Um whereas like immigrants, like say . . . Jewish people, came over this country and had, you know, they, it was like in their heads that they were going to do better. And that's why I think nowadays they own a lot of things. People who were persecuted against in other countries come here and do *real* well, but it you're here all along, well, for a long time, you get used to how you are. . . . (Interview # 6: 9)

Here Bob clearly states his belief that Blacks' family values are *inferior* to those of Whites. Black families are described as pathological, Black children as out of control, and Blacks in general as lacking the work ethic. In contrast, Bob views Whites as people who are entrepreneurial (mow yards even though they don't really need that extra money), can control their impulses (Blacks get their girlfriends "pregnant" and "get stuck in a rut"), and fight against all odds to overcome life's obstacles (White immigrants struggled but were able to overcome).

Although based on our analysis of the students' responses to the interview questions on affirmative action, interracial marriage, and the significance of discrimination for Blacks' life chances, most students were not racially tolerant (36 out of 41), we classified five of them as racial progressives. These racial progressives did not subscribe to the 'we-they' dichotomy, were more likely to find problems with the way in which Whites see Blacks, and were more understanding of the significance of discrimination in society. These students formulated their positions from alternative racial ideological frameworks (see

Table 5.5). For instance, Lynn, a student at a large midwestern university from a lower middle-class background who grew up in a small town, began her interview by acknowledging that her community was very racist. She said that her village was a "hick town" and that "there was a lot of stereotypes" (Interview # 196: 1). Whereas most White students felt quite comfortable with their segregated neighborhoods and did not even realize that they were segregated, racial progressives such as Lynn disliked the lack of diversity in their communities. In Lynn's words:

Um, I actually disliked it a lot because there was a lot of . . . um a lot of racist people and it was nothing for my friends to make very racist remarks . . . especially because they didn't know anybody of any other race, so it didn't bother them. And they were feeding off the stereotypes . . . that were really negative. (Interview # 196: 2)

Lynn also recognized that discrimination is central in explaining Blacks' status in the USA. For example, Lynn's response to a question on why there are so few minorities at the top of the occupational structure was the following:

Uh, discrimination. Um . . . just cuz they've had to come back from slavery and everything and . . . they're not fully integrated into . . . ya know . . . they just still aren't accepted. A lot of the old views are there. (Interview # 196: 10)

More significantly, although most Whites recognized that there are "racists out there," racial progressives such as Lynn were more likely to acknowledge that they themselves had problems. Lynn's response to a question on dealing with Blacks' claim that they face a great deal of racism in their daily lives elicited the following response:

I would say . . . I'd say yeah, they do, probably. Um . . . just, um, like I know . . . I do this, I've been trained to do this. Like, when I walk down the street at night . . . by myself, and I meet a White guy on the street, I'm not as scared as if I meet a Black guy on the street. I keep telling myself that's stupid, but . . . that's how I've been trained. I mean just little things like that, I mean, I don't think they're like discriminating, I guess, on a large scale every single day, but . . . yeah, in little ways like that. (Interview # 196: 9)

Although we believe that White progressives *tended* to formulate their views from an alternative racial ideology, they were not totally free from the influence of the dominant racial ideology. For instance, Lynn, who had agreed with the decision of a hypothetical ABZ company to hire an equally qualified Black applicant over a White to increase diversity "because obviously if they're 97 percent White . . . they've probably been discriminating in the past" (Interview # 196: 12), opposed hiring the Black candidate when the justification was that the ABZ company had discriminated in the past. Using a variety of semantic moves to shield her from being perceived as prejudiced, she stated:

I think I'd disagree because, I mean, even though it's kinda what affirmative action . . . well, it's not really, because . . . um . . . I don't think like . . . my generation should have to . . . I mean, in a way, we should, but we shouldn't be . . . punished really harshly for the things that our ancestors did, on the one hand. But on the other hand, I think that . . . how we should try and change the way we do things. So we aren't doing the same things that our ancestors did. (Interview # 196: 14)

Furthermore, although Lynn had stated that she supported affirmative action because "the White male is pretty instilled . . . very much still represses . . . um, people and other minorities" (Interview # 196: 12), she vented anger toward the program and even said that if she was involved in an affirmative action type of situation, "it would anger me. . . . I mean, because, ya know, *I* as an individual got . . . ya know, ripped off and, ya know, getting a job . . . even though, even if I thought I was more qualified" (Interview # 196: 14–15). Finally, although she expressed concern about the lack of diversity in the village where she grew up, had taken classes with racial minorities while at university, and had even reported having had Black acquaintances in her first year in college, all her primary associations at the time of the interview were with Whites. . . .

Mandy, a student at a large western university from a working-class background, . . . unlike most White students, believed that discrimination is a central reason why Blacks are worse off than Whites in the USA today. She even narrated a case of racial discrimination that she witnessed. Mandy said that while she was shopping in a store, the clerk totally ignored her as soon as a Black man entered the store and pointed out that she "could've stuck anything in my backpack if I wanted to" (Interview # 504: 10). Mandy narrated what happened after as follows:

> [The clerk] went over to the guns, picking out a gun, and I am standing there with money in my hand, and this guy goes "Can I help you?" to the guy. He says, "Do you need something, sir? Is there anything you need?" and just keep looking at him. And so I said, you know, "Here's my money (laughs) if you want to take it." And he's all "Sorry" and he is taking my money, but he's still keeping an eye on this guy, and I looked at the guy, and he had this look on his face that just broke my heart because you could tell . . . that he has to deal with this, and I had never had to deal with that. (Interview # 504: 10)

Whereas the typical White student interpreted Blacks' status as Blacks' own fault, Mandy acknowledged the role of discrimination and even understood the significance of White privilege. She states:

Oh, definitely [the overall inferior status of Black is] due to discrimination. It's not a coincidence . . . that a large population in this country lives in substandard housing, and, and, substandard jobs and schools . . . but I went to middle school in a richer neighborhood because my mom lied about where we lived, but I think that if you were Black in the community and tried to go over to a White school that was more wealthy . . . you wouldn't be able to do that because people would know exactly were you came from . . . and I just think that there is something at work keeping people in their spot. (Interview # 504: 11)

Finally, Mandy's answers concerning a hypothetical company's hiring practices, exemplifies how racial progressives framed racially perceived issues differently than reasonable racists. For example, Mandy supported the company's decision in the second case (White applicant scored 85 and Black applicant 80) and pointed out that "I thought that five percentage points wasn't enough of a difference in terms of a score" (Interview # 504: 18). When she was probed about whether these decisions could be construed as reverse racism, she said that "if the country [has] a history of hiring White people over Black people, then it's about damn time they hired a Black person, and if it's discriminatory toward the White person, too bad. They need a little dose of what it feels like" (Interview # 504: 17).

Discussion

Four points emerged from our examination of White college students' views on fundamental racial issues—affirmative action, interracial marriage, and the significance of discrimination. *First,* White students exhibited more prejudiced views in the interview than in their survey responses. . . .

Second, although, based on the interview data, the respondents were more prejudiced than in the survey, they used a variety of semantic moves to save face. Interview respondents consistently used phrases such as "I don't know," "I am not sure," "I am not prejudiced," or "I agree and disagree," rather than explicitly expressing their racial views. . . . The large degree to which respondents used semantic moves was astounding. Our respondents used these moves from 68 percent of the time on the affirmative action question to 85 percent on the direct intermarriage and significance of discrimination questions. This amounts to a new *racetalk*. Unlike during the Jim Crow period, when Whites openly expressed their racial views (Dollard, 1938; Johnson, 1943, 1946; Myrdal, 1944), today Whites express their racial views in a sanitized way. . . .

Third, we showed how useful a discursive approach is for deciphering the meaning of Whites' racial views. . . . As we showed, our respondents were not truly ambivalent about crucial racial issues. Their hesitations were part of a strategic talk to avoid appearing racist. Our respondents did not seem to experience cognitive dissonance (Festinger, 1957) because their opposition to affirmative action and other racially coded programs was couched *within* the discourse of liberalism. Thus, the apparent discursive contradictions and hesitations ("Yes and no" or "I am not sure about that one") were *resolved* by turning liberalism into an *abstract* matter. This strategy allowed them to feel that it is the government and Blacks who are being unfair. Moreover, the students' strong principled position collapsed when issues of past discrimination were raised. That is, students moved from the philosophical principles of liberalism into practical rationality (Billig et al., 1988; Wetherell and Potter, 1992). Virtually no policy alternatives were envisioned as feasible for addressing the profound inequality existing between Blacks and Whites. This casts serious doubt on arguments that suggest that class-based or color-blind

policies can unite Whites and racial minorities (Sniderman and Carmines, 1997; Wilson, 1987). Finally, 27 of the respondents used either "The past is the past" or "Present generations cannot be blamed for the mistakes of past generations" anti-egalitarian story lines in their responses to the question, "Do you believe that the history of oppression endured by minorities merits the intervention of the government on their behalf?" . . . This discursive flexibility in moving from strict liberalism to practical matters is central to racial ideology. In order to work, all ideologies must allow some "room" to handle contradictions, exceptions, and change. Rather than being eternally fixed, ideologies should be conceived as processes or as ideological practices (Jackman, 1994; Wetherell and Potter, 1992).

Fourth, based on the analysis of our data, we found that the students' defense of White supremacy is no longer based on the parameters of Jim Crow racism but is instead based on a new racial ideology. As many analysts have pointed out (Bobo et al., 1997; Bonilla-Silva and Lewis, 1999; Essed, 1996; Prager, 1982), the crux of the post civil rights racial ideology is twofold. First, Whites resolutely deny that racial inequality is structural and, second, they explain it as the result of Blacks' "cultural deficiency" (e.g. they are lazy, their families are in shambles, their communities are bursting with crime). . . . Thus, not surprisingly, most of our White respondents blamed Blacks themselves for their lower status. At best, the students felt pity for Blacks, at worst many openly expressed contempt and hostility toward Blacks. . . .

We want to conclude this article with a comment on the politics of color-blind racism. The interview data reveal that the liberal, free market, and pragmatic rhetoric of color-blind racism allows Whites to defend White supremacy in an apparently nonracial manner (Bobo and Hutchings, 1996; Bobo and Smith, 1994;

Carmines and Merriman, 1993; Kluegel and Bobo, 1993; Jackman, 1994). Color-blind racism allows Whites to appear "not racist" ("I believe in equality"), preserve their privileged status ("Discrimination ended in the sixties!"), blame Blacks for their lower status ("If you guys just work hard!"), and criticize any institutional approach—such as affirmative action—that attempts to ameliorate racial inequality ("Reverse discrimination!"). Hence, the task of progressive social analysts is to blow the whistle on color-blind racism. We must unmask color-blind racists by showing how their views, arguments, and lifestyles are (White) color-coded. We must also show how their color-blind rationales defend systemic White privilege. Analytically this implies developing new questions for our surveys and using new strategies for the analysis of contemporary racial attitudes. Politically it implies that we must concentrate our efforts in fighting the new racists, all the nice Whites who tell us "I am not a racist but . . ."

Notes

1. Semantic moves are "strategically managed relations between propositions" (Van Dijk, 1987: 86). They are called *semantic* because the strategic function of a proposition is determined by the "content of speech act sequences," that is, by the link between a proposition and a preceding or subsequent proposition. The overall goal of these moves, the *semantic strategy,* is to save face, that is, to avoid appearing "racist."

2. By racial ideology we mean the *changing* dogma that provides "the rationalization for social, political, and economic interactions between the races" (Bonilla-Silva, 1997: 474). The central function of racial ideology is explaining and, ultimately, justifying racial inequality (Prager, 1982). Unlike the notion of attitudes, which is bounded by methodological individualism, the notion of racial ideology regards the beliefs of actors as fundamentally shaped by their

group interests. Whereas attitudes ultimately represent degrees of affect toward non-Whites, racial ideology signifies the collective views and interests of Whites. Thus it is possible for Whites to have non-prejudiced attitudes and still subscribe to the central themes of the dominant racial ideology (Hartman and Husband, 1974: 54–5; Pettigrew, 1985).

3. This approach is congruent with the symbolic interaction tradition in sociology. As symbolic interactionists, we believe that "the meanings that things have for human beings are central in their own right," that those meanings "are socially produced through interaction with one's fellows, and that in the process of interaction, the meanings of things are interpreted and reinterpreted" (Blumer, 1969: 2–5). However, unlike many followers of this tradition, we pay attention to how the larger social system produces the themes and boundaries of the meanings produced through interaction.

4. Although we recognize that all people engage in what social psychologists label as *self-presentation,* it is clear that our subjects primarily resorted to *ideal* and *tactical* rather than *authentic* self-presentation (Baumeister, 1982; Swann, 1987).

5. The specific wording of the three questions was the following:

(a) Suppose that two candidates apply for a job at the ABZ company, a company that has a workforce that is 97% White. They take an examination and both applicants score 80 (70 was the minimum score required to pass the test). The company decides to hire the Black applicant over the White applicant because the company is concerned with the lack of diversity of its workforce. Under these conditions, do you agree or disagree with the decision of the ABZ company?

(b) Suppose that the black applicant in the above case scored 80 on the exam and the white candidate scored 85 (70 was the minimum score required to pass the test). The company, despite the fact that the White applicant did slightly better than the Black applicant, decided to hire the Black applicant because of its concern with the lack of diversity of its workforce. Under these conditions, do you agree or disagree with the decision of the ABZ company?

(c) Suppose that the decision of hiring the Black applicant over the White applicant in the previous two cases was justified by the ABZ company not in terms of the need to diversify its workforce but because the company had discriminated in the past against Blacks in terms of hiring. Under these conditions, would you agree or disagree with the decision of the ABZ company?

6. The specific wording of the three questions was the following:

(a) Suppose that two candidates apply for a job at the ABZ company, a company that has a workforce that is 97 percent White. They take an examination and both applicants score 80 (70 was the minimum score required to pass the test). The company decides to hire the Black applicant over the White applicant because the company is concerned with the lack of diversity of its workforce. Under these conditions, do you agree or disagree with the decision of the ABZ company?

(b) Suppose that the Black applicant in the above case scored 80 on the exam and the White candidate scored 85 (70 was the minimum score required to pass the test). The company, despite the fact that the White applicant did slightly better than the Black applicant, decided to hire the Black applicant because of its concern with the lack of diversity of its workforce. Under these conditions, do you agree with the decision of the ABZ company?

(c) Suppose that the decision of hiring the Black applicant over the White applicant in the previous two cases was justified by the ABZ company not in terms of the need to diversify its workforce but because the company had discriminated in the past against Blacks in terms of hiring. Under these conditions, would you agree or disagree with the decision of the ABZ company?

7. The specific wording of the questions was:

(1) Some Blacks claim that they face a great deal of racism in their daily lives. Many people claim that this is not the case. What do you think?

(2) Many Blacks and other minorities claim that they do not get access to good jobs because of discrimination and that, when they get the jobs, they are not promoted at the same speed and to the same jobs as their White peers. What do you think?

(3) On average, Blacks have worse jobs, income, and housing than Whites. Do you think that this is due to discrimination or something else?

(4) Many Whites explain the status of Blacks in this country today as a result of Blacks lacking motivation, not having the proper work ethic, or being lazy. What do you think?

(5) How do you explain the fact that very few minorities are at the top of the occupational structure in this country?

REFERENCES

Anderson, Barbara, Silver, Brian and Abramson, Paul (1988a) 'The Effects of Race of the Interviewer on Measures of Electoral Participation by Blacks in SRC National Election Studies,' *Public Opinion Quarterly* 52(1): 53–83.

Anderson, Barbara, Silver, Brian and Abramson, Paul (1988b) 'The Effects of the Race of Interviewer on Race-Related Attitudes of Black Respondents in SCR/CPS National Election Studies,' *Public Opinion Quarterly* 52(3): 289–324.

Baumeister, R. F. (1982) 'A Self-Presentational View of Social Phenomena,' *Psychological Bulletin* 91(1): 3–26.

Billig, Michael, Condor, Susan, Edwards, Derek, Gane, Mike, Middleton, David and Radley, Alan (1988) *Ideological Dilemmas: A Social Psychology of Everyday Thinking.* London: Sage.

Blauner, Bob (1989) *Black Lives, White Lives: Three Decades of Race Relations in America.* Berkeley and Los Angeles: University of California Press.

Blumer, Herbert (1967) *Symbolic Interactionism: Perspective and Method.* Englewood Cliffs, NJ: Prentice Hall.

Bobo, Lawrence, and Hutchings, Vincent (1996) 'Perceptions of Racial Competition in a Multiracial Setting,' *American Sociological Review* 61(6), December: 951–72.

Bobo, Lawrence and Kluegel, James R. (1993) 'Opposition to Race-Targeting: Self-Interest, Stratification Ideology, or Racial Attitudes?,' *American Sociological Review* 58: 443–64.

Bobo, Lawrence and Kluegel, James R. (1997) 'Status, Ideology, and Dimensions of Whites'

Racial Beliefs and Attitudes; Progress and Stagnation,' in Steven A. Tuch and Jack Martin (eds) *Racial Attitudes in the 1990s: Continuity and Change,* pp. 93–120. Westport, CT: Praeger.

Bobo, Lawrence, Kluegel, James and Smith, Ryan (1997) 'Laissez faire Racism: The Crystallization of a Kinder, Gentler, Antiblack Ideology,' in Steven A. Tuch and Jack Martin (eds) *Racial Attitudes in the 1990s: Continuity and Change,* pp. 15–42. Westport, CT: Praeger.

Bonilla-Silva, Eduardo (1997) 'Rethinking Racism: Toward a Structural Interpretation,' *American Sociological Review,* Vol. 62(3), June: 465–80.

Bonilla-Silva, Eduardo (1998) 'Racial Attitudes or Racial Ideology: Toward a New Paradigm for Examining Whites' Racial Views,' unpublished manuscript, Texas A&M University.

Bonilla-Silva, Eduardo and Lewis, Amanda E. (1999) 'The New Racism: Racial Structure in the United States, 1960s–1990s,' in Paul Wong (ed.) *Race, Ethnicity, and Nationality in the United States: Toward the Twenty-First Century,* pp. 55–101, Boulder, CO: Westview Press.

Brooks, Roy L. (1990) *Rethinking the American Race Problem.* Berkeley: University of California Press.

Brown, Gillian, and Yule, George (1983) *Discourse Analysis.* Cambridge, UK: Cambridge University Press.

Carmichael, Stokely and Hamilton, Charles V. (1967) *Black Power: The Politics of Liberation in America.* New York: Vintage Books.

Carmines, Edward G. and Merriman, W. Richard, Jr. (1993) 'The Changing American Dilemma: Liberal Values and Racial Polices,' in Paul M. Sniderman, Philip E. Tetlock and Edward G. Carmines (eds) *Prejudice, Politics, and the American Dilemma,* pp. 237–55. Stanford, CA: Stanford University Press.

Converse, Phillip E. (1964) 'The Nature of Belief Systems in Mass Publics,' in David E. Apter (ed.) *Ideology and Discontent,* pp. 206–61, London: Free Press of Glencoe.

Converse, Phillip E. (1970) 'Attitudes and Non-attitudes: Continuation of a Dialogue,' in E. R. Tufte (ed.) *The Quantitative Analysis of Social Problems,* pp. 168–89. Reading, MA: Addison-Wesley.

Converse, Phillip E. (1997) 'Comment: The Status of Nonattitudes.' *American Political Science Review* 68: 650–66.

Crenshaw, Kimberlé Williams (1997) 'Color-blind Dreams and Racial Nightmares: Reconfiguring Racism in the Post-Civil Rights Era,' in Toni Morrison and Claudia Brodsky Lacour (eds) *Birth of a Nation'hood,* pp. 97–68. New York: Pantheon.

Dollard, John (1937) *Caste and Class in a Southern Town.* London: Yale University Press.

Dovidio, John F. and Gaertner, Samuel L. (1986) 'How Do Attitudes Guide Behavior?' in R. M. Sorrentino and E.T. Higgins (eds) *The Handbook of Motivation and Cognition: Foundations of Social Behavior,* pp. 204–43. New York: Guilford Press.

Dovidio, John F., Mann, J. F. and Gaertner, Samuel L. (1989) 'Resistance to Affirmative Action: The Implications of Aversive Racism,' in F. Blanchard and F. Crosby (eds) *Affirmative Action in Perspective,* pp. 81–102. New York: Springer-Verlag.

Edley, Christopher Jr. (1996) *Not All Black and White: Affirmative Action and American Values.* New York: Hill and Wang.

Essed, Philomena (1996) *Diversity: Gender, Color, and Culture.* Amherst, MA: University of Massachusetts Press.

Fanon, Frantz (1967) *Black Skins, White Masks.* New York: Grove Press.

Feagin, Joe and Sikes, Melvin (1994) *Living With Racism: The Black Middle Class Experience.* Boston, MA: Beacon Press.

Feagin, Joe and Vera, Hernan (1995) *White Racism: The Basics.* New York: Routledge.

Festinger, Leon (1957) *A Theory of Cognitive Dissonance.* Evanston, IL: Row, Peterson, and Company.

Firebaugh, Glen and Davis, Kenneth E. (1988) 'Trends in Anti-Black Prejudice, 1972–1984: Region and Cohort Effects,' *American Journal of Sociology* 94: 251–72.

Glass Ceiling Commission (1995) *Good for Business: Making Full Use of the Nation's Human Capital.* Washington, DC: Government Printing Office.

Groves, Robert, Fultz, Nancy H. and Martin, Elizabeth (1992) 'Direct Questioning About Comprehension in a Survey Setting,' in Judith M. Tanur (ed.) *Questions About Questions: Inquiries Into the 4 Cognitive Bases of Surveys,* pp. 49–61. New York: Russell Sage Foundation.

Hartman, Paul and Husband, Charles (1974) *Racism and the Mass Media: A Study of the Role of the Mass Media in the Formation of White Beliefs and Attitudes in Britain.* London: David Porter.

Herring, Cedric, and Collins, Sharon (1995) 'Retreat from Equal Opportunity? The Case of Affirmative Action,' in Michael Peter Smith and Joe Feagin (eds) *The Bubbling Cauldron,* pp. 163–81. Minneapolis: University of Minnesota Press.

Hernton, Calvin C. (1988) *Sex and Racism in America.* New York: Anchor Books/Doubleday.

Hochschild, Jennifer (1995) *Facing Up to the American Dream: Race, Class, and the Soul of the Nation,* Princeton. NJ: Princeton University Press.

Hyman, Herbert H. and Sheatsley, Paul B. (1964) 'Attitudes Toward Desegregation,' *Scientific American* 195 (Dec): 85–9.

Jackman, Mary R. (1994) *Velvet Glove: Paternalism and Conflict in Gender, Class, and Race Relations.* Berkeley: University of California Press.

Johnson, Charles S. (1943) *Patterns of Negro Segregation.* New York: Harper and Brothers.

Johnson, Charles S. (1946) *Racial Attitudes: Interviews Revealing Attitudes of Northern and Southern White Persons of a Wide Range of Occupational and Educational Levels, Toward Negroes.* Nashville, TN: Social Science Institute, Fisk University.

Jordan, Winthrop D. (1977) *White Over Black: American Attitudes Toward the Negro, 1550–1812.* New York: W. W. Norton.

Kane, Emily and Macaulay, Laura (1993) 'Interviewer Gender and Gender Attitudes,' *Public Opinion Quarterly* 57(1): 1–28.

Katz, Irwin, Wackenhut, Joyce and Hass, R. Glen (1986) 'Racial Ambivalence, Value Duality, and Behavior,' in John Dovidio and Samuel L. Gaertner (eds) *Prejudice, Discrimination, and Racism,* pp. 35–60. Orlando, FL: Academic Press.

Kinder, Donald and Sanders, Lynn M. (1996) *Divided by Color: Racial Politics and Democratic Ideals.* Chicago and London: University of Chicago Press.

Kluegel, James R. (1990). 'Trends in Whites' Explanations of the Black-White Gap Socio-economic Status, 1977–1989,' *American Sociological Review* 55(4), August: 512–25.

Kluegel, James R. and Smith, Eliot R. (1982) 'Whites' Beliefs about Blacks' Opportunity,' *American Sociological Review* 47: 518–32.

Kluegel, James R. and Smith, Eliot R. (1986) *Beliefs About Inequality: Americans' Views of What Is and What Ought to Be.* New York: Aldine de Gruyter.

Kovel, Joel (1984) *White Racism: A Psychohistory.* New York: Columbia University Press.

Krysan, Maria (1998) 'Privacy and the Expression of White Racial Attitudes,' *Public Opinion Quarterly* 62(4): 506–44.

Lipset, Seymour M. (1996) *American Exceptionalism: A Double-Edged Sword.* New York and London: W. W. Norton.

Lipset, Seymour and Schneider, William (1978) 'The Bakke Case: How Would It Be Decided at the Bar of Public Opinion?' *Public Opinion* 1(1): 38–44.

MacLeod, Jay (1995) *Ain't No Makin' It: Aspirations and Attainment in a Low-Income Neighborhood.* Boulder, CO: Westview Press.

Massey, Douglas S. and Denton, Nancy A. (1993) *Segregation and the Making of the Underclass.* Cambridge, MA: Harvard University Press.

Myers, Samuel L. (1993) 'Measuring and Detecting Discrimination in the Post-Civil Rights Era,' in John H. Stanfield II and Rutledge M. Dennis (eds) *Race and Ethnicity in Research,* pp. 172–97. Newbury Park, CA: Sage.

Myrdal, Gunnar (1944) *An American Dilemma: The Negro Problem and Modern Democracy I.* New York and London: Harper and Brothers Publishers.

Nieme, Richard G, Mueller, John and Smith, Tom W. (1989) *Trends in Public Opinion: A Compendium of Survey Data.* New York: Greenwood Press.

Orfield, Gary and Eaton, Susan, E. (1996) *Dismantling Desegregation: The Quiet Reversal of Brown v. Board of Education.* New York: New York Press.

Pettigrew, Thomas F. (1985) 'New Black–White Patterns: How Best to Conceptualize Them?,' *Annual Review of Sociology* 11: 329–46.

Prager, Jeffrey (1982) 'American Racial Ideology as Collective Representation,' *Ethnic and Racial Studies* 5(1), January: 99–119.

Rieder, Jonathan (1985) *Canarsie: The Jews and Italians of Brooklyn against Liberalism.* Cambridge, MA: Harvard University Press.

Rubin, Lillian (1994) *Families on the Fault Line: America's Working Class Speaks about the Family, the Economy, Race, and Ethnicity.* New York: HarperCollins.

Schuman, Howard and Steeh, Charlotte (1996) 'The Complexity of Racial Attitudes in America,' in Silvia Pedraza and Ruben Rumbaut (eds) *Origins and Destinies,* pp. 455–69. Belmont, CA: Wadsworth.

Schuman, Howard, Steeh, Charlotte and Bobo, Lawrence (1988) *Racial Attitudes in America: Trends and Interpretations.* Boston, MA: Harvard University Press.

Schuman, Howard, Steeh, Charlotte, Bobo, Lawrence and Krysan, Maria (1997) *Racial Attitudes in America: Trends and Interpretations,* rev edn, Boston, MA: Harvard University Press.

Sigall, Harold and Page, Richard (1971) 'Current Stereotypes: A Little Fading, A Little Faking,' *Journal of Personality and Social Psychology* 18(2), January: 247–55.

Smith, Robert C. (1995) *Racism in the Post Civil Rights Period: Now You See It, Now You Don't.* Albany: State University of New York Press.

Smith, Tom W. and Sheatsley, Paul B. (1984) 'American Attitudes toward Race Relations,' *Public Opinion* 7(5): 14–15, 50–3.

Sniderman, Paul M. and Piazza, Thomas (1993) *The Scare of Race.* Boston, MA: Harvard University Press.

Sniderman, Paul M. and Carmines, Edward G. (1997) *Reaching Beyond Race.* Cambridge, MA: Harvard University Press.

Steeh, Charlotte and Krysan, Maria (1996) 'Affirmative Action and the Public, 1970–1995,' *Public Opinion Quarterly* 60: 128–58.

Swann, W. B., Jr. (1987) 'Identity Negotiation: Where Two Roads Meet,' *Journal of Personality and Social Psychology* 53(6): 1038–51.

Terkel, Studs (1993) *Race: How Blacks and Whites Think and Feel About The American Obsession.* New York: Doubleday.

Van Dijk, Teun A. (1977) *Text and Context: Explorations in the Semantics and Pragmatics of Discourse.* London and New York: Longman.

Van Dijk, Teun A. (1984) *Prejudice in Discourse: An Analysis of Ethnic Prejudice in Cognition and Conversation.* Amsterdam and Philadelphia, PA: John Benjamins Publishing Co.

Van Dijk, Teun A. (1987) *Communicating Racism: Ethnic Prejudice in Thought and Talk.* Beverly Hills, CA: Sage.

Van Dijk, Teun A. (1997) 'Political Discourse and Racism: Describing Others in Western Parliaments,' in Stephen Harold Riggins (ed.) *The Language and Politics of Exclusion: Others in Discourse,* pp. 31–64. Thousands Oaks, CA: Sage.

Weis, Lois, and Fine, Michelle (1996) 'Narrating the 1980s and 1990s: Voices of Poor and Working-Class White and African American Men,' *Anthropology and Education Quarterly* 27(4): 493–516.

Wellman, David (1977) *Portraits of White Racism.* Berkeley, CA: University of California Press.

Wetherell, Margaret and Jonathan Potter (1992) *Mapping the Language of Racism: Discourse and the Legitimation of Exploitation.* New York: Columbia University Press.

Wicker, Tom (1996) *Tragic Failure: Racial Integration in America.* New York: William Morrow and Company.

Wilson, William Julius (1987) *The Truly Disadvantaged.* Chicago, IL: University of Chicago Press.

SOURCE: From *Discourse and Society, 11:* 50-85. Copyright © Sage Publications Ltd., 2000. Reprinted by permission of Sage Publications Ltd. and the authors.

DISCUSSION QUESTIONS

1. What is the "new racetalk" that the authors' analysis reveals in this essay? Do these results indicate that prejudice has decreased, or has merely taken a new form that is equally, or even more, harmful?

2. Why do you think a sizeable group of whites say they support interracial marriages but lead segregated lives? Of the different possibilities in Table 5.4 for views on interracial marriage and type of life (integrated/segregated), where would you place yourself and why?

3. What is meant by "color-blind racism"? How can one be racist if one is "color-blind"? What are the alternatives?

4. Why do you think so many whites do not believe racial discrimination exists? What are the policy implications of this pattern?

RACE AND CRIMINALIZATION: BLACK AMERICANS AND THE PUNISHMENT INDUSTRY

Angela Davis

In this post-civil-rights era, as racial barriers in high economic and political realms are apparently shattered with predictable regularity, race itself becomes an increasingly proscribed subject. In the dominant political discourse it is no longer acknowledged as a pervasive structural phenomenon, requiring the continuation of such strategies as affirmative action, but rather is represented primarily as a complex of prejudicial attitudes, which carry equal weight across all racial boundaries. Black leadership is thus often discredited and the identification of race as a public, political issue itself called into question through the invocation of, and application of the epithet "black racist" to such figures as Louis Farrakhan and Khalid Abdul Muhammad. Public debates about the role of the state that once focused very sharply and openly on issues of "race" and racism are now expected to unfold in the absence of any direct acknowledgment of the persistence—and indeed further entrenchment—of racially structured power relationships. Because race is ostracized from some of the most impassioned debates of this period, their racialized character becomes increasingly difficult to identify by those who are unable—or do not want—to decipher the encoded language. This means that hidden racist arguments can be mobilized readily across racial boundaries and political alignments. Political positions once easily defined as conservative, liberal, and sometimes even radical therefore have a tendency to lose their distinctiveness in the face of the seductions of this camouflaged racism.

President Clinton chose the date of the Million Man March, convened by Minister Louis Farrakhan of the Nation of Islam, to issue a call for a "national conversation on race," borrowing ironically the exact words Lani Guinier (whose nomination for Assistant Attorney General in charge of civil rights he had previously withdrawn because her writings focused too sharply on issues of race).[1] Guinier's ideas had been so easily dismissed because of the prevailing ideological equation of the "end of racism" with the removal of all allusions to race. If conservative positions argue that race consciousness itself impedes the process of solving the problem of race—i.e., achieving race blindness—then Clinton's speech indicated an attempt to reconcile the two, positing race consciousness as a means of moving toward race blindness. "There are too many today, white and black, on the left and the right, on the street corners and radio waves, who seek to sow division for their own purposes. To them I say: 'No more. We must be one.'"

While Clinton did acknowledge "the awful history and stubborn persistence of racism," his remarks foregrounded those reasons for the "racial divide" that "are rooted in the fact that we still haven't learned to talk frankly, to listen carefully and to work together across racial lines." Race, he insisted, is not about government, but about the hearts of people. Of course, it would be absurd to deny the degree to which racism infects in deep and multiple ways the national psyche. However, the relegation of race to matters of the heart tends to render it increasingly difficult to identify the deep structural entrenchment of contemporary racism.

When the structural character of racism is ignored in discussions about crime and the rising population of incarcerated people, the racial imbalance in jails and prisons is treated as a contingency, at best as a product of the "culture of poverty," and at worst as proof of an assumed black monopoly on criminality. The high proportion of black people in the criminal justice system is thus normalized and neither the state nor the general public is required to talk about and act on the meaning of that racial imbalance. Thus Republican and Democratic elected officials alike have successfully called for laws mandating life sentences for three-time "criminals," without having to answer for the racial implications of these laws. By relying on the alleged "race-blindness" of such laws, black people are surreptitiously constructed as racial subjects, thus manipulated, exploited, and abused, while the structural persistence of racism—albeit in changed forms—in social and economic institutions, and in the national culture as a whole, is adamantly denied.

Crime is thus one of the masquerades behind which "race," with all its menacing ideological complexity, mobilizes old public fears and creates new ones. The current anti-crime debate takes place within a reified mathematical realm—a strategy reminiscent of Malthus's notion of the geometrical increase in population and the arithmetical increase in food sources, thus the inevitability of poverty and the means of suppressing it: war, disease, famine, and natural disasters. As a matter of fact, the persisting neo-Malthusian approach to population control, which, instead of seeking to solve those pressing social problems that result in real pain and suffering in people's lives, calls for the elimination of those suffering lives—finds strong resonances in the public discussion about expurgating the "nation" of crime. These discussions include arguments deployed by those who are leading the call for more prisons and employ statistics in the same fetishistic and misleading way as Malthus did more than two centuries ago. Take for example James Wooten's comments in the *Heritage Foundation State Backgrounder*:

> If the 55 percent of the estimated 800,000 current state and federal prisoners who are violent offenders were subject to serving 85 percent of their sentence, and assuming that those violent offenders would have committed 10 violent crimes a year while on the street, then the number of crimes prevented each year by truth in sentencing would be 4,000,000. That would be over 2/3 of the 6,000,000 violent crimes reported.[2]

In *Reader's Digest,* Senior Editor Eugene H. Methvin writes:

> If we again double the present federal and state prison population—to somewhere between 1 million and 1.5 million and leave our city and country jail population at the present 400,000, we will break the back of America's thirty-year crime wave.[3]

The real human beings—a vastly disproportionate number of whom are black and Latino/a men and women—designated by these numbers in a seemingly race-neutral way are deemed fetishistically exchangeable with the crimes they have already committed or will allegedly commit in the future. The real impact of imprisonment on their lives never need be examined. The inevitable part played by the punishment industry in the reproduction of crime never need be discussed. The dangerous and indeed fascistic trend toward progressively greater numbers of hidden, incarcerated human populations is itself rendered invisible. All that matters is the elimination of crime—and you get rid of crime by getting rid of people who, according to the prevailing racial common sense, are the most likely people to whom criminal acts will be attributed. Never mind that if this strategy is seriously and consistently pursued, the majority of young black men and a fast-growing proportion of young black women will spend a good portion of their lives behind walls and bars in order to serve as a reminder that the state is aggressively confronting its enemy.[4]

While I do not want to locate a response to these arguments on the same level of mathematical abstraction and fetishism I have been problematizing, it is helpful, I think, to consider how many people are presently incarcerated or whose lives are subject to the direct surveillance of the criminal justice system. There are already approximately 1 million people in state and federal prisons in the United States, not counting the 500,000 in city and county jails or the 600,000 on parole or the 3 million people on probation or the 60,000 young people in juvenile facilities. Which is to say that there are presently over 5.1 million people either incarcerated, on parole, or on probation. Many of those presently on probation or parole would be behind bars under the conditions of the recently passed crime bill. According to the Sentencing Project, even before the passage of the crime bill, black people were 7.8 times more likely to be imprisoned than whites.[5] The Sentencing Project's most recent report[6] indicates that 32.2 percent of young black men and 12.3 percent of young Latino men between the ages of twenty and twenty-nine are either in prison, in jail, or on probation or parole. This is in comparison with 6.7 percent of young white men. A total of 827,440 young African-American males are under the supervision of the criminal justice system, at a cost of $6 billion per year. A major strength of the 1995 report, as compared to its predecessor, is its acknowledgment that the racialized impact of the criminal justice system is also gendered and that the relatively smaller number of African-American women drawn into the system should not relieve us of the responsibility of understanding the encounter of gender and race in arrest and incarceration practices. Moreover, the increases in women's contact with the criminal justice system have been even more dramatic than those of men.

The 78 percent increase in criminal justice control rates for black women was more than double the increase for black men and for white women, and more than nine times the increase for white men. . . . Although research on women of color in the criminal justice system is limited, existing data and research suggest that it is the combination of race and sex effects that is at the root of the trends which appear in our data. For example, while the number of blacks and

Hispanics in prison is growing at an alarming rate, the rate of increase for women is even greater. Between 1980 and 1992 the female prison population increased 276 percent, compared to 163 percent for men. Unlike men of color, women of color thus belong to two groups that are experiencing particularly dramatic growth in their contact with the criminal justice system.[7]

It has been estimated that by the year 2000 the number of people imprisoned will surpass 2 million, a grossly disproportionate number of whom will be black people, and that the cost will be over $40 billion a year,[8] a figure that is reminiscent of the way the military budget devoured—and, continues to devour—the country's resources. This out-of-control punishment industry is an extremely effective criminalization industry, for the racial imbalance in incarcerated populations is not recognized as evidence of structural racism, but rather is invoked as a consequence of the assumed criminality of black people. In other words, the criminalization process works so well precisely because of the hidden logic of racism. Racist logic is deeply entrenched in the nation's material and psychic structures. It is something with which we all are very familiar. The logic, in fact, can persist, even when direct allusions to "race" are removed.

Even those communities that are most deeply injured by this racist logic have learned how to rely upon it, particularly when open allusions to race are not necessary. Thus, in the absence of broad, radical grassroots movements in poor black communities so devastated by new forms of youth-perpetrated violence, the ideological options are extremely sparse. Often there are no other ways to express collective rage and despair but to demand that police sweep the community clean of crack and Uzis, and of people who use and sell drugs and wield weapons. Ironically, Carol Moseley-Braun, the first black woman senator in our nation's

history, was an enthusiastic sponsor of the Senate Anticrime Bill, whose passage in November 1993 paved the way for the August 25, 1994, passage of the bill by the House. Or perhaps there is little irony here. It may be precisely because there is a Carol Moseley-Braun in the Senate and a Clarence Thomas in the Supreme Court—and concomitant class differentiations and other factors responsible for far more heterogeneity in black communities than at any other time in this country's history—that implicit consent to antiblack racist logic (not to speak of racism toward other groups) becomes far more widespread among black people. Wahneema Lubiano's explorations of the complexities of state domination as it operates within and through the subjectivities of those who are the targets of this domination facilitates an understanding of this dilemma.[9]

Borrowing the title of Cornel West's recent work, race *matters*. Moreover, it matters in ways that are far more threatening and simultaneously less discernible than those to which we have grown accustomed. Race matters inform, more than ever, the ideological and material structures of US society. And, as the current discourses on crime, welfare, and immigration reveal, race, gender, and class matter enormously in the continuing elaboration of public policy and its impact on the real lives of human beings.

And how does race matter? Fear has always been an integral component of racism. The ideological reproduction of a fear of black people, whether economically or sexually grounded, is rapidly gravitating toward and being grounded in a fear of crime. A question to be raised in this context is whether and how the increasing fear of crime—this ideologically produced fear of crime—serves to render racism simultaneously more invisible and more virulent. Perhaps one way to approach an answer to this question is to consider how this fear of crime effectively summons black people to imagine black people as the enemy. How many black people present at this conference have successfully extricated ourselves from the ideological power of the figure of the young black male as criminal—or at least seriously confronted it? The lack of a significant black presence in the rather feeble opposition to the "three strikes, you're out" bills, which have been proposed and/or passed in forty states already, evidences the disarming effect of this ideology.

California is one of the states that has passed the "three strikes, you're out" bill. Immediately after the passage of that bill, Governor Pete Wilson began to argue for a "two strikes, you're out" bill. Three, he said, is too many. Soon we will hear calls for "one strike, you're out." Following this mathematical regression, we can imagine that at some point the hardcore anti-crime advocates will be arguing that to stop the crime wave, we can't wait until even one crime is committed. Their slogan will be: "Get them before the first strike!" And because certain populations have already been criminalized, there will be those who say, "We know who the real criminals are—let's get them before they have a chance to act out their criminality."

The fear of crime has attained a status that bears a sinister similarity to the fear of communism as it came to restructure social perceptions during the fifties and sixties. The figure of the "criminal"—the racialized figure of the criminal—has come to represent the most menacing enemy of "American society." Virtually anything is acceptable—torture, brutality, vast expenditures of public funds—as long as it is done in the name of public safety. Racism has always found an easy route from its embeddedness in social structures to the psyches of collectives and individuals precisely because it mobilizes deep fears. While explicit, old-style racism may be increasingly socially unacceptable—precisely as a result of antiracist movements over the last forty years—this does not mean that US society has

been purged of racism. In fact, racism is more deeply embedded in socioeconomic structures, and the vast populations of incarcerated people of color is dramatic evidence of the way racism systematically structures economic relations. At the same time, this structural racism is rarely recognized as "racism." What we have come to recognize as open, explicit racism has in many ways begun to be replaced by a secluded, camouflaged kind of racism, whose influence on people's daily lives is as pervasive and systematic as the explicit forms of racism associated with the era of the struggle for civil rights.

The ideological space for the proliferations of this racialized fear of crime has been opened by the transformations in international politics created by the fall of the European socialist countries. Communism is no longer the quintessential enemy against which the nation imagines its identity. This space is now inhabited by ideological constructions of crime, drugs, immigration, and welfare. Of course, the enemy within is far more dangerous than the enemy without, and a black enemy within is the most dangerous of all.

Because of the tendency to view it as an abstract site into which all manner of undesirables are deposited, the prison is the perfect site for the simultaneous production and concealment of racism. The abstract character of the public perception of prisons militates against an engagement with the real issues afflicting the communities from which prisoners are drawn in such disproportionate numbers. This is the ideological work that the prison performs—it relieves us of the responsibility of seriously engaging with the problems of late capitalism, of transnational capitalism. The naturalization of black people as criminals thus also erects ideological barriers to an understanding of the connections between late twentieth-century structural racism and the globalization of capital.

The vast expansion of the power of capitalist corporations over the lives of people of color and poor people in general has been accompanied by a waning anticapitalist consciousness. As capital moves with ease across national borders, legitimized by recent trade agreements such as NAFTA [North American Free Trade Agreement] and GATT [General Agreement on Tariffs and Trade], corporations are allowed to close shop in the United States and transfer manufacturing operations to nations providing cheap labor pools. In fleeing organized labor in the US to avoid paying higher wages and benefits, they leave entire communities in shambles, consigning huge numbers of people to joblessness, leaving them prey to the drug trade, destroying the economic base of these communities, thus affecting the education system, social welfare—and turning the people who live in those communities into perfect candidates for prison. At the same time, they create an economic demand for prisons, which stimulates the economy, providing jobs in the correctional industry for people who often come from the very populations that are criminalized by this process. It is a horrifying and self-reproducing cycle.

Ironically, prisons themselves are becoming a source of cheap labor that attracts corporate capitalism—as yet on a relatively small scale—in a way that parallels the attraction unorganized labor in Third World countries exerts. A statement by Michael Lamar Powell, a prisoner in Capshaw, Alabama, dramatically reveals this new development:

> I cannot go on strike, nor can I unionize. I am not covered by workers' compensation of the Fair Labor Standards Act. I agree to work late-night and weekend shifts. I do just what I am told, no matter what it is. I am hired and fired at will, and I am not even paid minimum wage: I earn one dollar a month. I cannot even voice grievances or complaints, except at the risk of incurring arbitrary discipline or some covert retaliation.

> You need not worry about NAFTA and your jobs going to Mexico and other Third World countries. I will have at least five percent of your jobs by the end of this decade.

> I am called prison labor. I am the New American Worker.[10]

This "new American worker" will be drawn from the ranks of a racialized population whose historical superexploitation—from the era of slavery to the present—has been legitimized by racism. At the same time, the expansion of convict labor is accompanied in some states by the old paraphernalia of ankle chains that symbolically links convict labor with slave labor. At least three states—Alabama, Florida, and Arizona—have reinstituted the chain gang. Moreover, as Michael Powell so incisively reveals, there is a new dimension to the racism inherent in this process, which structurally links the superexploitation of prison labor to the globalization of capital.

In California, whose prison system is the largest in the country and one of the largest in the world, the passage of an inmate labor initiative in 1990 has presented businesses seeking cheap labor with opportunities uncannily similar to those in Third World countries. As of June 1994, a range of companies were employing prison labor in nine California prisons. Under the auspices of the Joint Venture Program, work now being performed on prison grounds includes computerized telephone messaging, dental apparatus assembly, computer data entry, plastic parts fabrication, electronic component manufacturing at the Central California Women's facility at Chowchilla, security glass manufacturing, swine production, oak furniture manufacturing, and the production of stainless steel tanks and equipment. In a California Corrections Department brochure designed to promote the program, it is described as "an innovative public-private partnership that makes good business sense."[11] According to the owner of Tower Communications, whom the brochure quotes,

> The operation is cost effective, dependable and trouble free. . . . Tower Communications has successfully operated a message center utilizing inmates on the grounds of a California state prison. If you're a business leader planning expansion, considering relocation because of a deficient labor pool, starting a new enterprise, look into the benefits of using inmate labor.

The employer benefits listed by the brochure include

> federal and state tax incentives; no benefit package (retirement pay, vacation pay, sick leave, medical benefits); long-term lease agreements at far below market value costs; discount rates on Workers Compensation; build a consistent, qualified work force; on call labor pool (no car breakdowns, no babysitting problems); option of hiring job-ready ex-offenders and minimizing costs; becoming a partner in public safety.

There is a major, yet invisible, racial supposition in such claims about the profitability of a convict labor force. The acceptability of the superexploitation of convict labor is largely based on the historical conjuncture of racism and incarceration practices. The already disproportionately black convict labor force will become increasingly black if the racially imbalanced incarceration practices continue.

The complicated yet unacknowledged structural presence of racism in the US punishment industry also includes the fact that the punishment industry which sequesters ever larger sectors of the black population attracts vast amounts of capital. Ideologically, as I have argued, the racialized fear of crime has begun to succeed the fear of communism. This corresponds to a structural tendency for capital that previously flowed toward the military industry

to now move toward the punishment industry. The ease with which suggestions are made for prison construction costing in the multibillions of dollars is reminiscent of the military build-up: economic mobilization to defeat communism has turned into economic mobilization to defeat crime. The ideological construction of crime is thus complemented and bolstered by the material construction of jails and prisons. The more jails and prisons are constructed, the greater the fear of crime, and the greater the fear of crime, the stronger the cry for more jails and prisons, ad infinitum. The law enforcement industry bears remarkable parallels to the military industry (just as there are anti-communist resonances in the anti-crime campaign). This connection between the military industry and the punishment industry is revealed in a May 1994 *Wall Street Journal* article entitled "Making Crime Pay: The Cold War of the '90s":

> Parts of the defense establishment are cashing in, too, scenting a logical new line of business to help them offset military cutbacks. Westinghouse Electric Corp., Minnesota Mining and Manufacturing Co., GDE Systems (a division of the old General Dynamics) and Alliant Techsystems Inc., for instance, are pushing crime-fighting equipment and have created special divisions to retool their defense technology for America's streets.

According to the article, a conference sponsored by the National Institute of Justice, the research arm of the justice Department, was organized around the theme "Law Enforcement Technology in the Twenty-first Century." The Secretary of Defense was a major presenter at this conference, which explored topics like "the role of the defense industry, particularly for dual use and conversion":

> Hot topics: defense-industry technology that could lower the level of violence involved in crime fighting. Sandia National Laboratories, for

instance, is experimenting with a dense foam that can be sprayed at suspects, temporarily blinding and deafening them under breathable bubbles. Stinger Corporation is working on "smart guns," which will fire only for the owner, and retractable spiked barrier strips to unfurl in front of fleeing vehicles. Westinghouse is promoting the "smart car," in which minicomputers could be linked up with big mainframes at the police department, allowing for speedy booking of prisoners, as well as quick exchanges of information.[12]

Again, race provides a silent justification for the technological expansion of law enforcement, which, in turn, intensifies racist arrest and incarceration practices. This skyrocketing punishment industry, whose growth is silently but powerfully sustained by the persistence of racism, creates an economic demand for more jails and prisons and thus for similarly spiraling criminalization practices, which, in turn, fuels the fear of crime.

Most debates addressing the crisis resulting from overcrowding in prisons and jails focus on male institutions. Meanwhile, women's institutions and jail space for women are proportionately proliferating at an even more astounding rate than men's. If race is largely an absent factor in the discussions about crime and punishment, gender seems not even to merit a place carved out by its absence. Historically, the imprisonment of women has served to criminalize women in a way that is more complicated than is the case with men. This female criminalization process has had more to do with the marking of certain groups of women as undomesticated and hypersexual, as women who refuse to embrace the nuclear family as paradigm. The current liberal-conservative discourse around welfare criminalizes black single mothers, who are represented as deficient, manless, drug-using breeders of children, and as reproducers of an attendant culture of poverty. The woman who does drugs is criminalized both because she is a drug user and because, as a

consequence, she cannot be a good mother. In some states, pregnant women are being imprisoned for using crack because of possible damage to the fetus.

According to the US Department of Justice, women are far more likely than men to be imprisoned for a drug conviction.[13] However, if women wish to receive treatment for their drug problems, often their only option, if they cannot pay for a drug program, is to be arrested and sentenced to a drug program via the criminal justice system. Yet when US Surgeon General Joycelyn Elders alluded to the importance of opening discussion on the decriminalization of drugs, the Clinton administration immediately disassociated itself from her remarks. Decriminalization of drugs would greatly reduce the numbers of incarcerated women, for the 278 percent increase in the numbers of black women in state and federal prisons (as compared with the 186 percent increase in the numbers of black men) can be largely attributed to the phenomenal rise in drug-related and specifically crack-related imprisonment. According to the Sentencing Project's 1995 report, the increase amounted to 828 percent.[14]

Official refusals to even consider decriminalization of drugs as a possible strategy that might begin to reverse present incarceration practices further bolsters the ideological staying power of the prison. In his well-known study of the history of the prison and its related technologies of discipline, Michel Foucault pointed out that an evolving contradiction is at the very heart of the historical project of imprisonment.

> For a century and a half, the prison has always been offered as its own remedy: . . . the realization of the corrective project as the only method of overcoming the impossibility of implementing it.[15]

As I have attempted to argue, within the US historical context, racism plays a pivotal role in sustaining this contradiction. In fact, Foucault's theory regarding the prison's tendency to serve as its own enduring justification becomes even more compelling if the role of race is also acknowledged. Moreover, moving beyond the parameters of what I consider the double impasse implied by his theory—the discursive impasse his theory discovers and that of the theory itself—I want to conclude by suggesting the possibility of radical race-conscious strategies designed to disrupt the stranglehold of criminalization and incarceration practices.

In the course of a recent collaborative research project with UC Santa Barbara, sociologist Kum-Kum Bhavnani, in which we interviewed thirty-five women at the San Francisco County jail, the complex ways in which race and gender help to produce a punishment industry that reproduces the very problems it purports to solve became dramatically apparent. Our interviews focused on the women's ideas about imprisonment and how they themselves imagine alternatives to incarceration. Their various critiques of the prison system and of the existing "alternatives," all of which are tied to reimprisonment as a last resort, led us to reflect more deeply about the importance of retrieving, retheorizing, and reactivating the radical abolitionist strategy first proposed in connection with the prison reform movements of the sixties and seventies.

We are presently attempting to theorize women's imprisonment in ways that allow us to formulate a radical abolitionist strategy departing from, but not restricted in its conclusions to, women's jails and prisons. Our goal is to formulate alternatives to incarceration that substantively reflect the voices and agency of a variety of imprisoned women. We wish to open up channels for their involvement in the current debates around alternatives to incarceration, while not denying our own role as mediators and interpreters and our own political positioning in these debates. We also want to distinguish explorations of alternatives from the spate of "alternative punishments" or what are now called "intermediate sanctions" presently being proposed and/or implemented by and through state and local correctional systems.

This is a long-range project that has three dimensions: academic research, public policy, and community organizing. In other words, for this project to be successful, it must build bridges between academic work, legislative and other policy interventions, and grassroots campaigns calling, for example, for the decriminalization of drugs and prostitution—and for the reversal of the present proliferation of jails and prisons.

Raising the possibility of abolishing jails and prisons as the institutionalized and normalized means of addressing social problems in an era of migrating corporations, unemployment and homelessness, and collapsing public services, from health care to education, can hopefully help to interrupt the current law-and-order discourse that has such a grip on the collective imagination, facilitated as it is by deep and hidden influences of racism. This late twentieth-century "abolitionism," with its nineteenth-century resonances, may also lead to a historical recontextualization of the practice of imprisonment. With the passage of the Thirteenth Amendment, slavery was abolished for all except convicts—and in a sense the exclusion from citizenship accomplished by the slave system has persisted within the US prison system. Only three states allow prisoners to vote, and approximately 4 million people are denied the right to vote because of their present or past incarceration. A radical strategy to abolish jails and prisons as the normal way of dealing with the social problems of late capitalism is not a strategy for abstract abolition. It is designed to force a rethinking of the increasingly repressive role of the state during this era of late capitalism and to carve out a space for resistance.

Notes

1. See coverage by the *Austin-American Statesman,* October 17, 1995.

2. Quoted in Charles S. Clark, "Prison Overcrowding," *Congressional Quarterly Researcher,* 4, no. 5 (February 4, 1994), 97–119.

3. Ibid.

4. Marc Mauer, *Young Black Men and the Criminal Justice System: A Growing National Problem* (Washington, DC: The Sentencing Project, February 1990).

5. Reported in an Alexander Cockburn article, *Philadelphia Inquirer,* August 29, 1994.

6. Marc Mauer and Tracy Huling, *Young Black Americans and the Criminal Justice System: Five Years Later* (Washington, DC: The Sentencing Project, October 1995).

7. Ibid., 18.

8. See Cockburn, *Philadelphia Inquirer,* August 29, 1994.

9. See Wahneema Lubiano, "Black Ladies, Welfare Queens, and State Minstrels: Ideological War by Narrative Means," in *Race-ing Justice, En-gendering Power: Essays on Anita Hill, Clarence Thomas, and the Construction of Social Reality,* ed. Toni Morrison (New York: Pantheon, 1992).

10. Michael Powell, "Modern Slavery American Style," 1995, unpublished essay (author's papers).

11. I wish to acknowledge Julie Brown, who acquired this brochure from the California Department of Correction in the course of researching the role of convict labor.

12. "Making Crime Pay: The Cold War of the '90s," *Wall Street Journal,* May 12, 1994.

13. Lawrence Rence, A. Greenfield, Stephanie Minor-Harper, *Women in Prison* (Washington DC: US Dept. of Justice, Office of Justice Programs, Bureau of Statistics, 1991).

14. Mauer and Huling, *Young Black Americans and the Criminal Justice System: Five Years Later,* 19.

15. Michel Foucault, *Discipline and Punish: The Birth of the Prison,* trans. Alan Sheridan (New York: Vintage, 1979), 395.

Discussion Questions

1. How is it possible that bills like "Three strikes, you're out" that do not mention race are evidence of antiblack racism, as the author suggests? What is meant by an ideology, and how does the role of ideology help explain why blacks such as Carol Moseley-Braun can also support such racist measures?

2. What is the relationship between the international expansion of capitalism and the proliferation of prisons in the United States, according to Davis? How have prisons-for-profit affected the rising numbers of blacks in prison?

3. What is the "female criminalization" process and how does it work? In solution to some of these problems, Davis suggests decriminalization of drugs. What would this look like, and how would treating drug use as an illness to be cured rather than a felony for which one is imprisoned change women's lives?

4. At the end of this essay, Davis suggests the abolition of the prison system. What would this look like, and how would it help the problems of racism and sexism she discusses?

THE ELEPHANT IN THE LIVING ROOM: THE ISSUE OF RACE IN CLOSE BLACK/WHITE FRIENDSHIPS

Kathleen Odell Korgen

I can't even think of any one thing that we've talked about in terms of race. Because it's just . . . You know, we're friends. That's where it is. That's the way it is. (Kofi, black, 35)

[Race does not come up] at all. Except for when we're like, ripping on each other. (Paul, white, 18)

I think race died down a long time ago in Vinnie's and my relationship. Now, it's personal [laughs]. It's just personal. . . . It just doesn't come up anymore except when talking about others and their deal with race. (Rod, black, 45)

There is no escaping the fact that we live in a race-conscious and divided society. All blacks and whites in close interracial friendships must somehow deal with this reality of race as they interact with their close friend. Consciously or not, the pair must agree upon and carry out a strategy to somehow "demilitarize" the topic of race and discuss it with defenses down or somehow find a way to sidestep the subject while still remaining close to one another.

An examination of forty pairs of close black/white friends reveals that cross-racial friends tend to handle the issue of race in one of three primary ways. In each case, the friends actively constructed a means to "disarm" the topic, so that it would not come between them and harm their friendship. Each pair developed its own means of handling this delicate task. However, it is possible to discern three basic behavioral patterns by which the friends dealt with the issue of race in their relationships:

1. Ignoring/avoiding the topic of race.

2. Joking about race.

3. Seriously discussing racial issues.

While some pairs exhibited traits from more than one category, one of the three strategies was clearly dominant in each of the dyads.

IGNORING/AVOIDING RACE

Just as race does not play a major role in the development of cross-racial friendships, it is not usually a topic of serious discussion in most close black/white friendships. As Walid Afifi and Laura Guerrero suggest, in their article "Some Things Are Better Left Unsaid II: Topic Avoidance in Friendships,"[1] the discussion of racial issues in cross-racial friendships is not necessarily an indication of the closeness of these relationships. Topic avoidance is not uncommon in close friendships. While self-disclosure is an integral part of these relationships,[2] researchers also now note that people consider some topics to be "taboo" and avoid discussing them even with close friends.[3]

Similar to platonic, cross-sex close friendships in which dating and sexual experiences are rarely discussed,[4] many close interracial friends do not talk to one another about racial issues. Afifi and Guerrero maintain that individuals in cross-sex friendships avoid discussing such topics as dating and sex at the "heart" of the tension in many such relationships. Friends in platonic, cross-sex relationships deal with what communication scholars Samter and Cupach describe as "the need to 'de-emphasize' sexuality."[5] The majority of these interracial friends deal with their racial differences by avoiding or ignoring the issue of race in their relationships. Whether consciously or not, the majority of these pairs have managed to avoid the volatile topic of race just as platonic, cross-sex friends stay away from the issue of sex.

Twenty of the forty pairs rarely discuss the issue of race. While there is no overt attempt to ignore or sidestep the topic, it seldom arises. When race does become a focus of conversation, the discussion usually consists of

a. discussions of what seem, at least to the white friend, seemingly isolated experiences of discrimination the black friend has faced,
b. brief debates about unavoidable, national, race-related incidents (e.g. O.J. Simpson's guilt or innocence), or
c. the topic of "light" conversation (e.g. importance of considering skin tones when purchasing clothes and makeup).

Kyle and Patrick provide a good example of how the first type of pair deals with the issue of race. As Kyle, a white, middle class, college student from a primarily white suburb in the Northeast puts it, race is "never" something that "enters into our relationship."

> It's not even like something that comes up in like conversation. Even now, it's like me and him, and just, and all my friends and stuff. We just, you know, Pat is Pat. We don't look at him as being black or whoever, you know. I never. I mean, obviously we know he is. But it just never, it never like enters into our relationship. (Kyle, white, 23)

One of the few times that Kyle remembers discussing race occurred when he, with Pat and some white friends, were pulled over by the police in a car.

> They'd [the police] pull him over and they, you know, they pulled me and my friends and he'd be in the car and they'd think we'd be up to you know . . . [We'd] say it's ridiculous. [We'd] say and Pat would say "the reason they're doing this and that, you know, [is] because I'm black." It's a typical, you know, stereotype that if you're black, you're some kind of criminal. You know, and I know he's encountered that, stuff like that. And it offends him, you know, it's ridiculous. It offends, you know, it offends me, it offends my friends. (Kyle, white, 23)

Those conversations, though, did not occur either outside such incidents or current news events.

Elizabeth and Louise, both middle class professionals and natives of Southern California, only discuss race during national news events such as the O.J. Simpson murder trial. As Louise describes,

> The only time we really got into something about race was during the O.J. Simpson trial and I thought he was not guilty and she thought he was guilty. . . . So, you know, we kind of. We discussed it for a while. And I told her my side, she told me her side. And ah, forget it. Let's go on to something else, and then we talked about something else. (Louise, black, 45)

While Louise and Elizabeth are very comfortable with one another, the O.J. Simpson trial provided one of the very few occasions where race entered into their friendship. When asked, individually, if race is ever an issue in their friendship, both brought up their discussion of O.J.'s guilt or innocence. Neither Louise nor Elizabeth agreed with the other's view and both realized that their disagreement was race-based. Like most white Americans, Elizabeth believed that he was guilty and like the majority of black Americans, Louise maintained that he was innocent.[6] However, they simply chose to agree to disagree and talk "about something else," rather than continue it and highlight the racial division that existed between them.

Dave and Kofi, two middle class professionals in their mid-thirties who have been best friends since meeting at their New England college, never discuss race. When asked if the topic of race comes up much between him and his friend Dave, Kofi, a native of Africa who came to the United States as a boy, said,

> No, it doesn't. . . . Hey, I know he's a Caucasian man. I know that. And I'm sure that he sees me as an African American person. But we don't. There are no issues. I mean, we don't talk about race per se. I can't even think of any one thing that we've talked about in terms of race. Because it's just . . . You know, we're friends. That's where it is. That's the way it is. (Kofi, black, 35)

Dave, who grew up in a predominantly white, New England neighborhood, echoed Kofi's statement when he tried to explain why he and Kofi do not discuss racial issues.

> Certainly it's not anything that I consciously avoided. I think we. I don't know, we're just two shallow guys. I don't know [laughs]. I don't know. Again, certainly, it's not anything that was consciously not brought up on my part. It's just ah, never been an issue with us. (Dave, white, 35)

The responses that both Kofi and Dave give to the question about whether they discuss race in their friendship reveals their unease with the topic. While Dave jokes that they just must e "two shallow guys" for not talking about race, Kofi describes him as the opposite of shallow, "not the kind of person that says a lot but . . . does things." Best friends since college, both men take their friendship very seriously and are clearly committed to one another. They have discussed extremely personal issues with each other and, as Kofi says, Dave is "not the type to open up [but] he opened up [to me]." Somehow, though, without conscious effort, the

two have never discussed the issue that divides so many black and white Americans from one another—race. Just as platonic cross-sex friends "de-emphasize" sexuality when they're together, Kofi and Dave, like the majority of the interracial friends, have "de-emphasized race" in their relationship.

JOKING ABOUT RACE

Ignoring or limiting discussions of race is one means of dealing with the "elephant in the living room." However, there are some pairs of friends who turn to their racial differences with humor as a means of cementing their relationship. The first time one makes fun of the other with a racial joke or slur and receives a good humored, similarly racist and abusive response, they know their friendship is on solid ground. These pairs of friends trade incessant racial barbs, yet rarely have a serious discussion about race or racial issues. Communication experts would not be surprised to learn that this is most common among young, male pairs of friends.

Nine of the forty pairs of friends fall chiefly into this category of black/white friends. Instead of generally ignoring the topic, this group deals with the issue of race by hurling racial insults at one another. Six of these pairs of friends consist of young men now in college. Three pairs of women also bring up race primarily through joking, though they also discuss individual incidents of racism that they have either faced or noticed.

Joe and Devin represent this second way close, black/white friends may deal with the issue of race. Joe, raised in a primarily white, upper-middle class, New York suburb, aptly sums up the role race plays in these friendships by saying,

> You know, when I look at friendships in general or specifically my friendship with Devin, it's

amazing how much race plays a role, but doesn't play a role. How much we joke about it, but we never talk about it seriously. (Joe, black, 18)

To them, racial stereotypes can be used as "in" jokes that bring them closer together. In many ways, their interactions are similar to those of the interracial buddy/partner characters Mel Gibson and Danny Glover play in the series of *Lethal Action* movies. As Devin, who grew up in a middle class, predominantly white, New England town describes it,

We make a weird fun of each other's ethnic backgrounds so much; it's incredible. . . . Like we found each other's stereotypes—I'm Irish and German—so we're, we're pretty bad with it. . . . Like I saw him at lunch, we were eating, and I saw him come back from one of the meal booths . . . and I was like 'What you got there—some fried chicken and Koolade?'" [He, in turn, might say something like] "Why don't you build a new gas chamber?" (Devin, white, 18)

Aware that people overhearing them are often aghast, Joe and Devin joke with each other in ways that they would never joke with others. They also readily admit that they would never permit others, outside their close circle of friends, to joke either with themselves or their close friend in a similar manner. Each expressed a strong willingness to defend their friend from any racial insults that others might deliver.

Vern and James, college students who both grew up in lower middle class, New Jersey neighborhoods, areas with increasing numbers of blacks, also use the topic of race as fodder for put-downs of one another. When asked if race has ever come up or been an issue in their friendship, Vern's succinct response was

No, not at all. Except for when we're, like, ripping on each other. (Vern, white, 18)

When asked the same question, separately, James's response was almost identical to Vern's:

Just like joking. We always joke about people's races all the time. (James, black, 18)

Like Joe and Devin, and the majority of the young male interracial friends, Vern and James use racial jokes as a means of both bonding and acknowledging the "elephant in the living room" without having to address, with any depth, the fact that race affects them both in different ways.

While in some friendship pairs the line may seem very far off, there is a line that the friends know to avoid crossing when joking with one another. As Steven describes it,

Well, you know, we talk about stuff, mostly joking. And, you know, it's a really open kind of friendship. You know, I'll say things and, you know, he'll say things and whenever those lines are crossed we know, you know, all you have to do is say "I'm not comfortable with that." And he backs off and I back off. . . .

When asked who crosses the line more often, Steven said,

On the issue of race? It's probably him crossing the line and me telling him that that's not something I'm comfortable with. But, I mean, it doesn't happen often. But, on the other hand, I don't think I've ever crossed a racial line with him, you know. And that just goes with the whole, you know, I think it's more serious . . . saying things that are offensive towards black people than it is saying things that are offensive towards white people. I guess it's just kind of society today. (Steven, black, 19)

The differing positions of the white and black "no crossing" line when it comes to racial jokes has nothing to do with political correctness. Young men who insult each other with as much wit and effort to disgust one another as these young men are not bound by current "adult" rules of verbal etiquette in their exchanges with one another. In some ways, they are carrying on the time-honored tradition of disparaging one another that male youths have acted out with each other for decades. Those who manage to deliver the most outrageous insults, while avoiding hitting a spot that is a little too sensitive and starting a fight, gain in stature among their friends.[7]

The reason that blacks are more sensitive than whites to racial jokes is intimately connected with the fact that blacks have been the butt of racial slurs and jokes associated with their devaluation, dehumanization, and lynching,[8] throughout the history of the United States. Today, as a group, blacks are still socially, politically, and economically in lower standing than whites. Whites, as a racial group, on the other hand, have not faced such abuse and still hold disproportionate economic, political, and social power in the United States. Just as it is easier to bear a "you are so ugly" joke when you are relatively good looking, it is much easier to take a racial insult when your race is in a position of power relative to those hurling the insults.

The fact that both friends feel comfortable, on the whole, trading race-based insults with one another is a sign of their closeness, despite their racial differences. Trading jokes and insults can also give the surface impression that the two friends are on an equal playing field. The only indication that the field is still slanted is the fact that racial insults are more likely to injure the black friend than the white one.

Seriously Discussing Race

The friends who openly discuss the different positions of blacks and whites in society are those who represent the third category of responses of close, interracial friends to the issue of race. These friends directly comment, with great seriousness, on the "elephant in the living room." Eleven of the friendship pairs have discussed race at length. They were deeply interested, usually near the beginning of their friendship, to discover all that they could about their friend's different racial background and perspective. Typically, the discussions would begin with the white friend asking the black friend questions. However, the conversations would almost always include multiple exchanges of opinions and information.

With each pair, however, the topic of race arose less frequently as time went by.[9] In all friendships, the differences in the friends that first seemed novel become normal, and less of a conversation maker as the friendship develops. The black/white friends who spent hours learning from each other's experiences and opinions on racial issues towards the beginning of their friendship, gradually turned to other topics as their friendship developed. After many years of friendship, the friends tended to talk about race only when discussing a news item or dealing with the racial issues of "others." Their lengthy talks about the subject earlier in their friendship often enable them to now feel confident that they know the other's thoughts on a current racial event or issue without having to ask.

Evan and Bob, friends now for many years, illustrate the third way in which many black/white friends deal with issues of race over time. While they eagerly discussed issues concerning race when they first became friends, their conversations now tend to focus on other topics. As Evan states,

> Well, I can tell you, Bob and I [spent] a lot of time just talking about race. Differences and attitudes, you know, things like that. . . . So, we've done a lot of exploring, he and I. Just questioning each other and talking in general. [But] we have a tendency now to focus on the similarities, instead of the differences. . . . We don't talk about it too much anymore now because we're past that. We've asked all the questions we want to ask. Or, we've covered that ground and we know the answer.
>
> [However], I would still not hesitate at all if a question came up about race or something like that. In fact, I've often thought to myself, if I ever have a problem, with an African American

employee, I'll call Bob first and run it by him to get his view on it before I took any action. (Evan, white, 41)

So, while, they have already "covered that ground," Evan and Bob have not decided to now simply ignore race. Instead, it has become just one of the many reasons, like guidance on work issues, jogging, marital issues, etc., for which they might turn to each other for advice. Evan and Bob value each other on multiple levels, and embrace the many identities, including racial, of each.

In some ways similar to Evan and Bob, Caroline turned to Janet for a sounding board when she dealt with issues of race in her work life. When Caroline a white, upper-middle class, midwestern professor and professional consultant, first started work at a company that, aside from her, was virtually all black, she was grateful to find her assistant, Janet, very willing to guide her through what for her was a new cultural environment. When asked how often she and Janet had discussions about racial issues, Caroline said,

> I think early on, a lot. You know, like typically every day something would be coming up. . . . Because I was surrounded, for the first time in my life, with African American women, working in [this] setting. And I truly wanted to understand their point of view. And I would say that Janet was sort of a, um, a critical person in helping me to understand a world that I had never experienced before. She was much more savvy in that world of employees that we had to work with that had problems and our clients, our residents and their families. . . . I mean, she was absolutely indispensable in helping me learn cultural ins and outs. (Caroline, white, 53)

Through the trust and rapport they developed through working together, Janet and Caroline have become very close friends and "part of one another's family" over the ten years they have known each other. Their relationship is markedly different than the hierarchical workplace relationships between whites and blacks that Hudson and Hines-Hudson described. While Caroline was, in reality, Janet's superior in the hierarchical structure of their company, Caroline repeatedly described their working relationship in terms that stressed their collaborative efforts. In the workplace Caroline depended upon Janet's willingness to share her knowledge of black culture. The fact that Caroline treated Janet as an equal at work in some ways balanced the playing field and most likely contributed to the ease with which their close friendship developed.

Caroline's and Janet's experience was rare. Approximately four-fifths of the friendship pairs in this sample are comprised of two people with similar educational and economic backgrounds. However, more than most other pairs of friends in this sample, the support Caroline and Janet gave each other dealing with issues of race was mutual. Because Janet was Caroline's assistant when they first met, and Caroline was educationally and financially in a superior situation, she was able to provide Janet much guidance and support in attaining further degrees in higher education and negotiating the predominantly white corporate world.

Typically among the friendship pairs, the teaching about culture was primarily one-sided. Black people, living in a white dominated society, are usually much more knowledgeable about white culture than whites are of black culture and therefore have less need of a tutorial about the other race. They, in many ways, must be bicultural, able to live in both black and white worlds. W. E. B. DuBois described this as having a "double consciousness" in *The Souls of Black Folk*.[10] Whites, on the other hand, while they may be fans of Michael Jordan and the Wayans brothers, do not often look into everyday black America. In the pairs in which race was an open topic, the white interviewees spoke appreciatively of their friend's assistance in their efforts to learn and understand the cultural differences that exist between many black and white Americans.

Given the American obsession with race, one might think that the vast majority of close black/white friends would discuss racial issues often. Yet, the overwhelming majority of friendship pairs (97.5%) did not make race the centerpiece of their friendship. Even pairs who have serious discussions about racism in US society concentrate on other aspects of their friendship. Rod describes this phenomenon within his friendship with Vinnie.

I think race died down a long time ago in Vinnie's and my relationship. Now, it's personal [laughs]. It's just personal. You know, this is so corny. I know he's a white guy, you know, and he knows I'm a black guy. But that's not a part of it. It's just the blood we've shed. You know, and the tears we've cried. I don't think it's. It just doesn't come up anymore except when talking about others and their deal with race. And how we see some people just doing some stupid things. And that's when, you know, they'll get our hair up. . . . Like we won't tolerate racial insensitivity or anything like that on our team. But it wouldn't manifest itself because, cause we're there. You know. So, I think, in response to, does race come up?, it comes up when dealing with others but not when dealing with each other. (Rod, black, 45)

Having grown completely comfortable with the racial differences between them, their attention towards race now focuses outward. Through the example of their friendship, and the way they coach together, Rod and Vinnie show their players and those around them that close friendships can be formed across the racial divide.

In their own ways, interracial friends develop strategies to keep race from consuming their friendship. The typical means, topic avoidance, is successful through the efforts of both the white and the black individuals in each of the pairs. The existence of these cross-racial friendships makes it clear that close friendships are possible across the racial divide. However, the fact that the

majority of close black/white friends do not seriously discuss issues of race is a testimony to the still painful and volatile separation that exists between black and white Americans.

Notes

1. See Afifi, Walid and Laura Guerrero (1998). "Some Things Are Better Left Unsaid II: Topic Avoidance in Friendships" *Communication Quarterly*, 46, 3, pp. 231–249.

2. See Monsour, M., Harris, B., Kurzweil, N. & Beard C. (1994). "Challenges Confronting Cross-Sex Friendships: 'Much Ado About Nothing?'" *Sex Roles*, 31, pp. 55–77; Parks, M. R. and Floyd, K. (1996). "Meanings for Closeness and Intimacy in Friendship." *Journal of Social and Personal Relationships*, 13, pp. 85–107; Derlega, V. J., Metts, S. Petronio, S. and Margulis, S. T. (1993). *Self-Disclosure*. Newbury Park, CA: Sage.

3. See Afifi, Walid and Laura Guerrero (1998). "Some Things Are Better Left Unsaid II: Topic Avoidance in Friendships" *Communication Quarterly*, 46, 3, pp. 231–249; Guerrero, Laura and Walid Affifi. (1995) "Some Things Are Better Left Unsaid: Topic Avoidance in Family Relationships." *Communication Quarterly*, 43, pp. 276–296.

4. See Afifi, Walid and Laura Guerrero (1998). "Some Things Are Better Left Unsaid II: Topic Avoidance in Friendships" *Communication Quarterly*, 46, 3, pp. 231–249.

5. See Samter, Wendy and William Cupach (1998). "Friendly Fire: Topical Variations in Conflict among Same and Cross-Sex Friends." *Communication Studies*, 49, 42, pp. 121–138.

6. Newport, Frank and Lydia Saad (1997). "Civil Trial Didn't Alter Public's View of Simpson Case." *Gallup News Service*, February 7, 1997. [http://www.gallup.com/poll/releases/pr970207.asp]

7. One of the anonymous reviewers pointed out that "this ritual is referred to in the black community as 'playing the dozens.' Hitting the hot spot usually means saying something derogatory about someone's mother."

8. The fact that these types of jokes are still told is evident in the fact that one white, twenty-four

year old interviewee related a joke her boyfriend recently heard as follows: "This one guy goes, 'I have no problem with black people. I've got one in my family tree.' And, and then someone goes 'Oh really' and he goes, 'Yah, he's hanging in my backyard.' " She was appalled both by the joke and that people could still be so "stupid" and "ignorant."

9. One pair, who met in grade school and are now in their late twenties, did not seriously discuss their different thoughts and experiences concerning race until they were in college. Since that time, they

have followed the trend of the other pairs in this category and have talked about racial issues less often as time passes.

10. DuBois, W. E. B. (1961). *The Souls of Black Folk: Essays and Sketches.* Greenwich: Fawcett.

SOURCE: From *From Black to Biracial: Transforming Racial Identity Among Americans* by Kathleen Odell Korgen. Copyright © 1998, 1999 Kathleen Odell Korgen. Reprinted with permission of Greenwood Publishing Group, Inc., Westport, CT.

DISCUSSION QUESTIONS

1. Why do you think certain close black-white friends use racial joking as part of their communication processes? Do you feel such joking is appropriate, and if so, under what conditions? What reasons does the author give for blacks being more sensitive to racial joking than whites? What does this tell us about the social nature of prejudice and its relationship to power?

2. Why did serious discussions of race tend to involve black people teaching whites about their culture, and not vice versa? Is it fair that blacks end up bearing the burden of being "teacher" in interracial

settings? What are the alternatives to whites expecting blacks to teach them about race?

3. Does the fact that most black-white friends do not seriously discuss race indicate that they have "gotten past" race, and thus indicate progress, or does it indicate a "painful and volatile" separation, as the author suggests? Do whites and blacks discuss race more honestly and openly in the presence of those who share their racial identity? What would need to change in society in order for people to feel comfortable discussing race with those unlike themselves?

CURRENT DEBATES

REPARATIONS

Should African Americans be compensated for the losses they suffered as a result of their kidnapping from Africa, their centuries of slavery, and their continuing oppression under de jure segregation? What, if anything, does American society owe for the centuries of uncompensated labor performed by African Americans and the oppression and coerced inequality of the Jim Crow era? Should present-day Americans be held accountable for the actions of their ancestors? What about the families and businesses that grew rich from the labor of blacks (and other minorities) in the past? To what extent are they responsible for the continuing racial gaps in income and wealth documented in this chapter?

The idea that America owes reparations to African Americans is not new but has been gaining momentum in recent years.[1] The movement has been spurred by a best-selling book,[2] and

---

1. Smith, V. (2001, August 27). Debating the wages of slavery. *Newsweek*, pp. 20–25.
2. Robinson, R. (2001). *The debt: What America owes to blacks.* New York: Plume.

in March of 2002, a reparations lawsuit was filed against several large U.S. corporations, including the Aetna insurance company, alleging that they had profited from slave labor. Also, the issue promises to receive a great deal of attention on college campuses, in part as a serious issue worthy of discussion and in part as a focus of activism, as students question the relationship between their schools' endowment and slavery.

In the excerpts below, Joe Feagin and Eileen O'Brien, while arguing for reparations, place the debate in a comparative and historical context. Manning Marable and John McWhorter present some of the central arguments for and against reparations. Both men are prominent African American academics.

REPARATIONS FOR AFRICAN AMERICANS IN HISTORICAL CONTEXT

Joe R. Feagin and Eileen O'Brien

Many discussions of reparation for African Americans seem to suggest that such compensation is a wild idea well beyond conventional U.S. practice or policy. This is not, however, the case. The principle of individual and group compensation for damages done by others is accepted by the federal government and the larger society in regard to some claims, but only grudgingly and incompletely for others, such as those by African Americans who have been harmed by racial oppression. For example, recent anti-crime legislation, in the form of the Victims of Crime Act, codifies the principle of compensation for victims of crime. In addition, as a nation, we now expect corporations to compensate the deformed children of mothers who took drugs without knowing their consequences . . . The fact that those who ran the corporation in the initial period of damage are deceased does not relieve the corporation from having to pay compensation to those damaged later on from the earlier actions. Injured children can sue for redress many years later. Clearly, in some cases monetary compensation for past injustices is accepted and expected.

Long after the Nazi party had been out of power and most of its leaders had grown old or died, the U.S. government continued to press the German government to make tens of billions of dollars in reparations to the families of those killed in the Holocaust and to the state of Israel. In recent years, the federal government has grudgingly agreed to (modest) reparations for those Japanese Americans who were interned during World War II. Federal Courts have also awarded nearly a billion dollars in compensatory damages to Native American groups whose lands were stolen in violation of treaties. Significantly, however, these slow moves to compensate some victims of racial oppression have not extended, even modestly, to African Americans . . .

In his 1946 book, *The World and Africa*, W.E.B. DuBois argued that the poverty in Europe's African colonies was "a main cause of wealth and luxury in Europe" (1965, p. 37). DuBois argued that the history of African colonization is omitted from mainstream histories of European development and wealth. A serious understanding of European wealth must *center* on the history of exploitation and oppression in Africa, for the resources of Africans were taken to help create Europe's wealth. To a substantial degree, Europeans were rich because Africans were poor. Africa's economic development—its resources, land, and labor—had been and was being sacrificed to spur European economic progress.

In our view, a similar argument is applicable to the development of the wealth and affluence of the white population in the United States. From its first decades, white-settler colonialism in North America involved the extreme exploitation of enslaved African Americans. European colonists built up much wealth by stealing the labor of African Americans and the land of Native Americans.

Racial oppression carried out by white Americans has lasted for nearly four centuries and has done great damage to the lives, opportunities, communities, and futures of African Americans. The actions of white Americans over many generations sharply reduced the income of African Americans, and thus their economic and cultural capital. Legal segregation in the South, where most African Americans resided until recent decades, forced black men and women into lower-paying jobs or into unemployment, where they could not earn incomes sufficient to support their families adequately, much less to save. In the 1930s, two-thirds of African Americans still lived in the South, and most were descendants of recently enslaved Americans. They were still firmly entrenched in the semi-slavery of legal segregation, which did not allow the accumulation of wealth. Significant property holding was not even available as a possibility to a majority of African Americans until the late 1960s . . .

Most whites do not understand the extent to which the racial oppression of the past continues to fuel inequalities in the present. Although affirmative action programs (where they still exist) attempt to redress discrimination by increasing job or educational opportunities for African Americans in a few organizations, such programs do little to address the large-scale wealth inequality between black and white Americans. All the "equal opportunity" programs and policies one could envisage would not touch the assets of whites who long ago reaped the benefits of not being subjected to legal segregation during the United States' most prosperous economic times in the 19th and 20th centuries . . .

Wealth transmission is a critical factor in the reproduction of racial oppression. Given the nature of whites' disproportionate share of America's wealth and the historical conditions under which it was acquired—often at the expense of African Americans—it is of little significance that legal discrimination and segregation do not exist today. The argument that "Jim Crow is a thing of the past" misses the point, because the huge racial disparities in wealth today are a *direct* outgrowth of the economic and social privileges one group secured unfairly, if not brutally, at the expense of another group.

SOURCE: From *When Sorry Isn't Enough: The Controversy Over Apologies and Reparations for Human Injustice*, edited by Roy L. Brooks. Copyright © 1999 by New York University. Reprinted by permission of New York University Press.

REPARATIONS ARE AN IDEA WHOSE TIME HAS COME

Manning Marable

In 1854 my great-grandfather, Morris Marable, was sold on an auction block in Georgia for $500. For his white slave master, the sale was just "business as usual." But to Morris Marable and his heirs, slavery was a crime against our humanity.

This pattern of human-rights violations against enslaved African Americans continued under Jim Crow segregation for nearly another century.

The fundamental problem of American democracy in the 21st century is the problem of "structural racism": the deep patterns of socioeconomic inequality and accumulated disadvantage that are coded by race, and constantly justified in public discourse by both racist stereotypes and white indifference. Do Americans have the capacity and vision to dismantle these structural barriers that deny democratic rights and opportunities to millions of their fellow citizens?

This country has previously witnessed two great struggles to achieve a truly multicultural democracy. The First Reconstruction (1865–1877) . . . briefly gave black men voting rights, but gave no meaningful compensation for two centuries of unpaid labor. The promise of "40 acres and a mule" was for most blacks a dream deferred.

The Second Reconstruction (1954–1968), or the modern civil-rights movement, outlawed legal segregation in public accommodations and gave blacks voting rights. But these successes paradoxically obscure the tremendous human costs of historically accumulated disadvantage that remain central to black Americans' lives.

The disproportionate wealth that most whites enjoy today was first constructed from centuries of unpaid black labor. Many white institutions, including Ivy League universities, insurance companies and banks, profited from slavery. This pattern of white privilege and black inequality continues today.

Demanding reparations is not just about compensation for slavery and segregation. It is, more important, an educational campaign to highlight the contemporary reality of "racial deficits" of all kinds, the unequal conditions that impact blacks regardless of class. Structural racism's barriers include "equity inequity," the absence of black capital formation that is a direct consequence of America's history. One third of all black households actually have negative net wealth. In 1998 the typical black family's net wealth was $16,400, less than one fifth that of white families. Black families are denied home loans at twice the rate of whites.

Blacks remain the last hired and first fired during recessions. During the 1990–91 recession, African Americans suffered disproportionately. At Coca-Cola, 42 percent of employees who lost their jobs were black. At Sears, 54 percent were black. Blacks have significantly shorter life expectancies, in part due to racism in the health establishment. Blacks are statistically less likely than whites to be referred for kidney transplants or early-stage cancer surgery.

In criminal justice, African Americans constitute only one seventh of all drug users. Yet we account for 35 percent of all drug arrests, 55 percent of drug convictions and 75 percent of prison admissions for drug offenses. . . .

White Americans today aren't guilty of carrying out slavery and segregation. But whites have a moral and political responsibility to acknowledge the continuing burden of history's structural racism.

A reparations trust fund could be established, with the goal of closing the socioeconomic gaps between blacks and whites. Funds would be targeted specifically toward poor, disadvantaged communities with the greatest need, not to individuals.

Let's eliminate the racial unfairness in capital markets that perpetuates black poverty. A national commitment to expand black homeownership, full employment and quality health care would benefit all Americans, regardless of race.

Reparations could begin America's Third Reconstruction, the final chapter in the 400-year struggle to abolish slavery and its destructive consequences. As Malcolm X said in 1961, hundreds of years of racism and labor exploitation are "worth more than a cup of coffee at a white cafe. We are here to collect back wages."

SOURCE: Originally titled "An Idea Whose Time Has Come . . . Whites Have an Obligation to Recognize Slavery's Legacy" from *Newsweek*, August 27, 2001. Reprinted by permission of the author.

BLOOD MONEY: WHY I DON'T WANT REPARATIONS FOR SLAVERY

John McWhorter

My childhood was a typical one for a black American in his mid-thirties. I grew up middle class in a quiet, safe neighborhood in Philadelphia. [My] mother taught social work at Temple University and my father was a student activities administrator there. My parents were far from wealthy, . . . but I had everything I needed plus some extras. . . .

Contrary to popular belief, I was by no means extraordinarily "lucky" or "unusual" among black Americans of the post-Civil Rights era. . . . [T]oday, there are legions of black adults in the United States who grew up as I did. As a child, I never had trouble finding black peers, and as an adult, meeting black people with life histories like mine requires no searching. In short, in our moment, black success is a norm. Less than one in four black families now live below the poverty line, and the black underclass is at most one out of five blacks. This is what the Civil Rights revolution helped make possible, and I grew up exhilarated at belonging to a race that had made such progress in the face of many obstacles.

Yet today, numerous black officials tell the public that lives like mine are statistical noise, that the overriding situation for blacks is one of penury, dismissal, and spiritual desperation. Under this analysis, the blood of slavery remains on the hands of mainstream America until it allocates a large sum of money to "repair" the . . . damage done to our race over four centuries. . . .

The shorthand version of the reparations idea is that living blacks are "owed" the money that our slave ancestors were denied for their unpaid servitude. But few black Americans even know the names or life stories of their slave ancestors; almost none of us have pictures or keepsakes from that far back. . . . Yes, my slave ancestors were "blood" to me; yes, what was done to them was unthinkable. But the 150 years between me and them has rendered our tie little more than biological. Paying anyone for the suffering of long-dead strangers . . . would be more a matter of blood money than "reparation." . . .

Perhaps recognizing this, the reparations movement is now drifting away from the "back salary" argument to justifications emphasizing the effects of slavery since Emancipation. It is said blacks deserve payment for residual echoes of their earlier disenfranchisement and segregation. This justification, however, is predicated upon the misconception that in 2001, most blacks are "struggling."

This view denies the stunning success that the race has achieved over the past 40 years. It persists because many Americans, black and white, have accepted the leftist notion which arose in the mid-1960s that blacks are primarily victims in this country, that racism and structural injustice hobble all but a few individual blacks. Based on emotion, victimologist thought ignores the facts of contemporary black success and progress, because they do not square with the "blame game."

Reparations cannot logically rely on a depiction of black Americans as a race still reeling from the brutal experience of slavery and its after effects. The reality is that, by any estimation, in the year 2001 there are more middle-class blacks than poor ones. The large majority of black Americans, while surely not immune to the slings and arrows of the eternal injustices of life on earth, are now leading dignified lives as new variations on what it means to be American. . . .

Any effort to repair problems in black America must focus on helping people to help themselves. Funds must be devoted to ushering welfare mothers into working for a living, so that their children do not grow up learning that employment is something "other people" do. Inner city communities should be helped to rebuild themselves, in part through making it easier for residents to buy their homes. Police forces ought to be trained to avoid brutality, which turns young blacks against the mainstream today, and to work with, rather than against, the communities they serve.

Finally, this country must support all possible efforts to liberate black children from the soul-extinguishing influence of ossified urban public schools, and to move them into experimental or all-minority schools where a culture of competition is fostered. This will help undo the sense that intellectual excellence is a "white" endeavor. Surely we must improve the public

schools as well, including increasing the exposure of young black children to standardized tests. But we also must make sure another generation of black children are not lost during the years it will take for these schools to get their acts together. . . .

Ultimately, a race shows its worth not by how much charity it can extract from others, but in how well it can do in the absence of charity. Black America has elicited more charity from its former oppressors than any race in human history—justifiably in my view. However, this can only serve as a spark—the real work is now ours.

SOURCE: From the July/August 2001 issue of *The American Enterprise*. Copyright © 2001. Reprinted with permission.

DEBATE QUESTIONS TO CONSIDER

1. Feagin and O'Brien justify reparations for African Americans, in part, by making comparisons to other situations in which victimized groups have been compensated. Are the situations they cite truly comparable to slavery and segregation? If so, what similarities make the situations comparable? If not, explain the differences that make the comparison invalid.

2. Feagin and O'Brien agree with Marable that whites share responsibility for the "continuing burden of history's structural racism." Explain this argument in light of the continuing racial gaps in income and education. (Data on race differences are available from the U.S. Bureau of the Census at www.census.gov.) Does McWhorter's assessment of black success make sense in terms of these gaps? Is the difference between Marable and McWhorter merely one of emphasis? Is Marable seeing the glass

"half empty" and McWhorter seeing it "half full"? Or, is there a deeper division between the two points of view? If so, what is it?

3. People often think of reparations for slavery in terms of cash payments to individuals. McWhorter opposes "reparations" but advocates programs of improvement (workfare, schools, etc.). How are these programs different from "reparations"?

4. Consider Marable's point that the reparations issue can be used as an educational tool. Could the campaign for reparations be used to counteract modern racism or white indifference? How?

5. Has any form of reparations been considered to compensate women for centuries of being excluded from the workplace and political life? Why or why not?

6

NATIVE AMERICANS

While African Americans lost their freedom under slavery, Native Americans lost their land, their resources, and their lives. Hostilities between Anglo-Americans and the Native tribes began shortly after the first white settlements were established, and continued for nearly 300 years. The tribes resisted the advances of white civilization as best they could, but eventually they succumbed to the superior power and larger size of the growing American society. At the end of armed hostilities, the tribes were forced into federally controlled reservations, often hundreds of miles from their traditional homelands. The reservations were typically on the least desirable, least productive land, and, for much of the past 100 years, Indians have had to struggle mightily to wrest from them even a meager subsistence.

Since the end of the Indian wars, federal policy toward the tribes has fluctuated between neglect and coerced acculturation. The federally controlled Indian school system exemplifies the latter. Indian children on the reservation were required to attend boarding schools where they were made to learn English, adopt Christianity, and follow other Anglo cultural practices. Mary Crow Dog, in the first Narrative Portrait, paints a grim picture of everyday life at the Indian schools. However, the efforts to Americanize Indians and exterminate their cultures was, at best, only partly successful. As illustrated in the second Narrative Portrait by John Lame Deer, Native American cultures and values survive into the present.

The three Readings for this chapter document the persistence of Native American cultures and the continuing discrimination and racism they face. Russell Thornton provides an overview of the situation of Native Americans and some background on present-day issues, including a summary of the effects of changing federal policy. Leonard Peltier examines the issues from a very personal point of view: he is currently in prison for his protest activities in support of Native American causes. Finally, Charon Asetoyer explains her attempts to address a broad range of women's and health-related issues on a Sioux reservation.

The Current Debates section raises an issue that might seem excessively "politically correct" to many: should Indian names and mascots be used by sports teams like the Cleveland Indians and Washington Redskins, for example? While some (non-Indians as well as Native Americans) are deeply offended by this practice, many regard it as a nonissue. After all, no one is directly injured or penalized by this practice, and it's all in good fun, right? Or is there something deeper and more meaningful involved in the debate?

Please visit the accompanying website to Race, Ethnicity, and Gender, second edition for the *Public Sociology Assignments* at http://www.pineforge.com/das2.

QUESTIONS TO CONSIDER IN THIS CHAPTER

1. What does this chapter reveal about anti-Native American prejudice and discrimination? What differences and similarities can you identify between anti-black and anti-Native American prejudice and discrimination? Why do these differences and similarities exist?

2. It has been said that Native Americans are the poorest and most powerless of American minority groups. Based on the material presented in this chapter, is this statement true? What historical and contemporary patterns might account for the present-day situation of this group?

3. Can you make a case for reparations for Native Americans? How about affirmative action? What factors would you cite for and against reparations and affirmative action? Are these factors different from those you might cite for African Americans (see Chapter 5)?

4. What gender dimensions can you identify in the issues raised in this chapter? How does gender impact (for example) prejudice, health care, and the selection of mascots and nicknames for sports teams?

NARRATIVE PORTRAITS

NATIVE AMERICANS' EXPERIENCES AND PERSPECTIVES

By the end of the 19th century, Native Americans had been defeated militarily, and those who survived the vicious conflicts were herded onto reservations where they remained isolated, impoverished, and powerless. Sometimes, in the 19th and 20th centuries, the tribes were subjected to various forms of coercive acculturation and attempts to "civilize" and Americanize them, experiences that left them bitter, resentful, and contemptuous of the cruel paternalism of the larger society. At other times, Native Americans were simply ignored and left to their own devices, experiences that permitted them to preserve some of their languages and many aspects of their traditional culture. The selection by Mary Crow Dog, a member of the Sioux tribe who became deeply involved in the Red Power movement that began in the 1960s, recounts one experience with coercive acculturation in the form of Indian boarding schools, and the selection by John Lame Deer, also a Sioux, illustrates the reality of a continuing, unassimilated Native American view of white society.

The boarding schools so vividly recalled by Mary Crow Dog have been much improved in recent decades. Facilities have been modernized and the faculty upgraded. The curriculum has been updated and often includes elements of Native American culture and language. Still, it was not that long ago that coercive acculturation at its worst was the daily routine—keep in mind that she was born in 1955 and started school in the early 1960s, only a generation or two ago.

In the 1972 interview summarized here, John Lame Deer gives his view of the technologically advanced society that surrounds him. Through his words, we can hear the voices of the Indian cultures that have survived and the strong suggestion that Native Americans are, in many ways, more advanced than the dazzling sophisticates of urban America.

LAKOTA WOMAN

Mary Crow Dog

It is almost impossible to explain to a sympathetic white person what a typical old Indian boarding school was like; how it affected the Indian child suddenly dumped into it like a small creature from another world, helpless, defenseless, bewildered, trying desperately to survive and sometimes not surviving at all. Even now, when these schools are so much improved, when . . . the teachers [are] well-intentioned, even trained in child psychology—unfortunately the psychology of white children, which is different from ours—the shock to the child upon arrival is still tremendous. . . .

In the traditional Sioux family, the child is never left alone. It is always surrounded by relatives, carried around, enveloped in warmth. It is treated with the respect due to any human being, even a small one. It is seldom forced to do anything against its will, seldom screamed at, and never beaten. . . . And then suddenly a bus or car arrives full of strangers, who yank the child out of the arms of those who love it, taking it screaming to the boarding school. The only word I can think of for what is done to these children is kidnapping. . . .

The mission school at St. Francis was a curse for our family for generations. My grandmother went there, then my mother, then my sisters and I. At one time or another, every one of us tried to run away. Grandma told me about the bad times she experienced at St. Francis. In those days they let students go home only for one week every year. Two days were used up for transportation, which meant spending just five days out of every 365 with her family. . . . My mother had much the same experiences but never wanted to talk about them, and then there was I, in the same place. . . . Nothing had changed since my grandmother's days. I have been told that even in the '70s they were still beating children at that school. All I got out of school was being taught how to pray. I learned quickly that I would be beaten if I failed in my devotions or, God forbid, prayed the wrong way, especially prayed in Indian to Wakan Tanka, the Indian creator. . . .

My classroom was right next to the principal's office and almost every day I could hear him swatting the boys. Beating was the common punishment for not doing one's homework, or for being late to school. It had such a bad effect upon me that I hated and mistrusted every white person on sight, because I met only one kind. It was not until much later that I met sincere white people I could relate to and be friends with. Racism breeds racism in reverse.

TALKING TO THE OWLS AND BUTTERFLIES

John Lame Deer

You have made it hard for us to experience nature in the good way by being part of it. Even here (a Sioux reservation in South Dakota) we are conscious that somewhere out in those hills there are missile silos and radar stations. White men always pick the few unspoiled, beautiful, awesome spots for these abominations. You have raped and violated these lands, always saying, "gimme, gimme, gimme," and never giving anything back. . . . . You have not only despoiled the earth, the rocks, the minerals, all of which you call "dead" but which are very much alive; you have even changed the animals, . . . changed them in a horrible way, so no one can recognize them. There is power in a buffalo—spiritual, magic power—but there is no power in an Angus, in a Hereford.

There is power in an antelope, but not in a goat or a sheep, which holds still while you butcher it, which will eat your newspaper if you let it. There was great power in a wolf, even in a coyote. You made him into a freak—a toy poodle, a Pekinese, a lap dog. You can't do much with a cat, which is like an Indian, unchangeable. So you fix it, alter it, declaw it, even cut its vocal cords so you can experiment on it in a laboratory without being disturbed by its cries. . . .

You have not only altered, declawed, and malformed your winged and four-legged cousins; you have done it to yourselves. You have changed men into chairmen of boards, into office workers, into time-clock punchers. You have changed women into housewives, truly fearful creatures. . . . You live in prisons which you have built for yourselves, calling them "homes," offices, factories. We have a new joke on the reservations: "What is cultural deprivation?" Answer: "Being an upper-middle-class white kid living in a split-level suburban home with a color TV." . . .

I think white people are so afraid of the world they created that they don't want to see, feel, smell, or hear it. The feeling of rain or snow on your face, being numbed by an icy wind and thawing out before a smoking fire, coming out of a hot sweat bath and plunging into a cold stream, these things make you feel alive, but you don't want them anymore. Living in boxes that shut out the heat of the summer and the chill of winter, living inside a body that no longer has a scent, hearing the noise of the hi-fi rather than listening to the sounds of nature, watching some actor on TV have a make-believe experience when you no longer experience anything for yourself, eating food without taste—that's your way. It's no good.

SOURCE: Reprinted with permission of Pocket Books, an imprint of Simon & Schuster Adult Publishing Group from *Lame Deer Seeker of Visions* by John (Fire) Lame Deer and Richard Erdoes. Copyright © 1972 by John (Fire) Lame Deer and Richard Erdoes.

READINGS

Native Americans are yet another minority group whose experiences have been profoundly shaped by whites as the dominant majority group. Once white settlers arrived on Native land, their stance toward Native Americans was based on a view that this group was a military threat that needed to be contained or eliminated. Whites' individualistic orientation and their exploitative approach toward the land contrasted sharply with Native Americans' collectivist orientation and deep respect for the connection between nature and humanity. Whites' devaluation of Native American values, combined with their stance of conquest and greater power over Native Americans, resulted in a situation of colonization and conquest whose effects are still being felt today. The first Reading, "Trends Among American Indians in the United States," examines some of these contemporary issues. After giving some background on estimated numbers of Native Americans and where they are located in the United States, author Russell Thornton discusses some of the U.S. government's policies toward them. We see that since 1976, Native Americans have had to assemble many documents to prove that they are a tribe before they can receive any kind of government recognition. Additionally, the government has had a long history of forcing Native Americans into federally run schools intended to "civilize" and to Christianize them. This view that Native Americans need to be civilized stems directly from the "savage" stereotype created by whites to rationalize their policies of termination and extermination of individual Native Americans and entire tribes. The legacy of this paternalistic relationship with the government can be seen today in the small number of educational institutions that are truly run by and for Native Americans. By the end of this Reading, however, Thornton seems to describe a more optimistic future by focusing on the Repatriation Movement and the successes they have had in reclaiming Native American artifacts and skeletal remains from museums to their proper descendants and communities.

A key organizer of the American Indian Movement (AIM), Leonard Peltier is the author of the second reading. The reading is an excerpt from his book, *Prison Writings,* which is written in diary-like vignettes reflecting back upon his life. Peltier is currently in a federal prison as a result of his role in a political protest organized by AIM. Although he is charged with the murder of a federal officer, the key witnesses used by the government to convict him have now confessed that they were coerced by federal officials into providing false testimony. However, this evidence has not been allowed to grant him a pardon or retrial, and he has been imprisoned for decades. This Reading begins with Peltier explaining why he sees himself as an Indian, and not an American, and continues to assert how prison has been just one way the government has sought to contain the Native American population. Peltier's reflections on his early years demonstrate the persistent poverty, dehumanizing "civilizing" education, and violent discrimination and prejudice that Native Americans faced, including Eisenhower's "termination and relocation" policy of the 1950s, which directly impacted the young Peltier. Peltier's writing shows the struggle Native Americans face just to speak their own language and practice their own religion—actions he describes as his "first crimes" in the eyes of authorities. We see how Indian culture and customs are a healing comfort to Peltier, and simultaneously we see how difficult it is just to be able to know and practice one's culture due to the dominant group's extermination efforts toward Native Americans.

Charon Asetoyer concurs with Peltier that the key issue facing Native Americans is survival. However, Asetoyer deals with survival in a biological sense and focuses on health care needs. She describes how what was supposed to be a temporary stay on her husband's Sioux reservation brought her face to face with a deplorable lack of basic health care, especially for women and children. She started a grassroots organization to address the issue, and she describes her struggles to make headway in providing even the most basic of services. Why have these problems not been addressed in the past? Why do minority group members—especially women and children—have such poor access to health care?

TRENDS AMONG AMERICAN INDIANS IN THE UNITED STATES[1]

Russell Thornton

Scholars debate the size of the aboriginal population north of present-day Mexico, and the magnitude of population decline beginning sometime after A.D. 1500 and continuing to about 1900. Early in the twentieth century, for the region north of the Rio Grande, James Mooney estimated individual indigenous tribal population sizes at first European contact, summed them by regions, then totaled them, arriving at an estimate of 1,152,950 aboriginal people in that region of what would become North America (Mooney, 1910, 1928). Subsequent scholars generally accepted Mooney's estimate, although one—Alfred L. Kroeber—suggested the number was excessive and lowered it.

In 1966, however, Henry Dobyns used depopulation ratios to assert an aboriginal population size, for this area, of between 9 and 12 million people (Dobyns, 1966). In 1983, Dobyns used depopulation ratios from epidemics along with possible carrying capacities to assert some 18 million native Americans for North America—i.e., northern Mexico as well as the present-day United States, Canada, and Greenland (Dobyns, 1983).

Most scholars now agree that Mooney's population estimate significantly underestimated aboriginal population size for the area north of the Rio Grande and, thus, the baseline from which the area's aboriginal population decline may be assessed.[2] By the same token, most scholars consider Dobyns's estimates to be excessive.[3] Other contemporary estimates, some of which are shown in Table 6.1, have varied from around 2 million to somewhat more than 7 million. The 7+ million estimate for north of present-day Mexico (Thornton, 1987) includes more than 5 million people in the present-day United States area and more than 2 million for present-day Canada, Alaska, and Greenland. Despite dissension about earlier population levels, there is no argument that substantial depopulation did occur after European arrival. The native population of the United States, Canada, and Greenland reached a nadir of perhaps 375,000 by 1900 (Thornton, 1987), although a somewhat larger nadir population has been argued (Ubelaker, 1988).

Trends in demographics, as well as in tribal sovereignty, economic development, education, and repatriation will be discussed here, with emphasis on change since the 1950s.

Table 6.1 Twentieth Century Estimates of the Aboriginal Population of North America

North America[a]	United States	Research (Date)
1,148,000	846,000	Mooney (1910)
1,148,000	—	Rivet (1924)
2–3,000,000	—	Sapper (1924)
1,153,000	849,000	Mooney (1928)
1,002,000	—	Wilcox (1939)
900,000	720,000	Kroeber (1931)
1,000,000	—	Rosenblatt (1945)
1,000,000	—	Steward (1949)
2–2,500,000	—	Ashbum (1947)
1,001,000	—	Steward (1949)
2,240,000	—	Aschmann (1959)
1–2,000,000	—	Driver (1961)
9.8–12,500,000	—	Dobyns (1966)
3,500,000	2,500,000	Driver (1969)
2,171,000	—	Ubelaker (1976)
4,400,000	—	Denevan (1976)
—	1,845,000	Thornton (1981)
18,000,000	—	Dobyns (1983)
5–10,000,000	—	Hughes (1983)
12,000,000	—	Ramenofsky (1987)
7,000,000	5,000,000	Thornton (1987)
1,894,000	—	Ubelaker (1988)
2–8,000,000	—	Zamberdino (1989)

a. North of Mesoamerica.

DEMOGRAPHIC AND RELATED TRENDS

Population Recovery

At the beginning of the twentieth century, the American Indian population of the United States and Canada began to increase. For the United States, census enumerations suggest almost continuous increase since 1900 (Table 6.2), a result of both decreases in mortality rates and increases in fertility rates. In fact, fertility has remained higher for American Indians than

Table 6.2 American Indian and Alaska Native[a] Population in the United States, 1900-1990

Year	Population
1900	237,000
1910	291,000
1920	261,000
1930	362,000
1940	366,000
1950	377,000
1960	552,000
1970	827,000
1980	1,420,000
1990	1,959,000
2000	2,475,956

a. American Indian, Inuit, and Aleut.
SOURCE: U.S. Bureau of the Census (1993).

for the U.S. population as a whole (see Thornton et al., 1991). The increase has also been a result of changes in the number of individuals self-identifying as "Indian" on recent U.S. censuses. Not including Inuits (Eskimo) and Aleuts, the American Indian population increased from 524,000 in 1960, to 793,000 in 1970, to 1.4 million in 1980, to more than 1.8 million in 1990, largely because of changing racial definitions from one census to another. It has been estimated that about 25 percent of the change from 1960 to 1970, about 60 percent of the change from 1970 to 1980, and about 35 percent of the change from 1980 to 1990 resulted from these changing identifications (Passel, 1976; Passel and Berman, 1986; Harris, 1994). Changing self-identification has generally been attributed to racial and ethnic consciousness-raising during the 1960s and 1970s, as well as American Indian political mobilization during the period.[4]

If Inuits and Aleuts are added to the more than 1.8 million American Indians enumerated in the 1990 Census, there was a total of more than 1.9 million native Americans in the United States in 1990 (U.S. Bureau of the Census, 1994). Adding in natives of Canada, the total in 1990 was approximately 2.75 million native Americans. This is obviously a significant increase over the 375,000 estimated for 1900 (Thornton, 1987); however, it is far less than the 7+ million in 1492. It is also only a very small fraction of the total population of the United States (more than 250 million in 1990) and Canada (more than 25 million in 1990).

U.S. census enumerations also provide self-reported tribal affiliations and ancestries. According to the 1990 Census, the 10 largest tribal affiliations in the United States are Cherokee, 308,000; Navajo, 219,000; Chippewa (Ojibwe), 104,000; Sioux, 103,000; Choctaw, 82,000; Pueblo, 53,000; Apache, 50,000; Iroquois, 49,000; Lumbee, 48,000; and Creek, 44,000 (U.S. Bureau of the Census, 1993: Figure 6.1).[5]

Tribal Enrollment

There are 317 American Indian tribes in the United States that are "recognized" by the federal government and receive services from the U.S. Bureau of Indian Affairs (BIA). There are also some 217 Alaska Native Village Areas identified in the 1990 Census, with populations of 9,807 American Indians, 32,502 Inuits, and 4,935 Aleuts (U.S. Bureau of the Census, 1992), some 125 to 150 tribes that are seeking federal recognition, and dozens of other groups who might do so in the future.

In 1990, some 437,079 American Indians, 182 Inuits, and 97 Aleuts lived on 314 reservations and trust lands; half of these—218,290 American Indians, 25 Inuits, and 5 Aleuts—lived on the 10 largest reservations and trust lands (Table 6.3; U.S. Bureau of the Census, 1993).

BIA has, generally, required a one-fourth degree of American Indian "ancestry" (blood

Table 6.3 The 10 Largest Reservations and Trust Lands

Navajo Reservations and Trust Lands	143,405
Pine Ridge Reservation and Trust Lands	11,182
Fort Apache Reservation	9,825
Gila River Reservation	9,116
Papago Reservation	8,480
Rosebud Reservation and Trust Lands	8,043
San Carlos Reservation	7,110
Zuni Pueblo	7,073
Hopi Pueblo and Trust Lands	7,061
Blackfeet Reservation	7,025

SOURCE: U.S. Bureau of the Census (1993).

quantum) and/or tribal membership to recognize an individual as American Indian.

Tribal membership requirements are typically set forth in tribal constitutions, approved by BIA. Each tribe also has a set of requirements for membership (enrollment) of individuals, generally including a blood-quantum requirement, and requirements vary widely (Table 6.4). The Walker River Paiute require at least a one-half Indian (or tribal) blood quantum, while many tribes—e.g., Navajo—require a one-fourth blood quantum. Some tribes, generally in Oklahoma or California, require a one-eighth or one-sixteenth or one-thirty-second blood quantum. Many tribes have no minimum blood-quantum requirement, but do require some degree of American Indian lineage

(Thornton, 1997). American Indian tribes on reservations tend to have higher blood-quantum requirements for membership than those not on reservations, as indicated in Table 6.4; and those with higher blood-quantum requirements tend to be slightly smaller than tribes with lower blood-quantum requirements.

The total membership of the more than 300 federally recognized tribes in the late 1980s was slightly more than 1 million; hence, only about 60 percent of the more than 1.8 million individuals self-identified as American Indian on the 1990 Census were actually enrolled in a federally recognized tribe (Thornton, 1997). Differences in self-identification and tribal enrollment varied considerably from tribe to tribe. For example, most of the more than 219,000 Navajo in the 1990 Census were enrolled in the Navajo Nation, but only about one-third of the more than 300,000 Cherokee were enrolled in one of the three Cherokee tribes—Cherokee Nation of Oklahoma, Eastern Band of Cherokee Indians, and United Keetoowah Band of Cherokee Indians.[6]

Redistribution and Urbanization

By the beginning of the twentieth century, American Indian groups that survived European contact had been redistributed (Figure 6.1). Much of this redistribution occurred during the nineteenth century with American Indian "removals," the establishment of the reservation

Table 6.4 Blood-Quantum Requirements by Reservation Basis and Membership Size

	More Than ¼	¼ or Less	No Minimum Requirement
Number of tribes	21	183	98
Reservation based	85.7%	83.1%	63.9%
Median number of individual members	1,022	1,096	1,185

SOURCES: Thornton (1987), U.S. Bureau of Indian Affairs (unpublished tribal constitutions and tribal enrollment data obtained by author).

NOTE: Information not available for 15 tribes.

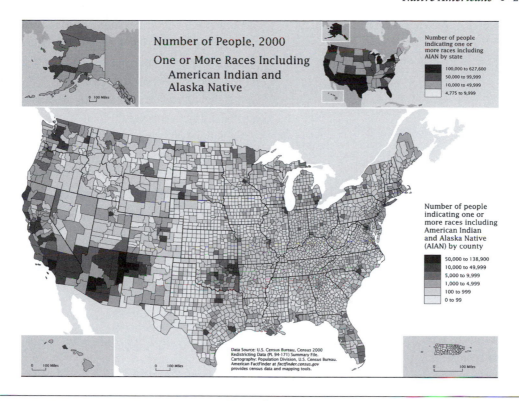

Figure 6.1 Native American Populations According to the 1990 Census

SOURCE: U.S. Bureau of the Census (2000). URL: http://tiger.census.gov/cgi-bin/mapbrowse.tbl.

system, and the subsequent elimination and allotment of some reservations. According to the 1990 Census, the 10 states with the largest American Indian populations were: Oklahoma, 252,000; California, 242,000; Arizona, 204,000; New Mexico, 134,000; Alaska, 86,000; Washington, 81,000; North Carolina, 80,000; Texas, 66,000; New York, 63,000; and Michigan, 56,000 (U.S. Bureau of the Census, 1993).

A redistribution of American Indians also occurred through urbanization in the United States and Canada. As shown in Table 6.5, only 0.4 percent of the American Indians in the United States lived in urban areas in 1900. By 1950, the number had increased to 13.4 percent; in 1990, 56.2 percent of American Indians lived in urban areas (U.S. Bureau of the Census, 1992; Thornton, 1997).

Important in this urbanization was the migration to cities and towns, some of which occurred under the BIA relocation program, which began in 1950 to assist American Indians in moving from reservations and rural areas to selected urban areas (Thornton, 1994). U.S. cities with the largest American Indian populations are New York City, Oklahoma City, Phoenix, Tulsa, Los Angeles, Minneapolis-St. Paul, Anchorage, and Albuquerque (Thornton, 1994).[7]

Issues in the Twenty-First Century

New demographic threats will be faced by American Indians in the twenty-first century because of urbanization and its partner, intermarriage. As populations of American Indians declined, and as they came into increased contact

Table 6.5 Percentage of Urban American Indian Population in the United States, 1900 to 1990

Year	Percentage Urban
1900	0.4
1910	4.5
1920	6.1
1930	9.9
1940	7.2
1950	13.4
1960	27.9
1970	44.5
1980	49.0
1990	56.2
2000	57.5

with Whites, Blacks, and others, American Indians increasingly married non-Indians, and this pattern has accelerated with the recent increase in urbanization. In the United States today, almost 60 percent of all American Indians (as defined by the Office of Management and Budget) are married to non-Indians (Sandefur and McKinnell, 1985; Eschbach, 1995). It has also been argued that those "Native Americans" by way of self-identification—or "'new' Native Americans" (Thornton, 1997)—are more likely to be intermarried (Eschbach, 1995; Nagel, 1995).

Urbanization has also created some decreased sense of tribal identity. In the 1970 Census, about 20 percent of American Indians overall reported no tribal affiliation. Only about 10 percent of those on reservations reported no affiliation, whereas 30 percent of those in urban areas reported no affiliation (Thornton, 1987). The 1980 and 1990 Censuses report no comparable urban/reservation data; however, 25 percent of the American Indians in the 1980 Census and 15 percent of those in the 1990 Census reported no tribal affiliation (Thornton, 1994; U.S. Bureau of the Census, 1994). The 1990 Census also indicates that only about one-fourth of all American Indians speak an Indian language at home (U.S. Bureau of the Census, 1992); census

enumerations indicate also that urban residents are far less likely than reservation residents to speak an Indian language or participate in cultural activities (Thornton, 1987).

If these trends continue, both the genetic and tribal distinctiveness of the total American Indian population will be greatly lessened. An American Indian population comprised primarily of "'old' Native Americans" strongly attached to their tribes will change to a population with a predominance of "'new' Native Americans" who may or may not have tribal attachments or even tribal identities. It may even make sense at some point in the future to speak mainly of Native American ancestry or ethnicity (Thornton, 1997).

SOVEREIGNTY AND POLITICAL PARTICIPATION

The idea of American Indian tribal sovereignty within the United States and the related issue of political participation within the larger American society have long been important issues for American Indians. They have, however, achieved new prominence in recent decades.

Sovereignty: Myth or Reality?

Chief Justice John Marshall described American Indian tribes as "domestic dependent nations" with "aspects of sovereignty" (Strickland, 1998). As Strickland pointed out (Strickland, 1998):

> [F]rom the beginning of the Republic, the courts have acknowledged that Native American government is rooted in an established legal and historical relationship between the United States and Native American tribes or nations. This is at the heart of Native American constitutionalism and grows from precontact tribal sovereignty. [Moreover] the rights and obligations of Native Americans, unique to Indian law, derive from a legal status as members or descendants of a sovereign Indian tribe, not from race. [Nevertheless] for the Native American, law and the courts

have been seen alternatively as shields of protection and swords of extermination, examples of balanced justice and instruments of a conquering empire (p. 248).

The federal government has a long history of defining, and thereby determining, the tribal status of both American Indian groups and American Indian individuals (Thornton, 1987). In 1871, Congress enacted legislation that basically destroyed tribal sovereignty, by ending the rights of American Indian groups to negotiate treaties with the United States. It said, "Hereafter no Indian Nation or Tribe within the Territory of the United States shall be acknowledged or recognized as an independent nation, tribe, or power with whom the United States may contract by treaty" (Blackwell and Mehaffey, 1983:53). Between then and 1934, American Indian tribes "became increasingly disorganized, in part because of other legislation passed in the late 1800s calling for the allotment of tribal lands" (Thornton, 1987:195). In 1934, the Indian Reorganization Act was passed, allowing that an American Indian group had "rights to organize for its common welfare," and delineated steps whereby this might occur (Cohen, 1982). Subsequently, though, "the U.S. government adopted policies more or less aimed at ending the special legal status of American Indian tribes, and in fact, 61 tribes were officially terminated" (Thornton, 1987:195)—i.e., no longer recognized by the federal government for the purposes of having relations.

Self-Determination Since Nixon

President Richard Nixon rejected the idea of terminating American Indian tribes, and in 1976 the Federal Acknowledgment was created, specifying seven mandatory criteria for an American Indian group to achieve federal recognition. It also placed the "burden of proof" on the American Indian group itself (Thornton, 1987). The seven criteria are:

1. A statement of facts establishing that the petitioner has been identified from historical times until the present on a substantially continuous basis, as "American Indian," or "aboriginal."

2. Evidence that a substantial portion of the petitioning group inhabits a specific area or lives in a community viewed as American Indian and distinct from other populations in the area, and that its members are descendants of an Indian tribe which historically inhabited a specific area.

3. A statement of facts which establishes that the petitioner has maintained tribal political influence or other authority over its members as an autonomous entity throughout history until the present.

4. A copy of the group's present governing document, or in the absence of a written document, a statement describing in full the membership criteria and the procedures through which the group currently governs its affairs and its members.

5. A list of all known current members of the group and a copy of each available former list of members based on the tribe's own defined criteria.

6 . The membership of the petitioning group is composed principally of persons who are not members of any other North American tribe.

7. The petitioner is not, nor are its members, the subject of congressional legislation which has expressly terminated or forbidden the federal relationship (U.S. Bureau of Indian Affairs, 1978).

Given that a tribe is federally recognized, however, "the courts have consistently recognized that one of an Indian tribe's most basic powers is the authority to determine questions of its own membership. A tribe has power to grant, revoke, and qualify membership" (Cohen, 1982).

Legal Status Today

Today, American Indian tribes as entities are healthy, if not thriving. Both tribes and individuals, however, are dominated by a maze of laws and their interpretation. Strickland (1998) notes:

> Much contemporary confusion results from the duality of traditional tribal law and federally enforced regulations. . . . The courts have powers of life-and-death proportion over tribal existence. The nature of U.S. constitutional law and public policy is such that legal issues loom large in even the smallest details of Native American cultural, economic, and political life. More than four thousand statutes and treaties controlling relations with Native Americans have been enacted and approved by Congress. Federal regulations and guidelines implementing these are even more numerous. The tribe's own laws, and some state statutes dealing with Indians, further complicate this legal maze (p. 252).

Importantly, American Indian tribes and individuals are unique in American society— they are the only segment of the U.S. population with a separate legal status, both as groups and as individuals.

> As Native American peoples prepare to move into the twenty-first century, the issues facing tribes are not substantially different from those faced over the last five centuries. . . . The miracle of the past 500 years is that Native American people and their values have survived in the face of the most unbelievable onslaughts. There is little question that the law and the courts have been, and will continue to be, a major battlefield in the struggle for sovereign survival (Strickland, 1998:255).

Increased Political Participation

Until the late nineteenth century, American Indians were the dominant "minority group" the U.S. government had to deal with on the national, political scene. From the Civil War until the 1980s, however, American Indians were a "moral" but not "powerful" minority political group.

With the reaffirmation and reestablishment of American Indian tribes as legal entities since the 1970s, and the accompanying economic well-being of some of these tribes, however, American Indian tribes are becoming increasingly important and increasingly sophisticated political actors, something we have not seen since the subjugation of the great Sioux Nations around 1890.

Economic Development and Economic Well-Being

One of the most intriguing developments since the 1970s is the increased economic development of American Indian tribes and the increased control of American Indian tribes over this development. As Snipp (1988) noted,

> Historically, American Indians have been one of the most economically deprived segments of American society. Joblessness and the accouterments of poverty, such as high infant-mortality rates and alcoholism, have been a traditional plague among Indian people (p. 1). . . . [A]s internal colonies, Indian lands are being developed primarily for the benefit of the outside, non-Indian economy (p. 3). [Thus] the tribes have been relatively unsuccessful in capturing the material benefits of development, and some observers claim that Indians are now exposed to subtle forms of economic exploitation, in addition to the political dominance they have experienced as captive nations.

Since Snipp made his arguments, the situation has changed partially; certainly not totally.

What Is Tribal Economic Development? Does It Translate to Tribal and Individual Well-Being?

Tribal economic development is generally conceived of as an increase in economic activities, particularly successful ones, on the part of the tribe itself as an entity, rather than increased economic well-being of tribal members per se. Individual economic well-being, nevertheless, is an important objective of tribal economic development; and American Indian tribes and individuals engage in virtually the entire spectrum of economic activities available in modern society, ranging from small service industries to manufacturing to extraction of natural resources—fishing, logging, hunting, etc. In some instances, the ability to exploit such resources has involved extensive legal issues engendered by American Indians' unique legal status in American society (Olson, 1988).

Tribes are also engaged in activities more specifically related to American Indian culture and themselves as American Indian peoples or peoples in rural areas. As is the case with many indigenous peoples worldwide, American Indian tribes are often involved in tourism, as objects of tourism or providers of facilities for tourists in tribal areas or both. Activities related to tourism on tribal lands include running museums, gift shops, gas stations, hotels, and restaurants; providing transportation and other direct services; and performing cultural plays, pow wows, dances, and, sometimes, ceremonies.

American Indian tribes have also engaged in economic activities available to them because of (rather than in spite of) their unique legal status in American society. First and foremost is legal gambling. In some instances, tribes have built and/or operate large, successful casinos that have brought some degree of prosperity to them and their members. Some of the more successful ones are operated by the Mississippi Choctaw in Philadelphia and Mississippi and by the Pequot in Connecticut.

Generally, tribal and individual economic well-being go hand in hand. It is not, however, always a simple, straightforward matter. For example, it is typically an issue of some discussion—and often dissension—as to how much of the "profits" from economic activities are to be either turned back into the business in question; used for tribal activities involving health, education, and welfare programs; distributed to tribal members individually; or used to fund other tribal activities. "Other activities" might include buying sacred tribal sites back from state governments (the Mississippi Choctaw considered buying their sacred mound from Mississippi), or giving donations to the National Museum of the American Indian (as did the Pequot), or making direct political campaign contributions (as was the case with the Southern Cheyenne of Oklahoma).

Conflicting Values and Traditions

Important in the decision to engage in economic activities is the issue of the type of activity to engage in and how chosen activities may or, typically, may not fit into the traditional cultural values of the tribe. Nowhere does more conflict occur than in considering the issue of gambling. Some tribes have explicitly decided not to engage in such activities—as profitable as they might be—because they conflict with important values. Wilma Mankiller, the former principal chief of the Cherokee Nation of Oklahoma, said that one of the most difficult decisions she made as principal chief was the decision that the Nation would not engage in gaming. "I literally cried when I made the decision," she said (personal conversation with the author). Gaming could have been very profitable for the Cherokee Nation and could have improved the economic well-being of tribal members, but it is also against Cherokee values.

There are American Indian communities who see economic development either as a return to old subsistence practices or as simply a reaffirmation of such practices. The attempt by the Makah Nation of Neah Bay, Washington, to return to traditional whaling practices is a case in point. Similarly, there are Inuit communities in Alaska who still cherish their traditional, subsistence lifestyles and are determined to preserve them.

EDUCATION OF AMERICAN INDIANS

Europeans sought to convert to Christianity and educate ("civilize," as they defined it) the native peoples of this hemisphere since, virtually, their first arrival. . . .

The efforts were very much a part of European colonization: "Indians could not be Christians until they first abandoned native habits and accepted 'civilized' customs. . . . 'Civilization and salvation' was the credo of nearly every North American missionary, which often proved to be a euphemism for cultural invasion and tribal decline" (Ronda and Axtell, 1978:30). Europeans' plans for the education of American Indians included not only mission schools but also colleges. The objectives were basically the same—train an elite group of natives who would then teach their own people "civilization and salvation." . . .

Government Schools

As Whites struggled with the idea of the new country they were creating, they sought to place American Indians within it. It became important for enlightened thinkers, like the revolutionary founding fathers, to believe that American Indians could attain equality with Whites through proper training. . . .

Thomas Jefferson advocated intermarriage as well as the adoption of White lifestyles through training. After telling a gathering of Indians to adopt farming and private property, he predicted to them, "you will become one people with us; your blood will mix with ours, and will spread with ours over this great island" (Jefferson). Thus, intermarriage with Whites would "uplift"

the entire American Indian race. The problem was those American Indians who insisted on being "Indians" and living un-"White" lifestyles. The solution became mandatory training and education for all American Indians.

. . .

Boarding and Other Schools

When one thinks of the history of the education of American Indians, one thinks first of the American Indian boarding and day schools provided by the U.S. government primarily for elementary and secondary education and vocational and technical training. The schools began generally after the Civil War, with many established in the 1870s through 1890s. Several were on reservations.

In 1878, a group of American Indian students were sent to Hampton Normal and Agricultural Institute (now Hampton University) in Virginia, established in 1868 for former slaves. The Indians were some of the Kiowa, Comanche, and Cheyenne former prisoners, members of southern plains tribes, involved in the "Outbreak of 1874" during the winter of 1874–1875. They had been imprisoned at Fort Marion, Florida.[8] Other American Indian students soon followed, and American Indians continued to attend Hampton until 1923.

Carlisle Indian School, of football and Jim Thorpe fame, established at Carlisle, Pennsylvania, in 1879, under Richard H. Pratt, was the first American Indian off-reservation boarding school. It restricted students' access to their families and gave them half a day of education and half a day of work. It also had an outing system, whereby students were placed with a White family to work for three years. Other boarding schools included Chilocco Industrial School in Oklahoma (1884), Albuquerque Indian School (1886), Santa Fe School (1890), Phoenix School (1892), Pipestone Indian

Table 6.6   Schools Under the Auspices of the Five Tribes

	Schools		*Orphan Homes/ Academies*	*Others*
	Day	*Boarding*		
Cherokee Nation	140	1	1	1 colored high school 2 seminaries
Creek Nation	52	6(2 colored)	1(1 colored)	
Choctaw Nation	190		5	
Chickasaw Nation	16	3	1	
Seminole Nation	Unknown number of schools			

NOTE: "Colored" denotes schools for former slaves of the Cherokee and Creek nations.
SOURCE: U.S. Bureau of Indian Affairs (1903).

Training School in Minnesota (1893), Chamberlain School in South Dakota (1898), and Riverside School in California (1902).

A 1903 report (U.S. Bureau of Indian Affairs, 1903) describes 221 government schools on reservations, 93 boarding schools, and 128 day schools, in addition to schools provided by states and schools in Indian Territory under the auspices of the Five Tribes (Table 6.6). Also listed are 26 off-reservation boarding schools and five off-reservation day schools.

A quarter-century later, it was realized that such schools were not providing the appropriate type of education. The Meriam Report of 1928 noted "that the whole Indian problem is essentially an educational one" (Meriam, 1928:348), and called for the redirection of the education of American Indians. As a result, the 1930s became a turning point, with educational objectives becoming more sympathetic to American Indians. Slowly, schools established for American Indians began to incorporate aspects of American Indian history and culture into their curricula. Following the Meriam Report, the number of boarding schools decreased, as students were increasingly channeled to day schools and, especially, public schools.

By the 1950s, public school education for American Indians had become more prevalent, following legislation terminating federal relationships with tribes and the relocation of American Indians to urban areas, "thus dumping many thousands of additional Indian students into the *public* school system" (Noriega, 1992:386). There were still, however, well over 200 American Indian schools run by the U.S. government. By 1968, the education of American Indians in the United States was, in the words of the U.S. Senate Special Subcommittee on Indian Education, "a national tragedy" (Prucha, 1975). The solution was greater involvement of American Indians in their own schools. Specific federal legislation was passed—the Indian Education Act of 1972 and the Indian Self-Determination and Educational Assistance Act of 1975. Also "survival schools" were established by the American Indian Movement, in urban areas primarily (Heart of the Earth in Minneapolis and The Red Schoolhouse in St. Paul, Minnesota), but also on reservations.

In 1999, there were almost 100 American Indian day and boarding schools.

Colleges

The first all-American Indian college in North America was Bacone College in Muskogee, Oklahoma, founded in 1880 by the Baptist Home

Mission Board. Several academies were then established to provide students for Bacone—the Cherokee Academy, the Choctaw Academy, the Seminole Female Academy, the Waco Baptist Academy for the Wichita (at Anadarko), and The Lone Wolf Mission among the Kiowa (Prucha, 1975).

Pembroke State University was established in 1887 at Lumberton, North Carolina, it, too, solely for the education of American Indians. Originally an elementary and secondary school, Pembroke became a two-year, then four-year college, then a university in 1969, and was the only four-year, state-supported university in the United States exclusively for American Indians. Both Bacone and Pembroke State eventually expanded their mandate to include non-American Indians.

Haskell Indian Nations University (formerly Haskell Institute) in Lawrence, Kansas, was first established as the U.S. Indian Industrial Training School in 1884 as a boarding school focused on agricultural education. A decade later it changed its name to Haskell Institute as it expanded its training. In 1970, it became Haskell Indian Junior College; its current nam was taken in 1993, after receiving accreditation to offer a bachelor's degree in education. It is still only for American Indians, and provides higher education to federally recognized tribal members. In 1995, it had the full-time equivalent of 890 students, representing some 147 tribes.

Since 1969, 29 tribal colleges have been established, either solely or primarily for American Indians. The first was the Navajo Community College in Tsaile, Arizona (1969). Typically, these schools are two-year community colleges offering associate degrees in academic, vocational, and technical areas; they also have programs in American Indian studies, frequently focused on their own tribe. As of 1996, there were three four-year colleges and one offering a master's degree (National Research Council, 1996:56). There are also other two-year community colleges, not wholly tribally run, that offer instruction in American Indian studies.

American Indian Studies

The Civil Rights Movement emerged fully in the 1960s. Accompanying it was heightened ethnic consciousness; not only Black became beautiful, any shade became beautiful and any ethnic origin became meaningful. Against these forces, the American academic system was changed. Students became important decision makers in their own education and educational institutions. Formerly all-male colleges became co-ed; and colleges and universities became more racially and ethnically integrated. As increasing numbers of minority students entered higher education, ethnic studies developed organizationally, if not intellectually. Ethnic studies courses found their way into curricula; and ethnic studies programs, departments, and degrees were created. A main driving force was the increased number of Black students calling for Black studies programs. Other groups followed their lead.

The impetus for the development of "Native American" studies was increased numbers of American Indian students. They formed organizations and associations and lobbied university faculties and administrators for academic programs to accompany the student support programs that were developing, and to receive their share of the ethnic studies impetus.

By the mid-1970s, 76 of 100 colleges and universities surveyed had courses dealing with American Indian concerns (Locke, 1974). When American Indian studies entered the academic system, however, it did so primarily as a reaction to the way American Indians were usually studied, rather than as a positive, worthy body of knowledge in its own right. Of particular concern, and inciting particular opposition, was the type of research conducted under the aegis of anthropology, and the "all inclusiveness" of anthropology as the discipline encompassing American Indian studies. An important problem had been anthropology's focus on American Indians at the point of the "ethnographic present," as if frozen in time with little prior history—and certainly no significant subsequent history—as "real" American Indians. In no small way, American Indian studies were also a protest against the technique of researchers establishing "friendships" with American Indians solely for research purposes.

American Indian studies also reacted against the history curriculum's lack of inclusion of American Indians as part of mainstream American history. What American Indian history was included, focused all too frequently on wars, battles, and American Indian warriors, and too little on American Indian views, philosophies, or the oral record. American Indian history was virtually limited to literature covering American Indian-White relationships, as though American Indians had no other history as a group or individually as nations. And, finally, American Indian studies reacted against the almost total lack of study of American Indian societies and cultures by other disciplines, such as sociology, political science, psychology, art, music, literature, religion, or philosophy. The main emphasis of the new area became American Indian history, a topic seemingly present in every American Indian studies program. Focusing on ethnic history was a means of going beyond the traditional anthropological approach, recognizing that American Indians were real people with significant pasts and futures. . . .

There was interest in presenting and describing native cultures, religions, art, music, customs, and practices; and a consideration of contemporary issues was ever-present. Other subjects included federal Indian law (typically not "Native American law," as traditionally practiced), the

education of American Indians, and American Indian languages and linguistics.

There is the same mix of topics 30 years later, although some have been added—e.g., economic development. "Native American" literature is at the forefront of the humanities facet of American Indian studies. American Indian history in the form of "ethnohistory" remains at the forefront of the social science component.[9] . . .

Despite all the activity, American Indian studies as a separate intellectual entity in higher education is underdeveloped. This does not mean that acceptable courses are not offered (though little innovation may be shown in the courses), that important community service and applied activities are not performed, that students are not adequately advised, or even that important research and writings have not been accomplished. All have, to one degree or another.[10] However, the full potential of American Indian studies is unrealized in most American Indian studies programs, in whatever fashion they are organized.

REPATRIATION . . .

The repatriation of American Indian human remains as well as the repatriation of funerary objects and other cultural objects, identified as "objects of patrimony"—i.e., something owned by the entire people—such as wampum belts, or sacred objects such as medicine bundles, is occurring today because of determined efforts by American Indians to achieve legal changes in American society.

Collecting Human Remains as Objects of Study

It has been estimated that objects obtained from graves and other sacred sites, and skeletal remains of "hundreds of thousands" of American

Indians are held in various universities, museums, historical societies, and even private collections in the United States and in other countries (Price, 1991). Whatever the actual figure, the estimates indicate a sizeable problem. It is also estimated that the skeletons, or more typically pieces of them, of several hundred American Indians and countless objects buried with them are uncovered every year in highway, housing, and other types of construction (Price, 1991).

American Indian remains and artifacts have been objects of study and intrigue to non-American Indians for centuries. Reported excavations of American Indian burial sites and mounds date from the eighteenth century. American Indian crania have been objects of particular scientific interest since the early nineteenth century. Various scholars actively collected American Indian remains, seeking to explain possible migration from Asia by comparing American Indians with Asians (Bieder, 1986). They also sought to explain physical and cultural differences between and among native peoples and others; often cultural differences were seen as a result of racial ones. In 1839, Morton published *Crania Americana,* reporting that Caucasians had larger brain capacities and therefore higher intelligence than American Indians, and the "science" of phrenology soon developed. Collecting crania became more widespread, as scholars attempted to relate intelligence, personality, and character to skulls and brains. . . .

Some of the human remains and objects subject to legal repatriation were obtained appropriately, with the permission if not actual support of American Indians at the time. Many, however, were not. The fact that many of the human remains and objects were obtained by grave robbing, theft, and fraudulent acts adds to American Indian discomfort and further legitimates claims for repatriation.

. . .

Important Research Findings

Research on American Indians' skeletal remains has generated much important knowledge about such diverse topics as population size and composition, cultural patterns of tooth mutilation, diseases among populations and customs of treatments for the diseases, life expectancies, growth patterns, population affinities, origins and migrations, and diets, including dates when corn was introduced into the diets of the native peoples of North America (Buikstra, 1992). From studying human remains of American Indians we now know, for example, that tuberculosis was present in this hemisphere prior to European contact, as were some other infectious diseases, especially treponema infections; that certain native groups had serious iron deficiencies from a diet heavily dependent on corn;[11] and that among some groups, males with more social prestige—as reflected by burial objects—were physically larger than males with less social prestige (perhaps because they had better diets, perhaps because bigger men were simply given more prestige).

. . .

Some scholars and others assert that the scientific knowledge to be gained from the remains and cultural objects outweigh claims American Indians may have on them. They argue that the scientific value is important not only to native peoples themselves but to the public at large as scholars attempt to reconstruct histories of American Indians. A related view is that the remains and objects now housed in museums and educational institutions belong not only to American Indians, but to all Americans, even to all peoples of the world, as part of the heritage of all humanity. Yet another view is that scholars are keeping and studying the remains because American Indians do not know what they are doing when requesting repatriation. Perhaps they think that someday American Indians will want this knowledge, and it is up to science to preserve it for them.

The Repatriation Movement

Many American Indians believe repatriation must occur despite any scholarly or general public good that may be derived from the study or display of the remains and objects. They assert that cultural and spiritual factors outweigh science and education. Furthermore, they point out that society and the government have already placed all sorts of restrictions on research deemed inappropriate. Particularly important, American Indians contend, is that Americans have been resolute in regard to returning to the United States the remains of American soldiers who died on foreign shores defending this country. American Indian skeletons obtained from battlefields, as many of those in the Army Medical Museum were, are remains of American Indians who died defending their homelands. It is felt that refusal to return the remains of American Indian warriors killed in battle implies that these fighters—and civilians killed in battles and massacres—are less deserving of an honorable burial than American servicemen and -women who died for the United States.

American Indians have attempted to legally prevent the collection of their human remains and cultural objects for more than a century (Cole, 1985). In the 1970s and 1980s, they increasingly demanded that ancestral remains and sacred objects be returned to them for proper disposal or care. . . .

The private sector also became involved in the repatriation movement, just as it did in the Civil Rights Movement. A major turning point was when Elizabeth Sackler purchased for $39,050 three Hopi and Navajo ceremonial masks in 1991. Her intent was to return them to the tribes. She then established the American Indian Ritual Object Repatriation Foundation to assist native groups in retrieving important cultural objects from private individuals and organizations.[12] The Foundation continues to be active in repatriation.

During the 1980s, the Pan-Indian Repatriation Movement began to experience some success through the passage of federal and state laws not only calling for the repatriation of human remains and objects to descendants, but also preventing the further disenfranchisement of remains and objects. Not only has the success of the repatriation movement revitalized Native America by providing new-found self-esteem, the task of actually repatriating human remains and cultural objects has also revitalized communities by bringing members together in the struggle as well as reaffirming important knowledge about many cultural and sacred objects. It is not always an easy undertaking, however; but the end result is worth it.

. . .

The repatriation process has great potential for bridging the gap between native worlds and larger society. As it developed, repatriation of human remains polarized advocates of reburial and advocates of study and preservation in repositories. Little compromise occurred between American Indian repatriation activists and researchers; yet, some degree of compromise is not only desirable, it is necessary. Science and scholarship have much to offer to American Indians, as American Indians attempt to recapture their lost histories. American Indians are no longer powerless in American society, but are important actors in shaping their own destinies. American Indian values, wishes, and perspectives must be respected by scholars. Although some disciplines such as anthropology have histories of applied work with American Indians, the repatriation process is providing new challenges for the application of scholarly disciplines to real-life concerns of American Indians.

. . .

Summary and Conclusions

Trends in demographics, tribal sovereignty, economic development, education, and repatriation are extremely important for American Indians in American society. Demographically, American Indians are now not only surviving in society, but also increasing in numbers. However, the ways American Indians define themselves, and are defined by our society, are changing; and this may have far-reaching implications for American Indians in the twenty-first century.

American Indian tribal sovereignty is alive if not well, and numerous court cases will continue to emerge as the legal relationships between American Indians and society continue to be debated, refined, and changed. Important, however, is the fact that American Indians may once again emerge as powerful political players on the national scene—not just as moral entities, but also as significant economic entities. This is in part because of the newly possible economic development of American Indian tribes. The twenty-first century holds much promise for American Indians in this regard.

Educationally, American Indians have gained some measure of control over the education of their youth, a trend unlikely to reverse itself in the new century. Also important, educationally, is the emergence of American Indian studies. It has the potential to fundamentally alter American conceptions about American Indians and bring important new knowledge bases within the realm of academe; unfortunately, that potential is largely unfilled.

Finally, the legally mandated repatriation of American Indian human remains and objects back to the native communities from which they came—and to which many would say they belong—is fundamentally altering the relationships of American Indians with society and academe. Important in this is the movement toward alleviating the traumas of history many American Indians experienced with colonialism and still find unresolved.

Notes

1. The sections of this paper on demography, education, and repatriation were drawn freely from my chapters on the same topics in Thornton (1998).

2. Dates for Mooney's regional estimates, from which his overall estimate was derived, varied from a.d. 1600 to a.d. 1845, depending on the region in question. A reason for his underestimate, scholars now realize, was Mooney's assumption that little population decline had occurred prior to his dates for the beginning of an extended European presence in a region. In fact, it seems that prior depopulation had occurred in most, if not all, regions.

3. There have been various criticisms of Dobyns's methodologies, particularly those in his 1983 book but also those in his 1966 paper.

4. Changing self-identification was perhaps also a result of individuals of mixed ancestry who formerly did not identify as American Indian because of the stigma attached to such an identity by the larger society. Clearly, however, some individuals with minimal, or no, Native American ancestry may have identified as American Indian because of the desire to affirm a marginal, or establish a nonexistent, ethnic identity.

5. It should be noted that about 11 percent of those individuals identifying as Native American in the 1990 Census did not report a tribal affiliation.

6. The situation in Canada is somewhat different. In Canada one must be registered under the Indian Act of Canada to be an "official" Indian. Categories of Canadian Indians include: (1) status (or registered) Indians, those recognized under the Act; and (2) nonstatus (or nonregistered) Indians, those never registered under the Act or those who gave up their registration (and became

"enfranchised"). Status Indians are subdivided into treaty and nontreaty Indians, depending on whether the group ever entered into a treaty relationship with the Canadian government. There are also the Métis—individuals of Indian and White ancestry not legally recognized as Indians. Some 500,000 of the 575,000 Canadian Indians in the mid-1980s were registered. About 70 percent of Canadian Indians live on one of the 2,272 reserves. There were 578 bands of Canadian Indians in the early 1980s, most containing fewer than 500 members. Only three bands had more than 5,000 members: Six Nations of the Grand River, 11,172; Blood, 6,083; and Kahnawake, 5,226.

7. Canadian provinces with the largest number of Native Americans are Ontario, British Columbia, Saskatchewan, and Manitoba. Approximately 40 percent of Canadian Native Americans lived in cities in the mid-1980s, particularly Vancouver, Edmonton, Regina, Winnipeg, Toronto, and Montreal. This was an increase from the 30 percent who lived in cities in the early 1970s, and the mere 13 percent who lived in cities in 1961. However, still only about 20 percent of Canadian Inuits live in cities, while only about 30 percent of the status Indians do.

8. This event is represented in the Dohasan Kiowa Winter Count with a picture of Big Meat, who was killed by soldiers. Above his head is a drawing of Fort Sill, Indian Territory (I.T., now Oklahoma), where some Kiowa were also imprisoned. (See A Chronicle of the Kiowa Indians (1832–1892). Berkeley: R. H. Lowie Museum of Anthropology, University of California, Berkeley, pp. 10, 18, footnote O.)

9. The repatriation of American Indian human remains, grave goods, sacred objects, and objects of cultural patrimony from museums, colleges, universities, and elsewhere as mandated by the Native American Graves Protection and Repatriation Act (NAGPRA) of 1990 as well as the National Museum of the American Indian (NMAI) Act of 1989 (which limited its provisions to the Smithsonian Institution) has greatly expanded the importance of ethnohistory, particularly to native peoples but also to museums and educational institutions. Critical to the repatriation process under both NAGPRA and the NMAI Act is the establishment of cultural

affiliation between contemporary groups and historic groups represented by the remains or objects. Thus, American Indian groups may, and often must, present different types of evidence to establish cultural affiliation—archaeological evidence, including physical anthropology, written history, oral traditions, ethnography, etc. For repatriation, archaeology and physical anthropology are important components of ethnohistory, along with anthropology and history. The archaeological record and the written record may be eventually reconciled with American Indian memories, in oral traditions, or otherwise.

10. There are journals devoted to Native American studies—e.g., American Indian Quarterly, Northeast Indian Studies, American Indian Culture and Research Journal, and Wicazo Sa Review.

11. These and other topics are discussed in Verano and Ubelaker (1992).

12. The Foundation has recently published Mending the Circle to assist native groups with their repatriation efforts; it is distributed free of charge to them.

REFERENCES

Bieder, R. 1986 Science Encounters the Indian, 1820–1880: The Early Years of American Ethnology. Norman: University of Oklahoma Press.

Blackwell, C., and J. Mehaffey 1983 American Indians, trust and recognition. In Non-recognized American Indian Tribes: An Historical and Legal Perspective, F. Porter, III, ed. Occasional Papers Series, no. 7. Chicago: The Newberry Library.

Buikstra, J. 1992 Diet and disease in late prehistory. Pp. 87–101 in Disease and Demography in the Americas, J. Verano and D. Ubelaker, eds. Washington, D.C.: Smithsonian Institution Press.

Cohen, F. 1982 [1942] Handbook of Federal Indian Law (reprint). New York: AMS Press.

Cole, D. 1985 Captured Heritage: The Scramble for Northwest Coast Artifacts. Seattle: University of Washington Press.

Dobyns, H. 1966 Estimating Aboriginal American population: An appraisal of techniques with a new hemispheric estimate. Current Anthropology 7:395–416.

——— 1983 Their Number Become Thinned: Native American Population Dynamics in Eastern North America. Knoxville: University of Tennessee Press.

Eschbach, K. 1995 The enduring and vanishing American Indian. Ethnic and Racial Studies 18:95.

Harris, D. 1994 The 1990 Census count of American Indians: What do the numbers really mean? Social Science Quarterly 15:583.

Jefferson, T. n.d. Thomas Jefferson address, War Department, National Archives.

Meriam, L. 1928 The Problem of Indian Administration. Baltimore: The Johns Hopkins Press.

Mooney, J. 1910 Population. In Handbook of American Indians North of Mexico, F. Hodge, ed. Washington, DC: U.S. Government Printing Office.

———. 1928 The aboriginal population of America north of Mexico. In Smithsonian Miscellaneous Collections, Vol. 80, J. Swanton, ed. Washington, DC: U.S. Government Printing Office.

Nagel, J. 1995 Politics and the resurgence of American Indian ethnic identity. American Sociological Review 60:953.

National Research Council 1996 Colleges of Agriculture at the Land Grant Universities: Public Service and Public Policy. Washington, D.C.: National Academy Press.

Noriega, J. 1992 American Indian education in the United States: Indoctrination for subordination to colonialism. In The State of Native America: Genocide, Colonization, and Resistance, M. Jaimes, ed. Boston: South End Press.

Olson, M. 1988 The legal road to economic development: Fishing rights in western Washington. Pp. 77–112 in Public Policy Impacts on American Indian Economic Development, C. Snipp, ed. Albuquerque: Institute for Native American Development, Development Series No. 4, University of New Mexico.

Passel, J. 1976 Provisional evaluation of the 1970 Census count of American Indians. Demography 13:397–409.

Passel, J., and P. Berman 1986 Quality of 1980 Census data for American Indians. Social Biology 33:986.

Price, H., III 1991 Disputing the Dead: U.S. Law on Aboriginal Remains and Grave Goods. Columbia: University of Missouri Press.

Prucha, F., ed. 1975 Documents of United States Indian Policy. Lincoln: University of Nebraska Press.

Ronda, J., and J. Axtell 1978 Indian Missions: A Critical Bibliography. Bloomington: Indiana University Press.

Sandefur, G., and T. McKinnell 1985 Intermarriage among Blacks, Whites and American Indians. Paper presented at the meetings of the American Sociological Association, Washington, DC.

Snipp, C. 1988 Public policy impacts and American Indian economic development. In Public Policy Impacts on American Indian Economic Development, C. Snipp, ed. Albuquerque: Institute for Native American Development, Development Series No. 4, University of New Mexico.

Strickland, R. 1998 The eagle's empire. In Studying Native America: Prospects and Problems, R. Thornton, ed. Madison: University of Wisconsin Press.

Thornton, R. 1987 American Indian Holocaust and Survival: A Population History since 1492. Norman: University of Oklahoma Press.

———. 1994 Urbanization. Pp. 670–671 in Native Americans in the Twentieth Century: An Encyclopedia, M. Davis, ed. New York: Garland.

———. 1997 Tribal membership requirements and the demography of "old" and "new" Native Americans. Population Research and Policy Review 7:9.

———. 1998 Studying Native America: Problems and Prospects. Thornton, R. ed. Madison: University of Wisconsin Press.

Thornton, R., G. Sandefur, and C. Snipp 1991 American Indian fertility history. American Indian Quarterly 15:359–367.

U.S. Bureau of the Census 1992 1990 Census of Population: General Population Characteristics: American Indian and Alaska Native Areas. Washington, DC: U.S. Government Printing Office.

1993 We the . . . First Americans. Washington, DC: U.S. Government Printing Office.

1994 1990 Census of the Population: Characteristics of American Indians by Tribe and Language. Washington, DC: U.S. Government Printing Office.

U.S. Bureau of Indian Affairs 1903 Statistics of Indian Tribes, Agencies, and Schools, 1903. Washington, DC: U.S. Government Printing Office.

1978 Guidelines for Preparing a Petition for Federal Acknowledgment as an Indian Tribe. Washington, DC. photocopy:3, 8–11, 17.

Ubelaker, D. 1988 North American Indian population size, A.D. 1500 to 1985. American Journal of Physical Anthropology 77:289–294.

Verano, J., and Ubelaker, D., eds. 1992 Disease and Demography in the Americas. Washington, DC: Smithsonian Institution Press.

SOURCE: Reprinted with permission from *America Becoming: Racial Trends and Their Consequences*, edited by N. Smelser, W. Wilson, and F. Mitchell. (Vol. 1, pp. 135-160). Copyright © 2001 by the National Academy of Sciences, courtesy of the National Academies Press, Washington, DC.

DISCUSSION QUESTIONS

1. Why do American Indian tribes have to meet a long list of criteria before they can be recognized as a tribe by the federal government? Why is this the only U.S. racial group that has to "prove" its identity for the purposes of federal recognition?

2. On the issue of gambling to bring economic development to Native Americans, what are the different views surrounding this activity? What do these differences tell us about the diversity within the category of "American Indian"?

3. The author suggests that repatriation should involve a fair compromise between the scientific community and American Indian communities in terms of how skeletal remains and artifacts should be used. Do you agree or disagree with this position? If other non-Indian families have to give permission for their families' remains and possessions to be used for science, why haven't Native Americans been accorded these same rights? Can the term "paternalism" be applied here, and if so, how?

GROWING UP INDIAN

Leonard Peltier

Like most Indian people, I have several names. In Indian Way, names come to you in the course of your life, not just when you're born. Some come during childhood ceremonies; others are given on special occasions throughout your life. Each name gives you a new sense of yourself and your own possibilities. And each name gives you something to live up to. It points out the direction you're supposed to take in this life. One of my names is Tate Wikuwa, which means "Wind Chases the Sun" in the Dakota language. That name was my great-grandfather's. Another name, bestowed on me by my Native Canadian brethren, is Gwarth-ee-lass, meaning "He Leads the People."

I find special inspiration in both of those names. The first, to me, represents total freedom—a goal even most of those outside prison walls never achieve. When I think that name to myself—Wind Chases the Sun—I feel free in my heart, able to melt through stone walls and steel bars and ride the wind through pure sunlight to the Sky World. No walls or bars or rolls of razor wire can stop me from doing that. And the second name—He Leads the People—to me, represents total commitment, a goal I strive for even within these walls, reaching out as best I can to help my people.

Maybe it seems presumptuous, even absurd—a man like me, in prison for two lifetimes, speaking of leading his people. But, like Nelson Mandela, you never know when you will suddenly and unexpectedly be called upon. He, too, knows what it's like to sit here in prison, year after year, decade after decade. I try to keep myself ready if ever I'm needed. I work at it within these walls, with my fellow inmates, with my supporters around the world, with people of good will everywhere. A strong leader shows mercy. He compromises for the good of all. He listens to every side and never makes hasty decisions that could hurt the people. I'm trying very hard to be the kind of leader I myself could respect.

So, in our way, my names tell me and others who I am. Each of my names should be an inspiration to me. Here at Leavenworth—in fact anywhere in the U.S. prison system—my official name is #89637-132. Not much imagination, or inspiration, *there.*

My Christian name, though I don't consider myself to be a Christian, is Leonard Peltier. The last name's French, from the French fur hunters and voyageurs who came through our country more than a century ago, and I take genuine pride in that holy blood, too. The name is a shortening of Pelletier, but has come to be pronounced, in the American fashion, Pel-teer. My first name was given to me by my grandmother, who said I cried so hard as a baby that I sounded like a "little lion." She named me Leonard, she said, because it sounded like "lion-hearted." I

don't know how she figured that out, but years later I looked it up in a dictionary of names and found that Leonard literally means "lion-hearted."

Though my bloodline is predominantly Ojibway and Dakota Sioux, I have also married into, and been adopted in the traditional way by, the Lakota Sioux people. All the Lakota/Dakota/Nakota people—also known as Sioux—are one great nation of nations. We Indians are many nations, but one People. I myself was brought up on both Sioux and Ojibway (Chippewa) reservations in the land known to you as America.

I would like to say with all sincerity—and with no disrespect—that I don't consider myself an American citizen. I am a native of Great Turtle Island. I am of the Ikce Wicasa—the Common People, the Original People. Our sacred land is under occupation, and we are now *all* prisoners, not just me.

Even so, I love being an Indian, for all of its burdens and all of its responsibilities. Being an Indian is my greatest pride. I thank Wakan Tanka, the Great Mystery, for making me Indian. I love my people. If you must accuse me of something, accuse me of that—being an Indian. To that crime—and to that crime alone—I plead guilty.

My crime's being an Indian.
What's yours?

. . .

When you grow up Indian you quickly learn that the so-called American dream isn't for you. For you that dream's a nightmare. Ask any Indian kid: you're out just walking across the street of some little off-reservation town and there's this white cop suddenly comes up to you, grabs you by your long hair, pushes you up against a car, frisks you, gives you a couple good jabs in the ribs with his nightstick, then sends you off with a warning sneer: "Watch yourself, Tonto!" He doesn't do that to white kids, just

Indians. You can hear him chuckling with delight as you limp off, clutching your bruised ribs. If you talk smart when they hassle you, off to the slammer you go. Keep these Injuns in their place, you know.

Truth is, they actually need us. Who else would they fill up their jails and prisons with in places like the Dakotas and New Mexico if they didn't have Indians? Think of all the cops and judges and guards and lawyers who'd be out of work if they didn't have Indians to oppress! We keep the system going. We help give the American system of injustice the criminals it needs. At least being prison fodder is *some* kind of reason for being. Prison's the only university, the only finishing school many young Indian brothers ever see. Same for blacks and Latinos. So-called Latinos, of course, are what white man calls Indians who live south of the Rio Grande. White man's books will tell you there are only 2.5 million or so of us Indians here in America. But there are more than 200 million of us right here in this Western Hemisphere, in the Americas, and hundreds of millions more indigenous peoples around this Mother Earth. We are the Original People. We are one of the fingers on the hand of humankind. Why is it we are unrepresented in our own lands, and without a seat—or many seats—in the United Nations? Why is it we're allowed to send our delegates only to prisons and to cemeteries?

Oddly enough, oppressed by the same people, we Indians often wind up fighting each other for what few perks are left to us in prison or society at large. "Set'm against each other and let'm fight it out while we rip them off!" That's been white man's strategy for five hundred years, and, hey, it's worked damned well for them! So, when you grow up Indian, you don't have to become a criminal, you already *are* a criminal. You never know innocence.

I was brought up into a world like that. It's a world most white people never see and will never know. When they do happen to drive by an Indian "rez" while out on vacation to see the four white presidential faces that desecrate the face of the holy mountain they call Mt. Rushmore, they gawk at us. They don't stop and say hello. They don't wave. They don't smile. They gawk. "Look!" the parents tell the kids as they pass by in their shiny car, pointing their finger at us—"There's an Indian!"

. . .

People drive through a reservation and see half a dozen junk cars in some Indian family's front yard and they shake their heads, saying, "These dirty Indians, how can they live like that? Why don't they get rid of those junkers?"

Maybe these people, so quick to judge, don't understand the higher mathematics of being poor. They don't realize that, when you can't afford to buy or commercially repair a car, it may take six or eight junkers out in the yard to keep one junker going on the road. Those yard junkers take on a special value in Indian eyes: they're the source of that hard-to-come-by and almost sacred commodity in Indian country—transportation. Without wheels out in the empty distances of the rez, you're utterly isolated. When the family's one working car breaks down, one of those yard junkers may provide precisely the part that's needed so that Pop can drive seventy miles to town each day to his menial job and help feed his often-hungry family. To such a family, those junkers out in the yard represent survival.

Besides, there's often some old auntie who sleeps, even lives, in those old wrecks. And, if you open the trunk or the glove compartment, you'll often see lovingly stacked rows of Indian corn and beans, sage, and sweetgrass, arranged in there like fine jewels. There's a poetry in those junkyards. Those old junkers can hold holy things in their rusted innards. Sort of like us Indians. Remember that next time you drive through a rez and see those junkers in the yard. They're holy, too.

. . .

I was born on September 12, 1944, in Grand Forks, North Dakota. My father, Leo, was three-fourths Chippewa (Ojibway) and—he always told us—one-fourth French. My mother, Alvina Showers, had a Dakota Sioux mother and a Chippewa father. When I was four my parents separated, then divorced, and my sister Betty Ann and I went to live with my father's parents, Alex and Mary Dubois-Peltier, on the Turtle Mountain Reservation, about four miles north of Belcourt, North Dakota. In Indian Way, the grandparents often bring up the kids; the old knowledge passes down not so much from parent to child as from grandparent to grandchild. That's in part why we honor our Elders. In our way, when you grow old, you *become* an Elder—and that's something to look forward to your whole life. So being raised by my grandparents—"Gramps" and "Gamma" we little kids called them—was one of the truly beautiful things in my life. Gamma taught me the old songs and stories, and even a little medicine. Gramps would take me out hunting, show me how to make things, how to survive all on your own out in the wild.

As a child, I became fluent in *métis*—a French-Indian mixture—as well as English, and I also spoke some Sioux, Ojibway, and French words. Since every language gives you a different view of reality, I soon saw that there were many realities you had to cope with in this life, most of them unpleasant.

At the time, our family used to work in the potato fields, migrating during harvest season from the reservation to the Red River Valley. You picked the spuds by hand, getting only 8 to 10 cents for a bushel. My job when I was small was to run up ahead and shake the spuds loose from the vines so the others could come along and pick them up more quickly. We lived at that time in a small log house, about twenty feet by fifteen feet. No water or electricity. We carried water from a distant spring or well. We cut and hauled wood for heat and cooking. I worked long hours, grew big and strong, and had no particular complaints about life, hard as it was. From my earliest years, living through each day was a matter of survival. That's just the way it was. It seemed natural. It made a survivor of me, that hard life. I've been a survivor ever since.

I was brought up with both Christian religion and Indian traditional religion. My grandmother believed in Indian traditional religion and also was a Catholic. Everyone knew that if you were Catholic, or at least Christian, you got more government assistance. I attended both kinds of services. Gamma didn't really get the spiritual relief she was seeking out of the Catholic's religion, so she never stopped going to Indian ceremonies. For medical problems she often went to a medicine man. That's how I was introduced to Indian religion. I was also introduced to Catholic religion, but that was something I lost faith in at an early age. I must have been about nine years old, I remember thinking to myself that I could never be a good, believing Catholic; it all seemed so harsh and far removed and devoid of human caring, at least where Indians were concerned. I don't want to criticize Catholics; that's just the way a child saw it. Maybe they were a lot harsher in my time than today. I understand there have been changes over the years, I don't know. For the sake of Indian children still in parochial care, I hope so.

In any case, I always felt more at home, more at ease, with Indian religion; it made me feel like I belonged, like I was wanted *as* an Indian and it also seemed loving and caring and wonderfully mystical and bound to our Mother the Earth and our Grandfather the Sky and to Wakan Tanka, the Great Mystery. And, in the sweat lodge and the Sun Dance, it taught you to deal with pain—something white man would always see that you as an Indian would have plenty of in this life. Our Elders spoke of the Original Instructions given to us by Wakan Tanka, and how the very first Instruction of all is to *survive!* Those same Elders taught us that we're not here to *preserve* our tradition, but to *live* it. Those lessons of the Elders have held me in good stead throughout my life. I've needed them often, and will no doubt continue needing them.

. . .

Around 1950, during particularly hard times on the rez, my grandfather took the family out to Montana, hoping to make some money working in the mines or logging camps there. We lived awhile in Butte, where, at age six, I got everyone in trouble by refusing to run away when three white kids started flinging rocks at me. "Go on home, you dirty Indian!" they laughed, using me for what they thought was a defenseless target. I got hit several times before I picked up a small rock, really just a large pebble, and sent it whistling back at them in defense. Damned if it didn't hit one of them smack on the temple. You could see the blood running down his face and he was screaming like he was about to die. I was terrified.

I ran home, hid under the bed, and prayed and prayed that that white boy wouldn't die. "Oh, let him live!" I remember crying. "Let him live!" A while later a big shiny automobile came pulling up in front of our little rented house. Big shiny automobiles always spelled trouble for Indians. A white woman got out. She was yelling and screaming and carrying on, warning she was going to have to put me away in the reformatory and calling Gamma dirty names like "stupid bitch" and "filthy squaw," things like that. When she left she shouted she was going right to the police, have the whole "dirty bunch" of us thrown in jail.

I listened to it all from under the bed, shivering the whole while. When Gamma came in and demanded to know what had happened, I was too scared to even talk. I just held my hand to my mouth. That was one of the few times Gramps ever spanked me; words and a hard look were

usually all that was necessary to keep discipline in our family. But that time Gramps really gave it to me with a horse strap. I kept my hand over my mouth the whole spanking so I wouldn't cry, and he really laid into me. Finally I told him what happened. He shook his head with tears welling up in the wrinkled corners of his eyes, and then he smiled the saddest smile and patted me on the head. He said I wasn't wrong, but that I still shouldn't have done it, throw that stone back at them. I should have thought of the family. Now we'd all have to pack up quick and get right out of there before the law came and made big trouble. "You're not s'posed to rile these white folks, boy," Gramps said. "They'll come back and get you every time. That's just the way they are." We packed up and headed back to North Dakota that very evening. Nobody chided me about it again. In fact, my sister clapped her hands and declared me a hero. "Not a hero," Gramps said, "he's a warrior!" I took tremendous pride in that.

After Gramps died of pneumonia when I was eight, life became really hard for us. My grandmother was left alone. She spoke hardly any English, had almost no income, and was trying to raise three small kids—me, my sister, and our cousin Pauline. I tried stocking the table with my slingshot, coming up with an occasional squirrel or maybe a small bird; mostly Gamma used them to flavor the otherwise vegetarian soup. I never could seem to catch a rabbit with my slingshot, like the big fat ones Gramps had gotten now and then with his single-shot 22 for Gamma's beloved rabbit stew. Given the cold North Dakota winters, hunger became a really big problem for us. We had no bread, no milk, hardly anything else. I thought that gnawing ache in my belly was just the way I was supposed to feel.

One day in the fall of 1953, a big black government car came and took us kids away to the Bureau of Indian Affairs boarding school in Wahpeton, North Dakota. I remember Gamma weeping in the doorway as she watched them take us off. We had no suitcases, just bundles. First thing after we got there, they cut off our long hair, stripped us naked, then doused us with powdered DDT. I thought I was going to die. That place, I can tell you, was very, very strict. It was more like a reformatory than a school. You were whacked on the butt with a yardstick for the smallest infraction, even if you so much as looked someone in the eye. That was considered insubordination, trying to relate to another person as a human being.

I consider my years at Wahpeton my first imprisonment, and it was for the same crime as all the others: being an Indian. We had to speak English. We were beaten if we were caught speaking our own language. Still, we did. We'd sneak behind the buildings, the way kids today sneak out to smoke behind the school, and we'd talk Indian to each other. I guess that's where I first became a "hardened criminal," as the FBI calls me. And you could say that the first infraction in my criminal career was speaking my own language. There's an act of violence for you!

. . .

After graduating from Wahpeton in 1957, I went to Flandreau, down in South Dakota, where I finished ninth grade. Then I went back home to Turtle Mountain Reservation, where my father had returned to live. I guess I was growing up to be a pretty normal teenager. I wanted a car, and built one out of spare parts. I got so good at it that later on, in Seattle, I would get into the body-and-fender shop business.

Living on the rez as a young teen, I attended lots of powwows and religious ceremonies, but I also went to the largely white school dances and listened to a lot of rock radio: Elvis, the Everly Brothers, Buddy Holly were some of my favorites. I was drawn to both cultures. I found myself spread-eagled between them, really, and, like many of my Indian brothers and sisters, I was nearly torn apart by the contradictions and conflicts between the two that I both saw in the outside world and felt within myself.

This was during the last years of the Eisenhower administration, when a resolution was passed by Congress and signed by President Eisenhower to "terminate" all Indian reservations and to "relocate" us off our lands and into the cities. Those suddenly became the most important, the most feared, words in our vocabulary: "termination" and "relocation." I can think of few words more sinister in the English language, at least to Indian people. I guess the Jews of Europe must have felt that way about Nazi words like "final solution" and "resettlement in the East." To us, those words were an assault on our very existence as a people, an attempt to eradicate us.

We were given two choices: either relocate or starve. Later, court decisions would declare this compulsory policy totally illegal, which it was, but that was no comfort to us at the time. We pleaded with the government to let us stay on our land and to create some employment on the reservation, as they had promised to do, but all that was in vain. The ones we went to for help, the Bureau of Indian Affairs, were the last ones, it seemed, with any intention of helping us. It's no accident that the BIA started off back in the 1800s as part of the Department of War. They're still waging war on us today.

To implement their inhuman policy, the federal government in the late 1950s cut off the reservations' already meager supply of food and commodities—the pitiful little "payment" they'd promised us in those treaties to recompense us for all the vast and holy continent they'd stolen. Hunger was the only thing we had plenty of; yeah, there was plenty of that to go around, enough for everybody. When frantic mothers took their bloated-bellied children to the clinic, the nurses smiled and told them the children just had "gas." A little girl who lived right near us on the reservation died of malnutrition. Sounds like "termination" to me.

"Termination" was nothing new in red-white relations, really. They'd been trying to terminate us since 1492. They've always wanted to get rid of us, and I suppose they'll never stop trying. Indian people were offered money to get off the rez and move to cities like Minneapolis, Milwaukee, Cleveland, Los Angeles, and Chicago, where all those wonderful inner-city slums and mean streets were waiting for us. With the reservation under threat of termination, housing was severely limited. Our lands were being leased right out from under us by white ranchers and mining interests, or annexed by the U.S. government. My family, like many others, wound up with nowhere to stay. We were being all but forced off the rez to go to the newly sprouting urban "red ghettos" the government was so keen on sending us to. Sometimes we shuttled between relatives, sometimes we slept in the car.

. . .

I was about fourteen at the time. My dad, who'd returned to live with us, had started attending community meetings on the reservation to discuss the government's decision to terminate Turtle Mountain. I went along with him to those meetings, more to eat the few little snacks they served on such occasions than to hear the political arguments. But at one of those meetings I chanced to do a little listening for a change, and something started stirring deep inside me—even deeper than the hunger in my belly. Some women were weeping aloud about having starving children at home. One Ojibway lady, a cousin of mine—I'll always remember it—stood up angrily and asked in a loud, emotional, tear-filled voice, "Where are our warriors? Why don't they stand up and fight for their starving people?"

That sent electric vibrations from my scalp all the way down my spine to the soles of my feet. It was like a revelation to me—that there was actually something worthwhile you could *do* with your life, something more important than living your own selfish little life day by day. Yes, there was something more important than your poor miserable self—your *People*. You could actually

stand up and fight for them! Now *that* was something I had never learned in school or heard about on the radio. I'd only learned in school and from society at large that being Indian was something I was supposed to be ashamed of, something I was supposed to cast aside for my own well-being. "Kill the Indian to save the man!" was their official motto! Now here was this woman challenging me to the roots of my being with the notion of the *People*. Yes, the People, the Tiospaye as the Lakota call the extended family, and by extension, as I would come to see in later years, *all* Indian people, all indigenous people, all human beings of good heart. I vowed right then and there that I would become a warrior and that I'd always work to help my people. It's a vow I've done my best to keep.

About that same time, I renewed my interest in Indian religion and Indian Way, taking part in ceremonies and sensing something echoing deep inside myself. One night in 1958, a few friends and I sneaked out to watch the Sun Dance at Turtle Mountain, which was held secretly because piercing went on, which was illegal at the time. We got a few close-up glimpses of the Sun Dancers, with the rivulets of blood running down their chests. I was impressed that no one was screaming or hollering or whimpering. Those guys looked fiercely proud; I envied them and vowed that someday I would be a Sun Dancer. Then, my friends and I were actually arrested by BIA police as we came out of the Sun Dance grounds. They claimed we were drunk—a total lie—and jailed us overnight. They were afraid to arrest the Sun Dancers, who would surely have put up a fight, but we young teenagers were there, and we were Indian, so why not arrest us? They did. Here I was, not yet fifteen, and already I was getting firsthand experience in government-fabricated criminal charges and false imprisonment. I began to realize that my real crime was simply being who I was—an Indian.

So speaking my language was my first crime, and practicing my religion was the second.

When I was also arrested that winter for siphoning some diesel fuel from an army reserve truck to heat my grandmother's freezing house, I was arrested again and spent a couple of weeks in jail. That was my first stretch of hard time. So trying to keep my family from freezing was my third crime, the third strike against me. Henceforth, I would be considered "incorrigible." My career as a "hardened criminal" was already well on its way.

SOURCE: From *Prison Writings* by Leonard Peltier. Copyright © 1999 by Leonard Peltier. Reprinted by permission of St. Martin's Press, LLC.

DISCUSSION QUESTIONS

1. Why does Peltier say he does not consider himself an American? When your people grow up for centuries on certain land, and then it is overtaken by people who rename it "America" and treat you as a foreigner in your own land, what kinds of emotions might you experience?

2. What do you think was the rationale behind converting American Indians to Catholicism and sending children to prison-like boarding school? How might this treatment make a young child feel about his or her heritage? When, as a child, Peltier's family had to pick up and move because he fought back against racial slurs, what messages might this have communicated to him about the differences between whites and Indians in American society?

3. What are some of the cultural values and traditions that warm Peltier's heart despite society's disparagement of them? What might be the effect on a group of people for the dominant group to strip away such sources of pride and dignity? Are there ways to annihilate a people without killing them directly? If so, what are some ways to do this, according to Peltier? Are the underestimated counts of Native Americans' population in the United States a part of this process?

FROM THE GROUND UP

Charon Asetoyer

My Husband is Dakota Sioux from the Yankton Sioux reservation, located in the south central part of South Dakota. His father passed away in 1983, and in 1985 we moved to his reservation in order to fulfill our traditional commitment. It is tradition to hold a memorial on the anniversary of a loved one's death for the following four years. It was to be a temporary stay, until our commitment was over. We had planned to move to Oklahoma so I could work for my tribe.

After we had moved to South Dakota, I applied for a job with the Yankton Sioux Tribe. The tribe is small and jobs were held by members of the tribe; it was not likely that I would be hired. I was turned down. But word got around that Clarence Rockboy had married a Comanche woman and had returned home with her, and people were curious to meet me.

Women in particular started to drop by, and I took that opportunity to invite others to come and talk. Before long a group of women were meeting regularly in my home to talk about "women's things." We moved the meetings to an empty bedroom in our basement.

Our conversations centered around problems that women and children were having in the community and what we might do to address them.

By 1986 we were incorporated as a nonprofit organization. My small basement bedroom turned into an office. Women would stop in to have coffee and talk about the problems at home. Early one morning a woman came by to ask me what I knew about Fetal Alcohol Syndrome (FAS). She told me that she had gone on drinking during her pregnancy and that her child, now a teenager, was having many learning problems. She wanted to know where she could get the child tested for FAS. She was frustrated and had nowhere to turn for support or help. Before long we were meeting on a regular basis; she began bringing other mothers to join in. Soon we had a community task force on FAS, the beginning of our first project, "Women and Children in Alcohol."

It was natural that health issues should come up first: in reservation communities across the U.S., health problems are devastating, and some of the worst are on the Yankton Sioux Reservation. The infant mortality rate has been as high as 23.8 per thousand. Diabetes affects 70 percent of the people over the age of 40, and the rates of secondary health conditions caused by diabetes, such as kidney failure, heart attacks, stroke, amputations and blindness, are alarmingly high. Alcoholism is out of control and contributes to many of these health problems, including domestic abuse and fetal alcohol births—one out of four children has FAS. Many health problems are related to poor nutrition, caused by years and even generations of eating government commodity foods that are high in salt, sugars and fat and low in fiber.

Native activists have brought the Indian Health Service under fire for years for their neglect and mistreatment of Native women. In the 1960s sterilization abuses surfaced, as they did again in the eighties when it was revealed that the Indian Health Service had used Depo-Provera on Native women who were developmentally disabled before it was FDA approved. Today the Indian Health Service is still abusing Native women's reproductive rights by limiting our contraception choices. They are promoting contraceptives like Depo Provera and Norplant, as well as sterilization. When the Hyde Amendment took away federal funding for abortion, Native women lost their access to abortion altogether: the Indian Health Service, our primary health care provider, is a division of the U.S. Public Service—that is, the Federal government.

The direction our programs have taken has been determined by the women who have come through our doors. I was sitting at my desk one afternoon working on an article for our newsletter when the phone rang. "Is it true that a tubal ligation can be temporary and that I can have it reversed when I want to have a child?" the caller asked. When I asked her why she wanted the information, she said an Indian Health Service doctor had recommended that she have her tubes tied. The procedure, he told her, could be reversed later if she wanted. Incidents like this spurred us to create a reproductive health program.

Other issues evolved after we started doing workshops in the community. One Saturday morning a young woman came to my front door, banging for someone to let her in. I opened the door and she ran in. I recognized the look of fright and helplessness on her face, and locked the door behind her. During my first marriage I too had been a victim of domestic violence. There I was, standing in the hallway of my home faced with something that I had wanted to leave behind. Only this time I was not the one in need of someone to take me in.

In the course of time we created a program to assist women like this one and their children. We started out with a safe house program, sheltering women in local motels. In 1991, after a long court battle over zoning, the Native American Community Board opened a shelter for women and children fleeing from domestic violence and sexual assault. It now houses eighteen women and children and has provided services for over 900 women and children over the past two and a half years.

As more concerns were brought forward, we needed additional programming and additional staff. The office had grown too small for the organization. Several months earlier I had visited the National Black Women's Health Project in Atlanta, Georgia. The Project was located in a large house which seemed ideal: there was room to grow in, space for program work, a kitchen, a yard, and a strong sense of pride among the staff in their unique working environment. It all seemed so right: why not for us too? We wanted to do nutrition work to address diabetics, so we needed a place to prepare food; we wanted to work with children, so we needed space for them as well as for office work. And if we could buy a house we would no longer have to pay rent to a landlord.

Owning our own place seemed like a good idea but no more than a dream at that point, so I put it in the back of my mind. Who would fund a group of women to buy a house anyway, especially a group of Native American women living on a reservation in South Dakota? I had no idea what the cost of real estate might be in Lake Andes, South Dakota. But I kept thinking about the idea. A friend mentioned a small house she knew of, a fixer-upper, around $5,000 to $7,000. I went to look at it: it did seem to suit our needs.

Shortly after, I was invited to a conference sponsored by the National Women's Health Network, a health advocacy organization based in Washington, D.C. At a networking reception the first evening, I met another woman of color, Luz Alveolus Martinets, the director of the National Latina Health Organization. We talked about the work we were doing, and I eventually told her about our dream of buying a house for our project. When I told her what it would cost, she thought I meant the down payment. But $6,000 was the price for the entire house.

Luz told me that most of the women attending the conference were working women and could afford to make a contribution toward the house. All I had to do was to get up during the next day, when we all had to introduce ourselves, and make an appeal for donations. At lunch I tried to avoid Luz: it seemed too hard to stand up in a crowded room of women I really did not know and ask for money. But Luz found me. Still, when it was my turn to introduce myself, I started to sit down without making my request for donations. Luz kept encouraging me to go ahead and make my request. Before long, all the women in the room wanted to know what we were arguing about. So I went ahead and asked for their help. Then I saw Byllye Avery of the National Black Women's Health Project, across the room, reach into her pocketbook and pull out her checkbook. Byllye held up the first check and announced to the room, "I donate $100." The pocketbooks opened and the checks piled up. It was like a dream: the house was soon to become a reality. I left the conference with about half of the money we needed.

Soon after we purchased the house, people from the community came to help clean, paint and panel the walls. A few weeks of hard work transformed the little brick house across from my home into a warm environment where women and children could come together to share in health education activities and to organize around issues confronting our community. In February 1988, the doors opened on the first Native American Women's Health Education Resource Center based on a reservation, located in Lake Andes, South Dakota, on the Yankton Sioux Reservation.

Not long after the Resource Center opened a young Yankton Sioux woman walked in, introduced herself and asked if she could do her college internship with us. She was interested in working with children. It was time, we decided, for us to examine how we could provide services for children with special needs. The Child Development Program was our answer.

The Program brought children with special needs together to work, play and learn in an after-school program. Fetal alcohol-affected children, latchkey children, gifted children, and children from highly stressed families participate in the program. Today the program has evolved into a Dakota Cultural program in which elders of the Yankton Sioux tribe work with children, teaching them Dakota language, values and spirituality.

An Adult Education Program was not something we had even thought about developing—until one day a call came in from one of the local high school counselors, asking if a sixteen-year-old pregnant student could continue her schooling at the Resource Center with tutoring from our staff. "She's getting too big to sit in class all day long," he said. We said "Sure," and the next week we had a student. Soon after that a mother of one of the children in our Child Development Program asked if we could show her how to use a computer. She said that she already knew how to type, and she could get a job if she knew how to use a computer. This was the beginning of a program that offered job readiness skills and GED completion.

As more women heard about the work and the services that the Resource Center was providing, a feeling of trust was established. Women turned to us for help concerning sterilization abuse, and for information about sexually transmitted diseases, AIDS, family planning and abortion. A high school student came into the Resource Center one afternoon wanting information about pregnancy, AIDS and condoms. She asked if we could get her a home pregnancy test kit, since she thought that

she might be pregnant, but if she went down to the local drugstore for it, the clerk would recognize her and call her mother.

It was not long before we were going into the schools with AIDS and contraception information, and conducting AIDS workshops in the community. We hired four high school students, two girls and two boys, and trained them to be AIDS peer counselors, so they could go back into the community and schools to give out accurate information to other young people.

It became obvious to us that no one else in our community, and no other Native women's groups on other reservations, were doing this kind of work. As women turned to us for information about abortion and issues of reproductive health, we knew that we needed to organize our reproductive health work more formally. Our next move was to bring Native women together in a project that would address our unmet health care needs and the reproductive abuses committed by the Indian Health Service. In 1990, 36 Native women met in Pierre, South Dakota, to form the first Native Women's Reproductive Rights Coalition. The Coalition has developed a reproductive rights agenda that defines the issues of reproductive rights and health as Native women ourselves understand them.

Over the past three years the Native Women's Reproductive Rights Coalition has grown to involve over 150 women from eight states, and it continues to grow each year. It organizes Native women to address such concerns as Norplant and Depo-Provera abuse, environmental issues, abortion, and the oppressive effects of organized religion in reservation communities.

Another central part of the Coalition's work has been to include the teachings of our elders. The passing down of traditional methods of birthing, child spacing, abortion, parenting and "becoming a woman" ceremonies is an important issue for Native women and has become a major mission of the Coalition. Through its work, combined with the direct services of our Resource Center, we can bring into the national and international arena practices and policies that we ourselves have shaped and that truly represent the issues confronting us.

SOURCE: From *Women's Review of Books 11* (July 1994): 22. Reprinted by permission of the author.

DISCUSSION QUESTIONS

1. Research online the women's health groups listed in this article, including the National Black Women's Health Project, the National Latina Health Organization, the Native Women's Reproductive Rights Coalition, and the National Women's Health Network. What are some of the unique issues that these groups attempt to address, and why aren't they currently being addressed by mainstream private or government-funded health programs?

2. Other scholars have noted how race plays an important role in what reproductive health issues are most important to women: while white privileged women fight to be able to have abortions, poor women of color struggle for the right to have children. What is "sterilization" and why is it such an important health issue for Native American women and other women of color?

3. Funds for Asetoyer's programs for Native American women are raised by "passing the hat" at meetings of other women of color's health organizations. After the centuries of government-sanctioned theft of Native lands and resources, why isn't the government playing a more active role in rebuilding these communities?

4. As you read about the health and other educational issues that Asetoyer's programs seek to address, many of them are certainly of concern to all women, not just women of color. Brainstorm and/or research the ways in which concerns like fetal alcohol syndrome, AIDS, and child development are addressed in race-specific programs. How might race-specific programs address these concerns more effectively than programs simply directed toward women at large?

CURRENT DEBATES

ARE INDIAN SPORTS TEAM MASCOTS OFFENSIVE?

Native Americans face many challenges as they address persistent problems like unemployment and poverty. Some of the issues they face are not about money and jobs but are, rather, symbolic and perceptual. How are Native Americans seen by the larger society? What stereotypes linger in American popular culture? How might these stereotypes affect the ability of Native Americans to argue their causes?

The controversies over using Indian mascots for athletic teams illustrate these symbolic battles. What's the harm in using team names like Indians, Seminoles, or Braves? Isn't this just another case of political correctness and ethnic sensitivities being carried too far?

The excerpts below present both sides of this argument. Journalists Price and Woo, in the lead article in the March 4, 2002 issue of *Sports Illustrated* (SI), argue that the team names are not offensive to sports fans or, in fact, to most Native Americans. The opposing point of view is presented by a group of five academics and Indian activists. They raise a number of issues about the SI article, including its use of polling and what they see as a profound bias on the part of the authors and the magazine. In this selection, their analysis of stereotypes and Native Americans is presented.

Indian Symbols and Mascots Are Not Offensive

S. L. Price and Andrea Woo

The thorniest word problem in sports today is the use of Native American names and mascots by high school, college and professional teams. For more than 30 years the debate has been raging over whether names such as Redskins, Braves, Chiefs and Indians honor or defile Native Americans, whether clownish figures like the Cleveland Indians' Chief Wahoo have any place in today's racially sensitive climate and whether the sight of thousands of non-Native Americans doing the tomahawk chop at Atlanta's Turner Field is mindless fun or mass bigotry. It's an argument that, because it mixes mere sports with the sensitivities of a people who were nearly exterminated, seems both trivial and profound . . .

The case of Betty Ann Gross, a member of the Sisseton-Wahpeton Sioux tribe, illustrates how slippery the issue can be. She grew up on a reservation in South Dakota and went to Sisseton High, a public school on the reservation whose teams are called the Redmen. Gross, 49, can't recall a time when people on the reservation weren't arguing about the team name, evenly divided between those who were proud of it and those who were ashamed. Gross recently completed a study that led the South Dakota state government to change the names of 38 places and landmarks around the state, yet she has mixed feelings on the sports issue. She wants Indian mascots and the tomahawk chop discarded, but she has no problem with team names like the Fighting Sioux (University of North Dakota) or even the Redskins. "There's a lot of division," Gross says.

. . .

Although most Native American activists and tribal leaders consider Indian team names and mascots offensive, neither Native Americans in general nor a cross-section of U.S.

sports fans agree. That is one of the findings of a poll conducted for SI. . . . The pollsters interviewed 351 Native Americans (217 living on reservations and 134 living off) and 743 fans. Their responses were weighted according to U.S. census figures for age, race and gender and for distribution of Native Americans on and off reservations. With a margin of error of ± 4%, 83% of the Indians said that professional teams should not stop using Indian nicknames, mascots or symbols, and 79% of the fans agreed with them. . . . When pollsters asked about the Washington Redskins, they found no great resentment toward the name. Instead, they again found agreement between Native Americans and fans (69% of the former and 74% of the latter do not object to the name) . . .

Regardless, the campaign to erase Indian team names and symbols nationwide has been a success. Though Native American activists have made little progress at the highest level of pro sports . . . their single-minded pursuit of the issue has literally changed the face of sports in the U.S. Since 1969 . . . more than 600 school teams and minor league professional clubs have dropped nicknames deemed offensive by Native American groups. . . .

While those who support names such as Seminoles (Florida State) and [Atlanta] Braves can argue that the words celebrate Native American traditions, applying that claim to the Redskins is absurd. Nevertheless, Redskins vice president Karl Swanson says the name "symbolizes courage, dignity and leadership and has always been employed in that manner"—conveniently ignoring the fact that in popular usage dating back four centuries, the word has been a slur based on skin color. . . . Many experts on Native American history point out that . . . the word redskin was first used by whites who paid and received bounties for dead Indians. . . .

However, what's most important, Swanson counters, is intent: Because the Redskins and their fans mean nothing racist by using the nickname, it isn't racist or offensive. Not so, says Suzan Harjo (a Native American activist): "There's no more derogatory word that's used against us . . . in the English language. . . . Everyone knows that it has never been an honorific. It's a terrible insult." . . .

That the name is offensive to Native Americans is easy for non-Natives to presume. It resonates when an Olympic hero and former Marine Corps captain such as Billy Mills (a Native American and a Gold Medal winner in the 1964 Olympics), who speaks out against Indian names and mascots at schools around the country, insists that a team named Redskins in the capital of the nation that committed genocide against Native Americans is the equivalent of a soccer team in Germany being called the Berlin Kikes.

Somehow that message is lost on most of Mills's fellow Native Americans. Asked if they were offended by the name Redskins, 75% of Native American respondents in SI's poll said they were not, and even on reservations, where

Native American culture and influence are perhaps felt most intensely, 62% said they weren't offended. . . . Only 29% of Native Americans . . . thought [the owner of the Redskins] should change his team's name. Such indifference implies a near total disconnect between Native American activists and the general Native American population on this issue. . . .

The Utes' experience with the University of Utah might serve as a model for successful resolution of conflicts over Indian nicknames. Four years ago the council met with university officials, who made it clear that they would change their teams' name, the Running Utes, if the tribe found it objectionable. . . . The council was perfectly happy to have the Ute name continue to circulate in the nations' sports pages . . . Florida State, likewise, uses the name Seminoles for its teams with the express approval of the Seminole nation. . . . Like the Ute tribe, most Native Americans have no problem with teams using [Indian] names . . .

SOURCE: Reprinted courtesy of *Sports Illustrated.* "Poles Apart," by Andrea Woo and "The Indian Wars," by S. L. Price from *Sports Illustrated*, March 4, 2002. Copyright © 2002, Time, Inc. All rights reserved.

MASCOTS ARE OFFENSIVE

C. Richard King, Ellen J. Staurowsky, Lawrence Baca,
R. Davis, and Cornel Pewewardy

To fully understand both the SI article and ongoing controversy about mascots, one must grasp the history of Indian symbols in sports. . . . Native American mascots emerged (mainly) in the early 1900s, after [the end of military hostilities] . . . These mascots were part of a larger phenomena [sic] of increased prevalence of Native American images in U.S. popular culture, including Western movies, symbols for beer and butter,

and art in homes. One of the reasons why most Americans find the mascots unremarkable . . . is because of the prevalence of similar images throughout U.S. popular culture. . . .

Historically, the most popular sport mascots have been animals associated with aggression (e.g., Tigers) and Native Americans (e.g., Indians, Chiefs, Braves, and so forth). Although other ethnic groups have been occasionally used as mascots, these mascots differ from Native American mascots in several ways: [these mascots] are often (a) a people that do not exist today (e.g., Spartans); (b) less associated with aggression (e.g., Scots); (c) selected by people from the same ethnicity (e.g., Irish Americans at Notre Dame); and (d) not mimicked to nearly the same degree.

Native American mascots emerged in a context in which many non-Native Americans were "playing Indian." Still today, children don "Indian" costumes at Halloween, "act like Indians" during "Cowboy and Indian" games, "become Indian Princesses" at the YMCA, and perform "Indian rituals" at summer camps. Adults belong to organizations that involve learning "Indian ways" and performing "Indian rituals." Non-Native Americans have created an imaginary version of Indianness that they sometimes enact, and they expect real Native Americans to either ignore, affirm, or validate such myths and practices. Similar practices applied to other races/ethnicities, such as "playing Black" or "playing Jewish," would not be accepted in our society today.

Activism against Native American mascots has been evident for more than 30 years. Since the early 1990s, this activism has become more widespread [and] emerged from Native American individuals, groups, and communities that work on a variety of other issues, such as treaty, economic, cultural, environmental, health, and educational issues. Although many U.S. citizens see the mascot issue as emerging "out of the blue," many Native American organizations see the elimination of such mascots as part of a larger agenda of reducing societal stereotyping about Native Americans (in the media, school curriculums, and so forth) and informing the public about the realities of Native American lives. An increase in accurate information about Native Americans is viewed as necessary for the achievement of other goals such as poverty reduction, educational advancements, and securing treaty rights.

Anti-mascot activists articulate many different arguments against the mascots. First, they assert that the mascots stereotype Native Americans as only existing in the past, having a single culture, and being aggressive fighters. Second, they hold that these stereotypes influence the way people perceive and treat Native Americans. Such imagery is seen as affecting Native American images of themselves, creating a hostile climate for many Native Americans, and preventing people from understanding current Native American realities, which affects public policy relative to Native Americans. Third, the activists state that no racial/cultural group should be mimicked (especially in regard to sacred items/practices), even if such mimicking is "culturally accurate." And fourth, they argue that Native Americans should have control over how they are represented. . . .

Native American mascots are rooted in the bloodthirsty savage stereotype, as it is this stereotype that is linked to desirable athletic qualities such as having a fighting spirit and being aggressive, brave, stoic, proud, and persevering . . .

Of course, even [this] so-called positive stereotype [is] ultimately negative. [All] stereotypes fail to recognize diversity among the people who are being stereotyped. . . . Most people deny that they believe any racial stereotypes . . . When we do notice our own stereotyping, it is often because our beliefs are very negative (e.g., believing that African Americans are criminal or Puerto Ricans are lazy). When our stereotypes are "positive" (e.g., Jews as good at business or Asians as smart), we tend to think that these beliefs are not stereotypical and thus not racist.

Sport mascots are based on what is today perceived as "positive" ideas about Native Americans: that they are brave, principled, persevering, good fighters. This "positive cast" to the mascot stereotype leads most to conclude that the mascots are not racist. In fact, it is this "positive cast" to the mascot stereotype that leads many mascot supporters to think that the mascots actually counter racism by "honoring" Native Americans. . . .

It is not surprising that some Native Americans embrace "positive" stereotypes of Native Americans, and thus that some are not critical of Native American mascots. There are several factors that encourage Native Americans to accept, internalize, celebrate, and even capitalize on, "positive" stereotypes of Native Americans. First, many people do not define so-called positive stereotypes as stereotypes or racist. In fact, a group that experiences a great deal of inequality may be especially attracted to any imagery that is positive, as such imagery might be a relief from the negative. Second, throughout much of U.S. history, Native people have faced intense pressures to acculturate and have been exposed to many of the same stereotypical images of Native Americans as non-Natives have. These pressures have certainly resulted in some Natives adopting "dominant/White/outsider views" of Native Americans. Third, given the destruction of native economies

and the resulting economic destitution, some Native people have turned to the marketing of their ethnicity, or an acceptable Hollywood version of their ethnicity, to survive, including teaching "Native spirituality" to non-Native Americans; selling Native jewelry and art; and managing Native tourist establishments.

In conclusion, to understand the Native American mascot issue, and the SI article, one needs to understand the social context surrounding the mascots. Most important, one must understand the historically rooted, but contemporarily alive, stereotypes of Native Americans. Native American mascots emerged from these stereotypes, and these mascots continue to reinforce these stereotypes. The continued prevalence of these stereotypes inhibits social changes that would better contemporary Native American lives.

SOURCE: Originally titled "Of polls and race prejudice: Sports Illustrated's errant 'Indian Wars'," from *Journal of Sport and Social Issues, 26:* 381–403. Copyright © 2002. Reprinted with permission of Sage Publications, Inc.

DEBATE QUESTIONS TO CONSIDER

1. Price and Woo argue that the majority of Native Americans polled did not object to the use of Indian team mascots. How relevant is this point to the debate? Should questions such as these be decided by "popular vote" or are there deeper principles that should guide public policy? If so, what are those principles and how should they be applied?

2. Price and Woo quote an official of the Washington Redskins franchise as arguing that the team uses the term to honor Native Americans for their courage and dignity. Should "intent" matter in deciding if a term is insulting or offensive? Who should decide these matters? The team? The tribes? Someone else?

3. What arguments do King et al. make about why these matters are important? What *real* harm

comes from using Indian team mascots? Are their arguments convincing? Why or why not?

4. Is there a gender dimension to these arguments? Price and Woo mention the controversy about a South Dakota High School using "Redmen" as a team name. What do you suppose the women's teams at this school were called? Lady Redmen? Redwomen? How is this handled on your campus? Are the women's athletic teams distinguished by adding the modifier "Lady" or "Women"? What issues arise from this (very common) pattern? How do these issues matter?

5. Ultimately, is all of this just a matter of political correctness? What is at stake here (if anything)?

7

HISPANIC AMERICANS

Hispanic Americans are an extremely diverse group. They trace their origins to scores of different nations and vary from each other in culture, physical characteristics, dialect, and other ways. Mexicans living in the Southwest and West in the early 1800s were the first to become a Hispanic American minority group as a result of the U.S. expansion and the military defeat of Mexico. Since that time, the group has been augmented by immigrants from Mexico, especially during the past several decades, and, today, Mexican Americans are the largest Hispanic American group.

Puerto Ricans, the second largest Hispanic American group, began migrating in large numbers in the 1940s and 1950s and settled predominantly in the urban Northeast. Although both Puerto Ricans and Mexican Americans can be found at all levels of U.S. class structure, they average well below national standards in education, income, and prosperity. Cuban Americans are the third largest Hispanic group. They began immigrating just 40 years ago, fleeing the socialist revolution of Fidel Castro. They settled in southern Florida and especially in the Miami area, where a thriving Cuban American local economy has raised their average social class position relative to Mexican Americans and Puerto Ricans. Other sizeable Hispanic American groups come from Colombia, the Dominican Republic, El Salvador, Nicaragua, Peru, and several other nations. Immigration has been particularly heavy since the mid-1960s, and Hispanic Americans, taken as a single entity, are now the largest U.S. minority group.

Many Hispanic Americans face the same kinds of problems as African Americans: urban poverty, racism and discrimination, crime, failing school systems, and the prospect of a continuing disconnection from the mainstream economy. In addition, a large percentage of Hispanic Americans are recent immigrants or the children of immigrants and must cope with language barriers and lack of familiarity with U.S. customs. Taken together, these problems create formidable challenges for Hispanic Americans.

This chapter begins with two Narrative Portraits. In the first, journalist Rose Guilbault examines the concept of "macho," a term that changed its meaning from positive to negative as it moved from the Hispanic to the Anglo community. In the second, Professor Judith Cofer analyzes the gendered stereotype attached to Hispanic women. The focus on stereotypes and prejudice continues in the Reading by Jane Hill. She analyzes "Mock Spanish" and shows how this seemingly innocent and playful language pattern sustains negative images and expresses disdain and contempt, although in an indirect and "socially acceptable" way. The reading by Elizabeth Martinez argues for a shift in the U.S. racial paradigm away from the "black/white" dichotomy to a more encompassing (and realistic) vision that explicitly incorporates Hispanic Americans and other groups. This expanded view of American group relations is particularly necessary as the number and percentage of peoples who are both nonwhite and nonblack increase. The selection by O'Brien elaborates on the potential impacts of the growing number of nonwhites and mixed-race people on the racial structure of the United States. What will happen to the simple, dichotomized black-white racial order? Will whites become the minority group? Will a new racial democracy emerge? Or will Latinos (and Asians) find a way to join the white dominant group and preserve the exclusion of nonwhites?

The Current Debate at the end of the chapter takes up some of the issues raised by O'Brien but from a different angle. Is immigration a threat to the American way of life and American values? Will the newcomers—especially Latinos—change American culture and weaken traditional American values such as individualism, democracy, and the rule of law? Or will the immigrants find themselves, in time, Americanized and forever changed by the larger society?

Please visit the accompanying website to Race, Ethnicity, and Gender, second edition for the *Public Sociology Assignments* at http://www.pineforge.com/das2.

Questions to Consider in This Chapter

1. In what ways are anti-Hispanic prejudice and discrimination different from and the same as prejudice and discrimination directed at other minority groups? What stereotypes does this chapter reveal and how do these stereotypes differ from those maintained for other groups? Why do these differences exist? What role do language and immigration play in these patterns?

2. What do you see as the future for America's traditional, dichotomous racial order? Will the rapid growth of Latino groups change the ways Americans think about race and ethnicity? Why or why not? What is an "honorary white" and why might this be an important concept?

3. What gender dimensions can you identify in the issues raised in this chapter? How does gender impact (for example) stereotypes, language, assimilation, and equality?

NARRATIVE PORTRAIT

THE MEANING OF MACHO

The selections below speak to two different dimensions of minority group experience.

Rose Guilbault, a newspaper editor and columnist, reflects on the meaning of a term that has become central to the dominant group's view of Hispanic males. The image evoked by the term *macho* changed from positive to negative as it found its way into American English, a process that reflects dominant-minority relations and partly defines them. This passage reminds us that words as well as people can immigrate, and in both cases, the process can be transforming.

In the second selection, Judith Ortiz Cofer, a writer, poet, professor of English, and a Puerto Rican, describes some of the images and stereotypes of Latinas with which she has had to struggle and some of the dynamics that have created and sustained those images. She writes from her own experiences, but the points she makes illustrate that one part of the minority group experience is learning to deal with the stereotypes, images, and expectations of the larger society. Of course, everyone (even white males) has to respond to the assumptions of others, but given the realities of power and status, minority group members have fewer choices and a narrower range in which to maneuver. The images imposed by the society are harder to escape and more difficult to deny.

AMERICANIZATION IS TOUGH ON MACHO

Rose Del Castillo Guilbault

What is macho? That depends on which side of the border you come from. . . . The negative connotations of macho in this country are troublesome to Hispanics.

The Hispanic macho is manly, responsible, hardworking, a man in charge, a patriarch. A man who expresses strength through silence. . . .

The American macho is chauvinist, a brute, uncouth, loud, abrasive, capable of inflicting pain, and sexually promiscuous.

Quintessential macho models in this country are Sylvester Stallone, Arnold Schwarzenegger, and Charles Bronson. . . . They exude toughness, independence, masculinity. But a closer look reveals their machismo is really violence masquerading as courage, sullenness disguised as silence and irresponsibility camouflaged as independence. . . .

In Spanish, macho ennobles Latin males. In English it devalues them. This pattern seems consistent with the conflicts ethnic minority males experience in this country. Typically the cultural traits other societies value don't translate as desirable characteristics in America.

I watched my own father struggle with these cultural ambiguities. He worked on a farm for 20 years. He laid down miles of irrigation pipe, carefully plowed long, neat rows in fields, . . . stoically worked 20-hour days during the harvest season, accepting the long hours as part of agricultural work. When the boss complained or upbraided him for minor mistakes, he kept quiet, even when it was obvious that the boss had erred.

He handled the most menial tasks with pride. At home he was a good provider. . . . Americans regarded my father as decidedly unmacho. His character was interpreted as non-assertive, his loyalty, non-ambition, and his quietness, ignorance. I once overheard the boss's son blame him for plowing crooked rows. . . . My father merely smiled at the lie, knowing the boy had done it, . . . confident his good work was well-known. . . . Seeing my embarrassment, my father dismissed the incident, saying "They're the dumb ones. Imagine me fighting with a kid."

I tried not to look at him with American eyes because sometimes the reflection hurt. . . .

In the United States, I believe it was the feminist movement of the early '70s that changed macho's meaning. Perhaps my generation of Latin women was in part responsible. I recall Chicanas complaining about the chauvinistic nature of Latin men and the notion they wanted their women barefoot, pregnant, and in the kitchen. The generalization that Latin men embodied chauvinistic traits led to this . . . twist of semantics. Suddenly a word that represented something positive in one culture became a negative stereotype in another. . . .

The impact of language in our society is undeniable. And the misuse of macho hints at a deeper cultural misunderstanding that extends beyond mere word definitions.

SOURCE: *The San Francisco Chronicle,* August 20, 1989. Copyright © 1989. Reprinted with permission via Copyright Clearance Center.

NARRATIVE PORTRAIT

GENDER IMAGES OF LATINAS

THE ISLAND TRAVELS WITH YOU

Judith Ortiz Cofer

On a bus trip from London to Oxford University . . . a young man, obviously fresh from a pub, spotted me and as if struck by inspiration went down on his knees in the aisle. With both hands over his heart he broke into an Irish tenor's rendition of "Maria" from West Side Story. My politely amused fellow passengers gave his lovely voice the round of gentle applause that it deserved. Though I was not quite as amused, I managed my version of an English smile: no show of teeth, no extreme contortions of the facial muscles—I was at this time in my life practicing reserve and cool. . . . But Maria had followed me to London, reminding me of a prime fact of my life: You can leave the island, master the English language, and travel as far as you can, but if you are a Latina, . . . the Island travels with you.

This is sometimes a very good thing—it may win you the extra minute of somebody's attention. But with some people, the same things can make you an island—not so much a tropical paradise as an Alcatraz, a place nobody wants to visit. As a Puerto Rican girl growing up in the United States and wanting like most children to "belong," I resented the stereotypes that my Hispanic appearance called forth from many people I met.

Our family lived in a large urban center in New Jersey during the sixties, where life was designed as a microcosm of my parents' casas on the island. We spoke Spanish, we ate Puerto Rican food bought at the bodega, and we practiced strict Catholicism. . . .

As a girl, I was kept under strict surveillance, since virtue and modesty were, by cultural equation, the same as family honor. As a teenager, I was instructed on how to behave as a proper senorita. But it was a conflicting message girls got, since the Puerto Rican mothers also encouraged their daughters to look and act like women and to dress in clothes our Anglo friends found too "mature" for our age. . . . At a Puerto Rican festival, neither the music nor the colors we wore could be too loud. I still experience a vague sense of letdown when I'm invited to a "party" and it turns out to be a marathon conversation in hushed tones rather than a fiesta with salsa, laughter, and dancing—the kind of celebration I remember from my childhood. . . .

Mixed cultural signals have perpetuated certain stereotypes—for example, that of the "Hot Tamale" or sexual firebrand. It is a . . . view that the media have found easy to promote. In their special vocabulary, advertisers have designated "sizzling" and "smoldering" as the adjectives of choice for describing not only the foods but the women of Latin America. . . .

It is custom, however, not chromosomes, that leads us to choose scarlet over pale pink. As young girls, we were influenced in our decisions about clothes and colors by the women . . . who had grown up on a tropical island where the natural environment was a riot of primary colors, where showing your skin was one way to keep cool as well as to look sexy. Most important of all, on the island, women perhaps felt freer to dress and move more provocatively, since . . . they were protected by the traditions, mores, and laws of a Spanish/Catholic system of morality and machismo whose main rule was: You may look at my sister, but if you touch her I will kill you. The extended family and church structure could provide a young woman with a circle of safety in her small pueblo on the Island; if a man "wronged" a girl, everyone would close in to save her family honor. . . .

Because of my education and proficiency with the English language, I have acquired many mechanisms for dealing with the anger I experience. This was not true for my parents, nor is it true for the many Latin women working at menial jobs who must put up with stereotypes about our ethnic group such as: "They make good domestics." This is another facet of the myth of the Latin women in the United States. . . . The myth of the Hispanic menial has been maintained by the same media phenomenon that made "Mammy" from *Gone With the Wind* America's idea of a black woman for generations: Maria, the housemaid or counter girl, is now indelibly etched into the national psyche. The big and little screens have presented us with the picture of the funny Hispanic maid, mispronouncing words and cooking up a spicy storm in the kitchen. . . .

I am one of the lucky ones. My parents made it possible for me to acquire a stronger footing in the mainstream culture by giving me the chance at an education. . . . There are thousands of Latinas without the privilege of an education or the entrée into society that I have. For them, life is a struggle against the misconceptions perpetuated by the myth of the Latina as whore, domestic, or criminal. My personal goal in my public life is to try to replace the old pervasive stereotypes and myths about Latinas with a much more interesting set of realities. Every time I give a reading [of my poetry], I hope the stories I tell, the dreams and fears I examine in my work, can achieve some universal truth which will get my audience past the particulars of my skin color, my accent, or my clothes.

SOURCE: From "The Myth of the Latin Woman: I Just Met a Girl Named Maria," in *The Latin Deli: Prose and Poetry* by Judith Ortiz Cofer. Copyright © 1993 by Judith Ortiz Cofer. Reprinted by permission of The University of Georgia Press.

READINGS

The first two readings for this section both explore the meaning of prejudice and racism for Latinos in U.S. society today. The first reading, "Mock Spanish," demonstrates how butchered uses of the Spanish language function to reproduce negative stereotypes about Hispanic Americans, especially Mexicans. From advertisements and greeting cards to movies and political campaigns, author Jane Hill provides numerous examples of how Mock Spanish is used to conjure up these stereotypical images of Latinos as sneaky, untrustworthy, and cheap. Hill uses the term *dual indexicality* to refer to the two meanings behind the mock Spanish utterances. The first meaning is the conscious intent of the speaker to convey humor and even warmth toward Hispanic people and culture, while the second meaning is the negative racial stereotypes unacknowledged by the speaker. The Reading raises important questions about racial humor and the process by which we assess whether or not a joke is racist, because our criteria for assessment often tend to privilege the intent of the (white) speaker rather than the effect on the (nonwhite) targets of the joke, and Hill presents a strong critique of this power dynamic. That is, even when the speaker claims not to be prejudiced and even has Latino friends, the joke he or she tells can still be racist in its effects, by perpetuating negative ideas about Hispanic culture unknowingly. Hill characterizes Mock Spanish as *elite racist discourse,* since the speakers are not overt in expressing prejudice, but communicate racist stereotypes in more subtle ways, especially through the mass media, which normalize the images. The evidence presented here is yet another reminder of the *modern racism* we have been reviewing throughout this volume. Additionally, Hill points to negative stereotypical depictions of Latinos such as the caricatures of "Mexicans hidden under huge sombreros" and others as seen in the film *Encino Man,* and asks why comparable images of African Americans (like Mammy in a kerchief or Sambo with a slice of watermelon) elicit more outrage today than these similar anti-Hispanic images. These parallels between the racism faced by Hispanic Americans and African Americans that often seem to go literally unseen in the United States raise questions that are explored further in the second reading.

Elizabeth Martinez's "Seeing More Than Black and White" poses a direct challenge to the black/white model of racism from a Latina woman's perspective. She points out that the media focus almost exclusively on the racism faced by African Americans rather than comparable atrocities that are also directed at Hispanic Americans. This amounts to a divide-and-conquer or "Oppression Olympics" dynamic, which Martinez argues keeps minorities competing with each other rather than uniting together into one stronger force against white racism. Expanding the black/white model will become increasingly important as the United States becomes a majority nonwhite nation, and the largest percentage of that nonwhite majority will be Latinos of various ethnicities, rather than blacks.

Martinez also refutes the claim that Latinos face "national minority" oppression (or discrimination based on *ethnicity*) rather than oppression based on *race,* citing numerous examples of race-based anti-Latino discrimination. Often times African Americans are not aware that they share such common historical experiences with Hispanic Americans, such as lynchings and police brutality. Moreover, Martinez critiques the dualistic thinking that limits racism to a black/white issue as the same limited frame of mind that perpetuates racism in general. Latinos' mixed racial heritage (*mestizaje*) that combines Native American, European, and African ancestry is a striking piece of evidence for the limits of such dualistic frameworks. This reading takes the stance that as long as racism is conceived as solely a black/white issue, it will never be fully conquered or eliminated. Multiple racial realities are the wave of the future, and Latinos stand in the forefront of that optimistic complexity.

O'Brien uses the results of in-depth interviews with Latinos and Asians to raise questions about the future of U.S. group relations and the ways that people will perceive and discuss the changes that are in the making. She sketches several alternative racial futures for American society and then analyzes the potential impact of "honorary whites" not only for the evolving racial order but for the way people think about issues of race and ethnicity. Her analysis uses several of the concepts developed in previous chapters, most notably the concept of "color-blind" racism introduced by Bonilla-Silva and Forman in Chapter 5.

Mock Spanish: A Site for the Indexical Reproduction of Racism in American English

Jane H. Hill

I was first drawn to the study of "Mock Spanish"[1] by a puzzle. In the southwestern United States, English speakers of "Anglo"[2] ethnic affiliation make considerable use of Spanish in casual speech, in spite of the fact that the great majority of them are utterly monolingual in English under most definitions. However, these monolinguals both produce Spanish and consume it, especially in the form of Mock Spanish humor. Mock Spanish has, I believe, intensified during precisely the same period when opposition to the use of Spanish by its native speakers has grown, reaching its peak in the passage of "Official English" statutes in several states during the last decade.[3]

As I began to explore this question, I realized that I had also engaged a larger one: In a society where for at least the last 20 years to be called a "racist" is a dire insult, and where opinion leaders almost universally concur that "racism" is unacceptable, how is racism continually reproduced? For virulent racism unquestionably persists in the United States. People of color feel it intensely in almost every dimension of their lives. Studies by researchers of every political persuasion continue to show substantial gaps between the several racialized groups and so-called "whites" on every quantifiable dimension of economic prosperity, educational success, and health (including both infant mortality and life expectancy). I argue here that everyday talk, of a type that is almost never characterized (at least by Anglos) as "racist," is one of the most important sites for the covert reproduction of this racism. "Mock Spanish," the topic of this paper, is one example of such a site.

"Mock Spanish" exemplifies a strategy of dominant groups that I . . . call . . . "incorporation" (Hill, 1995). By incorporation, members of dominant groups expropriate desirable resources, both material and symbolic, from subordinate groups. Through incorporation, . . . "whiteness" is elevated. Qualities taken from the system of "color" are reshaped within whiteness into valued properties of mind and culture. This process leaves a residue that is assigned to the system of color, consisting of undesirable qualities of body and nature. These justify the low position of people of color in the hierarchy of races, and this low rank in turn legitimates their exclusion from resources that are reserved to whiteness. By using Mock Spanish, "Anglos" signal that they possess desirable qualities: a sense of humor, a playful skill with a foreign language, authentic regional roots, an easy-going attitude toward life. The semiotic function by which Mock Spanish assigns these qualities to its Anglo speakers has been called "direct indexicality" by Ochs (1990). "Direct indexicality" is visible to discursive consciousness. When asked about a specific instance of Mock Spanish, speakers will often volunteer that it is humorous, or shows that they lived among Spanish speakers and picked up some of the language, or is intended to convey warmth and hospitality appropriate to the Southwestern region. They also easily accept such interpretations when I volunteer them.

The racist and racializing residue of Mock Spanish is assigned to members of historically Spanish-speaking populations by indirect indexicality (Ochs 1990). Through this process, such people are endowed with gross sexual appetites, political corruption, laziness, disorders of language, and mental incapacity [and this identity] restricts Mexican-Americans and Puerto Ricans largely to the lowest sectors of the regional and national economies. This indexicality is "indirect" because it is not acknowledged, and in fact is actively denied as a possible function of their usage, by speakers of Mock Spanish. . . .

The purpose of this paper is to argue for this semiotic analysis of "dual indexicality." The argument, in summary, is that speakers and hearers can only interpret utterances in Mock Spanish insofar as they have access to the negative residue of meaning. Those who hear Mock Spanish jokes, for instance, cannot possibly "get" them—that is, the jokes will not be funny—unless the hearer has instant, unreflecting access to a cultural model of "Spanish speakers" that includes the negative residue.

Furthermore, I suggest that Mock Spanish usages actively produce this residue.

They carry with them, of course, a debris of racist history that is known to most speakers: they presuppose . . . a racist and racialized image. But insofar as speakers laugh at Mock Spanish jokes, or, indeed, interpret Mock Spanish expressions in any of the several appropriate ways, such imagery is also entailed, locally reproduced in the interaction, and thus made available in turn as a presupposition of ensuing interactions.

I suggest that Mock Spanish is a new (at least to the theory of racist discourse) type of what van Dijk (1993) has called "elite racist discourse." . . . [T]he most productive usage of the system is, I have found, among middle-and upper-income, college-educated whites. Mock Spanish is not heard, nor are printed tokens of it usually encountered, at truck stops, country-music bars, or in the "Employees Only" section of gas stations. Instead, the domain of Mock Spanish is the graduate seminar, the boardroom, the country-club reception. It is found issuing from the mouths of working-class whites only in the mass media, and is placed there by writers who come from elite backgrounds.

I am, myself, a "native speaker" of Mock Spanish. I grew up in West Los Angeles, in a neighborhood where the notoriously wealthy districts of Westwood, Brentwood, and Bel-Air come together. On school playgrounds populated by the children of film directors, real estate magnates, and university professors I learned to say "Adios" and "el cheapo" and "Hasty banana." The explosion of Mock Spanish that can be heard today in mass media is produced by the highly-paid Ivy-Leaguers who write "The Simpsons," "Roseanne," "Northern Exposure," and "Terminator Two: Judgment Day," and by the more modest literati who compose greeting-card texts and coffee-cup slogans. This suggests an extremely important

property of the large structure of racism—that it is "distributed" within the social system of whiteness.

Racist practice in its crudest forms—the obscene insult, the lynching—is assigned within this larger structure to the trailing edge of the upwardly-mobile social continuum of "whiteness." People who overtly manifest such practices are often defined by opinion makers as a minority of "white trash" or "thugs" (even when many surface signs suggest that they are members of the social and economic mainstream). Those who aspire to advancement within whiteness practice instead what is often called "New Racism," the various forms of exclusion and pejoration that are deniable, or justifiable as "fair" or "realistic." The covert practices of Mock Spanish can even be contributed to the system of whiteness by people who are not, personally, racist in any of the usual senses. However, by using Mock Spanish they play their part in a larger racist system, and contribute to its pernicious and lethal effects. I first review the history of Mock Spanish. I then illustrate contemporary Mock Spanish usage, emphasizing that it constitutes a linguistic system of substantial regularity. In the course of exemplifying this system, I argue for the semiotic interpretation of Mock Spanish as manifesting "dual indexicality" by which desirable qualities are assigned to Anglos, and undesirable qualities are assigned to members of historically Spanish-speaking populations. . . . I conclude with a brief discussion of additional evidence, beyond the semiotic analysis, that Mock Spanish constitutes a racist discourse.

A Brief History of Mock Spanish

Mock Spanish is quite old in American English. The earliest attestation I have found is from the *Dictionary of American Regional English*

(Cassidy 1985:508; henceforth, DARE), where we are told that the jail in the city of Mobile was called, in 1792, the "calaboose." This word is from Spanish *calabozo* "prison" (especially, a subterranean cell, or an isolation cell within a prison). . . . DARE (p. 411) [also] attests . . . awareness of what I call Mock Spanish as a pejorating and vulgar register at an early period, in a citation for "buckaroo" from Hart's Vigilante Girl, set in Northern California: "I can talk what they call 'buckayro' Spanish. It ain't got but thirteen words in it, and twelve of them are cuss words. . . ."

Today, I think it would be fair to speak of an "explosion" of Mock Spanish. I hear it constantly, and it is especially common at what I call "sites of mass reproduction": films, television shows, including the Saturday morning cartoons watched religiously by most children, greeting cards, video games, political cartoons, coffee-cup slogans intended for display on the office desk, bumper stickers, refrigerator magnets, and the like. These items are marketed far beyond the Southwest.

. . .

Mock Spanish as a System of Strategies for Borrowing

. . . Mock Spanish is only one of at least three registers of "Anglo Spanish." . . . "Cowboy" Spanish is a register of loan words for plants (mesquite), animals (coyote), land forms (mesa), food (tamale), architecture (patio), legal institutions (vigilante), and (the source of my name for it), an extensive terminology associated with the technology of managing range cattle from horseback, among which the words "lariat" and "bronco" are among the best known. "Cowboy" Spanish is largely restricted to the U.S. Southwest, but has some overlap, in both lexicon and usage patterns, with Mock Spanish.

The second register is "Nouvelle" Spanish.[4] This is used in marketing the Southwest as "the land of mañana," a place for a relaxing vacation or a peaceful retirement. It produces luxury hotels named "La Paloma," street names in upscale Anglo neighborhoods like "Calle Sin Envidia," and restaurant placemats that wish the diner "Buenas Dias." . . . [B]oth Cowboy Spanish and Nouvelle Spanish share with Mock Spanish a more or less complete disregard for the grammatical niceties of any dialect of Spanish itself. . . .

Mock Spanish itself is a system of four major strategies for the "incorporation" of Spanish-language materials into English. These strategies yield expressions that belong to a pragmatic zone bounded on one end by the merely jocular, and on the other by the obscene insult. They include . . . (1) "Semantic derogation": the borrowing of neutral or positive Spanish loan words which function in Mock Spanish in a jocular and/or pejorative sense and (2) "Euphemism": the borrowing of negative, including scatological and obscene, Spanish words, as euphemisms for English words, or for use in their own right as jocular and/or pejorative expressions, . . . and (3) "Hyperanglicization": absurd mispronunciations, that endow commonplace Spanish words or expressions with a jocular and/or pejorative sense and can create vulgar puns.

Strategy I: Mock Spanish Semantic Derogation

In "semantic derogation"[5] a positive or neutral Spanish word is borrowed as a Mock Spanish expression and given a humorous or negative meaning. [Consider two examples using] the Spanish greeting *Adios*. In Spanish *Adios* is an entirely neutral farewell. While it includes the root *Dios* "God," it has about as much to do with "God" for most Spanish speakers as English "goodbye," a contraction of "God be with ye," does for English speakers. But it is at the very least polite, and, like "Goodbye," it is not in the least slangy. [The first example] is a greeting card. . . . On the front of the card a small figure coded as "Mexican" by his big sombrero and striped serape says, "Adiós."[6] Turning to the inside of the card we find [not a standard "Best of luck in your new job/house/etc." message but, instead,] "That's Spanish for, sure, go ahead and leave your friends, the only people who really care about you, the ones who would loan you their last thin dime, give you the shirts off their backs, sure. Just take off."

The second, even more obvious, [example] of the semantic pejoration of "Adios" *is* [the expression] "Adios, cucaracha" with a picture of a fleeing roach, a bus-bench advertisement for a Tucson exterminating company. The bench is . . . in one of the most exclusive Anglo neighborhoods, so it is highly unlikely that the ad is addressed to a Spanish-speaking audience. Note that Spanish cucaracha is chosen over English "cockroach," to convey heightened contempt.

The final example of "Adios" appears in . . . "Terminator 2: Judgment Day," a film which made heavy use of Mock Spanish. In the film . . . the child John Connor must live, because thirty years into the future he will successfully lead a bedraggled band of human survivors in the final war against machines. The machines have twice sent an evil cyborg, a "Terminator," into the past to kill him. But the humans of the future send a good terminator, played by Arnold Schwarzenegger, into the past to protect the boy. The "Adios" scene is at the end of the film. . . . The Good Terminator has finally destroyed his evil opponent. . . . The Good Terminator, John Connor, and Connor's heroic mother Sarah have stolen the arm of the first Terminator . . . [and] the arm must be destroyed, so that the Terminator technology can never threaten humanity. As young Connor [destroys] the evil artifact . . . , he says "Adios." Then we realize that the Good Terminator,

whom the humans have come to love and admire, must also destroy himself—his futuristic metal body is as dangerous as those of his evil opponents. Sarah must lower him into the steel. As he descends, he looks one last time at his human friends and says, "Goodbye." The contrast could not be more clear: "Adios" for evil, "Goodbye" for good.

These uses of "Adios" cannot be understood except under the "dual indexicality" analysis. By direct indexicality they project variously humor, a streetwise acquaintance with Spanish, a sense of Southwestern regional identity (especially for the greeting card and the advertising sign), and, for the "Terminator 2" screenwriters, a representation of what they take to be the appropriate speech for a white street kid from Los Angeles.[7] Finally, they are all obviously intended as insults. Neither the humor nor the insult is available as a meaning unless a second, indirect, set of indexicals is present. By indirect indexicality these instances of "Adios" evoke . . . a greeting that would be uttered by an untrustworthy and insincere person, the kind of person who might stab you in the back, the kind of person who would use a word to mean its opposite. The person thus conjured up is, clearly, a speaker of Spanish. And of course this stereotype, of the sneaky and untrustworthy "Latin lover" or the sneering "Mexican bandit," is undeniably available to American English speakers. Only this presence makes possible the humorous and/or insulting quality of "Adios" in these usages.[8]

A second derogated Spanish greeting, "Hasta la vista, baby" also appears in "Terminator 2," from which origin it became an immensely popular slogan that continues to circulate in American usage, in a variety of variants including "Hasta la bye-bye," "Hasta la pasta," and "Hasta la baby, vista."[9] [There are] two occurrences in the film. In the first scene, the Good Terminator is driving John Connor and his mother to a desert hideout. The dialogue is as follows:

Mother:	Keep it under sixty-five, we don't want to be pulled over.
Terminator:	Affirmative (in a clipped, machine-like tone)
John Connor:	No no no no no no. You gotta listen to the way people talk. You don't say "Affirmative," or some shit like that, you say "No problemo." And if someone comes off to you with an attitude, you say "Eat me." And if you want to shine them on, you say, "Hasta la vista, baby."
Terminator:	Hasta la vista, baby. (still in a machine-like voice)
John Connor:	Yeah, "Later, dickwad." And if someone gets upset, you say, "Chill out," or, you can do combinations.
Terminator:	Chill out, dickwad. (in a machine-like voice)
John Connor:	That's great! See, you're getting it.
Terminator:	No problemo. (in a somewhat more natural voice)

This fascinating scene clearly locates Mock Spanish in the same register with extremely vulgar English expressions. But notice that this register, and its Mock Spanish component, is "the way people talk." If the Terminator is to become human, to be redeemed from his machine nature, he must learn to talk this way too. By learning Mock Spanish, the Terminator becomes more like the witty, resourceful young John Connor, and gains the boy's approval. This is a superb demonstration of the direct indexicality of Mock Spanish: it recruits positive qualities to whiteness. However, the indirect indexicality is also made vivid in this passage. [In] associating "Hasta la vista" with "Eat me" and "Dickwad," . . . Spanish speakers [are associated with] filth and obscenity, [as is] their language. . . . In the next scene we see the most famous token of "Hasta la vista, baby," when

Schwarzenegger utters his newly-acquired line as he destroys the evil terminator with a powerful gun.[10] During the 1992 presidential campaign Schwarzenegger, a Republican stalwart, appeared on many occasions in support of President George Bush, uttering the famous line as a threat against Bush's opponents. Bush himself also used the line occasionally. . . . Thus it was clearly judged by campaign managers and consultants as highly effective, resonating deeply with public sentiment.[11] This suggests that the simultaneous pleasures of feeling oneself streetwise and witty, while accessing an extremely negative image of Spanish and its speakers, are widely available to American politicians and voters.

[Several] further examples illustrate the strategy of semantic derogation. [One] is a political cartoon from the *Arizona Daily Star,* caricaturing Ross Perot, running for President in 1992 against George Bush and Bill Clinton on a third-party ticket. Perot, who is much given to speaking from charts, holds a list that urges support for him because (among other reasons), there are "Bucks flyin' into my 'Perot for El Presidente' treasure trove." Here, the direct indexicality is humorous, and permits the comprehending reader to feel cosmopolitan and streetwise. However, the expression is clearly intended to criticize Perot, to suggest that he is pompous and absurd. In order to interpret the insult, the reader must have access to a highly negative image of the sort of person who might be called "El Presidente." This is, of course, the classic tin-horn Latin American dictator, dripping with undeserved medals and presiding in a corrupt and ineffectual manner over a backwater banana republic. Through indirect indexicality, the Mock Spanish expression reproduces this stereotype.

[Another example, from] a "Calvin and Hobbes" comic strip, shows Calvin and his tiger friend Hobbes in one of their endless silly debates about who will be the highest officer in their tree-house club. Hobbes proclaims himself "El Tigre Numero Uno." This is not, however, mere self-aggrandizement: mainly, the locution satirizes the grandiose titles that Calvin makes up for himself, like "Supreme Dictator for Life." Again, by direct indexicality, "El Tigre Numero Uno" is funny, and is also part of Hobbes' cool and witty persona. But to capture the absurdity and the insult, we must also have access to indirect indexicality, which picks out, again, the stereotype of the tinhorn Latin American dictator.

[A third example] illustrates a very common Mock Spanish usage, of Spanish nada "nothing." In Mock Spanish the word has been pejorated from this merely neutral meaning into a more extreme sense, meaning "absolutely nothing." One formulaic usage, "Zip, zero, nada" (and minor variants) has become wildly popular; I have seen it in television commercials for free drinks with hamburgers, in newspaper announcements for no-fee checking accounts, and, most recently, in an editorial piece in the *Arizona Daily Star* (August 20, 1995) in which an urban planner chastises the Pima County Board of Supervisors for spending "zero dollars—*nada,* zip" on improving a dangerous street intersection. . . .

Finally, [to] illustrate a common use of semantic derogation, the use of Mock Spanish to express "cheapness" [I have a] a newspaper advertisement for a sale at Contents, an exclusive furniture store in Tucson. The deep price cuts are announced under the headline "Contemporary and Southwestern Dining, For Pesos." Here, the direct indexicality is not only "light" and jocular; it is almost certainly also invoking regional ambiance. The store flatters its clientele by suggesting that they are "of the Southwest," able to interpret these Spanish expressions. However, in order to understand how these customers could interpret "For Pesos" (which is surely not intended literally), we must assume that the indirect indexicality

presupposed and/or entailed here is that the peso is a currency of very low value. "For Deutschemarks" or "For Yen" would hardly serve the same purpose! This advertisement is dense with Mock Spanish, driving home the message about bargains with, "Si our menu of fine southwestern and contemporary dining tables and chairs at prices that are muy bueno, now during our Winter Sale . . . Plus, caramba, there's Masterplan, our interior design service that helps you avoid costly decorating errors. . . . Hurry in today before we say adios to these sale savings, amigo."

The strategy of semantic derogation is highly productive, and includes such well-known expressions as "macho," "the big enchilada," and "No way, José," in addition to the examples above. For every one of these usages, in order to understand how the expression can be properly interpreted, we must assume the division between a set of direct indexes (such as "humorous," "streetwise" "light-hearted," and "regional identity") and a set of indirect indexes which presuppose or entail a highly negative image of the Spanish language, its speakers, and the culture and institutions associated with them.

STRATEGY II: MOCK SPANISH EUPHEMISM

The second strategy borrows Spanish words that have highly negative connotations even in the original language, including scatological and obscene expressions. The Mock Spanish form serves as a euphemism for the corresponding rude English word, or creates a new, especially negative semantic space. The first [example] illustrating this strategy is of a coffee cup [which] was purchased . . . in a card and gift shop only a few doors from the University of Arizona campus (the source of many of the items discussed here; the store is, of course, targeting its merchandise at the campus community, thus supporting my claim that Mock Spanish is part of elite usage). The cup bears the slogan, "Caca de Toro," obviously a euphemism for the English expression, "Bullshit." There exist, of course, coffee cups that say "Bullshit," but it seems clear that the "Caca de toro" coffee cup would be more widely acceptable, seen as less vulgar and insulting, than a cup with the English expression. Again, the direct indexicality of this cup is that its owner is a person with a sense of humor, the independence of mind to express a negative attitude, and enough sophistication to understand the Spanish expression (although this expression is not formulaic in Spanish; it is a translation from English). The indirect indexicality required for understanding why the slogan is in Spanish, however, must be that this language is particularly suited to scatology, and that its speakers are perhaps especially given to its use, failing to make the fine distinctions between the polite and the vulgar that might be made by an English speaker.[12]

The second illustration of the strategy of borrowing negative Spanish words is of a gift coffee cup bearing the expression "Peon." Unlike "Caca de Toro," which does not exist as an idiom in Spanish, *peón* is well-established in that language in a negative meaning . . . and referring . . . to people in low occupations. . . . In Latin America it came to designate a person held in debt servitude in a low occupation. . . . It is highly unlikely that the anticipated owner of the cup would be "an unskilled laborer." Instead, the owner could even be a manager, but would be expressing an ironic complaint about being exploited and maltreated. . . .

[The next example] . . . of the . . . strategy . . . is not at all humorous. [It appeared on] the cover of the *Tucson Weekly*, a weekly free newspaper (paid for by advertising) known for its outspoken, even radical, point of view. The cover shows a young Mexican-American man

along with the title of the feature article: *Gang-Bangers: La Muerte y la Sangre en el Barrio Centro* ("Death and Blood in the *Barrio Centro*"). What is curious here is the unusual choice of Spanish for the language of the subtitle; I cannot remember another case where the *Tucson Weekly* used such a long expression in Spanish. Unfortunately, the Spanish title . . . suggests a stereotyped association between gang membership and Chicano ethnicity that is not borne out by the facts; many young people in gangs in Tucson are Anglos (and there are also a few African-American gangs). I believe that the Spanish title intends to convey the special direness of the gang threat: "La Muerte y la Sangre" has a sort of Hemingwayesque ring, suggesting that the author of the essay will plumb the most profound depths of the human condition.

However, at the same time, the Spanish title has a softening effect—just as "Caca de Toro" is less offensive than "bullshit," "La Muerte y la Sangre" is somehow more distant, less immediate for the English-speaking reader than "Blood and Death." "La Muerte y la Sangre," in short, is something that happens to "Mexican" kids. Here, the direct indexicality thus is probably the sophistication, the ethnographic depth, enjoyed by the author and, in turn, by the reader of the essay. The indirect indexicality is that "muerte" and "sangre" are at the same time more horrible, and yet less serious, than "death" and "blood"—they are, in short, a peculiarly "Spanish" condition capturing some quality of existence in the lower depths that is not available to Anglos in their own language.

The final example of the strategy of euphemism is illustrated by . . . the 1992 film *Encino Man*. This film was obviously aimed at young people, and carried, astonishingly, a "PG" rating. The hip (white) teenage subculture of Southern California is apparently viewed by young people across the country as highly attractive, and the film features the actor Pauly

Shore, a former MTV announcer, who exemplifies it. Shore is famous for using the variety of English that is closely associated with this subculture, a variety that makes heavy use of Mock Spanish.[13] Indeed, there are far more instances of Mock Spanish in the film than I have space to include. The example that I have chosen is an elaborate and extraordinarily vulgar and obscene joke at the expense of a Chicana character that is acceptable in a film aimed at children because it is uttered in Spanish. It is an especially clear and dramatic attestation of the Mock Spanish strategy of euphemism.

The plot of *Encino Man* is that two teenage boys who live in Encino (a wealthy suburb of Los Angeles) dig a swimming pool in their backyard and find a Cro-Magnon man encased in a block of ice. They thaw him out, name him "Linc" (as in "Missing"), and take him to high school. The clip opens as "Stoney," Pauly Shore's character, escorts "Linc" to his Spanish class. "Spanish," explains Stoney, "is guacamole, chips, and salsa." Stoney then raises his leg and makes a farting noise. The stereotyped and racist vision of Spanish-speaking culture thus conveyed needs no further comment. Stoney continues in "Spanish": "The dia es mi hermanos, the day is beautiful." (The stereotype reproduced here is that Spanish is a language studied by the dimmest scholars.) . . .

[Later in the film,] Stoney and his friend have taken Linc to a bar frequented by cholos, stereotyped as absurd in dress and manner. As the scene opens, the lead cholo threatens Stoney and Dave, warning them not to bother his "muchacha," or he will make sure that they are "no longer recognizable as a man." Linc does not hear the threat, because he is already approaching the cholo's girlfriend, shown as a ridiculous Latin sexpot, writhing hotly in time to the salsa beat of the dance music. Linc grabs the girl and carries her off-screen in classic cave-man style. The cholo finds them dancing together and pulls a knife on Linc, saying (with

subtitles), "Te dije, si yo veo a alguién con mi mujer, lo mato." ("I told you, if I see anybody with my woman, I kill him"). Linc extricates himself from the situation by using the two lines from the morning's Spanish class: "El queso está viejo y podrido. ¿Donde está el sanitario?" ("The cheese is old and moldy. Where is the bathroom?").

The astounded cholo gapes at him and then begins to laugh. "You're right, *ese,*" he chuckles. "She's not worth it!" The girl slaps the cholo, who collapses, weeping, into the arms of his supporters. Just as when, in "Terminator 2: Judgment Day," the Good Terminator becomes fully human when he learns Mock Spanish, Linc the cave-man is at his most clever and resourceful when he uses the language. While the direct indexicality of Linc's vulgar joke is positive, enhancing his image, the indirect indexicality . . . is almost entirely negative. Indeed, here the indirect indexicality is really not indirect, but fully expressed in the visual images that accompany the talk. The film is trivial and deeply sexist.

But what is especially striking about the film is its casual racism: Here, the indirect indexicality . . . is amply reinforced by the grossly racist depictions of the cholo and his girlfriend. If similar depictions of African-American characters were to appear in a release from a major studio, there would almost certainly be public outcry. However, as far as I know, "Encino Man" passed quite unnoticed. The implications of this fact for the socialization of white youth are quite horrifying.

There are, of course, innumerable examples of this second strategy. . . . Like semantic pejoration, Mock Spanish euphemism is highly productive, and every case of it I have ever encountered requires the dual-indexicality analysis: Speakers express their sense of humor and cosmopolitanism by direct indexicality, while pejorating and denigrating Spanish language and culture by indirect indexicality, the latter being absolutely required for successful interpretation and appreciation of the humor.

HYPERANGLICIZATION AND BOLD MISPRONUNCIATION

For those readers of this paper who have never heard Mock Spanish, it is important to know that it is almost always pronounced in entirely English-language phonology; Mock Spanish cannot be understood as "code-switching" in the usual sense. However, Mock Spanish forms are often more than merely Anglicized. Instead, they undergo what I call (Hill 1993) "hyperanglicization," yielding pronunciations that are widely known to be ludicrous departures from their Spanish originals. These absurd mispronunciations provide a rich source of vulgar puns, some of them best rendered in writing, as in the following examples.

[The first example is] a Christmas card, the front of [which] says "Pablo, the Christmas Chihuahua, has a holiday wish for you" over a drawing of a ludicrously ugly little dog wearing a huge sombrero and scratching frantically at the many fleas visibly jumping around on his hairless body. The greeting inside the card . . . is "Fleas Navidad," a pun on the Spanish Christmas salutation, *Feliz Navidad*. The second example . . . is of a thank-you card, [the front of which] shows . . . a tiny mouse crouching in a sea of grass, and the word "Muchas" ("Many"). Opening the card, we find more grass and the word "Grass-ias," a hyperanglicized version of Spanish *gracias* "Thanks" that yields the pun.[14] . . .

[Another example consists] of a menu from a Mexican restaurant in Tucson. . . . Baja Bennie's, the source for this menu, is . . . in an area that is notoriously almost exclusively Anglo. It is a favorite place for young Anglo professionals. The Baja Bennie's menu parodies the menus in legitimate Mexican-food venues with

silly Mock Spanish section headings like "El Figuro Trimmo." This section is explained as "Bennie's answer to the Border Patrol, sort of our Mex-er-size area . . . ," a note that would be interpreted as the grossest sort of insult by almost any Chicano. . . .

FURTHER EVIDENCE FOR RACISM IN MOCK SPANISH

Thus far, I have argued that Mock Spanish is ineluctably racist because it can only be understood by speakers insofar as they have access to its indirect indexical force, of relentless denigration of the Spanish language, culture, and people. However, there is additional evidence that Mock Spanish is a racist discourse.

Occasionally Mock Spanish usage reveals its fundamental character by being embedded in grossly racist texts. I owe one example to Jodi Goldman, who found an article from *The Koala*, the University of California at San Diego student satirical newspaper, from April 6, 1994. This satirical piece requires contextualization: college students from institutions along the border often choose to spend "Spring Break" at beach resorts in Mexico, a dislocation which many take as an excuse to go on an alcohol-fueled orgy of misbehavior that is a source of exasperation to Mexicans and enormous concern to college officials and parents in the United States (serious injuries and even deaths are unfortunately not rare).

The article in *The Koala* is a fantasy about being arrested on a beer-sodden Spring Break at Rosarita Beach in Baja California, and is entitled "¿Que pasa en tus pantalones?" The author provides a parodic "pronunciation guide" to her name: "By Pamela Benjamin (pronounced: Pahm-eh-lah Ben-haam-een)." The article features many elaborate instances of Mock Spanish, but I will restrict myself to one revealing paragraph, which the author introduces by noting that "I have no knowledge of Spanish." She continues:

"My brother taught me a few phrases: 'Cuanto cuesta es tu Madre?' (How much does your mother cost?), 'Que pasa en tus pantalones?' (What's happening in your pants?), and the answer for that question, 'Una fiesta en mi pantalones, y tu invito,' (There's a party in my pants, and you're invited.)

"These phrases were of no help to me when captured by Mr. Hideous, Huge-sweat-rings-on-his-uniform, Body-oder[sic]-of-a-rotting-mule, Must-eat-at-least-10-tortas-a-day, Mexican Federale guy. I thought I was going to die, not only from his smell, but from the killer cockroaches the size of hamsters in the back seat. I thought to myself, "No problem, Pam. You can deal with this. Stay calm, don't scream, and say something in Spanish. He'll notice your amazing brilliance and let you go." Unfortunately, the first thing that popped out was, "Cuanto Cuesta es tu Madre?" My doom was sealed.

Here, one hardly needs the "dual indexicality" analysis: Mexico is clearly depicted as a corrupt and filthy country, where the only Spanish one needs are the few phrases necessary to buy the services of a prostitute.

Mock Spanish in print is very frequently associated with patently racist imagery, [including "bean jokes," images of stereotyped "Mexicans" shown barefoot and wearing huge sombreros, etc.]. Many Mexican-Americans find caricatures of Mexicans hidden under huge sombreros to be grossly offensive. They have precisely the force for them that the picture of a grinning black boy with a slice of watermelon, or a fat-cheeked mammy with her head done up in a kerchief, have for African Americans. Following many years of effort by Latino citizens' groups, this image has been largely eliminated from mainstream advertising and mass media (an important example was the agreement by the Frito-Lay Corporation to give up its trademark caricature of the "Frito Bandito"). However, it survives vigorously in a variety of minor media such as on . . . greeting cards.[15]

Teun van Dijk, in *Elite Discourse and Racism*, argues that in a theory of racist discourse it is essential to take into account what he calls "minority competence," the assessment of a situation, as racist or nonracist, by "those who experience racism as such, that is, the competent or 'conscious' members of minority groups" (van Dijk 1993:18). This is a fundamental departure from the tradition that regards the views of the targets of racism as unreliable, because biased. Instead, it suggests that we view competent members of minority communities as especially likely to be able to make nuanced discriminations between racist and nonracist or anti-racist practice, because it is precisely they who have the most at stake in making such distinctions.

Van Dijk recognizes that there may be wide variation among minority-group members in general. I have never addressed an audience on this topic without having an Anglo member of the audience tell me that my analysis is incorrect, because a Mexican-American or Puerto Rican friend of theirs once sent them a card, or told them a joke, with Mock Spanish content. I have no doubt that they are telling the truth about their experiences. Certainly some Mexican-Americans find the tokens of Mock Spanish that I have shown them (including many of the items described above) to be entertaining. However, I find that those Mexican-Americans who laugh at Mock Spanish are generally very young (many of them have been college freshmen or sophomores) or relatively naive and uneducated. Older people are almost unanimous in immediately reacting negatively to these tokens. Many of them recognize the Mock Spanish genre immediately, and volunteer stories about times that Anglos have offended them by using Mock Spanish to them, such as calling them "Amigo" or asking them "Comprende?" . . . In summary, thoughtful people among the Latino and Chicano population in the Southwest usually define Mock Spanish as a racist practice.[16]

CONCLUSION: MOCK SPANISH IS A NEW KIND OF ELITE RACIST DISCOURSE

I have shown that Mock Spanish usages cannot be interpreted unless interlocutors reproduce, through indirect indexicality, very negative images of Spanish and its speakers. It functions, therefore, as a racist discourse in itself. I have also shown that uses of Mock Spanish often occur with grossly racist imagery. . . . Furthermore, I have shown that many Mexican-Americans . . . concur that it is racist, and I have argued, following van Dijk (1993), that their views must be taken very seriously. However, I have found in discussing this work that many Anglos find my conclusions implausible. How, they argue, can Mock Spanish be racist? They use it, and they are not racist. . . . How could anyone call "Calvin and Hobbes" a racist comic strip, or "Terminator 2: Judgment Day" a racist film?

I would argue, along with many contemporary theorists of racism . . . that to find that an action or utterance is "racist," one does not have to demonstrate that the racism is consciously intended. Racism is judged, instead, by its effects: of successful discrimination and exclusion of members of the racialized group from goods and resources enjoyed by members of the racializing group. It is easy to demonstrate that such discrimination and exclusion not only has existed in the past against Mexican Americans and other members of historically Spanish-speaking populations in the United States, but continues today.

Furthermore, the semiotic analysis that I have proposed above demonstrates that

Mock Spanish is discriminatory and denigrating in its indexical meaning, that it cannot be understood without knowing about the stereotypes that such indexes presuppose and entail, even if speakers believe that what they are doing is inoffensive joking. Mock Spanish is effective precisely because of its relative deniability, because people are not aware of "being racist," even in a mild way, let alone in a vulgar way. Through its use, the "upwardly mobile system of whiteness" is created covertly, through the indirect indexicality of hundreds of taken-for-granted commonplace utterances that function to "racialize" their targets, constructing them as members of a human group represented as essentially inferior. . . . [I]t is through these covert indexes that the deepest structures of the self, those that are least accessible to inquiry and modification, are laid down. Indeed, . . . covert semiosis is at least as, if not more, powerful than overt meaning in the construction of the world through linguistic practice. . . .

A second argument that is often used against my analysis is that there are in American English many expressions that mock other languages besides Spanish. This is, of course, correct. . . . It seems to me obvious, however, that these other "mock" usages are today scattered and relatively unproductive, in stark comparison with Mock Spanish. . . .

Finally, I suggest that "Mock Spanish" constitutes a new type of racist discourse.

The kinds of examples that van Dijk (1993) treats as illustrations of "elite racist discourse" are nearly all far more overt, addressing directly whether privileges and rights (such as immigration, or access to public housing) should be extended to members of racialized populations. For instance, van Dijk points out that elite racist discourse can be identified when it is accompanied by qualifying expressions. Someone might say: "Of course I don't dislike foreigners, some of them are fine people, but our country has already admitted too many immigrants." Even though such a speaker would deny that the statement "Our country already has too many immigrants" was racist, the qualifying statement shows that the speaker knows that it could be heard in that way, rather than only an absolutely neutral scientific judgment that shows that the speaker is in control of statistical evidence about what percentage of immigrants is optimal for national development.

People who use Mock Spanish do not use such qualifying expressions. Nobody would say, "Of course Arnold Schwarzenegger has many Mexican-American friends, but he said 'Hasta la vista, baby' at the rally for Bush," or, "I have the highest respect for the Mexican people, but no problemo." . . . These facts enlarge our understanding of the continuum of racist discourse. A picket sign that says "Wetbacks go home!" is obvious vulgar racism. Van Dijk has demonstrated that expressions like, "I don't have anything against Mexicans as such. But we can't pay to deliver the baby of every pregnant lady in Mexico who wants her kid to be an American citizen" constitute clear cases of "elite racist discourse." To these two types we need to add a third, at the most covert end of the continuum, reproducing racism almost entirely through indirect indexicality. This type is exemplified by cases like "Hasta la vista, baby." The first is easily identifiable as racist and is almost always avoided by the powerful; indeed, public vulgar racism precisely indexes powerlessness. The second sounds sleazy and weasely to many thoughtful Anglos. But the last seems to most Anglos to be utterly innocent, even delightful and clever. I would argue, however, that this last is the most powerful of the three. Because of its seeming innocence, it can find its way into a film seen by literally hundreds of millions of people, and can become a clever new casual expression, functioning in that useful range of meanings that range between light talk and insult, that is used by everyone from six-year-olds to senatorial candidates. And each time that it is used, it inexorably reproduces a highly negative stereotype of speakers of Spanish.

American racism almost certainly includes other, similar strategic systems that might be identified by careful research. Especially, similar devices that function to pejorate and racialize African Americans and Asian Americans should be sought and analyzed. Furthermore, many questions remain about Mock Spanish itself. For instance, its history needs more careful investigation. We need to develop techniques by which to show when it has been more, and when less, intense and productive, and whether this ebb and flow of productivity coincides with economic cycles or other possibly related phenomena. More information is needed about who uses Mock Spanish. I have concluded, on the basis of limited and informal observation, that it is largely an elite usage, but it may be extending its reach across the social organization of the system of Whiteness. What are its functions in parts of the English-speaking world like Canada and Ireland . . . , where Spanish-speaking populations are minuscule and largely irrelevant to the local racist system?

Furthermore, Mock Spanish raises a whole range of fascinating questions about the role of humor in discrimination. One of the most compelling arguments of conservative foes of what is called "Political Correctness" is that the "politically correct" have no sense of humor.[17] It strikes me that vulgar racism, for those who practice it, also seems to be fun, full of shared humor. Signs saying "No Mexicans or Dogs served here" were obviously intended to be hilarious. The Good Old Boys at a recent weekend retreat of "law enforcement officers" featured on the national news probably found the "Nigger Check Point" sign (assuming that it was really there, and not faked by their enemies) to be a real thigh-slapper. The drunken laughter of the lynch mob is a stereotype of American history. Unlike the deadly serious, careful register of "elite racist discourse" that van Dijk has identified, systems like Mock Spanish share humor uncomfortably with the cackling of the mob, in the snickering of the corner boys as one of their number sticks out a foot and trips up a black man. How important is humor and joking in the reproduction of racism? (And, of course, of sexism, anti-Semitism, and other systems of discrimination and exclusion.)

In summary, much remains to be done. I believe that linguistic anthropologists are especially well-qualified by the power and subtlety of the analytical tools that are available to us today, to make progress in these matters that are so important to the health of our society.

NOTES

1. In some previous papers on this phenomenon . . . , and in several lectures, I referred to this system as "Junk Spanish." I found that this term was very frequently misunderstood as a reference to so-called "Border Spanish," the code-switching, somewhat Anglicized forms of Spanish that can be heard from some speakers in the U.S. Southwest. I am indebted to James Fernandez for a very convincing explanation of why this misunderstanding was so pervasive, and for the suggestion of "Mock Spanish." Fernandez points out that for English speakers the association between "junk"—ruin and decline—and the Mediterranean areas of Europe (and their colonial offshoots) is hundreds of years old. The use of "junk" plays into this system. "Mock" both avoids this metaphorical system and makes clearer the central function and social location of the register of English that I address here.

2. The term "Anglo" is widely used in the Southwest for "white people." It is an all-encompassing term that includes Italians, Greeks, Irish, etc. Its existence (it is a short, monomorphemic element) is eloquent testimony to the social reality of this group, the members of which often like to argue that they are too diverse internally for such a single label. I will use this term for this social unit in the remainder of the paper.

3. In Arizona, "Official English" legislation, pushed by the national organization U.S. English, took the form of an amendment to the state constitution that included particularly restrictive language, that in the business of "the state and all its dependencies" (which include the University of Arizona), officers of the state (which includes me), "shall act in English and in no other language." The only exclusions were for the criminal courts, the teaching of foreign languages, and health and safety emergencies. Both the federal district court and the Ninth Circuit Court of Appeals have held this amendment to be in violation of the first and fourteenth amendments of the U.S. Constitution. . . .

4. This name borrows from "Nouvelle Southwest Cuisine." . . .

5. I take this expression from the work of Muriel Schulz (1975) on the historical semantic trajectory of words with female referents, such as "queen" (which has acquired the sense of "transvestite," in contrast to "king") and "housewife" (which has the contracted offshoot "hussy," in contrast to "husband," which has no such derogated relative).

6. The correct use of the accent mark on the *o* here is nothing short of astonishing. Written Mock Spanish is usually orthographically absurd.

7. "John Connor" has been "raised up rough" by an aunt and uncle, since his mother is locked in a lunatic asylum because she keeps talking about the first terminator. He is represented at the beginning of the film as running wild in the streets. I have no idea whether working-class white kids in Los Angeles today actually talk like John Connor. I do know, however, that the exposure of the screenwriters of such a film to the talk of kids is far more likely to be at the catered birthday party in Bel Air or in the parking lot of the Montessori School than on the actual mean streets of L.A.

8. There is no doubt that "Adios" is also used, at least in the Southwest, when speakers wish merely to be "warm" rather than funny and insulting. In this case, the stereotype of "Mexicans" (or perhaps the stereotype is of some gruff old Anglo rancher from the 1860's who has helped you fight off the Apaches) is that of generosity and hospitality. This usage does not, of course, cancel out the force of the very common use of "Adios" to convey insult.

9. I owe the "Hasta la baby, vista" example to Jodi Goldman, who found it in *The Koala*, a satirical newspaper published by UCSD students, in the March 8, 1993 Edition. The phrase appears in an ad parodying the advertising for "Terminator 2: Judgment Day." I thank Kathryn Woolard for sending me the work of Ms. Goldman and other students.

10. In the film, the miraculous properties of the terminator metal permit the pieces of the evil terminator's shattered body to flow together and reconstitute him; he comes after Schwarzenegger and his charges again! This detail is neglected by politicians who use "Hasta la vista, baby" as an expression for final dismissal.

11. In Texas, the Democratic candidate Robert Krueger used "Hasta la vista, baby" in a television commercial where he dressed in a peculiar black suit apparently intended to allude to "Zorro," a . . . Mexican bandit from 1950's television. . . .

12. Spanish is, of course, by no means the only European language that is used as a source of "softened" scatological and obscene expressions for English speakers; one thinks immediately of Yiddish *dreck* and French *merde*. But Mock Spanish is a far more productive source. Another example along the same lines is a Mock Spanish version of the widely-distributed slogan "Shit Happens," seen on bumper stickers and other paraphernalia. Bumper stickers are available that read "Caca Pasa."

13. I am indebted to Jay Sanders for drawing my attention to the use of Mock Spanish by Southern California teens; he contributed to a course in Discourse Analysis tapes of young female friends of his (who were from Thousand Oaks, not Encino), chatting casually on the phone using unusually high frequencies of Mock Spanish. Pauly Shore has made several films since "Encino Man" that probably deserve attention as well.

14. There is another, more vulgar version of this greeting that I have not seen. I owe the description of it to Barbara Babcock, who received a card where the front showed Hawaiian hula dancers, face forward, and the word "Muchas." Opening the card revealed a rear view of the dancers, buttocks clearly visible through their grass skirts, and the word "Grassy-ass."

15. Susan Philips found a card that actually shows a "Mexican" sleeping under an enormous sombrero, under the question, "¿Cómo esta frijol?" (Punctuation as in the original). Inside, the card reads: "[English translation] How ya bean?" (Of course it is printed on "100% recycled paper".)

16. Dominique Louisor-White and Dolores Valencia Tanno (1994), of the Communications department at California State University at San Bernardino, found that Mexican-American television newscasters in the Los Angeles area were increasingly likely to choose fully Spanish pronunciations of names when reading the news, starting with the pronunciation of their own names, since they regarded the usual Anglicized pronunciations as disrespectful. (They often encountered opposition to their pronunciation from Anglo station managers.)

17. I do make a claim to a sense of humor. But I have stopped using Mock Spanish, and I urge others to avoid it as well. As soon as Spanish is used within English in such a way that *de lujo* is as common as *de luxe*, that *camarones en mojo de ajo* are as prestigious a dish as *truite a la muniére*, and that *señorita*, like *mademoiselle*, can allude to good breeding as much as to erotic possibility, I'll go back to being as funny as possible with Spanish loan materials. Given the present context, I think that Mock Spanish is harmful—it is humor at the expense of people who don't need any more problems.

REFERENCES

Cassidy, Frederic G. 1985. *Dictionary of American Regional English*. Cambridge, MA: Harvard University Press.

Hill, Jane H. 1993. Hasta la vista, baby: Anglo Spanish in the American Southwest. *Critique of Anthropology* 13:145–176.

Hill, Jane. 1995. "Language, History, and Identity: Ethnolinguistic Studies of the Arizona Tewa." *American Indian Culture and Research Journal,* 19:205–210.

Louisor-White, Dominique and Dolores Valencia Tanno. 1994. Code-switching in the public forum: New expressions of cultural identity and persuasion. Paper presented at the

Conference on Hispanic Language and Social Identity, University of New Mexico, Albuquerque NM, February 10–12, 1994.

Ochs, E. 1990. "Indexicality and Socialization." In J. W. Stigler, R. A. Shweder, & G. Herdt (Eds.). *Cultural Psychology* (pp. 287–308). Cambridge, UK: Cambridge University Press.

Schulz, Muriel. 1975. The semantic derogation of women. In B. Thorne and N. Henley (eds.),

Language and Sex: Difference and Dominance, pp. 64–73. Rowley, MA: Newbury.

Van Dijk, Teun Adreianus. 1993. *Elite Discourse and Racism.* Newbury Park, CA: Sage.

SOURCE: *Mock Spanish: A Site for the Indexical Reproduction of Racism in America English* by Jane H. Hill. Reprinted by permission of the author.

DISCUSSION QUESTIONS

1. If racism is covert and unintended, is it still racism? How does Hill make the case that Mock Spanish helps to reproduce and sustain racism in the larger society? Is her case convincing? What evidence does she cite? If she is correct, under what conditions would it *not* be racist to tell an "ethnic" joke? Is ethnic or racial humor always racist?

2. What is "dual indexicality" and how does it work? What's the difference between direct and indirect indexicality? Cite and explore an example from your own discourse, the conversations of others, or from the mass media (TV, movies, and so on).

SEEING MORE THAN BLACK AND WHITE: LATINOS, RACISM, AND THE CULTURAL DIVIDE

Elizabeth Martinez

. . .

When [Henry] Kissinger [Secretary of State under President Nixon] said years ago "nothing important ever happens in the south," he articulated a contemptuous indifference toward Latin America, its people, and their culture which has long dominated U.S. institutions and attitudes. Mexico may be great for a vacation, and some people like burritos but the usual image of Latin America combines incompetence with absurdity in loud colors. My parents, both Spanish teachers, endured decades of being told kids were better off learning French.

U.S. political culture is not only Anglo-dominated but also embraces an exceptionally stubborn national self-centeredness, with no global vision other than relations of domination. The U.S. refuses to see itself as one nation sitting on a continent with 20 others all speaking languages other than English and having the right not to be dominated.

Such arrogant indifference extends to Latinos within the U.S. The mass media complain, "people can't relate to Hispanics"—or Asians, they say. Such arrogant indifference has played an important role in invisibilizing La Raza (except where we become a serious nuisance or a handy scapegoat). It is one reason the U.S. harbors an exclusively white-on-Black concept of racism. It is one barrier to new thinking about racism which is crucial today. There are others.

GOOD-BYE WHITE MAJORITY

In a society as thoroughly and violently racialized as the United States, white-Black relations have defined racism for centuries. Today the composition and culture of the U.S. are changing rapidly. We need to consider seriously whether we can afford to maintain an exclusively white/Black model of racism when the population will be 32 percent Latin/Asian/Pacific American and Native American—in short, neither Black nor white—by the year 2050. We are challenged to recognize that multicolored racism is mushrooming, and then strategize how to resist it. We are challenged to move beyond a dualism comprised of two white supremacist inventions: Blackness and Whiteness.

At stake in those challenges is building a united anti-racist force strong enough to resist contemporary racist strategies of divide-and-conquer. Strong enough in the long run, to help defeat racism itself. Doesn't an exclusively Black/white model of racism discourage the perception of common interests among people of color and thus impede a solidarity that can challenge white supremacy? Doesn't it encourage the isolation of African Americans from potential allies? Doesn't it advise all people of color to spend too much energy understanding our lives in relation to Whiteness, and thus freeze us in a defensive, often self-destructive mode?

No "Oppression Olympics"

For a Latina to talk about recognizing the multicolored varieties of racism is not, and should not be, yet another round in the Oppression Olympics. We don't need more competition among different social groupings for that "Most Oppressed" gold. We don't need more comparisons of suffering between women and Blacks, the disabled and the gay, Latino teenagers and white seniors, or whatever. We don't need more surveys like the recent much publicized Harris Poll showing that different peoples of color are prejudiced toward each other—a poll patently

designed to demonstrate that us coloreds are no better than white folk. (The survey never asked people about positive attitudes.)

Rather, we need greater knowledge, understanding, and openness to learning about each other's histories and present needs as a basis for working together. Nothing could seem more urgent in an era when increasing impoverishment encourages a self-imposed separatism among people of color as a desperate attempt at community survival. Nothing could seem more important as we search for new social change strategies in a time of ideological confusion.

My call to rethink concepts of racism in the U.S. today is being sounded elsewhere. Among academics, liberal foundation administrators, and activist-intellectuals, you can hear talk of the need for a new "racial paradigm" or model. But new thinking seems to proceed in fits and starts, as if dogged by a fear of stepping on toes, of feeling threatened, or of losing one's base. With a few notable exceptions, even our progressive scholars of color do not make the leap from perfunctorily saluting a vague multiculturalism to serious analysis. We seem to have made little progress, if any, since Bob Blauner's 1972 book *Racial Oppression in America*. Recognizing the limits of the white-Black axis, Blauner critiqued White America's ignorance of and indifference to the Chicano/a experience with racism.

Real opposition to new paradigms also exists. There are academics scrambling for one flavor of ethnic studies funds versus another. There are politicians who cultivate distrust of others to keep their own communities loyal. When we hear, for example, of Black/Latino friction, dismay should be quickly followed by investigation. In cities like Los Angeles and New York, it may turn out that political figures scrapping for patronage and payola have played a narrow nationalist game, whipping up economic anxiety and generating resentment that sets communities against each other.

So the goal here, in speaking about moving beyond a bipolar concept of racism, is to build stronger unity against white supremacy. The goal is to see our similarities of experience and needs. If that goal sounds naive, think about the hundreds of organizations formed by grassroots women of different colors coming together in recent years. Their growth is one of today's most energetic motions and it spans all ages. Think about the multicultural environmental justice movement. Think about the coalitions to save schools. Small rainbows of our own making are there, to brighten a long road through hellish times.

It is in such practice, through daily struggle together, that we are most likely to find the road to greater solidarity against a common enemy. But we also need a will to find it and ideas about where, including some new theory.

The West Goes East

Until very recently, Latino invisibility—like that of Native Americans and Asian/Pacific Americans—has been close to absolute in U.S. seats of power, major institutions, and the non-Latino public mind. Having lived on both the East and West Coasts for long periods, I feel qualified to pronounce: an especially myopic view of Latinos prevails in the East. This, despite such data as a 24.4 percent Latino population of New York City alone in 1991, or the fact that in 1990 more Puerto Ricans were killed by New York police under suspicious circumstances than any other ethnic group. Latino populations are growing rapidly in many eastern cities and the rural South, yet remain invisible or stigmatized—usually both.

Eastern blinders persist. I've even heard that the need for a new racial paradigm is dismissed in New York as a California hang-up. A black Puerto Rican friend in New York, when we talked about experiences of racism common to

Black and brown, said "People here don't see Border Patrol brutality against Mexicans as a form of police repression," despite the fact that the Border Patrol is the largest and most uncontrolled police force in the U.S. It would seem that an old ignorance has combined with new immigrant bashing to sustain divisions today.

While the East (and most of the Midwest) usually remains myopic, the West Coast has barely begun to move away from its own denial. Less than two years ago in San Francisco, a city almost half Latino or Asian/Pacific American, a leading daily newspaper could publish a major series on contemporary racial issues and follow the exclusively Black-white paradigm. Although millions of TV viewers saw massive Latino participation in the April 1992 Los Angeles uprising, which included 18 out of 50 deaths and the majority of arrests, the mass media and most people labeled that event "a Black riot."

If the West Coast has more recognition of those who are neither Black nor white, it is mostly out of fear about the proximate demise of its white majority. A second, closely related reason is the relentless campaign by California Governor Pete Wilson to scapegoat immigrants for economic problems and pass racist, unconstitutional laws attacking their health, education, and children's future. Wilson has almost single-handedly made the word "immigrant" mean Mexican or other Latino (and sometimes Asian). Who thinks of all the people coming from the former Soviet Union and other countries? The absolute racism of this has too often been successfully masked by reactionary anti-immigrant groups like FAIR [the Federation for American Immigration Reform] blaming immigrants for the staggering African-American unemployment rate. . . .

As this suggests, what has been a regional issue mostly limited to western states is becoming a national issue. If you thought Latinos were just "Messicans" down at the border, wake up— they are all over North Carolina, Pennsylvania and 8th Avenue Manhattan now. A qualitative change is taking place. With the broader geographic spread of Latinos and Asian/Pacific Islanders has come a nationalization of racist practices and attitudes that were once regional. The west goes east, we could say.

Like the monster Hydra, racism is growing some ugly new heads. We will have to look at them closely.

THE ROOTS OF RACISM AND LATINOS

A bipolar model of racism—racism as white on Black—has never really been accurate. Looking for the roots of racism in the U.S. we can begin with the genocide against American Indians which made possible the U.S. land base, crucial to white settlement and early capitalist growth. Soon came the massive enslavement of African people which facilitated that growth. As slave labor became economically critical, "blackness" became ideologically critical; it provided the very source of "whiteness" and the heart of racism. Frantz Fanon would write, "colour is the most outward manifestation of race."

If Native Americans had been a crucial labor force during those same centuries, living and working in the white man's sphere, our racist ideology might have evolved differently. "The tawny," as Ben Franklin dubbed them, might have defined the opposite of what he called "the lovely white." But with Indians decimated and survivors moved to distant concentration camps they became unlikely candidates for this function. Similarly, Mexicans were concentrated in the distant West; elsewhere Anglo fear of them or need to control was rare. They also did not provide the foundation for a definition of whiteness.

Some anti-racist left activists have put forth the idea that only African Americans experience racism as such and that the suffering of other people of color results from national minority rather than racial oppression. From this viewpoint, the exclusively white/Black model for racism is correct. Latinos, then, experience exploitation and repression for reasons of culture and nationality—not for their "race." (It should go without saying . . . that while racism is an all-too-real social fact, race has no scientific basis.)

Does the distinction hold? This and other theoretical questions call for more analysis and more expertise than one article can offer. In the meantime let's try on the idea that Latinos do suffer for their nationality and culture, especially language. They became part of the U.S. through the 1846–48 war on Mexico and thus a foreign population to be colonized. But as they were reduced to cheap or semi-slave labor, they quickly came to suffer for their "race"— meaning, as non-whites. In the Southwest of a super-racialized nation the broad parallelism of race and class embraces Mexicans ferociously.

The bridge here might be a definition of racism as "the reduction of the cultural to the biological," in the words of French scholar Christian Delacampagne now working in Egypt. Or: "racism exists wherever it is claimed that a given social status is explained by a given natural characteristic." We know that line: Mexicans are just naturally lazy and have too many children so they're poor and exploited.

The discrimination, oppression and hatred experienced by Native Americans, Mexicans, Asian/Pacific Islanders, and Arab Americans are forms of racism. Speaking only of Latinos, we have seen in California and the Southwest especially along the border, almost 150 years of relentless repression which today includes Central Americans among its targets. That history reveals hundreds of lynchings between 1847 and 1935, the use of counter-insurgency armed forces beginning with the Texas Rangers, random torture and murder by Anglo ranchers, forced labor, rape by border lawmen, and the prevailing Anglo belief that a Mexican life doesn't equal a dog's in value.

But wait. If color is so key to racial definition, as Fanon and others say, perhaps people of Mexican background experience racism less than national minority oppression because they are not dark enough as a group. For White America, shades of skin color are crucial to defining worth. The influence of those shades has also been internalized by communities of color. Many Latinos can and often want to pass for whites; therefore, White America may see them as less threatening than darker sisters and brothers.

Here we confront more of the complexity around us today, with questions like: What about the usually poor, very dark Mexican or Central American of strong Indian or African heritage? (Yes, folks, 200,000–300,000 Africans were brought to Mexico as slaves, which is far, far more than the Spaniards who came.) And what about the effects of accented speech or foreign name, characteristics that may instantly subvert "passing"?

What about those cases where a Mexican-American is never accepted, no matter how light-skinned, well-dressed or well-spoken? A Chicano lawyer friend coming home from a professional conference in suit, tie and briefcase found himself on a bus near San Diego that was suddenly stopped by the Border Patrol. An agent came on board and made a beeline through the all-white rows of passengers direct to my friend. "Your papers." The agent didn't believe Jose was coming from a U.S. conference and took him off the bus to await proof. Jose was lucky; too many Chicanos and Mexicans end up killed.

In a land where the national identity is white, having the "wrong" nationality becomes grounds for racist abuse. Who would draw a sharp line between today's national minority oppression in the form of immigrant-bashing, and racism?

None of this aims to equate the African American and Latino experiences; that isn't necessary even if it were accurate. Many reasons exist for the persistence of the white/Black paradigm of racism; they include numbers, history, and the psychology of whiteness. In particular they include centuries of slave revolts, a Civil War, and an ongoing resistance to racism that cracked this society wide open while the world watched. Nor has the misery imposed on Black people lessened in recent years. New thinking about racism can and should keep this experience at the center.

A DEADLY DUALISM

The exclusively white/Black concept of race and racism in the U.S. rests on a western, Protestant form of dualism woven into both race and gender relations from earliest times. In the dualist universe there is only black and white. A disdain, indeed fear, of mixture haunts the Yankee soul; there is no room for any kind of multi-faceted identity, any hybridism.

As a people, La Raza combines three sets of roots—indigenous, European, and African—all in widely varying degrees. In short, we represent a profoundly un-American concept: *mestizaje* (pronounced mess-tee-zah-hey), the mixing of peoples and emergence of new peoples. A highly racialized society like this one cannot deal with or allow room for *mestizaje*. It has never learned to do much more than hiss "miscegenation!" Or, like that Alabama high school principal who recently denied the right of a mixed-blood pupil to attend the prom, to say: "your parents made a mistake." Apparently we, all the millions of La Raza, are just that—a mistake.

Mexicans in the U.S. also defy the either-or, dualistic mind in that, on the one hand, we are a colonized people displaced from the ancestral homeland with roots in the present-day U.S. that go back centuries. Those ancestors didn't cross the border; the border crossed them. At the same time many of us have come to the U.S. more recently as "immigrants" seeking work. The complexity of Raza baffles and frustrates most Anglos; they want to put one neat label on us. It baffles many Latinos too, who often end up categorizing themselves racially as "Other" for lack of anything better. For that matter, the term "Latino" which I use here is a monumental simplification; it refers to 20-plus nationalities and a wide range of classes.

But we need to grapple with the complexity, for there is more to come. If anything, this nation will see more *mestizaje* in future, embracing innumerable ethnic combinations. What will be its effects? Only one thing seems certain: "white" shall cease to be the national identity.

A glimpse at the next century tells us how much we need to look beyond the white/Black model of race relations and racism. White/Black are real poles, central to the history of U.S. racism. We can neither ignore them nor stop there. But our effectiveness in fighting racism depends on seeing the changes taking place, trying to perceive the contours of the future. From the time of the Greeks to the present, racism around the world has had certain commonalties but no permanently fixed character. It is evolving again today, and we'd best labor to read the new faces of this Hydra-headed monster. Remember, for every head that Hydra lost it grew two more.

Sometimes the problem seems so clear. Last year I showed slides of Chicano history to an Oakland high school class with 47 African Americans and three Latino students. The images included lynchings and police beatings of Mexicans and other Latinos, and many years of resistance. At the end one Black student asked, "Seems like we have had a lot of experiences in common—so why can't Blacks and Mexicans get along better?" No answers, but there was the first step: asking the question.

. . .

SOURCE: From *De Colores Means All of Us: Latina Views for a Multi-Colored Century* by Elizabeth Martinez. Reprinted by permission of the author.

DISCUSSION QUESTIONS

1. What does Martinez mean by the "Oppression Olympics"? Why is it destructive, from her point of view, to compete for the "most oppressed" gold? What should nonwhites be pursuing instead? What can minority groups learn from each other? How would (white) America change if nonwhite groups learned to "get along better"?

2. Martinez argues that the dualistic white/black model of racism encourages people of color "to spend too much energy understanding our lives in relation to Whiteness." What does she mean by this? What is "whiteness" and how does it relate to nonwhite groups? Is Martinez addressing a psychological process only, or are there political or economic (or other) dimensions?

3. Martinez discusses the struggle of nonwhite and dispossessed groups against "a common enemy." Who is that enemy? White people? Whiteness?

4. What are some specific ways discussed by Martinez in which nonwhites and Hispanic Americans in general are "invisibilized" and scapegoated?

5. Is the oppression and discrimination faced by Latinos mainly based on race or ethnicity, culture, and language? How would Martinez answer this question? What difference does it make? How?

Not White or Black, but In Between: Latinos and Asian Americans Expanding the Language of Colorblind Racism

Eileen O'Brien

Population experts predict that the percentage of Americans in "minority groups" will increase radically by the middle of this century with Latinos and Asian Americans leading the way. U.S. society has largely been defined by a dichotomous racial order: blacks vs. whites. What will happen to this simple structure as America becomes more "brown" and "yellow"? Will the ancient racial order find a way to perpetuate itself or will it be transformed? What changes can we expect in the way race and group membership are discussed and perceived?

Some scholars predict that the growth of Latinos and Asians signifies the impending end of white domination (the "coming white minority"), and foreshadows the coming of a new racial democracy (e.g., Feagin 2000; Feagin and O'Brien 2003). I will call this the "pluralism" or "browning" prediction. These scholars point to the similarities of black, Latino, and Asian experiences with discrimination. In effect, the browning argument posits that Latinos and Asians are "people of color" too and thus more like blacks than like whites.

A second interpretation is that Latinos and Asians will actually eventually "whiten" as did immigrant ethnic groups such as Irish, Italians, and Russian Jews before them. This "whitening thesis" is supported by George Yancey (2003) with survey data, demonstrating how Latinos' and Asians' residential, intermarriage, and voting patterns are more like whites than blacks. According to this school of thought, the black-white dichotomy will remain the paradigmatic structure of US race relations, with Latinos and Asians falling on the white, or "nonblack," side of the dichotomy. This perspective not only posits that Latinos and Asians are more

"like whites," but it follows the classic model of assimilation (Gordon 1964) that states that immigrant groups should model themselves after the dominant group if they expect to reap the advantages of all their new society is to offer them.

However, it could be that the racial reality that eventually emerges will be more complex than either model suggests. The basic predictions that Latinos and Asians will simply become "white" or "black" simplify the possibilities.

To acknowledge this complexity, Eduardo Bonilla-Silva has developed what he calls the Latin-Americanization of race relations thesis (Bonilla-Silva and Embrick 2006). This third perspective takes a middle ground by proposing a "trichotomy" of groups: whites, honorary whites, and the "collective black." Bonilla-Silva predicts that about 25% of Latinos and Asians will be allowed to become "honorary whites," at least partially substantiating Yancey's "whitening" claim (though "honorary white" status is tenuous and not as solid as the "white" status that the Irish and Jews have been able to achieve). The other 75%, the large majority, of Latino and Asian Americans are predicted to fall into a "collective black" category, where they will share the common experiences of discrimination and alienation that blacks currently face. This perspective offers the most promise in terms of acknowledging a middle ground for Latinos and Asians that would be qualitatively different than either that experienced by blacks or that experienced by whites. While no data has been presented yet to empirically document the "honorary white" experience, it suggests a degree of assimilation, with skin tone and ethnicity still limiting full access to the privileges of whiteness.

What is missing from all three of these perspectives is a consideration of how the intermediate space of "honorary white" would be distinct, not just due to lack of full structural access to the material benefits of whiteness, but due also to the more unique racialized space. How will "honorary whites" think of themselves? How will they distinguish themselves from blacks? Will their self conceptions and emerging ideologies bolster or challenge white supremacy?

Colorblind Racism's Ideology

Research has identified *colorblind racism* as the dominant racial ideology of the late twentieth and early twenty-first centuries (Bonilla-Silva 2003; Carr 1997; Frankenberg 1993). Through colorblind racism (Bonilla-Silva 2003; Carr 1997) or color and power evasiveness (Frankenberg 1993), people discourage overt references to "color" as reasoning for why certain racial groups are "ahead" or "behind." We may continue to communicate racism through code words (e.g., "at-risk" children, "welfare mothers," "ghetto," the "bad part of town") or through language that minimizes the significance of systemic racism and instead "blames the victims" for their plight.

By studying the discourse of U.S. blacks and whites, Bonilla-Silva (2003) identified four frames of colorblind racism, and various other rhetorical styles and storylines common to its usage. The first frame is abstract liberalism, an individualistic discourse which evaluates people's success or lack thereof as a result of their individual motivations, talents and free choice, downplaying any structural limitations. Quotes about "people are people" and "I don't see color" would be demonstrative of this frame. The second frame is naturalization, which views social facts such as racial segregation as race-neutral results of "human nature" and a benign desire for people to be with others most like themselves. The third frame is cultural racism, which interprets a social fact such as racial differences in income as a result of cultural factors not having to do with discrimination—such as lack of work ethic, lack of education, or lack of "family values"—"anything but race." The fourth frame is minimization, which largely dismisses claims that people of color face discrimination, often by way of rhetorical devices like distancing (e.g., "I'm not black, so I don't really know . . .") or projection (e.g., "blacks are the only ones I see discriminating").

Due to its focus on blacks and whites, the research on colorblind racism leaves open the question of how Latinos and Asians might make use of its ideological framework to make sense of U.S. race relations. Leslie Carr's (1997) survey of students found that 77 percent of students agreed with the statement "I am colorblind when it comes to race" while only 40 percent of black students agreed. Bonilla-Silva's (2003) study reports that, on the four frames of colorblind racism analyzed, blacks used them from 6 to 35 percent of the time, while whites used them 43 to 96 percent of the time (Bonilla-Silva 2003: 153). Moreover, while a small minority (12 to 15 percent) of whites is racially progressive by Bonilla-Silva's criteria (they support intermarriage, affirmative action, and recognize the significance of contemporary racial discrimination), about three-quarters of blacks share these progressive (and non-colorblind) views. If Latinos and Asians are "browning" or joining the "collective black" we would expect them to use colorblind rhetoric sparingly, but if they are indeed "whitening" we would expect them to use it often, much in the same way that whites do.

RESEARCH METHODS AND SAMPLE INFORMATION

The data gathered for this project come from twenty in-depth interviews with Latinos and Asian Americans about their racial and ethnic related experiences in the United States. This sample was purposefully selected to represent a diverse range of ethnicities, ages, generation of migration, and both genders. The sample includes nine Asian/Pacific Islander respondents and eleven Hispanic/Latino respondents. Their ages range from 18 to 60—six are under thirty, eight are in their thirties, five are in their forties, and one is sixty. They share a range of ethnicities, generations, geographic locations, levels of education, and occupations. Respondents were interviewed using an in-depth interview method with an interview guide.

My sample suggests that Latinos and Asians are neither completely like blacks nor completely like whites. A full 50% of my sample would actually be classified as progressive by Bonilla-Silva's standards above, quite higher than the 12 to 15 percent typical of whites, and thus supporting the "browning" thesis. Yet more than half of them use colorblind racism, which partly supports the "whitening" position. However, it will be my contention that, rather than simply parroting the dominant discourse of colorblind racism, some Latinos and Asians are indeed perpetuating the discourse of colorblind racism, but in ways that are not only unique to them, but arguably accessible only to

them. This positions them in a decidedly middle ground not reducible to black or white Americans' racial ideologies.

LATINOS, ASIANS, AND COLORBLIND RACISM

At first glance, counting up percentages of our own respondents' usage of the 4 frames of colorblind racism, Latinos and Asians seem to fit neatly in between blacks' and whites' percentages, ranging from 35 to 65 percent, but share more overlap with whites, as Yancey's whitening thesis might predict. In Table 7.1, I use Bonilla-Silva's (2003) results for whites and blacks, and my own results for the Latino/Asian column. Although these are not entirely comparable data sources, they serve as a good beginning point from which to springboard to a more detailed analysis of our qualitative data.

For all frames, we can see that Latinos and Asians seem to use colorblind racism more than blacks do. For three out of four frames, their usage is closer to whites than blacks (echoing Yancey's findings on other outcomes), and in the case of naturalization, their rate of usage is nearly identical to whites. However, it is important to note that on abstract liberalism, Latinos and Asians talk much more like blacks. Thus, even upon this cursory glance, we can see that the whitening thesis is partially substantiated in Latinos' and Asians' racial attitudes, although not entirely. The browning thesis is more correct only when it comes to abstract liberalism.

Table 7.1   Comparison of Usage of Colorblind Racism Frames, by Race

	Whites	*Latinos/Asians*	*Blacks*
Abstract Liberalism	96%	35% (7/20)	35%
Cultural Racism	88%	65% (13/20)	24%
Naturalization	43%	40% (8/20)	24%
Minimization	84%	50% (10/20)	6%

The picture gets even more complex once we take note of an important aspect that differentiates both Latinos and Asians from the bipolar black/white comparison. When whites discuss the factors they perceive as responsible for racial differences, they typically are either referring mainly to blacks, or else they are lumping all people of color together. Likewise, when blacks use colorblind language, they are usually referring to their own group. However, when Latinos and Asians use the two frames of cultural racism and minimization in particular, they are much more likely to either be talking about their own specific ethnic group or another nonblack racial/ethnic group, rather than about blacks. If we restrict our analysis of cultural racism to instances of *antiblack* colorblind racism, the percentage jumps down from 72% to only 33% of the respondents. Likewise, if we restrict our analysis of the minimization frame to the times when our respondents are talking about how *blacks* over-exaggerate discrimination (or, for instance, how blacks "use it as a crutch") the percentage again jumps down, from 56% to just 17% of the respondents. What is clear from this breakdown is that Latinos and Asians seem to be more willing to use colorblind racism when referring to their own and other "intermediate" racial groups, rather than towards blacks. However, a more detailed qualitative analysis reveals that sometimes, even when blacks are not mentioned, they are the actual "unmentioned" target of racism. Blacks end up being the unspoken reference point through which other groups are evaluated and compared.

ANTI-BLACK RACISM—VEILED AND UNVEILED

Latino and Asian respondents do discuss antiblack racism explicitly at times, while other times it is "veiled" through reference to another racial or ethnic group. Demonstrating colorblind racism, this Dominican American woman

recalls her daughter's relationship with an African American young man, which was unacceptable to her and other members of the family, although she insists it was not because of his "race":

> Well, one of my daughters, she had a relationship with an African American, and I didn't judge him because of his ethnicity, I judged him because of his actions, that's what I didn't like, his actions. . . . [Interviewer: how did the other people in the family react when your daughter was dating an African American? Did they have mixed feelings?] Yes, they did, they had mixed feelings. They had mixed feelings because he was older than her, and didn't have the same goals as she had. And but also I'm not going to lie. There was unkind, when they found out it was black. But that didn't come from me, it came from my mother. [Interviewer: she didn't really like it?] She didn't like it. [Interviewer: it's just because she has a view of—] She has a view of—that African Americans—like she is scared. But it's something that me and my brother and sister have tried to teach her, that no it's not like that.

In this exchange, our respondent uses some discourse familiar to Bonilla-Silva's white respondents who express some back-and-forth resistance to interracial relationships. They may approve of them in the abstract, but once they are pressed to discuss details, and how it impacts their own families, they discuss their resistance by valorizing a view that blacks are "just different" in terms of values, and in this case "goals" and "actions." She also uses a common storyline that Bonilla-Silva identifies when she distances herself from a racist family member to prove her own nonracism.

However, the unique "intermediate" dimension to this respondent's negative view of African Americans comes out later in the interview, when she is asked which racial or ethnic group she identifies with most and the least. She states she feels furthest away from Ecuadorians because:

I don't know, because maybe how they also have relationship with black community. Well not all of them, some of them. I don't know I don't know maybe I'm wrong.

This respondent uses some of the rhetorical styles Bonilla-Silva identifies to distance herself from her own views by using the "I don't know, maybe I'm wrong" maneuver. Yet because the respondent never goes as far as to say that she herself feels negatively towards the black community, rather she says she cannot identify with another Hispanic group because of their perceived ties to the "black community." Ecuadorians serve as the "veil" through which this respondent feels comfortable enough to express her disdain for African Americans without having to do it more explicitly. There is a sense that, in the unwritten rules of racial discourse, it is within the realm of nonracist acceptability for her to be able to make negative judgments about Ecuadorians without seeming racist, since she is somewhat of an insider by being Latino just like them. Non-Hispanic whites would be more likely to either find both references inappropriate, or to go ahead and make generalizations about both blacks and Hispanics. When they do refer to the "intermediate groups" alone, they are more likely to single them out for more positive stereotyping than blacks. They tend to choose other code words, rather than words that were explicitly ethnic, to cast negative light on what they believed to be black-associated behaviors.

Similarly, this Filipino respondent separates herself out from others in her own group, especially those whom she characterizes as more like blacks. However, unlike the above respondent, she never mentions blacks explicitly. Instead, she divides her own ethnic group into categories that are either more or less like blacks, as indicated by the racial code words of "hip-hop" and "ghetto." The subgroup of Filipinos that she considers to be more like whites, though, she does actually describe as "more white":

I know a lot of Asians that grew up in communities that are predominantly white and that's because most Asians in terms of economics they just tend to be more affluent because it's like you know they're just hardworking. . . . they're much more white. And at the same time I know a lot of like Filipinos and Koreans that are really like ghetto, I mean really like into the hip hop culture. . . . So Filipinos are either really white or really ghetto [laughs] it's weird.

Elsewhere in this interview, this respondent points out that she was unlike most Filipinos at her school growing up in that she did not identify with "hip-hop" and "ghetto" culture. In the above quote, though, she characterizes Asians on the whole as "more white" because of their "hardworking nature." The adjectives she chooses like "secure" and "well off" cast a more positive light on this group. Here, veiled antiblack racism operates by essentially saying, "I look down upon/distance myself from X group because they are too much like blacks." Being culturally "like blacks" is cast as a negative, but other ethnic groups (here, one's own ethnic group) get substituted as a proxy for blacks.

I'M OK, YOU'RE NOT OK—SELECTIVE DECONSTRUCTION OF STEREOTYPES

As indicated by the above quote, several of the interviews touched upon stereotypical generalizations about particular racial and/or ethnic groups—whether they were groups in which the respondent claimed membership or not. Sometimes respondents reflected upon stereotypes that *others* held about their own group, while other times they admitted to holding stereotypes of their own. Recall that half of our sample would be categorized as progressive based upon the conceptual definition in prior related research. When these progressive respondents discussed stereotypes, they were quite consistent in breaking them down as faulty overgeneralizations and treating them as problematic. In contrast, our other (non-progressive) respondents would tend to display an interesting pattern—within the same interview, they would use progressive racial ideology to deconstruct a particular stereotype, yet elsewhere throw these analytical skills out the window by agreeing with other stereotypes.

Recall the Filipino student quoted above, relying upon the stereotype of Asians as "well off" due to their "hardworking nature." One could actually present a more progressive critique of this "model minority" generalization, as indeed another Asian respondent, a statistician originally from India, does in the following quote:

> They think that, the perception now, because Indians do so well is that they are really smart and that they are all educated and they are very successful and that's not true because there are a lot of dumb Indians in India. It's just that the ones that come here, the smart ones come here to go to school. Those that are not career oriented, not very smart stay in India. So you got the crème of the crop, and you know that [the stereotype]'s not necessarily true.

As it turns out, however, her sophisticated understanding of the structural factors operating to create a certain group's experience do not extend much past Indians. She indeed uses a stereotypical cultural racism frame to interpret the experience of her Chinese coworker, and contrasts it with her own experience as an Indian:

> We are so diverse within India because each state is so different . . . not like China were everyone is Chinese and speaks the same language and stuff like that. . . . Most Indians will integrate, you know, they have white friends, they, you know first of all with the language, everyone speaks English so that makes a difference. You know the Chinese don't. I know this girl at work . . . she's been here since she was 2 years old . . . can you believe is living in the heart of New York and she can't even speak English?! . . . Everything is in Chinatown—Chinese hospitals, Chinese food . . . Chinese libraries . . . Chinese friends . . . you will never find that with Indians. . . . It's bizarre. I'm shocked.

While she acknowledges Indians are not monolithic, she speaks with sweeping generalizations about "the Chinese." Instead of exploring the structural factors that account for why Indians already speak English upon arrival to the US (colonization by the British, higher education, etc.), she poses it as her Chinese coworker's own lack of effort, interest, or motivation that she does not speak English as well as herself. Her argument is very similar to the one often used by whites about blacks "segregating themselves," especially when she contrasts with Indians who "integrate" and "have white friends." Elsewhere in her interview, she continues on extolling the virtues of the great diversity of India, and this time contrasts it with Hispanics: "The Hispanic culture has a very strong culture and representation. Indians are very divided even among themselves in terms of culture." While we might give Trina some benefit of the doubt in characterizing India as more diverse than China, nation to nation, clearly, her overgeneralization about dozens of Latin American cultures shows that she is more willing to challenge white supremacist notions about her own group, while she uncritically accepts them about others'.

In contrast to the above respondent's glossing over ethnic differences among Latinos, this white-Cuban biracial man, who is well-traveled in many Latin American countries due to his occupation, makes sharp distinctions among them. In particular, he singles out his own ethnic group as more deserving of the "model minority" stereotype than many of the others:

> I say this not because I'm Cuban, but as my observation, and I think the statistics bear it out as well, but—Cubans are seen in higher status than most Latins that have come to the United States, compared to let's say Puerto Ricans, Dominicans, and Central Americans for the most part. And even to an extent maybe even Venezuelans and Colombians—though maybe it starts to blur there. Cubans are very industrious. They've done extremely well for themselves compared to the other Latin American populations . . . doing especially better than the Nicaraguans, or Salvadorians . . . Cubans are very crafty, they're very industrious, they'll think outside the box. I mean who else would take a 1960 Chevrolet something or other and turn it into a boat in order to cross the Florida straits. I mean really!? You know—a boat! And it worked, but that's how they are.

The phrase "that's how they are" sounds familiar as stereotypical language whites tend to use to generalize about blacks and/or other minorities, but here it is being used by someone who identifies as white/Cuban, so theoretically he is speaking about "his own" group (using the third person pronoun *they*). Perhaps he uses this voice to position himself as an objective observer, since he begins by saying that he is not just saying it because he is Cuban. The kind of structural analysis that the Indian respondent quoted earlier used to critique the model minority stereotype (analyzing human capital factors, economic conditions of each country and its migrants, government/refugee assistance unique to Cubans, etc.) could certainly have been applied to the various Latino groups listed in the above quote. However, this respondent instead relies on a combination of naturalization and cultural racism to explain the differences in these various Latino groups'

socioeconomic positions. The hardworking/ "industrious" generalization that the Filipino student used to describe Asians comes up again here, and posited as an essential trait of Cubans this time.

However, this Cuban respondent understands at the abstract level that generalizations about an entire group only go so far when he makes this comment:

> I could care less if who lives next door to me, or across the street, or behind me is black, Hispanic, Asian, Muslim, as long as they're good people. That's what I care about. I just want to live next to people that are good people. Because you know, I could live next door to a Cuban guy and he could be a jack ass. Right [laughter] And there's plenty of them too, plenty of Cuban jackasses.

Here we see the abstract liberalism frame of "I could care less . . . as long as they're good people." By making the point that there are "good" and "jackass" people in every ethnic group (particularly his own) he demonstrates that he could potentially have the ability to deconstruct stereotypical generalizations about his own group. But he fails to do so in the previous example.

More to the point, this respondent can recall personal family experiences attesting to how painful it can be to be the victim of unjustly applied stereotypes. He remembers how difficult it was for their family to leave Miami and relocate to a Midwestern state where it was constantly assumed that his Cuban father was a drug dealer. Even though at some level this respondent critiques the unfairness of such stereotypes, ultimately he finds them as inevitable and even justified:

> So if you got a lot of Cubans in the drug trade, and you're Cuban then unfortunately you may be associated with that. Is it fair? Maybe not, probably not . . . Mexican groups are seen as kinda being lazy. I don't think that's necessarily fair.

I mean they work . . . back breaking work. But Mexico is seen generally in terms of government as being corrupt . . . That's a fact . . . Is it fair for that to reflect on all Mexicans? No. But when you have something that's going on . . . until you get it cleaned up that's kinda what you're gonna have to be prepared to live with . . . Are all people of the Islamic faith terrorists? Of course not, no. But right now they've got a small minority of people . . . doing heinous crimes in the name of the Islamic religion. Well, until they get that cleaned up, they're going to have live with the repercussions of that.

The usage of the pronoun "they" is interesting here, because while he acknowledges that stereotypes are true of only a "small minority" of any given group, "they" have to "live with the repercussions" since "they" have not "cleaned up." Here the "they" is one and the same—it is as if those who do not live out the stereotype are still at fault, guilty by association. Those who erroneously apply a stereotype to all members of a group are somehow not at all at fault in this equation.

Conclusion

Occupying an intermediate position in the US racial hierarchy does not simply mean that one is somewhat like whites and somewhat like blacks. While certainly the above quotes demonstrate that several Latino and Asian American respondents use colorblind ideology in ways similar to that which has been documented in research on whites, they additionally make use of colorblind racism in ways unique to them. Indeed, whites particularly have been reported to be a bit more simplistic in their usage of colorblindness than my respondents are. Whites typically use blacks as their nonwhite group of comparison, and "intermediate" groups are often lumped together with all people of color. If whites do separate out intermediate groups in

their discussions, they tend to be singled out for more "positive" stereotyping than blacks. For instance, some elite white men in Feagin and O'Brien's (2003) study praised the work ethic of Mexicans and Asian Americans as a whole while viewing negatively that of blacks. They are held up as "model minorities" if only to cast a negative comparison with African Americans. From a white perspective, a distinct hierarchy seems to emerge on a scale of valued to devalued—whites, Asians/Latinos, blacks—consistent with social distance studies done (on whites) since the 1920s. In contrast, from the viewpoint of Latinos and Asians themselves, the situation is more complex. Latinos and Asians seem to resist racialized generalizations about their own groups, stressing the ethnic distinctions among them that are sometimes lost on other whites, and even on members of other "outsider" nonwhite groups. In the process of stressing these ethnic distinctions, they use them both to deconstruct racist ideology for some groups (especially their own) and to reify it for others.

Since racist ideology has been constructed for the benefit of the dominant group (whites), in order to make it work towards their advantage, Latinos and Asians must be much more sophisticated about how they use it, since in its most commonly used forms it does not address them directly. While the fact that racist ideology has been constructed for the benefit of whites might suggest that there is less flexibility in its usage for Latinos and Asians, actually in some ways there is more flexibility for them to make use of it. Specifically, they have room to exercise antiblack racism in ways even more camouflaged than whites do by using these ethnic distinctions between themselves and other racially-similar groups through which to "veil" their negative sentiments about blacks. We saw a Dominican respondent "veil" her antiblack racism through Ecuadorians, and a Filipino respondent "veil" her antiblack racism through

Filipinos who are "ghetto" or like hip-hop. This veiling dynamic demonstrates that as "insiders," Latinos and Asians can exercise an ideological option which makes them more comfortable casting negative light upon African Americans if they combine their own racial group along with it.

If colorblind racism has been characterized as a more sophisticated and savvy form of racism than the more overt racism that pre-ceded it historically, then clearly Latinos and Asians, as intermediate groups, have taken this sophistication to an even more elevated level. Bonilla-Silva and Embrick (2006) discuss this more complex manifestation of colorblind racism as they compare Latin American race relations to that of the United States. My research suggests that both Latinos and Asians, as intermediate racial groups in the US racial hierarchy, may indeed contribute to these new dimensions of racism. The challenge for antiracist scholars and activists will be to also research the unique forms of racial progres-sivism among US Latinos and Asians in order to demonstrate how an intricate form of racism can also be undone.

References

Bonilla-Silva, Eduardo and David G. Embrick. 2006. "Black, Honorary White, White: The Future of Race in the United States?" Pp. 33–48 in David L. Brunsma, ed. *Mixed Messages: Multiracial Identities in the "Color-Blind" Era.* Boulder, Colorado: Lynne Rienner.

Bonilla-Silva, Eduardo. 2003. *Racism without Racists.* Lanham, Maryland: Rowman and Littlefield.

Carr, Leslie. 1997. *Colorblind Racism.* Thousand Oaks, California: Sage.

Feagin, Joe R. 2000. *Racist America.* New York: Routledge.

Feagin, Joe R. and Eileen O'Brien. 2003. *White Men on Race.* Boston: Beacon Press.

Frankenberg, Ruth, 1993. *White Women, Race Matters: The Social Construction of Whiteness.* Minneapolis: University of Minnesota Press.

Gordon, Milton. 1964. *Assimilation in American Life.* New York: Oxford University Press.

Yancey, George. 2003. *Who Is White? Latinos, Asians, and the New Black/Nonblack Divide.* Boulder, Colorado: Lynne Rienner.

SOURCE: Reprinted by permission of the author.

Discussion Questions

1. What makes both Latinos and Asians dif-ferent from whites in terms of how they express color-blind racism?

2. Latinos are now a slightly larger percentage of the U.S. population than African Americans. Due to the ethnic diversity among Latinos (and Asians), what kinds of ethnic distinctions do they make when discussing race relations that often do not appear in blacks' or whites' discourse?

3. We might expect people who are able to use their sociological imaginations to debunk *some* racial-ethnic stereotypes to also apply that logic to others. Why does this expectation not hold true with the respondents quoted here? Have you known others who seem open-minded about one group yet prejudiced about another? How and why do you think this happens, and what might be done to change it?

4. Elizabeth Martinez's reading in this chapter is optimistic about people of color coming together and realizing the common struggles with racism that they share. What challenges does O'Brien's reading suggest would need to be overcome before such cross-racial and cross-ethnic coalitions could be built?

CURRENT DEBATES

IS AMERICANIZATION THREATENED BY "HISPANIZATION"?

Immigration from Latin America—and especially from Mexico—is voluminous and shows no sign of slowing. How will these new immigrations shape American culture? Will traditional American values such as individualism, the Protestant Ethic, democracy, and loyalty and patriotism be compromised? Are we developing into two nations, one Anglo and the other Hispanic?

Many people are deeply concerned that American culture cannot survive in its present form. For example, political scientist Samuel Huntington, in his influential book *Who Are We?* (2004), argues that large-scale immigration (particularly from Mexico) is leading the United States away from its historical roots and its central values. Others have taken up his argument and, in the article below, John Fonte presents a case for patriotic assimilation as an antidote to the threats presented by our growing cultural diversity.

In opposition to the alarms raised Huntington and Fonte, Professor Francis Fukuyama, a leading American academic, argues that the immigrants are the true carriers of the "Protestant Ethic" and that the United States is corrupting their stronger family and traditional values, not the other way around.

HOW TO MAKE AN AMERICAN

John Fonte

Browsing through my grandmother's citizenship textbook from the 1930s one day, I found Lesson 61 on the Americanization policies of Theodore Roosevelt:

[Roosevelt] loved America above all else and his last public message was a plea for the "complete Americanization" of our people in which he said: ". . . [if] the immigrant who comes here in good faith becomes an American and assimilates himself to us, he shall be treated on an exact equality with everyone else, for it is an outrage to discriminate against any such man because of creed, or birthplace, or origin. But this is predicated upon the man's becoming an American, and nothing but an American. There can be no divided allegiance here. We have room for but one soul (sic) loyalty and that is loyalty to the American people."

The textbook captured the spirit of Americanization—that immigrants are expected to assimilate patriotically and become loyal Americans. More than one hundred years earlier George Washington had written to John Adams that he envisioned immigrants "assimilated to our customs, measures, and laws," and because of this, Washington declared, native-born citizens and immigrants would "soon become one people."

This sentiment is roughly the view of the majority of Americans today, but clearly not the opinion of many American elites. As Samuel Huntington argues . . . , elites in government, business, education, academia, and the media have for decades been actively involved in efforts to "deconstruct"* the American nation and its traditional concepts of assimilation and citizenship.

Huntington explains in his new book, *Who Are We?*, that arguments over multiculturalism, bilingualism, ethnic and gender group preferences, dual citizenship, history standards, transnationalism—and immigration and assimilation—are all part of the same conflict over the nature of the American liberal democratic regime. He is right to maintain that a "deconstructionist coalition" challenges the core principles of the American nation on all fronts. At the end of the day, the deconstructionists would transform an American nation based on the principles of individual citizenship, equality of opportunity, and self-government within Constitutional limits, into a new form of regime built on ethnic, racial, and gender group rights with decision-making increasingly in the hands of unelected elites. . . . What is ultimately at stake is whether the traditional American regime will be transmitted to future generations intact or wholly transformed.

Clearly, all of this means that the issue of immigration/assimilation (and these two issues should always be considered as one) must be examined within the broader context of the leftist assault on traditional American political principles. To help clarify the problem, let us explore a series of assimilation-related issues that will soon confront both elite and popular opinion. These include initiatives to revise the oath of allegiance [and] design a new citizenship test. . . .

Implicit in Huntington's thesis is that just below the surface of the policy debate there exists unapologetic public support for vigorous Americanization policies that would explicitly promote the patriotic integration of immigrants into what was once called "the American way of life." Besides public support, there appears to be a bloc in Congress . . . strongly interested in patriotic, as well as economic and linguistic, integration. Last year when the United States Citizenship and Immigration Services (USCIS) wanted to simplify the citizenship oath, some members of Congress immediately protested, and the USCIS pulled back. Worried that the

traditional oath (in which new citizens promise to "renounce" their old allegiances and "bear arms" on behalf of the United States) will be weakened, Senator Lamar Alexander (R-TN) and Congressman Jim Ryun (R-KS) have introduced legislation to codify it into law.

In addition, it appears that the forces of patriotic renewal are being heard in discussions over the development of a new citizenship test. . . . Advocates of patriotic integration in veterans groups, think tanks, and Congress . . . declare that we must start with first principles by asking: What is the purpose of the history/government citizenship test?

The law states that applicants for citizenship must have: (1) "a knowledge and understanding of the history, and of the principles and form of government of the United States" and (2) possess "good moral character, attachment to the principles of the Constitution, and be well disposed to the good order and happiness of the United States." This leads naturally to the conclusion that the purpose of the test as a whole is not merely to get new citizens to know certain facts, but also to be "attached" to the principles of the Constitution—evidence of the explicit normative purpose of naturalization.

The citizenship naturalization process should be a life-altering experience, a rite of passage, such as a wedding, graduation, first communion, or bar mitzvah, which fosters emotional attachment to our nation and strengthens patriotism. . . . The oath is especially crucial to American democracy, because citizenship in America is not based on race, religion, or ethnicity, but on political loyalty. In taking the oath, the new citizen transfers allegiance from the land of his birth to the United States.

Oath-takers have a moral obligation to give up all political loyalty to their birth nations. . . . The oath of allegiance, like wedding vows, represents not only a moral obligation for individuals, but a norm for our democracy. . . .

If it becomes routine for large numbers of new citizens to keep old political loyalties, the nature of American citizenship will be transformed, just as, say, legal polygamy would transform the nature of marriage. The principle that we are a people united by political allegiance rather than the ascriptive characteristics of race, ethnicity, and birth would be effectively repudiated.

"Patriotic Renewalists" on Capitol Hill could very well demand that . . . we should get serious about patriotic assimilation. . . . Like Theodore Roosevelt . . . , we should insist that immigration policy be combined with serious Americanization initiatives and that immigration levels remain dependent on how well we integrate newcomers patriotically. After all, we are a nation, not just a market.

---

* In this context, to "deconstruct" means to critically analyze values and traditions in order to expose contradictions and inconsistencies.

SOURCE: From the September 2004 issue of *The American Enterprise*. Copyright © 2004. Reprinted with permission.

WHY WE SHOULDN'T WORRY ABOUT THE "HISPANIZATION" OF THE UNITED STATES

Francis Fukuyama

It is not politically correct today to say that America is fundamentally a Protestant country, or that a specific form of religion is critical to its success as a democracy. Yet as historical facts, these statements are undoubtedly true, and they are the premise of *Who Are We?*, Samuel Huntington's new book. The United States, he argues, is a liberal democracy based on certain universal political principles regarding liberty and equality, summed up traditionally as the American Creed. But the country's success as a free and prosperous democratic society was not due simply to the goodness of these principles or the strength of America's formal institutions. There was a crucial supplement: cultural values that Huntington describes as "Anglo-Protestant." . . .

Huntington is following in the path of innumerable observers of the United States [who] have noted that the dissident, sectarian nature of the Protestantism transplanted to North America was critical to shaping American values like individualism, anti-statism, tolerance, moralism, the work ethic, the propensity for voluntary association, and a host of other informal habits and customs that augment our Constitution and legal system. *Who Are We?* is also perfectly consistent with Huntington's [work] in arguing that liberal democracy is less a universalistic system for organizing political life than an outgrowth of a certain northern European Christian culture, the appeal and feasibility of which will be limited in other cultural settings.

Huntington goes on to argue that . . . immigration [is a] threat to that traditional American identity. In his view, the American elite, from corporate executives to professors to journalists, sees itself as cosmopolitan, secular, and attached to the principle of diversity as an end in itself. That elite no longer feels emotionally attached to America and is increasingly out of touch with the vast majority of non-elite Americans who remain patriotic, morally conservative, and Christian. . . .

On no issue are elites and ordinary Americans further apart than on immigration, and Huntington takes the latter's concerns about the threat posed by Mexican immigration very seriously. This is because of the numbers involved, . . . the concentration of Mexican immigrants in a few Southwestern states and cities, and the proximity of their country of origin. The wave has occurred, moreover, at a time when American elites have lost confidence in their own cultural values and are no longer willing to use the public school system to assimilate these new immigrants to Anglo-Protestant culture. Huntington worries that unchecked immigration will sow the seeds of a later backlash, and may even lead one day to something new in the American experience, an ethnolinguistic minority with strong ties to a neighboring country that could potentially make territorial claims on much of the Southwest.

I am glad that a scholar like Huntington has raised these issues, since they deserve serious discussion. . . . Huntington poses some real questions about whether the large Mexican immigrant population will assimilate as other immigrant groups have done before them. . . . He is right that "culture matters" and he is right that the thoughtless promotion of multiculturalism and identity politics threatens important American values. But his book, ironically, offers grist for a rather different perspective on the problem: *Who Are We?* suggests that the more serious threat to American culture comes perhaps from its own internal contradictions than from foreigners.

Let's begin with the question of who the true bearers of "Anglo-Protestant" values are. . . . His chapter describing "core" Anglo-Protestant values ends up focusing almost entirely on the work ethic: "from the beginning," he writes, "America's religion has been the religion of work." But who in today's world works hard? Certainly not contemporary Europeans with their six-week vacations. The real Protestants are those Korean grocery-store owners, or Indian entrepreneurs, or Taiwanese engineers,

or Russian cab drivers working two or three jobs in America's free and relatively unregulated labor market. I lived in Los Angeles for nearly a decade, and remember passing groups of Chicanos gathered at certain intersections at 7 a.m. waiting for work as day laborers. No lack of a work ethic here: That's why Hispanics have pushed native-born African-Americans out of low-skill jobs in virtually every city where they compete head-to-head. . . .

There are a number of grounds for thinking that the United States will assimilate Hispanic immigrants just as it has earlier ethnic groups. Most important is the fact that they are Christian—either Catholic or, to an increasing degree, Evangelical Protestant. When controlling for socioeconomic status, they have stronger traditional family values than their native-born counterparts. This means that culturally, today's Mexican immigrants are much less distant from mainstream "Anglos" than were, say, the southern Italian immigrants or Eastern European Jews from mainstream WASPs at the beginning of the 20th century. Their rates of second- and third-generation intermarriage are much closer to those of other European groups than for African-Americans. And, from Gen. Ricardo Sanchez on down, they are serving honorably today in the U.S. armed forces in numbers disproportionate to their place in the overall population.

The problem . . . is not that Mexican and other Latino immigrants come with the wrong values, but rather that they are corrupted by American practices. Many young Hispanics are absorbed into the underclass culture of American inner cities, which has then re-exported gang violence back to Mexico and Central America; or else their middle-class leaders have absorbed the American post-civil rights era sense of victimization and entitlement. There is a sharp divide between elites—organizations like the National Council of

La Raza, or the Mexican-American Legal Defense Fund—and the general population of Hispanic immigrants. The latter, overall, tend to be socially conservative, want to learn English and assimilate into the American mainstream, and were even supportive initially of California's Proposition 187 (denying benefits to illegal immigrants) and 227 (ending bilingualism in public education). . . .

If it is the case that high levels of immigration are inevitable for developed societies, then what we need to do is to shift the focus from immigration per se to the issue of assimilation. . . .

This will be a huge challenge for the United States, but I am more confident than Huntington that we can meet it. Indeed, Hispanic immigrants will help to reinforce certain cultural values like the emphasis on family and work, and the Christian character of American society.

DEBATE QUESTIONS TO CONSIDER

1. Is "patriotic assimilation" a reasonable policy to deal with the concerns over "Hispanization"? What would this policy look like if implemented in schools and other institutions?

2. What points does Fukuyama make in response to the arguments presented by Fonte and Huntington? What evidence does he present to back up his points? How convincing is the evidence?

3. Is it fair to say that Fonte is a pessimist and Fukuyama is an optimist about the future of American culture? Does immigration really threaten traditional American values?

8

ASIAN AMERICANS AND PACIFIC ISLANDERS

The term "Asian Americans and Pacific Islanders" imposes a label on a variety of groups that in reality have very little in common. These groups differ from each other in language, religion, cuisine, physical appearance, and in countless other ways. The category includes people who trace their origins to countries as diverse as China, Japan, the Philippines, Pakistan, Samoa, Vietnam, India, and scores of others. Some members of the group have American roots going back nearly 200 years, while others are the newest of newcomers.

Even considered as a whole, Asian Americans and Pacific Islanders are few in number and comprise about 4 percent of the national population. Because of high rates of immigration, however, these groups are growing rapidly, as is their impact on American society, and they are projected to make up 10 percent of the population by 2050.

Of all the groups in this category, Chinese Americans and Japanese Americans have the longest histories in the United States. Immigrants from China began arriving in the early 1800s to fill jobs in the burgeoning economy of the west coast, and immigrants from Japan began arriving in significant numbers at the end of the 1800s. Both groups faced intense, bitter campaigns of discrimination and racism and, as a result, formed ethnic enclaves or separate, largely self-contained subeconomies (for example, Chinatowns). The Narrative Portrait in this chapter provides some insight into the World War II relocation of Japanese Americans, a massive act of discrimination and one of the most serious violations of civil rights in the nation's history.

Other groups of Asian Americans and Pacific Islanders began immigrating in large numbers after the 1965 change in U.S. immigration laws. This immigration stream is extremely diverse and includes highly educated professionals, refugees fleeing warfare or persecution, unskilled laborers, and large numbers of illegal immigrants. Some of these immigrants are attracted by jobs at the highest levels of American society and are medical practitioners, engineers, college faculty, and scientists. Others provide a cheap workforce for the ethnic enclaves and take jobs that are poorly paid, have few if any benefits, and little security. Although Asian Americans and Pacific Islanders can be found at every level of the economy, there is a tendency for these groups to be "bipolar" and occupy positions at the very top and the very bottom of the job market.

One thing that Asian Americans and Pacific Islanders do share is the widespread perception that they are successful and well-behaved: a "model minority." This stereotype is supported by the fact that many Asian American and Pacific Islander groups are at or above national norms on such indicators of success as average income and years of education. The Current Debates section explores the realities of the "model minority" image and some of the reasons for the relative success of some of these groups. Harry Kitano argues that the key to success lies in the value systems Asian immigrants bring with them, while Alejandro Portes and Min Zhou attribute the relative success to the enclave economies. Finally, Ronald Takaki explores some of the not-so-hidden political agendas that underlie the attribution of success to Asian Americans.

Of course, the perception of Asian success is greatly exaggerated and certainly does not apply to many recent immigrants, especially the refugee groups and those who find themselves at the bottom of the ethnic enclave economies. The readings for this chapter, in fact, explore the ugly realities faced by many Asian Americans and Pacific Islanders. Victor Hwang analyzes hate crimes against the group and explores some of the problems that Asian Americans and Pacific Islanders share with other minority groups of color. In the second reading, reporter Salim Jiwa describes the ongoing trade in sexual slaves from South Korea to North America, a trade in human beings that has counterparts linking many more affluent nations with other Asian nations, Eastern Europe, and many other places.

Please visit the accompanying website to Race, Ethnicity, and Gender, second edition for the *Public Sociology Assignments* at http://www.pineforge.com/das2.

QUESTIONS TO CONSIDER IN THIS CHAPTER

1. How can images of a group that seem positive (for example, the "model minority" image often applied to Asian Americans) actually be negative? What stereotypes characterize the relationships between Asian American groups and the larger society? How do these differ from or resemble the images applied to other groups?

2. Are Asian American groups really successful? If you think the answer is yes, how did these racial minorities accomplish this feat? How can this image of success be maintained in light of massive discrimination both historically (e.g., the relocation camps) and in the present (hate crimes and sex trafficking from Asia)? If you think the answer is no, why is the image of success and good behavior so popular? What political agendas might be at work just under the surface?

3. What gender dimensions can you identify in the issues raised in this chapter? How does gender impact (for example) anti-Asian violence, sexual slavery, and the image of the "model minority"?

NARRATIVE PORTRAIT

THE RELOCATION

Joseph Kurihara was born in Hawaii in 1895. He moved to California at age 20 and served with the U.S. Army in World War I, completed a college education, and was a businessman working within the Japanese American enclave until World War II. He worked actively to promote acculturation and better relations with the larger society during the interwar years. He was sent to the relocation camp at Manzanar, California, in the spring of 1942 and continued to play an active role in the dislocated Japanese American community. Although he had never visited Japan and had no interest or connection with the country of his parents' birth, his experiences in the camp were so bitter that he renounced his American citizenship and expatriated to Japan following the war.

WE WERE JUST JAPS

Joseph Kurihara

[The evacuation] . . . was really cruel and harsh. To pack and evacuate in forty-eight hours was an impossibility. Seeing mothers completely bewildered with children crying from want and peddlers taking advantage and offering prices next to robbery made me feel like murdering those responsible without the slightest compunction in my heart.

The parents may be aliens but the children are all American citizens. Did the government of the United States intend to ignore their rights regardless of their citizenship? Those beautiful furnitures (sic) which the parents bought to please their sons and daughters, costing hundreds of dollars were robbed of them at the single command, "Evacuate!" Here my first doubt of American Democracy crept into the far corners of my heart with the sting that I could not forget. Having had absolute confidence in Democracy, I could not believe my very eyes what I had seen that day. America, the standard bearer of Democracy had committed the most heinous crime in its history. . . .

[The camp was in an area that is largely desert] The desert was bad enough. The . . . barracks made it worse. The constant cyclonic storms loaded with sand and dust made it worst. After living in well furnished homes with every modern convenience and suddenly forced to live the life of a dog is something which one can not so readily forget. Down in our hearts we cried and cursed this government every time when we were showered with sand. We slept in the dust; we breathed the dust; and we ate the dust. Such abominable existence one could not forget, no matter how much we tried to be patient, understand the situation, and take it bravely. Why did not the government permit us to remain where we were? Was it because the government was unable to give us the protection? I have my doubt. The government could have easily declared Martial Law to protect us. It was not the question of protection. It was because we were Japs! Yes, Japs!

After corralling us like a bunch of sheep in a hellish country, did the government treat us like citizens? No! We were treated like aliens regardless of our rights. Did the government think we were so without pride to work for $16.00 a month when people outside were paid $40.00 to $50.00 a week in the defense plants? Responsible government officials further told us to be loyal and that to enjoy our rights as American citizens we must be ready to die for the country. We must show our loyalty. If such is the case, why are the veterans corralled like the rest of us in the camps? Have they not proven their loyalty already? This matter of proving one's loyalty to enjoy the rights of an American citizen was nothing but a hocus-pocus.

My American friends . . . no doubt must have wondered why I renounced my citizenship. This decision was not that of today or yesterday. It dates back the day when General DeWitt (*the office in charge of the evacuation*) ordered evacuation. It was confirmed when he flatly refused to listen even to the voices of the former World War Veterans and it was doubly confirmed when I entered Manzanar. We who already had proven our loyalty by serving in the last World War should have been spared. The veterans asked for special consideration but their requests were denied. They too had to evacuate like the rest of the Japanese people, as if they were aliens.

I did not expect this of the Army. . . . I expected that at least the Nisei would be allowed to remain. But to General DeWitt, we were all alike. "A Jap's a Jap. Once a Jap, always a Jap." . . . I swore to become a Jap 100 percent and never to do another day's work to help this country fight this war. My decision to renounce my citizenship there and then was absolute.

Just before he left for Japan (in 1946), Kurihara wrote:

> It is my sincere desire to get over there as soon as possible to help rebuild Japan politically and economically. The American Democracy with which I was infused in my childhood is still unshaken. My life is dedicated to Japan with Democracy my goal.

SOURCE: From *The Spoilage* by Thomas Swaine and Richard S. Nishimoto. Copyright © 1946 University of California Press. Reprinted with permission.

READINGS

Like Hispanic Americans, Asian Americans belong to a racial category within the United States that lumps together many diverse peoples with vastly differing experiences. Yet, unlike Latinos, Asian Americans and Pacific Islanders do not share a common language or religion. What this group does have in common is a shared experience of how the dominant group (whites) in the United States perceives them. Their coming together under one pan-ethnic racial rubric is a clear example of how race is a social construction, usually based on the perceptions of those in power. Although their national origins may even make them enemies to each other, Asian Americans face certain common prejudices in the eyes of whites, particularly the "model minority" stereotype, a perception that means that they are not included in some much-needed social programs.

Also, this so-called positive stigma has some severely negative and even deadly consequences, as it has made Asian Americans the target of hate crimes, usually committed by whites who are angry about and envious of their supposed success.

The first reading explores this issue in depth. Victor Hwang discusses two different incidents, each highlighting different aspects of hate crimes and the multiple layers of injury that they cause. In the first incident, a 63-year-old Korean American woman is brutally beaten just because of her race, and Hwang argues that this woman's injuries are not only physical but emotional as well. The way people react to her after the attack only adds insult to injury in various ways when certain well-meaning individuals assault her humanity. The beating and its aftermath cause a transformation in the victim, who had heretofore internalized the model minority stereotype and developed a false consciousness as a result. She abandons her antagonistic views toward blacks, fueled by this model-minority idea, and for the first time realizes the common experiences they share as racial minorities. In the second incident, swastikas are painted on Asian-owned and Asian-related businesses, signed by the "Sunset White Boys." Again, the author finds exploring the aftermath of the incident to be just as meaningful as the incident itself. From institutions to individuals, the initial desire to minimize the significance of the racist attacks and the delay in efforts to respond to the crime are clear. Further, although the town seems to give lip service to condemning the actual attacks, the sentiment behind them is shared by many, as evidenced in a town meeting where venting about people of color "taking over" the area becomes more important than expressing concern for the business owners who were attacked. Hwang asks us to consider anti-Asian prejudice not just as isolated violent acts of bigotry but as social products for which we are collectively responsible. In doing so, he takes a decisively different turn than most popular media representations of hate crimes, and ultimately shows us how a seemingly positive stereotype can have severely harmful consequences.

The second reading deals with another pattern that calls the model minority stereotype into question: sex trafficking from Korea to the United States. Young South Korean women are recruited for the American sex industry, often by false promises of legitimate jobs such as domestic workers or nannies, and then forced into a status that closely resembles slavery. South Koreans can enter Canada without a visa and are then smuggled into the United States, where their illegal status helps to keep them powerless and exploitable.

This trade in sex workers is part of a global movement of population from less developed to more developed nations. The movement is enormous and fueled by a complex set of forces including the displacement of rural populations in the third world and the unquenchable thirst for cheap labor in the first world. From the standpoint of the United States, immigrants tend to be seen as threats to the moral and cultural stability of America (see the Current Debates in Chapter 7) or, especially since the terrorist attacks of September 11, 2001, as security risks and potential terrorists. Either way, the dominant response to immigration has been to make it more difficult to cross the border. Given that borders can never be completely secure and that the pressure to enter the United States is intense and unyielding, these efforts force immigrants to enter illegally and fuel an entire industry dedicated to smuggling people over the border. What forces propel these women into international sex trafficking? What is the real problem: the immigrant "others" or our own policies that force them into seeking illegal means to enter the country? What would change for these women if they were seen as people in need of economic and political empowerment rather than as hapless victims or threats to morality or security?[1]

THE INTERRELATIONSHIP BETWEEN ANTI-ASIAN VIOLENCE AND ASIAN AMERICA

Victor M. Hwang

The concept of the Asian Pacific American community is unique in the field of American race relations. Our community is neither united by a common experience such as slavery or by a common language such as Spanish. We are individually Vietnamese Amerasians, second generation South Asian Americans, kibei, third generation Sansei, . . . 1.5 generation Korean Americans, . . . Pilipino seniors, Taiwanese nationalists, and more. . . . Our community encompasses differences in ethnicity, religion, language, culture, class, color, immigration history, politics and even race.

What we obviously do have most in common is the way that we look to those outside our community and the way we are treated in America based upon the way we look. Our commonality begins with a recognition that . . . you are constantly at risk of being killed without warning or provocation based upon the belief that you are a foreign "Jap." Whether you are second generation South Asian American or a fifth generation Chinatown native, we are faced constantly with the implicit and explicit question, "No, really, where are you from?"

Yet, while anti-Asian violence forces individuals to band together at times for physical or political protection, it plays a much greater role in shaping the Asian Pacific American [APA] community than simply acting as the outside threat which drives the flock together. It is not the action of anti-Asian violence which is so important to the development of our community as much as it is the reaction to the incident. For "Asian America" lives not in the Chinatowns or the Little Tokyos, but in the hearts of those who recognize that incidents of anti-Asian violence are not isolated attacks, but are part of the historical treatment of Asians in America for the past two hundred years.

. . . [T]he pattern of anti-Asian violence dictates the role and character of our community and its relationship to mainstream society. . . . [T]he unspoken policy and history of America has been to erase the experience of Asians in America and to silence the voice of the community. Thus, we have been displaced from our role in American history, from our place in America, and more than two hundred years after the first Asians came to America, we are still being collectively told to go back to where we came from.

It is in our struggle against this pattern of violence and its underlying message of physical, political, and historical exclusion that we find ourselves as Asian Pacific Americans. Not every Asian in America is a member of the Asian Pacific American community. . . . [W]e become Asian Americans as we begin to recognize that we share a common bond and experience with all other Asians in America based upon our history, our treatment and our status as a racial minority in the United States. The formation of the community begins not when ten Asian families happen to live in the same neighborhood, but when one family has been attacked and the other nine rally to their assistance.

The Asian American community is based on an understanding and appreciation of the fact that we have struggled for nearly two centuries against this violence and exclusion. . . . From the early organizing efforts of the Chinese Six Companies in San Francisco to protect the Chinese workers from nativist attacks to the more recent campaign to bring justice to the killers of Vincent Chin and Kao Kuan Chung, Asian Americans have not always been the silent victims of hate crimes, but have strived to defend and empower our communities in the American tradition.

This paper will discuss the role of anti-Asian violence as a foil and as a catalyst in the development of an Asian American identity and a community. Our community lives in the contradiction, in the friction between competing notions of ethnicity and nationality, in the margins and as a wedge between black and white in American society. It is not a physical community, but one that exists in flashes, in movements, in speeches, in hearts and minds, and in struggle. It is within the heat of the response to these incidents of extreme racial violence that we continue to forge our identity and our sense of community. We build our community in times of crisis by speaking out against the incidents of anti-Asian violence and claiming our piece of history.

However, in times of racial tension, it is sometimes difficult to process the elements of the hate crime to craft a . . . response which serves both the needs of the individual victim as well as empowering the community. In this paper, I will explore two recent incidents of anti-Asian violence as a framework to discussing the crafting and mis-crafting of a progressive community response. I believe we should approach hate crimes in the same way a doctor would approach a medical problem. Prior to making a diagnosis, we need to understand the nature of the injury as well as who has been hurt. Further, without an understanding of the history of anti-Asian violence, hate crimes, and the community, we can do little for either the protection of the individual or the development of Asian America.

ANTI-ASIAN VIOLENCE AND THE INDIVIDUAL: WHAT IS THE INJURY?

Individual victims of hate crimes and their families often suffer injuries far beyond the physical wounds inflicted upon them. It is both the sticks and stones which break our bones and the accompanying words and hateful intent which hurt us. Like a snake's bite, the venomous injuries of anti-Asian violence go far deeper than the physical injury because they are intended to inject a poison to strike at the core of our being. As advocates, we must recognize the injury to the internal psyche as well as the physical injury in crafting a remedy for the individual and the community. Just as you cannot treat a snake bite with a Band-Aid, you cannot treat the hate crime as either a simple crime or an accident.

The Incident

Sylvia is a 63 year old Korean American who came to the United States as a teenager. She grew up in Washington, D.C., the daughter of a Korean minister and attended an all-white segregated high school. She spent most of her adult years in Arizona . . . where, as she describes it, she never thought she experienced much racism. . . . ""Oh, every once in a while, my kids would tell me that someone had called them a Chinaman in school or had tried to put them down on account of their race," she said. "But I always told them just to work harder and prove to every one else that they were superior. I knew that we were descendants of a proud people with many centuries of culture and civilization. I never worried much about what the other people thought. I knew we were better."

She never had much contact with African Americans, but says that she always sort of looked down her nose at them since she felt that they tended to complain too much about racism and did not adopt the Asian work ethic to work twice as hard when confronted with racist behavior.

Sylvia moved to California a number of years ago and ironically it was in San Francisco that she experienced her first taste of anti-Asian violence. She was coming out of the Borders Bookstore in Union Square when a 6-foot tall "Timothy McVeigh"-looking Caucasian man ran up to her and said "My mother is not Chinese but yours is." Sylvia was somewhat taken aback, but tried to ignore him while she passed him.

He repeated the remark from behind her and when she did not react, he picked her up from behind and threw her against a nearby concrete wall, shattering her hip. Her assailant then ran away. As she lay there in shock, she was assaulted again in a much more painful and personal way as two Caucasian tourists walked by and in an attempt to be helpful, asked her if she spoke English.

Sylvia noted afterwards that even in an emergency situation, the first thought that crossed the minds of these Caucasians upon seeing an injured Asian woman was not the injury, but the race. "I was so outraged then, I couldn't even respond. Here I lay, on the ground, I was beaten, my hip was shattered, and the first thing they asked me was if I spoke English, not if I was ok, if I needed help, or if they should call an ambulance. The first thing they asked me was if I spoke English. . . . I was so shocked, I couldn't even say anything."

Sylvia was eventually taken to the hospital and underwent extensive surgery to have her entire hip replaced. But as her physical injuries were treated by the doctors, her psychological injuries remained unattended, festering as she fell into a deep depression. "My co-workers, who were mostly Caucasian, came by to see me and I guess that they were trying to be funny. One of them said something like 'Well, at least you got a new hip.' At that moment, I just felt so angry because they couldn't understand that I was almost killed because of my race. I just didn't think I could ever see them in the same light again."

. . . Her friends felt that she was obsessed with the racial nature of the attack and that she should not dwell on the incident. Sylvia, on the other hand, felt like she was unable to talk with them anymore.

The police . . . were unable to develop any substantive leads and, in the opinion of the family, discouraged them from pursuing an active criminal investigation. Time and time again, Sylvia was told by the officer in charge of the investigation it was not worth her while to pursue the assailant, suggesting it was better to forget the incident and simply let old wounds heal. . . .

But as time progressed, Sylvia did not just "get over" the racial attack. Her mental health continued to deteriorate. . . . [Her family was] frustrated over the lack of police response, angry over the racist nature of the attack, and distressed over Sylvia's deepening depression. . . .

The Response: What Is the Injury?

In treating only her physical injuries, the doctors . . . were able to replace her shattered hip, [but] they were unable to give her a replacement for her shattered frame of reference which had helped her in life to interpret, deflect, and respond to racism. . . . In failing to address the underlying cause of the injury, the doctors failed to treat the most serious injury of all—the one to her psyche. As such, Sylvia was left feeling confused and powerless, without the ability to either explain or prevent another unprovoked attack.

The isolated hate crime is particularly venomous because of its seemingly random nature and the inability of the victim to rationalize its occurrence. Even as children, we learn to create mental defenses and white lies to guard against the mental attacks from others. Rationalization is an important defense in our logical world and, as thinking beings, it is important for us to believe that the world is controlled by rationality. . . . The inability to explain the incident subjects the victim to further trauma because if you can't explain it, there's nothing you can do to prevent it from happening again. . . .

Victims of burglary may rationalize that they did not take enough safety precautions and install a better alarm system. Someone who is involved in an automobile accident will try to remember to look both ways next time before crossing the street. But there is nothing you can do to hide your race, skin color, gender, or sexual orientation. There is simply no escape or change in behavior possible for victims of hate crimes and they understand that they have to live with the possibility of reoccurrence without warning. In Sylvia's case and in other similar cases, this helplessness may be exacerbated by the fact that the actual perpetrators are rarely caught.

Moreover, this may be compounded by the fact that victims of hate crimes may have never even viewed themselves as representatives of the community, but in the hate crime they are subject to attack, not as individuals, but as symbols. They are stripped of their individuality and reduced to their race. . . . Sylvia was not attacked for anything about her, anything she stood for, but on the basis of her birth. Her "crime" in the eyes of the attacker was . . . the crime of her ancestors . . . being born "Chinese." The message was direct and terrifying—you are different from me and so you must be hurt.

This is the poison of hate crimes which distinguishes it from other types of victimization. The consistent message of [Anti-Asian] violence . . . is that you . . . do not belong here, you are not an American. This message was one that Sylvia was not prepared to receive. . . . Like many immigrants, Sylvia always believed in the ideal of America as the land of equality and opportunity. If you worked hard, you could get ahead, blend in, and be considered an equal. In the instances where she or her family were confronted with racist attitudes, her external response was to work twice as hard to go around the wall of racism, to work harder to prove her worth as an American.

In coming to America, Asians accept the unspoken racial hierarchy which will allow them to succeed up to the point where they hit the glass ceiling. They do not even carry the expectations of parity with whites. As such, they are identified as the "model minority," willing to accept a second-class standard of living as opposed to the African Americans whose civil rights paradigm has demanded an equal playing field. As in Sylvia's case, it is precisely due to this reason that many immigrants look down upon African Americans, because they themselves have made the difficult choice to swallow their pride and accept their status to provide their children with a better future. Sylvia believed that African Americans chose to complain too much and did not work hard enough to fight their way through the wall of racism.

The attack shook Sylvia to the core not only due to the extreme violence, but because it forced her to confront the fact that . . . the years of work that she put into proving herself . . . offered little protection . . . from either the attacker or the tourists who did not view her as an equal American. In an incident lasting less than a minute, one man stripped her of her veneer, her status as an honorary white, and reduced her to her race. Despite years of sacrifice and hard work to form a protective layer of class, assimilation, and privilege, she understood now that she was still as vulnerable as the newly-arrived Asian immigrant or the African American. . . . [Y]ou could not just turn your back and try to ignore the racism because it would just follow you and haunt you. The advice that she had given herself and her children for years simply did not work and failed to protect her from the brutal assault.

The attack also undermined Sylvia's second learned form of psychological defense of internally strengthening herself against racist attacks by relying upon her heritage as a Korean immigrant. . . . [I]n America, as a guest or sojourner, she could accept second class citizenship . . . [by] saying, "I don't deserve to be treated like a regular American and I don't need to respond to these demeaning attitudes because I have another home in Korea where they treat me like an equal." This is a standard form of mental gamesmanship that we all engage in to protect our sense of pride when denied a certain goal; we always create a lie that we didn't really want it anyway.

However, [after the attack] . . . she was no longer able to ignore the fact that her rights had been violated and that she was not respected as an equal in the country where she had spent the majority of her life. . . . [S]he was viewed as a foreigner, as an outsider, told physically and orally that she did not belong.

The inability to use her birthplace heritage as a source of comfort was a first step towards establishing an identity as an Asian American. . . . Lost and feeling abandoned, Sylvia fell into a depression over the realization that she was homeless, neither Korean nor American. In this nether world, she could no longer claim the protection of her cultural heritage or the promises of American equality.

Sylvia's Response: Knocking Down Walls

Metaphorically speaking, Sylvia was thrown against the concrete wall of racial reality, which forced her to re-examine her internal and external defenses which were previously erected to deny or mitigate the existence of racism in her life. . . . The life-threatening nature of her injuries forced her to take a second look not only at racism, but her own responses and attitudes in the past.

Sylvia's response . . . was to build an entirely new frame of reference in relating to American society incorporating elements of Asian American and cross-cultural studies. Ironically, at the time that she was subject to this hate violence, Sylvia had been taking a class in cross-cultural studies to become a certified ESL [English as a Second Language] instructor. . . . She tells me that initially she . . . found many of the African American attitudes to be tiresome. "Why couldn't they just work harder?" I thought, "Why do they always complain so much?"

. . . [T]he attack prompted Sylvia to reexamine her beliefs and attitudes towards all of race relations with a particular emphasis on African Americans. By turning to the theories she acquired through cross-racial studies courses, she found a framework for recovery, a new structure for re-evaluating her own life and experiences through the lens of race. After her attack, that which had been theoretical and incomprehensible found form and substance. What had previously existed outside her reality now became her point of view. She read books on Martin Luther King Jr. and other African American leaders, looking to them for answers.

As she began to understand the broader context of racism and race relations in the United States, her incident of hate violence began to seem less a random occurrence. At the same time, it became less painful as she read about the history of African Americans in the U.S. "I just stopped feeling sorry for myself. After all, it had just happened to me for a few times. But this sort of thing was happening to African Americans all the time."

Talking with her children and others about her experiences and newfound framework, she eagerly embraced learning about new cultures and ideas. It was as if she were born again at the age of 63. . . .

"In a way, my biggest regret is that this beating I suffered didn't happen to me 60 years earlier," she laughs. "I now look back on my life and think how blind I was. I now spend time reflecting on my whole life and I think what I might have done different if only my eyes had been opened sooner to the racism in our society. I wish I had been able to do more; to do something about it."

Sylvia credits her exploration and increased understanding of the African American struggle with providing her with the strength and context to fight her way out of her pit of depression. "I don't hate white people. I still don't know that much about black people, but I know more now about where I fit in than I did before."

Sylvia has recovered both physically and psychologically and now continues to attend classes in exploring race relations and cultural studies. After the release of the 1996 National Asian Pacific American Legal Consortium report on violence against Asian Pacific Americans, Sylvia was profiled widely by the media including an appearance on the Lehrer News Hour. She hopes to be certified as an ESL instructor soon and intends to teach new immigrants not only about English, but about America.

Swastikas in the Sunset: Who Is the Victim?

The Incident

The Sunset District of San Francisco is an affordable, residential and small business community located in the western section of the city. . . . It is a culturally diverse and middle-class neighborhood with a long-established Irish, Jewish and Russian community and a rapidly growing Asian American immigrant population. The Asian American population of the Sunset District has doubled in recent years and many now refer to the area as the "New Chinatown." The area has historically prided itself on its neighborhood "mom and pop" stores and has been highly resistant to the influx of chain stores and fast food franchises.

In 1996, a Chinese American business owner opened a Burger King franchise in the area, which was immediately met with community resistance, both reasoned and racist. While some residents protested the change in the neighborhood character, others posted flyers calling for "Chinks and Burger King Out of the Sunset." The Burger King was subject to a barrage of vandalism, graffiti, and protests through the following months, continuing to this day.

In February of 1997, . . . the "SWB" or "Sunset White Boys" carved swastikas into the glass storefronts of nearly two dozen Asian American businesses [located in the Sunset District]. The placement and selectivity of the swastikas was particularly ominous in that primarily Asian-owned businesses were targeted and non-Asian businesses were passed over. . . . The clinical precision exercised in the choice of the targets indicated a familiarity with the community, leading people to suspect that this was an "inside" job. There were also the biblical overtones of genocide and divine retribution.

The vandalism ranged from small, red spray-painted swastikas accompanied by the initials "SWB" to three-foot high swastikas carved with some sharp instrument into the glass storefronts of several Asian-owned businesses. . . .

Surprisingly, many of the store owners were immigrants from China and Vietnam who confessed ignorance at the significance of the swastikas. All they knew was that they were vandalized once again, and due to the indifferent or hostile treatment that they had received at the hands of the police in previous cases . . . , most failed to even report the occurrence. Many did not even realize that other Asian businesses along the street had suffered similar etchings and more than a week went by without any action being taken. During this time, the swastikas remained prominently displayed to the public.

The swastikas were finally brought to the attention of a Chinese American officer in another jurisdiction who decided to look into it on his own. The Asian Law Caucus was notified . . . and immediately responded to the location to document the hate vandalism, interview the targeted merchants and offer assistance. . . .

Even after I spoke with them, some of the store owners indicated that they did not intend to replace the glass panes defaced with swastikas since vandalism was rampant and they would just be hit again after spending the money. . . . In fact, many were surprised that what they viewed as another routine round of vandalism had attracted outside attention. After speaking with the merchants and documenting the incidents, we alerted the mainstream press. Both print and broadcast media ran widespread coverage on the swastikas even though the vandalism had taken place a week earlier. In response to the media coverage and subsequent public outcry, police and elected officials flocked to the community.

The Response: Who Is the Victim?

The response to a hate crime must be carefully tailored to address both the needs and concerns of the primary victim and also that of the community. A directed and strategic response works to counter the hateful message of exclusion and intimidation. However, in many cases it is unclear at the outset who the

primary victim is and towards whom the communal remedy should be directed. Was the true victim of the hate crime the more established Jewish community at large which was forced to confront the painful reminder of the Holocaust? Or was the victim the potential APA . . . store owner, resident, or customer considering coming into the Sunset District but who was then scared away by the prospect of being racially targeted because of his/her ethnicity? Or was it the San Francisco community at large? The responses of various authorities in this case differed depending upon their determinations on the identity of the victim. While all were successful in achieving some measure of combating hate crimes, no one fully addressed the underlying tensions which created the hate-filled environment.

The Police Response

Typically, the police are focused solely on the apprehension of the criminal and exhibit little sympathy or understanding of the needs of the victim or community. Generally, they are reluctant to categorize any case as a hate crime, perhaps out of an unwillingness to invest the extra time into conducting additional investigation, or perhaps due to a resistance to taint their jurisdiction with an insinuation of racism.

In this case, the police responded exceptionally poorly, which was surprising given the fact that San Francisco Police Department Chief Fred Lau is Chinese American and for years the department maintained a separate investigative unit specifically trained and devoted to working on hate crimes. In response to press inquiries, the police captain incredulously countered that these carvings were not hate crimes since swastikas are anti-Semitic in nature and not anti-Asian. While this initial statement was quickly retracted, the captain then adopted the position that these acts of vandalism were the acts of juveniles and therefore, should not be taken seriously. The acts were dismissed and somehow excused as childish pranks and therefore, not worthy of community discussion and intervention.

Under increasing scrutiny and public pressure, Chief Fred Lau intervened. Several bilingual officers were re-assigned to patrol the Sunset District, the case was turned over to the special hate crimes unit, and general police presence in the area was increased over the short term in an attempt to apprehend the perpetrator(s).

Several juveniles were soon arrested and the newspaper headlines reported that the responsible parties had been found. Conveniently, one of the youths was Pilipino and so the police took the opportunity to declare that this was clearly not a hate crime since one of the suspects was Asian. Weeks later, with smaller fanfare, it was reported that the youths who were arrested—while admitting to general tagging in the neighborhood—did not actually have anything to do with the swastikas. After a few weeks when community and media pressure died down, nothing further was heard from the police regarding their efforts to find the perpetrators.

Asian American Merchants as Victims?

One Asian American San Francisco county supervisor organized a highly successful volunteer clean-up day and recruited elected officials, union labor, community members and donations of materials to clean up all of the graffiti, sweep the streets, and replace the glass at no charge to the merchants. Volunteers turned out from all parts of the city and the media flocked. The event removed the obvious signs of hate and arguably sent a message to the perpetrators and the community that such hate violence would not be tolerated and that San Francisco was united in stamping out the signs of racism. The clean-up day was successful in removing the swastikas from public view, in giving the

community a chance to directly demonstrate its commitment to fighting hate crimes, and bringing together diverse communities for a day to take a joint stand against hate crimes.

However, . . . it is questionable as to how successful [the clean-up day] was in addressing the underlying attitudes that lead to acts of hate. In addressing the problem as one of vandalism, the effort failed to acknowledge that the swastikas were reflective of ideas and beliefs held much closer to heart of the community. The focus upon the physical element of the hate crime overlooked the intangible factors of prejudice and racial tensions which had created an environment conducive to the racist expression of the swastikas.

On the other hand, one may argue the lesson learned in bringing together diverse communities to tackle a common goal was that the volunteer physical labor itself served as a symbol of the community coming together to fight anti-Asian violence. Undoubtedly, a major part of this effort was intended to impart upon the individual merchants that they were a part of the community and to demonstrate that in times of crisis they could rely upon the community to come to their assistance.

The focus upon these individual merchants was perhaps misplaced in that many of them were unaware of the historical and genocidal significance of the swastikas. Given their political naiveté, it is debatable as to whether or not they were truly the victims of a hate crime and whether or not they could appreciate the reasons for the volunteer response. . . .

Certainly, the store owners were economically and physically the victims of vandalism, but can they also be considered the victims of a hate crime if some failed to understand the intended message of the perpetrator(s)? Given that several did not understand the importance of the symbols, was it critical for the people and politicians to rally behind them in a show of community support?

According to the traditional principles of criminal law and specifically the law around hate crimes, these store owners are the victims of a hate crime. Generally, the definition of a hate crime turns on the intent of the perpetrator and not the understanding of the victim. For example, many jurisdictions hold that a man who is attacked because he is perceived to be gay—even if he is not—would be the victim of a hate crime and the perpetrator could be subject to enhanced penalties. On the other hand, a person who fights with a gay person motivated solely by a dispute over a parking space, would not be subject to a hate crime even if the gay person was subjectively afraid that the dispute was over his sexual orientation. This follows the general principles of criminal law that focuses on the intent of the perpetrator.

However, what makes hate crimes punishable above and beyond the physical act of criminality is the recognition that hate violence carries levels of psychological and emotional impact well beyond the simple commission of the crime. The penalties for hate crimes are more severe because we recognize that based upon a history of racial intolerance, the victims are particularly vulnerable and suffer levels of injuries far beyond the physical and objective damages. A cross-burning on an African American lawn is much more than an act of arson or vandalism. It carries with it the clear threat of further escalation of violence when considered in the context of historical precedent. Thus, when the victim does not understand or is unaware of the message of hate, much of the psychological trauma and venom of the crime is not present and from the individual victim's viewpoint, it becomes indistinguishable from a simple act of vandalism. . . .

Therefore, should some of the merchants who did understand the message of intimidation and racial hatred and suffered the psychological consequences be considered hate violence victims while the other merchants are not? . . . Clearly, the focus on the individual level makes little sense because the bottom line is that property-based hate crimes such as these are clearly an attack upon the community. Common sense dictates that the use of a swastika defines the incident as one of hate violence given its symbolism for racial hatred and violence regardless of the understanding of the owner of the property. But if the merchants were not particularly intimidated by this act, then was the clean-up perhaps for the benefit of the community as opposed to assisting these particular individuals? After all, the older neighborhood is predominantly Jewish and was certainly put on notice . . . once the swastikas were carved into their community stores. A more cynical and jaded viewpoint would be that the clean-up was not directed at helping the Asian American merchants at all but rather at the larger Jewish community which had to be confronted with these symbols every day.

The Neighborhood/Geographic Community as Victim?

A second Asian American county supervisor organized two town hall meetings to facilitate discussions on the placement of swastikas in the community. The events were advertised in several languages to both the Asian merchants and the Sunset community at large. Myself and several other volunteers conducted outreach to the merchants along the Irving corridor in an attempt to encourage their participation in the hearings. A non-Asian leader in hate crimes coalition work was selected to lead the discussions and hate crimes "experts," police, elected officials, media, and community groups were invited to attend.

Nearly two hundred people attended the first town hall meeting, but virtually none of the Asian merchants attended either of the sessions.

The discussions were mostly dominated by a number of neighborhood conservation and watch groups from the Sunset community—many of whom were involved and continued to be involved in the efforts to drive the Burger King out of the Sunset District.

The first forum was opened with statements of support from local elected officials and presentations by the hate crimes experts. However, as the discussions progressed and the floor was opened up to those in attendance, the talk quickly turned to combating vandalism generally in the community and the changing character of the neighborhood. The changing character of the neighborhood, of course, was a euphemism for the rapid growth of the Asian American community in the Sunset district. . . . More neighborhood watch groups and closer cooperation with the police were proposed, a vandalism task force and hotline were discussed, and after the opening few minutes, the discussion of "hate" had been dropped and the audience spoke only of the "crimes."

In a more disturbing segment of the town hall meeting, audience members testified that the real problem contributing to the rise in crime was the fact that the community had changed so much that they did not feel that this was their community anymore. Some attendees remarked that Asian-language signs dominated the streets and you no longer heard English being spoken. Others commented that these "new" residents packed too many family members in a house, did not try to assimilate, hung out only with their own, did not participate in the civic affairs of the community, and generally did not fit into the Sunset character.

It is important to note that this was as much a case of ethnic conflict as it was a dispute between long time residents and newcomers. Some of those who spoke out against the transformation of the neighborhood included established Japanese Americans who could not read the Chinese language signs or understand the foreign languages being spoken on the street.

In an ironic twist, several residents complained that the merchants were at fault for not acting quickly to eradicate the swastikas once they appeared. These residents stated that they were offended that the stores did not act responsibly and rapidly to remove these signs of hate once they were carved on their front windowpanes. The residents who appeared at this public forum indicated that the problem was that the Asians did not participate in the neighborhood watches and other civic duties of the "community" and thus, hate crimes and vandalism were allowed to flourish. In a loosely-controlled forum, the audience had come full circle in scape-goating the victims as the perpetrators, and these were the voices and faces heard that night on the eleven o'clock news. . . .

In earlier discussions, the Asian American merchants expressed a general disinterest in attending such a forum and noted that the scheduled times conflicted with their business hours. . . . I think the true reason why many failed to attend was a premonition that their issues, concerns and needs were not going to be addressed in this public setting. Perhaps the merchants thought they would not be able to communicate the depth of their hopes and fears through an interpreter. Many expressed a fear in becoming involved and subjecting themselves to potential future retaliation. And maybe they already knew who their neighbors were and did not want to walk into a hostile trap.

In trying to open up discussions with the community, the officials had allowed the content of the discourse to shift without moderation and granted legitimacy and press to a particular viewpoint of the community. In empowering a certain segment of the community which was hostile to the "Asian invasion," the town hall meetings served to further divide and separate the community. . . .

All of a sudden, it became clear "who killed Vincent Chin,"[1] these community leaders who had turned out to ostensibly combat hate crimes were in fact perpetuating much of the hate crimes messages in their own homes. No doubt, it was some juvenile that had committed the physical act of vandalism, but the hate was something being taught at home. The town hall meetings ended with the second forum. Nothing ever came of those meetings.

. . .

The Asian Pacific American Community as Victim?

The swastikas were only a symptom of a more deeply rooted problem. The vandalism was neither a juvenile prank, nor a simple act of vandalism, but rather a powerful symbol of communities in conflict and a visible mark of the underlying tensions around a changing demographic in the Sunset District.

. . . [T]he intent behind the swastikas was not a childish thought, but one shared by a large segment of the community. Asian Americans in the Sunset district were being told both by symbol and by comments made in community forums that they were threatening the integrity and character of the neighborhood. . . . And, in the town hall discussions, while many residents repudiated the specific action taken in this case, no one spoke against the underlying message of racial intolerance and disharmony.

Anti-Asian violence is the friction generated from two communities beginning to rub up against each other where there is no discussion or relationship between the communities. Viewing this situation in a historical context, what happened in the Sunset District was identical to what happened in countless other cities . . . where a fast-growing Asian American immigrant population began to threaten the character of an "older" neighborhood. . . .

Because we are perceived as new, because we are seen as foreign, we are interpreted as a threat. . . . As our community continues to grow, we can only expect to see a greater incidence of hate violence directed against us.

Conclusion

. . . The Asian American identity is based upon an understanding that anti-Asian violence has played an integral part in the history of both America and Asian America and that it has always served to exclude and deny us our rightful place. . . . [I]n combating anti-Asian violence, we fight the message that we do not belong. It is a recognition that the attack upon the individual is an attempt to silence us all and therefore, to break our silence, we must speak up for the individual. Thus, while the community may be defined by the isolation and exclusion by the mainstream, it is also created from the response to anti-Asian violence.

But more than exclusion, it is a recognition that Asian America lives in the hearts of those in our community. The history of Asian Americans reflects the struggle for recognition and equality. Our forefathers planted seeds in the cracks of mountains and they planted dynamite high above the railroads, in concentration camps located in the deserts of Wyoming and Arizona, across the oceans on flotsam and refugee boats, parachuted in from modern jets and seared in the fires of Koreatown. The acres of history that we have tilled have not been welcoming or fertile, but we have persevered and out of the desert we have taken seed and we have grown. The promise of America is not happiness or equality, but the pursuit of happiness and the opportunity to advocate for equality. In order for us to be recognized as equals, we must struggle to assert our right to sit at the table.

NOTE

1. "Who killed Vincent Chin?" is a question raised in the documentary by the same name directed by Renee Tajima-Pena and Christine Choy. Vincent Chin was killed by two unemployed autoworkers on June 19, 1982, a week before he was to be wed. The two murderers yelled at Chin "It's because of motherf***ers like you that we are out of work," chased him down the street and one held him while the other beat his head in with a baseball bat. His murderers never served a day in jail and were sentenced to three years probation and a $3000 fine. The case became a symbol for anti-Asian violence in America and the filmmakers raised in their documentary the question of societal responsibility for Chin's death. The high level of Japan-bashing and Asian-bashing promulgated by the auto manufacturers, especially in this period, created an environment conducive to violence and anti-Asian American violence.

SOURCE: Originally published in *Chicano-Latino Law Review 17* (2000). Reprinted with permission.

DISCUSSION QUESTIONS

1. What, role according to Hwang, does violence play in creating an Asian Pacific community? What does he mean when he says that violence is a "foil and catalyst" in the development of community?

2. How does Sylvia illustrate the "false consciousness" of Asian Americans? How does the attack change the way she thinks about herself, her place in American society, and her view of African Americans?

3. How does the image of APA communities presented by Hwang differ from the image of the "model minority"?

4. How did the various responses to the vandalism in the Sunset District illustrate anti-Asian prejudice? Did the strength of the Asian community increase as a result of these attacks? Did the larger society develop a deeper understanding of Asian Americans? Why or why not?

SOUTH KOREAN SEX SLAVES IN THE UNITED STATES AND CANADA

Salim Jiwa

For South Korean women looking for a new life, a one-way ticket to Vancouver can be a journey into a sordid world of sexual slavery and indebtedness with no way out.

"There has been a clear increase in people coming over and being enslaved as a result of the fact they don't need a visa to enter Canada," Assistant U.S. Attorney Ye-Ting Woo said.

The women are bonded into sex slavery and traded like cattle to brothels in Los Angeles and other U.S. cities, Woo said.

She said Vancouver has become a smuggling capital, with flights arriving daily from Seoul. South Koreans do not need a visa to enter Canada.

"Within the prostitution industry, or these brothels or massage parlors, you will usually find someone who is called an enforcer—and it could be a woman and it could be a man—who will either physically or by coercion cause these women to have to stay," said Woo, who prosecuted people smuggler Young Pil (Ricky) Choi last month.

Choi was sentenced to three years in prison and three years of supervised release for conspiracy to transport more than 100 aliens to the United States, bringing immigrants to the United States for financial gain and three counts of harbouring illegal aliens.

"The demand is from the sex industry, so you have bars in Los Angeles and outcall services and they need women to work in them and they advertise in Korea for women who want to come over and they look at their pictures and see if they would be suitable and their ages and then bring them over. It's just horrible, just stunning."

Assistant U.S. Attorney Tessa Gorman said the women work in bars from Seattle to Los Angeles and as far away as Houston.

"These women work as companions for the evening and when you have one of these girls work with you and stay with you during the evening, the price of your liquor goes up," Gorman said. "Then you can also have them come home with you."

Woo said some of the women coming from South Korea are prostitutes, but others are innocent women who were promised other jobs. They are eventually forced into prostitution to pay off their smuggling debt.

"Even after they pay off their smuggling debt, it's like they apply an interest to the debt so it almost makes it impossible for you pay it off," Woo said. "That is one way they hold or enslave women." They also force the women to sign contracts.

Others, she said, are threatened. They are told unless the contract is paid off "something bad will happen to your family."

"But the family may not even know of the contract back in Korea," she said.

Authorities say they believe another sex slave ring is in operation after the arrests of 18 Korean women spirited into Idaho from British Columbia.

"To me the fact that all the Koreans we arrested this fiscal year so far are women once again indicates there is sex trafficking going on," said a border intelligence official in Spokane, Wash., who did not want to be identified.

Since the destruction of Choi's smuggling network, U.S. authorities say smugglers are moving away from heavy enforcement zones in B.C., such as Blaine, Sumas and Aldergrove and are driving deeper into eastern B.C.

Vancouver resident Sang Yoon Kim, a Canadian citizen of Korean origin, and Bum Suk Kim of Korea were arrested April 3 and accused of smuggling 13 South Koreans across the border.

A tip from Canadian officials led U.S. border patrol agents to stop a recreational vehicle with steamed up windows, well past the border. Inside, lying on the floor and on a side bed, were 13 women. The women will be returned to South Korea once released.

DISCUSSION QUESTIONS

1. Since September 11, 2001, the news media has focused mainly on border control as a means of thwarting terrorism, and we rarely hear of sex trafficking as a border control issue. Why do you think the U.S. government has not taken a more vocal, active stance on this problem?

2. One border official in Washington states, "all the Koreans we arrested this fiscal year so far are women." Why do you think sex trafficking so heavily involves Korean women in particular? Could it be economic factors, sexually charged stereotypes about Asian women, or other factors? Do some

research on sex trafficking to find out what other nations are most often implicated in this migration issue. Are there other Asian nations involved? Are there non-Asians also participating in the export of women for sexual services? What do these other nations and South Korea have in common?

3. Why do you think U.S. men turn to these illegal immigrant prostitutes as opposed to domestic women's services (or do you think they are even aware of the women's legal status)? Are the reasons behind this kind of low-wage exploitation identical to other immigrant work-related concerns (they will work for less than legal immigrants and permanent residents), or are there additional factors unique to women that are important for analyzing this problem?

4. Many scholars and activists studying sex work advocate legalizing prostitution (as Canada has done) to reduce the kind of exploitation that goes on within this currently illegal industry in the United States. Do you think legalizing prostitution in the United States would curb some of this sex trafficking/immigration problem? Why or why not? If not, what additional problems would remain and how could they be addressed?

5. The most lucrative types of jobs often available to illegal immigrants tend to be filled by men—farm and manufacturing labor, restaurant work. Could eliminating or reducing the gender wage gap, even among low-wage work, alleviate some of the sex trafficking in immigrant women? How might this be done?

CURRENT DEBATES

ASIAN AMERICAN "SUCCESS"—WHAT ARE THE DIMENSIONS, CAUSES, AND IMPLICATIONS FOR OTHER MINORITY GROUPS?

The following selections continue the discussion of the causes of Asian American success. The first selection, from the writings of sociologist Harry Kitano, is consistent with cultural explanations for the upward mobility of Asian groups. It argues that the success of the Japanese in America is due in part to their culture and in part to their strength of character, resiliency, and flexibility.

In opposition to Kitano's views are two other selections. The first counterargument, by sociologists Alejandro Portes and Min Zhou, presents a structural analysis that links the success of Chinese Americans to their enclave economy. Portes and Zhou also draw some provocative comparisons between Chinese Americans and African Americans, suggesting that the "thorough acculturation" of the African American community has weakened its economic vitality.

The second counterargument, by sociologist Ronald Takaki, sharply questions the whole notion of the "model minority" and points out the limits and qualifications that need to be observed when comparing Asian Americans with other groups. Takaki also points to a hidden agenda of those who single out Asian Americans as a "model minority": the chastisement of other minority groups, particularly African Americans.

THE SUCCESS OF JAPANESE AMERICANS IS CULTURAL

Harry Kitano

Social interaction among Japanese Americans is governed by behavioral norms such as enryo and amae. These derive from Confucian ideas about human relationships and define the dimensions of interaction and exchange between superior and inferior members of a social group. Although these forms of behavior were brought over by Issei immigrants, they still survive in attenuated form among the Nisei and even the Sansei.

Enryo prescribes the way in which a social inferior must show deference and self-abnegation before a superior. Hesitancy to speak out at meetings, the automatic refusal of a second helping, and selecting a less desired object are all manifestations of enryo. . . .

Amae behavior softens a power relationship through the acting out of dependency and weakness, and expresses the need for attention, recognition, acceptance, and nurture. A child displays amae to gain the sympathy and indulgence of a parent. A young, anxious-to-please employee in a business firm will act with exaggerated meekness and confusion to give his superior an opportunity to provide paternal advice and treat him as a protégé. Through the ritual display of weakness and dependency, reciprocal bonds of loyalty, devotion, and trust are formed. In this way amae creates strong emotional ties that strengthen cohesion within the family, business organization, and community.

Japanese Americans inherit an almost reverential attitude toward work. Their ancestors struggled for survival in a crowded island country with limited natural resources and they placed great value on industry and self-discipline. Certain traditional attitudes encourage resilient behavior in the face of setbacks and complement the moral imperative to work hard. Many Japanese Americans are familiar with the common expressions gaman and gambotte which mean "don't let it bother you," "don't give up." These dicta, derived from Buddhist teachings, encourage Japanese people to conceal frustration or disappointment and to carry on. A tradition that places great value on work and persistence has helped many Japanese Americans to acquire good jobs and to get ahead.

The submerging of the individual to the interest of the group is another basic Japanese tradition, and one that produces strong social cohesion

and an oblique style of behavior, one manifestation of which is the indirection or allusiveness of much communication between Japanese; another is the polite, consensual behavior expected in all social contacts. Both are common in Japan and visible among Japanese Americans. Today, even third- and fourth-generation Japanese Americans are apt to be seen by others as agreeable, unaggressive, willing to accept subordinate roles, and reluctant to put themselves forward. . . .

The history of the Japanese Americans in the United States is one of both resilience and adaptation. Suffering from discriminatory laws and racial hostility in the first half of the 20th century, Japanese Americans were nonetheless able to create stable ethnic communities and separate, but vital, social organizations. Since the end of World War II, with the disappearance of legal discrimination and the weakening of social restrictions, they have assimilated more readily into American society and shown rapid economic progress. Scholars have searched for the key to their remarkable record of adaptation. Some have pointed to the Japanese family, others to a strong group orientation, and still others to Japanese moral training; all of these theories often tend to overemphasize the degree to which Japanese traditions have been maintained. Japanese Americans have displayed a pragmatic attitude toward American life. [Rather] than rigidly maintaining their traditions, Japanese Americans have woven American values and behavior into the fabric of their culture and have seized new social, cultural, and economic avenues as they have become available, extending the limits of ethnicity by striking a workable balance between ethnic cohesion and accommodation.

SOURCE: Reprinted by permission of the publisher from *Harvard Encyclopedia of American Ethnic Groups,* edited by Stephen Thernstrom, Ann Orlov and Oscar Handlin, pp. 570-571, Cambridge, MA.: The Belknap Press of Harvard University Press. Copyright © 1980 by the President and Fellows of Harvard College.

The "Success" of Chinese Americans Is Structural

Alejandro Portes and Min Zhou

[What lessons for ethnic poverty can we find in the experiences of Chinese Americans and other groups that have constructed ethnic enclaves?] A tempting option—and one to which many experts have not been averse—is to resort to culturalistic explanations. According to these interpretations, certain groups do better because they possess the "right" kind of values. This view is, of course, not too different from assimilation theory except that, instead of learning the proper values after arrival, immigrants bring them ready made. A moment's reflection suffices to demonstrate the untenability of this explanation. . . .

The very diversity of [the] groups [which have constructed enclave economies] conspires against explanations that find the roots of economic mobility in the unique values associated with a particular culture. If we had to invoke a particular "ethic" to account for the business achievements of Chinese and Jews, Koreans and Cubans, Lebanese and Dominicans, we would wind up with a very messy theory. In terms of professed religions alone, we would have to identify those unique values leading Confucianists and Buddhists, Greek Orthodox and Roman Catholics into successful business ventures. In addition, culturalistic explanations have little predictive power since they are invoked only after a particular group has demonstrated its economic prowess. . . .

There is no alternative but to search for the relevant causal process in the social structure of the ethnic community. [Several] common aspects in the economic experience of the immigrant communities [are] relevant. . . .

[First is] the "bounded solidarity" created among immigrants by virtue of their foreignness and being treated as [different]. As consumers, immigrants manifest a consistent preference for items associated with the country of origin, both for their intrinsic utility and as symbolic representations of a distinct identity. As workers, they often prefer to work among "their own," interacting in their native language even if this means sacrificing some material benefits. As investors, they commonly opt for firms in the country of origin or in the ethnic community rather than trusting their money to impersonal outside organizations.

Bounded solidarity [is accompanied by] "enforceable trust" against malfeasance among prospective ethnic entrepreneurs. Confidence that business associates will not resort to double-dealing is cemented in something more tangible than generalized cultural loyalty since it also relies on the ostracism of violators, cutting them off from sources of credit and opportunity. [Enforceable trust] is the key mechanism underlying the smooth operation of rotating credit associations among Asian immigrant communities.

Bounded solidarity and enforceable trust as sources of social capital do not inhere in the moral convictions of individuals or in the value orientations in which they were socialized. [These benefits] accrue by virtue of [the group's] minority [status] in the host country and as a result of being subjected to mainstream pressure to accept their low place in the ethnic hierarchy. Such pressures prompt the revalorization of the symbols of a common nationality and the privileging of the ethnic community as the place where the status of underprivileged menial labor can be avoided. . . .

Black Americans, Mexican Americans, and mainland Puerto Ricans today lag significantly behind the immigrant groups in their entrepreneurial orientation. [This] lack of entrepreneurial presence is even more remarkable because of the large size of these minorities and the significant consumer market that they represent. . . .

We believe that the dearth of entrepreneurship among these groups is related to the dissolution of the structural underpinnings of the social capital resources noted above: bounded solidarity and enforceable trust. A thorough process of acculturation among U.S.-born members of each of these groups has led to a gradual weakening of their sense of community and to a re-orientation towards the values, expectations, and preferences of the cultural mainstream. [Complete] assimilation among domestic minorities leads to identification with the mainstream views, including a disparaging evaluation of their own group. . . .

[Even] groups with a modest level of human capital have managed to create an entrepreneurial presence when the necessary social capital, created by specific historical conditions, was present. This was certainly the case among turn-of-the-century Chinese. [It] was also true of segregated black communities during the same time period. The current desperate conditions in many inner-city neighborhoods have led some black leaders to recall wistfully the period of segregation. [As one black leader said]:

[T]he same kind of business enclave that exists in the Cuban community or in the Jewish community existed in the black community when the consumer base was contained [i.e., segregated from the larger society] and needed goods and services that had to be provided by someone in the neighborhood. Today, blacks will not buy within their neighborhood if they can help it; they want to go to the malls and blend with mainstream consumers.

Hence, thorough acculturation and the formal end of segregation led to the dissipation of the social capital formerly present in restricted black enclaves and the consequent weakening of minority entrepreneurship. As blacks attempted to join the mainstream, they found that lingering discrimination barred or slowed down their progress in the labor market, while consumption of outside goods and services undermined their own community business base.

SOURCE: Originally titled "Gaining the Upper Hand: Economic Mobility Among Immigrant and Domestic Minorities" from *Ethnic and Racial Studies, 15:* 513-518. Copyright © 1992. Reprinted with permission of Routledge, Ltd.

THE SUCCESS OF ASIAN AMERICANS HAS BEEN EXAGGERATED, IN PART, TO CRITICIZE OTHER MINORITY GROUPS

Ronald Takaki

African American "failure" has been contrasted with Asian American "success." In 1984, William Raspberry of the Washington Post noted that Asian Americans on the West Coast had "in fact" "outstripped" whites in income. Blacks should stop blaming racism for their plight, he argued, and follow the example of the self-reliant Asian Americans. In 1986, NBC Nightly News and McNeil/Lehrer Report aired special segments on

Asian Americans and their achievements. U.S. News and World Report featured Asian American advances in a cover story, and Newsweek focused a lead article on "Asian Americans: A 'Model Minority'" while Fortune applauded them as "America's super minority."

But in their celebration of this "model minority," these media pundits have exaggerated Asian American "success." Their comparisons of income between Asians and whites fail to recognize the regional location of the Asian American population. Concentrated in California, Hawaii, and New York, most Asian Americans reside in states with higher incomes but also higher costs of living than the national average. . . .

Asian American families have more persons working per family than white families. Thus, the family incomes of Asian Americans indicate the presence of more workers in each family rather than higher individual incomes. Actually, in terms of personal incomes, Asian Americans have not reached equality.

While many Asian Americans are doing well, others find themselves mired in poverty: They include southeast-Asian refugees such as the Hmong, as well as immigrant workers trapped in Chinatowns. Eighty percent of the people in New York Chinatown, 74% of San Francisco Chinatown, and 88% of Los Angeles Chinatown are foreign born. Like the nineteenth century Chinese immigrants in search of Gold Mountain, they came here to seek a better life. But what they found instead was work in Chinatown's low wage service and garment industries. . . .

The myth of the Asian American "model minority" has been challenged, yet it continues to be widely believed. One reason for this is its instructional value. For whom are Asian Americans supposed to be a "model"? . . .

Asian Americans are being used to discipline blacks. If the failure of blacks on welfare warns Americans in general how they should not behave, the triumph of Asian Americans affirms the deeply rooted values of the Protestant ethic and self-reliance. Our society needs an Asian American "model minority" in an era anxious about a growing black underclass. If Asian Americans can make it on their own, why can't other groups? . . .

Betraying a certain nervousness over the seeming end of the American dream's boundlessness, praise for this "super minority" has become society's most recent jeremiad—a call for a renewed commitment to the traditional values of hard work, thrift, and industry. After all, it has been argued, the war on poverty and affirmative action were not really necessary. Look at the Asian Americans! They did it by pulling themselves up by their bootstraps. For blacks shut out of the labor market, the Asian American model provides the standards for acceptable behavior: Blacks should not depend on welfare or affirmative action. While congratulating Asian Americans for their family values, hard work, and high incomes, President Ronald Reagan chastised blacks for their dependency on the "spider's web of welfare" and their failure to recognize that the "only barrier" to success was "within" them.

SOURCE: From *A Different Mirror* by Ronald Takaki. Copyright © 1993 by Ronald Takaki. Reprinted by permission of Little, Brown and Company, Inc.

DEBATE QUESTIONS TO CONSIDER

1. If Kitano's analysis is correct, what could other minority groups learn from the Japanese experience? If Portes and Zhou are correct, what could other minority groups learn from the Chinese experience? Do Portes and Zhou use cultural factors as part of their explanation? How? Are Portes and Zhou advocating segregation? Pluralism? Assimilation?

2. Why would the United States "need" a "model minority"? How would you answer Takaki's question: "For whom are Asian Americans supposed to be a 'model'?" Whose interests are being served by these comparisons? Do Asian Americans gain anything from these labels and comparisons? Do they lose anything?

9

NEW AMERICANS

Immigration and Assimilation

The United States is a nation of immigrants, but the rate of immigration has not been constant. Since the founding of the nation, immigration has waxed and waned from year to year, and there have been two periods of mass immigration that have been especially significant in their impact on American society. The first wave came in the century between the 1820s and 1920s and consisted mostly of Europeans. These immigrants shaped the nation in countless ways, and we discuss them in Chapter 10 of this book. The second wave began in the 1960s, and it may ultimately be as monumental in its effects as the first.

Well over 20 million immigrants (not counting undocumented or illegal immigrants) have arrived in the United States over the past four decades. This yearly rate of about half a million is actually higher than the rate of the European immigration that ended in the 1920s, and there are many important differences between immigration then and immigration now. For example, contemporary immigrants are much more diverse. They come, literally, from all over the world and represent every conceivable culture, language, race, ethnicity, and religion. They also include people from every station in life, from poorly educated, Spanish-speaking, undocumented Mexican laborers to highly skilled neurosurgeons from India, more fluent in English than most Americans.

Some of the diversity within these groups is suggested by the two Narrative Portraits in this chapter. The first is from Ho Yang, who immigrated decades ago and entered an ethnic enclave. The second, by Vo Thi Tam, recounts the experiences of a refugee who arrived much more recently and with very few resources or connections to assist her adjustment to American life. Moving from personal accounts to broad national trends, the reading by Martin and Midgley provides an overview of the contemporary stream of immigrants and discusses some of their differences from 19th- and early 20th-century immigrants. They also discuss several of the issues stimulated by the high rate of influx, including issues of assimilation and pluralism and bilingual education.

Marvasti and McKinney supplement this broad overview with a focused look at immigrants from the Middle East, a very significant group of "new Americans." This study focuses on the "American Dream"—the lofty goals of fairness and justice that the United States holds for itself—and how that dream is perceived by Middle Eastern immigrants, especially in the light of the events of September 11, 2001.

Can the United States absorb these sundry, disparate groups? Should the newcomers be pressured to Americanize or should they be encouraged to preserve their traditions and language? What policy would be most logical for the larger society? What would be fairest and most humane for the immigrants? Some of these issues are further discussed in the Current

Debates section. Peter Brimelow argues that the number of immigrants should be lowered because contemporary immigrants are an economic burden on the larger society. Reynolds Farley takes the opposite point of view, and George Borjas argues for a different way of approaching the question.

While the society wrestles with these myriad issues, it must also take account of another new feature of contemporary immigration: it is occurring at a time of rapid globalization. Indeed, contemporary immigration is one response to the shrinking of the globe and the porosity of national boundaries. Globalization has stimulated a number of counter trends, including attempts to preserve traditional cultures and systems of privilege such as paternalism and male dominance. The reading by Kimmel explores some of the social forces that have stimulated racist and nativist social movements. He also draws what might be some surprising parallels between lower middle class white males in the United States and Scandinavia and fundamentalist Islamic terrorists. The similarities between them are driven largely by class and gender: they feel emasculated by their changed economic prospects in an increasingly global society.

Please visit the accompanying website to Race, Ethnicity, and Gender, second edition for the *Public Sociology Assignments* at http://www.pineforge.com/das2.

QUESTIONS TO CONSIDER IN THIS CHAPTER

1. How will immigration change American society? Does immigration threaten U.S. values and the American way of life? Do immigrants take jobs away from native-born people? How do they impact local schools and health and welfare systems? Also consider how the United States will affect the immigrants: how will they be changed by Americanization and the values of this consumer-oriented, materialistic society? In thinking about this question in this chapter, be sure to refer back to materials introduced in previous chapters (for example, the Current Debates in Chapter 7).

2. The American Dream, as discussed by Marvasti and McKinney, presents goals and values (fairness, justice, equality) that would be difficult for any society to achieve and maintain. With regard to minority groups, immigrants, women, and working-class people, isn't the society setting itself up for inevitable failure and disappointment by claiming these goals? The "dream" can't be equally available to everyone and every group (right?), so wouldn't our society be more peaceful and less alienating if we lowered our sights and set less difficult goals? Wouldn't immigrants and minority groups expect less and suffer less disappointment and anger? Wouldn't society be more stress free?

3. How are the issues of immigration affected by globalization? How has globalization affected lower-middle-class males across the globe and stimulated movements that reject the "other" and ideologies of gender equality? How have these same changes affected women? What groups lose as a result of globalization and how do they react?

NARRATIVE PORTRAITS

TWO STORIES OF IMMIGRATION

The following accounts illustrate some of the variety in Asian American experiences. The first recounts the experiences of Ho Yang, who immigrated to San Francisco's Chinatown as a young boy in 1920. He describes some of the dynamics of the enclave community he grew to be a part of. At the time of the interview (1980), he was an officer in one of the family associations that helped to organize and structure the Chinese American community.

The second account is from Vo Thi Tam, a Vietnamese refugee whose husband had been an officer in the South Vietnamese Air Force. She describes a harrowing passage to America during which she became separated from her husband, was attacked by pirates, and gave birth in a refugee camp. These two Asian immigrants arrived in the United States under vastly different circumstances. What consequences will their different modes of incorporation have?

LIFE IN THE ENCLAVE

Ho Yang

My village in Kwantung Province is very small, only about a hundred people, and it was really poor. . . . We used cows for plows, you know, because buffaloes were expensive. A whole life would depend on a cow. In fact, when a cow died there, I think the family wept more than when a relative died. . . .

My father went to Canton and worked there, and after a while, he saved up enough money and he came to the United States. And when I was 13, he came back to China and got me. He couldn't bring my mother for some legal reason, and my sister wanted to stay with her, so I was the only one he brought back. . . .

Later, I went back to China to get married. I had a friend over here who said, "You want to get married? Maybe I'll write a letter to my niece in China." And I said, "Well, all right, you can try. It won't hurt." And it turned out to be all right with her. . . . and we've been together for more than 40 years now. . . .

There's really two reasons people like to live in Chinatown. One is the language. Some Chinese have been here for thirty years and they've never been out of Chinatown and they can't speak English. The other reason is the work here. People own little shops. There must be over 200 shops in Chinatown. Little butcher shops, little curio shops, noodle shops, all those

kinds of shops. It's usually just a husband and wife, and the kids work in there. And the small restaurants are family style. Everybody helps; washing dishes, waiters and waitresses, and all that. The money isn't too good but it's all in the family.

Many of the Chinese ladies, they go to the garment factory. . . . My wife did that. . . . [The] main reason ladies go in them is this: If you don't understand English, you can't go to work in an American place. Also, Americans pay you by the hour and you can't go too slow. Too slow and they fire you, you know. But in Chinatown, they go by piecework—so much a dozen. . . . And ladies with children, it's good for them, too, because they can bring their little kids with them and can run around there. And if the ladies need to leave, they're free to go to take their kids to school, because by the piece, the less time you spend there, the less money you get. Sometimes they call those companies sweatshops, because the pay is so low, but they're better now than they were before.

SOURCE: "Ho Yang, from China, 1920," is reprinted from *American Mosaic: The Immigrant Experience in the Words of Those Who Lived It* by Joan Morrison and Charlotte Fox Zabusky. Copyright © 1980, 1993. Reprinted by permission of the University of Pittsburgh Press.

LIFE AS A REFUGEE

Vo Thi Tam

[To escape] we got together with some other families and bought a big fishing boat. . . . Altogether there were about 37 of us that were to leave. I was five months pregnant.

[On the day of the escape, we were to rendezvous with my husband and another man outside the harbor] but there was no one there. [A patrol boat was approaching] and there was a discussion aboard the boat and the end of it was the people on our boat decided to leave without my husband and the other man. (Long pause)

When we reached the high seas, we discovered that the water container was leaking and only a little was left. So we had to ration the water from then on. We had brought some rice and some other food. . . . but the sea was so wavy that we could not cook anything at all. So all we had was raw rice and a few lemons and very little water. After seven days we ran out of water, so all we had to drink was the sea water. . . . Everyone was sick and, at one point, my mother and my little boy, four years old, were in agony, about to die. And the other people on the boat said that if they were agonizing like that, it would be better to throw them overboard so as to save them pain. . . .

[While we] were discussing throwing my mother and son overboard, we could see [a] ship coming and we were very happy. . . . When the boats came together, the people came on board . . . and made all of us go aboard the bigger boat. They began to search us—cutting off our blouses, our bras, searching everywhere. . . . Finally, they pried up the planks of our boat, trying to see if there was any gold or jewelry hidden there. And when they had taken everything, they put us back on our boat and pushed us away.

[We were attacked twice more by pirates before finally reaching land in Malaysia. Once ashore, yet another group attacked us and one of the women was raped. We were finally rescued by Malaysian police and taken to a refugee camp on Bidong Island.] Perhaps in the beginning it was all right there, maybe for ten thousand people or so, but when we arrived, there were already fifteen to seventeen thousand crowded onto thirty acres. There was no facilities, no housing, nothing. . . .

The Malaysian authorities did what they could but . . . there were no sanitary installations, and many people had diarrhea. It was very hard to stop sickness under those conditions. . . . When the monsoons came, the floor of our shelter was all mud. We had one blanket and a board to lie on, and that was all. . . . After four months, it was time for my baby to come. Fortunately, we had many doctors among us, because many . . . had escaped from Vietnam, so we had medical care but no equipment. There was no bed, no hospital, no nothing, just a wooden plank to lie down on and let the baby be born. . . . After the delivery I had to get up and . . . make room for the next one to be born.

[After seven months in the camp, we finally came to the United States.] It was like waking up after a bad nightmare. Like coming out of hell into paradise. [Shortly after her arrival, Vo Thi Tam learned that her husband had been recaptured and was a prisoner in Vietnam.]

SOURCE: "Vo Thi Tam, from Vietnam, 1979," is reprinted from *American Mosaic: The Immigrant Experience in the Words of Those Who Lived It* by Joan Morrison and Charlotte Fox Zabusky. Copyright © 1980, 1993. Reprinted by permission of the University of Pittsburgh Press.

READINGS

The readings in this section illustrate very different approaches to the study of contemporary immigration. Martin and Midgley provide a general overview while Marvasti and McKinney supply a "case study" of Middle Eastern immigrants. Kimmel takes the broadest view and links immigration to globalization and some of the most profound economic and social trends shaping modern society.

Martin and Midgley cite many of the similarities and differences between immigration in the 19th and early 20th centuries and the current wave of immigration. These comparisons provide a useful context for appreciating and understanding immigration today. On one hand, the similarities reassure us that U.S. society has successfully met the challenges created by high rates of immigration in the past and, thus, has a basis for addressing the challenges of today. On the other hand, the differences between then and now suggest that perhaps the solutions of the past may not be particularly relevant to the present. Language assimilation is one of the key challenges facing immigrants today, and Martin and Midgley point out the importance of learning English, especially in a post-industrial, consumer-oriented economy, and review the typical public school programs designed to deal with non-English-speaking students. Of course, learning English is just one aspect of assimilation and, as the authors point out, it raises a host of other questions about inclusion and integration. America is, as Martin and Midgley state, an "unfinished nation," and contemporary immigrants face an uncertain future.

Marvasti and McKinney report on their in-depth interviews with 20 immigrants from a variety of Middle Eastern nations. While the immigrants view the American promises of freedom, safety, opportunity, and material comfort very positively, they are also concerned with the preservation of their heritage, a very common and often agonizing trade-off that is faced by virtually every immigrant group. How can the frequent contradictions between the values of America and the Middle East be negotiated? The interviews report some of the attempts to deal with these conflicts, especially in the context of the attacks of September 11 and the labeling of Middle Easterners as "public enemy number one." The intense reaction of the larger society to the terrorist attacks has increased the ambivalence of many Middle Eastern Americans about the American Dream and their sense of marginalization in the larger society.

Michael Kimmel takes a different approach to immigration and the increasing numbers of "new Americans" and frames the issues in the context of globalization and changing social class structures and gender relations. He argues that the same social forces—in particular, the decline of the lower middle class—have stimulated white supremacist movements in the United States and Scandinavia that reject a host of "others" (including immigrants, women, gays, nonwhites, and Jews) and Islamic terrorists. The sense that they are being denied their just and deserved positions in the larger society motivates these sons to furiously reject modernity and attempt to return to an earlier time before globalization displaced the social class of their fathers and disrupted rigidly unequal gender relations. As Kimmel notes, these are movements of restoration, not of revolution.

IMMIGRANTS IN AMERICAN SOCIETY

Philip Martin and Elizabeth Midgley

During the 19th and early 20th centuries, the leading metaphor for the incorporation of newcomers to America was a fusion of peoples in a "smelting pot" (Ralph Waldo Emerson), "cauldron" (Henry James), or "crucible" in which, historian Frederick Jackson Turner noted, "immigrants were Americanized, liberated, and fused into a mixed race, English in neither nationality nor characteristics."[1] The hero of Israel Zangwill's popular play of 1908, "The Melting Pot," echoed this sentiment when he cried out, "Germans and Frenchmen, Irishmen and Englishmen, Jews and Russians— into the Crucible with you all! God is making the American!"

Reality was more complex. There is always a tension between the newcomers' desires to keep alive the culture and language of the community they left behind, and their need and wish to adapt to new surroundings and a different society. The balance between these competing forces changed over time, but three principles have guided what is now called integration:

• America was to be open to all kinds of immigrants. As George Washington said, "The bosom of America is open to receive not only the Opulent and respectable Stranger, but the oppressed and persecuted of all Nations and Religions; whom we shall welcome to a participation of all our rights and privileges."[2]

• No ethnic group should establish a formally recognized political identity. Nothing bars the formation of a Mexican American political party, but the two-party tradition and the belief that American citizens act politically as individuals, not as members of officially defined ethnic groups, has discouraged such political parties.

• No ethnic or national origin group would be required to give up its character and distinctive qualities. Each immigrant group was free to maintain what it could of its cultural heritage and institutions.

At no time in American history has the process of integration been easy or trouble-free. The open hostility that was expressed toward certain racial and ethnic groups in the past is surprising by today's standards. In 1930, for example, President Herbert Hoover rebuked New York Congressman Fiorella La Guardia by saying that "the Italians are predominantly our murderers and bootleggers," and invited La Guardia and his Italian-American supporters to "go back to where you belong" because "like a lot of other foreign spawn, you do not appreciate this country which supports you and tolerates you."[3] Today, no public official is likely to offer such advice to Chinese-American Gary Locke, who was elected governor of Washington in 1996. Governor Locke, like La Guardia, is the son of immigrants.

Integration can be regarded as a glass half full or half empty. The "Changing Relations" study, which investigated immigrant communities in six cities in the 1980s, found that— despite segregation in jobs and housing and the lack of a common language—newcomers and natives in a number of U.S. cities were cooperating to achieve local goals, such as obtaining government benefits or improving their neighborhoods.[4] The report also noted that, in cities with large immigrant populations, immigrants were not integrating into the broader community. Economic restructuring had created fears in many communities that immigrants threatened the jobs of longer-term residents.

Integrating immigrants is likely to be different in the early 21st century than it was in the early 20th century. In the early 1900s, many U.S.-born Americans first interacted with immigrants when the U.S.-born left their farms for jobs in the cities, where both they and the immigrants were newcomers.[5] Now, immigrants are moving into and sometimes transforming established communities.

In 1997, the U.S. Commission on Immigration Reform (CIR) recommended that the federal government do more to "Americanize immigrants" to help them integrate into U.S. society. The CIR emphasized that Americanization is a two-way street. The United States expects immigrants to "obey our laws, pay our taxes, respect other cultures and ethnic groups. At the same time, [we] also incur obligations to provide an environment in which newcomers can become fully participating members of our society." The CIR recommended that federal grants be given to communities with large numbers of immigrants to create resource centers in which immigrants and the native-born could interact. The CIR also urged U.S. businesses to do more to help integrate immigrants: "Those business groups in particular who lobby for high levels of immigration must make a far greater effort not only to support immigration, but also to support immigrants, through English classes, naturalization and civic education."[6]

LANGUAGE AND EDUCATION

The 2000 U.S. Census reported that 47 million residents older than age 5 spoke a language other than English at home, 15 million more than in 1990. Spanish was the most common non-English language, spoken by 28.1 million, while 2.0 million spoke Chinese, 1.6 million spoke French, 1.4 million spoke German,

Table 9.1

Language Spoken at Home	Population Age 5 or Older (Thousands)
Speak only English	215,424
Speak a language other than English	46,952
Spanish or Spanish Creole	28,101
Chinese	2,022
French (Incl. Patois, Cajun)	1,644
German	1,383
Tagalog	1,224
Vietnamese	1,020
Italian	1,008
Korean	894
Total	**262,375**

SOURCE: U.S. Census Bureau, Summary Tables on Language Use and English Ability: 2000, PRC- T-20 (Feb. 23, 2003): table 5

1.2 million spoke Tagalog, and 1.0 million each spoke Italian and Vietnamese (see table).

In the United States, the shift from speaking another language to speaking English has usually occurred over three generations. Adult immigrants commonly did not learn English well. Their children were usually bilingual, using their parents' language at home and English at school. English often became dominant as the children of immigrants entered the workplace. The grandchildren of immigrants—the third generation—typically speak only English.[7]

The shift to English may be accelerating among recent immigrants and may occur within just two generations.[8] Most immigrants settle in U.S. cities, where they are more likely to be exposed to English than were workers in farms and factories earlier in the century. A recent study found that the children of immigrants in Miami, for example, preferred English for their everyday communication.[9] Another survey found that even though most Mexican-born U.S. residents spoke Spanish at home, almost two-thirds of U.S.-born people of Mexican ancestry used English at home.[10]

Immigrants and their children would benefit from acquiring English language ability even more rapidly. Poor English skills are associated with lower earnings in a high-tech society. Earlier immigrants could farm or work in factories or build railroads without speaking English. But in today's service-dominated economy, the ability to speak English is required for nearly all but the lowest-paying jobs. One study found that among immigrant men who did not speak English at home, those who were not fluent in English earned only about half as much as those who were.[11] Another study concluded that those in the United States "who speak English 'well' or 'very well' have 17 percent higher earnings than those with less fluency."[12]

Most immigrants want to learn English. A survey of residents of Mexican, Cuban, and Puerto Rican origins found that more than 90 percent agreed that all U.S. citizens and residents should learn English.[13] But acquiring a new language is a difficult undertaking for adults, particularly those who work long hours. There are frequently long waiting lists for English classes for adults. There is no federally financed program to teach English to adult speakers of other languages, although states use federal adult education grants along with their own funds to provide English instruction.

PUBLIC EDUCATION

Lack of English language skills is also a major issue for the nation's schools. Students who have difficulty understanding an all-English curriculum are often referred to as limited-English proficient (LEP), a term whose definition varies from state to state and between federal agencies. These students are referred to as English language learners.

In the 2000–2001 school year, there were 3.4 million students in primary and secondary schools receiving LEP services, including 1.5 million in California and 570,000 in Texas.[14] There are two major approaches to teaching English to students fluent in another language: English-as-a-second-language (ESL) instruction for rapid acquisition of English, and bilingual education, which includes instruction in a limited-English student's native language. Each approach has its own philosophy and assumptions about what is appropriate for students with different linguistic backgrounds. With the ESL approach, children of various language backgrounds receive instruction in English for all subjects, but the English is modified by specially trained teachers so English-learners can more easily understand it. Teachers provide an appropriate context for the students to help them with the new language.

With bilingual education, children are taught to read and write in their home languages before shifting their language of instruction gradually to English. Older children who are new to English are taught such core subjects as math, science, and history in their home languages while they are learning English. The aim of bilingual education is to ensure that limited-English students are taught material with the same intellectual content as other students while these students gain competence in English.

Educators do not agree on which method is best. A report on limited English students by the NRC [National Research Council] concluded that the most successful school programs have three similar characteristics: some native language instruction initially for most students; relatively early phasing-in of English instruction; and teachers specially trained in instructing English-language learners.[15]

These three characteristics are lacking in many school programs. Schools with bilingual programs—most are Spanish—may continue instruction in a non-English language for as long as seven years. In other schools, limited English children are taught in English by teachers who have had no special training in teaching children in a language that is not their own.

Most non-English-speaking students come from disadvantaged socioeconomic backgrounds, which presents other handicaps for excelling in school. The NRC report found that 77 percent of English-language learners in a sample of schools were eligible for free or reduced-price lunches, compared with 38 percent of all students in the sample.

The debate about bilingual education is especially vociferous in California, which has about 45 percent of the nation's limited-English school children. In June 1998, California voters approved Proposition 227, the English for the Children initiative, 61 percent to 39 percent, ending bilingual education and requiring most non-English speaking children to be placed in special English classes for one year and then shifted to regular classes. Since then, students in English immersion classes have scored higher on math and reading than students in bilingual programs. In 2002, 32 percent of the LEP students in the immersion program passed the California English proficiency test, compared with just 9 percent the previous year. Students in bilingual programs showed less dramatic improvement, from 3 percent to 16 percent.[16] Arizona and Massachusetts also ended bilingual education by voter initiative, but Colorado voted to continue teaching LEP children in their native language.[17]

The debate about bilingual education involves much broader issues than the best way to teach non-English-speaking children. One issue is whether newcomers should quickly be integrated into mainstream America, or whether newcomers should be encouraged to retain their distinctive cultural attributes and their native languages—and whether the public schools should help immigrants maintain their language and culture. If schools give priority to English-language learning, does that show concern for immigrants' future success in the United States, or is it "Anglo cultural imperialism"? Is bilingual education a form of minority patronage that creates public employment for members of particular ethnic groups? Should U.S. immigration policy be changed to favor people who already know English, as it does in Australia and New Zealand?

Strong feelings about the role of English often overwhelm educational considerations in the debate over bilingual education. Should the United States establish English as its official language? Would a prohibition against the government's use of other languages be a beneficial affirmation that English is the common language of the United States, or would establishing English as the official language be a rebuff to speakers of other languages and a handicap to the work of government? Such questions involve the public education system in much broader issues and feelings about immigrants, integration, and national character.

AN UNFINISHED NATION

Past immigration flows to the United States resemble waves, with the number of immigrants increasing to peak levels and then falling into troughs. The fourth wave of U.S. immigration, which began in 1965, has been climbing since the early 1980s. Now, in the early 21st century, 1 million immigrants a year are being admitted, with no end in sight. Many Americans want the federal government to take steps to reduce immigration. If the flow were reduced, the current period would be the peak of the fourth wave. Other Americans are comfortable with current levels of immigration, so the fourth wave might continue.

The United States is a nation of immigrants that first welcomed all newcomers, later excluded certain types, and since the 1920s has limited the number of immigrants with an annual ceiling. Immigrants and refugees continue to arrive through America's front door, which was opened wider in 1990 to accommodate more relatives of U.S. residents and more workers desired by U.S. employers. But the fastest growth in entries in the 1990s was through side and back doors, as nonimmigrant tourists, foreign workers and students, and unauthorized foreigners arrived in larger numbers.

Research on the economic, social, and political effects of immigration does not provide clear guidelines for policy. Overall, immigrants have minor effects—for better or worse—on the huge American economy and labor market. Most immigrants are better off financially in America than they were at home, but many arrive with minimal education and skills and find it hard to advance to better jobs in the American labor market. State and local governments, meanwhile, point out that the taxes paid by immigrants go mostly to the federal government, while state and local governments bear the brunt of the costs of providing services to the immigrants.

Most immigrants to the United States do not become naturalized citizens. Instead, they live as permanent residents and keep their original nationality. Laws enacted in 1996 made noncitizens ineligible for some welfare benefits, which prompted a record 1 million foreigners to naturalize. The U.S. constitution makes U.S. born children of immigrants citizens at birth, whether their parents are naturalized citizens, legal immigrants, or illegal immigrants.

U.S. immigrants are often isolated from native-born Americans, as they were in previous periods of mass immigration. Their isolation is reinforced by housing and job segregation and language barriers. There are many examples of cooperation between natives and immigrants, however, as well as signs that immigrant children may be acquiring English faster than did previous immigrants.

For the foreseeable future, America seems likely to remain the world's major destination for immigrants. Our history and traditions suggest that, within a few decades, most of today's immigrants will be an integral part of the ever-changing American community. But past success does not guarantee that history will repeat itself. There are concerns about the size and nature of today's immigrant population. As the nation searches for an immigration policy for the 21st century, the United States, and the immigrants on their way here, are on a journey to an uncertain destination.

SOURCE: Reprinted by permission of Population Reference Bureau.

Notes

1. Frederick Jackson Turner. *The Frontier in American History.* (New York: Henry Holt, 1920).

2. George Washington. "Address to the Members of the Volunteer Association and Other Inhabitants of the Kingdom of Ireland Who Have Lately Arrived in the City of New York." (Dec. 2, 1783). Accessed online at www.pbs.org/george-washington/collection/other_1788dec2.html, on May 3, 2003.

3. E. Digby Baltzell. *The Protestant Establishment: Aristocracy and Caste in America.* (New York: Vintage Books. 1964): 30.

4. Robert Bach. *Changing Relations: Newcomers and Established Residents in U.S. Communities.* (New York: Ford Foundation, 1992): 49.

5. Only 35% of the 75 million Americans in 1900 lived in urban areas. The small communities

where most Americans lived in the early 1900s could be homogeneous even as the country as a whole was becoming more diverse. Immigrants and Americans interacted in a common "new land"— cities. Thomas Archdeacon. "Reflections on Immigration to Europe in the light of U.S. Immigration History, *International Migration Review* 26, no. 2(1992): 525–48.

6. U.S. Commission on Immigration Reform, "Becoming an American: Immigration and Immigrant Policy (1997), accessed online at http://migration.ucdavis.edu/mn/cir/97Reort1/titlepgs/titlepgs.htm, on May 12, 2003.

7. Francois Gosjean. Life with Two Languages: An Introduction to Bilingualism. (Cambridge, MA: Harvard University Press, 1982): chapter 2.

8. Calvin Veltmann. The Future of the Spanish Language in the United States (Washington, DC and New York: Hispanic Policy Development Project, 1988): Chapter 8.

9. Alejandro Portes and Richard Schauffler, "Language and the Second Generation: Bilingualism Yesterday and Today," in *The Second Generation,* ed. Alejandro Portes (New York: Russell Sage Foundation, 1996): Chapter 2.

10. Rodolfo de la Garza, et al. *Latino Voices* (Boulder, CO: Westview Press, 1992): 42.

11. Portes and Schauffler, "Language and the Second Generation": 8–29.

12. Joseph R. Meisenheimer II, "How do Immigrants Fare in the U.S. Labor Market?" *Monthly Labor Review* 115, no. 12 (1992): 17; and Barry Chiswick and Paul Miller, "Language in the Immigrant Labor Market," in *Immigration, Language, and Ethnicity: Canada and the U.S.,* ed. Barry Chiswick (Washington, DC: The AEI Press, 1992): 27.

13. de la Garza et al., *Latino Voices:* 98.

14. U.S. Department of Education, National Center for Educational Statistics, Common Core of Data, "Public Elementary/Secondary School Universe Survey" (2000–2001), and "Local Education Agency Universe Survey" (2000–2001), accessed online at http://nces.ed.gov/pubs2002/overview/x;s/table10/xls, on Jan. 26, 2003.

15. National Research Council, *Improving Schooling for Language-Minority Children: A Research Agenda.* (Washington, DC: Commissions on Behavioral and Social Sciences and Education, 1997).

16. Nanette Asimov, "English-Only Students Do Better on State Test," *San Francisco Chronicle,* March 26, 2003.

17. Massachusetts on Right Track With English Immersion, Results in California are Encouraging, Says U.S. ENGLISH,: *U.S. Newswire,* may 5, 2003; and Jim Boulet, "Win Some, Lose Some," *National Review Online,* Nov. 7, 2002.

DISCUSSION QUESTIONS

1. The authors raise issues of assimilation and pluralism, questions that should be familiar at this point in the text. Should we stress our common traits or celebrate and preserve our differences? Which course is more just and fair? Why?

2. According to the authors, what educational programs for non-English-speaking children are common in American schools? How do these programs work and how are they related to the larger issues raised in the first question? Did the schools you attended have special programs for non-English speakers? How did these programs work? How would you evaluate their success?

3. The authors mention that the Commission on Immigration Reform recommended the awarding of federal grants to communities to establish resource centers to increase interaction between immigrants and the native born. What good could such centers do? What objections—from both immigrants and native born—would you anticipate to the success of these centers? If you were the head of such a center, what specific programs would you recommend? Why?

DISCRIMINATION AND THE AMERICAN DREAM: THE CASE OF MIDDLE EASTERN AMERICANS

Amir Marvasti and Karyn D. McKinney

The American Dream assumes that certain values, like equality, freedom, and justice, are available to any person in the United States. Social scientists have long been interested in the validity of this assumption. As early as the 1930s, Swedish social scientist Gunnar Myrdal and his colleagues wrote about an "American dilemma" in a work by that title. This "dilemma" was the failure of U.S. society to live up to its stated values of equality and justice for everyone regardless of race. These researchers saw a great deal of conflict in the fact that although Americans held lofty ideals about fairness and equal opportunity, racism and segregation characterized the social structure of the country.

In this article, we examine three dimensions of how Middle Eastern Americans see the American Dream. First, we explore the respondents' perceptions of the promises offered by the American Dream. Second, we examine the strategies respondents have used to attempt to fulfill the promise of the American Dream. Finally, we show contradictions in the American Dream, as our respondents experienced them, especially in the wake of the attacks of September 11, 2001. In particular, our respondents' understanding of discrimination was manifested in relation to how they experienced the United States and its promises of equal opportunity and prosperity (i.e., the "American Dream").

METHODS AND DATA

From May 2002 to May 2004, we conducted 20 in-depth interviews with 12 male and 8 female respondents whose ages ranged from 18 to 55. All were enrolled in college or had earned a four-year degree or higher. Eighteen were naturalized citizens and 2 were longtime immigrants who had lived and worked in the United States for more than 10 years and planned to become citizens. Respondents were interviewed in three states (Florida, Pennsylvania, and Virginia) about how they manage being Middle Eastern, particularly when faced with discrimination. Our data collection took the form of "active interviewing," or a process in which both the participants and the researcher contribute to meaning-making. We began our interviews with demographic questions about age, country of origin, and education. We then followed with questions about whether respondents had experienced any form of ethnic discrimination at work, in school, or in their communities due to their religion, names, accents, appearance, or style of dress.

Participants were recruited using snowball sampling, which is considered especially useful when dealing with a sensitive topic that can best be understood from an insider's perspective. Respondents were our relatives, friends, and professional colleagues, who in turn referred us to other potential research participants. The respondents (Pakistanis, Iranians, Egyptians, a Turk, and a Lebanese) all self-identified as Middle Eastern American. This method of self-identification is the norm for most studies of ethnicity and race. Even the U.S. census, an ostensibly objective population count, is based on self-identification. In other words, when answering ancestral background questions in the U.S. census, respondents are free to choose from a number of categories (e.g., "Arab or Arabic," "Middle Eastern," and "North African").

In fact, according to a census report, from 1990 to 2000 the number of people who self-identified as "Middle Eastern" quadrupled.

EMBRACING THE AMERICAN DREAM

When asked what they considered to be a positive aspect of life in the United States, almost all of our respondents referred to the abundance of financial and educational opportunities and the freedom to pursue them, particularly in comparison to what was available in their home countries. A Pakistani man whose parents immigrated to the United States when he was 10 states the following about the positive aspects of his immigration experience:

> The opportunities that are available here, that's the whole reason our parents came here. To provide for us and to give us opportunities they never had. It's definitely a blessing coming here. You really don't notice it until you go back home.

An Iranian man specifically praises the educational opportunities in the United States and notes how he made the decision to become a naturalized citizen:

> When I came to the United States, I actually was never thinking about staying here. . . . I had my Bachelors of Science before I came to the States. I thought I come here and go through my Masters and Ph.D. and then one day I would go back home. But after many years, knowing what the situation is like back home [Iran], . . . I really thought that this is a better place to stay and this is a better place to live and this is a better place to establish my life. And that's why I made the decision to become a citizen and stay in this country.

Aside from the educational opportunities, some cited personal freedoms, such as freedom of speech. For example, an Iranian American man stated that the most positive aspect of living in the United States is "Freedom of speech . . . that you can say what comes to your mind without being punished."

Other respondents had a very positive view of the material comforts of life in the United States. For example, a Pakistani man notes, "Most positive aspect is that I have all the material benefits that I ever imagined. Most of them are within my reach." For this man, the American Dream is as much about the potential for material success (things that are within one's reach) as it is about its actual achievement. This, certainly, is the definition of the American Dream, and is what many believe to be the most beneficial part of being in this country.

Finally, for some, the most important part of the American Dream is the assurance of physical safety from war and political persecution. For example, a Lebanese American professor who had lived through the wars that devastated his country in the 1980s has this to say about his immigration experience:

> There is intensity to war, which you survive. It is unparalleled to anything else in life. It [Beirut] was insanely intense. I mean you would be teaching your classes, and there was bombing and you would run to the shelter and come back and finish your lecture. It's a dangerous city, it's a wild city and you live or you don't. I didn't want to leave; I left because I had to. So immigration was really salvation. I had no alternative. And I would say for a lot of immigrants, immigration is not easy because you come into a different environment. . . . I would say, from the people that I know, that immigration is a way of hope. Because, as I said, it's not easy. . . . it's not easy because it's different. . . . People have to do it because it is salvation, it's hope. It always saddens me in that the host countries don't realize that it's not easy for the immigrants. They are desperate and they're looking for a way out. . . . There's despair, there's hopelessness.

For this respondent, the promise of the American Dream is not the material or educational opportunities per se, but the simple possibility of leading an ordinary life. Note that for this respondent, the real cultural misunderstanding between the immigrants and natives is not about language or customs but the reasons and motives that bring millions to the United States in search of a better life. Immigrants are often confronted with the question, "Why do you people come here?" The answer is typically "To live the American Dream." Admittedly, this is a simplistic response. Nonetheless, it points to the heart of the problem. Namely, what is the American dream, who does it belong to, and how should it be lived? Questions about discrimination and injustice invariably point to the gap between fundamental American ideals and their practice in everyday life.

AMBIVALENCE ABOUT THE AMERICAN DREAM

The second part of our discussion about the relationship between perceptions of the American Dream and discrimination involves the personal sacrifices that Middle Eastern Americans have to make to participate in the dream. All of our respondents spoke of ambivalence about having to give up parts of their heritage and about adopting new customs. For example, as seen in the following excerpt from a respondent in a focus group, a preoccupation with one's native culture and the possibility of its loss competes with the desire to fulfill the American Dream. As one respondent notes,

> The funny thing with that is our kids won't have the joy of growing up with parents that speak the language. The language, the accents, that kind of stuff won't be there for them and they miss out on what we enjoy thoroughly.

Despair about loss of cultural heritage is particularly evident when raising children in a new environment is concerned. We posed a question about the importance of language to a Lebanese American man, and his response reflects the importance that many Middle Eastern Americans place on transmitting their cultural heritage to their children.

Interviewer: Your children speak Arabic?

Respondent: They understand but they don't like it. The older one now is a little bit more interested. The younger one is rebellious. . . . . But they understand and we're trying annually to send them to Lebanon so they keep their ears alive, as it were.

Here the use of the metaphor "keep their ears alive" is particularly enlightening. Becoming distant from one's culture is akin to having part of oneself die.

Similarly, an Iranian American man speaks of losing his cultural traditions and the problems he faces with raising his child. As he stated, the most negative aspect is

> . . . . missing the culture. Missing the day-to-day activities that we have back home. It's difficult to try to accept a new culture, it's different from what you believe and you have to go out there and face that every day. And now that I have a child, it's really about how can I raise him so that he can keep most of the traditions that I believe in and my wife believes in? And that's really the toughest question, the toughest part I have to face.

The problems of adapting to a new culture while maintaining one's own also manifest themselves in the way continuity of family experience is disrupted. In the following excerpt, a Lebanese American father speaks of cultural displacement as he compares his own childhood experiences with that of his sons:

I think it [coming to America] does change you and it does challenge you when you have a family when you have kids because then you realize the gap that is growing between you and your children. . . . I think the challenge and difficulty of immigration particularly becomes apparent, at least to me, when I have to relate to my children who are growing up as Americans. They love me and obviously understand me, but we have a lot of miscommunication because I don't relate to some of the values that they have. . . . I would also point out inability on my part to convey my own cultural experience. For example, my neighbor he has always been fishing so he takes out his son fishing and there's a continuity of cultural experience there. This is his land; he is very familiar with it. He's grown up on hamburgers so his son will grow up on hamburgers. For us, obviously it's different. My wife always insists on cooking Arabic food and the kids are horrified and say: "What is this junk?" And from that to the rest of the social and personal goals that this society kind of encourages, which to me are devastating behaviors. So that's where it comes in. It's not typical generational gap between a father and his children. . . . So, that's where the gap is . . . That's where the challenge is. How do you cope with things like that?

Here the problem is not simply that one has to adapt to a new way of life; rather, the cultural resources that gave meaning to one's identity and family experiences have become fragments of a distant life. At the same time, the new cultural resources for defining oneself and one's family may contradict deeply held convictions.

As a whole, while the American Dream of a more successful life is something that our respondents subscribe to in one form or another, their participation in the American Dream also raises questions about navigating two cultural realms that sometimes have contradictory values. For Middle Eastern Americans, their struggle with being different has become significantly difficult in recent years, especially after the events of September 11, 2001.

REALIZING THE CONTRADICTIONS IN THE AMERICAN DREAM IN THE WAKE OF SEPTEMBER 11

Difficulty with cultural assimilation is a common experience for most ethnic groups, but being designated public enemy number one is not. In the hours following the tragic attacks of September 11, 2001, being or just looking Middle Eastern became an instant offense. For members of this group, this was a turning point in terms of both the way they were viewed by others and the way they defined themselves. While the feeling of shock is similar to what everyone must have felt that day, in the case of Middle Eastern Americans, there was also a feeling of impending doom, the knowledge that their lives would never be exactly the same. Many of our respondents stated that after their sense of initial shock and sadness, the next thought they remember was that they hoped that the incident was perpetrated by domestic terrorists, as was the case with the Oklahoma City bombing. One Pakistani American stated,

I was on my way to the gym listening to radio when it happened. And I thought it was a hoax. And then I got to the gym and it was on TV and I was like "Oh my God, please don't let it be Muslims." That was the first thing came to my mind, "God please don't let this be one of us."

As the day went by, a chasm began to form between Middle Eastern Americans and their fellow citizens. The perception that Middle Easterners were the aggressors and Americans the victims began to take hold, and out of this perception grew anger.

Respondent: I went to class that day and came back and from then on for two days, I was glued to CNN. . . . Wherever you went you always— that day even among my friends there was talk about anger and they looked really angry. . . .

There was talk about "We should bomb Palestine." And "Who cares about these people now." In a way, I understood their anger because of what had just happened. I guess it was kind of lonely that day.

In the days following the attacks, Middle Eastern Americans had to accept the fact that they were seen by many as legitimate targets of anger. The news media were full of messages about hate being an acceptable emotion under the circumstances. In that atmosphere it was indeed very "lonely" to be Middle Eastern American. What was most striking was the ordinary tone with which retaliatory violence was talked about. For example, in an introductory race and ethnicity course taught by the first author, a young man passionately exclaimed, "I say we go bomb the Taj Mahal!" Although others in the class corrected his error in terms of his misplaced target, his general idea of bombing buildings where civilians would be the primary casualties was not disputed.

Some Middle Eastern Americans also felt a strong sense of impending doom related to this tragedy. As indicated here, in the aftermath of September 11, perhaps the most significant realization for many Middle Eastern Americans was the awareness that their right to be part of the American Dream could be taken away for actions that they were not in any way responsible for. With this realization came the sense of not belonging and the real possibility of being physically separated from the rest of society and placed in an internment camp. One young Middle Eastern American remembered,

> I really thought I was going to be sent to like a camp. . . . It didn't—for those couple of days—it didn't feel like we were going to be back to normal again. Like I really didn't feel like—along with going to internment camp—I thought my life was never going to be the same. I no longer had a home here.

As this respondent puts it, realizing that one no longer has a home here was tantamount to realizing that the American Dream applied to some more than others, or that some groups were more vulnerable and more likely to be disenfranchised than others.

RETHINKING THE AMERICAN DREAM

Despite the purported pluralism of the contemporary U.S. ethnic landscape, it becomes obvious to immigrants that to achieve success in the United States, they must conform to standards of Americanization. September 11 was an important turning point in the psyche of Middle Eastern Americans to the extent that it caused them to reevaluate their place in American society and its promises of freedom and equality. Consider, for example, how this Pakistani American woman (who was born in Pennsylvania) rethinks her status as an American in light of how she and her family have been treated since September 11:

> My brother was assaulted three days after September 11th. It was part of the backlash. And I'm worried for my parents more than I am for myself. They've been here since 1968, longer than they ever lived in Pakistan. But they are still very much considered outsiders, and it's because of their accents largely. I feel I'm even considered an outsider a lot of the times. I sound just as American as anyone else, and I was born and raised here. . . . [After September 11] I think a lot of people thought that if you're not going to consider me American, why am I going to consider myself an American. If you're not going to protect me like other Americans, if you are going to create laws that are going to undermine me, then I shouldn't be trying so hard to fit into a culture that consistently and perpetually rejects me.

According to this respondent, after September 11, and particularly after a brutal physical attack on her younger brother, it became particularly apparent that the ideals of equality in the American Dream did not apply to her and her family. Her ethnicity transcends her identity as an American and places her in the position of a second-class citizen.

Many also worry about the future of their U.S.-born children. In the following excerpt, an Iranian American woman expresses her worries about her son's future, who was born in Florida just days after the terrorist attacks.

> Sometimes I think if my son is going to school and in first grade, you know, the kids talk and they really don't know anything. . . . I don't know what is going to happen . . . how he's going to react. I know he was born here but still. I hope everything is going to be okay with him. . . . Some kid who doesn't know anything and the first thing they notice is your parents are from Iran, or the Middle East, and they call you a terrorist. He [my son] doesn't understand that or get upset. . . . I would tell any kid from Iran don't get into a fight. Deep down you know that you are not a terrorist, something like that. . . . Hopefully this thing will end soon.

As was the case with the previous respondent, this woman also expresses doubt about how much protection her son's identity as a born American will provide against prejudice and stereotypes. Her advice for young Iranians to remember that deep down they are not terrorists shows how keeping in mind the authentic meaning of one's ethnic identity protects that identity from corruption by the discrimination of others.

One of the most profound effects of September 11 on the lives of Middle Eastern Americans was the realization that their daily routines (i.e., the mundane tasks of going on a trip or even to a grocery store) would be subjected to scrutiny and potentially make them vulnerable to acts of violence. An Iranian American man describes how September 11 affected his life:

> I actually canceled a trip. We usually take a trip on Thanksgiving with about 30–40 Iranian Americans. And that's when I realized there's a difference in this war [War on Terrorism]. There is a new order. We've been doing this [going on trips] for the past seven or eight years. . . . Now that year, . . . I thought there was too much risk in taking 40 people on a trip, and most of them were thinking the same way. We can't go somewhere and not play our own music. We like our own music, we like our own dance, we like our own food and tradition so we couldn't do that therefore I canceled that trip. That's when it occurred to me there's a difference.

Interviewer: Did you put any other limitations on your life because of it? Did you restrict your life in any other way?

Respondent: I'm more alert these days about how I answer people. . . . In the past I wouldn't mind if they asked right off the bat where I'm from . . . But now most of the time I say "God, please don't let them ask the question." . . . I don't volunteer information. . . . I'm more guarded about what I say.

For many Middle Eastern Americans, September 11 meant restricting their personal freedoms (e.g., the right to travel, go to various public places, attend mosques, or practice Islam). While many of these were self-imposed restrictions, they were nonetheless in direct response to real or perceived threats of persecution and violence. Being "more guarded" about personal speech and travel became the new way of life.

Middle Eastern Americans have experienced discrimination and prejudice for at least the past two decades; however, September 11 gave new legitimacy and justification to a level of mistreatment that many had never experienced before. As a Pakistani American woman puts it,

[It happened before] but not with this magnitude, and not with the accusatory tone, and not with the same attitude as they did before. Before it was just out of curiosity, and it was incidental, but this is an even more demanding tone of "Who are you? And why did your people do this?" And we need to protect ourselves.

Collectively, these post-9/11 experiences have caused some Middle Eastern Americans to question the meaning of the American Dream and the extent to which its lofty promises apply to them. They have recognized that full assimilation into American culture will not provide protection against acts of ignorance and that their future in this country is uncertain. One Pakistani woman stated, "Policies are being passed very quietly, foundation is being laid that makes it a little bit scary." This outlook is eloquently summarized by one of our Lebanese American respondents:

I for one imagine that every immigrant coming to this country comes with at least the impression that this is a country that has laws—laws which are civil. But suddenly to realize, as I have seen it, this is a veneer, a very thin veneer of civility. At the moment that something threatening happens, that veneer is gone. For instance, the Patriot Act is horrific. And, of course, the bigotry and the xenophobia that flooded the media is appalling. That again was disappointing to me because, as I said, all immigrants who are coming to America are coming to an America they have seen in the movies. And, in a sense, because that's the only thing we know about America, we believe that. We come with these high values, discipline, honesty, hard work, and of course, the rule of law, justice, all these values. We have seen them in the movies, the good guys always winning at the end. . . . And suddenly when something horrific happens, that veneer is gone. . . . So my faith is shaken.

The very value of civility is that it should offer protection when things are the most tense. If it fails to do so, then it is in fact, just a "veneer." Similarly, laws, as this man suggests, are of no value unless they defend those who are least able to protect themselves (e.g., the newest immigrants) at times when they are most vulnerable. For this respondent, the fact that the immigrants' constitutional rights (i.e., due process protections) are undermined with the passage of new laws, such as the Patriot Act, further reveals how thin this "veneer of civility" really is.

CONCLUSION

For many immigrants, the American Dream is not an all-or-nothing proposition, but a multifaceted experience. It means both opportunities and unfulfilled promises. Like most immigrants, many Middle Eastern Americans are not only pushed out of their own countries due to conflict, poverty, and oppression, but are pulled to the United States by the promise of a better life. To take advantage of new opportunities, most sacrifice parts of their culture and even identity. However, many discover that what is presented as "freedom" and "opportunity" for all is a thinly veiled system of discrimination that often excludes them.

DISCUSSION QUESTIONS

1. What is the American dream, as defined by the authors and by the respondents in their study? Given the information presented in the article, which parts of the dream may be accessible to them, if any, and which parts may be inaccessible, if any?

2. What do the authors mean by characterizing some of their respondents as "ambivalent" about the American dream? Is it possible to embrace parts of the American dream but not others? Would you say Middle Eastern Americans are unique in their "partial" endorsement of the American dream, or are there other groups/individuals who may feel this way? If you can think of others, explain why these others might feel this way.

3. Why do some immigrants struggle more than others when ensuring that subsequent generations retain cultural traditions like language and food? Are there groups who have an easier time finding support in American culture for passing on their family traditions? If so, who are they, and why? Be mindful of geographic variations in the United States in your answer.

4. What are the advantages and disadvantages of Middle Eastern and other U.S. immigrants losing these cultural traditions? (Include advantages and disadvantages for both majority and minority groups.) If you were (or are) in the position of being a recent-generation immigrant, what choices would you (or do you) make in how much of your cultural traditions you pass on, and how are those choices constrained by outside factors?

5. How did the events of September 11, 2001, affect the experiences of Middle Eastern Americans in the United States? How did this affect their embracing of the American dream? Is there anything the United States could or should have done differently to minimize the negative impact of this event on its new immigrants?

GLOBALIZATION AND ITS MAL(E)CONTENTS: THE GENDERED MORAL AND POLITICAL ECONOMY OF TERRORISM

Michael S. Kimmel

Globalization changes masculinities—reshaping the arena in which national and local masculinities are articulated, and transforming the shape of men's lives. Globalization disrupts and reconfigures traditional, neocolonial or other national, regional or local economic, political and cultural arrangements, and thus transforms local articulations of both domestic and public patriarchy (see Connell, 1998). The marketplace, multinational corporations and transnational geopolitical institutions (World Court, United Nations, European Union) and their attendant ideological principles (economic rationality, liberal individualism) express a gendered logic. As a result, the impact of global economic and political restructuring is greater on women. At the national and global level, the world gender order privileges men in a variety of ways, such as unequal wages, unequal labor force participation, unequal structures of ownership and control of property, unequal control over one's body, as well as cultural and sexual privileges.

The patterns of masculinity embedded within these gendered institutions also are rapidly becoming the dominant global hegemonic model of masculinity, against which all local, regional and national masculinities are played out and increasingly refer. The processes of globalization and the emergence of a global hegemonic masculinity have the ironic effect of increasingly "gendering" local, regional and national resistance to incorporation into the global arena as subordinated entities. Gender becomes one of the chief organizing principles of local, regional and national resistance to globalization, whether expressed in religious or secular, ethnic or national terms. These processes involve flattening or eliminating local or regional distinctions, cultural homogeniza-tion as citizens and social heterogenization as new ethnic groups move to new countries in labor migration efforts. Movements thus tap racialist and nativist sentiments at the same time as they can tap local and regional protec-tionism and isolationism. They become gen-dered as oppositional movements also tap into a vague masculine resentment of economic displacement, loss of autonomy and collapse of domestic patriarchy that accompany further integration into the global economy. Efforts to reclaim economic autonomy, to reassert politi-cal control and revive traditional domestic dominance thus take on the veneer of restoring manhood.

It is the lower middle class—that stratum of independent farmers, small shopkeepers, craft and highly skilled workers and small-scale entrepreneurs—who have been hardest hit by the processes of globalization. This has resulted in massive male displacement—migration, downward mobility. And it has been felt the most not by the adult men who were the trades-men, shopkeepers and skilled workers, but by their sons, by the young men whose inheritance has been seemingly stolen from them. They feel entitled and deprived—and furious. These angry young men are the foot soldiers of the armies of rage that have sprung up around the world.

Here I discuss white supremacists and Aryan youth in both the US and Scandinavia, and compare them briefly with the terrorists of Al

Qaeda who were responsible for the attack on the US on 11 September 2001. All these groups, I argue, use a variety of ideological and political resources to re-establish and reassert domestic and public patriarchies. These movements look backward, nostalgically, to a time when they— native-born white men and Muslim men in a pre-global era—were able to assume the places in society to which they believed themselves entitled. They seek to restore that unquestioned entitlement, both in the domestic sphere and in the public sphere. They are movements not of revolution, but of restoration.

By examining far right Aryan white supremacists in the US, and their counterparts in Scandinavia, we can see the ways in which masculinity politics may be mobilized among some groups of men in the economic North; and while looking at the social origins of the Al Qaeda terrorists, we can see how they might work out in Islamic countries. Although such a comparison in no way effaces the many differ-ences that exist among these movements, and especially between the movements in the eco-nomic South and North, a comparison of their similarities enables us to explore the political mobilization of masculinities, and map the ways in which masculinities are likely to be put into political play in the coming decades.

RIGHT-WING MILITIAS: RACISM, SEXISM, AND ANTI-SEMITISM AS MASCULINE REASSERTION[1]

In an illustration in a 1987 edition of WAR, the magazine of the White Aryan Resistance, a working-class white man, in hard hat and flak jacket, stands proudly before a suspension bridge while a jet plane soars overhead. "White Men Built This nation!!" reads the text, "White Men Are This nation!!!" Here is a moment of fusion of racial and gendered discourses, when both race and gender are made visible.

"This nation," we now understand, "is" neither white women, nor non-white.

The White Aryan Resistance that produced this illustration is situated on a continuum of the far right that runs from older organizations such as the John Birch Society, Ku Klux Klan and the American Nazi Party, to Holocaust deniers, neo-Nazi or racist skinheads, White Power groups like Posse Comitatus and White Aryan Resistance, and radical militias, like the Wisconsin Militia or the Militia of Montana. The Southern Poverty Law Center cites 676 active hate groups in the US, including 109 Klan centers, 209 neo-Nazi groups, 43 racist skinheads groups and 124 neo-Confederate groups, and more than 400 US-based websites (*Intelligence Report,* Spring 2002).

These groups are composed of young white men, the sons of independent farmers and small shopkeepers.[2] Buffeted by the global political and economic forces that have produced global hegemonic masculinities, they have responded to the erosion of public patriarchy (displacement in the political arena) and domestic patriarchy (their wives now work away from the farm) with a renewal of their sense of masculine entitlement to restore patriarchy in both arenas. That patriarchal power has been both surrendered by white men—their fathers—and stolen from them by a federal government controlled and staffed by legions of the newly enfranchised minorities, women and immigrants, all in service to the omnipotent Jews who control international economic and political life. Downwardly mobile rural white men—those who lost the family farms and those who expected to take them over—are squeezed between the omnivorous jaws of capital concentration and a federal bureaucracy which is at best indifferent to their plight, and at worse, facilitates their further demise. What they want, says one, is to "take back what is rightfully ours" (cited in Dobratz and Shanks-Meile, 2001:10).

In many respects, the militias' ideology reflects the ideologies of other fringe groups on the far right, from whom they typically recruit, especially racism, homophobia, nativism, sexism and anti-Semitism. These discourses of hate provide an explanation for the feelings of entitlement thwarted, fixing the blame squarely on "others" who the state must now serve at the expense of white men. The unifying theme of these discourses, which have traditionally formed the rhetorical package Richard Hoftsadter labeled "paranoid politics," is gender. Specifically, it is by framing state policies as emasculating and problematizing the masculinity of these various "others" that rural white militia members seek to restore their own masculinity. One issue of *The Truth at Last* put it this way:

> Immigrants are flooding into our nation willing to work for the minimum wage (or less). Super-rich corporate executives are flying all over the world in search of cheaper and cheaper labor so that they can "lay off" their American employees. . . . Many young White families have no future! They are not going to receive any appreciable wage increases due to job competition from immigrants. (cited in Dobratz and Shanks-Meile, 2001: 115)

White supremacists see themselves as squeezed between global capital and an emasculated state that supports voracious global profiteering. NAFTA took away American jobs; the "Burger King economy" leaves no room at the top, so "many youngsters see themselves as being forced to compete with nonwhites for the available minimum wage, service economy jobs that have replaced their parents' unionized industry opportunities" (Coplon, 1989: 84).

In their foreboding futuristic vision, communalism, feminism, multi-culturalism, homosexuality and Christian-bashing are all tied together, part and parcel of the New World Order. Multicultural textbooks, women in government and legalized abortion can individually be taken as signs of the impending New World Order. Increased opportunities for women can only lead to the oppression of men. The feminist now represents the confusion of gender boundaries and the demasculinization of men, symbolizing a future where men are not allowed to be real men.

White men not involved in the movement are often referred to as "sheeple" while feminist women, it turns out, are more masculine than men are. Not only does this call the masculinity of white men into question, but it uses gender as the rhetorical vehicle for criticizing "other" men. Thus in the logic of militias and other white supremacist organizations, gay men are both promiscuously carnal and sexually voracious and effete fops who do to men what men should only have done to them by women. Black men are both violent hyper-sexual beasts, possessed of an "irresponsible sexuality," seeking white women to rape (*WAR*8(2), 1989: 11) and less than fully manly, "weak, stupid, lazy" (*NS Mobilizer,* cited in Ferber, 1998: 81). Blacks are primal nature—untamed, cannibalistic, uncontrolled, but also stupid and lazy—and whites are the driving force of civilization. "American and all civilized society are the exclusive products of White man's mind and muscle," is how *The Thunderbolt* put it (cited in Ferber, 1998: 76), "the White race is the Master race of the earth. . . . the Master Builders, the Master Minds, and the Master warriors of civilization. What can a black man do but clumsily shuffe off, scratching his wooley [*sic*] head, to search for shoebrush and mop" (*New Order,* cited in Ferber, 1998: 91).

Most interesting is the portrait of the Jew. One the one hand, the Jew is a greedy, cunning, conniving, omnivorous predator; on the other, the Jew is small, beady-eyed and incapable of masculine virtue. By asserting the hyper-masculine power of the Jew, the far right can support capitalism as a system while decrying the actions of capitalists and their corporations. According to militia logic, it is not the capitalist corporations that have turned the government against them, but the international cartel of Jewish bankers and financiers, media moguls and intellectuals who have already taken over the US state and turned it into ZOG (Zionist Occupied Government). Jews are seen as the masterminds behind the other social groups who are seen as dispossessing rural American men of their birthright. And toward that end, they have coopted blacks, women and gays and brainwashed cowardly white men to do their bidding. In a remarkable passage, white supremacists cast the economic plight of white workers as being squeezed between non-white workers and Jewish owners:

> It is our RACE we must preserve, not just one class. . . . White Power means a permanent end to unemployment because with the non-Whites gone, the labor market will no longer be overcrowded with unproductive niggers, spics and other racial low-life. It means an end to inflation eating up a man's paycheck faster than he can raise it because OUR economy will not be run by a criminal pack of international Jewish bankers, bent on using the White worker's tax money in selfish and even destructive schemes. (*The Thunderbolt*, cited in Ferber, 1998: 140)

Since Jews are incapable of acting like real men—strong, hardy, virtuous manual workers and farmers—a central axiom of the international Jewish conspiracy for world domination is their plan to "feminize White men and to masculinize White women" (*Racial Loyalty,* No. 72, 1991: 3). If the state and capital emasculate them, and if the masculinity of the "others" is problematic, then only real white men can rescue this American Eden from a feminized, multicultural androgynous melting pot. The militias seek to reclaim their manhood gloriously, violently.

WHITE SUPREMACISTS IN SCANDINAVIA

While significantly fewer in number than their American counterparts, white supremacists in the Nordic countries have also made a significant impact on those normally tolerant social democracies. Norwegian groups such as Bootboys, NUNS 88, the Norsk Arisk Ungdomsfron (NAUF), Varg and the Vikings; the Green Jacket Movement (Gronjakkerne) in Denmark; and the Vitt Ariskt Motstand (VAM, or White Aryan Resistance), Kreatrivistens Kyrka (Church of the Creator, COTC) and Riksfronten (National Front) in Sweden have exerted an impact beyond their modest numbers, Norwegian groups number a few hundred, while Swedish groups may barely top 1000 adherents, and perhaps double that number in supporters and general sympathizers.

Their opposition seems to come precisely from the relative prosperity of their homelands, a prosperity that has made the Nordic countries attractive to ethnic immigrants from the economic South. Most come from lower middle-class families; their fathers are painters, carpenters, tilers, brick-layers, road maintenance workers. Some come from small family farms. Several fathers own one-person businesses, are small capitalists or self-employed tradesmen (Fangen, 1999b: 36). All the sons were downwardly mobile; they work sporadically, have little or no control over their own labor or workplace, and none owns his own business. Almost all members are between 16 and 20 (Fanger, 1996b: 84). Youth unemployment has peaked, especially in Sweden, just as the number of asylum seekers has peaked, and with it attacks on centers for asylum seekers. Like the American white supremacists, Scandinavian

Aryans understand their plight in terms of masculine entitlement which is eroded by state immigration policies, international Zionist power and globalization. All desire a return to a racially and ethnically homogeneous society, seeing themselves, as one put it, as a "front against alienation, and the mixing of cultures" (Fangen, 1998a: 214).

Anti-gay sentiments also unite these white supremacists. "Words are no use; only action will help in the fight against homosexuals," says a Swedish magazine, *Siege*. "With violence and terror as our weapons we must beat back the wave of homosexual terror and stinking perversion whose stench is washing over our country" (cited in Bjorgo, 1997: 127). And almost all have embraced anti-Semitism, casting the Jews as the culprits for immigration and homosexuality. According to the group Vitt Ariskt Motstand, the Jew represents a corrupt society that "poisons the white race through the immigration of racially inferior elements, homosexuality, and moral disorder" (cited in Loow, 1998b: 86). As *Storm*, the magazine of the Swedish White Aryan Resistance, put it:

> In our resistance struggle for . . . the survival of the white race . . . we must wield the battle axe against our common enemy—the Zionist Occupation Government (ZOG) and the liberal race traitors, the keen servants of the hook noses who are demolishing our country piece by piece. (cited in Bjorgo, 1997: 219)[3]

The anti-Semitism, however, has also inhibited alliances across the various national groups in Scandinavia. Danish and Norwegian Aryans recall the resistance against the Nazis, and often cast themselves as heirs to the resistance struggle against foreign invasion. Some Swedish groups, on the other hand, openly embrace Nazism and Nazi symbols. In order to maintain harmony among these different national factions of the Nordic Aryan movement, the Danish groups have begun to use Confederate flags and other symbols of the racist US south, which all sides can agree signifies the Ku Klux Klan and the "struggle against Negroes, communists, homosexuals and Jews" (cited in Bjorgo, 1997: 99).

Like their American counterparts, Scandinavian white supremacists also exhibit the other side of what Connell calls "protest masculinity"—a combination of stereotypical male norms with often untraditional attitudes respecting women. All these Nordic groups experience significant support from young women, since the males campaign against prostitution, abortion and pornography—all of which are seen as degrading women (see Durham, 1997). On the other hand, many of these women soon become disaffected when they feel mistreated by their brethren, "unjustly subordinated," or just seen as "mattresses" (in Fangen, 1998a). Often sexualized images of women are used to recruit men. In one comic strip for Vigrid's newspaper, a topless woman with exaggerated breasts is hawking the newspaper on the streets. "Norway for Norwegians!" she shouts. She's arrested by the police for "selling material based on race discrimination"; meanwhile caricatures of blacks and Pakistanis burn the city and loot a liquor store.

One significant difference between the American and the Scandinavian Aryan movements concerns their view of the environment. While American Aryans support right-wing and conservative Republican efforts to discard environmental protection in the name of job creation in extractive industries, and are more than likely meat-eating survivalists, Nordic white supremacists are strong supporters of environmentalism. Many are vegetarians, some vegan. Each group might maintain that their policies flow directly from their political stance. The Nordic groups claim that the modern state is "impure," "perverted" and full of "decay and decadence" and that their environmentalism is a means to cleanse it.

The Restoration of Islamic Masculinity Among the Terrorists of September 11

Although it is still too soon, and too little is known to develop as full a portrait of the terrorists of Al Qaeda and the Taliban regime in Afghanistan, certain common features warrant brief comment. For one thing, the class origins of the Al Qaeda terrorists appear to be similar to these other groups. Virtually all the young men were under 25, well educated, lower middle class, downwardly mobile (see also Kristof, 2002a). Other terrorist groups in the Middle East appear to have appealed to similar young men. . . .

Several of the leaders of Al Qaeda are wealthy. Ayman al-Zawahiri, the 50-year-old doctor who was the closest advisor to Osama bin Laden, is from a fashionable suburb of Cairo; his father was dean of the pharmacy school of the university there. Bin Laden was a multi-millionaire. By contrast, many of the hijackers were engineering students, for whom job opportunities had been dwindling dramatically. . . . Most of these Islamic radical organizations developed similar political analyses. All were opposed to globalization and the spread of western values; all opposed what they perceived as corrupt regimes in several Arab states (notably Saudi Arabia and Egypt), which were mere puppets of US domination. Central of their political ideology is the recovery of manhood from the devastatingly emasculating politics of globalization. Over and over, Nasra Hassan writes, she heard the refrain "The Israelis humiliate us. They occupy our land, and deny our history" (Hassan, 2001: 38). The Taliban saw the Soviet invasion and westernization as humiliations. Osama bin Laden's 7 October videotape describes the "humiliation and disgrace" that Islam has suffered for "more than 80 years."

This fusion of anti-globalization politics, convoluted Islamic theology and virulent misogyny has been the subject of much speculation. Viewing these through a gender lens, though, enables us to understand the connections better. The collapse of public patriarchal entitlement led to a virulent and violent reassertion of domestic patriarchal power. "This is the class that is most hostile to women," said the scholar Fouad Ajami (cited in Crossette, 2001: 1). But why? Journalist Barbara Ehrenreich (2001) explains that while "males have lost their traditional status as farmers and bread-winners, women have been entering the market economy and gaining the marginal independence conferred even by a paltry wage." As a result, "the man who can no longer make a living, who has to depend on his wife's earnings, can watch Hollywood sexpots on pirated videos and begin to think the world has been turned upside down."

Taliban policies were designed to both remasculinize men and to refeminize women. Thus, not only were policies of the Afghani republic that made female education compulsory immediately abandoned, but women were prohibited from appearing in public unescorted by men, from revealing any part of their body, or from going to school or holding a job. Men were required to grow their beards, in accordance with religious images of Mohammed. Beards especially symbolically reaffirm biological natural differences between women and men, even as they are collapsing in the public sphere. Such policies removed women as competitors and also shored up masculinity, since they enabled men to triumph over the humiliations of globalization, and as well to triumph over their own savage, predatory and violently sexual urges that would be unleashed in the presence of uncovered women.

Perhaps this can be best seen paradigmatically in the story of Mohammed Atta, apparently the mastermind of the entire operation and the pilot of the first plane to crash into the World Trade Center Tower. The youngest child of an ambitious lawyer father and pampering mother, Atta grew up a shy and polite boy. "He was so gentle," his father said. "I used to tell him 'Toughen up, boy!'" (cited in *The New York Times Magazine,* 7 October). Atta spent his youth in a relatively shoddy Cairo neighborhood. Both his sisters are professionals—one is a professor, the other a doctor. Atta decided to become an engineer, but his "degree meant little in a country where thousands of college graduates were unable to find good jobs."[4] His father had told him he "needed to hear the word 'doctor' in front of his name. We told him your sisters are doctors and their husbands are doctors and you are the man of the family." After he failed to find employment in Egypt, he went to Hamburg, Germany, to study to become an architect. . . .

But his ambitions were constantly thwarted. His only hope for a good job in Egypt was to be hired by an international firm. He applied and was constantly rejected. He found work as a draftsman—highly humiliating for someone with engineering and architectural credentials and an imperious and demanding father—for a German firm involved with razing lower-income Cairo neighborhoods to provide more scenic vistas for luxury tourist hotels. Defeated, humiliated, emasculated, a disappointment to his father and a failed rival to his sisters, Atta retreated into increasingly militant Islamic theology. By the time he assumed the controls of American Airlines flight 11, he evinced a gendered hysteria about women. In the message he left in his abandoned rental car, he made clear what really mattered to him in the end. "I don't want pregnant women or a person who is not clean to come and say good-bye to me," he wrote. "I don't want women to go to my funeral or later to my grave" (on CNN, 2 October 2001).

MASCULINE ENTITLEMENT AND THE FUTURE OF TERRORISM

Of course such fantasies are the fevered imagination of hysteria; Atta's body was without doubt instantly incinerated, and no funeral would be likely. But the terrors of emasculation experienced by the lower middle classes all over the world will no doubt continue to resound for these young men whose world seems to have been turned upside down, their entitlements snatched from them, their rightful position in their world suddenly up for grabs. And they may continue to articulate with a seething resentment against women, "outsiders," or any other "others" perceived as stealing their rightful place at the table.

The common origins and common complaints of the terrorists of September 11 and their American counterparts were not lost on American white supremacists (see also Kristof, 2002b). In their response to the events of September 11, American Aryans said they admired the terrorists' courage, and took the opportunity to chastise their own compatriots. Bill Roper of the National Alliance publicly wished his members had as much "testicular fortitude" (*Intelligence Report*, Winter 2001). "It's a disgrace that in a population of at least 150 million White/Aryan Americans, we provide so few that are willing to do the same," bemoaned Rocky Suhayda, Nazi Party chairman from Eastpointe, Michigan. "A bunch of towel head/sand niggers put our great White Movement to shame" (cited in Ridgeway, 2001: 41). It is from that gendered shame that mass murderers are made.

NOTES

This article is part of an ongoing research project, "The Stony Brook Study of Gender and Globalization." Earlier essays based on this research were published in *A Man's World* (eds. K. Pringle and B. Pease, Zed Press, 2002), and serve as the basis for a chapter in the Handbook on the Study of Men and Masculinities (eds. M. Kimmel

R. W. Connell and J. Hearn, Sage, forthcoming). Every effort has been made to trace all third party copyright holders but if any have not been contactable prior to publication or have been inadvertently overlooked, the publishers will be pleased to make the necessary arrangement at the first opportunity.

1. This section is based on collaborative work with Abby Ferber, and appears in Kimmel and Ferber (2000).

2. Of course, women play an important role in many of these groups, ranging from a Ladies' Auxiliary to active participants as violent skinheads. See Blee (2001) and see also my review of Blee's book in Contexts 1(2), 2002.

3. Interestingly, Loow (1994: 21) found that the localities with the highest numbers of attacks on asylum seekers in the early 1990s had the highest concentrations of national socialist or racist organizations in the 1920–40s.

4. All unattributed quotes come from a fascinating portrait of Atta (Yardley, 2001).

REFERENCES

Abrahamian, E. (1982) *Iran Between the Revolutions.* Princeton, NJ: Princeton University Press.

Bakhash, S. (1984) *The Reign of the Ayatollahs: Iran and the Islamic Revolution.* New York: Basic Books.

Barber, B. (1995) *McDonalds and Jihad.* New York: Simon and Schuster.

Bjorgo, Tore (1997) *Racist and Right-Wing Violence in Scandinavia: Patterns, Perpetrators, and Responses.* Leiden: University of Leiden.

Bjorgo, Tore (1998) "Entry, Bridge-Burning, and Exit Options: What Happens to Young People Who Join Racist Groups—and Want to Leave?," in J. Kaplan and T. Bjorgo (eds) Nation and Race. Boston, MA: Northeastern University Press.

Blee, Katherine (2001) *Inside Organized Racism: Women in the Hate Movement.* Berkeley: University of California Press.

Connell, R. W. (1987) *Gender and Power.* Stanford, CA: Stanford University Press.

Connell, R. W. (1995) *Masculinities.* Berkeley: University of California Press.

Connell, R. W. (1998) "Masculinities and Globalization," *Men and Masculinities* 1(1).

Coplon, J. (1989) "The Roots of Skinhead Violence: Dim Economic Prospects for Young Men," *Utne Reader* May/June.

Crossette, B. (2001) "Living in a World Without Women," *New York Times* 4 October.

Dobratz, B. and Shanks-Meile, S. (2001) *The White Separatist Movement in the United States: White Power! White Pride!* Baltimore, MD: Johns Hopkins University Press.

Durham, Martin (1997) "Women and the Extreme Right: A Comment," *Terrorism and Political Violence* 9: 165–8.

Ehrenreich, B. (2001) "Veiled Threat," *Los Angeles Times* 4 November.

Fangen, Katrine (1998a) "Living Out our Ethnic Instincts: Ideological Beliefs among Rightist Activists in Norway," in Jeffrey Kaplan and Tore Bjorgo (eds) *Nation and Race: The Developing Euro-American Racist Subculture*, pp. 202–30. Boston, MA: Northeastern University Press.

Fangen, Katrine (1998b) "Right-Wing Skinheads: Nostalgia and Binary Opposition," *Young* 6(2): 33–49.

Fangen, Katrine (1999a) "Pride and Power. A Sociological Interpretation of the Norwegian Radical Nationalist Underground Movement," PhD dissertation, Department of Sociology and Human Geography, University of Oslo.

Fangen, Katrine (1999b) "Death Mask of Masculinity," in Soren Ervo (ed.) *Images of Masculinities: Moulding Masculinities.* London: Ashgate.

Fangen, Katrine (1999c) "On the Margins of Life: Life Stories of Radical Nationalists," *Acta Sociologica* 42: 359–63.

Ferber, A. L. (1998) *White Man Falling: Race, Gender and White Supremacy.* Lanham, MD: Rowman and Littlefield.

Frank, Andre Gunder (1968) *The Development of Underdevelopment.* New York: Monthly Review Press.

Griffith, V., P. Spiegel and H. Williamson (2001) "The Hijackers' Tale: How the Men of September 11 Went Unnoticed," *The Financial Times* 30 November.

Hassan, Nasra (2001) "An Arsenal of Believers," *The New Yorker* 19 November.

Jurgensmeyer, Mark (1993) *The New Cold War? Religious Nationalism Confronts the Secular State.* Berkeley: University of California Press.

Jurgensmeyer, Mark (2000) *Terror in the Mind of God: The Global Rise of Religious Violence.* Berkeley: University of California Press.

Kaplan, Jeffrey (1995) "Right Wing Violence in North America," in Tore Bjorgo (ed.) *Terror from the Extreme Right.* London: Frank Cass.

Kimmel, M. (1989) "New Prophets' and 'Old Ideals': Charisma and Tradition in the Iranian Revolution," *Social Compass* 36(4).

Kimmel, M. (1996a) *Manhood in America: A Cultural History.* New York: The Free Press.

Kimmel, M., Ed. (1996b) *The Politics of Manhood.* Philadelphia, PA: Temple University Press.

Kimmel, M. and Ferber, A. (2000) "'White Men Are This Nation': Right Wing Militias and the Restoration of Rural American Masculinity," *Rural Sociology.*

Kristof, N. (2002a) "What Does and Doesn't Fuel Terrorism," *The International Herald Tribune* 8 May: 13.

Kristof, N. (2002b) "All-American Osamas," *New York Times* 7 June: A-27.

Lewis, B. (2001) "The Revolt of Islam," *The New Yorker* 19 November.

Loow, Helene (1994) "'Wir sind wieder da'—From National Socialism to Militant Race Ideology: The Swedish Racist Underground in a Historical Context," paper presented at the XIII World Congress of Sociology, Bielefeld, July.

Loow, Helene (1998a) "Racist Youth Culture in Sweden: Ideology, Mythology, and Lifestyle," in C. Westin (ed.) *Racism Ideology and Political Organisation*, pp. 77–98. Stockholm: CEIFO Publications, University of Stockholm.

Loow, Helene (1998b) "White Power Rock and Roll: A Growing Industry," in J. Kaplan and T. Bjorgo (eds) *Nation and Race*. Boston, MA: Northeastern University Press.

Marrs, T. (1993) *Big Sister is Watching You: Hillary Clinton and the White House Feminists Who Now Control America—And Tell the President What To Do*. Austin, TX: Living Truth Publishers.

Marsden, P. (2002) *The Taliban: War and Religion in Afghanistan*. London: Zed Books.

Messner, M. (1998) *Politics of Masculinities: Men and Movements*. Newbury Park, CA: Pine Forge Press.

Moore, Barrington (1966) *The Social Origins of Democracy and Dictatorship: Lord and Peasant in the Making of the Modern World*. Boston, MA: Beacon Press.

Pedersen, W. (1996) "Working Class Boys at the Margins: Ethnic Prejudice, Cultural Capital and Gender," *Acta Sociologica* 39: 257–79.

Pierce, W. (1978) *The Turner Diaries*. Hillsboro, VA: National Vanguard Books.

Ridgeway, J. (2001) "Osama's New Recruits," *The Village Voice* 6 November.

Rubin, L. (1994) *Families on the Fault Line*. New York: HarperCollins.

Sinha, M. (1995) *Colonial Masculinity: The Manly Englishman and the Effeminate Bengali in the Late Nineteenth Century*. Manchester: Manchester University Press.

Stern, K. S. (1996) *A Force Upon The Plain: The American Militia Movement and the Politics of Hate*. New York: Simon and Schuster.

Tiger, L. (2001) "Osama bin Laden's Man Trouble," *Slate* 28 September.

Westin, Charles, ed. (1998) *Racism, Ideology and Political Organisation*. Stockholm: CEIFO Publications, University of Stockholm.

Willner, A. (1984) *The Spellbinders: Charismatic Political Leadership*. New Haven, CT: Yale University Press.

Witte, R. (1995) "Racist Violence in Western Europe," *Journal of Ethnic and Migration Studies* 21(4).

Yardley, J. (2001) "A Portrait of the Terrorist: From Shy Child to Single-Minded Killer," *New York Times* 10 October.

SOURCE: From *International Sociology*, September 2003, vol. 18(3): 603-620. Reprinted by permission of Sage Publications, Ltd. and the author.

Discussion Questions

1. Although through a narrow lens of "race" one may not regard white supremacist terrorists and Arab Islamic terrorists in the same category, Kimmel argues that from a class and gender lens, globalization has impacted these two groups similarly. Discuss the economic effects of globalization to which both groups are reacting.

2. How do women, "homosexuals," "Jews," and various "others" become blamed for the economic and cultural consequences of globalization in the eyes of these men? Thinking back to the Rosenblum and Travis essay in Chapter 1, what kind of us-them dichotomy is being set up here for these men's groups?

3. As immigration regulations take center stage in the U.S. political sphere, what kind of gendered dynamics enter into the debate? Do you notice those who advocate for harsher restrictions on immigration positing U.S. workers as men whose manhood is taken away when jobs are scarce? How else is the kind of discourse Kimmel identifies used even outside of extremist circles, into the mainstream?

4. Do some empirical research to find out how globalization has differentially impacted men and women, people of color and whites, industrialized and nonindustrialized nations. Although lower-middle-class and working-class men seem most vocal in their discontent, who actually has been hit hardest by recent global changes?

CURRENT DEBATES

IS IMMIGRATION HARMFUL OR HELPFUL TO THE UNITED STATES?

The continuing debate over U.S. immigration has generated plenty of arguments but little consensus. Following are three positions in the debate. The first, a passionate argument against immigration, was presented by Peter Brimelow, a journalist and an immigrant himself, in his best seller *Alien Nation* (1995). The rejoinder is excerpted from sociologist Reynolds Farley's book *The New American Reality* (1996), an analysis of many issues and social problems besides immigration. Farley's analysis is generally pro-immigration and is stated in more objective and scholarly terms—which does not, of course, mean that it is any more correct than Brimelow's argument. Third, George Borjas (1999) looks at the way in which immigration issues are typically raised in the United States and argues for a new approach.

IMMIGRATION IS HARMFUL

Peter Brimelow

Today, immigration . . . is not determined by economics; it is determined—or at least profoundly distorted—by public policy. . . . [The] effect of the 1965 reform [in immigration policy] has been to uncouple legal immigration from the needs of the U.S. economy. A low point was reached in 1986, when less than 8 percent of over 600,000 legal immigrants were admitted on the basis of skills. [Most of the remainder were admitted under family reunification provisions.] Of course, some of the family-reunification immigrants will have skills. But it is purely an accident whether their skills are wanted in the U.S. economy. The family-reunification policy inevitably contributes to two striking characteristics of the post-1965 flow:

• Firstly: The post-1965 immigrants are, on average, less skilled than earlier immigrants. And getting even less so. As George Borjas [a leading immigration researcher] put it: "The skill level of successive immigrant waves

admitted to the U.S. has declined precipitously in the last two or three decades."

• Secondly: The post-1965 immigrants unmistakably display more mismatching between what they can do and what America needs. They seem not to be fitting as well into the economy as did earlier immigrants. Instead, they are showing a greater tendency to become what used to be called a "public charge."

[In] 1970 the average recent immigrant had 0.35 less years of schooling than native-born Americans. By 1990, the average recent immigrant had 1.32 years less schooling. . . . [Economists] view education as a proxy for skills. And the relative decline in immigrant education seems to be confirmed by the relative decline in their earnings that has occurred in the same period.

In 1970, immigrants on average actually earned some 3 percent more than native-born

Americans. . . . But in 1990, the immigrant achievement had disappeared: Immigrants on average earned 16.2 percent less than native-born Americans.

The second striking characteristic of the post-1965 immigrant flow: increased mismatching with the U.S. labor market. This shows up in the immigrants' increasing tendency to go on welfare.

In the early 1980s, immigration researchers were generally pretty complacent about immigration's impact on the United States. It became an article of faith . . . that immigrants earned more, and went on welfare less, than native-born Americans.

The reason for this complacency, of course: The researchers were looking at old data. It still substantially reflected pre-1965 immigrants.

By the early 1990s, the scene had changed completely. It was becoming clear that, among the post-1965 immigrants, welfare participation rates were sharply higher. Immigrant welfare participation was, on average, higher than native-born Americans (9.1 vs. 7.4 percent). And

what's more, immigrant households on welfare tended to consume more, and increasingly more, than native-born households on welfare. (In 1970, 6.7 percent of all welfare cash benefits went to immigrants; in 1990, 13.1 percent.)

(And note that "welfare" means just cash programs like Aid to Families with Dependent Children, Supplementary Security Income, and general assistance—not non-cash programs like Food Stamps and Medicaid, for which there are no good numbers.) . . .

Examining the group of immigrants arriving in the five years before 1970 reveals even more depressing news: Welfare participation actually increased the longer they stayed in the United States. Originally, their rate was 5.5 percent; the 1990 census reported it at 9.8 percent. All waves of immigrants show a similar drift. The conclusion is unavoidable: Immigrants are assimilating into the welfare system.

SOURCE: From *Alien Nation* by Peter Brimelow. Copyright © 1995 by Peter Brimelow; Maps & Illustrations copyright © 1995 by John Grimwade. Used by permission of Random House, Inc. and The Wylie Agency.

IMMIGRATION IS NOT HARMFUL

Reynolds Farley

During the 1980s, the native-born labor force with a high school education or less fell from 55 million to 48 million, reflecting the shift toward greater educational attainment and the retirement of older workers who had less schooling. But 3 million immigrants who arrived in the 1980s had high school educations or less. Isn't it obvious that this high volume of immigration depresses employment opportunities and lowers wages for native-born Americans who lack college training? Wouldn't wages rise if we immediately terminated the flow of immigrants? Can't we blame the high level of immigration for the declining wages [of American workers]?

Because of the importance of immigration, this issue receives a great deal of attention. While there are still disagreements about the details, there is consensus that the effects of immigration on the employment prospects and wages of natives are modest. Summarizing several dozen studies based on the 1970 and 1980 census, Fix and Pascal (1994, p. 49) conclude that if immigrants as a share of the labor force in a metropolis went up from 10 percent . . . to 20 percent, the labor force participation rate of natives would drop only 1 percent, net of all other factors. . . .

This seems counterintuitive. How can the presence of many immigrants not depress employment opportunities and lower wages for natives? The economists who model these processes report that four factors explain this puzzle. First, immigration is concentrated in metropolises that are growing rapidly, most of them in the South and Southwest. Booming populations and economic growth in these places create thousands of jobs each year, and a fraction are filled by immigrants. Migrants, to a large degree, are fitting into occupational slots created by economic and demographic growth. Second, the presence of immigrants . . . may permit industries [that would otherwise move offshore] to thrive. . . . In recent years, the garment industry has prospered in New York, Los Angeles, and Miami largely because immigrants from China and the Caribbean are willing to work long hours for small paychecks, producing the costly dresses and suits that highly educated women need as they pursue careers. . . . And it is clear that quite a few new arrivals set up their own businesses, thereby hiring workers. . . .

Third, many immigrants fill jobs that native-born Americans are reluctant to accept—for example, the stoop labor traditionally needed in agriculture [or the jobs as nannies created] as women increasingly devote themselves to full-time jobs. . . .

There may be a fourth reason: employers may prefer illegals to citizens. Recent immigrants may, perhaps, be easily exploited and are unlikely to file suits about violations of minimum wage laws [or health] violations.

[Opposition to immigration will continue despite the evidence that immigration does little harm to the employment and wage prospects of natives.] Opposition . . . will come from those states and cities whose budgets are greatly impacted by the high volume of recent immigration. Several studies have investigated the financial consequences of undocumented immigration, especially in the seven states most affected. There were approximately three million illegals in those states in 1992 who paid an estimated $1.9 billion annually in state sales taxes, state and local property taxes, and state income taxes (Clark, Passel, Zimmerman, & Fix, 1994). The investigators considered the three most expensive state programs used by illegal aliens: the costs of emergency medical care, public schools, and prisons. These charges came to about $4 billion, implying that illegals imposed a burden of $2 billion upon taxpayers in these seven states. Although $2 billion is a very large sum and gives a clear indication of the substantial cost illegals place on local governments, the total expenditure of the governments in these seven states in 1992 was approximately $245 billion, so the termination of all undocumented immigrants would produce only a very modest reduction in state spending.

WE NEED TO REFRAME THE IMMIGRATION DEBATE

George Borjas

As the 21st century begins, the United States is about to embark once again upon a historic debate about the type of immigration policy that the country should pursue. As in the past, the cost-benefit calculus frames the terms of the debate: Who loses from immigration, and by how much? Who wins from immigration, and by how much? . . .

[These costs and benefits] are also symptoms of pursuing particular immigration policies.

By arguing over . . . these symptoms—whether immigrants use a lot of welfare, whether consumer prices are lowered by immigration—the immigration debate is, in a sense, worrying about the height of trees in the forest, rather than the shape of the forest.

Typically, those who argue over . . . a particular social policy take sides by grasping onto a specific fact, and from that fact they immediately infer some policy reform that the country should pursue. In my view, this [approach] is just plain wrong.

To see why, single out a particular symptom of immigration over which there is little disagreement: Immigrant use of welfare is high. The policy implications of this fact depend crucially on what the U.S. is trying to accomplish. If the goal of immigration policy is to ensure that immigration did not place a fiscal burden on the native population, this symptom [implies] that the U.S. should take steps to restrict the entry of potential welfare recipients. If, in contrast, the goal of immigration policy is to help the poorest people in the world, this symptom has no relevance—it is the price that the country must pay to achieve a particular humanitarian objective.

In the end, a debate over the policy implications of . . . immigration cannot be based on the evidence alone. Any policy discussion requires explicitly stated assumptions about what constitutes the national interest. It is the combination of the evidence with an assumption about what Americans desire that permits an informed debate. . . . [First, the American people must] answer the bigger question: What should immigration policy accomplish?

Of course, answering this question is very difficult, even when the debate is restricted purely to . . . economic issues. To see why, divide the world into three distinct constituencies: the current population of the U.S., the immigrants themselves, and those who remain in the source countries. To draw policy implications . . . one has to know whose economic welfare the U.S. should try to improve. . . .

By framing the issue in this fashion, the tradeoffs . . . are made crystal clear. The native population probably benefits . . . when high-quality scientific workers [are admitted] but the people left behind in the source country probably lose a lot. Similarly, immigrants benefit when . . . policy favors the entry of their relatives, but natives may lose because the policy . . . might let in many persons who qualify for social services.

It is probably impossible to come up with an immigration policy where all relevant parties benefit. As a result, the U.S. will have to make difficult choices.

SOURCE: From *Heaven's Door: Immigration Policy and the American Economy* by George J. Borjas. Copyright © 1999 Princeton University Press. Reprinted by permission of Princeton University Press.

DEBATE QUESTIONS TO CONSIDER

1. Consider the nature of the arguments presented by Brimelow and Farley. To what extent do they appeal to emotion? To what extent do they base their arguments in evidence and logic? What specific disagreements over "facts" can you identify? What information would you need to resolve these disagreements?

2. What does Borjas add to the debate? Does his approach offer a way to resolve the disagreements between the other two authors? In Borjas's terms, what constituencies do Brimelow and Farley have in mind (native population, immigrants, or those left behind)? How might their arguments change if they considered a different constituency?

10

WHITE ETHNIC GROUPS

During the century between the 1820s and 1920s, nearly 40 million people immigrated to the United States from Europe. This mass migration, the largest in human history, began in the nations of Northern and Western Europe (including Ireland, Norway, and Germany) and spread, over the course of the 19th century, to the nations of Southern and Eastern Europe (including Italy, Poland, and Russia). The immigrants came from every nook and cranny of European society and included people from every conceivable background: aristocrats, paupers, criminals, peasants, artisans, skilled professionals, and everything in between. Some looked on the United States as the Promised Land and vowed never to leave. Some wanted only the chance to work and save money and return to their home villages as quickly as possible. Their impact on the young nation was vast: they swelled the population, farmed the Midwest, made uncountable contributions to American art, music, literature, and architecture, and supplied a massive labor force for the industrialization of the United States. When this immigration stream began, the United States was a small, agricultural nation on the periphery of world events. When this period of mass immigration ended in the 1920s, the United States was industrialized and one of the strongest, most robust nations in the world, a transformation that is linked to the contributions of these immigrants in an infinite variety of ways, both direct and subtle.

Although all immigrants had their own unique reasons for coming to the United States, most were motivated by the simple desire to find work that could sustain them and their families. They entered the economy in a variety of roles, but most took jobs in factories, mills, and mines and became the workforce for the Industrial Revolution that propelled the United States to world preeminence. These immigrant laborers carved out a place for themselves in the American economy—even though at the bottom rung of the job structure—from which their children and grandchildren were able to climb higher and, over the course of generations, eventually be assimilated into the great suburban middle class. Today, the descendants of the European immigrants are generally equal to national norms in terms of education, income, and other measures of equality.

As assimilation progressed over the generations, ethnic identity and the sense of a connection with "old country" traditions weakened and faded. For present-day descendants of the immigrants, ethnicity is largely symbolic and optional. That is, their ethnicity is a minor part of their self-image (if that) and has little effect on their values, voting habits, diet, friendships, place of residence, or job prospects. They may acknowledge their ethnicity on occasion (for example, St. Patrick's Day for the Irish), but, otherwise, they are free to ignore it or celebrate it, as they choose. Increasingly, it seems that the sense of ethnicity for these groups has been merged into a broad, generalized identity based on whiteness—not specific to any particular white ethnic group—that follows the racial contours that run through so much of our society.

The Narrative Portrait that begins this chapter is part of a sociological memoir of growing up in the 1930s, at a time when ethnic identity was still strong. David Gray discusses how he gradually became aware of the dividing lines that ran through the community of his boyhood and how he came to understand the difference between "us" and "the others." He also discusses how the Irish in his hometown used the local machinery of government to protect their own during the Great Depression. The Irish, and virtually every other white ethnic group, found ways to use the city government, labor unions, private businesses, the church, and other institutions—including organized crime and sports—to abet their rise to acceptance and equality.

The Readings in this chapter view the process of assimilation from a variety of perspectives. Karen Brodkin looks at some of the factors that helped Jewish Americans (but not African Americans and other minority groups of color) achieve acceptance in the larger society. Peggy McIntosh examines the dynamics of white privilege, the advantaged position now shared by the descendants of the European immigrants, and Michèle Lamont explores the dividing lines between white and black members of the working class. The Current Debate extends the examination of white racial identity and discusses the meaning of whiteness in contemporary society.

Please visit the accompanying website to Race, Ethnicity, and Gender, second edition for the *Public Sociology Assignments* at http://www.pineforge.com/das2.

QUESTIONS TO CONSIDER IN THIS CHAPTER

1. Are prejudice and discrimination still problems for white ethnic groups? Compare these groups with the minority groups covered in previous chapters. How do the dynamics and content of prejudice and discrimination differ from group to group? Why do these differences exist?

2. How did the descendant of this wave of immigrants from Europe make their way into mainstream American society? Was their successful assimilation a result of their actions or more a result of the behavior of the dominant group? How do white ethnic groups help to sustain the sense of "us" and "them" along the white-nonwhite racial divide?

3. Why is it important to study "whiteness"? What do we gain from analyzing the dominant group and its sense of identity? How does this contribute to our understandings of the situations of minority groups?

4. What class and gender dimensions can you identify for the issues raised in this chapter? For white ethnic groups, do class and gender operate in ways similar to those for other minority groups we have considered? What differences can you identify? Why do these differences exist?

NARRATIVE PORTRAIT

ETHNICITY, PREJUDICE, AND THE IRISH POLITICAL MACHINE

David Gray grew up a Welsh Protestant in the city of Scranton, Pennsylvania, during the 1930s and 1940s. At that time, this coal-mining town was split along ethnic lines, and Gray (1991) recounts his gradual socialization into the realities of in-groups and out-groups in this memoir. He also describes how Scranton's Irish Catholic community responded to the Great Depression and how they used the local political machine to protect their own. Gray reflects on the consequences of these experiences for his own personal prejudices and sense of social distance.

Gray eventually left Scranton and earned a Ph.D. in sociology. He became a college professor and an accomplished and respected sociologist. Among his many admiring students was one of the editors of this book, who grew up in Scranton's Irish Catholic community a generation after Gray.

SHADOW OF THE PAST

David Gray

C. Wright Mills (an American sociologist) [stressed] the intimate relationship of "history, social structure, and biography." . . . Though he did not say so directly, the logic of Mills' position would surely indicate that, for self-knowledge, no biography is more important than one's own. Born within a social context not of our own making, subject to social forces we did not create, in retrospect, we attempt to understand. . . .

Personally, then, I did not ask to be born Welsh Protestant in Scranton, Pennsylvania. No more than Eddie Gilroy, with whom I attended . . . school, asked to be born Irish Catholic. But there we both were in the heart of the anthracite coal region . . . during the years of the Great Depression. . . . We were friends, good friends. During recess and after 3:00 p.m., he played second base and I played shortstop in the shrunken, dirt diamond in the schoolyard. . . . We thought we made a good double-play combination and, beyond the baseball field, we respected and liked each other as well.

But, there was something wrong with Eddie Gilroy. At age ten I didn't know exactly what it was. He didn't make many errors and we often shared whatever pennies we had . . . at the corner candy store. Still, there was something wrong with him—vague, general, apart from real experience, but true all the same.

His fundamental defect came into sharper focus at the age of twelve. Sunday movies had just arrived in Scranton and . . . I wanted to go with Eddie and Johnny Pesavento [but] I couldn't.

"Why?"

"Because Protestants don't go to the movies on Sunday—nor play cards, football, or baseball."

"How come Eddie and Johnny can go?"

"They're Catholic."

No one quite used the word "immoral" but . . . anyone who attended Sunday movies was certainly close to sinful. And the implication was clear: If Catholics did such bad things on Sunday, they surely did a lot of bad things on other days as well.

No matter, then, that Gilroy might sacrifice for even a Protestant runner to go to second, or let you borrow his glove, or share his candy. . . . His Catholicism permeated his being, . . . muting his individual qualities. Eddie wasn't the point, his Catholicism was.

[The] deeply held beliefs . . . of the adult world were visited upon the young. Most often subtly . . . but persistently and effectively, little Welsh Protestant boys and girls learned that Catholics were somehow the enemy. . . .

Unfortunately, from their vantage point, the Welsh of Scranton were not the only ones in town. While they had come to the coal regions in large numbers, others, in even larger numbers, had come also. Irish, Italian, Polish, German, many from eastern European countries, fewer who were Jewish—all constituted Scranton's ethnic portion of broader 19th century immigrant waves. With [some] obvious exceptions, most were Catholic.

In this communal setting—a very ethnically and religiously distinct one—the Great Depression arrived with particular force. [The region suffered from massive unemployment and began to lose population as people left in search of work elsewhere.] The coal industry, upon which the economy of Northeastern Pennsylvania essentially rested, was gone. The private sector, initially hard-hit, did not recover [until after the 1960s]. The public sector consequently became the primary possibility for often meager, by no means high-paying jobs.

And the Irish, their political talents augmented by the fact that they were the largest single ethnic group in town, controlled political power. Allied with others of Catholic faith, the Irish did their best to take care of their religiously affiliated, politically important, own.

In Scranton's political life, the intimate relationship of religion, politics, and economics was clear for all to see. The mayor was Jimmy Hanlon, . . . the political boss, Mickey Lawlor, . . . McNulty ran the post office, and Judge Hoban the courts. From the mayor's office to trash collectors, with policemen, firemen, school teachers, truant officers, and dog catchers in between, the public payroll included the names of O'Neill, Hennigan, Lydon, Kennedy, Walsh, Gerrity, and O'Hoolihan. As the depression persisted, Welsh Protestants came to know (with reason but also as an act of faith) that Lewis, Griffiths, and Williams need not apply.

Pale shades of contemporary Northern Ireland, but with political power reversed. No shots were fired, perhaps because American democratic traditions compel accommodation and compromise. Nonetheless, among the Welsh, the general feeling of resentment on more than one occasion was punctuated with: "Those goddam Irish Catholics."

Whatever may have been true in pre-depression years, however tolerant or intolerant individuals may have been, . . . that Welsh sentiment was not at all limited to individuals guilty of irrational prejudice. It was communally shared. Jobs, homes, and lives were at stake, and religious affiliation was relevant to them all. Irish Catholic political power was a fact from which Welsh Protestant resentment followed. Prejudice there certainly was—deeply felt, poignantly articulated, subjectively often going beyond what facts would justify and, unfortunately, communicated to the young. . . .

The public sector was vulnerable to Irish Catholic control. The Welsh knew that. The private sector (banks, small businesses) simultaneously retained a diminished but tightened, now more consciously Protestant, ownership and/or control. Though the musically inclined Welsh never composed it, their regional battle hymn surely was: If Irish politicians were using their political power to control what they could, it was essential for Protestants to protect what they privately had.

SOURCE: From *American Journal of Economics and Sociology*, 50, 33-39. Copyright © 1991. Reprinted by permission of Blackwell Publishing Ltd.

READINGS

An examination of the experiences of white Americans from their initial immigration to the United States to modern times provides a good illustration of the difference between ethnicity and race. While ethnicity refers to a shared national origin and/or cultural heritage, race is a social construction denoting boundaries between the powerful and less powerful and thus often defined by the dominant group. Thus, there are many different ethnicities that make up the racial group of "white Americans," "Hispanic Americans," "Asian Americans," and so forth. When we investigate the situation of white Americans, it is evident that various ethnicities have gradually been incorporated into the dominant racial category of white over time, provided they met certain cultural, physical, and socioeconomic criteria. Our first Reading, "How Jews Became White," presents a case study of how one white ethnic group, Jewish Americans, succeeded in this process. For nearly two centuries of United States history, author Karen Brodkin documents the court rulings and laws that restricted the status of "white," and the rights of full citizenship that went along with it, to only northwestern Europeans. This excluded Jews and many other ethnic groups. However, the achievement of a certain degree of socioeconomic success, thanks to the postwar economic boom of the late 1940s and early 1950s, allowed Jewish Americans like Brodkin (who was growing up right around this time) to be considered white Americans for the first time. What is useful about Brodkin's essay is her detailed analysis of the U.S. government's economic and social programs during this time period—policies she calls "affirmative action" for white males—which demonstrates how certain groups, particularly African Americans, were legally excluded from these unparalleled generous government subsidies of education and housing. In this way, she challenges the argument (typified by her parents' explanations) that Jews' cultural work ethic is responsible for their assimilation success story, pointing instead to these structural factors that allowed them to "become white" where other groups were not permitted to do so.

In an individualistic society such as the United States, we want to believe that factors such as hard work and motivation are responsible for certain groups' relative success. It is this "myth of meritocracy" that Peggy McIntosh seeks to challenge in our second Reading, "White Privilege and Male Privilege." Recall that in Part I of this book, we reviewed the concepts of privilege and stigma, and noted that members of minority groups are usually much more aware of their stigma than members of dominant groups are of their privilege. McIntosh illustrates this point writing from the perspective of a white woman who is quite aware of male privilege, being female and knowing all too well the limits she faces that her male counterparts do not have to face, yet utterly ignorant about her racial privilege as a white person until she challenged herself to study it. Upon doing so, she comes up with a now widely cited list of 46 white privileges covering many areas of life, from housing and employment to shopping and media representation. By definition, these privileges are unearned. People of color, compared to similarly situated whites in terms of class, gender, or age, cannot count on receiving such advantages even if they work just as hard as or even harder than their white counterparts.

Another crucial point McIntosh makes about privilege is that members of dominant groups are kept oblivious about its existence. No matter how obvious it is to members of minority groups, these advantages are something that whites have often never stopped to consider. Every time throughout history that the government has somehow limited nonwhites in the ways we have read about in this text, whites receive a corresponding privilege as a result. Even whites who are not discriminatory or prejudiced benefit from these privileges. This reading sheds additional light upon why the socially constructed boundaries of whiteness are so closely guarded—because those who permeate them become the beneficiaries of all these privileges that McIntosh describes.

It is difficult to accept the idea of white privilege, especially for members of the white working class, who are struggling to make ends meet themselves. In our third

Reading, Michèle Lamont explores the perceptions that white and black working-class Americans have of each other. She demonstrates that the racial boundaries are deeply conflated with moral boundaries and that the groups use relational "us" versus "them" logic to separate their identities. The white workers claim a moral high ground around their conception of the work ethic and "the disciplined self." In contrast, blacks generally argue for racial equality—not superiority—based on more universalistic notions.

It is important to keep in mind that an oppositional white identity is not the only way to be white. As we move into Part IV of this book, we will consider other antiracist ways of being white that affirm and celebrate the advent of a multiracial society.

How Jews Became White

Karen Brodkin

The American nation was founded and developed by the Nordic race, but if a few more million members of the Alpine, Mediterranean and Semitic races are poured among us, the result must inevitably be a hybrid race of people as worthless and futile as the good-for-nothing mongrels of Central America and Southeastern Europe.

—Kenneth Roberts, qtd. in Carlson & Colburn (1972:312)

It is clear that Kenneth Roberts did not think of my ancestors as white like him. The late nineteenth and early decades of the twentieth centuries saw a steady stream of warnings by scientists, policymakers, and the popular press that "mongrelization" of the Nordic or Anglo-Saxon race—the real Americans—by inferior European races (as well as inferior non-European ones) was destroying the fabric of the nation. I continue to be surprised to read that America did not always regard its immigrant European workers as white, that they thought people from different nations were biologically different. My parents, who are first-generation U.S.-born eastern European Jews, are not surprised. They expect anti-Semitism to be a part of the fabric of daily life, much as I expect racism to be part of it. They came of age in a Jewish world in the 1920s and 1930s at the peak of anti-Semitism in the United States

(Gerber 1986). They are proud of their upward mobility and think of themselves as pulling themselves up by their own bootstraps. I grew up during the 1950s in the Euroethnic New York suburb of Valley Stream where Jews were simply one kind of white folks and where ethnicity meant little more to my generation than food and family heritage. Part of my familized ethnic heritage was the belief that Jews were smart and that our success was the result of our own efforts and abilities, reinforced by a culture that valued sticking together, hard work, education, and deferred gratification. Today, this belief in a Jewish version of Horatio Alger has become an entry point for racism by some mainstream Jewish organizations against African Americans especially, and for their opposition to affirmative action for people of color (Gordon 1964; Sowell 1981; Steinberg 1989: chap. 3).

It is certainly true that the United States has a history of anti-Semitism and of beliefs that Jews were members of an inferior race. But Jews were hardly alone. American anti-Semitism was part of a broader pattern of late-nineteenth-century racism against all southern and eastern European immigrants, as well as against Asian immigrants. These views justified all sorts of discriminatory treatment including closing the doors to immigration from Europe and Asia in the 1920s.[1] This picture changed radically after World War II. Suddenly the same folks who promoted nativism and xenophobia were eager to believe that the Euro-origin people whom they had deported, reviled as members of inferior races, and prevented from immigrating only a few years earlier were now model middle-class white suburban citizens.

It was not an educational epiphany that made those in power change their hearts, their minds, and our race. Instead, it was the biggest and best affirmative action program in the history of our nation, and it was for Euromales. There are similarities and differences in the ways each of the European immigrant groups became "whitened." I want to tell the story in a way that links anti-Semitism to other varieties of anti-European racism, because this foregrounds what Jews shared with other Euroimmigrants and shows changing notions of whiteness to be part of America's larger system of institutional racism.

EURORACES

The U.S. "discovery" that Europe had inferior and superior races came in response to the great waves of immigration from southern and eastern Europe in the late nineteenth century. Before that time, European immigrants—including Jews—had been largely assimilated into the white population. The twenty-three million European immigrants who came to work in U.S. cities after 1880 were too many and too concentrated to disperse and blend. Instead, they piled up in the country's most dilapidated urban areas, where they built new kinds of working-class ethnic communities. Since immigrants and their children made up more than 70 percent of the population of most of the country's largest cities, urban America came to take on a distinctly immigrant flavor. The golden age of industrialization in the United States was also the golden age of class struggle between the captains of the new industrial empires and the masses of manual workers whose labor made them rich. As the majority of mining and manufacturing workers, immigrants were visibly major players in these struggles (Higham 1955:226; Steinberg 1989:36).[2]

The Red Scare of 1919 clearly linked anti-immigrant to anti-working-class sentiment—to the extent that the Seattle general strike of native-born workers was blamed on foreign agitators. The Red Scare was fueled by economic depression, a massive postwar strike wave, the Russian revolution, and a new wave of postwar immigration. . . .

Not surprisingly, the belief in European races took root most deeply among the wealthy U.S.-born Protestant elite, who feared a hostile and seemingly unassimilable working class. By the end of the nineteenth century, Senator Henry Cabot Lodge pressed Congress to cut off immigration to the United States; Teddy Roosevelt raised the alarm of "race suicide" and took Anglo-Saxon women to task for allowing "native" stock to be outbred by inferior immigrants. In the twentieth century, these fears gained a great deal of social legitimacy thanks to the efforts of an influential network of aristocrats and scientists who developed theories of eugenics—breeding for a "better" humanity—and scientific racism. Key to these efforts was Madison Grant's influential *Passing of the Great*

Race, in which he shared his discovery that there were three or four major European races ranging from the superior Nordics of northwestern Europe to the inferior southern and eastern races of Alpines, Mediterraneans, and, worst of all, Jews, who seemed to be everywhere in his native New York City. Grant's nightmare was race mixing among Europeans. For him, "the cross between any of the three European races and a Jew is a Jew" (qtd. in Higham 1955:156). He didn't have good things to say about Alpine or Mediterranean "races" either. For Grant, race and class were interwoven: the upper class was racially pure Nordic, and the lower classes came from the lower races.

Far from being on the fringe, Grant's views resonated with those of the nonimmigrant middle class. A *New York Times* reporter wrote of his visit to the Lower East Side:

> This neighborhood, peopled almost entirely by the people who claim to have been driven from Poland and Russia, is the eyesore of New York and perhaps the filthiest place on the western Continent. It is impossible for a Christian to live there because he will be driven out, either by blows or the dirt and stench. Cleanliness is an unknown quantity to these people. They cannot be lifted up to a higher plane because they do not want to be. If the cholera should ever get among these people, they would scatter its germs as a sower does grain. (qtd. in Schoener 1967:58)[3]

Such views were well within the mainstream of the early-twentieth-century scientific community. Grant and eugenicist Charles B. Davenport organized the Galton Society in 1918 in order to foster research and to otherwise promote eugenics and immigration restriction.[4] . . .

By the 1920s, scientific racism sanctified the notion that real Americans were white and real whites came from northwest Europe. Racism animated laws excluding and expelling Chinese in 1882, and then closing the door to immigration by virtually all Asians and most Europeans in 1924 (Saxton 1971, 1990). Northwestern European ancestry as a requisite for whiteness was set in legal concrete when the Supreme Court denied Bhagat Singh Thind the right to become a naturalized citizen under a 1790 federal law that allowed whites the right to become naturalized citizens. Thind argued that East Indians were the real Aryans and Caucasians, and therefore white. The Court countered that the United States only wanted blond Aryans and Caucasians, "that the blond Scandinavian and the brown Hindu have a common ancestor in the dim reaches of antiquity, but the average man knows perfectly well that there are unmistakable and profound differences between them today" (Takaki 1989:298–299). A narrowly defined white, Christian race was also built into the 1705 Virginia "Act concerning servants and slaves." This statute stated "that no negroes, mulattos and Indians or other infidels or jews, Moors, Mahometans or other infidels shall, at any time, purchase any christian servant, nor any other except of their own complexion" (Martyn 1979:111).[5]

The 1930 census added its voice, distinguishing not only immigrant from "native" whites, but also native whites of native white parentage, and native whites of immigrant (or mixed) parentage. In distinguishing immigrant (southern and eastern Europeans) from "native" (northwestern Europeans), the census reflected the racial distinctions of the eugenicist-inspired intelligence tests.[6]

Racism and anti-immigrant sentiment in general and anti-Semitism in particular flourished in higher education. Jews were the first of the Euroimmigrant groups to enter colleges in significant numbers, so it wasn't surprising that they faced the brunt of discrimination there.[7] The Protestant elite complained that Jews were unwashed, uncouth, unrefined, loud, and pushy. Harvard University President A. Lawrence Lowell, who was also a vice president of the Immigration

Restriction League, was openly opposed to Jews at Harvard. The Seven Sisters schools had a reputation for "flagrant discrimination." . . .

Anti-Semitic patterns set by these elite schools influenced standards of other schools, made anti-Semitism acceptable, and "made the aura of exclusivity a desirable commodity for the college-seeking clientele" (Synott 1986: 250; and see Karabel 1984; Silberman 1985; Steinberg 1989: chaps. 5, 9). Fears that colleges "might soon be overrun by Jews" were publicly expressed at a 1918 meeting of the Association of New England Deans. In 1919 Columbia University took steps to decrease the number of entering Jews by a set of practices that soon came to be widely adopted. . . .

Columbia's quota against Jews was well known in my parents' community. My father is very proud of having beaten it and of being admitted to Columbia Dental School on the basis of his sculpting skill. In addition to demonstrating academic qualifications, he was asked to carve a soap ball, which he did so well and fast that his Protestant interviewer was willing to accept him. Although he became a teacher instead because the dental school tuition was too high, he took me to the dentist every week of my childhood and prolonged the agony by discussing the finer points of tooth filling and dental care. My father also almost failed the speech test required for his teaching license because he didn't speak "standard"—that is, nonimmigrant, nonaccented—English. For my parents and most of their friends, English was a second language learned when they went to school, since their home language was Yiddish. They saw the speech test as designed to keep all ethnics, not just Jews, out of teaching. . . .

My parents' conclusion is that Jewish success, like their own, was the result of hard work and of placing a high value on education. They went to Brooklyn College during the Depression. My mother worked days and started school at night, and my father went during the day. Both their families encouraged them. More accurately, their families expected this effort from them. Everyone they knew was in the same boat, and their world was made up of Jews who advanced as they did. The picture of New York—where most Jews lived—seems to back them up. In 1920, Jews made up 80 percent of the students at New York's City College, 90 percent of Hunter College, and before World War I, 40 percent of private Columbia University. By 1934, Jews made up almost 24 percent of all law students nationally, and 56 percent of those in New York City. Still, more Jews became public school teachers, like my parents and their friends, than doctors or lawyers (Steinberg 1989:137, 227). Steinberg has debunked the myth that Jews advanced because of the cultural value placed on education. This is not to say that Jews did not advance. They did.

> Jewish success in America was a matter of historical timing. . . . [T]here was a fortuitous match between the experience and skills of Jewish immigrants, on the one hand, and the manpower needs and opportunity structures, on the other" (1989:103).

Jews were the only ones among the southern and eastern European immigrants who came from urban, commercial, craft, and manufacturing backgrounds, not least of which was garment manufacturing. They entered the United States in New York, center of the nation's booming garment industry, soon came to dominate its skilled (male) and "unskilled" (female) jobs, and found it an industry amenable to low-capital entrepreneurship. As a result, Jews were the first of the new European immigrants to create a middle class of small businesspersons early in the twentieth century. Jewish educational advances followed this business success and depended upon it, rather than creating it (see also Bodnar 1985 for a similar argument about mobility).

In the early twentieth century, Jewish college students entered a contested terrain in which the elite social mission was under challenge by a newer professional training mission. Pressure for change had begun to transform the curriculum and reorient college from a gentleman's bastion to a training ground for the middle-class professionals needed by an industrial economy. "The curriculum was overhauled to prepare students for careers in business, engineering, scientific farming, and the arts, and a variety of new professions such as accounting and pharmacy that were making their appearance in American colleges for the first time" (Steinberg 1989:229). Occupational training was precisely what drew Jews to college. In a setting where disparagement of intellectual pursuits and the gentleman's C were badges of distinction, it was not hard for Jews to excel.

How we interpret Jewish social mobility in this milieu depends on whom we compare Jews to. Compared with other immigrants, Jews were upwardly mobile. But compared with that of nonimmigrant whites, their mobility was very limited and circumscribed. Anti-immigrant racist and anti-Semitic barriers kept the Jewish middle class confined to a small number of occupations. Jews were excluded from mainstream corporate management and corporately employed professions, except in the garment and movie industries, which they built. Jews were almost totally excluded from university faculties (and the few that made it had powerful patrons). Jews were concentrated in small businesses, and in professions where they served a largely Jewish clientele (Davis 1990:146 n. 25; Silberman 1985: 88–117; Sklare 1971:63–67). . . .

My parents' generation believed that Jews overcame anti-Semitic barriers because Jews are special. My belief is that the Jews who were upwardly mobile were special among Jews (and were also well placed to write the story). My generation might well counter our parents'

story of pulling themselves up by their own bootstraps with, "But think what you might have been without the racism and with some affirmative action!" And that is precisely what the postwar boom, the decline of systematic public anti-immigrant racism and anti-Semitism, and governmental affirmative action extended to white males.

EUROETHNICS INTO WHITES

By the time I was an adolescent, Jews were just as white as the next white person. Until I was eight, I was a Jew in a world of Jews. Everyone on Avenue Z in Sheepshead Bay was Jewish. I spent my days playing and going to school on three blocks of Avenue Z, and visiting my grandparents in the nearby Jewish neighborhoods of Brighton Beach and Coney Island. There were plenty of Italians in my neighborhood, but they lived around the corner. They were a kind of Jew, but on the margins of my social horizons. Portuguese were even more distant, at the end of the bus ride, at Sheepshead Bay. . . . We left that world in 1949 when we moved to Valley Stream, Long Island, which was Protestant, Republican, and even had farms until Irish, Italian, and Jewish exurbanites like us gave it a more suburban and Democratic flavor. Neither religion nor ethnicity separated us at school or in the neighborhood. Except temporarily. In elementary school years, I remember a fair number of dirt-bomb (a good suburban weapon) wars on the block. Periodically one of the Catholic boys would accuse me or my brother of killing his God, to which we would reply, "Did not" and start lobbing dirt-bombs. Sometimes he would get his friends from Catholic school, and I would get mine from public school kids on the block, some of whom were Catholic. Hostilities lasted no more than a couple of hours and punctuated an otherwise friendly relationship. They ended by junior high years, when other things became more important. Jews, Catholics, and Protestants, Italians, Irish, Poles, and "English" (I don't remember hearing WASP as a kid) were mixed up on the block and in school. We thought of ourselves as middle class and very enlightened because our ethnic backgrounds seemed so irrelevant to high school culture. We didn't see race (we thought), and racism was not part of our peer consciousness, nor were the immigrant or working-class histories of our families.

Like most chicken and egg problems, it's hard to know which came first. Did Jews and other Euroethnics become white because they became middle class? That is, did money whiten? Or did being incorporated in an expanded version of whiteness open up the economic doors to a middle-class status? Clearly, both tendencies were at work. Some of the changes set in motion during the war against fascism led to a more inclusive version of whiteness. Anti-Semitism and anti-European racism lost respectability. The 1940 census no longer distinguished native whites of native parentage from those, like my parents, of immigrant parentage, so that Euroimmigrants and their children were more securely white by submersion in an expanded notion of whiteness. (This census also changed the race of Mexicans to white [U.S. Bureau of the Census, 1940:4].) Theories of nurture and culture replaced theories of nature and biology. Instead of dirty and dangerous races who would destroy U.S. democracy, immigrants became ethnic groups whose children had successfully assimilated into the mainstream and risen to the middle class. In this new myth, Euroethnic suburbs like mine became the measure of U.S. democracy's victory over racism. Jewish mobility became a new Horatio Alger story. In time and with hard work, every ethnic group would get a piece of the pie, and the United States would be a nation with equal opportunity for all its people to become part of a prosperous middle-class majority. And it seemed that Euroethnic immigrants and their children were delighted to join middle America.[8]

This is not to say that anti-Semitism disappeared after World War II, only that it fell from fashion and was driven underground. . . .

Although changing views on who was white made it easier for Euroethnics to become middle class, it was also the case that economic prosperity played a very powerful role in the whitening process. Economic mobility of Jews and other Euroethnics rested ultimately on U.S. postwar economic prosperity with its enormously expanded need for professional, technical, and managerial labor, and on government assistance in providing it. The United States emerged from the war with the strongest economy in the world. . . . The postwar period was a historic moment for real class mobility and for the affluence we have erroneously come to believe was the U.S. norm. It was a time when the old white and the newly white masses became middle class.

The GI Bill of Rights, as the 1944 Serviceman's Readjustment Act was known, was arguably the most massive affirmative action program in U.S. history. It was created to develop needed labor-force skills, and to provide those who had them with a life-style that reflected their value to the economy. The GI benefits ultimately extended to sixteen million GIs (veterans of the Korean War as well) included priority in jobs—that is, preferential hiring, but no one objected to it then; financial support during the job search; small loans for starting up businesses; and, most important, low-interest home loans and educational benefits, which included tuition and living expenses (Brown 1946; Hurd 1946; Mosch 1975; *Postwar Jobs for Veterans* 1945; Willenz 1983). This legislation was rightly regarded as one of the most revolutionary postwar programs. I call it affirmative action because it was aimed at and disproportionately helped male, Euro-origin GIs. . . .

EDUCATION AND OCCUPATION

It is important to remember that prior to the war, a college degree was still very much a "mark of the upper class" (Willenz 1983:165). Colleges were largely finishing schools for Protestant elites. Before the postwar boom, schools could not begin to accommodate the American masses. Even in New York City before the 1930s, neither the public schools nor City College had room for more than a tiny fraction of potential immigrant students.

Not so after the war. The almost eight million GIs who took advantage of their educational benefits under the GI Bill caused "the greatest wave of college building in American history" (Nash et al. 1986:885). White male GIs were able to take advantage of their educational benefits for college and technical training, so they were particularly well positioned to seize the opportunities provided by the new demands for professional, managerial, and technical labor. "It has been well documented that the GI educational benefits transformed American higher education and raised the educational level of that generation and generations to come. With many provisions for assistance in upgrading their educational attainments veterans pulled ahead of nonveterans in earning capacity. In the long run it was the nonveterans who had fewer opportunities" (Willenz 1983:165).[9] . . .

Even more significantly, the postwar boom transformed the U.S. class structure—or at least its status structure—so that the middle class expanded to encompass most of the population. Before the war, most Jews, like most other Americans, were working class. Already upwardly mobile before the war relative to other immigrants, Jews floated high on this rising economic tide, and most of them entered the middle class. Still, even the high tide missed some Jews. As late as 1973, some 15 percent of New York's Jews were poor or near-poor, and in the 1960s, almost 25 percent of employed Jewish men remained manual workers (Steinberg 1989:89–90).

Educational and occupational GI benefits really constituted affirmative action programs for white males because they were decidedly not extended to African Americans or to women of any race. White male privilege was shaped against the backdrop of wartime racism and postwar sexism. During and after the war, there was an upsurge in white racist violence against black servicemen in public schools, and in the KKK, which spread to California and New York (Dalfiume 1969:133–134). The number of lynchings rose during the war, and in 1943 there were antiblack race riots in several large northern cities. Although there was a wartime labor shortage, black people were discriminated against in access to well-paid defense industry jobs and in housing. In 1946 there were white riots against African Americans across the South, and in Chicago and Philadelphia as well. Gains made as a result of the wartime Civil Rights movement, especially employment in defense-related industries, were lost with peacetime conversion as black workers were the first fired, often in violation of seniority (Wynn 1976:114, 116). White women were also laid off, ostensibly to make jobs for demobilized servicemen, and in the long run women lost most of the gains they had made in wartime (Kessler-Harris 1982). We now know that women did not leave the labor force in any significant numbers but instead were forced to find inferior jobs, largely nonunion, parttime, and clerical.

Theoretically available to all veterans, in practice women and black veterans did not get anywhere near their share of GI benefits. Because women's units were not treated as part of the military, women in them were not considered veterans and were ineligible for Veterans' Administration (VA) benefits (Willenz 1983: 168). The barriers that almost completely shut

African-American GIs out of their benefits were more complex. In Wynn's portrait (1976:115), black GIs anticipated starting new lives, just like their white counterparts. Over 43 percent hoped to return to school and most expected to relocate, to find better jobs in new lines of work. The exodus from the South toward the North and far West was particularly large. So it wasn't a question of any lack of ambition on the part of African-American GIs.

Rather, the military, the Veterans' Administration, the U.S. Employment Service, and the Federal Housing Administration (FHA) effectively denied African-American GIs access to their benefits and to the new educational, occupational, and residential opportunities. Black GIs who served in the thoroughly segregated armed forces during World War II served under white officers, usually Southerners (Binkin and Eitelberg 1982: Dalfiume 1969; Foner 1974; Johnson 1967; Nalty and MacGregor 1981). African-American soldiers were disproportionately given dishonorable discharges, which denied them veterans' rights under the GI Bill. Thus between August and November 1946, 21 percent of white soldiers and 39 percent of black soldiers were dishonorably discharged. Those who did get an honorable discharge then faced the Veterans' Administration and the U.S. Employment Service. The latter, which was responsible for job placements, employed very few African Americans, especially in the South. This meant that black veterans did not receive much employment information, and that the offers they did receive were for low-paid and menial jobs. "In one survey of 50 cities, the movement of blacks into peacetime employment was found to be lagging far behind that of white veterans: in Arkansas 95 percent of the placements made by the USES for Afro-Americans were in service or unskilled jobs" (Nalty and MacGregor 1981:218, and see 60–61). African Americans were also less likely than whites,

regardless of GI status, to gain new jobs commensurate with their wartime jobs, and they suffered more heavily. For example, in San Francisco by 1948, black Americans "had dropped back halfway to their pre-war employment status" (Wynn 1976:114, 116).[10]

Black GIs faced discrimination in the educational system as well. Despite the end of restrictions on Jews and other Euroethnics, African Americans were not welcome in white colleges. Black colleges were overcrowded, and the combination of segregation and prejudice made for few alternatives. About twenty thousand black veterans attended college by 1947, most in black colleges, but almost as many, fifteen thousand, could not gain entry. Predictably, the disproportionately few African Americans who did gain access to their educational benefits were able, like their white counterparts, to become doctors and engineers, and to enter the black middle class (Walker 1970).

SUBURBANIZATION

In 1949, ensconced at Valley Stream, I watched potato farms turn into Levittown and into Idlewild (later Kennedy) Airport. This was a major spectator sport in our first years on suburban Long Island. A typical weekend would bring various aunts, uncles, and cousins out from the city. After a huge meal we would pile in the car—itself a novelty—to look at the bulldozed acres and comment on the matchbox construction. During the week, my mother and I would look at the houses going up within walking distance.

Bill Levitt built a basic 900–1,000-square-foot, somewhat expandable house for a lower-middle-class and working-class market on Long Island, and later in Pennsylvania and New Jersey (Gans 1967). Levittown started out as two thousand units of rental housing at sixty dollars a month, designed to meet the low-income housing needs of returning war vets, many of whom, like my Aunt Evie and Uncle Julie, were living in quonset huts. By May 1947, Levitt and Sons had acquired enough land in Hempstead Township on Long Island to build four thousand houses, and by the next February, he'd built six thousand units and named the development after himself. After 1948, federal financing for the construction of rental housing tightened, and Levitt switched to building houses for sale. By 1951 Levittown was a development of some fifteen thousand families. . . .

At the beginning of World War II, about 33 percent of all U.S. families owned their houses. That percentage doubled in twenty years. Most Levittowners looked just like my family. They came from New York City or Long Island; about 17 percent were military, from nearby Mitchell Field; Levittown was their first house; and almost everyone was married. The 1947 inhabitants were over 75 percent white collar, but by 1950 more blue-collar families moved in, so that by 1951, "barely half" of the new residents were white collar, and by 1960 their occupational profile was somewhat more working class than for Nassau County as a whole. By this time too, almost one-third of Levittown's people were either foreign-born or, like my parents, first-generation U.S. born (Dobriner 1963:91, 100).

The FHA "[Federal Housing Authority]" was key to buyers and builders alike. Thanks to it, suburbia was open to more than GIs. People like us would never have been in the market for houses without FHA and VA low-down-payment, low-interest, long-term loans to young buyers.[11] . . .

The FHA believed in racial segregation. Throughout its history, it publicly and actively promoted restrictive covenants. Before the war, these forbade sale to Jews and Catholics as well as to African Americans. The deed to my house in Detroit had such a covenant, which theoretically prevented it from being sold to Jews or

African Americans. Even after the Supreme Court ended legal enforcement of restrictive covenants in 1948, the FHA continued to encourage builders to write them against African Americans. FHA underwriting manuals openly insisted on racially homogeneous neighborhoods, and their loans were made only in white neighborhoods. I bought my Detroit house in 1972 from Jews who were leaving a largely African-American neighborhood. By that time, after the 1968 Fair Housing Act, restrictive covenants were a dead letter (although blockbusting by realtors was rapidly replacing it).

With the federal government behind them, virtually all developers refused to sell to African Americans. Palo Alto and Levittown, like most suburbs as late as 1960, were virtually all white. Out of 15,741 houses and 65,276 people, averaging 4.2 people per house, only 220 Levittowners, or 52 households, were "nonwhite." In 1958 Levitt announced publicly at a press conference to open his New Jersey development that he would not sell to black buyers. This caused a furor, since the state of New Jersey (but not the U.S. government) prohibited discrimination in federally subsidized housing. Levitt was sued and fought it, although he was ultimately persuaded by township ministers to integrate. . . .

The result of these policies was that African Americans were totally shut out of the suburban boom. An article in *Harper's* described the housing available to black GIs.

> On his way to the base each morning, Sergeant Smith passes an attractive air-conditioned, FHA-financed housing project. It was built for service families. Its rents are little more than the Smiths pay for their shack. And there are half-a-dozen vacancies, but none for Negroes (qtd. in Foner 1974:195).

Where my family felt the seductive pull of suburbia, Marshall Berman's experienced the brutal push of urban renewal. In the Bronx in the 1950s, Robert Moses's Cross-Bronx Expressway erased "a dozen solid, settled, densely populated neighborhoods like our own; . . . something like 60,000 working- and lower-middle-class people, mostly Jews, but with many Italians, Irish and Blacks thrown in, would be thrown out of their homes. . . . For ten years, through the late 1950s and early 1960s, the center of the Bronx was pounded and blasted and smashed" (1982:292).

Urban renewal made postwar cities into bad places to live. At a physical level, urban renewal reshaped them, and federal programs brought private developers and public officials together to create downtown central business districts where there had formerly been a mix of manufacturing, commerce, and working-class neighborhoods. Manufacturing was scattered to the peripheries of the city, which were ringed and bisected by a national system of highways. Some working-class neighborhoods were bulldozed, but others remained (Greer 1965; Hartman 1975; Squires 1989). In Los Angeles as in New York's Bronx, the postwar period saw massive freeway construction right through the heart of old working-class neighborhoods. In East Los Angeles and Santa Monica, Chicano and African-American communities were divided in half or blasted to smithereens by the highways bringing Angelenos to the new white suburbs, or to make way for civic monuments like Dodger Stadium (Pardo 1990; Social and Public Arts Resource Center 1990:80, 1983:12–13).

Urban renewal was the other side of the process by which Jewish and other working-class Euroimmigrants became middle class. It was the push to suburbia's seductive pull. The fortunate white survivors of urban renewal headed disproportionately for suburbia, where they could partake of prosperity and the good life. . . .

If the federal stick of urban renewal joined the FHA carrot of cheap mortgages to send masses of Euros to the suburbs, the FHA had a different kind of one-two punch for African Americans. Segregation kept them out the suburbs, and redlining made sure they could not buy or repair their homes in the neighborhoods where they were allowed to live. The FHA practiced systematic redlining. This was a system developed by its predecessor, the Home Owners Loan Corporation (HOLC), which in the 1930s developed an elaborate neighborhood rating system that placed the highest (green) value on all-white, middle-class neighborhoods, and the lowest (red) on racially nonwhite or mixed and working-class neighborhoods. High ratings meant high property values. The idea was that low property values in redlined neighborhoods made them bad investments. The FHA was, after all, created by and for banks and the housing industry. Redlining warned banks not to lend there, and the FHA would not insure mortgages in such neighborhoods. Redlining created a self-fulfilling prophecy. "With the assistance of local realtors and banks, it assigned one of the four ratings to every block in every city. The resulting information was then translated into the appropriate color [green, blue, yellow, and red] and duly recorded on secret 'Residential Security Maps' in local HOLC offices. The maps themselves were placed in elaborate 'City Survey Files,' which consisted of reports, questionnaires, and workpapers relating to current and future values of real estate" (Jackson 1985:197).[12]

FHA's and VA's refusal to guarantee loans in redlined neighborhoods made it virtually impossible for African Americans to borrow money for home improvement or purchase. Because these maps and surveys were quite secret, it took the 1960s Civil Rights movement to make these practices and their devastating consequences public. As a result, those who fought urban renewal or who sought to make a home in the urban ruins found themselves locked out of the middle class. They also faced an ideological assault that labeled their neighborhoods slums and called those who lived in them slum dwellers (Gans 1962).

The record is very clear that instead of seizing the opportunity to end institutionalized racism, the federal government did its best to shut and double seal the post-war window of opportunity in African Americans' faces. It consistently refused to combat segregation in the social institutions that were key for upward mobility: education, housing, and employment. Moreover, federal programs that were themselves designed to assist demobilized GIs and young families systematically discriminated against African Americans. Such programs reinforced white/nonwhite racial distinctions even as intrawhite racialization was falling out of fashion. This other side of the coin, that white men of northwestern or southeastern European ancestry were treated equally in theory and in practice with regard to the benefits they received, was part of the larger postwar whitening of Jews and other eastern and southern Europeans.

The myth that Jews pulled themselves up by their own bootstraps ignores the fact that it took federal programs to create the conditions whereby the abilities of Jews and other European immigrants could be recognized and rewarded rather than denigrated and denied. The GI Bill and FHA and VA mortgages were forms of affirmative action that allowed male Jews and other Euro-American men to become suburban homeowners and to get the training that allowed them—but not women vets or war workers—to become professionals, technicians, salesmen, and managers in a growing economy. Jews' and other white ethnics' upward mobility was the result of programs that allowed us to float on a rising economic tide. To African Americans the government offered the cement boots of segregation, redlining, urban renewal, and discrimination.

Those racially skewed gains have been passed across the generations, so that racial inequality seems to maintain itself "naturally," even after legal segregation ended. Today, in a shrinking economy where downward mobility is the norm, the children and grandchildren of the postwar beneficiaries of the economic boom have some precious advantages. For example, having parents who own their own homes or who have decent retirement benefits can make a real difference in young people's ability to take on huge college loans or to come up with a down payment for a house. Even this simple inheritance helps perpetuate the gap between whites and nonwhites. Sure Jews needed ability, but ability was not enough to make it. The same applies even more in today's long recession.

Notes

This is a revised and expanded version of a paper published in *Jewish Currents* in June 1992 and delivered at the 1992 meetings of the American Anthropological Association in the session *Blacks and Jews, 1992: Reaching across the Cultural Boundaries* organized by Angela Gilliam. I would like to thank Emily Abel, Katya Gibel Azoulay, Edna Bonacich, Angela Gilliam, Isabelle Gunning, Valerie Matsumoto, Regina Morantz-Sanchez, Roger Sanjek, Rabbi Chaim Seidler-Feller, Janet Silverstein, and Eloise Klein Healy's writing group for uncovering wonderful sources and for critical readings along the way.

1. Indeed, Boasian and Du Boisian anthropology developed in active political opposition to this nativism; on Du Bois, see Harrison and Nonini 1992.

2. On immigrants as part of the industrial work force, see Steinberg 1989:36.

3. I thank Roger Sanjek for providing me with this source.

4. It was intended, as Davenport wrote to the president of the American Museum of Natural History, Henry Fairfield Osborne, as "an anthropological

society . . . with a central governing body, self-elected and self-perpetuating, and very limited in members, and also confined to native Americans who are anthropologically, socially and politically sound, no Bolsheviki need apply" (Barkan 1991:67–68).

5. I thank Valerie Matsumoto for telling me about the Third case and Katya Gibel Azoulay for providing this information to me on the Virginia statute.

6. "The distinction between white and colored" has been "the only racial classification which has been carried through all the 15 censuses." "Colored" consisted of "Negroes" and "other races": Mexican, Indian, Chinese, Japanese, Filipino, Hindu, Korean, Hawaiian, Malay, Siamese, and Samoan. (U.S. Bureau of the Census, 1930:25, 26).

7. For why Jews entered colleges earlier than other immigrants, and for a challenge to views that attribute it to Jewish culture, see Steinberg 1989.

8. Indeed, Jewish social scientists were prominent in creating this ideology of the United States as a meritocracy. Most prominent of course was Nathan Glazer, but among them also were Charles Silberman and Marshall Sklare.

9. The belief was widespread that "the GI Bill . . . helped millions of families move into the middle class" (Nash et al. 1986:885). A study that compares mobility among veterans and nonveterans provides a kind of confirmation. In an unnamed small city in Illinois, Havighurst and his colleagues (1951) found no significant difference between veterans and nonveterans, but this was because apparently very few veterans used any of their GI benefits.

10. African Americans and Japanese Americans were the main target of wartime racism (see Murray 1992). By contrast, there were virtually no anti-German American or anti-Italian American policies in World War II (see Takaki 1989:357–406).

11. See Eichler 1982:5 for homeowning percentages; Jackson (1985:205) found an increase in families living in owner-occupied buildings, rising from 44 percent in 1934 to 63 percent in 1972; see Monkkonen 1988 on scarcity of mortgages; and Gelfand 1975, esp. chap. 6, on federal programs.

12. These ideas from the real estate industry were "codified and legitimated in 1930s work by University of Chicago sociologist Robert Park and real estate professor Homer Hoyt" (Jackson 1985:198–199).

REFERENCES

Berman, Marshall. 1982. *All That Is Solid Melts into Air: The Experience of Modernity.* New York: Simon and Schuster.

Binkin, Martin, and Mark J. Eitelberg. 1982. *Blacks and the Military.* Washington, DC: Brookings.

Bodnar, John. 1985. *The Transplanted: A History of Immigrants in Urban America.* Bloomington: Indiana University Press.

Brody, David. 1980. *Workers in Industrial America: Essays of the Twentieth Century Struggle.* New York: Oxford University Press.

Brown, Francis J. 1946. *Educational Opportunities for Veterans.* Washington, DC: Public Affairs Press, American Council on Public Affairs.

Carlson, Lewis H., and George A. Colbum. 1972. *In Their Place: White America Defines Her Minorities, 1850–1950.* New York: Wiley.

Dalfiume, Richard M. 1969. *Desegregation of the U.S. Armed Forces: Fighting on Two Fronts, 1939–1953.* Columbia: University of Missouri Press.

Davis, Mike. 1990. *City of Quartz.* London: Verso.

Dobriner, William M. 1963 *Class in Suburbia.* Englewood Cliffs, N.J.: Prentice Hall.

Eichler, Ned. 1982. *The Merchant Builders.* Cambridge: MIT Press.

Fields, Barbara Jeanne. 1990. Slavery, Race, and Ideology in the United States of America. *New Left Review* 181:95–118.

Foner, Jack. 1974. *Blacks and the Military in American History: A New Perspective.* New York: Praeger.

Gans, Herbert. 1962. *The Urban Villagers.* New York: Free Press.

_____. 1967. *The Levittowners.* New York: Pantheon.

Gordon, Milton. 1964. *Assimilation in American Life.* New York: Oxford University Press.

Hartman, Chester. 1975. *Housing and Social Policy.* Englewood Cliffs, N.J.: Prentice Hall.

Higham, John. 1955. *Strangers in the Land.* New Brunswick, N.J.: Rutgers University Press.

Hurd, Charles. 1946. *The Veterans' Program: A Complete Guide to Its Benefits, Rights, and Options.* New York: McGraw-Hill.

Jackson, Kenneth T. 1985. *Crabgrass Frontier: The Suburbanization of the United States.* New York: Oxford University Press.

Johnson, Jesse J. 1967. *Ebony Brass: An Autobiography of Negro Frustration amid Aspiration.* New York: Frederick.

Karabel, Jerome. 1984. Status-Group Struggle, Organizational Interests, and the Limits of Institutional Autonomy. *Theory and Society* 13:1–40.

Kessler-Harris, Alice. 1982. *Out to Work: A History of Wage-Earning Women in the United States.* New York: Oxford University Press.

Martyn, Byron Curti. 1979. Racism in the U.S.: A History of Anti-Miscegenation Legislation and Litigation. Ph.D. diss., University of Southern California.

Mosch, Theodore R. 1975. *The GI Bill: A Breakthrough in Educational and Social Policy in the United States.* Hicksville, N.Y.: Exposition.

Nalty, Bernard C., and Morris J. MacGregor, eds. 1981. *Blacks in the Military: Essential Documents.* Wilmington, Del.: Scholarly Resources.

Nash, Gary B., Julie Roy Jeffrey, John R. Howe, Allen F. Davis, Peter J. Frederick, and Allen M. Winkler. 1986. *The American People: Creating a Nation and a Society.* New York: Harper and Row.

Pardo, Mary. 1990. Mexican-American Women Grassroots Community Activists: "Mothers of East Los Angeles." *Frontiers* 11: 1–7.

Postwar Jobs for Veterans. 1945. *Annals of the American Academy of Political and Social Science* 238 (March).

Saxton, Alexander. 1971. *The Indispensable Enemy.* Berkeley and Los Angeles: University of California Press.

_____. 1990. *The Rise and Fall of the White Republic.* London: Verso.

Silberman, Charles. 1985. A *Certain People: American Jews and Their Lives Today.* New York: Summit.

Sklare, Marshall. 1971. *America's Jews.* New York: Random House.

Sowell, Thomas. 1981. *Ethnic America: A History.* New York: Basic.

Steinberg, Stephen. 1989. *The Ethnic Myth: Race, Ethnicity, and Class in America.* 2d ed. Boston: Beacon.

Synott, Marcia Graham. 1986. Anti-Semitism and American Universities: Did Quotas Follow the Jews? In *Anti-Semitism in American History,* ed. David A. Gerber. Urbana: University of Illinois Press, 233–274.

Takaki, Ronald. 1989. *Strangers from a Different Shore.* Boston: Little, Brown.

Tobin, Gary A., ed. 1987. *Divided Neighborhoods: Changing Patterns of Racial Segregation.* Beverly Hills: Sage.

U.S. Bureau of the Census. 1930. *Fifteenth Census of the United* States. Vol. 2. Washington, DC: U.S Government Printing Office.

_____. 1940. *Sixteenth Census of the United States.* Vol. 2. Washington, DC: U.S. Government Printing Office.

Walker, Olive. 1970. The Windsor Hills School Story. *Integrated Education: Race and Schools* 8(3): 4–9.

Willenz, June A. 1983. *Women Veterans: America's Forgotten Heroines.* New York: Continuum.

Wynn, Neil A. 1976. *The Afro-American and the Second World War.* London: Elek.

Discussion Questions

1. How was it that in just a few decades, Jews in America went from being excluded from the full privileges of whiteness to being included? How do ethnicity and class combine to define who is "white" in the United States? What role does the government play in solidifying this definition?

2. Why weren't women and blacks able to take full advantage of their GI benefits, when they too had served their country in war? What were the processes by which blacks were excluded from post–World War II suburbanization? Why don't we learn about these more recent acts of black exclusion in our history lessons?

3. How are these exclusions of blacks from economic opportunities related to how Jews became white? What is meant by the author's calling these opportunities an "affirmative action" program for white males? How does this information affect what we take into account when comparing the experiences of white immigrant and other immigrant groups?

WHITE PRIVILEGE AND MALE PRIVILEGE

Peggy McIntosh

Through work to bring materials and perspectives from Women's Studies to the rest of the curriculum, I have often noticed men's unwillingness to grant that they are overprivileged in the curriculum, even though they may grant that women are disadvantaged. Denials that amount to taboos surround the subject of advantages that men gain from women's disadvantages. These denials protect male privilege from being fully recognized, acknowledged, lessened, or ended.

Thinking through unacknowledged male privilege as a phenomenon with a life of its own, I realized that since hierarchies in our society are interlocking, there was most likely a phenomenon of white privilege that was similarly denied and protected, but alive and real in its effects. As a white person, I realized I had been taught about racism as something that puts others at a disadvantage, but had been taught not to see one of its corollary aspects, white privilege, which puts me at an advantage.

I think whites are carefully taught not to recognize white privilege, as males are taught not to recognize male privilege. So I have begun in an untutored way to ask what it is like to have white privilege. This paper is a partial record of my personal observations and not a scholarly analysis. It is based on my daily experiences within my particular circumstances.

I have come to see white privilege as an invisible package of unearned assets that I can count on cashing in each day, but about which I was "meant" to remain oblivious. White privilege is like an invisible weightless knapsack of special provisions, assurances, tools, maps, guides, codebooks, passports, visas, clothes, compass, emergency gear, and blank checks.

Since I have had trouble facing white privilege, and describing its results in my life, I saw parallels here with men's reluctance to acknowledge male privilege. Only rarely will a man go beyond acknowledging that women are disadvantaged to acknowledging that men have unearned advantage, or that unearned privilege has not been good for men's development as human beings, or for society's development, or that privilege systems might ever be challenged and *changed*.

I will review here several types or layers of denial that I see at work protecting, and preventing awareness about, entrenched male privilege. Then I will draw parallels, from my own experience, with the denials that veil the facts of white privilege. Finally, I will list forty-six ordinary and daily ways in which I experience having white privilege, by contrast with my African American colleagues in the same building. This list is not intended to be generalizable. Others can make their own lists from within their own life circumstances.

Writing this paper has been difficult, despite warm receptions for the talks on which it is based.[1] For describing white privilege makes one newly accountable. As we in Women's Studies work reveal male privilege and ask men to give up some of their power, so one who writes about having white privilege must ask, "Having described it, what will I do to lessen or end it?"

The denial of men's overprivileged state takes many forms in discussions of curriculum change work. Some claim that men must be central in the curriculum because they have done most of what is important or distinctive in life or in civilization. Some recognize sexism in the curriculum but deny that it makes male students seem unduly important in life. Others agree that certain *individual* thinkers are male oriented but deny that there is any *systemic* tendency in disciplinary frameworks or epistemology to overempower men as a group. Those men who do grant that male privilege takes institutionalized and embedded forms are still likely to deny that male hegemony has opened doors for them personally. Virtually all men deny that male overreward alone can explain men's centrality in all the inner sanctums of our most powerful institutions. Moreover, those few who will acknowledge that male privilege systems have overempowered them usually end up doubting that we could dismantle these privilege systems. They may say they will work to improve women's status, in the society or in the university, but they can't or won't support the idea of lessening men's. In curricular terms, this is the point at which they say that they regret they cannot use any of the interesting new scholarship on women because the syllabus is full. When the talk turns to giving men less cultural room, even the most thoughtful and fair-minded of the men I know will tend to reflect, or fall back on, conservative assumptions about the inevitability of present gender relations and distributions of power, calling on precedent or sociobiology and psychobiology to demonstrate that male domination is natural and follows inevitably from evolutionary pressures. Others resort to arguments from "experience" or religion or social responsibility or wishing and dreaming.

After I realized, through faculty development work in Women's Studies, the extent to which men work from a base of unacknowledged privilege, I understood that much of their oppressiveness was unconscious. Then I remembered the frequent charges from women of color that white women whom they encounter are oppressive. I began to understand why we are justly seen as oppressive, even when we don't see ourselves that way. At the very least, obliviousness of one's privileged state can make a person or group irritating to be with. I began to count the ways in which I enjoy unearned skin privilege and have been conditioned into oblivion about its existence, unable to see that it put me "ahead" in any way, or put my people ahead, overrewarding us and yet also paradoxically damaging us, or that it could or should be changed.

My schooling gave me no training in seeing myself as an oppressor, as an unfairly advantaged person, or as a participant in a damaged culture. I was taught to see myself as an individual whose moral state depended on her individual moral will. At school, we were not taught about slavery in any depth; we were not taught to see slaveholders as damaged people. Slaves were seen as the only group at risk of being dehumanized. My schooling followed the pattern which Elizabeth Minnich has pointed out: whites are taught to think of their lives as morally neutral, normative, and average, and also ideal, so that when we work to benefit others, this is seen as work that will allow "them" to be more like "us." I think many of us know how obnoxious this attitude can be in men.

After frustration with men who would not recognize male privilege, I decided to try to work on myself at least by identifying some of the daily effects of white privilege in my life. It is crude work, at this stage, but I will give here a list of special circumstances and conditions I experience that I did not earn but that I have been made to feel are mine by birth, by citizenship, and by virtue of being a conscientious law-abiding "normal" person of goodwill. I have chosen those conditions that I think in my case *attach somewhat more to skin-color privilege* than to class, religion, ethnic status, or geographical location, though these other privileging factors are intricately intertwined. As far as I can see, my Afro-American co-workers, friends, and acquaintances with whom I come into daily or frequent contact in this particular time, place, and line of work cannot count on most of these conditions.

1. I can, if I wish, arrange to be in the company of people of my race most of the time.

2. I can avoid spending time with people whom I was trained to mistrust and who have learned to mistrust my kind or me.

3. If I should need to move, I can be pretty sure of renting or purchasing housing in an area which I can afford and in which I would want to live.

4. I can be reasonably sure that my neighbors in such a location will be neutral or pleasant to me.

5. I can go shopping alone most of the time, fairly well assured that I will not be followed or harassed by store detectives.

6. I can turn on the television or open to the front page of the paper and see people of my race widely and positively represented.

7. When I am told about our national heritage or about "civilization," I am shown that people of my color made it what it is.

8. I can be sure that my children will be given curricular materials that testify to the existence of their race.

9. If I want to, I can be pretty sure of finding a publisher for this piece on white privilege.

10. I can be fairly sure of having my voice heard in a group in which I am the only member of my race.

11. I can be casual about whether or not to listen to another woman's voice in a group in which she is the only member of her race.

12. I can go into a book shop and count on finding the writing of my race represented, into a supermarket and find the staple foods that fit with my cultural traditions, into a hairdresser's shop and find someone who can deal with my hair.

13. Whether I use checks, credit cards, or cash, I can count on my skin color not to work against the appearance that I am financially reliable.

14. I could arrange to protect our young children most of the time from people who might not like them.

15. I did not have to educate our children to be aware of systemic racism for their own daily physical protection.

16. I can be pretty sure that my children's teachers and employers will tolerate them if they fit school and workplace norms; my chief worries about them do not concern others' attitudes toward their race.

17. I can talk with my mouth full and not have people put this down to my color.

18. I can swear, or dress in secondhand clothes, or not answer letters, without having people attribute these choices to the bad morals, the poverty, or the illiteracy of my race.

19. I can speak in public to a powerful male group without putting my race on trial.

20. I can do well in a challenging situation without being called a credit to my race.

21. I am never asked to speak for all the people of my racial group.

22. I can remain oblivious to the language and customs of persons of color who constitute the world's majority without feeling in my culture any penalty for such oblivion.

23. I can criticize our government and talk about how much I fear its policies and behavior without being seen as a cultural outsider.

24. I can be reasonably sure that if I ask to talk to "the person in charge," I will be facing a person of my race.

25. If a traffic cop pulls me over or if the IRS audits my tax return, I can be sure I haven't been singled out because of my race.

26. I can easily buy posters, postcards, picture books, greeting cards, dolls, toys, and children's magazines featuring people of my race.

27. I can go home from most meetings of organizations I belong to feeling somewhat tied in, rather than isolated, out of place, outnumbered, unheard, held at a distance, or feared.

28. I can be pretty sure that an argument with a colleague of another race is more likely to jeopardize her chances for advancement than to jeopardize mine.

29. I can be fairly sure that if I argue for the promotion of a person of another race, or a program centering on race, this is not likely to cost me heavily within my present setting, even if my colleagues disagree with me.

30. If I declare there is a racial issue at hand, or there isn't a racial issue at hand, my race will lend me more credibility for either position than a person of color will have.

31. I can choose to ignore developments in minority writing and minority activist programs, or disparage them, or learn from them, but in any case, I can find ways to be more or less protected from negative consequences of any of these choices.

32. My culture gives me little fear about ignoring the perspectives and powers of people of other races.

33. I am not made acutely aware that my shape, bearing, or body odor will be taken as a reflection on my race.

34. I can worry about racism without being seen as self-interested or self-seeking.

35. I can take a job with an affirmative action employer without having co-workers on the job suspect that I got it because of my race.

36. If my day, week, or year is going badly, I need not ask of each negative episode or situation whether it has racial overtones.

37. I can be pretty sure of finding people who would be willing to talk with me and advise me about my next steps, professionally.

38. I can think over many options, social, political, imaginative, or professional, without asking whether a person of my race would

be accepted or allowed to do what I want to do.

39. I can be late to a meeting without having the lateness reflect on my race.

40. I can choose public accommodation without fearing that people of my race cannot get in or will be mistreated in the places I have chosen.

41. I can be sure that if I need legal or medical help, my race will not work against me.

42. I can arrange my activities so that I will never have to experience feelings of rejection owing to my race.

43. If I have low credibility as a leader, I can be sure that my race is not the problem.

44. I can easily find academic courses and institutions that give attention only to people of my race.

45. I can expect figurative language and imagery in all of the arts to testify to experiences of my race.

46. I can choose blemish cover or bandages in "flesh" color and have them more or less match my skin.

I repeatedly forgot each of the realizations on this list until I wrote them down. For me, white privilege has turned out to be an elusive and fugitive subject. The pressure to avoid it is great, for in facing it I must give up the myth of meritocracy. If these things are true, this is not such a free country, one's life is not what one makes it; many doors open for certain people through no virtues of their own. These perceptions mean also that my moral condition is not what I had been led to believe. The appearance of being a good citizen rather than a trouble-maker comes in large part from having all sorts of doors open automatically because of my color.

A further paralysis of nerve comes from literary silence protecting privilege. My clearest memories of finding such analysis are in Lillian Smith's unparalleled *Killers of the Dream* and Margaret Andersen's review of Karen and Mamie Fields' *Lemon Swamp*. Smith, for example, wrote about walking toward black children on the street and knowing they would step into the gutter. Andersen contrasted the pleasure that she, as a white child, took on summer driving trips to the south with Karen Fields' memories of driving in a closed car stocked with all necessities lest, in stopping, her black family should suffer "insult, or worse." Adrienne Rich also recognizes and writes about daily experiences of privilege, but in my observation, white women's writing in this area is far more often on systemic racism than on our daily lives as light-skinned women.[2]

In unpacking this invisible knapsack of white privilege, I have listed conditions of daily experience that I once took for granted, as neutral, normal, and universally available to everybody, just as I once thought of a male-focused curriculum as the neutral or accurate account that can speak for all. Nor did I think of any of these perquisites as bad for the holder. I now think that we need a more finely differentiated taxonomy of privilege, for some of these varieties are only what one would want for everyone in a just society, and others give license to be ignorant, oblivious, arrogant, and destructive. Before proposing some more finely tuned categorization, I will make some observations about the general effects of these conditions on my life and expectations.

In this potpourri of examples, some privileges make me feel at home in the world.

Others allow me to escape penalties or dangers that others suffer. Through some, I escape fear, anxiety, insult, injury, or a sense of not being welcome, not being real. Some keep me from having to hide, to be in disguise, to feel sick or crazy, to negotiate each transaction from the position of being an outsider or, within my group, a person who is suspected of having too close links with a dominant culture. Most keep me from having to be angry.

I see a pattern running through the matrix of white privilege, a pattern of assumptions that were passed on to me as a white person. There was one main piece of cultural turf; it was my own turf, and I was among those who could control the turf. I could measure up to the cultural standards and take advantage of the many options I saw around me to make what the culture would call a success of my life. *My skin color was an asset for any move I was educated to want to make.* I could think of myself as "belonging" in major ways and of making social systems work for me. I could freely disparage, fear, neglect, or be oblivious to anything outside of the dominant cultural forms. Being of the main culture, I could also criticize it fairly freely. My life was reflected back to me frequently enough so that I felt, with regard to my race, if not to my sex, like one of the real people.

Whether through the curriculum or in the newspaper, the television, the economic system, or the general look of people in the streets, I received daily signals and indications that my people counted and that others *either didn't exist or must be trying, not very successfully, to be like people of my race.* I was given cultural permission not to hear voices of people of other races or a tepid cultural tolerance for hearing or acting on such voices. I was also raised not to suffer seriously from anything that darker-skinned people might say about my group, "protected," though perhaps I should more accurately say *prohibited,* through the habits of my economic class and social group, from living in racially mixed groups or being reflective about interactions between people of differing races.

In proportion as my racial group was being made confident, comfortable, and oblivious, other groups were likely being made unconfident, uncomfortable, and alienated. Whiteness protected me from many kinds of hostility, distress, and violence, which I was being subtly trained to visit in turn upon people of color.

For this reason, the word "privilege" now seems to me misleading. Its connotations are too positive to fit the conditions and behaviors which "privilege systems" produce. We usually think of privilege as being a favored state, whether earned, or conferred by birth or luck. School graduates are reminded they are privileged and urged to use their (enviable) assets well. The word "privilege" carries the connotation of being something everyone must want. Yet some of the conditions I have described here work to systemically overempower certain groups. Such privilege simply *confers dominance,* gives permission to control, because of one's race or sex. The kind of privilege that gives license to some people to be, at best, thoughtless and, at worst, murderous should not continue to be referred to as a desirable attribute. Such "privilege" may be widely desired without being in any way beneficial to the whole society.

Moreover, though "privilege" may confer power, it does not confer moral strength. Those who do not depend on conferred dominance have traits and qualities that may never develop in those who do. Just as Women's Studies courses indicate that women survive their political circumstances to lead lives that hold the human race together, so "underprivileged" people of color who are the world's majority have survived their oppression and lived survivors' lives from which the white global minority can and must learn. In some groups, those dominated have actually become strong through *not* having all of these unearned advantages, and this gives them a great deal to teach the others. Members of so-called privileged groups can seem foolish, ridiculous, infantile, or dangerous by contrast.

I want, then, to distinguish between earned strength and unearned power conferred systemically. Power from unearned privilege can look like strength when it is, in fact, permission to escape or to dominate. But not all of the privileges on my list are inevitably damaging. Some, like the expectation that neighbors will be decent to you, or that your race will not count against you in court, should be the norm in a just society and should be considered as the entitlement of everyone. Others, like the privilege not to listen to less powerful people, distort the humanity of the holders as well as the ignored groups. Still others, like finding one's staple foods everywhere, may be a function of being a member of a numerical majority in the population. Others have to do with not having to labor under pervasive negative stereotyping and mythology.

We might at least start by distinguishing between positive advantages that we can work to spread, to the point where they are not advantages at all but simply part of the normal civic and social fabric, and negative types of advantage that unless rejected will always reinforce our present hierarchies. For example, the positive "privilege" of belonging, the feeling that one belongs within the human circle, as Native Americans say, fosters development and should not be seen as privilege for a few. It is, let us say, an entitlement that none of us should have to earn; ideally it is an *unearned entitlement*. At present, since only a few have it, it is an *unearned advantage* for them. The negative "privilege" that gave me cultural permission not to take darker-skinned Others seriously can be seen as arbitrarily conferred dominance and should not be

desirable for anyone. This paper results from a process of coming to see that some of the power that I originally saw as attendant on being a human being in the United States consisted in *unearned advantage* and *conferred dominance,* as well as other kinds of special circumstance not universally taken for granted.

In writing this paper I have also realized that white identity and status (as well as class identity and status) give me considerable power to choose whether to broach this subject and its trouble. I can pretty well decide whether to disappear and avoid and not listen and escape the dislike I may engender in other people through this essay, or interrupt, answer, interpret, preach, correct, criticize, and control to some extent what goes on in reaction to it. Being white, I am given considerable power to escape many kinds of danger or penalty as well as to choose which risks I want to take.

There is an analogy here, once again, with Women's Studies. Our male colleagues do not have a great deal to lose in supporting Women's Studies, but they do not have a great deal to lose if they oppose it either. They simply have the power to decide whether to commit themselves to more equitable distributions of power. They will probably feel few penalties whatever choice they make; they do not seem, in any obvious short-term sense, the ones at risk, though they and we are all at risk because of the behaviors that have been rewarded in them.

Through Women's Studies work I have met very few men who are truly distressed about systemic, unearned male advantage and conferred dominance. And so one question for me and others like me is whether we will be like them, or whether we will get truly distressed, even outraged, about unearned race advantage and conferred dominance and if so, what we will do to lessen them. In any case, we need to do more work in identifying how they actually affect our daily lives. We need more down-to-earth writing by people about these taboo subjects. We need more understanding of the ways in which white "privilege" damages white people, for these are not the same ways in which it damages the victimized. Skewed white psyches are an inseparable part of the picture, though I do not want to confuse the kinds of damage done to the holders of special assets and to those who suffer the deficits. Many, perhaps most, of our white students in the United States think that racism doesn't affect them because they are not people of color; they do not see "whiteness" as a racial identity. Many men likewise think that Women's Studies does not bear on their own existences because they are not female; they do not see themselves as having gendered identities. Insisting on the universal "effects" of "privilege" systems, then, becomes one of our chief tasks, and being more explicit about the *particular* effects in particular contexts is another. Men need to join us in this work.

. . .

One factor seems clear about all of the interlocking oppressions. They take both active forms that we can see and embedded forms that members of the dominant group are taught not to see. In my class and place, I did not see myself as racist because I was taught to recognize racism only in individual acts of meanness by members of my group, never in invisible systems conferring racial dominance on my group from birth. Likewise, we are taught to think that sexism . . . is carried on only through intentional, individual acts of discrimination, meanness, or cruelty, rather than in invisible systems conferring unsought dominance on certain groups. Disapproving of the systems won't be enough to change them. I was taught to think that racism could end if white individuals changed their attitudes; many men think sexism can be ended by individual changes in daily behavior toward women. But a man's sex provides advantage for him whether or not he approves of the way in which dominance has been conferred on his group. A "white" skin in the United States opens many doors for whites whether or not we approve of the way dominance has been conferred on us. Individual acts can palliate, but cannot end, these problems. To redesign social systems, we need first to acknowledge their colossal unseen dimensions. The silences and denials surrounding privilege are the key political tool here. They keep the thinking about equality or equity incomplete, protecting unearned advantage and conferred dominance by making these taboo subjects. Most talk by whites about equal opportunity seems to me now to be about equal opportunity to try to get into a position of dominance while denying that *systems* of dominance exist.

Obliviousness about white advantage, like obliviousness about male advantage, is kept strongly inculturated in the United States so as to maintain the myth of meritocracy, the myth that democratic choice is equally available to all. Keeping most people unaware that freedom of confident action is there for just a small number of people props up those in power and serves to keep power in the hands of the same groups that have most of it already. Though systemic change takes many decades, there are pressing questions for me and I imagine for some others like me if we raise our daily consciousness on the perquisites of being light-skinned. What will we do with such knowledge? As we know from watching men, it is an open question whether we will choose to use unearned advantage to weaken invisible privilege systems and whether we will use any of our arbitrarily awarded power to try to reconstruct power systems on a broader base.

NOTES

1. This paper was presented at the Virginia Women's Studies Association conference in

Richmond in April, 1986, and the American Educational Research Association conference in Boston in October, 1986, and discussed with two groups of participants in the Dodge seminars for Secondary School Teachers in New York and Boston in the spring of 1987.

2. Andersen, Margaret, "Race and the Social Science Curriculum: A Teaching and Learning Discussion." *Radical Teacher,* November, 1984,

pp. 17–20. Smith, Lillian, *Killers of the Dream,* New York: W. W. Norton, 1949.

SOURCE: *From White Privilege and Male Privilege: A Personal Account of Coming to See Correspondences Through Work in Women's Studies* by Peggy McIntosh. Copyright © 1988 Peggy McIntosh. Permission to reprint must be obtained from author, Peggy McIntosh, Wellesley College Center for Research on Women, Wellesley, MA.

Discussion Questions

1. Why do we tend to conceptualize racism and sexism as systems of disadvantage rather than as systems of advantage? Who stands to gain, and how, by this ideological framework? When you signed up to take a course in race and ethnicity, did you ever think that one of the groups you would learn about would be whites? Why or why not?

2. Examining McIntosh's list of 46 privileges, how many had you considered before? How many had you not considered before? Do any stand out to

you in particular? Can you add more? Can you construct a similar list for male privileges?

3. What are the options the author suggests that someone can do once she or he recognizes the unearned privilege she or he receives? If people work to end negative privileges and make positive privilege exist for all, will this be enough to end inequality? Can inequality be ended through policies aimed at rectifying disadvantage, but not advantage? Why or why not?

Euphemized Racism: Moral qua Racial Boundaries

Michèle Lamont

The white professionals and managers I [interviewed] . . . in [a] previous study very rarely mentioned race when they were asked to compare themselves to others and to talk about their likes and dislikes. They were more likely to mention people like themselves, that is, white middle class people who are highly educated. Their feelings of superiority and inferiority were often organized around income and around their children's educational and occupational success. By contrast, workers read such questions as pertaining directly to race,

although I did not mention race in questioning them on these issues. . . .

This chapter will show that moral and racial boundaries are intertwined, and that white workers repeatedly and spontaneously referred to blacks when drawing moral boundaries. This pattern also generally holds when black workers discuss whites, although their racial boundaries are much weaker: while some are quite critical of whites, many offer a wide range of arguments supporting the view that races are equal. . . .

Both groups define their collective identity in opposition to one another, in an "us" versus "them" relational logic. While this relational dynamic is a well-documented feature of racism,[1] our analysis puts flesh on it by documenting inductively the building blocks of boundaries: we will see that a number of whites criticize blacks for not stressing the disciplined self they value and believe themselves to embody. In turn, blacks emphasize the caring self they privilege when evaluating whites whom they describe as domineering and egotistical: By doing so, each group places itself above the other and defines its collective identity.[2] . . .

It makes a difference that workers, whites and blacks alike, use moral criteria to evaluate the other racial group: these criteria are purportedly universalistic—that is, apply to the whole of humanity and transcend individual groups or ascribed characteristics.[3] They are an extension of the criteria workers use to evaluate everyone. . . . Thus, their racist feelings appear justified in their eyes instead of reflective of their own personal biases.[4]

To get at the boundary ideologies of whites and blacks, I asked workers to describe "my type of folks" and "the type I don't like much."[5] In analyzing the interviews, I systematically traced the relative salience of different themes in the full repertoire of arguments and types of evidence used to demonstrate that racial groups are above one another or equal—what I call their rhetoric of racism and antiracism.[6] My research contributes several novel findings. First, I document which norms whites perceive blacks as violating instead of predefining these norms, as does the survey work on this question (the symbolic racism literature in particular). Second, I provide evidence about the antiracism of ordinary white Americans, a topic unexplored to date.[7] I find that the most popular form of antiracism in academia, multiculturalism, is absent from the worldview of these

workers. Third, . . . I characterize simultaneously racist and antiracist discourse across populations and thus illuminate new aspects of racial boundary work (e.g., specific types of evidence, such as earning capacity, are used to demonstrate both racial equality and inequality). Fourth, I address another crucial, yet largely neglected, topic: how contemporary ordinary blacks construe whites and understand the differences between blacks and whites.[8] We will see that blacks employ a much broader set of arguments to demonstrate equality between the two races, perhaps in response to their everyday experience of racism. For instance, only blacks find support for equality in our common origin as children of God, our common physiology, and in a shared American citizenship. . . .

I will refer to a number of factors to explain the prevalence of moral arguments in the drawing of racial boundaries and to explain differences in the arguments used by white and black workers. I focus less on psychological factors than on how institutions such as churches, political parties, and the media shape the cultural repertoires to which blacks and whites have access. I also focus on how workers' life conditions, such as economic insecurity and the frequency of interracial encounters, lead them to draw on specific aspects of these repertoires rather than others.[9] I argue that the difficulties experienced by white workers in providing for their families and "keeping on" make them more likely to buy into the depiction of blacks by some media and politicians as violating the norms of American individualism.[10]

This chapter first examines the moral standards white workers use to evaluate blacks. . . . I show that their work ethic and the defense of traditional morality are the main criteria white workers use to place themselves above blacks. In contrast, white antiracism is primarily grounded in earning capacity and in the notion that human nature is universal, that is, that there are "good and bad people in all races." The second part of the chapter turns to blacks' perceptions of whites. Blacks point to their earning capacity, buying power, and competence (i.e., the "disciplined self") to establish racial similarity. Drawing on more collective conceptions of morality, they describe whites as domineering. In addition, they use non-moral evidence of racial equality, such as basic human needs, lineage, physiological similarities, and citizenship. . . .

WHITES ON BLACKS

The "Nigger" and "The Kind That Work Like You and Me": Work Ethic and Responsibility

Many white Americans describe blacks as lazy and irresponsible. Surveys suggest that whites' perceptions of black moral failures center first and foremost on work ethic, self-reliance, and socioeconomic status.[11] . . . Many of the white workers I interviewed associated blacks with welfare, dependency, and affirmative action, just as they think of their own identity as organized around responsibility and hard work.[12]

Vincent Marchesi, [a] white electronics technician, associates [blacks] with laziness and welfare and with claims to receiving special treatment at work, through programs such as affirmative action. He says:

> Blacks have a tendency to . . . try to get off doing less, the least possible . . . to keep the job, where whites will put in that extra oomph. . . . A lot of the blacks on welfare have no desire to get off it. Why should they? It's free money. I can't stand to see *my hard-earned money* [said with emphasis] going to pay for someone who wants to sit on his ass all day long and get free money.

Vincent's . . . self-identity as hardworking is tied to his depiction of blacks as being the opposite of himself. . . .

Other white workers complain that blacks do not want to take responsibility for their situations and that they claim special privileges because of their past exploitation. For Vincent, "you hear it on TV all the time: [blacks say] 'we don't have to do this because we were slaves 400 years ago. You owe it to us.' I don't owe you shit, period! I had nothing to do with that and I'm not going to pay for it." . . . For these white workers, their perceptions of African Americans take their meaning against the backdrop of their own incessant efforts to struggle for survival. In their view, this situation is unbearable because "not giving up" is so central to their own senses of self. They underscore a concrete link between the perceived dependency of blacks, their laziness, and the taxes that are taken from their own paychecks.

Whites also cite special privileges associated with affirmative action. . . . Whites view it as particularly unfair because they believe they can count only on themselves to get ahead in life. This is essential to their class identity as they believe that it differentiates them from the middle class: they rarely get a break and no one is trying to pass on advantages to them.[13] They are angry that they have to work harder than blacks to be promoted while they also go through great pain to remain self-reliant. . . .

The central role of work performance in the racial attitudes of whites is also supported by the claims of whites who argue for the equality of the races. They say that they have real respect for blacks who know their job and pull their weight. For instance, Joe Lasco, the Elizabeth police officer, expresses this in criticizing white southerners he knows who think that every black is a "nigger": "I tell them no. There is two different kinds. The kind that work like you and me and then you have your 'nigger.'" Men like

Joe believe they apply the same criteria of evaluation to all, criteria grounded in the universalistic principles of hard work by which they judge themselves and by which others give them status. These universal criteria lead some of these men to feel justified in evaluating blacks negatively and to perceive themselves as moral people who are not racists, but realistic.

Blacks as Collective Violators of Traditional Morality

A remarkably large number of Americans believe that . . . we are witnessing a unique crisis in black America, and that the destruction of the black family is to blame for it because "morals don't get taught." This theme is echoed by a number of moralist books published over the last few years that lament the moral crisis of society, of the black family, and "of our times,"[14] and by academic books that depict the United States as split by a deep moral divide.[15] Similarly, the workers I talked to come to the defense of traditional morality while drawing racial boundaries.

Talk of family values by politicians and other public figures offers workers important points of reference, and indeed these workers often discuss "family values," a theme central to media discourse at the time I conducted the interviews.[16] In the eyes of Stan Morley, a pipe fitter, "I could have ended up stealing cars and stuff too if I wanted. I was brought up better than that . . . I think [blacks] have less family values. . . . Today the kids, the blacks, they don't even have respect for their parents today and it's getting bad. . . ." . . .

White workers also readily associate blacks with violence. For instance, Larry Relles, the policeman . . . , explains that he is prejudiced against blacks because "it's pretty much from bad experiences through work and as a kid. Blacks were always the perpetrators of crime . . ." . . .

If white workers are so anxious about black violation of moral boundaries, it is in part because . . . they feel that their world is threatened on various fronts simultaneously. Studies have often linked racism to the dominant group's perceptions of economic threat.[17] These threats affect not only workers' economic and social position, as is generally suggested, but also their general sense of social order. . . . Workers often condemn the moral failings of blacks in the same breath that they lament the downfall of American society.

White workers frame their own racism in patriotic terms when they argue that blacks threaten what is good about American society. They are particularly upset by this because being an American is one of the few high-status characteristics they claim. . . .

My white respondents explain racial differences by a mix of natural, historical, psychological, and cultural arguments. Several suggest that laziness is part of the "nature" of blacks or comes from a culture that is so deeply ingrained and rooted in history that it is not easily changed and is passed on from one generation to the next in an almost unalterable manner.

A few workers offer genetic explanations of perceived racial differences in intelligence. For instance, a warehouse worker believes that "you can't make [blacks] learn" and that "white people pick it up much faster." Another warehouse worker believes that blacks have less practical intelligence than whites—a dimension of intelligence particularly valued by workers.

To summarize: for white workers moral and racial boundaries are inseparable from one another. Whether they focus on differences in the areas of work ethic, responsibility, family values, or traditional morality, interviewees move seamlessly from morality to race, extending their moral distinctions to broad racial categories. They view these moral boundaries as legitimate because they are based on the same *universal criteria* of evaluation that are at the center of their larger worldviews. They are thus able to make racist arguments and still feel that they are fundamentally *good, fair people.* They also avoid feelings of responsibility toward the disadvantaged while defining themselves as whites, that is, disciplined and moral. By doing so, they contribute to the formation of racial inequality.

White Antiracism: Market Arguments and the Universality of Human Nature

There are, to be sure, white workers who express antiracist positions. They privilege two types of arguments to demonstrate that whites and blacks are equal, and these have to do with earning ability and human nature.

In the American workplace, where an ideology of meritocracy prevails and where ascribed characteristics are in principle irrelevant in the assessment of employees' performances, money is often used, paradoxically, as a basis for equalization.[18] Just as racists use work ethic and self-reliance to criticize blacks, non-racists argue that earning capacity makes people equal, market mechanisms being the ultimate arbitrator of the value of people. . . . In fact, the legitimacy of earning capacity as a criterion of evaluation is one of the few assumptions shared by American racists and nonracists. . . . Having high-status occupations can make blacks equal to whites, but otherwise, at least in the eyes of John Bridges the warehouse worker, there is no such equality. He explains that "most of the black people I get along with either come from parents who are professionals or families where there were both parents. [They are] more stable. Not the street niggers. They're different. They live more off the land." This claim about racial equality, a form of antiracism, is classist as it correlates people's worth with their class position.

White workers often offer as additional evidence of the equality of races the universality of human nature across races. While racists treat the black individuals they know well—their coworkers or neighbors—as exceptions, stating that "you might not like the race but you like the person,"[19] nonracists argue that good and bad people are found in all races. In the words of Billy Taylor, the foreman in a cosmetics company, "I could have a problem with you as a black but I could have the same problem if you were white, or green, or yellow, or whatever. People are people. . . ."

These men posit that human nature is universal and that one should not generalize about blacks or any other races since there are so many differences among people.[20] . . .

Note that only one . . . respondent . . . promotes the principle of multiculturalism by celebrating the importance of "exposing our children to a diversity of people so that when they hear slurs, they can ward off these preconceptions [better] than others who don't have experience with people from different backgrounds." Cultural relativism, multiculturalism, or the celebration of racial differences, which are widely viewed in academic circles as effective antidotes to racism,[21] are absent from the worldviews of the workers with whom I spoke.[22]

Morality, Racial Boundaries, and the Broader Context

Theories of racism that emerged in the last 20 years have generally been concerned with new forms of racism that are moral in character, and that are contrasted with the old-fashioned racism prevalent under Jim Crow segregation that was more explicit and often stressed the biological inferiority of blacks. Most notably, social scientists have proposed the terms "symbolic racism"[23] . . . and "modern racism,"[24] to point out that racism now takes the following form: white Americans value individualism, self-reliance, a work ethic, obedience, and discipline, and they believe that blacks violate these values. Thus, they say that their racism is motivated not by a dislike of blacks but by a concern for key American values.[25] While these contributions all focus on the importance of whites' beliefs concerning the moral qua cultural failings of blacks, they generally posit such beliefs or predefine a few of them as particularly important.[26] My interviews complement this influential work by documenting inductively whites' perceptions of the differences between themselves and the "racial other." . . . Thus, by using as a point of departure the general moral worldviews of workers, rather than racism itself, we can get at the very framework through which they think about racial differences. . . .[27]

That white workers struggle to keep the world in moral order in the face of adversity and uncertainty explains why they would be particularly concerned with those whom they perceive as upsetting this order. That they come to single out blacks as the main source of disturbance, and that they generalize specific observations to encompass the group as a whole, has to do with a number of cultural and structural factors.

At the cultural level, guided by survey responses documenting what political platform would appeal to workers, the Republican Party has had a profound impact in influencing how this group thinks about racial differences. This party's position toward blacks resembles that of Democrat George Wallace, who combined an antigovernment position with a rejection of racial desegregation policies to win white working class votes in the sixties.[28] The ascendancy of the Republican Party in the eighties and the move of the Democratic Party to the right in the nineties meant that justifying social policies in the name of solidarity among all human beings, as promoted by progressive forces, became increasingly difficult.[29] This same Republican ascendancy has emphasized family values to attack both welfare programs and race-targeted policies. Public figures, such as political commentator Rush Limbaugh, increase the availability of a racialized moral language through the mass media.[30] This language often treats blacks as a useful explanation for all that is wrong with American society.

Some of the main characteristics of the antiracism of the workers can also be accounted for by cultural factors, such as the growing legitimacy of egalitarian strands of thought in American culture over the last 30 years. Support for egalitarianism, defined as equality in the opportunity to compete, is alive and well in American society. Indeed, 98% of whites responding to a national survey agreed with the statement "everyone in America should have equal opportunities to get ahead."[31] . . . This support for egalitarianism makes it increasingly difficult for individuals to promote old-fashioned racism that affirms biological inequality between races or to assert racial discrimination in the name of blatantly bigoted beliefs. That market performance is used as evidence of racial equality is also not surprising, given the centrality of market ideology in American society.

At the structural level, economic recession, such as that in the early 1990s, the time of the interviews, fosters among workers a sense of economic insecurity, lack of opportunity, and racial threat, especially in the context of personal and national downward mobility. The increase in black teenage pregnancy also supports the view that, demographically, blacks are "taking over" and pushing the country downhill. These structural factors, along with the relative availability of specific cultural repertoires discussed above, have combined to perpetuate to some extent the lasting impact of slavery and Jim Crow segregation on the way white Americans understand and evaluate black Americans. This structural and cultural account of the construction of blackness by white workers centers on their environment and as such eschews elements of psychological reductionism found in some influential studies of the construction of blackness.[32]

I mentioned at the beginning of the chapter that blacks play little role in the mental maps of professionals and managers. This is in part because blacks are even less present in upper middle class neighborhoods and workplaces than they are in those of white workers.[33] The low salience of blacks to professionals may also be accounted for by the fact that the latter have learned to conceal racist attitudes. This hypothesis is supported by research showing that (1) compared to the noncollege-educated, the college-educated express subtle, as opposed to blatant, racism, and hence are less likely to make explicitly racist statements[34] (and, indeed, high school graduates are repeatedly found to express more prejudiced attitudes than the college-educated);[35] and (2) opposition to race-targeted policies is weakest among the college-educated and strongest among the self-identified working class.[36]

BLACKS ON WHITES

How do blacks think about whites? This has rarely been studied. White and black folks have "stomach equality," I was told by a black textile industry worker. They have similar needs but also similar dreams: "a decent paying job, a few credit cards, a car that's decent and a nice place to live. I think people in a certain age, a certain income bracket, their thinking is just about equal or the same." . . .

These men share with the white non-racists a belief in the universality of human nature. However, they also have to confront the fact that the principles of "stomach equality" or "common human nature" do not translate into equal treatment. They turn to arguments having to do with market performance (as producers and consumers) to ground equality, making worth conditional on individual achievement and class. They also mobilize criteria of evaluation related to the "disciplined self" valued by whites, suggesting the pervasiveness of the criteria whites take to be universal. However, exemplifying the tension between assimilation and separation that has historically divided the black community, black workers also offer a critical perspective on whites by describing them as domineering and antithetical to the caring qualities blacks value. In doing so, some rebut the notion of racial inequality not by showing that races are equal but by showing that blacks are superior to whites.

"Money Makes You Equal": Earnings, Consumption, and Competence as Bases of Cultural Membership

John Lamb is a black worker employed by a recycling plant in Paterson. . . . John has often had to deal with racial discrimination at work and has given much thought to racial equality. In his theory of how the world works, money is what gives everyone voice, including blacks. He says: "Money separates people . . . It gives you power in the world, it gives you an ability to do anything you want in the world . . . That's the way the world's set up. Regardless of what you hear on this or that, money means everything." John also believes that money is the key to respect and, implicitly, to equality and social membership (i.e., to being construed as "belonging"): "If you ain't got no money, you got no respect at all. . . . Money gets you places. . . . Money's basically everything, without a doubt."

For John, competence is the other key to access to mainstream society and to social membership:

. . . once you prove yourself that you're just as good as [your white coworkers] . . . then people respect you, they kind a back away from you. I'm kind of quiet, I just go there, I don't miss a day on the job, I do what I gotta do, and I'm one of the best throughout the whole plant at what I do.

Competence is a particularly legitimate piece of evidence of equality in a blue-collar world where coworkers are often direct witnesses of each other's expertise on the job and where physical proximity leaves little room for hiding mistakes. Accordingly, skilled workers often express pride in their know-how and respect for those who do their work properly.

Tyrone Smith, a chemical plant worker, shares John's perspective, though he extends it to cultural membership and stresses consumption over production. He says:

I'm accepted [at work] and I work with really white people. I think . . . [that] it doesn't really matter [what color you are], because then the money makes it equal . . . I'm overcoming [the limits put on me because of my race] because I am achieving the same thing [as my coworkers] money-wise. If I was poor and on welfare, they would just call me another nigger on the street. I may not be as equal as them, but they know it's not too much below. If they buy a house, I could buy a house too.

It is this reasoning about money that leads Tyrone to say that class is a greater divider than race in American society. . . .

These workers put less emphasis on production than consumption as evidence of equality. Under slavery and Jim Crow, the ability to work did not give African Americans cultural, let alone civic, membership. They indeed produced but could not consume. Today, work gives access to consumption, that is, to external signals that one is "in" (a bike, new shoes, and, later, a car, a house). Working and consuming are individual strategies for coping with racism, in that they signal that one "belongs."[37]

However, these strategies of equalization perpetuate particularism, in the sense that they are unevenly spread across groups, even though they are in principle available to all.[38]

When using market performance as a criterion to establish equality, workers follow in the footsteps of black leaders . . . Indeed, both Booker T. Washington and W. E. B. Du Bois advocated work as a means to establish the worth of blacks. . . . This universalistic strategy of claiming equal status can be opposed to a particularistic one that consists of reversing the racial hierarchy "that would place formerly subordinate groups in a position of dominance over their erstwhile superior."[39] It is to this latter strategy that I now turn.

The Moral Failings of White People and the Superiority of Black People

John Lamb . . . [has] much to say about the moral flaws of white people. . . . John thinks that white people . . . are inherently domineering. Blacks, he says, "didn't create the bomb, we didn't play with gunpowder, . . . The interest of white America was always to build and be better and be competitive, and in doing that, that's more reading and sitting and studying and being more manipulative, and more deceiving, and more, you know, whereas we weren't." . . .

In describing moral differences between whites and blacks, black workers often point to whites' individualistic worldviews and their lack of caring. A truck driver contrasts the domineering tendencies of whites with the playfulness of blacks when he says that "white people are always looking for a way to beat you . . . [Blacks] enjoy having a good time, hanging out in the park, playing sports, stuff like that." . . . Blacks are also more caring and intimate, especially when compared to whites. . . . Whites' overly disciplined self is defined in opposition to "black soul," which is manifested in the black religious experience and has been defined as natural "primal spiritual energy and joy available only to members of the exclusive racial confraternity."[40]

In sum, blacks . . . define the identities of the two groups relationally, and they value most those aspects of the self that they perceive whites as valuing less. This resonates with a key finding in social psychology concerning the dynamics between in-group and out-group: one of the mechanisms by which members of stigmatized groups protect their self-esteem from negative feedback is by "selectively devaluing, or regarding as less important for their self-definition, those performance dimensions on which they or their group fare poorly and selectively valuing those dimensions on which they or their group excel."[41]

Hence, the white individualist, domineering, and disciplined self is opposed to the caring black self. These black perspectives on whites are not surprising given African Americans' experience of slavery, segregation, discrimination, and racism, which do not sustain a "kinder, gentler" view of whites. . . .

Black constructions of whites are correctly described in the historical literature as part of a process of resistance to the domination of whites.[42] However, I view them above all as an expression of blacks' sense of common identity and the standards (the "caring self") they invest in, independently of the unintended consequences of this process for resistance. These men "feel" a racial difference, and this feeling comes out of their understanding of their everyday experience and the repertoires to which they have access—such as those provided by the black nationalist movements—as much as from the need to preserve their dignity and integrity. My interviews shed light on how contemporary black resistance is framed by spelling out some of the underexplored categories through which black collective identity is defined in opposition to that of whites.[43]

How can we account for differences in the boundaries drawn by whites toward blacks and blacks toward whites that have been described so far? Social psychologists have identified fundamental psychological processes suggesting that the combination of moral and racial boundaries just described is universal: they argue that there is a universal tendency for members of all groups, including racial groups, to have in-group biases and to be discriminatory toward out-groups. There is also a tendency to attribute behavior to enduring dispositions, such as attitudes and personality traits (often moral traits), instead of to situation and to associate high-status social identity with worthiness.[44] This may explain why white workers rarely use structural explanations to account for racial differences (but not why blacks do use such explanations): white workers seldom refer to the socioeconomic situation of blacks or to their lasting experience of discrimination and white domination to explain their plight. They interpret the alleged economic "failure" of blacks as a consequence of moral failure. They use much the same explanation to account for poverty generally . . . [45] The existence of such universal psychological mechanisms, however, does not account for the specific moral themes that I have documented for whites and blacks. . . . . To account for these patterns, we have to refer to structural and cultural conditions that have characterized American . . . society over the last decades.

The institutions that played an important role in diffusing black collectivist conceptions of morality . . . have an impact here—for instance, the black church. The civil rights movement has also given blacks a collective experience of a kind that whites rarely share. Hence, the notions of solidarity and egalitarianism resonate with their shared past. Finally, the less collectivist aspects of their understanding of racial equality can also be linked to their group experience. For instance, that they use consumption (as opposed to production) as a proof of equality has to be related to the historical meaning of production for them as dislocated from citizenship.

What Brings Us Together: Children of God, Family of Man, Physiology, and Citizenship

To rebut the notion of racial inequality, blacks mobilize other pieces of evidence than those used by whites. Unlike most of the evidence analyzed so far, these are not articulated around the notions of the "disciplined self" and the "caring self" or around the notion that blacks are superior to whites. It is useful to examine these pieces of evidence because they suggest that blacks use a wider range of antiracist arguments than whites. We will see that blacks rebut racism by adopting universalistic strategies: they provide evidence having to do with whites' and blacks' shared status as children of God, common physiology, and common status as Americans. However, some also appear to take for granted the predominance of a culture of particularism when they affirm that protecting your own kind is a universal human tendency.

Reflecting on the importance of divine intervention in black narratives of emancipation, W. E. B. Du Bois pointed out that historically the church played an important role in affirming equality and providing blacks with tools for spiritual empowerment.[46] The biblical notion that "God created men equal" was also alluded to by Martin Luther King, and it rests on a notion of basic humanity for all, with love as a basis for similarity.[47] Accordingly, blacks use religion to demonstrate that we all share something fundamental.[48] . . .

[Religious] arguments are appealing to blacks in part because they offer a useful counterpoint to racist evolutionary accounts, according to which blacks are lower on the scale of human development. For instance, a photo technician combines God's creation ("we all come from Adam and Eve"), physiological evidence ("we all come out one way"), and a lineage account that stresses common descent ("family of man")[49] to refute both evolutionism and Afrocentrist views. . . . This view was not expressed among whites and goes unmentioned in survey-based studies of antiracism. . . .

African Americans also rebut racism by pointing to diversity in levels of intelligence among whites, as if they presume that they have to refute what they perceive to be the widely held notion of white intellectual superiority. . . . A phone technician . . . refers to his personal experience attending school with whites to contest the myth of their superior intelligence. He explains that . . . ". . . When I went to school, I found that there were dumb white people, you understand? There were poor white people . . . there was no differences in their learning ability. It made me proud." . . .

The Culture of Particularism

While these pieces of counterevidence to the myth of racial inequality are universalistic (in the sense that they point to what is universally common among all human beings—or all Americans), a few black workers also take for granted a culture of particularism: they do so when they explain racism by referring to the view that "preferring and protecting your own kind" is ingrained in human nature. . . . Some, like John Lamb, explain it by a need to create a pecking order: "Whites influence what district, what state, what county gets the proper money it takes to run the school system. The people you look out for is your own people. . . . Whites is going to look out for whites for schooling, and whites not going to look out for blacks." . . .

Within this culture of particularism, black workers think of racism as a universal and unavoidable phenomenon, and this reinforces a zero sum approach to group positioning: dominant groups will always maximize their position to the detriment of others, and this will occur whether whites or blacks are "on top." It is as if the discourse of universalism had not deeply penetrated the worlds inhabited by these workers, as if a number of them saw universal claims as merely rhetorical, given their own experience of America.[50] . . . Universal human rights, the American Constitution, cultural relativism, and multiculturalism are not salient in their discourse, as if they were not commonsensical realities and as if they had great cultural distance from these languages. Arguments having to do with our common lineage as children of God, the universality of our physiological needs and characteristics, and a shared American citizenship are more readily used, perhaps because they emerge from everyday experience. These latter themes were not salient among white workers, perhaps because whites do not confront the task of disproving racial inequality in their daily lives and are not forced to (or concerned with) developing a large battery of arguments. . . .

THE POLICING OF RACIAL BOUNDARIES

This chapter showed that whites and blacks alike subtly move from drawing moral boundaries to drawing racial boundaries. Whites' moral standards center around a work ethic, responsibility, and the defense of traditional morality ("family values" and anticrime). Hence, the "disciplined self" is absolutely at the center of the rationale that leads white workers to view blacks as moral violators. Similarly, blacks' condemnations of whites have to do with their perceived lack of caring and with their domineering tendencies: whites are too competitive and imperialistic and less human, caring, and spiritual than blacks.[51] They also have less moral fortitude, as illustrated by their inferior ability to handle hardship. This "us" versus "them" dynamic animated by two different conceptions of morality is closely associated with the collective identities of the two groups.

[The combination of] racist rhetoric [and] . . . moral boundaries . . . makes us understand better the internal coherence of workers' worldviews and helps us comprehend why racist views can make sense to them, given the cultural and structural contexts in which they live. This, of course, is not to justify racism. . . . However, we can see why white workers blame blacks for their lack of work ethic and violations of traditional morality: the centrality of these values in their own lives . . . , the sense of threat to their group position, the fear of being demographically outnumbered, and of losing status as Americans, as well as the cultural repertoires provided by the Republican Party, all contribute to making this possible. Similarly, a number of factors make it possible for some blacks to view whites as domineering and uncaring. These include the factors that led them to emphasize the "caring self" . . . , their common experience of slavery, segregation, and discrimination, and the continuous supply of Afrocentrist repertoires.

There are also similarities and differences in the rhetoric of antiracism used by white and black workers. White "racists" and "antiracists" as well as blacks use market performance to define worth. A notion of equality based on a common dignity as human beings is conspicuously absent from the interviews.[52] This suggests the growing influence of neoliberalism, which defines cultural membership in terms of middle class status. While white workers ground racial equality exclusively in earning capacity and the universality of human nature, blacks mobilize a much broader range of arguments to show that they are equal to whites because they are more concerned with rebutting racism than whites. Some point to their competence at work and to their own ability to earn money and consume, responding to white racism on its own terms by demonstrating a "disciplined self." Others rebut racism by showing that blacks are superior to whites because they are less domineering and more caring and "sensitive to the human thing." Yet others draw on a wide range of evidence-common lineage, physiological characteristics, *or* citizenship.

This comparative study of boundaries not only makes visible the unexplored territories of ordinary white and black antiracism: by looking specifically at how workers define similarities and differences, including racial ones, we are able to identify and explain the presence and absence of different arguments that had gone unnoticed to date. For instance, we find that whites and blacks alike use evidence drawn from everyday experience—such as the commonsensical notion that human nature is universal—to rebut the notion of racial inequality. Their rhetoric is in stark contrast with that produced in academia, and popularized by school curricula, which stresses multiculturalism. The latter appeals less to workers than to professionals due to their desire to keep the world in moral order and to distinguish clearly what is permissible and "normal" from what is not.

We are witnessing the ascendancy of the "disciplined self" over the "caring self" and collectivist logics, which shape the dominant representations of whites and blacks. The notion that whites are uncaring and domineering is not widely available in American society the way representations of blacks as lazy and violent are. Whites are in general better able to communicate through the mass media and political discourse their standards of evaluation. . . . Whites are also successful at asserting their own definition of moral legitimacy in the workplace . . .[53]

The ascendancy of these dominant criteria is revealed by surveys showing that a relatively large number of blacks agree that they are unintelligent, prefer welfare, and are hard to get along with.[54] It is also revealed by the fact that many Americans reject affirmative action in the name of individualism and oppose collective rights.[55] Such rights are in line with the collectivist logic of black solidarity. By opposing these rights, whites naturalize the ideal traits that they value most ("the disciplined self") and pressure dominated groups to adopt them.

The asymmetry in the ability of the two groups to disseminate a demonized view of the other is key to understanding the crucial role that culture plays in the reproduction of racial inequality in American society. The definitions of moral worth, on which these demonized views are based, are not only different; they also have very unequal impact on American mainstream culture. They are central to the construction of white and black racial identity and to American racism. They contribute directly to the growing inequality in the resources that whites and nonwhites have access to.[56] As taken-for-granted "cultural structures," they define the frames of human life as thoroughly as material resources.[57]

At the same time, the extent to which whites are ignorant of the complexities of black culture, and vice versa, should not be underestimated. That Craig Patterson, the assistant cable splicer, describes white people as typically having nannies is evidence of this gap, as is the dismay of the medical supply worker, Tony Clark, when he finds that his white colleagues think that he resembles the lanky television personality Arsenio Hall although he himself is fat and short. Though talk of racism is pervasive in American public discourse, it is easy to forget how little contact, overall, blacks and whites have with one another due to segregation in housing and employment. With the increase in the level of education of African Americans, many are now closer to white culture than they were 20 years ago.[58] Yet many still live in communities that are almost exclusively black and enter into contact with white culture primarily through the mass media. The relative isolation of blacks from whites and whites from blacks plays a role in sustaining racial stereotypes and an impoverishment of understanding of the culture of the other in both groups. The spatial distance reinforces a social and cultural distance that remains largely understudied, and this chapter is one step toward filling this gap.

NOTES

1. Racism is defined here as "an ethnic group's assertion of . . . a privileged or protected status vis-a-vis members of another group or groups who are thought . . . to possess a set of socially relevant characteristics that disqualify them from full membership in a community or citizenship in a nation state" (Fredrickson 1997, p. 85). Goldberg (1993, p. 98) defines racism similarly, as a rhetoric aimed at promoting exclusion based on racial membership and produced by a dominant group against a dominated group. I use the term "racist rhetoric" broadly to refer to exclusive discourse aimed at racial or ethnic groups.

On racism and the boundary between in-group and out-group or between "us" and "them," see Sumner (1906); Merton (1972); Banton (1983); Guillaumin (1972); and Memmi (1965). Social psychologists working on group categorization also focus on "us" and "them" segmentations (for instance, Moscovici 1984 and Tajfel and Turner 1985). The works of Barth (1969) and Horowitz (1985) also center on the strength of boundaries and on how feelings of communality are defined in opposition to the perceived identity of other racial and ethnic groups.

This relational approach is akin to closure approaches in the fields of nationalism, citizenship, and immigration, which attempt to establish rules of membership and boundary work (for instance,

Brubaker 1992; Favell 1997a; and Zolberg and Woon 1999). This approach is also close to that of sociologists who, following Herbert Blumer, understand racism as resulting from threats to group positioning. This approach "shifts study and analysis from a preoccupation with feelings as lodged in individuals to a concern with the relationship of racial groups . . . [and with] the collective process by which a racial group comes to define and redefine another racial group" (Blumer 1958, p. 3). Influential scholars using related approaches include Bobo and Hutchings (1996); Sidanius (1993); Feagin and Vera (1995); Rieder (1985); Roediger (1991); and Wellman (1993). On race and cultural membership, see Praeger (1987).

2. This is part of an internal identification process, which, along with group categorization, are the two processes central to the formation of group identity (Jenkins 1996).

3. Following Patterson (1977, p. 197), I define the tradition of universalism as "the idea of the brotherhood of mankind, the psychic unity of the human race, and the equality of [people's] worth."

4. A similar argument is made by Wellman (1993) and Feagin and Vera (1995).

5. Following Sniderman and Hagen (1985), I consider these descriptions of categories of individuals to be revealing of broader social and political attitudes. They write: "The average citizen, though he (or she) may know little about politics, knows whom he likes, and still more important perhaps, whom he dislikes. This can be a sufficient basis for figuring out a consistent policy stance" (p. 16). In their view this is particularly true of racial attitudes and of race-targeted policies.

Again, the bulk of the interviews I have conducted concern how individuals draw boundaries between the people they like and dislike, feel inferior and superior to, and feel similar to and different from. Respondents were encouraged to answer these questions in reference to people in general and to concrete individuals they know at work and elsewhere. Discussions of racism generally emerged while exploring these issues, but some interviewees were also probed specifically on racial differences and racism at the end of our meeting.

6. I use Aptheker's (1992) definition of anti racism as rhetoric aimed at disproving racial inferiority.

7. However, we do have a survey-based literature on whites' and blacks' accounts of racial inequality (Schuman et al. 1997); a historical literature on the struggle against racism in the abolitionist and the civil rights movements (Aptheker 1992; McAdams 1988; and McPherson 1975); and a study of contemporary antiracist organizations (Omi 1998).

8. The social-psychological and survey-based literatures on race exhibit a clear bias toward examining whites' stereotypes of racial minorities. This point is made by Sigelman and Welch (1991, p. 3); Roediger (1998); and hooks (1997). I am not aware of any contemporary ethnographic and interview-based studies of blacks' perceptions of whites beside Fordham (1996), which deals with this topic only tangentially.

9. I particularly point to competing historical frames that are part of the rhetorical resources that American society makes available to its citizens. In this, I follow Wetherell and Potter (1992, p. 197), who write that social scientists should focus not on whether there is conflict "between a feeling and a value, or between psychological drive and socially accepted expressions, or between emotions and politics, but between competing frameworks for articulating social, political, and ethical questions," such as those offered by liberal and egalitarian ideologies. Jackman (1994, p. 268) is also concerned with the importance of available repertoires for analyzing racism.

10. This argument resonates with that of Rubin (1976, p. 7), who argues that many of the behaviors and attitudes of working class individuals are realistic responses to, and results of, their structural position.

11. Using the 1990 General Social Survey, Smith (1990, p. 90) shows that blacks are perceived by whites and members of other ethnic groups as being most different from whites in their ability to be self-supporting. Along the same lines, 21 percent of non-blacks who participated in a 1993 national survey agreed that African American men enjoy living on welfare (National Conference, 1994, p. 72).

12. Similarly, Wellman (1993) shows that white racist rhetoric describes properties blacks are lacking, calls blacks responsible for current problems, and demands changes in blacks (not in whites). Contrary to Wellman, I emphasize workers' affirmation of their identity by blaming blacks rather than their defensive responses.

13. On the central role of "passing on advantages" in the reproduction of racial and class inequality, see the ongoing work of DiTomaso (2000).

14. See Bennett (1993). For a discussion of this literature, see Sandel (1996, pp. 324–328).

15. Hunter (1991; 1994) argues that American society is deeply divided between relativists and traditionalists. In contrast, sociologists like Wolfe (1997, p. 276) and DiMaggio, Evans, and Bryson (1996) argue that although Americans have moral principles for themselves, they are fairly tolerant on most moral issues. The latter study concludes that any culture war that exists in American society is largely a creation of the media and not of irreconcilable moral differences among citizens.

16. For a description of debates about family values during the Clinton administration, see Stacey (1996, chapters 3 and 4). For an analysis of the impact of conceptions of family morality on the conservative/liberal political divide, see Lakoff (1996).

17. Rieder (1985) understands the moral criticisms of blacks by middle and working class white ethnic Italians in terms of resistance to black demands. He views these criticisms as expressions of a defense of traditional values, family, and neighborhood (p. 42), a form of nostalgia (p. 93), and a desire to defend their territory in the context of more frequent physical encounters that are perceived to threaten law and order (p. 67). He suggests that for these white Italians, race is a "metaphor for vague indignities" (p. 93), which are considered to be incompatible with family life and patriotic devotion. The presence of blacks threatens their precarious middle class status (p. 97). A similar argument is made by Rubin (1994). She explains white workers' racism as a result of the anger and resentment generated by the deterioration of their condition (p. 239). See also Bobo and Hutchings (1996). My explanation for white racism is more multidimensional than those proposed by these authors as it takes into consideration the supply of cultural repertoires as well as the structural conditions that push workers to draw on aspects of these repertoires.

18. Accordingly, Simmel (1978, pp. 442–443) wrote that money is a "basically democratic leveling social form" that functions in "complete indifference to individual qualities."

19. In contrast, nonracists are not willing to generalize from the individual to the entire race—a categorization process typical of racial stereotyping (Hamilton and Trolier 1986). For a more general review of the literature on stereotyping, see Stangor and Lange (1994).

20. This position is different from rationalist universalism, which considers people to be equal because of their perfectibility and ability to make moral judgments. Patterson (1977, p. 215) links rationalist universalism to the Stoics and Alexander the Great; Alexander would have developed this notion to ground the unity of a multitude of people and races in their perfectibility through rationality.

21. On cultural relativism, see Levi-Strauss (1973, pp. 367–422) and Taguieff (1988). On multiculturalism, see Taylor (1992). For an excellent overview of American debates surrounding multiculturalism, see Lacorne (1997).

22. Along these lines, fully 65 percent of the respondents to the 1993 General Social Survey conducted by the National Opinion Research Corporation agreed or strongly agreed with the statement that "it is a shame when traditional American literature is ignored while other works are promoted because they are by women or by members of minority groups" (DiMaggio and Bryson 1995). Verter (1994) finds that the majority of Americans uphold a traditional canon to the exclusion of alternatives.

23. Symbolic racism "represents a form of resistance to change in the racial status quo based on moral feelings that blacks violate such traditional American values as individualism and self-reliance, the work ethic, obedience and discipline" (Kinder and Sears 1981, p. 416).

24. McConahay (1986) defines the principal tenets of modern racism as follows: "(1) Discrimination is a thing of the past because blacks now have the freedom to compete on the marketplace and to enjoy those things they can afford; (2) blacks are pushing too hard, too fast, and into places where they are not wanted; (3) these tactics and demands are unfair; (4) therefore recent gains are undeserved and the prestige granting institutions of society are giving blacks more attention and the concomitant status than they deserve. Two other tenets are added to this psychological syllogism: Racism is bad and the other beliefs do not constitute racism because these beliefs are empirical facts" (pp. 92–93). In an earlier text McConahay and Hough (1976) associated this form of racism not with a sense of threat to the personal welfare of whites but to fears for the survival of the nation. These fears translate into symbolic acts like voting against black candidates. For these authors, American civil Protestantism (hard work, individualism, sexual repression, delay of gratification), negative feelings toward blacks, and socialization in laissez-faire political conservatism are central in defining that which is rejected by modern racism.

25. Bobo and Smith (1998, pp. 20–21) also proposed the term "laissez-faire racism" to label new patterns of belief that involve "acceptance of negative stereotypes of African-Americans, a denial of discrimination as a current societal problem, and attribution of primary responsibility for blacks' disadvantage to blacks themselves."

26. Using Likert scales, theorists of symbolic racism measure how strongly people believe in certain statements representative of symbolic racism. McConahay and Hough (1976) identify several dimensions of symbolic racism without providing empirical evidence of their levels of salience. Elsewhere, Kinder and Sears write that symbolic racism rests on traditional Protestant values, including "hard work, individualism, thrift, punctuality, sexual repression and delay of gratification, as opposed to laziness, seeking favoritism and handouts, impulsivity, and so on" (1981, p. 72). However, the importance of these values is not documented within the context of a broader set of racial representations. In their more recent work, Kinder and Sanders (1996, p. 106) prefer the concept of racial resentment to that of racial symbolism, highlighting the notion that whites resent blacks for wanting favors while not trying hard enough. Symbolic racism is contrasted with "old-fashioned racism" through the ideas of the divine origin of racial differences, lower ability of blacks, support for housing

and school segregation, and opposition to interracial marriage (p. 26). One of the many criticisms of this theory is that "the traditional American value of individualism does not foster either antipathy to blacks or opposition to public policies intended to help them: on the other hand, traditional authoritarian values like obedience and conformity promote both" (Sniderman and Piazza 1993, p. 6).

27. Sears et al. (1997, p. 49) recognize that they have yet to unravel which nonracial dispositions are involved in symbolic racism.

28. Thompson (1998).

29. Ehrenreich (1989, chapter 3) has also argued that the Republican Party has fueled working class resentment of the new class by bringing together racism, antiintellectualism, and populism while promoting the moral concerns of the New Right relative to family values, abortion, patriotism, private schooling, and religion.

30. See also Entman (1992).

31. McClosky and Zaller (1984, p. 83). The authors do not provide information concerning the year the survey was conducted.

32. Roediger (1991, pp. 13–14) explains white workers' construction of blacks as libidinous by their need to cope with fear of dependency. In this account, workers' fear is not sufficiently grounded in the cultural and structural context in which workers live.

33. On the importance of perceptual salience in framing comparisons, see Stanger and Lange (1994). On the isolation of professionals, see Laumann (1973). Note that upper middle class isolation can encourage tolerance, indifference, or stereotyping, as it may leave individuals "susceptible to propaganda, rumor, and their own stereotypes—to 'fears of imagination,'" as Gordon Allport once put it (Kinder and Mendelberg 1995, p. 420).

34. Meertens and Pettigrew (1997, p. 67).

35. In a 1992 national survey of 800 American adults aged 18 and older, the least prejudiced group included 67 percent of those with post-graduate degrees, 54 percent of those with college degrees, and 38 percent of those with high school degrees or less (Anti-Defamation League of B'Nai B'rith 1993, p. 19).

36. Bobo and Kluegel (1993).

37. For political philosopher Judith Shklar (1991, p. 3), American citizenship has primarily involved the right to earn a living.

38. Hochschild (1995a, p. 26) describes this as a tenet of the American dream: "people start the pursuit of success with varying advantages, but no one is barred from the pursuit."

39. Meier, Rudwick, and Broderick (1971, p. II).

40. Van Deburg (1992, p. 195). This soul style is also defined in opposition to the "robot-like mannerisms of 'uptight' white people" (p. 197). On the meaning of "soul" as an expression of essential black identity and belonging, see Hannerz (1968).

41. The Washington, DC, African-American high school students studied by Fordham and Ogbu (1986) also point to the disciplined self of whites when they define the meaning of "acting white." Indeed, these students view the following behaviors as distinctively white: spending a lot of time in the library studying, working hard to get good grades in school, getting good grades in school, and being on time. Other cultural practices labeled "acting white" include listening to white music, classical music, and white radio stations, having a party with no music, going to the opera, ballet, and the Smithsonian, reading and writing poetry, going to a Rolling Stones concert at the Capital Center, doing volunteer work, camping, hiking, or mountain climbing, having cocktails or a cocktail party, speaking standard English, and putting on airs. The authors of the study argue that blacks "develop a sense of collective identity and a sense of people-hood in opposition to the social identity of white Americans because of the way white Americans treat them in economic, political, social, and psychological domains." See also Fordham (1996).

42. Classical discussions of resistance in the context of black/white relations are found in Levine (1977); Lewis (1991); and Stuckey (1987). Building on the work of Williams (1980), it has been suggested that black popular culture is more alternative than oppositional, since it generally does not attack the social hegemony of whites.

43. My findings complement those of historian Robin Kelley, Jr. (1994) and others who have advocated the importance of analyzing black identity by considering how feelings of mutuality and fellowship were constructed and what is viewed as distinctively black by blacks. This includes pleasures derived from black popular culture (p. 45).

44. Brewer's (1986) social identity theory suggests that "[p]ressures to evaluate one's own group positively through in-group/out-group comparison lead social groups to attempt to differentiate themselves from each other." This process of differentiation aims "to maintain and achieve superiority over an out-group on some dimension" (Tajfel and Turner 1985, pp. 16–17). Sidanius (1993) argues that this in-group bias operates more for higher status groups than for lower status ones.

45. This resonates with Newman's (1993) study of downward mobility among New Jersey residents. She writes: "American culture is allergic to the idea that impersonal forces control individual destiny. Rather we prefer to think of our lives as products of our own efforts. Through hard work, innate ability, and competition, the good prosper and the weak drop by the wayside. Accordingly, the end results in peoples' lives—their occupation, material possessions, and the recognition accorded by friends and associates—are proof of the underlying stuff of which they are made. Of course, when the fairy tale comes true, the flip side of meritocratic individualism emerges with full force. Those who prosper— the morally superior—deserve every bit of their material comfort" (p. 89).

46. Du Bois (1935, p. 124). Cited by Kelley (1994, p. 42). See also Harding (1981).

47. Condit and Lucaites (1993, p. 192).

48. Lincoln and Mamiya (1990, p. 4) describe differences in emphasis in black and white worship by pointing to "the greater weight given [by blacks] to the biblical view of the importance of human personality and human equality implicit in 'children of God.' The trauma of being officially defined by the U.S. Constitution as 'three-fifths' human and treated in terms of that understanding, the struggle of the African-American people to affirm and establish their humanity and their worth as persons has a long history."

49. Miles (1989, chapter I) suggests that this account gained in popularity between the sixteenth and nineteenth centuries, after which it was superseded by scientific racism viewing the human species as divided into permanent and discrete groups.

50. The term "universalism" is used differently across sociological literatures. The functionalist literature compares cultural orientations cross-nationally using the "universalistic/particularistic" pattern variable. Universalists believe that "all people shall be treated according to the same criteria (for instance, equality in and before the law)," while particularists believe that "individuals shall be treated differently according to their personal qualities or their particular membership in a class or group" (Lipset 1979, p. 209). In the French literature on racism, universalism is opposed not to particularism but to differentialism. For instance, Taguieff (1988, p. 164) opposes a universalistic racism (which posits that *we* are the humanity) and a differentialist racism (which posits that *we* are the best). The anthropological literature opposes a universalism that declares an absolute and shared human essence—including the Enlightenment notions of freedom and equality—to a relativism that affirms the diversity of cultural identities. Finally, the philosophical literature juxtaposes a universalism defined through shared moral orientations or Platonic ideals (the good, the right, the just) and communitarianism, which stresses moral norms that emerge from the collective life of groups (see, for instance, Rasmussen 1990).

51. As suggested by Scott (1985), morality provides individuals in dominating positions with suitable tools to confront and adapt to their situations.

52. For a discussion of the meaning of egalitarianism in American political culture, see McClosky and Zaller (1984, chapter 3). These authors show that even in the late seventies Americans tended to interpret the egalitarian principle as having more to do with equality of opportunity than with equality as resulting from a common humanity (p. 74).

53. Kirschenman and Neckerman (1990).

54. In a survey based on a large sample of whites, blacks, Hispanics, and Asians residing in Los Angeles, respondents were asked to rate each ethnic group according to these criteria, with a high score reflecting more prejudice. Blacks rate themselves at 3.60 for "unintelligent"; blacks received scores of 3.77 from Hispanics, 4.05 from whites, and 4.27 from Asians. On the welfare issue, blacks gave themselves a score of 3.98 and received scores of 4.10 from whites, 0.84 from Asians, and 5.22 from Hispanics. In terms of difficulty to get along with, blacks gave themselves a score of 3.57 and received

scores of 3.81 from whites, 4.02 from Asians, and 4.55 from Hispanics (Bobo and Zubrinski 1996).

55. Jackman (1994, pp. 73–93 and 314). For this analysis as it applies to reactions to the civil rights movement, see Omi and Winant (1986, p. 126).

56. On the widening inequality of wealth between whites and nonwhites between 1983 and 1990, see Wolff (1995).

57. To paraphrase Durkheim (1965).

58. The college-educated population continues to show a high degree of similarity in its cultural practices and attitudes over a wide range of areas. See Collins (1979) and Davis (1982). Eleven percent of blacks had a college degree in 1990, compared to 22 percent of whites (United States Bureau of Census of Population 1990b, pp. 151–154).

REFERENCES

Anti-Defamation League of B'Nai B'rith. 1993. "Highlights from an Anti-Defamation League Survey on Racial Attitudes in America." New York: Unpublished report.

Apetheker, Herbert. 1992. *Anti-Racism in U. S. History: The First Two Hundred Years.* New York: Greenwood.

Banton, Michael. 1983. *Racial and Ethnic Competition.* Cambridge, UK: Cambridge University Press.

Barth, Fredrik. 1969. "Introduction." In *Ethnic Groups and Boundaries: The Social Organization of Culture Difference,* edited by Fredrik Barth, pp. 9–38. London: George Allen and Unwin.

Bennett, William J. 1993. *The Book of Virtues: A Treasury of Great Moral Stories.* New York: Simon and Schuster.

Blumer, Herbert. 1958. "Race Prejudice as a Sense of Group Position." *Pacific Sociological Review* 1:3–7.

Bobo, Lawrence, and Camille L. Zubrinksi. 1996. "Attitudes on Residential Integration: Perceived Status Differences, Mere In-Group Preference, or Racial Prejudice?" *Social Forces* 74(3): 883–909.

Bobo, Lawrence, and James R. Kluegel. 1993. "Opposition to Race-Targeting: Self-Interest, Stratification Ideology, or Racial Attitudes?" *American Sociological Review* 58:443–464.

Bobo, Lawrence, and Ryan A. Smith. 1994. "Antipoverty Policy, Affirmative Action, and Racial Attitudes." In *Confronting Poverty: Prescriptions for Change,* edited by Sheldon H. Danzinger, Gary D. Sandefur, and Daniel H. Weinberg, pp. 365–395. New York: Russell Sage Foundation.

Bobo, Lawrence, and Vincent L. Hutchings. 1996. "Perceptions of Racial Group Competitions: Extending Blumer's Theory of Group Position to a Multiracial Social Context." *American Sociological Review* 61(6): 951–972.

Brewer, Marilynn B. 1986. "The role of Ethnocentrism in Intergroup Conflict. In *Psychology of Intergroup Relations,* edited by Stephen Worchel and William G. Austin, pp. 88–102. Nelson-Hall Publishers.

Brubaker, Rogers. 1992. *Citizenship and Nationhood in France and Germany.* Cambridge: Harvard University Press.

Collins, Randall. 1979. *The Credential Society.* New York: Academic Press.

Condit, Celeste Michelle, and John Louis Lucaites. 1993. *Crafting Equality: America's Anglo-African Word.* Chicago: University of Chicago Press.

Davis, James. 1982. "Achievement Variables and Class Cultures: Family, Schooling, Jobs and Forty-Nine Dependent Variables in the Cumulative GSS." *American Sociological Review* 47: 569–586.

DiMaggio, Paul and Bethany Bryson. 1995. "Americans' Attitudes towards Cultural Diversity and Cultural Authority; Culture Wars, Social Closure, or Multiple Dimensions. General Social Survey Topical Report no. 27. Chicago: National Opinion Research Center.

DiMaggio, Paul, John Evans, and Bethany Bryson. 1996. "Have Americans' Social Attitudes Become More Polarized?" *American Journal of Sociology* 102(3): 690–755.

DiTomaso, Nancy. 2000. "Why Anti-Discrimination Policies Are Not Enough: The Legacies and

Consequences of Affirmative Inclusion for Whites." Paper presented at the meeting of the American Sociological Association, Washington D.C., August 12–16.

Du Bois, W. E. B. 1935. *Black Reconstruction in America: An Essay toward a History of the Part Which Black Folk Played in the Attempt to Reconstruct Democracy in America, 1860–1880.* New York: Harcourt Brace.

Durkheim, Emile. 1965. *The Elementary Forms of Religious Life.* New York: The Free Press.

Ehrenreich, Barbara. 1989. *Fear of Falling: The Inner Life of the Middle Class.* New York: Pantheon Books.

Entman, Robert. 1992. "Blacks in the News: Television, Modern Racism, and Cultural Change." *Journalism Quarterly* 69(2): 341–361.

Favell, Adrian. 1997a. *Philosophies of Integration: Immigration and the Idea of Citizenship in France and Britain* London: MacMillan.

Feagin, Joe R. and Hernan, Vera. 1995. *White Racism: The Basics.* New York: Routledge.

Fordham, Signithia, and John Ogbu. 1986. "Black Students' School Success: Coping with the Burden of 'Acting White,'" *Urban Review* 18(3): 176–206.

Fordham, Signithia. 1996. *Blacked Out: Dilemmas of Race, Identity and Success at Capital High.* Chicago: University of Chicago Press.

Fredrickson, George. 1997. "Race and Empire in Liberal Thought: The Legacy of Tocqueville." In *The Comparative Imagination: On the History of Racism, Nationalism, and Social Movements,* edited by George Fredrickson, pp. 98–116. Berkeley: University of California Press.

Goldberg, David. 1993. *Racist Culture: Philosophy and the Politics of Meaning.* New York: Blackwell.

Guillaumin, Colette. 1972. *L'idéologie raciste: Genèse et langage actuel.* Paris/La Haye: Mouton.

Hamilton, David, and Tina Trolier. 1986 "Stereotypes and Stereotyping: An Overview of the Cognitive Approach." In *Prejudice, Discrimination, and Racism,* edited by John F. Dovidio and Samuel L. Gaertner, pp. 127–164. New York: Academic Press.

Hannerz, Ulf. 1968. "The Rhetoric of Soul: Identification in Negro Society." *Race* 9(4): 453–465.

Harding, Vincent. 1981. *There Is a River: The Black Struggle for Freedom in America.* New York: Harcourt Brace Jovanovich.

Hochschild, Jennifer L. 1995a. *Facing Up to the American Dream: Race, Class, and the Soul of the Nation.* Princeton: Princeton University Press.

hooks, bell. 1997. "Representing Whiteness in the Black Imagination." In *Displacing Whiteness: essays in Social and Cultural Criticism,* edited by Ruth Frankenburg, pp. 165–179. Durham: Duke University Press.

Horowitz, Donald L. 1985. *Ethnic Groups in Conflict.* Berkeley: University of California Press.

Hunter, James Davison. 1991. *Culture War: The Struggle to Define America.* New York: Basic Books.

———. 1994. *Before the Shooting Begins: Searching for Democracy in America's Culture War.* New York: Free Press.

Jackman, Mary R. 1994. *The Velvet Glove: Paternalism and Conflict in Gender, Class, and Race Relations.* Berkeley: University of California Press.

Jenkins, Richard. 1996. *Social Identity.* London: Routledge.

Kelley, Robin D. G. 1994. *Race Rebels: Culture, Politics and the Black Working Class.* New York: Free Press.

Kinder, Donald R., and David O. Sears. 1981. "Prejudice and Politics: Symbolic Racism versus Racist Threats to the Good Life." *Journal of Personality and Social Psychology* 40(3): 414–431.

Kinder, Donald R., and Tali Mendelberg. 1995. "Cracks in American Apartheid: The Political Impact of Prejudice among Desegregated Whites." *Journal of Politics* 57(2): 402–424.

Kirschenman, Joleen, and Kathryn M. Neckerman. 1990. "'We'd Love to Hire Them , but . . . ': The Meaning of Race for Employers." In *The Urban Underclass,* edited by Christopher Jencks and Paul E. Peterson, pp. 203–233. Washington, D.C.: Brookings Institute.

Lacorne, Denis. 1997. *Le crise de l'identité américaine: Du melting-pot au multiculturalisme.* Paris: Fayard.

Laumann, Edward O., ed. 1973. *Bonds of Pluralism: The Form and Substance of Urban Social Networks.* New York: John Wiley.

Levine, Lawrence. 1977. *Black Culture and Black Consciousness: Afro-American Folk thought from Slavery to Freedom.* New York: Oxford University Press.

Lévi-Strauss, Claude. 1973. *L'anthropologie structurale,* vol. II. Paris: Plon.

Lewis, Earl. 1991. *In Their own Interests: Race, Class, and Power in Twentieth Century Norfork, Virginia.* Berkeley: University of California Press.

Lincoln, C. Eric, and Lawrence H. Mamiya. 1990. *The Black Church in African American Experience.* Durham: Duke University Press.

Lipset, Seymour Martin. 1979. *The First New Nation: The United States in Historical and Comparative Perspective.* New York: Norton.

McAdams, Doug. 1988. *Freedom Summer.* New York: Oxford University Press.

McClosky, Herbert, and John Zaller. 1984. *The American Ethos: Public Attitudes toward Capitalism and Democracy.* Cambridge, MA: Harvard University Press.

McConahay, John B. 1986. "Modern Racism, Ambivalence, and the Modern Racism Scale." In *Prejudice, Discrimination, and Racism,* edited by Samuel L. Gaertner and John F. Dovidio, pp. 91–126. New York: Academic Press.

McConahay, John B. and Joseph C. Hough, Jr. 1976. "Symbolic Racism." *Journal of Social Issues* 32(2): 23–45.

McPherson, James M. 1975. *The Abolitionist Legacy: From Reconstruction to the NAACP.* Princeton, NJ: Princeton University Press.

Meertens, Roel W., and Thomas F. Pettigrew. 1997. "Is Subtle Prejudice Really Prejudice?" *Public Opinion Quarterly* 61:54–71.

Meier, August, Elliott Rudwick, and Francis L. Broderick. 1975. *Black Protest Thought in the Twentieth Century.* Indianapolis: Bobbs-Merrill Co.

Memmi, Albert. 1965. *The Colonizer and the Colonized.* Boston: Beacon Press.

Merton, Robert K. 1972. "Insiders and Outsiders: A Chapter in the Sociology of Knowledge." *American Journals of Sociology* 18: 9–47.

Miles, Robert. 1989. *Racism.* New York: Routledge.

Moscovici, Serge. 1984. 'The Phenomenon of Social Representations." In *Social Representations,* edited by Robert M. Farr and Serge Moscovici, pp. 3–69. Cambridge, UK: Cambridge University Press.

National Conference of Christians and Jews. 1994. "Taking America's Pulse: The Full Report of the National Conference Survey on Inter-Group Relations." New York: National Conference of Christians and Jews.

Newman, Katherine. 1993. *Declining Fortunes: The Withering of the American Dream.* New York: Basic.

Omi, Michael, and Howard Winant. 1986. *Racial Formation in the United States from the 1960s to the 1980s.* New York: Routledge.

Omi, Michael. 1998. "(E)racism: Emergent Practices of Anti-Racist Organizations." Paper presented at the meeting of the American Sociological Association, San Francisco, August.

Patterson, Orlando. 1977. "The Universal and the Particular in Western Social Thought." In *Ethnic Chauvinism: The Reactionary Impulse,* pp. 197–229. New York: Stein and Dayle.

Praeger, Jeffery. 1987. "American Political Culture and the Shifting Meaning of Race." *Ethnic and Racial Studies* 10(1): 62–81.

Rasmussen, David, ed. 1990. *Universalism vs. Communitarianism. Contemporary Debates in Ethics.* Cambridge, Mass.: MIT Press.

Rieder, Johnathan. 1985. *Canarsie: The Jews and Italians of Brooklyn and Liberalism.* Cambridge: Harvard University Press.

Roediger, David. 1991. *The Wages of Whiteness: Race and the Making of the American Working Class.* London: Verso.

———. 1998. *Black on White: Black Writers on What It Means to Be White.* New York: Schocken Books.

———. 1994. *Families on the Faultline: America's Working Class Speaks about the Family, the*

Economy, Race, and Ethnicity. New York: HarperCollins.

Rubin, Lillian B. 1976. *Worlds of Pain: Life in the Working Class Family.* New York: Basic Books.

Sandel, Michael J. 1996. *Democracy's Discontent: America in Search of a Public Philosophy.* Cambridge: Harvard University Press.

Schumann, Howard, Charlotte Steeh, Lawrence Bobo, and Maria Krysan. 1997. *Racial Attitudes in America: Trends and Interpretation,* rev. ed. Cambridge: Harvard University Press.

Scott, James C. 1985. *Weapons of the Weak.* New Haven: Yale University Press.

Sears, David O., Colette Van Laar, Mary Carillo, and Rick Kosterman. 1997. "Is It Really Racism? The Origins of White Americans' Opposition to Race-Targeted Policies." *Public Opinion Quarterly* 61:16–53.

Shklar, Judith N. 1991. *American citizenship: The Quest for Inclusion.* Cambridge, Mass: Harvard University Press.

Sidanius, James. 1993. "The Psychology of Group Conflict and the Dynamics of Oppression: A Social Dominance Perspective." In *Explorations in Political Psychology,* edited by Shanto Iyengar and William McGuire, pp. 183–219. Durham: Duke University Press.

Sigelman, Lee, and Susan Welch. 1991. *Black Americans' Views of Racial Inequality: A Dream Deferred.* Cambridge: Cambridge University Press.

Simmel, Georg. 1978. *The Philosophy of Memory.* Boston: Routledge and Kegan Paul.

Smith, Tom W. 1990. *Ethnic Images.* GSS Topical Report no. 19. Chicago: National Opinion Research Center, University of Chicago.

Sniderman, Paul M., and with Michael Gray Hagen. 1985. *Race and Inequality: A Study in American values.* Chatham, NJ: Chatham House Publishers.

Stacey, Judith. 1996. *In the Name of the Family: Rethinking Family Values in the Postmodern Age.* Boston: Beacon Press.

Stangor, Charles, and James E. Lange. 1994. "Mental Representations of Social Groups: Advances in Understanding Stereotypes and Stereotyping." *Advances in Experimental Social Psychology* 26:357–416.

Stuckey, Sterling. 1987. *Slave Culture: Nationalist Theory and the Foundation of Black America.* New York: Oxford University Press.

Sumner, William Graham. 1906. *Folkways.* New York: Ginn.

Taguieff, Pierre-André. 1988. *La force du préjugé: Essai sure le racisme et ses doubles.* Paris: La Découverte.

Tajfel, Henri, and John C. Turner. 1985. "The Social Identity Theory of Intergroup Behavior." In *Psychology of Intergroup Relations,* edited by Stephen Worchel and William G. Austin, pp. 7–24. Chicago: Nelson-Hall.

Taylor, Charles. 1992. "The Politics of Recognition." In *Multiculturalism: Examining the Politics of Recognition,* Edited by Charles Taylor and Amy Gutmann, pp. 25–74. Princeton: Princeton University Press.

Thompson, J. Phillip III. 1998. "Universalism and Deconcentration: Why Race Still Matters in Poverty and Economic Development." *Politics and Society* 26(2):181–219.

United States Bureau of the Census of Population. (1990b). *Statistical Abstracts of the United States 1990,* 110th ed. Washington, D.C.: U.S. Government Printing Office.

Van Deburg, William L. 1992. *New Day in Babylon: The Black Power Movement and American Culture, 1965–1975.* Chicago: University of Chicago Press.

Verter, Bradford. 1994. "Aiming the Canon: A preliminary Investigation into the Determinants of Public Opinion in the Curriculum Debate." Paper presented at the meeting of the American Sociological Association, Los Angeles.

Wellman, David. 1993. *Portraits of White Racism,* 2nd ed. New York: Cambridge University Press.

Wetherell, Margaret, and Jonathan Potter. 1992. *Mapping the Language of Racism: Discourse and the Legitimation of Exploitation.* New York: Harvester Wheatsheaf.

Williams, Raymond. 1980. "Base and Superstructure in Marxist Cultural Theory." In *Problems in Materialism and Culture: Selected Essays,* pp. 31–49. London: Verso.

Wolff, Edward N. 1995. *Top Heavy: A Study of the Increasing Inequality of Wealth in America.* New York: Twentieth Century Fund Press.

Zollberg, Aristide R., and Long Litt Woon. 199. "Why Islam Is Like Spanish: /Cultural Incorporation in Europe and the United States." *Politics and Society* 27 (1): 5–38.

SOURCE: From *The Dignity of Working Men: Morality and the Boundaries of Race, Class and Immigration* by Michele Lamont. Copyright © 2000 by The Russell Sage Foundation. Co-published with Harvard University Press. Reprinted with permission.

DISCUSSION QUESTIONS

1. When examining the quotes from white working class respondents, how would you say the language and rhetoric of racism differ from that of more formally educated, middle- to upper-class whites (like those featured in "I Am Not a Racist But . . ." in Chapter 5, for example)? In what ways is the discourse of racism similar across class lines for whites despite some of these above-discussed differences?

2. What kinds of arguments do white workers make for an antiracist worldview, and how do they differ from those made in the middle- to upper-class environment of academia?

3. How does the issue of "morals" enter into the transmission of racism, and how does the concept of "morals" differ depending on whether black workers or white workers are discussing it?

4. Why does the author describe black workers' construction of whites' morality as an act of resistance?

5. How might gender be coming into play with these male workers as they construct who is morally superior along racial lines? Does the notion of a "good provider" role for males factor into the moral evaluations discussed here? How might moral assessments of racial "others" be differently articulated if those being alternatively critiqued and praised for their "morals" or lack thereof were female rather than male? What commonalities and differences might white and black female workers see in each other?

CURRENT DEBATES

THE RACIAL IDENTITIES OF WHITES AND BLACKS

Earlier, we referred to the merging of the separate white ethnic identities (Irish American, Polish American, Italian American, and others) into a single, all-encompassing, generalized "European American" identity. In the selections below, we go beyond this assimilative process to consider some broader issues of racial identity in the United States today. A growing number of scholars have been exploring contemporary white racial identity, examining its nature and analyzing how it differs from the racial identity of nonwhites. In the first selection, Dyer argues that whites see themselves in nonracial terms, as the norm against which all other groups are compared. The perception of whiteness as "normal" distances all other groups and reinforces the power relationships that have dominated American society virtually since its inception.

Waters points out that "symbolic ethnicity," the ability to choose the extent to which one identifies with one's ancestral groups, is a luxury available only to whites. Members of racial and colonized groups are not free to excuse themselves from their groups, and those memberships continue to shape and limit their lives. Furthermore, argues Waters, the way whites think about their own ethnicity limits their ability to understand the situation and reactions of non-whites, even when they are motivated by genuine acceptance of and interest in members of other groups.

Unlike other Current Debates, these selections are not opposed to each other. Rather, both challenge some "taken-for-granted" assumptions that are deeply embedded in the consciousness of white Americans, including, increasingly, the descendants of the white ethnic groups.

THE NEED TO UNDERSTAND WHITENESS

Richard Dyer

Racial imagery is central to the organization of the modern world. . . . Whose voices are listened to at international gatherings, who bombs and who is bombed, who gets what jobs, housing, access to health care and education . . . these are all largely inextricable from racial imagery. . . . Race is not the only factor governing these things . . . but it is never not a factor, never not in play. . . .

There has been an enormous amount of analysis of racial imagery in the past decades. . . . Yet, until recently, a notable absence from such work has been the study of images of white people. Indeed, to say that one is interested in race has come to mean that one is interested in any racial imagery other than that of white people.

This essay is about the racial imagery of white people. . . . This is not done merely to fill a gap in the analytical literature, but because there is something at stake in looking at . . . white racial imagery. As long as race is something only applied to non-white peoples, as long as white people are not racially seen and named, they/we function as a human norm. Other people are raced, we are just people. There is no more powerful position than that of being "just" human. The claim to power is the claim to speak for the commonality of humanity. Raced people can't do that—they only speak for their own race.

The sense of white as non-raced is most evident in the absence of reference to whiteness in the habitual speech and writing of white people. . . . Whites will speak of, say, the blackness or Chineseness of friends, neighbors, colleagues . . . and it may be in the most genuinely friendly and accepting manner, but we don't mention the whiteness of white people we know. An old style white comedian will often start a joke: "There's this bloke walking down the street and he meets a black geezer," never thinking to race the bloke as well as the geezer. . . .

The assumption that white people are just people, which is not far off from saying that whites are people whereas other colors are something else, is endemic to white culture. . . . The invisibility of whiteness as a racial position in white (which is to say dominant) discourse is of a piece with its ubiquity. . . . Whites are everywhere in representation. Yet precisely because of this and their placing as the norm they seem not to be represented to themselves as whites but as people who are variously gendered, classed, sexualized, and abled. At the level of racial representation, in other words, whites are not of a certain race, they're just the human race. . . .

This is why it is important to come to see whiteness. . . . [As] long as whiteness is felt to be the human condition, then it alone defines normality. . . . [The] equation of being white with being human secures a position of power. White people have power and believe that they think, feel, and act like and for all people; white people, unable to see their particularity, cannot take account of other people's [particularity].... White power ... reproduces itself ... overwhelmingly because it is not seen as whiteness but as normal. White people need to learn to see themselves as white, to see their particularity. In other words, whiteness needs to be made strange.

SOURCE: From *White: Essays on Race and Culture* by Richard Dyer. Copyright © 1987. Reprinted by permission of Routledge.

SYMBOLIC AND INVOLUNTARY ETHNICITY

Mary Waters

[Symbolic ethnicity is] confined to White Americans of European origin. Black Americans, Hispanic Americans, Asian Americans, and American Indians do not have the option of a symbolic ethnicity at present.... For all of the ways in which ethnicity does not matter for White Americans, it does matter for non-Whites. Who your ancestors are does affect your choice of spouse, where you live, what job you have, who your friends are, and what your chances are for success in American society, if those ancestors happen not to be from Europe. The reality is that White ethnics have a lot more choice and room to maneuver than they themselves think they do. The situation is very different for members of racial minorities, whose lives are strongly influenced by their race or national origin regardless of how much they choose to identify themselves in terms of their ancestries.

When white Americans learn the stories of how their [ancestors] triumphed ... over adversity, they are usually told in terms of their individual efforts.... The important role of labor unions and other organized political and economic factors in their social and economic success are left out of the story in favor of a story of individual Americans rising up against ... Old World intolerance and New World resistance. As a result, the "individualized" voluntary, cultural view of ethnicity for Whites is what is remembered....

The symbolic ethnic tends to think that all groups are equal: Everyone has a background that is their right to celebrate and pass on to their children. This leads to the conclusion that all identities are equal.... The important thing is to treat people as individuals and all equally. However, this assumption ignores the very big difference between an individualistic symbolic identity and a socially enforced and imposed racial identity.... When White Americans equate their own symbolic ethnicities with the socially enforced identities of non-White Americans, they obscure the fact that the experiences of Whites and non-Whites have been qualitatively different ... and that the current identities of individuals partly reflect their unequal history....

An example of the kind of misunderstanding that can arise because of the different understandings of the meaning and implications of symbolic versus [involuntary] identities concerns questions [college] students ask one another ... in the dorms about personal appearance and customs. A very common type of interaction in the dorms concerns questions Whites ask Blacks about their hair.... Whites are generally quite curious about Black student's hair [and] wonder to themselves whether they should ask ... questions. One thought experiment Whites perform is to ask themselves whether a particular question would upset them. Adopting a "do unto others" rule, they ask themselves, "If a Black person was curious about my hair would I get upset?" The answer is usually "No, I would be happy to tell them." [So, assuming that everyone would be equally open, they proceed to ask their questions and are surprised when their] innocent questions . . . lead to resentment. The . . . stereotypes about Black Americans and the assumption that all Blacks are alike . . . has . . . power to hurt and offend a Black person.

The innocent questions about Black hair also bring up the asymmetries between Black and White experience. Because Blacks tend to have more knowledge about Whites than vice versa, there is not an even exchange going on. . . . Because of the [historical] differences [between the groups], there are some connotations to Black hair that don't exist about White hair. (For instance, is straightening your hair a form of assimilation, . . . How is this related to looking "White"?) Finally, even a Black student who cheerfully disregards . . . these asymmetries will soon slam into another asymmetry if she willingly answers every innocent question asked of her. In a situation where Blacks make up only 10 percent of the student body, if every non-Black needs to be educated about hair, she will have to explain it to nine other students. As one Black student explained to me, after you've been asked a couple of times about something so personal you begin to feel like you are an attraction in a zoo, that you are at the university for the education of White students.

SOURCE: Originally titled "Optional Ethnicities: For Whites Only?" from *Origins and Destinies: Immigration, Race and Ethnicity in America,* 1st ed., edited by Sylvia Pedraza and Rueben Rumbaut. Copyright © 1996. Reprinted with permission of Wadsworth, a division of Thomson Learning: www.thomsonrights.com. Fax 800-730-2215.

DEBATE QUESTIONS TO CONSIDER

1. Is Dyer right about the tendency to "race" only nonwhites? Can you detect this pattern in the everyday conversations of people around you? What are the implications of this tendency for people's perceptions of each other and the possibilities for honest, clear communication across group lines? What does he mean when he says that we need to make whiteness strange?

2. Can you extend Dyer's point to gender relations? Do only females have gender? How?

3. Is Waters saying that it's wrong to treat people equally and as individuals? How can it be wrong to be "color-blind"? What does she mean by the distinction she makes between an "individualistic symbolic identity" and an "imposed racial identity"?

Part IV

CONCLUSIONS

11

ANTIRACIST AND FEMINIST SOLUTIONS

Courses about inequality often leave students feeling depressed about the state of dominant-minority relations. Often the problems have been going on for much longer, and are much more widespread, than many students have considered or believed. In this final chapter, we present a diversity of writings that consider possible solution strategies for the problems of sexism and racism that we have encountered throughout this book. Obviously, there is no single answer, and scholars and activists alike have struggled with different approaches to ending inequality. In introducing just a few key perspectives here, we hope to invite you as the reader to consider where you fit into the struggle to end oppression, and what measures you might be willing to support to this end. In this way, we can end on a positive, proactive note rather than one of despair and inaction.

The first reading comes from legal scholar Patricia Williams. Williams makes it clear that any strategy of color blindness is a "childish" fiction. Using various examples from her life as an African American woman living in U.S. society, she demonstrates how color blindness is a myth that we prop up to pretend we do not see differences. Although she agrees that color blindness is an eventual ideal, she argues that we must first start where we are by acknowledging our different histories and the reality of the power that separates us. In other words, we must begin with looking at color in order to get to the point where color no longer matters. Williams concludes by reviewing some common excuses people use to assert that racism is permanent and therefore unsolvable. She challenges these positions, and suggests some ways to begin approaching solutions.

Although he is also an African American legal scholar, Derrick Bell, author of the second reading, takes a different position by asserting the permanence of racism in U.S. society. Bell uses a writing style from the "critical race studies" approach that appears in law journals, in which legal points are laid out in dialogue between fictional characters. In this selection, the narrator is questioning "Geneva" about a policy proposal she has created called the "Racial Preference Licensing Act," and the rationale behind it. Through the discussion, Bell points out that racism is maintained not only through overt acts of exclusion, but through whites' "racial nepotism," whereby they hire and promote individuals with whom they feel more comfortable—namely, other whites. Rather than assuming whites are predominantly nondiscriminating and structuring the law to punish the occasional aberration of discrimination, Bell suggests a different approach, which acknowledges that racial nepotism is the norm. With the Racial Preference Licensing Act, individual places of business purchase a license that will allow them to maintain racially segregated workplaces, hiring people only like themselves, for a fee that will be put toward educational and economic opportunities for people of color. Bell's innovative approach comes out of recognizing that through these several decades of civil rights legislation, rampant discrimination has continued to occur, only now under the guise of "equal opportunity for all." He echoes the sentiment of many people of color that overt racism is sometimes preferable to the subtle modern racism of today, because at least people of color know whom to avoid. With the racial preference license, that would be very clear. Rather than wasting any more time changing white hearts, from a realist position Bell deals solely with actions—actions he argues will help people of color directly, unlike the poorly enforced civil rights legislation currently in use.

Bell's permanence of racism thesis is often characterized as cynical, yet often those who have worked within public policy circles come to such a position through their real experiences in such venues. One such experience is chronicled through the next reading, coauthored by two white pro-feminists, one a pro-labor sociologist and the other an activist with the Feminist Majority Foundation. Ronnie Steinberg and Jennifer Hickman chronicle one of the pioneering struggles to correct for sex and race inequality in earnings—comparable worth in New York state. As academics in university classrooms, we often consider solutions for inequality in the abstract, but this particular reading engages us to envision the power struggles inherent in implementing such solutions. In particular, we see that a feminist organization must engage other key players that do not always share their interests. Indeed, any entity attempting to address inequality must enlist allies outside of its sphere of influence. They rarely possess enough societal power to do it alone. Steinberg and Hickman stress that the outcome of these kinds of alliances is seldom likely to be significant enough to impact the centuries of inequality it was meant to undo. This reading gives us some history behind how reforms that attempt to redress prior discrimination got enacted, and the difficulties reformers faced along the way. It also alerts us to the importance of having majority group members "on one's team," so to speak, in order for inequality focused policy reform to be successfully implemented.

Pursuing this focus on majority group allies, the next reading is by two white sociologists—one white antiracist and one male pro-feminist—who each studied activist groups who confronted racism and sexism from dominant group perspectives. This piece is a unique treatment of the similarities and differences between fighting racism and sexism. Although parallels are often drawn between the two forms of oppression, it becomes evident through their interview data that convincing majority group members that they should participate in the struggle is notably different depending on whether racism or sexism is the topic in question. Specifically, because so many more men have close personal relationships with women than whites do with people of color, men become motivated to participate in feminism out of a personal interest in bettering their relationships with women in a way that whites typically do not stress when considering how fighting racism will impact their personal lives. At the movement level, though, the similarities are striking in how social movement organizations dictate how the problem will be defined. Particularly, both movements stress the notion of privilege, and how the entire culture is implicated in privileging whites or men over "others." The idea of overt bigots/racists or male chauvinists/rapists being the main problem is clearly discouraged and debunked by both movements, which focus instead upon how all are implicated as covert participants in perpetuating sexism or racism. However, the authors raise some interesting conclusions about the challenges of building coalitions between antiracists and feminists at large because of the limits of the parallels that can be drawn between them.

The remainder of the readings for this chapter move from the larger policy and social movement levels of society to the more micro aspects of confronting racism and sexism in one's everyday life. Our next reading is by two white historians, Noel Ignatiev and John Garvey, editors of the journal *Race Traitor,* who disagree with "antiracism" and have a different proposal for what whites can do to end racism. They have called their strategy "new abolitionism," since they argue that the "white race" as a social construction must be abolished, and this can be done if whites become "race traitors." The way they can do this is by refusing to accept the privileges that come with whiteness, or the "white club." One example they touch upon is the polite warnings whites often receive from traffic cops who pull them over, as opposed to the often hostile treatment people of color encounter in the same scenario. It would obviously take a bold commitment on the part of those who appear white to the police officer to refuse to accept any privileges by letting the officer know, "I'm not really 'white.'" This new abolitionist strategy is based on the premise that race has no biological basis and is completely socially created. Thus, abolishing the white race means destroying the social meanings attached to it, not the physical bodies that seem to represent it. This conceptualization alerts us to why so many solution strategies for racism focus upon what whites can do: because whites' actions and inactions are so often what keeps the system of racism in motion.

Following this attention to whites, white educator Paul Kivel takes a different tack, arguing that the task for a white person is to be an *ally* to people of color. Kivel writes that being an ally includes listening to people of color, avoiding the tendency to be defensive, and examining one's own actions that may perpetuate power and privilege. He also lists 13 "basic tactics" that an ally can use, then presents a hypothetical conversation between Roberto and a teacher, demonstrating how an ally validates a person of color's report of discrimination and offers to help rather than second-guessing or minimizing the incident. This reading ends by pointing out that allies must be committed for the long haul, requiring patience and humility as eventual interracial trust is established.

Our final two selections are brief checklists by white social justice activists and educators Judith Katz and Chris Crass, each a sort of personal inventory by which you, the reader, can evaluate your own life and actions. Katz's suggestions focus more squarely on strategies for ending racism, which are particularly geared toward college students but also appropriate to any age group. Katz's strategies can be practiced by majority and minority group members alike. Crass's suggestions are directed more at majority group members but encompass both race and gender dynamics. Both authors outline techniques for observing and taking inventory of one's own local environment, noting the everyday ways racism and sexism can manifest themselves around us and how we can intervene to minimize them. Whether you are an optimist, a realist, an antiracist, a feminist, a pro-feminist, a race traitor, or an ally, there is undoubtedly someplace on this list where you can begin in the struggle to end oppression. As Margaret Mead once said, "Never doubt that a group of thoughtful committed citizens can change the world; indeed, it is the only thing that ever has."

Please visit the accompanying website to Race, Ethnicity, and Gender, second edition for the *Public Sociology Assignments* at http://www.pineforge.com/das2.

THE EMPEROR'S NEW CLOTHES

Patricia Williams

My son used to attend a small nursery school. Over the course of one year, three different teachers in his school assured me that he was color-blind. Resigned to this diagnosis, I took my son to an ophthalmologist who tested him and pronounced his vision perfect. I could not figure out what was going on until I began to listen carefully to what he was saying about color.

As it turned out, my son did not misidentify color. He resisted identifying color at all. "I don't know," he would say when asked what color the grass was; or, most peculiarly, "It makes no difference." This latter remark, this assertion of the greenness of grass making no difference, was such a precociously cynical retort, that I began to suspect some social complication in which he was somehow invested.

The long and the short of it is that the well-meaning teachers at his predominantly white school had valiantly and repeatedly assured their charges that color makes no difference. "It doesn't matter," they told the children, "whether you're black or white or red or green or blue." Yet upon further investigation, the very reason that the teachers had felt it necessary to impart this lesson in the first place was that it *did* matter, and in predictably cruel ways: some of the children had been fighting about whether black people could play "good guys."

My son's anxious response was redefined by his teachers as physical deficiency. This anxiety redefined as deficiency suggests to me that it may be illustrative of the way in which the liberal ideal of color-blindness is too often confounded. That is to say, the very notion of blindness about color constitutes an ideological confusion at best, and denial at its very worst. I recognize, certainly, that the teachers were inspired by a desire to make whole a division in the ranks. But much is overlooked in the move to undo that which clearly and unfortunately matters just by labeling it that which "makes no difference." The dismissiveness, however unintentional, leaves those in my son's position pulled between the clarity of their own experience and the often alienating terms in which they must seek social acceptance.

There's a lot of that in the world right now: someone has just announced in no uncertain terms that he or she hates you because you're dark, let's say, or Catholic or a woman or the wrong height, and the panicked authority figures try to patch things up by reassuring you that race or gender or stature or your heartfelt religion doesn't matter; means nothing in the calculation of your humanity; is the most insignificant little puddle of beans in the world.

While I do want to underscore that I embrace colorblindness as a legitimate hope for the future, I worry that we tend to enshrine the notion with a kind of utopianism whose naïveté will ensure its elusiveness. In the material world ranging from playgrounds to politics, our ideals perhaps need more thoughtful, albeit more complicated, guardianship. By this I mean something more than the "I think therefore it is" school of idealism. "I don't think about color, therefore your problems don't exist." If only it were so easy.

But if indeed it's not that easy then the application of such quick fixes becomes not just a shortcut but a short-circuiting of the process of resolution. In the example of my son's experience at school, the collective aversion to confronting the social tensions he faced resulted in their being pathologized as his individual physical limitation. This is a phenomenon that happens all too frequently to children of color in a variety of contexts. In both the United States and the United Kingdom, the disproportionate numbers of black children who end up in special education or who are written off as failures attest to the degree to which this is a profound source of social anxiety.

In addition, the failure to deal straightforwardly with the pervasive practices of exclusion that infect even the very young allowed my son's white schoolmates to indulge in the false luxury of a prematurely imagined community. By this I mean that we can all be lulled rather too easily into a self-congratulatory stance of preached universalism—"We are the world! We are the children!" was the evocative, full-throated harmony of a few years ago. Yet nowhere has that been invoked more passionately than in the face of tidal waves of dissension, and even as "the" children learn that "we" children are not like "those," the benighted creatures on the other side of the pale.

This tension between material conditions and what one is cultured to see or not see—the dilemma of the emperor's new clothes, we might call it—is a tension faced by any society driven by bitter histories of imposed hierarchy. I don't mean to suggest that we need always go about feeling guilty or responsible or perpetually burdened by original sin or notions of political correctness. I do wish, however, to counsel against the facile innocence of those three notorious monkeys, Hear No Evil, See No Evil, and Speak No Evil. Theirs is a purity achieved through ignorance. Ours must be a world in which we know each other better.

To put it another way, it is a dangerous if comprehensible temptation to imagine inclusiveness by imagining away any obstacles. It is in this way that the moral high ground of good intentions knows its limits. We must be careful not to allow our intentions to verge into outright projection by substituting a fantasy of global seamlessness that is blinding rather than just color-blind.

This is a dilemma—being colored, so to speak, in a world of normative whiteness, whiteness being defined as the absence of color. The drive to conform our surroundings to whatever we know as "normal" is a powerful force—convention in many ways is more powerful than reason, and customs in some instances are more powerful than law. While surely most customs and conventions encode the insights of ancient wisdom, the habits of racial thought in Western society just as surely encapsulate some of the greatest mistakes in human history. So how do we rethink this most troubled of divisions, the fault line in our body politic, the fault line in ourselves? The ability to remain true to *one* self, it seems to me, must begin with the ethical project of considering how we can align a sense of ourselves with a sense of the world. This is the essence of integrity, is it not, never having to split into a well-maintained "front" and a closely guarded "inside."

Creating community, in other words, involves this most difficult work of negotiating real divisions, of considering boundaries before we go crashing through, and of pondering our differences before we can ever agree on the terms of our sameness. For the discounted vision of the emperor's new clothes (or a little boy's color) is already the description of corrupted community.

Perhaps one reason that conversations about race are so often doomed to frustration is that the notion of whiteness as "race" is almost never implicated. One of the more difficult legacies of slavery and of colonialism is the degree to which racism's tenacious hold is manifested not merely in the divided demographics of neighborhood or education or class but also in the process of what media expert John Fiske calls the "exnomination" of whiteness as racial identity. Whiteness is unnamed, suppressed, beyond the realm of race. Exnomination permits whites to entertain the notion that race lives "over there" on the other side of the tracks, in black bodies and inner-city neighborhoods, in a dark netherworld where whites are not involved.

At this level, the creation of a sense of community is a lifelong negotiation of endless subtlety. One morning when my son was three, I took him to his preschool. He ran straight to a pile of Legos and proceeded to work. I crossed the room and put his lunchbox in the refrigerator, where I encountered a little girl sitting at a table, beating a mound of clay into submission with a plastic rolling pin. "I see a Mommy," she said to me cheerfully. "That must mean that your little boy is here somewhere, too."

"Yes, he's here," I answered, thinking how sweetly precocious she was. "There, he's over by the Legos."

She strained to see around the bookcases. "Oh yes," she said. "Now I see that black face of his."

I walked away without responding, enraged—how can one be so enraged at an innocent child—yet not knowing what to say just then, rushing to get the jaggedly dangerous broken glass of my emotions out of the room.

I remember being three years old so well. Three was the age when I learned that I was black, the colored kid, monkeychild, different.

What made me so angry and wordless in this encounter forty years later was the realization that none of the little white children who taught me to see my blackness as a mark probably ever learned to see themselves as white. In our culture, whiteness is rarely marked in the indicative *there! there!* sense of my bracketed blackness. And the majoritarian privilege of never noticing themselves was the beginning of an imbalance from which so much, so much else flowed.

But that is hard to talk about, even now, this insight acquired before I had the words to sort it out. Yet it is imperative to think about this phenomenon of closeting race, which I believe is a good deal more widespread than these small examples. In a sense, race matters are resented and repressed in much the same way as matters of sex and scandal: the subject is considered a rude and transgressive one in mixed company, a matter whose observation is sometimes inevitable, but about which, once seen, little should be heard nonetheless. Race thus tends to be treated as though it were an especially delicate category of social infirmity—so-called—like extreme obesity or disfigurement.

Every parent knows a little of this dynamic, if in other contexts: "Why doesn't that lady have any teeth?" comes the child's piping voice. "Why doesn't that gentleman have any hair?" And "Why is that little boy so black?" *Sssshhhh!* comes the anxious parental remonstrance. The poor thing can't help it. We must all pretend that nothing's wrong.

And thus we are coached upon pain of punishment not to see a thing.

Now, to be sure, the parent faces an ethical dilemma in that moment of childish vision unrestrained by social nicety. On the one hand, we rush to place a limit on what can be said to strangers and what must be withheld for fear of imposition or of hurting someone's feelings. As members of a broad society, we respect one another by learning not to inflict every last intimate, prying curiosity we may harbor upon everyone we meet.

That said, there remains the problem of how or whether we ever answer the question, and that is the dimension of this dynamic that is considerably more troubling.

"Why is that man wearing no clothes?" pipes the childish voice once more. And the parent panics at the complication of trying to explain. The naked man may be a nudist or a psychotic or perhaps the emperor of the realm, but the silencing that is passed from parent to child is not only about the teaching of restraint; it is calculated to circumnavigate the question as though it had never been asked. *"Stop asking such silly questions."*

A wall begins to grow around the forbidden gaze; for we all know, and children best of all, when someone wants to change the subject, forever. And so the child is left to the monstrous creativity of ignorance and wild imagination.

Again, I do believe that this unfortunate negotiation of social difference has much in common with discussions about race. Race is treated as though it were some sort of genetic leprosy or a biological train wreck. Those who privilege themselves as Un-raced—usually but not always those who are white—are always anxiously maintaining that it doesn't matter, even as they are quite busy feeling pity, no less, and thankful to God for their great good luck in having been spared so intolerable an affliction.

Meanwhile, those marked as Having Race are ground down by the pendular stresses of having to explain what it feels like to be You—why are you black, why are you black, why are you black, over and over again; or, alternatively, placed in a kind of conversational quarantine of muteness in which any mention of racial circumstance reduces all sides to tears, fears, fisticuffs, and other paroxysms of unseemly anguish.

This sad, habitual paralysis in the face of the foreign and the anxiety-producing. It is as though we are all skating across a pond that is not quite thoroughly frozen. Two centuries ago, or perhaps only a few decades ago, the lake was solidly frozen, and if for those skating across the surface things seemed much more secure, it was a much more dismal lot for those whose fates were frozen at the bottom of the pond. Over time, the weather of race relations has warmed somewhat, and a few of those at the bottom have found their way to the surface; we no longer hold our breath, and we have even learned to skate. The noisy, racial chasm still yawns darkly beneath us all, but we few brave souls glide gingerly above, upon a skim of hope, our bodies made light with denial, the black pond so dangerously and thinly iced with the conviction that talking about it will only make things worse.

And so the racial divide is exacerbated further by a welter of little lies that propel us foolishly around the edges of our most demanding social stresses: Black people are a happy people and if they would just stop complaining so much, they would see how happy they are. Black people who say they're unhappy are leftist agitators whose time would be better spent looking for a real job. White people are victims. Poor Bangladeshis are poor because they want to be. Poor white people are poor because rich Indians stole all the jobs under the ruse of affirmative action. There is no racism in the marketplace—"each according to his merit" goes the cant, even as the EEOC has a backlog of 70,000 cases by the most conservative estimates; even as top executives funnel the jobs to school chums and their next of kin, or chief executives at major corporations are captured on tape destroying subpoenaed records of ongoing discriminatory practices. Immigrants are taking over the whole world, but race makes no difference. If sixty percent of young black men are unemployed in the industrialized world, well, let them watch Oprah. If some people are determined to be homeless, well then let them have it, if homelessness is what they like so much. . . .

Anthropologist Michael Taussig has written about the phenomenon of public secrets. He writes of a ritual in Tierra del Fuego in which the men come out of the men's hut wearing masks. The women hail them by singing "Here come the spirits!" On some level, everyone must know that these are not spirits but husbands and brothers and fathers and sons, but so powerful is the ritual to the sense of community that it is upon pain of death that the women fail to greet them as spirits.

In our culture, I think that the power of race resembles just such a public secret. I understand the civic ritual that requires us to say in the face of all our differences, We are all one, we are the world. I understand the need for the publicly reiterated faith in public ideals as binding and sustaining community. Such beliefs are the very foundation of institutional legitimacy and no society can hold itself together without them. Yet such binding force comes from a citizenry willing to suspend disbelief for the sake of honoring the spiritual power of our appointed ideals. And where suspicion, cynicism, and betrayal have eaten away at a community to the degree that the folk parading from the men's hut look like just a bunch of muggers wearing masks—or badges, as the case may be—then hailing the spirit will sound like a hollow incantation, empty theater, the weary habit of the dispossessed.

There is a crisis of community in the United States no less than in the rest of the world, of specific and complicated origin perhaps, but in this moment of global upheaval, worth studying for possibilities both won and lost. Whites fear blacks, blacks fear whites. Each is the enemy against whom the authorities will not act.

If racial and ethnic experience constitutes a divide that cannot be spoken, an even greater paradox is the degree to which a sense of commonality may be simultaneously created as well as threatened by notions of ethnicity and race.

It is no wonder we end up deadlocked with so many of our most profound political problems. The "O. J. divide" (as it's come to be known in America) is merely a convenient metaphor for everything else we disagree about. Are you one of "us" or one of "them"? When I say "we," am I heard as referring only to other black people? When I employ the first person, will it only be heard as an exercise of what might be called the "royal I"—me as representative stand-in for all those of my kind. . . .

Certainly the great, philosophically inspiring quandary of my life is that despite the multiculturalism of my heritage and the profundity of my commitment to the notion of the "usness" of us all, I have little room but to negotiate most of my daily lived encounters as one of "them." How alien this sounds. This split without, the split within.

Yet in this way the public secret of human fallibility, whose silence we keep to honor our symbolic civic unity, is vastly complicated by the counter-secret of palpitating civil discord. Hail the spirit of our infallibly peaceful coexistence. Hail our common fate (even as young white men are forming their own private militias complete with grenade launchers and one in three young black men are in jail or on probation. . . . But shush, don't stare. . . .)

Such is the legacy of racism in the modern world. Perhaps it is less and less fashionable these days to consider too explicitly the kinds of costs that slavery and colonialism exacted, even as those historical disruptions have continued to scar contemporary social arrangements with the transcendent urgency of their hand-me-down grief.

I realize therefore that it might be considered impertinent to keep raising the ghost of slavery's triangle trade and waving it around; there is a pronounced preference in polite society for just letting bygones be bygones. And I concede that a more optimistic enterprise might be to begin any contemporary analysis of race with

the Civil Rights Movement in the United States, or the Notting Hill riots in the United Kingdom. Beginning at those points is a way of focusing one's view and confining one's reference to the legitimately inspiring ideals that coalesced those movements: the aims of colorblindness, the equality of all people, and the possibility of peaceful coexistence.

Yet if that well-chosen temporal slice allows us to be optimistic about the possibility of progress, there are nonetheless limitations to such a frame. First, it is the conceptual prehistory of those movements that explains the toll of racism and its lingering effects. There can be no adequate explanation without reference to it. Second, the diasporic complexity of today's social problems requires an analysis that moves those ideals of the social movements of the 1960s and 1970s beyond themselves, into the present, into the future—to a more complex, practical grappling with such phenomena as the hybridizing of racial stereotypes with the fundamentalisms of gender, class, ethnicity, religion. Third, the problem of race is overlaid with crises in environmental and resource management that have triggered unparalleled migrations from rural to urban locations within national boundaries, and that have impassioned debates about immigration across national boundaries. Finally, not a few aspects of our New Age global economics, much like the commercial profiteering of colonialisms past, threaten to displace not just the very laws to which we persistently make such grand appeal but the nation-state itself. I believe that a genuine, long-term optimism about the future of race relations depends on a thorough excavation of the same.

A memory slips into my mind. I was riding the train from New York to Washington, DC, some years ago on my way to some lawyers' conference or other; I was accompanied by two black colleagues. An hour into the trip, the train stopped in the city of Philadelphia. A young white woman got on whom my colleagues knew. She was also a lawyer, headed to the same conference. She joined us, sitting among us in a double row of seats that faced each other. A little while later, the conductor came along. The new woman held up her ticket, but the conductor did not seem to see her. He saw four of us seated and only three ticket stubs.

"One of you hasn't paid," he said, staring at me, then at each of my two black friends. I remember pointing to the white woman, and someone else said, "Over there." But the conductor was resolute.

"Which one of you hasn't paid?" he asked again. Two of us kept saying, "Our receipts, see?" and the white woman, speaking *very* clearly said, "Here. I am trying to give you my ticket."

The conductor was scowling. He still did not hear. "I am not moving till one of you pays up."

It was the longest time before the conductor stopped staring in all the wrong directions. It was the longest time before he heard the new woman, pressing her ticket upon him, her voice reaching him finally as though from a great distance, passing through light-years of understanding as if from another universe. The realization that finally lit his face was like the dawning of a great surprise.

How precisely does the issue of color remain so powerfully determinative of everything from life circumstance to manner of death, in a world that is, by and large, officially "color-blind"? What metaphors mask the hierarchies that make racial domination frequently seem so "natural," so invisible, indeed so attractive? How does racism continue to evolve, post-slavery and post-equality legislation, across such geographic, temporal, and political distance?

No, I am not saying that this is the worst of times. But neither will I concede that this is the best of all possible worlds. And what a *good* thing, is it not, to try to imagine how much better we could be. . . .

"I had a dream," said my son the other morning. Then he paused. "No," he said, "it was more of a miracle. Do you know what a miracle is?"

"Tell me," I said, thunderstruck, and breathless with maternal awe.

"A miracle is when you have a dream and you open your eyes in it. It's when you wake up and your dream is all around you."

It was a pretty good definition, I thought. And even though my son's little miracle had something to do with pirates meeting dinosaurs, I do think that to a very great extent we dream our worlds into being. For better or worse, our customs and laws, our culture and society are sustained by the myths we embrace, the stories we recirculate to explain what we behold. I believe that racism's hardy persistence and immense adaptability are sustained by a habit of human imagination, deflective rhetoric, and hidden license. I believe no less that an optimistic course might be charted, if only we could imagine it. What a world it would be if we could all wake up and see all of ourselves reflected in the world, not merely in a territorial sense but with a kind of nonexclusive entitlement that grants not so much possession as investment. A peculiarly anachronistic notion of investment, I suppose, at once both ancient and futuristic. An investment that envisions each of us in each other.

. . .

Finally, I would like to return to what I think is one of the greatest obstacles to progress at this moment—the paralyzing claim that racism *has* no solution. Resembling often the schoolyard game of bullies tormenting those deemed wimps, this argument takes a number of forms:

Racism is not a problem, because racism is "universal"; all cultures are racist and xenophobic. Circling the wagons around one's own is just a "human thing."

Or: *Racism is not a problem because even if it is a problem, it's a* social *problem, and law, politics, and economic regulation have no place in the social realm. "People" will just have to deal with it "by themselves." Let them intermarry.* Not quite let them eat cake, but rather a romantic resolution to palpable political disparity.

Or: *Racism isn't a problem, because while white people used to hate black people, now it's black people who hate white people, so it's only fair for white people to hate black people in return.* And so the argument sloshes back and forth, forth and back, like a pendulum, like a lullaby, like the tolling of a knell.

Or: *Racism is a problem, but it's not* our *problem. Black people ought to help themselves before they lay claim to the sympathies of good white people.* I must say, I always wonder at this sifting out of the presumed responsibility of black people for their own fate that so casually overlooks the long history of self-help and intracommunity networks that do exist. Such self-help structures—churches, for example—are neither wealthy nor philanthropic in a way that matches those of some other groups, but much political rhetoric treats them as nonexistent. And while no one can argue that black self-help is not a fine thing, I wonder about its meaning when it is used as an injunction that black concerns be severed from the ethical question of how we as a society operate. These debates make me suspicious when they are raised so as to be at the core of arguments about black people overreaching, even as black people earn only two-thirds of what similarly educated and qualified white people do. These arguments fuel characterizations of antidiscrimination remedies as only having helped those who were already overprivileged to begin with; they feed images of those who speak publicly of racial discrimination as those who are merely "shaking down" the establishment, exploiting white guilt for personal profit.

With regard to all these configurations, let me just say that I am certain that the solution to racism lies in our ability to see its ubiquity but not to concede its inevitability. It lies in the collective and institutional power to make change, at least as much as with the individual will to change. It also lies in the absolute moral imperative to break the childish, deadly circularity of centuries of blindness to the shimmering brilliance of our common, ordinary humanity.

· · ·

SOURCE: From *Seeing a Color-Blind Future: The Paradox of Race* by Patricia Williams. Copyright © 1997 by Patricia J. Williams. Reprinted by permission of Farrar, Straus & Giroux, LLC.

THE RACIAL PREFERENCE LICENSING ACT

Derrick Bell

Racial nepotism rather than racial animus is the major motivation for much of the discrimination blacks experience.

—Matthew S. Goldberg

It was enacted as the Racial Preference Licensing Act. At an elaborate, nationally televised signing ceremony, the President—elected as a "racial moderate"—assured the nation that the new statute represented a realistic advance in race relations. "It is," he insisted, "certainly not a return to the segregation policies granted constitutional protection under the stigma-inflicting 'separate but equal' standard of *Plessy* v. *Ferguson* established roughly a century ago.[1]

"Far from being a retreat into our unhappy racial past," he explained, "the new law embodies a daring attempt to create a brighter racial future for all our citizens. Racial realism is the key to understanding this new law. It does not assume a nonexistent racial tolerance, but boldly proclaims its commitment to racial justice through the working of a marketplace that recognizes and seeks to balance the rights of our black citizens to fair treatment and the no less important right of some whites to an unfettered choice of customers, employees, and contractees."

Under the new act, all employers, proprietors of public facilities, and owners and managers of dwelling places, homes, and apartments could, on application to the federal government, obtain a license authorizing the holders, their managers, agents, and employees to exclude or separate persons on the basis of race and color. The license itself was expensive, though not prohibitively so. Once obtained, it required payment to a government commission of a tax of 3 percent of the income derived from whites employed, whites served, or products sold to whites during each quarter in which a policy of "racial preference" was in effect. Congress based its authority for the act on the commerce clause, the taxing power, and the general welfare clause of the Constitution.

License holders were required both to display their licenses prominently in a public place and to operate their businesses in accordance with the racially selective policies set out on their license. Specifically, discrimination had to be practiced in accordance with the license on a nonselective basis. Licenses were not available to those who, for example, might hire or rent to one token black and then discriminate against other applicants, using the license as a shield against discrimination suits. Persons of color wishing to charge discrimination against a facility not holding a license would carry the burden of proof, but such burden might be met with statistical and circumstantial as well as with direct evidence provided by white "testers."* Under the act, successful complainants would be entitled to damages set at ten thousand dollars per instance of unlicensed discrimination, including attorneys' fees.

The President committed himself and his administration to the effective enforcement of the Racial Preference Licensing Act. "It is time," he declared, "to bring hard-headed realism rather than well-intentioned idealism to bear on our long-standing racial problems. Policies adopted because they seemed right have usually failed. Actions taken to promote justice for blacks have brought injustice to whites without appreciably improving the status or standards of living for blacks, particularly for those who most need the protection those actions were intended to provide.

"Within the memories of many of our citizens, this nation has both affirmed policies of racial segregation and advocated polices of racial integration. Neither approach has been either satisfactory or effective in furthering harmony and domestic tranquillity." Recalling the Civil Rights Act of 1964[3] and its 1991 amendments,[4]

---

* Testing is an effective, but too little utilized, technique to ferret out bias in the sale and rental of housing or in employment practices. Generally, in testing, people who are alike in virtually every way except race or ethnicity are sent to apply for jobs, housing, or mortgages. The results are then analyzed for how differently whites are treated compared with blacks or Hispanics seeking college and vocational education. To counter charges that black people, as under *Plessy*, would be both segregated and never gain any significant benefit from the equality fund, the act provided that five major civil rights organizations (each named in the statute) would submit the name of a representative who would serve on the commission for one, nonrenewable three-year term.

the President pointed out that while the once-controversial public-accommodation provisions in the original 1964 act received unanimous judicial approval in the year of its adoption,[5] even three decades later the act's protective function, particularly in the employment area, had been undermined by both unenthusiastic enforcement and judicial decisions construing its provisions ever more narrowly.

"As we all know," the President continued, "the Supreme Court has now raised grave questions about the continued validity of the 1964 Act and the Fair Housing Act of 1968[6]—along with their various predecessors and supplemental amendments as applied to racial discrimination. The Court stopped just short of declaring unconstitutional all laws prohibiting racial discrimination, and found that the existing civil rights acts were inconsistent with what it viewed as the essential 'racial forgiveness' principle in the landmark decision of *Brown* v. *Board of Education* of 1954.[7] The Court announced further that nothing in its decision was intended to affect the validity of the statutes' protection against discrimination based on sex, national origin, or religion.

"This is, of course, not an occasion for a legal seminar, but it is important that all citizens understand the background of the new racial preference statute we sign this evening. The Supreme Court expressed its concern that existing civil rights statutes created racial categories that failed to meet the heavy burden of justification placed on any governmental policy that seeks to classify persons on the basis of race. In 1989, the Court held that this heavy burden, called the 'strict scrutiny' standard, applied to remedial as well as to invidious racial classifications.[8] Our highest court reasoned that its 1954 decision in the landmark case of *Brown* v. *Board of Education* did not seek to identify and punish wrongdoers, and the implementation order in *Brown II*[9] a year later did not require immediate enforcement. Rather, *Brown II* asserted that

delay was required, not only to permit time for the major changes required in Southern school policies, but also—and this is important—to enable accommodation to school integration which ran counter to the views and strong emotions of most Southern whites.

"In line with this reasoning," the President continued, "the Court referred with approval to the views of the late Yale law professor Alexander Bickel, who contended that any effort to enforce *Brown* as a criminal law would have failed, as have alcohol prohibition, antigambling, most sex laws, and other laws policing morals. Bickel said, 'It follows that in achieving integration, the task of the law ... was not to punish law breakers but to diminish their number.'[10]

"Now the Court has found Professor Bickel's argument compelling. Viewed from the perspective provided by four decades, the Court says now that *Brown* was basically a call for a higher morality rather than a judicial decree authorizing Congress to coerce behavior allegedly unjust to blacks because that behavior recognized generally acknowledged differences in racial groups. This characterization of *Brown* explains why *Brown* was no more effective as an enforcement tool than were other 'morals-policing' laws such as alcohol prohibition, antigambling, and sex laws, all of which are hard to enforce precisely because they seek to protect our citizens' health and welfare against what a legislature deems self-abuse.

"Relying on this reasoning, the Court determined that laws requiring cessation of white conduct deemed harmful to blacks are hard to enforce because they seek to 'police morality.' While conceding both the states' and the federal government's broad powers to protect the health, safety, and welfare of its citizens, the Court found nothing in the Constitution authorizing regulation of what government at any particular time might deem appropriate 'moral' behavior. The exercise of such authority, the Court feared, could lead Congress to control the perceptions of what some whites believe about the humanity of some blacks. On this point," the President said, "I want to quote the opinion the Supreme Court has just handed down: 'Whatever the good intentions of such an undertaking, it clearly aimed for a spiritual result that might be urged by a religion but is beyond the reach of government coercion.'

"Many of us, of both political persuasions," the President went on, "were emboldened by the Court to seek racial harmony and justice along the route of mutual respect as suggested in its decision. This bill I now sign into law is the result of long debate and good-faith compromise. It is, as its opponents charge and its proponents concede, a radical new approach to the nation's continuing tensions over racial status. It maximizes freedom of racial choice for all our citizens while guaranteeing that people of color will benefit either directly from equal access or indirectly from the fruits of the license taxes paid by those who choose policies of racial exclusion.

"A few, final words. I respect the views of those who vigorously opposed this new law. And yet the course we take today was determined by many forces too powerful to ignore, too popular to resist, and too pregnant with potential to deny. We have vacillated long enough. We must move on toward what I predict will be a new and more candid and collaborative relationship among all our citizens. May God help us all as we seek with His help to pioneer a new path in our continuing crusade to bring justice and harmony to all races in America."

* * *

Well, Geneva, you've done it again, I thought to myself as I finished this second story well after midnight. After all our battles, I thought I'd finally pulled myself up to your advanced level of racial thinking—but the Racial Preference Licensing Act is too much.

"You still don't get it, do you?"

I looked up. There she was—the ultimate African queen—sitting on the small couch in my study. The mass of gray dreadlocks framing

Geneva's strong features made a beautiful contrast with her smooth blue-black skin. She greeted me with her old smile, warm yet authoritative.

"Welcome," I said, trying to mask my shock with a bit of savoir-faire. "Do you always visit folks at two o'clock in the morning?"

She smiled. "I decided I could not leave it to you to figure out the real significance of my story."

"Well," I said, "I'm delighted to see you!" As indeed I was. It had been almost five years since Geneva disappeared at the close of the climatic civil rights conference that ended my book *And We Are Not Saved.* Seeing her now made me realize how much I had missed her, and I slipped back easily into our old relationship.

"Tell me, Geneva, how can you justify this law? After all, if the Fourteenth Amendment's equal protection clause retains any viability, it is to bar government-sponsored racial segregation. Even if—as is likely—you convince me of your law's potential, what are civil rights advocates going to say when I present it to them? As you know, it has taken me years to regain some acceptance within the civil rights community—since I suggested in print that civil rights lawyers who urge racial-balance remedies in all school desegregation cases were giving priority to their integration ideals over their clients' educational needs.[11] Much as I respect your insight on racial issues, Geneva, I think your story's going to turn the civil rights community against us at a time when our goal is to persuade them to broaden their thinking beyond traditional, integration-oriented goals."

"Oh ye of little faith!" she responded. "Even after all these years, you remain as suspicious of my truths as you are faithful to the civil rights ideals that events long ago rendered obsolete. Whatever its cost to relationships with your civil rights friends, accept the inevitability of my Racial Preference Licensing Act. And believe—if not me—yourself.

"Although you maintain your faith in the viability of the Fourteenth Amendment, in your writings you have acknowledged, albeit reluctantly, that whatever the civil rights law or constitutional provision, blacks gain little protection against one or another form of racial discrimination unless granting blacks a measure of relief will serve some interest of importance to whites.[12] Virtually every piece of civil rights legislation beginning with the Emancipation Proclamation supports your position.[13] Your beloved Fourteenth Amendment is a key illustration of this white self-interest principle. Enacted in 1868 to provide citizenship to the former slaves and their offspring, support for the amendment reflected Republicans' concern after the Civil War that the Southern Democrats, having lost the war, might win the peace. This was not a groundless fear. If the Southern states could rejoin the union, bar blacks from voting, and regain control of state government, they might soon become the dominant power in the federal government as well.[14]

"Of course, within a decade, when Republican interests changed and the society grew weary of racial remedies and was ready to sacrifice black rights to political expediency, both the Supreme Court and the nation simply ignored the original stated purpose of the Fourteenth Amendment's equal protection guarantee. In 1896, the *Plessy* v.

Ferguson precedent gave legal validity to this distortion and then to a torrent of Jim Crow statutes. 'Separate but equal' was the judicial promise. Racial subordination became the legally enforceable fact."

"Well, sure," I mustered a response, "the Fourteenth Amendment's history is a definitive example of white self-interest lawmaking, but what is its relevance to your Racial Preference Licensing Act? It seems to me—and certainly will seem to most civil rights advocates—like a new, more subtle, but hardly less pernicious 'separate but equal' law. Is there something I'm missing?"

"You are—which is precisely why I am here."

"I could certainly," I said, "use more of an explanation for a law that entrusts our rights to free-market forces. The law and economics experts might welcome civil rights protections in this form,* but virtually all civil rights professionals will view legalizing racist practices as nothing less than a particularly vicious means of setting the struggle for racial justice back a century. I doubt I could communicate them effectively to most black people."

"Of course you can't! Neither they nor you really want to come to grips with the real role of racism in this country."

"And that is?"

---

* These law and economics experts, especially Richard Posner and John J. Donohue, accept Gary Becker's theory that markets drive out discriminating employers because discrimination tends to minimize profits.[15] The essence of Posner and Donohue's debate on Title VII (the Equal Employment Opportunity Act) is whether "[l]egislation that prohibits employment discrimination . . . actually enhance[s] rather than impair[s] economic efficiency."[16] Donohue argues that the effects of the Title VII statutory scheme are to increase the rate at which discriminators are driven out of the market from the base rate, which many economists steeped in the neoclassical tradition would argue is the optimal rate. Posner questions whether this effect (the increased rate) occurs; and, significantly, also raises questions about whether the regulatory scheme, designed to decrease discrimination against blacks in employment decisions and thereby increase the net welfare of blacks, actually succeeds in doing so. If neither assumption is accurate, he states that the costs of enforcement and all other costs associated with administering Title VII "are a dead weight social loss that cannot be justified on grounds [not only of efficiency but] of social equity."[17]

Posner and David A. Strauss both make statements that would seem to indicate openness to such measures as the Racial Preference Licensing Act. Posner writes that "it might be that a tax on those whites [who discriminate because of an aversion to blacks and therefore would seek a license] for the benefit of blacks would be justifiable on the grounds of social equity [although this is not an *efficiency* justification in the wealth maximization sense]."[18] And Strauss asks, "Why would the objectives of compensatory justice and avoiding racial stratification not be better served, at less cost, if the legal system permitted statistical discrimination; captured the efficiency gains (and the gains for reduced administrative costs) through taxation, and transferred the proceeds to African Americans?"[19]

"My friend, know it! Racism is more than a group of bad white folks whose discriminatory predilections can be controlled by well-formed laws, vigorously enforced. Traditional civil rights laws tend to be ineffective because they are built on a law enforcement model. They assume that most citizens will obey the law; and when law breakers are held liable, a strong warning goes out that will discourage violators and encourage compliance. But the law enforcement model for civil rights breaks down when a great number of whites are willing—because of convenience, habit, distaste, fear, or simple preference—to violate the law. It then becomes almost impossible to enforce, because so many whites, though not discriminating themselves, identify more easily with those who do than with their victims."

"That much I understand," I replied. "Managers of hotels, restaurants, and other places of public accommodation have complied with antidiscrimination laws because they have discovered that, for the most part, it is far more profitable to serve blacks than to exclude or segregate them. On the other hand, these same establishments regularly discriminate against blacks seeking jobs."

"Precisely right, friend. A single establishment, often a single individual, can be inconsistent for any number of reasons, including the desire not to upset or inconvenience white customers or white employees. More often, management would prefer to hire the white than the black applicant. As one economist has argued, 'racial nepotism' rather than 'racial animus' is the major motivation for much of the discrimination blacks experience."[20]

"But nepotism," I objected, "is a preference for family members or relatives. What does it have to do with racial discrimination?"

Geneva gave me her "you are not serious" smile. Then it hit me. "Of course! You're right, Geneva, it is hard to get out of the law enforcement model. You're suggesting that whites tend to treat one another like family, at least when there's a choice between them and us. So that terms like 'merit' and 'best qualified' are infinitely manipulable if and when whites must explain why they reject blacks to hire 'relatives'—even when the only relationship is that of race. So, unless there's some pressing reason for hiring, renting to, or otherwise dealing with a black, many whites will prefer to hire, rent to, sell to, or otherwise deal with a white—including one less qualified by objective measures and certainly one who is by any measure better qualified."

"Lord, I knew the man could figure it out! He just needed my presence."

"Well, since a little sarcasm is the usual price of gaining face-to-face access to your insight, Geneva, I am willing to pay. Actually, as I think about it, racial licensing is like that approach adopted some years ago by environmentalists who felt that licensing undesirable conduct was the best means of dealing with industry's arguments that it could not immediately comply with laws to protect the environment. The idea is, as I recall, that a sufficiently high licensing fee would make it profitable for industry to take steps to control the emissions (or whatever), and that thereby it would be possible to reduce damage to health and property much more cheaply than an attempt to control the entire polluting activity.[21]*

"Come to think of it, Geneva, there's even a precedent, of sorts, for the Equality Fund. College football's Fiesta Bowl authorities no doubt had a similar principle in mind when

---

* A similar economically based principle underlay the action of the Connecticut Legislature when in 1973 it enacted a statute mandating penalties equal to the capital and operating costs saved by not installing and operating equipment to meet applicable regulatory limits.[22] In 1977, Congress added "noncompliance penalties" patterned after the Connecticut compliance program to section 120 of the Clean Air Act.[23] As of 1988, section 173(1)(A) of the Clean Air Act in effect permits the introduction of new pollution sources if "total allowable emissions" from existing and new sources are "sufficiently less than total emissions from existing sources allowed under the applicable implementation plan."[24]

they announced in 1990 that they would create a minority scholarship fund of one hundred thousand dollars or endow an academic chair for minority students at each competing university; the aim was to induce colleges to participate in the Fiesta Bowl in Arizona, a state whose populace has refused to recognize the Martin Luther King, Jr., holiday.[25] Sunkist Growers, Inc., the event's sponsor, agreed to match the amount. Further 'sweetening the pot,' one university president promised to donate all net proceeds to university programs benefiting minority students."[26]

"Both examples," remarked Geneva, "illustrate how pocketbook issues are always near the top of the list of motives for racial behavior. That's why compliance with traditional civil rights laws is particularly tough during a period of great economic uncertainty, white nepotism becoming most prevalent when jobs and reasonably priced housing are in short supply. During such times, racial tolerance dissolves into hostility."

"Just as during the 1890s," I interjected, "when economic conditions for the working classes were at another low point, and there was intense labor and racial strife.[27] Today, whites have concluded, as they did a century ago, that the country has done enough for black people despite the flood of evidence to the contrary. The Supreme Court's civil rights decisions reflect the public's lack of interest. In the meantime, enforcement of civil rights laws, never vigorous, has dawdled into the doldrums, and this inertia encourages open violation and discourages victims from filing complaints they fear will only add futility and possible retaliation to their misery."

"All true," Geneva agreed.

"But given the already strong anti-civil rights trends," I argued, "wouldn't the Racial Preference Licensing Act simply encourage them?"

"You are resistant," Geneva replied. "Don't you see? For the very reasons you offer, urging stronger civil rights laws barring discrimination

in this period is not simply foolhardy; it's the waste of a valuable opportunity."

"Well," I acknowledged, "I have no doubt that a great many white people would prefer the Racial Preference Licensing Act to traditional civil rights laws. The licensing feature provides legal protection for their racially discriminatory policies—particularly in employment and housing—which whites have practiced covertly, despite the presence on the books of civil rights laws and Court decisions declaring those practices unlawful."

"It is even more attractive," Geneva said, "in that thoughtful whites will view the new law as a means of giving moral legitimacy to their discriminatory preferences by adopting the theory[28] that whites have a right of non-association (with blacks), and that this right should be recognized in law."

"On those grounds," I put in, "the act could expect support from white civil libertarians who think racial discrimination abhorrent but are troubled by the need to coerce correct behavior. Whites will not be happy about the Equality Fund, though these provisions might attract the support of black separatists who would see the fund as a fair trade for the integration they always distrusted.[29] But, believe me, Geneva, no such benefits will assuage the absolute opposition of most civil rights professionals—black and white. They remain committed—to the point of obsession—with integration notions that, however widely held in the 1960s, are woefully beyond reach today."

"Don't start again!" Geneva threw up her hands. "I understand and sympathize with your civil rights friends' unwillingness to accept the legalized reincarnation of Jim Crow. They remember all too well how many of our people suffered and sacrificed to bury those obnoxious signs 'Colored' and 'White.' I think that even if I could prove that the Racial Preference Licensing Act would usher in the racial millennium, civil rights professionals would be unwilling to—as they might put it—'squander our high principles in return for a mess of segregation-tainted pottage.' Victory on such grounds is, they would conclude, no victory at all."

"You mock them, Geneva, but integration advocates would see themselves as standing by their principles."

"Principles, hell! What I do not understand—and this is what I really want to get clear—is what principle is so compelling as to justify continued allegiance to obsolete civil rights strategies that have done little to prevent—and may have contributed to—the contemporary statistics regarding black crime, broken families, devastated neighborhoods, alcohol and drug abuse, out-of-wedlock births, illiteracy, unemployment, and welfare dependency?"

She stopped to take a deep breath, then went on. "Racial segregation was surely hateful, but let me tell you, friend, that if I knew that its return would restore our black communities to what they were before desegregation, I would think such a trade entitled to serious thought. I would not dismiss it self-righteously, as you tell me many black leaders would do. Black people simply cannot afford the luxury of rigidity on racial issues. This story is not intended to urge actual adoption of a racial preference licensing law, but to provoke blacks and their white allies to look beyond traditional civil rights views. We must learn to examine every racial policy, including those that seem most hostile to blacks, and determine whether there is unintended potential African Americans can exploit.

"Think about it! Given the way things have gone historically, if all existing civil rights laws were invalidated, legislation like the Racial Preference Licensing Act might be all African Americans could expect. And it could prove no less—and perhaps more—effective than

those laws that now provide us the promise of protection without either the will or the resources to honor that promise."

"Most civil rights advocates," I replied, "would, on hearing that argument, likely respond by linking arms and singing three choruses of 'We Shall Overcome.'"

"You're probably right, friend—but it is your job, is it not, to make them see that racist opposition has polluted the dream that phrase once inspired? However comforting, the dream distracts us from the harsh racial reality closing in around you and ours."

As I did not respond, Geneva continued. "You have to make people *see*. Just as parents used to tell children stories about the stork to avoid telling them about sex, so for similarly evasive reasons many black people hold to dreams about a truly integrated society that is brought into being by the enforcement of laws barring discriminatory conduct. History and—one would hope—common sense tells us that dream is never coming true."

"Dreams and ideals are not evil, Geneva."

"Of course they aren't, but we need to be realistic about our present and future civil rights activities. The question is whether the activity reflects and is intended to challenge the actual barriers we face rather than those that seem a threat to the integration ideology."

"That's all very high-sounding, Geneva, and I agree that we need a more realistic perspective, but how can I bring others to recognize that need?"

"We might begin by considering the advantages of such a radical measure as the Racial Preference Licensing Act. First, by authorizing racial discrimination, such a law would, as I suggested earlier, remove the long-argued concern that civil rights laws deny anyone the right of non-association.* With the compulsive

---

* Herbert Wechsler, for example, has suggested the decision in *Brown* v. *Board of Education* might be criticized as requiring "integration [that] forces an association upon those for whom it is unpleasant or repugnant."[30]

element removed, people who discriminate against blacks without getting the license authorized by law may not retain the unspoken but real public sympathy they now enjoy. They may be viewed as what they are: law breakers who deserve punishment.

"Second, by requiring the discriminator both to publicize and to pay all blacks a price for that 'right,' the law may dilute both the financial and the psychological benefits of racism. Today even the worst racist denies being a racist. Most whites pay a tremendous price for their reflexive and often unconscious racism, but few are ready to post their racial preferences on a public license and even less ready to make direct payments for the privilege of practicing discrimination. Paradoxically, gaining the right to practice openly what people now enthusiastically practice covertly will take a lot of the joy out of discrimination and replace that joy with some costly pain.

"Third, black people will no longer have to divine—as we have regularly to do in this antidiscrimination era—whether an employer, a realtor, or a proprietor wants to exclude them. The license will give them—and the world— ample notice. Those who seek to discriminate without a license will place their businesses at risk of serious, even ruinous, penalties."

"It seems crazy," I began.

"Racism is hardly based on logic. We need to fight racism the way a forest ranger fights fire with fire."

NOTES

The epigraph is from Matthew S. Goldberg, "Discrimination, Nepotism, and Long-Run Wage Differentials," *Quarterly Journal of Economics* 97 (1982): 307.

1. *Plessy* v. *Ferguson*, 163 U.S. 537 (1896) (upholding statute requiring segregated railway coaches).

2. *Havens Realty Co.* v. *Coleman*, 455 U.S. 363 (1982).

3. Civil Rights Act of 1964, 42 U.S.C. Secs. 1971, 1975a–1975d, 2000a–2000h-6 (1988).

4. Civil Rights Act of 1991, Public Law No. 102–166, 105 Stat. 1071 (1991).

5. See, for example, *Heart of Atlanta Motel, Inc.* v. *United States,* 379 U.S. 241 (1964), and *Katzenbach* v. *McClung,* 379 U.S. 294 (1964) (both cases upholding the public facilities provisions of Title II).

6. Fair Housing Act of 1968, Pub. L. 90–284, Title VIII, sections 801–19, 42 U.S.C. SS 3601–19 (1970) (as amended 1988, Section 13(a) of Pub. L. 100–430, short title "Fair Housing Amendments Act of 1988").

7. *Brown* v. *Board of Education,* 347 U.S. 483 (1954).

8. See *City of Richmond* v. *J. A. Croson Co.,* 488 U.S. 469 (1989).

9. *Brown v. Board of Education II,* 349 U.S. 294 (1955).

10. Alexander Bickel, *The Least Dangerous Branch: The Supreme Court at the Bar of Politics* (1962), 247–54.

11. Derrick Bell, "Serving Two Masters: Integration Ideals and Client Interests in School Desegregation Litigation," *Yale Law Journal* 85 (1976): 470.

12. Comment, "Brown v. Board of Education and the Interest-Convergence Dilemma," *Harvard Law Review* 93 (1980): 518.

13. See Derrick Bell, *Race, Racism and American Law,* 2nd ed. (1980), 2–44.

14. Ibid., 33.

15. Gary Becker, *The Economics of Discrimination,* 2nd ed. (1971). See, for example, Richard Epstein, *Forbidden Grounds: The Case Against Employment Discrimination Laws* (1992); Richard A. Posner, *Economic Analysis of Law,* 3rd ed. (1986), 621–23; John J. Donohue, "Is Title VII Efficient?" *University of Pennsylvania Law Review* 134 (1986): 1411; Richard A. Posner, "The Efficiency and Efficacy of Title VII," *University of Pennsylvania Law Review* 136 (1987): 513; John J. Donohue, "Further Thoughts on Employment Discrimination Legislation: A Reply to Judge Posner," *University of Pennsylvania Law Review* 136 (1987): 523; and Strauss, "Law and Economics." See also John J.

Donohue and Peter Siegelman, "The Changing Nature of Employment Discrimination Litigation," *Stanford Law Review* 43 (1991): 983; John J. Donohue and James J. Heckman, "Re-Evaluating Federal Civil Rights Policy," *Georgetown Law Journal* 79 (1991): 1713.

16. Donohue, "Is Title VII Efficient?" 1411–12.

17. Posner, "Efficiency and Efficacy of Title VII, 513, 521.

18. Ibid., 516.

19. David A. Strauss, "The Law and Economics of Racial Discrimination in Employment: The Case for Numerical Standards" *Georgetown Law Journal* 79 (1991): 1619, 1630.

20. Matthew Goldberg, "Discrimination, Nepotism, and Long-Run Wage Differentials," *Quarterly Journal of Economics* 97 (1982): 307.

21. See *Economic Report of the President*, H.R. Doc. No. 28, 92d Cong., 1st Sess. 119 (1971).

22. See Conn. Gen. Stat. Sec. 22a-6b (West Supp. 1990).

23. Act of 7 August 1977, Pub. L. No. 95–96, 91 Stat. 714, codified as amended at 42 U.S.C. Sec. 7420(2)(A) (1988 & Supp. 1990).

24. Act of 7 August 1977, as amended at 42 U.S.C. Sec. 7503(1)(A) (1988).

25. "There's Another Way to Honor King," *Chicago Tribune,* 18 November 1990, sec. 4, p. 3.

26. George Will, "Bush's Blunder on Racial Scholarships," *Newsday* 27 December 1990, p. 95 (characterizing Fiesta Bowl officials' actions as a "penance for the sin of playing football in Arizona").

27. See Nell Painter, *Standing at Armageddon: The United States, 1877–1919* (1987), 110–44, 163–69.

28. Herbert Wechsler, "Toward Neutral Principles of Constitutional Law," *Harvard Law Review* 73 (1959): 1 (suggesting that the *Brown* decision may have arbitrarily traded the rights of whites not to associate with blacks in favor of the rights of blacks to associate with whites).

29. For a summary of black reparations efforts in both the nineteenth and the twentieth centuries, see Bell, *Race, Racism,* 44–47.

30. Herbert Wechsler, "Toward Neutral Principles," *Harvard Law Review* 73 (1959): 1, 34.

The Redefinition and Subversion of Comparable Worth in New York State: "We Did It Our Way"

Ronnie Steinberg and Jennifer Hickman

The state of New York and the state's largest union, the Civil Service Employees Association (CSEA), agreed in 1982 to conduct a comparable worth study. The study came about largely as a result of pressure from feminists working in coalition with supporters inside both labor and management. Over one year later, in 1983, a contract to conduct the study was awarded to the Center for Women in Government (CWG), a university-based research and advocacy organization that had been an active proponent of comparable worth since 1979. Comparable worth, with this decision, ostensibly had been placed on the political agenda in New York State.

Over two years later, in late 1985, CWG completed the study. The Center's study was the largest study of wage differentials undertaken up to that time and the first to consider both sex and race bias in compensation practices. The study also was the first to assess the extent of wage discrimination on the basis of a set of job evaluation procedures designed and implemented by feminist technical proponents. All other studies had used off-the-shelf gender-biased job evaluation systems. Yet, to the surprise of many and given the Center's pro-feminist, pro–comparable worth reputation, the study results yielded perhaps the lowest estimates of wage discrimination of any study that had been completed. Although these results could have indicated that New York compensation practices embedded little discrimination, the low estimates, in fact, reflected the sophisticated political maneuvering of those intent on protecting the status quo in relative wages between male and female employees and on minimizing the cost of wage adjustments made in the name of pay equity. Indeed, the Center's low estimates of discrimination only foreshadowed subsequent events.

It was not until April 1987—some five years later—that wage adjustments to incumbents of undervalued, historically female and minority jobs were distributed. These wage adjustments were even lower than those projected by the CWG. Calling the CWG study an interim report, management, with labor's support, undertook a second study not only to estimate the extent of wage discrimination but also to design a new set of compensation practices that would apply to all state jobs. The results of this second technical exercise produced pay equity adjustments that were even smaller than those originally recommended by the CWG study.

Moreover, the majority of New York State nonmanagerial employees were organized into two competing unions. The CSEA represented employees without college degrees. Its rival, the Professional Employee Association (PEA) represented nonmanagerial employees whose jobs required a college degree. When announcing the specific pay equity adjustments, they varied by union. Adjustments recommended for job classes represented by CSEA were low, but those announced for job classes represented by PEA were even lower, and, in some cases, the state asserted that historically female and minority jobs represented by PEA were "overvalued," or paid more than their job complexity warranted. By this time, however, many years had passed, and both CSEA and PEA leadership had few options open to them, short of throwing out five years of effort and thus losing face with their membership. As a result, the unions were placed in a defensive bargaining posture, with management holding virtually all of the power in these negotiations. The low pay adjustments and the differences by union remained intact.

Thomas Hartnett, the Director of New York State's Governor's Office of Employee Relations (GOER), in an April 1987 *GOER News* editorial following announcement of the final so-called comparable worth adjustments, proclaimed that "we did it our way." Management certainly did. In the name of pay equity, New York State distributed a small portion of what incumbents of historically female and minority job classes were due for having suffered years of discrimination in their wage rates. New York State also managed to implement a new set of wage practices that maintained all but the most extreme forms of wage discrimination.

How did these outcomes result from such a promising comparable worth initiative? This article chronicles the competing agendas and conflicting alliances that, taken together, resulted in significantly limited wage increases. This is a story about the significance of differential power resources—both material and symbolic—between management, on the one hand, and labor and feminists, on the other hand. While in 1982 these interests converged in the decision to actually undertake a comparable worth study, this convergence of interests was sporadic and short-lived. In the political battle to achieve pay equity in New York State, the real losers were both the women and the men in historically female and minority jobs in New York State and in other locales that used the New York State initiative as precedent.

Origins of the New York State Comparable Worth Study

In the late 1970s and early 1980s, comparable worth emerged as a prominent issue for feminists, public sector personnel, labor relations managers, and unions. In New York State, the CWG was the pivotal force crystallizing interest in a New York State comparable pay initiative and keeping it moving forward. CWG, housed at the State University of New York-Albany at Rockefeller College's Institute for Government and Policy Studies and financed by private and state grants, was established in January 1978 to conduct research, training, and public education to achieve labor market equality for women and minorities.

Comparable worth was a personal and organizational priority of the Center's leadership. . . . The CWG sought to strategically locate itself at the center of national pay equity activities politically and technically. From the perspective of the Center, the primary goal of comparable worth was to revalue women's work economically through changing compensation practices to remove gender and race biases that artificially depress wages paid to those performing work in historically female and minority job classes. Gender neutrality could only be achieved if jobs were rewarded on a consistent basis and if characteristics of work performed by women and minorities were recognized and positively valued. In New York State, CWG wanted to conduct a study that would meet technical standards of gender neutrality.

CWG also saw the New York State study as being a potential model for the nation. The New York State study would be the first to focus on discrimination as well as sex. Since New York State was the third largest government employer in the nation and had twice as many job titles as jurisdictions that had conducted prior studies, this study would be the largest ever undertaken.

This study also would be the first to use new statistical techniques for uncovering the discriminations embedded in state jobs and salary structure.[1]

Funding the Study

The Center knew that to move the New York State comparable worth initiative forward would require the support of both labor and management. A first step toward achieving their commitments was to invite representatives of labor and management to join the Center's Board of Directors. This strategy worked. In 1980, both management and labor were present when the Center's Board endorsed, as its top priority, the New York State comparable worth study. Although the Center was unaware of it at the time, both labor and management had agreed to undertake a state comparable worth study for different reasons. These divergent priorities would lead to the reform's demise.

The New York State study was thought of as a "pay equity partnership" between labor and management. In reality, it actually constituted an uneasy alliance of opponents who saw pay equity as a way to achieve other, long-standing agenda items of greater significance. Labor and management committed to moving this initiative forward. To some degree, CSEA and GOER shared the Center's agenda for women's equality. But this "partnership" hinged on a mutual commitment to reshape their archaic compensation structure. For management, pay equity was a route toward a struggle with CSEA to demonstrate that clerical workers were *not* underpaid.

By contrast, for the unions, comparable worth was a way to separate the wages paid to the clerical workers it represented to keep these members from defecting from the union. Their fear was grounded in the prior defection of the states as professional employees, who formed a second union, PEA, some years earlier. Previous pay equity initiatives in other states had resulted in pay raises for clerical workers. Their commitment to increasing the wages of clerical workers was *not* a commitment to achieving pay equity for all their women members, including the approximately 20,000 Mental Hygiene Therapy Aides it represented. . . . Moreover, while GOER controlled the study for management, there were actually three sets of management officials involved in the study—the Civil Service department, human relations or the GOER, and the Division of the Budget. They too operated in uneasy alliance with one another.

Because a majority of the New York State legislature would oppose a pay equity study, for a variety of reasons the Center decided to fund its study through the collective bargaining process. As a result of various behind-the-scenes maneuvers between labor and management, the CSEA President and Research Director introduced the study proposal during negotiations, and to their surprise, management agreed. In April 1982, CSEA and the state agreed to spend $500,000 for the pay equity study. But this study would focus only on CSEA employees. PEA, which represented nurses, librarians, and social workers, wanted nothing to do with the study.

MAKING COMPARABLE WORTH REASONABLE

As the study began, labor and management claimed the study as their own. . . . But, the mixed motives for conducting the comparable worth study translated into varied visions about the extent to which the study results should alter the existing wage structure. The Center's approach involved rigorous methodologies to produce results that would remedy gender- and race-based pay disparities. Despite their public announcements, however, management and labor wanted only "reasonable

comparable worth"—reform that would bring about only short-term and limited increases to workers in female-dominated and significantly minority jobs. Management defined "reasonable" in terms of minimal cost to the state after management estimated that adjustments would be 1% of payroll. GOER had anticipated comparable worth adjustments in the range of a 5% increase in the payroll. Labor defined "reasonable" as wage adjustments that would not upset its white male union members.

Some state labor leaders did not believe that their female workers were underpaid. Men were more powerful within the union and had historically been opposed to pay equity. Some state union leaders went along with the study because their national organization supported it.

At every step of the Center's study, the state worked to assure that the outcomes would not exceed these "reasonable" criteria. As GOER's Hartnett said as he announced the final wage adjustments, "both [labor and management] recognized the need to establish comparable worth. Both knew the bottom line of resources available." . . . But while the Center viewed their approach as the first step to further wage adjustments, to management, the research technique offered a scientific rationale for maintaining the status quo.

DIVIDE AND DELAY: EARLY CONTAINMENT STRATEGIES

One of management's primary nontechnical strategies to control the study outcomes was to play the two public employee unions off against each other and against the feminist Center. They began by encouraging CSEA to cosponsor the study, while playing off of PEA's lack of receptivity to the study. PEA leaders perceived the Center as a "management advocate." They believed that the Center's close relationships with management and with CSEA would compromise PEA.

Second, different groups within management attempted to stop the study. It took 18 months before the state signed the contract with the Center, largely due to the different reservations voiced by labor, management, and GOER, including that they either opposed it or feared it would be expensive and/or controversial.

Third, management and labor engaged in a preemptive strategy to counter the Center's anticipated results by funding a second joint labor-management study, conducted by Arthur Young Associates, a management consulting firm. This second study would serve as a fallback in the event that the Center's findings were not "reasonable."

Even after the study contract was signed, the Center's dual roles as pay equity advocacy organization and as research institute continued to be contentious. Indeed, GOER hired a high-level manager whose sole job was to oversee the Center's study. Questions were raised as to whether the Center was "fulfilling the role of researcher" and "working for us [management] or promoting a concept." Yet, as an explicitly feminist organization, the Center gave the study symbolic legitimacy. Management could oversee the study on a daily basis and CSEA could pacify its female clerical workers. . . .

[B]y making the Center responsible for the pay equity study, the most active and visible comparable worth proponent organization was now accountable largely to management. This co-optation effectively silenced the Center from criticizing its own study or the subsequent state implementation study publicly.

The Structures and Methodology of Compromise

The Center began work on the study in June 1983. By February 1984, the Center had completed the survey design, and by June 1984, a pilot survey of 1,550 employees in 60 titles was finished. During this phase, several technical restrictions imposed by management laid the groundwork for severely restricting final study outcomes. Because technical decisions were so far removed from public accountability, they presented vast opportunities for managerial manipulation. Furthermore, the highly technical nature of the comparable worth study rendered it inaccessible to those employees who would benefit from the final results. Indeed, redefining political decisions as technical decisions was a key management strategy that both successfully limited labor participation and kept true comparable worth off the agenda.

Because labor offered little input into technical decisions, the Center tried repeatedly to compensate by keeping CSEA apprised both of the status of the study and of the material consequences of technical choices. The Center sent monthly study updates to both CSEA and the management. The Center never received any response from the union. Management, on the other hand, reviewed each monthly report in great detail, responding with guidelines for the study design. Without CSEA serving as a counterbalance to management, the Center had no external allies who could question managerial perspectives.

For example, a major technical conflict took place over what constituted a female-dominated or a significantly minority job. There are several ways to define these concepts. The Center recommended classifying jobs as female-dominated if they comprised 70% or more women, as mixed female if they included 50–69% women, as minority-dominated if they were 30% or more minority, and as mixed minority if 20–29% of job occupants were minority. GOER's Hartnett disagreed. He instructed the Center to *only* examine titles that were 70% or more female and 30% or more minority. Labor's role in these discussions remains ambiguous beyond arguing that certain jobs be included as female-dominated or significantly minority. As a compromise, the Center was allowed to make a case for including jobs that were "obviously impacted by historical association with women and minorities" but fell below the percentage cutoffs. Whether or not to include these jobs when estimating wage discrimination was made on a job-by-job basis. The smaller the number of jobs for which wage adjustments were estimated, the lower the cost of the study.

The completion of the Center's pilot study served as a wake-up call for the state because the results suggested that their wage structure embedded significant wage discrimination by gender and race. Upon receiving these results, the management monitor for the study established a Management Advisory Committee (MAC), including GOER, the division of the Budget, and the Department of Classification and Compensation in August 1984. At the same time, management rejected the Center's recommendation for a public advisory committee comprised of labor, management, and representatives from the legislature, women's organizations, and civil rights groups. As a result, MAC became the primary forum for debate over the direction of the study and the site of disagreements among divergent elements of the Administration. The MAC simply set a ceiling on the amount of money to spend on comparable worth and saw to it that the results stayed within these limits, as discussed below.

After the distribution of the results of the pilot study, the Division of Budget stopped payments to the Center. . . . The action by the Budget Division delayed survey distribution by two months. However, Budget was unable to fully derail the study. The Center's careful methodology proved to be beyond reproach. No significant changes in the study design resulted from the consultant recommendations. Also, the Center mobilized GOER to override Budget's obstruction to the study. Finally, labor applied its own pressure to continue the study, expressing concern that further delays in the study would make union leadership "a laughing stock."

As a result of this delay, the study was not completed by the March 1985 end date of the contract. This delay forced CSEA to enter negotiations without the results in hand, and publicly blamed management for the delays. Despite the lack of data on the extent of wage discrimination, in late March 1985, CSEA and GOER agreed upon a new three-year contract that allocated $34 million for comparable worth adjustments, the equivalent of 1% of payroll. The contract was ratified by union members in May 1985. CSEA called the negotiated agreement on comparable worth "a real breakthrough."

DISPARATE RESOURCES AND OUTCOMES

Four months later, in September 1985, the Center submitted its final report to labor and management. The Center found that the wages of 60,000 state employees in 185 titles were undervalued because these titles were female-dominated or significantly minority. The Center's study found that jobs with 100% women incumbents were paid two full salary grades or 10% less than jobs held only by men simply because of the gender of job incumbents. And, the Arthur Young Associates' wage discrimination study reached similar conclusions. The Arthur Young Associates study attributed 80% of pay disparities to sex- and race-based undervaluation.

In its report, the Center followed the standard approach to determining the extent of wage discrimination for each female-dominated or significantly minority job. Specifically, wage discrimination was defined as the difference between predicted pay for a job (with gender bias removed) and the actual pay rate. That difference in dollars specified the amount the wages for that job should be raised. But, at that time and even today, there are several ways to calculate the predicted pay. The Center calculated wage adjustments using three different approaches to obtaining predicted pay.

The first approach, the one recommended by the Center, is that predicted pay be the pay policy in place for jobs held by white men, on the assumption that, by definition, there is no race or gender bias in the wages paid for work historically performed by white males. This pay policy yields the highest wage adjustments. A second approach is to remove statistically the effect of "femaleness" and "minorityness" on average wages. The second approach would have yielded adjustments of about 7.5 percent. A third approach involves even more restricted assumptions about how to calculate predicted wages. Accordingly, wage adjustments using this third approach were around 4 percent.

Not surprisingly, the state preferred the third approach. They got their way by withholding monies the Center needed to finish the study.

In the summer of 1984, the Center ran out of money to complete the study. It had not anticipated in its budget the long delays the state would impose on its timeline. The Center's Director requested $168,000 in additional funding from GOER's Director Hartnett. The Center would receive the fund under one condition: that it would calculate wage adjustments using the third and most conservative approach to calculating wage adjustments. The Center Director agreed. What were the consequences of this decision? The results of the Center's study would *appear* to be eliminating wage discrimination, but would, instead, retain gender bias in wages. Specifically, by accepting these terms, the study would "cost" state employees in historically female or minority jobs approximately 10 percent of their "true" salary adjustment. By applying this third approach, for example, incumbents of jobs that involved working with difficult clients or dying patients or involved fine finger dexterity would actually lose money for performing this work because of its association with women's work. Moreover, the technical model

chosen by the state lessened the significance of education and experience requirements to job pay. This decision to devalue education and experience also lowered final wage adjustments because most female jobs require more education than male jobs with the same wages.

Management was satisfied with the Center's study results. As they put it, the study "reflect[ed] favorably on the state and the unions," without the numbers "get[ting] out of hand." CSEA was also pleased with the study results, although they wanted the pay of every female and minority-dominated title to be adjusted. The other union, PEA, however, was less enthusiastic with the Center's results since their titles had not been included in the study.

IMPLEMENTATION AND INEQUALITY: THE FINAL CONTAINMENT

Following completion of the Center's study, the state spent two years completing another in-house study that further diluted the original findings. This final stage would serve as the basis of implementation. This in-house study was based on the data collected by the Center for Women in Government, but manipulated the significance of specific job characteristics to pay in order to come up with predetermined findings. Although both CSEA and PEA were paying for a portion of the in-house study, they knew nothing about these political maneuvers. In other words, the state study team successfully managed to remove comparable worth from the results, but to claim that the results were based on the Center's study. Accordingly, the Center bore most of the discontent associated with a minimal implementation plan in which they played no role.

How did the state do this? First, a project team oriented to the status quo was set up to develop a quantitative wage model and use it to determine pay increases for a wage discrimination compensation system. The new compensation system would not alter the current hierarchy of wages.

Second, feminists inside the state bureaucracy were resistant to merging management into a single voice. They correctly feared that, as a minority, they lacked the institutional power to be effective. And they weren't. The in-house study was conducted within a department led by a very visible feminist unable to influence the study outcome because of her position. Other feminist bureaucrats were strategically unable to obtain any information about this study.

Third, labor was also at a disadvantage because it had neither the technical expertise nor the resources available to the study team. Further, the unions, and especially CSEA, were willing to abandon comparable worth if the state study team addressed hazardous duty pay, an issue of particular concern to male union members. GOER promised CSEA that the hazardous pay issue would be resolved before the union's October 1986 convention. Hazardous duty adjustments cost $7 million of $75 million set aside for implementation of the new compensation system.

The study team would actually change the survey response of job incumbents. They would change the impact or weight of job characteristics on pay.

Two results of the state's maneuvers are especially noteworthy. One was that management claimed some PEA titles, such as Registered Nurse and Occupational and Physical Therapists, were "overvalued" under their compensation system. Doctors and dentists were also found to be overpaid, as were correction officers.

In announcing these new results, Tom Hartnett wrote an editorial in the *GOER News*, entitled, "We Did It Our Way": "implementation will once and for all end the double standard of financial remuneration. Women and minorities will no longer be in the shadows of a white male majority. We can now move forward together, secure in the knowledge that New York State compensates its employees fairly for the work that they do . . . The resolve of the state and its public employee unions together, without outside interference has established a national model for labor-management cooperation." In a subsequent labor management press release, Hartnett said that he was "especially pleased that we have achieved comparable worth in the negotiations process, without mandate from the courts, and without employee lawsuits. Together the State and the unions have cooperated on an important, complex and timely issue in a responsive way." Of course, the question is responsive to whom?

NOTE

1. Ronnie Steinberg. (1981, April 17). The Feasibility of a Comparable Worth Pay Study of New York State Government Employment: A Proposal for Research. Final Report Prepared for the Legislative Committee on Economy and Efficiency in Government, State of New York.

BUILDING CONNECTIONS BETWEEN ANTIRACISM AND FEMINISM

Eileen O'Brien and Michael P. Armato

To overturn the vast inequalities that characterize U.S. society, members of the "dominant" groups, including white American men and women, will have to actively engage in the fight for racial and gender justice. Such actions are not unprecedented in U.S. history. Some men voiced support for women's equality as far back as the late 1800s,[1] and in the 1970s radical and socialist feminist men's groups emerged in response to the U.S. women's movement.[2] Moreover, white abolitionists voiced their opposition to the enslavement of black Americans in the nineteenth century.[3] In the early twentieth century when the political and social rights of formerly enslaved blacks were denied, white Americans helped to establish, and financially sponsored, the National Association for the Advancement of Colored People (NAACP), an interracial organization, which has been the leading organization combating racial discrimination in the United States. Whites also played a central role in the black civil rights movement, particularly in freedom schools, civil disobedience, and voter registration drives.[4]

Continuing this tradition of what we call "dominant group activism" today are white antiracist and male profeminist activists in North America who see their involvement as necessary to the struggle for social justice. In recent decades, numerous "men's movements" have appeared throughout the United States, typically as small local grassroots organizations. Although some, like The Promise Keepers and certain strands of Robert Bly's Mythopoetic Men's Movement, are antifeminist, others such as Men's Rape Prevention Project, Men Stopping Violence, Men as Peacemakers, Men Stopping Rape, RAVEN, and many others support feminist goals. Moreover, whites are active in antiracist groups such as Antiracist Action, founded in the 1990s, with over one hundred North American chapters and an estimated 100,000 core members, and the People's Institute which has trained thousands in its "Undoing Racism" workshops since 1980.[5]

In this essay, we analyze the similarities and differences in the way white antiracists and male profeminists practice activism, concluding with a consideration of the potential for coalition building across these groups. The data are from Eileen O'Brien's study of white antiracists and Michael Armato's study of male profeminists. The antiracist participants came primarily from two organizations: Antiracist Action (ARA) and the People's Institute (PI) for Survival and Beyond.

Eileen O'Brien used participant-observation methods, including "tabling" (providing information about the group and recruiting members at a concert) and protesting at a Ku Klux Klan rally with ARA, and participating in a two-and-a-half-day Undoing Racism workshop offered by PI. She interviewed twenty-four white antiracists (thirteen women and eleven men) from one Canadian city and a variety of regions in the United States. Nine were under the age of thirty, but the majority were thirty to sixty years old; one was over eighty.

Michael Armato's study included interviews with ten profeminist activists. Seven were affiliated with four profeminist organizations from the East, Southeast, and Midwest of the United States: Men Can Stop Rape (formerly known as Men's Rape Prevention Project) in Washington, D.C., Men Stopping Violence (MSV) in Atlanta, Georgia, Men Stopping Rape (MSR) in Madison, Wisconsin, and Men as Peacemakers (MP) in Duluth, Minnesota. Three were not associated with any organization but actively worked for feminist causes, two as abortion clinic escorts in Florida and one as a feminist campus activist in the state of Washington. The men's ages ranged from twenty-five to fifty, with a relatively equal distribution of men in their twenties, thirties, and forties. Armato also participated in a Mens Rape Prevention Project (MRPP) weekend training workshop in July 1999. Additionally, both authors analyzed the literature of these groups, including pamphlets, newsletters, and web sites.

ORGANIZATIONAL FRAMES OF ACTIVISM

Collective action "frames" have been popular in recent work on social movements.[6] Originally proposed by Snow and Benford, framing refers to the way movement actors develop shared understandings of what their goals are and how to achieve them.[7] The concept is an attempt to incorporate interpretive sociology into social movement theory, a response to its previously highly structural focus.[8] Framing becomes part of a shared organizational culture that is drawn upon regularly by movement members.

Frames are not necessarily shared across an entire movement. Within the feminist movement, debates abound over how to frame feminism. For example, whether U.S. professor Mary Daly's exclusion of men from her feminist seminars is indeed a feminist practice would be debated from the position of radical and liberal feminists because of the different ways the two groups frame what feminism is and what its practices should be. Here we want to examine the frames that dominant group activists use to direct their profeminist and antiracist practices. Those practices flow directly from the way they frame what sexism and racism means for them and their organizations.

ARE ALL MEN (POTENTIAL) RAPISTS?

As suggested by names such as Men's Rape Prevention Project, Men Stopping Violence, and Men Stopping Rape, profeminist groups focus on violence in general and sexual violence in particular. This grows directly out of their theoretical orientation toward gender and culture. In contrast to many "rape prevention" programs, which target women and make use of a risk-reduction model of rape prevention—and therefore inadvertently place the culpability primarily on the victims of sexual assault— these profeminist men's groups target what they call the "rape culture" in the United States.[9] Instead of conceptualizing violence as the behavior of exceptional, dysfunctional individuals, they view cultural expectations of manhood in this society as contributing to sexual violence. Peter, an activist from MRPP, explains:

> All of these behaviors, even if they don't directly lead to rape—that you know, every ten times I call a woman a bitch someone else gets raped. It's not that direct—and if we lived in a society in which it didn't occur to people to think of women as there for my sexual gratification exclusively, then it would be impossible for us to imagine that we were in a society that has a million rapes of women and girls a year, impossible.

Another activist, Rob, when asked about how his organization initially determined where to focus its energies, answered:

> We thought the roles that men play in society have a large part in why men commit most of the violence. So the way they are raised to look out and do things and behave are the major part of the problem.

Peter offered a similar sentiment:

> Our name says rape because we see sexual assault as sort of the touchstone of so many other issues that radiate out from it. But ultimately we see our project as redefining what it means to be a man. And sort of creating less destructive modes of masculinity.

Both Rob's and Peter's comments typify the general goal of most of the profeminist organizations: to develop a new, nonviolent paradigm of masculinity.

The culture of rape approach leads these groups to focus on making men (and women) aware of the relationships between everyday language/practices and sexual violence toward women in the hope that it will make individuals more likely to speak out against behaviors that propagate rape culture. Peter explained it quite succinctly:

> Our particular take on our work is that we need to address the bystander issues. Every rapist has a friend, and if we can reach that friend, whether that friend is male or female, then we can reach the rapist. It's sort of [a] male peer support model. You know [the] MADD [Mothers against Drunk Driving] model, "Friends don't let friends drive drunk." Well, friends don't let friends rape either.

Indeed, a central tenet of the ideologies of these groups is that bystanders need to become more active in challenging those behaviors that support rape culture. Rob echoed this sentiment:

> So the idea is really by training those young men to ask questions, ethical questions, about the appropriateness of their behavior, not their own behavior, but it's really built on looking as a bystander at what's happening and making a decision about whether or not you should step in and do something.

In keeping with the notion of bystander responsibility, the culture of rape approach does not distinguish between "good" and "bad" men, arguing that all men (and women) play a role in the continuance (or cessation) of rape culture. Peter traced the development of his thoughts:

> And so I've moved from rapists are all crazy and dangerous and all strangers hiding in the bushes and predominantly black, of course, and on down the line to OK rapists look like me, rapists act like me, rapists talk to me, and so maybe I have a role here. Maybe there's something that I can do.

He continued by recounting the words of an elder of his who was instrumental in the founding of his organization: "We live in a society in which bad men rape, good men do nothing, and I can't tell the difference."

In order to reach their target audience, nearly all these groups conduct discussions with high school and college-aged men (and women) about gender, especially masculinity, and its relationship to violence, using a series of exercises as well as personal anecdotes. MSV, based in Atlanta, runs discussion groups to educate batterers and violent men and teenaged boys. Although most participants are court-ordered, all must agree that they have a problem in order to participate. MSV also pushes for better legislation and law enforcement where men's violence is concerned. MRPP has evolved from a support group for profeminist men to an outreach program that makes presentations in area schools. MSR does similar educational work. MP works with a battered women's shelter to provide emergency transport of women to the shelter and to care for children at the shelter to give women a break. They also run various outreach and education programs with area schools, including the "playbook" program, which gives male college athletes a list of alternatives to sexual violence and sexist banter. In all these groups' practices, careful attention is paid to the message that *all* men participate to some extent in a "rape culture."

ARE ALL WHITES RACIST?

In contrast with the profeminist male activists, the white antiracist activists did not agree on where to focus their energies. While the focus of PI members was similar to that of profeminist men—that their own propagation of white racism was of central importance to their activism—ARA members' frame of racism as consisting mostly of overt acts like police brutality and neo-Nazi terrorism meant that their own relationship to white racism was not of primary concern.

PI was founded in New Orleans by two black American men as a training institute for those in social service professions that served communities of color. It has a white subsidiary group called European Dissent ("dissenting what has been done in the European name") of which all the PI respondents here are members. PI is most noted for its Undoing Racism workshops, which serve as transformative experiences for whites confronting racism and are now offered on a national and global scale. Focusing on institutionalized racism as a barrier to community organizing and activism, the workshops delve into historical and contemporary race relations and rely on a Malcolm X-like philosophy that whites should be doing separate work in their own communities. PI defines racism as "race prejudice plus power" and states that all whites are racist under this definition. A PI member, Pam, described what it was like to accept this frame of antiracism and incorporate it into her own self-concept:

> That was tough for me to swallow at the training, that [I'm a racist] . . . because I don't wanna believe that of myself. But if you look at the true historical definition of it then *yes,* I'm a racist. I'm white. I take advantage of the privileges that I have as a white person.

For white PI members, the antagonist is themselves and other whites. As in the "rape culture" frame of the profeminist men, there are no "good whites" and "bad whites" in the framework of PI.

After members complete the Undoing Racism training, they are encouraged to create antiracist change in the white-dominated organizations and groups in which they participate. Such practices include Pam's successful implementation of a "multicultural arts" program at the elementary school where she teaches predominantly impoverished students of color and Kendra's work to get her religious denomination (Unitarian Universalists) to adopt an antiracist agenda at the national level. Kendra described how she used her position as a religious educator at her church to educate children about whites' involvement in racism:

> I was teaching a Sunday school class to ten-year-olds last week and they said to me, "Everyone's a racist. Everyone's a little bit racist." And I said, "No, everyone's *not* a little bit racist. Everyone has some racial prejudice, because of racism. But really, not everybody is a racist." I said, "Racism is something that is when the whole society is set up for one group." I said, "Which [group] is this?" and they could *tell me* that it was white people. . . . *They know* that society is set up by and for white people, they can see it in their experience. And so we talked about some of those things. We talked about who it is that runs the government, who it is that owns most of the banks, who it is that runs the schools, and who it is that makes up standardized tests, and we talked about testing and things like that—things that are in their experience—and they *can* understand the difference, that it is white people who've been given power in this nation.

Kendra's method of practicing antiracism here is not to point out 'good whites' and 'bad whites,' but rather to emphasize whites' position in the system. PI trainers point out that many whites are "gatekeepers" of white-dominated institutions. Rather than saying whites are "bad" by virtue of their positions in these institutions, PI trainers encourage whites to use those positions to usher in institutional change.

The "all whites are racist" frame of antiracism used by PI differs considerably from that used by ARA, and their practices clearly reflect this difference. ARA was started in the cities of Columbus, Minneapolis, and Toronto by mostly white individuals to counteract Ku Klux Klan and neo-Nazi activity in their communities.[10] Counterdemonstrations at Klan rallies drew initial memberships, and youths wanting to protest right-wing hate groups that were forming at their schools followed suit. ARA focuses predominantly on front-line activism. Its newest project is Copwatch, a system of videotaping and police misconduct litigation to "police the police" in urban neighborhoods.

ARA's frames target overt acts of racism such as neo-Nazi atrocities, police brutality, and, as their mission statement reads, "hate in any form." Members do not generally see themselves as "hateful" human beings. When asked about successes in their antiracist work, most talked about a victory over the Nazis (driving them out of a "territory" such as a concert or a street), or successful cases in which perpetrators of police brutality were convicted. ARA member Tim, for instance, was one of the leaders of the outspoken opposition to the white supremacist "White Power Hour" TV show on his local cable access station. He narrowly escaped arrest when he and some others staged a protest outside the apartment of the host of the show. He credits the actions of ARA with raising awareness about the presence of racist hate and violence in his community. These kinds of antiracist practices, which focus on extremists, are typical of ARA members.

The only exception to this pattern within ARA was veteran organizer and key informant Steve who saw himself within the definition of racism:

> So I started trying to be not racist, and was totally unsuccessful at it, and still I am not skilled at it, because you get programmed at an early age and then deprogramming your uncontrollable mental processes as a white person that grew up in this culture—or as a male, for that matter—is not that easy! So this is why it's a lifelong kind of evolution.

While Steve understood himself to be a part of "racism," the practices of ARA do not include the notion of "deprogramming" ordinary whites. Similarly, although members of PI at one time banded together to protest the overtly racist flyers posted by a local fraternity, this is not a regularly occurring practice of the whites in the group. PI members' frame of "all whites are racist" and its related practices of targeting the white-dominated institutions of which they are a part most closely mirrors the profeminist men's "rape culture" frame, while ARA members frame racism as overt acts of hostility in which they cannot imagine themselves participating.

DOMINANT GROUP ACTIVISTS AND PRIVILEGE

Dominant group activists face the issue of how to deal with privilege in their organizing efforts. This issue arose in three ways in the profeminist men's groups and the white antiracist groups: in the definition of privilege, the cost of privilege to dominant group members, and the price of dominant group activism.

The Question of Privilege

First, profeminist men and white antiracists had to decide how they understood gender and racial privilege. While feminist discourse tends to use a language of oppression, power, and privilege, most profeminist men's discourse, surprisingly, is not one of male privilege and female oppression. Although they are sensitive to the notion of gendered oppression, they avoid language that might seem accusatory or offensive to men or ineffective for communicating their message to a wider audience. Consider the following statements made by Rob about his organization's (MRPP's) approach to social change:

> I think it's a very positive kind of a thing. It's not finger pointing. We have been very clear in our organization that we are not going to point fingers at men, which is one of the things that sometimes profeminist groups get into is the finger pointing. We say very clearly, men commit 90 percent of the

violence—that's why we're in this. They commit a lot of that violence against women, but they also commit an incredible amount against other men.

One notable exception to this pattern was Andy from MSV who explained that one of his biggest challenges was recognizing and giving up his privilege as a white male in U.S. society. When asked what he meant by that, he offered the following anecdote:

> I remember like when I was really pretty young in [an activist organization for the homeless and poor]. I was probably maybe there for like two months at this point, and I was really getting comfortable and there was one of the women who had helped start it. This was her last meeting and she was sort of giving her final thoughts. And she was leaving and she just said, "You know, I think this organization has a lot to learn and think about as far as like internal sexism and how men handle themselves during group conversations. I feel that men are dominating group conversations. They don't give women a chance to speak or listen to women when they do." And that was like falling on virgin ears for *me*. Like I was just like blown away by that. And feel like I didn't talk for like the next year, until I learned that was not the way to respond because then that is leaving most of the responsibility and organizational work to women. And so, and just like that process. Figuring out, you know, first of all identifying your privilege. I mean I know like one of, and I don't know if this necessarily came from MSV, but it's like the metaphor that's used a lot there talking about men and privilege is like talking about fish in a fish tank and the water around them. I mean it's just what you live in.

More typical is the position of Robert Jensen who argues that feminism is more compelling to men if it focuses on how it can improve *their* lives. His emphasis is *not* on how sexism privileges men, but rather on how it makes men "miserable," with careful attention to the idea that "being miserable, however, is not the same as being oppressed."[11] Drawing upon personal experience, Jensen believes that bringing men to feminist politics requires a "self-interest" argument rather than a "justice" argument, since "a justice argument does not always persuade people in power to give up some of that power."[12]

Steve, a member of ARA, made an argument similar to Jensen's when he argued that emphasizing the negative effects of racism on whites was an effective antiracist organizing tactic. He was careful, however, to argue that although whites were "victims" of racism, they were not themselves oppressed by racism:

> Racism is not good for most white people. It's good for a few people, most of whom are white, but it could theoretically be better for some nonwhite people as well . . . It's a benefit we'd be better off without by far. Still doesn't mean that white people on average don't do better than black people in almost every circumstance [because] they do, 'cause of this institution that's put on everybody. But seeing most white people as victims of it as well is more accurate than to emphasize the privilege element of white racism in the United States.

Steve's position was unusual among white antiracist activists. Most white antiracists subscribed to the notion of privilege as a means of conceptualizing their position in the movement. In fact, ARA members Kristin and Claire both recognized that whites in their group could take more risks at marches and demonstrations than could people of color and were less likely to be arrested. Lori, a nonorganizational activist, concurred and remarked that "if a person of color expresses an antiracist opinion, they're just being overly sensitive" yet, as a white person with privilege, people would "listen to [her] more" because she is a member of the dominant group.

PI members also were also well-versed in the concept of white privilege. Their definition of racism (race prejudice plus power equals racism) recognizes power and privilege as central. To "undo" racism in their own lives and in their positions as "gatekeepers," they believe they must be aware of their racial privilege.

Costs of Privilege

Second, antiracist whites and profeminist men had to decide how to assess whether there were costs to dominant groups of racial and gender privilege. Profeminist men's organizations see both women and men as casualties of contemporary gender arrangements. Although they do not claim that men are as oppressed as women, profeminist men devote a significant amount of time to exploring the challenges they face as men. In so doing, they seek to address what Michael A. Messner terms the "costs of masculinity" to men who try to live up to a masculine norm, such as shallow relationships, poor health, and early death.[13] Indeed, the desire to mitigate these costs strongly motivates their involvement in profeminist organizations. Their activism is not merely selfless devotion to ending gender inequality, but rather a search for a less harmful version of manhood. One member, Jim, explained that he felt totally liberated when he finally got involved with the profeminist organization in his town because it provided him with close male friendships that were unlike any he had ever had, suggesting that one benefit of profeminist men's groups for their members is a sense of community.

Although white antiracists generally emphasize the *power* inherent in privilege rather than its costs, PI expresses concern about the lack of awareness of community and culture among whites. Included in its Undoing Racism workshop is an evening of "cultural sharing" in which everyone brings a show-and-tell object representing his or her culture. Relative to people of color, whites have a harder time recognizing

their racial culture. In one exercise, participants are asked to say what they like about being white or black. Typically, almost all answers by whites are about power (for example, "I like that I am represented adequately in history books, that people don't look past me because of my race," and so on) and nearly all answers by black Americans are about culture (for example, "I like our music, feeling like a family/sense of unity," and so on). PI trainers claim that one barrier to building a multiracial movement is this lack of a sense of belonging to a larger collective among whites. This lack of cultural identity among whites is also seen as a barrier to change, leading some antiracist whites to dissociate themselves from racist whites in their lives rather than working for change.

However, white antiracists do not refer to this sense of community as a major motivation for their antiracist activism in the way that profeminist men do. Although losing an individualistic orientation is one step on the path of "undoing racism" for whites, it does not seem to provide the lasting inspiration and staying power for white antiracists that it does for male profeminists. Rather, white antiracists cite the oppression of people of color and their privileged racial position as their reason for remaining in the struggle. For example, Mike had previously signed up to teach elementary school in an inner city community for a limited number of years, but his involvement with antiracism in the community motivated him to make a lifetime commitment to the city. Thus, after his mandatory contract was over, he chose a life of antiracist activism despite having a "hundred choices" of working in communities that would have been more financially beneficial to him. PI member Lisa concurred with Mike's sentiments:

> Every single day I have to recommit myself to that process. . . . just being very aware of that privilege that I *can*, I can leave this city, I can

leave this process, and so, every single day, just making that recommitment that this is something that I believe in and this is something that I want to work for.

Rather than relying on a sense of community that she feels with other whites to keep her motivated, Lisa compared her situation with that of the impoverished people of color in her community and the privilege that she has relative to them. Although there might be costs to being privileged, recognizing them is not what sustains white antiracists.

Paying the Price

Third, dominant group activists struggle with the costs of their activist practices. Profeminist men often cited their frustration with the work that remains to be done, as did Peter, despite the few serious negative consequences of being profeminist for men:

> On a personal level, I don't sleep any more. I'm so full with the experience of frustration that I'm seeing in men and women about this work, about the ravages that masculinity has committed against our society that I don't sleep. It just keeps going over and over again in my mind. I feel I'm not doing enough, and so I'm exhausted most of the time. . . . I often feel like I can't do any more and then I get the next phone call and I can do more; I have to. So, I think the sign of an old activist, right, are the bags under the eyes [laughs], and I see myself heading there; I'm only thirty!

In contrast, the activist practices of white antiracists often had serious costs, particularly for those not affiliated with any organization. For challenging a fraternity's racist paraphernalia, Lori ended up receiving death threats and eventually had to change schools to finish her degree.

We were going to hang signs that said . . ."The Confederate Flag: Four Hundred Years of Oppression or a [fraternity name] Tradition? You Decide." And we hung them up all over campus one night when everyone was asleep. . . . like an idiot, I wrote; "For more information, contact [Lori]" [laughs]. And I wrote my number on it, right?! And my PO Box, so of course, what do I get? Millions of harassing phone calls, and [frat name]'s telling me they're going to sue me for defamation! And I'm like, well, it's true, it was their symbol! I don't know what they thought they were going to sue me for, but so I had all these people like calling me up, and all these people leaving me notes in my mailbox telling me I was going to die and I started getting death threats and stuff, whatever, people saying they were going to burn a cross and shoot me.

Some white antiracists have lost jobs by performing acts of antiracism in isolation. Before joining PI, Paul was fired from his job as a teacher when he took his students on a field trip to a civil rights march. Betty's career as a journalist ended when she exposed local incidents of racism:

> I wrote a story about healthcare, what the blacks were getting and not getting in [the] county, and I included the fact that the local hospital wasn't serving any black people. Because we also complained to Washington after that happened and they sent somebody in, and the hospital straightened up. But anyway, I got fired. [Interviewer: You got fired? For what?] It turned out the publisher was on the hospital board.

POSSIBILITIES FOR COALITION BUILDING

This study suggests three lessons about dominant group activism. First, it is important to conceptualize *all* dominant group members as implicated in oppression, not to settle for targeting only extremists. In this study, the similarity between the male profeminists' "rape culture" frame and the PI white antiracists' "all whites are racist" frame was striking. Both viewed dominant group members as part of the structure of oppression they were seeking to abolish. Because this frame was not shared by ARA white antiracists, it may be hard to build coalitions across the two dominant antiracist movements. We argue that ARA needs to broaden its focus to incorporate antiracist practices focused on everyday racism, rather than just on overt acts of racism.

Second, we conclude that for dominant group activists, approaches to privilege should vary based on whether racism or sexism is the issue. Male profeminists tend to emphasize the cost of men's participation in hegemonic masculinity rather than the privileges that sexism affords them. Some white antiracists (particularly PI members) also see the costs that whites pay in a racist society, but it is not a central aspect of their movement, which is more focused on racial privileges. This difference may reflect a difference in the way racism and sexism operate in North American societies and, therefore, it may not be to the two movements' advantage to become more alike on this dimension. Profeminist men's emphasis on costs can help build a stronger sense of community among men as well as improve relationships between men and women. In contrast, because of the fear of intimate interracial relationships in North American society, whites are less likely to experience a cost in their relationships with people of color. The possibility of heightened intimacy with people of color is not likely to attract more whites to antiracism.

Finally, the question of the costs of antiracist and profeminist activism for dominant group members needs further exploration. Our data suggest that while profeminist men are occasionally accused of being gay, for the most part they are lauded for being profeminist. White antiracists, on the other hand, are commonly stigmatized as "race traitors." However, we find

that being affiliated with an organization can be a buffer against serious repercussions. Many of our sample of profeminist men worked in organizations, which may explain their decreased sense of the costs of activism.

It is also important to note that although our interviews focused on individuals' own "dominant" status, activists often linked racism and sexism. For example, MRPP explicitly points out how race plays into common myths of rape in the United States and therefore bolsters both gender and race oppression. One of ARA's principles is that members should address many other "isms" besides racism (among which sexism is included). Yet the organizations varied in how explicit they were in addressing the connection between racism and sexism. PI prefers not to have its attention diverted to other issues of oppression unless they are addressed specifically in an antiracist framework. As PI member Lisa put it: "Too often we focus on other issues as escapism, like trying to get out of [focusing on] racism." Such sentiments may prove an additional challenge to coalition building across dominant group activist organizations.

Acknowledgments

The authors would like to thank all the wonderful activists who shared their time and energy with us for this project, and Kathleen Blee and France Winddance Twine for their helpful comments and editing of our essay. Michael Armato is also grateful to his life partner Amanda for enriching his understanding of feminism.

Notes

1. Michael S. Kimmel, "From 'Conscience and Common Sense' to 'Feminism' for Men," in *Feminism and Men,* ed. Steven P. Schacht and Doris W. Ewing (New York: New York University Press, 1998), 21–42.

2. Michael A. Messner, "Radical Feminist and Socialist Feminist Men's Movements in the United States," in *Feminism and Men,* ed. Steven P. Schacht and Doris W. Ewing (New York: New York University Press, 1998), 67–85; Michael A. Messner, *Politics of Masculinities: Men in Movements* (Thousand Oaks. Calif.: Sage, 1997).

3. Herbert Aptheker, *Antiracism in U.S. History: The First Two Hundred Years* (New York: Greenwood Press, 1992).

4. Doug McAdam, *Freedom Summer* (New York: Oxford University Press, 1988).

5. Michael Novick, "Antiracist Action on the Move," *Turning the Tide: Journal of Antiracist Activism Research and Education,* vol. 10, no. 2 (1997): 1–2; Ronald Chisom and Michael Washington, *Undoing Racism: A Philosophy of International Social Change* (New Orleans: People's Institute Press, 1997).

6. Hank Johnston and Bert Klandermans, *Social Movements and Culture* (Minneapolis: University of Minnesota Press, 1995); Enrique Larana, Hank Johnston, and Joseph R. Gusfield, *New Social Movements: From Ideology to Identity* (Philadelphia: Temple University Press, 1994).

7. Scott A. Hunt, Robert D. Benford, and David A. Snow, "Identity Fields: Framing Processes and the Construction of Social Identities," in *New Social Movements: From Ideology to Identity,* ed. Enrique Larana, Hank Johnston, and Joseph R. Gusfield (Philadelphia: Temple University Press, 1994), 185–208; David A. Snow and Robert D. Benford, "Master Frames and Cycles of Protest," in *Frontiers in Social Movement Theory,* ed. Aldon D. Morris and Carol McClurg Mueller (New Haven: Yale University Press, 1992), 133–55.

8. Johnston and Klandermans, *Social Movements and Culture.*

9. Emilie Buchwald, Pamela Fletcher, and Martha Roth, *Transforming a Rape Culture* (Minneapolis: Milkweed, 1993).

10. Novick, "Antiracist Action on the Move," 1–2; Jonathan Franklin, "Skinnin' Heads," *Vibe* (June-July 1998): 84–85.

11. Robert Jensen, "Men's Lives and Feminist Theory," *Race, Class and Gender,* vol. 2 (1995): 114.

12. Jensen, "Men's Lives and Feminist Theory," 115.

13. Messner, *Politics of Masculinities,* 5–6.

ABOLISH THE WHITE RACE BY ANY MEANS NECESSARY

Noel Ignatiev and John Garvey

The white race is a historically constructed social formation—historically constructed because (like royalty) it is a product of some people's responses to historical circumstances; a social formation because it is a fact of society corresponding to no classification recognized by natural science.

The white race cuts across ethnic and class lines. It is not coextensive with that portion of the population of European descent, since many of those classified as "colored" can trace some of their ancestry to Europe, while African, Asian, or American Indian blood flows through the veins of many considered white. Nor does membership in the white race imply wealth, since there are plenty of poor whites, as well as some people of wealth and comfort who are not white.

The white race consists of those who partake of the privileges of the white skin in this society. Its most wretched members share a status higher, in certain respects, than that of the most exalted persons excluded from it, in return for which they give their support to the system that degrades them.

The key to solving the social problems of our age is to abolish the white race. Until that task is accomplished, even partial reform will prove elusive, because white influence permeates every issue in U.S. society, whether domestic or foreign.

Advocating the abolition of the white race is distinct from what is called "antiracism." The term "racism" has come to be applied to a variety of attitudes, some of which are mutually incompatible, and has been devalued to mean little more than a tendency to dislike some people for the color of their skin. Moreover, antiracism admits the natural existence of "races" even while opposing social distinctions among them. The abolitionists maintain, on the contrary, that people were not favored socially because they were white; rather they were defined as "white" because they were favored. Race itself is a product of social discrimination; so long as the white race exists, all movements against racism are doomed to fail.

The existence of the white race depends on the willingness of those assigned to it to place their racial interests above class, gender, or any other interests they hold. The defection of enough of its members to make it unreliable as a determinant of behavior will set off tremors that will lead to its collapse.

Race Traitor aims to serve as an intellectual center for those seeking to abolish the white race. It will encourage dissent from the conformity that maintains it and popularize examples of defection from its ranks, analyze the forces that hold it together and those that promise to tear it apart. Part of its task will be to promote debate among abolitionists. When possible, it will support practical measures, guided by the principle, *treason to whiteness is loyalty to humanity.*

DISSOLVE THE CLUB

The white race is a club that enrolls certain people at birth, without their consent, and brings them up according to its rules. For the most part the members go through life accepting the benefits of membership, without thinking about the costs. When individuals question the rules, the officers are quick to remind them of all they owe to the club, and warn them of the dangers they will face if they leave it.

Race Traitor aims to dissolve the club, to break it apart, to explode it. Some people who sympathize with our aim have asked us how we intend to win over the majority of so-called whites to anti-racism. Others, usually less friendly, have asked if we plan to exterminate physically millions, perhaps hundreds of millions, of people. Neither of these plans is what we have in mind. The weak point of the club is its need for unanimity. Just as the South, on launching the Civil War, declared that it needed its entire territory and would have it, the white race must have the support of all those it has designated as its constituency, or it ceases to exist.

Before the Civil War, the leading spokesmen for the slaveholders acknowledged that the majority of white northerners, swayed above all by the presence of the fugitive slave, considered slavery unjust. The Southerners also understood that the opposition was ineffective; however much the white people of the north disapproved of the slave system, the majority went along with it rather than risk the ordinary comforts of their lives, meager as they were in many cases.

When John Brown attacked Harpers Ferry, Southern pro-slavery leaders reacted with fury: they imposed a boycott on northern manufacturers, demanded new concessions from the government in Washington, and began to prepare for war. When they sought to portray John Brown as a representative of northern opinion, Southern leaders were wrong; he represented only a small and isolated minority. But they were also right, for he expressed the hopes that still persisted in the northern population despite decades of cringing before the slaveholders. Virginia did not fear John Brown and his small band of followers, but rather his soul that would go marching on, though his body lay a-mould'rin' in the grave.

When the South, in retaliation for Harpers Ferry, sought to further bully northern opinion, it did so not out of paranoia but out of the realistic assessment that only a renewal of the national pro-slavery vows could save a system whose proud facade concealed a fragile foundation. By the arrogance of their demands, the Southern leaders compelled the people of the north to resist. Not ideas but events were in command. Each step led inexorably to the next: Southern land-greed, Lincoln's victory, secession, war, blacks as laborers, soldiers, citizens, voters. And so the war that began with not one person in a hundred foreseeing the end of slavery was transformed within two years into an anti-slavery war.

It is our faith—and with those who do not share it we shall not argue—that the majority of so-called whites in this country are neither deeply nor consciously committed to white supremacy; like most human beings in most times and places, they would do the right thing if it were convenient. As did their counterparts before the Civil War, most go along with a system that disturbs them, because the consequences of challenging it are terrifying. They close their eyes to what is happening around them, because it is easier not to know.

At rare moments their nervous peace is shattered, their certainty is shaken, and they are compelled to question the common sense by which they normally live. One such moment was in the days immediately following the Rodney King verdict, when a majority of white Americans were willing to admit to polltakers that black people had good reasons to rebel, and some joined them. Ordinarily the moments are brief, as the guns and reform programs are moved up to restore order and the confidence that matters are in good hands and they can go back to sleep. Both the guns and the reform programs are aimed at whites as well as blacks—the guns as a warning and the reform programs as a salve to their consciences.

Recently, one of our editors, unfamiliar with New York City traffic laws, made an illegal right turn there on a red light. He was stopped by two cops in a patrol car. After examining his license, they released him with a courteous admonition. Had he been black, they probably would have ticketed him, and might even have taken him down to the station. A lot of history was embodied in that small exchange: the cops treated the miscreant leniently at least in part because they assumed, looking at him, that he was white and therefore loyal. Their courtesy was a habit meant both to reward good conduct and induce future cooperation.

Had the driver cursed them, or displayed a bumper sticker that said, "Avenge Rodney King," the cops might have reacted differently. We admit that neither gesture on the part of a single individual would in all likelihood be of much consequence. But if enough of those who looked white broke the rules of the club to make the cops doubt their ability to recognize a white person merely by looking at him or her, how would it affect the cops' behavior? And if the police, the courts, and the authorities in general were to start spreading around indiscriminately the treatment they normally reserve for people of color, how would the rest of the so-called whites react?

How many dissident so-called whites would it take to unsettle the nerves of the white executive board? It is impossible to know. One John Brown—against a background of slave resistance—was enough for Virginia. Yet it was not the abolitionists, not even the transcendent John Brown, who brought about the mass shifts in consciousness of the Civil War period. At most, their heroic deeds were part of a chain of events that involved mutual actions and reactions on a scale beyond anything they could have anticipated—until a war that began with both sides fighting for slavery (the South to take it out of the Union, the North to keep it in) ended with a great army marching through the land singing, "As He died to make men holy, let us fight to make men free."

The moments when the routine assumptions of race break down are the seismic promise that somewhere in the tectonic flow a new fault is building up pressure, a new Harpers Ferry is being prepared. Its nature and timing cannot be predicted, but of its coming we have no doubt. When it comes, it will set off a series of tremors that will lead to the disintegration of the white race. We want to be ready, walking in Jerusalem just like John.

SOURCE: From *Race Traitor* by Noel Ignatiev and John Garvey. Copyright © 1996. Reproduced by permission of Routledge/Taylor and Frances Group, LLC.

BEING AN ALLY

Paul Kivel

WHAT DOES AN ALLY DO?

Being allies to people of color in the struggle to end racism is one of the most important things that white people can do. There is no one correct way to be an ally. Each of us is different. We have different relationships to social organizations, political processes, and economic structures. We are more or less powerful because of such factors as our gender, class, work situation, family, and community participation. Being an ally to people of color is an ongoing strategic process in which we look at our personal and social resources, evaluate the environment we have helped to create, and decide what needs to be done.

This book is filled with things to do and ways to get involved. These suggestions are not prioritized because they cannot be. Times change and circumstances vary. What is a priority today may not be tomorrow. What is effective or strategic right now may not be next year. We need to be thinking with others and noticing what is going on around us so we will know how to put our attention, energy, time, and money toward strategic priorities in the struggle to end racism and other injustices.

This includes listening to people of color so that we can support the actions they take, the risks they bear in defending their lives and challenging white hegemony. It includes watching the struggle of white people to maintain dominance and the struggle of people of color to gain equal opportunity, justice, safety, and respect.

We don't need to believe or accept as true everything people of color say. There is no one voice in any community, much less in the complex and diverse communities of color spanning our country. We do need to listen carefully to the voices of people of color so that we understand and give credence to their experience. We can then evaluate the content of what they are saying by what we know about how racism works and by our own critical thinking and progressive political analysis.

It is important to emphasize this point because often we become paralyzed when people of color talk about racism. We are afraid to challenge what they say. We will be ineffective as allies if we give up our ability to analyze and think critically, if we simply accept everything that a person of color states as truth.

Listening to people of color and giving critical credence to their experience is not easy for us because of the training we have received. Nevertheless, it is an important first step. When we hear statements that make us want to react defensively, we can instead keep the following points in mind as we try to understand what is happening and determine how best to be allies.

We have seen how racism is a pervasive part of our culture. Therefore we should always assume that racism is at least part of the picture. In light of this assumption, we should look for the patterns involved rather than treating most events as isolated occurrences.

Since we know that racism is involved, we know our whiteness is also a factor. We should look for ways we are acting from assumptions of white power or privilege. This will help us acknowledge any fear or confusion we may feel. It will allow us to see our tendencies to defend ourselves or our tendencies to assume we should be in control. Then we may want to talk with other white people both to express our feelings and to get support so our tendencies towards defensiveness or controlling behavior don't get in the way of our being effective allies.

We have many opportunities to practice these critical listening and thinking skills because we are all involved in a complex web of interpersonal and institutional relationships. Every day we are presented with opportunities to analyze what is going on around us and to practice taking direct action as allies to people of color.

People of color will always be on the front lines fighting racism because their lives are at stake. How do we act and support them effectively, both when they are in the room with us and when they are not?

Basic Tactics

Every situation is different and calls for critical thinking about how to make a difference. Taking the statements above into account, I have compiled some general guidelines.

1. **Assume racism is everywhere, every day.** Just as economics influences everything we do, just as our gender and gender politics influence everything we do, assume that racism is affecting whatever is going on. We assume this because it's true and because one of the privileges of being white is not having to see or deal with racism all the time. We have to learn to see the effect that racism has. Notice who speaks, what is said, how things are done and described. Notice who isn't present. Notice code words for race, and the implications of the policies, patterns, and comments that are being expressed. You already notice the skin color of everyone you meet and interact with— now notice what difference it makes.

2. **Notice who is the center of attention and who is the center of power.** Racism works by directing violence and blame toward people of color and consolidating power and privilege for white people.

3. Notice how racism is denied, minimized, and justified.

4. **Understand and learn from the history of whiteness and racism.** Notice how racism has changed over time and how it has subverted or resisted challenges. Study the tactics that have worked effectively against it.

5. Understand the connections between racism, economic issues, sexism, and other forms of injustice.

6. **Take a stand against injustice.** Take risks. It is scary, difficult, and may bring up feelings of inadequacy, lack of self-confidence, indecision, or fear of making mistakes, but ultimately it is the only healthy and moral human thing to do. Intervene in situations where racism is being passed on.

7. **Be strategic.** Decide what is important to challenge and what's not. Think about

strategy in particular situations. Attack the source of power.

8. **Don't confuse a battle with the war.** Behind particular incidents and interactions are larger patterns. Racism is flexible and adaptable. There will be gains and losses in the struggle for justice and equality.

9. **Don't call names or be personally abusive.** Since power is often defined as power over others—the ability to abuse or control people—it is easy to become abusive ourselves. However, we usually end up abusing people who have less power than we do because it is less dangerous. Attacking people doesn't address the systemic nature of racism and inequality.

10. **Support the leadership of people of color.** Do this consistently, but not uncritically.

11. **Learn something about the history of white people who have worked for racial justice.** There is a long history of white people who have fought for racial justice. Their stories can inspire and sustain you.

12. **Don't do it alone.** You will not end racism by yourself. We can do it if we work together. Build support, establish networks, and work with already established groups.

13. Talk with your children and other young people about racism.

GETTING INVOLVED

It can be difficult for those of us who are white to know how to be strong allies for people of color when discrimination occurs. In the following interaction, imagine that Roberto is a young Latino just coming out of a job interview with a white recruiter from a computer company. Let's see how one white person might respond.

Roberto is angry, not sure what to do next. He walks down the hall and meets a white teacher who wants to help.

Teacher: Hey, Roberto, how's it going?

Roberto: That son of a bitch! He wasn't going to give me no job. That was really messed up.

Teacher: Hold on there, don't be so angry. It was probably a mistake or something.

Roberto: There was no mistake. The racist bastard. He wants to keep me from getting a good job. Rather have us all on welfare or doing maintenance work.

Teacher: Calm down now or you'll get yourself in more trouble. Don't go digging a hole for yourself. Maybe I could help you if you weren't so angry.

Roberto: That's easy for you to say. This man was discriminating against me. White folks are all the same. They talk about equal opportunity, but it's the same old shit.

Teacher: Wait a minute. I didn't have anything to do with this. Don't blame me, I'm not responsible. If you wouldn't be so angry maybe I could help you. You probably took what he said the wrong way. Maybe you were too sensitive.

Roberto: I could tell. He was racist. That's all. (He storms off.)

What did you notice about this scene? The teacher is concerned and is trying to help, but his intervention is not very effective. He immediately downplays the incident, discounting Roberto's feelings and underestimating the possibility of racism. He seems to think that racism is unlikely—that it was just a misunderstanding, or that Roberto was being too sensitive.

The teacher is clearly uncomfortable with Roberto's anger. He begins to defend himself, the job recruiter, and white people. He ends up feeling attacked for being white. Rather than talking about what happened, he focuses on Roberto's anger and his generalizations about white people. He threatens to get Roberto in trouble himself if Roberto doesn't calm down. As he walks away, he may be thinking it's no wonder Roberto didn't get hired for the job.

You probably recognize some of the tactics described. . . . The teacher denies or minimizes the likelihood of racism, blames Roberto, and eventually counterattacks, claiming to be a victim of Roberto's anger and racial generalizations.

This interaction illustrates some of the common feelings that can get in the way of intervening effectively where discrimination is occurring. First is the feeling that we are being personally attacked. It is difficult to hear the phrases "all white people" or "you white people." We want to defend ourselves and other whites. We don't want to believe that white people could intentionally hurt others. Or we may want to say, "Not me, I'm different."

There are some things we should remember when we feel attacked. First, this is a question of injustice. We need to focus on what happened and what we can do about it, not on our feelings of being attacked.

Second, someone who has been the victim of injustice is legitimately angry and may or may not express that anger in ways we like. Criticizing the way people express their anger deflects attention and action away from the injustice that was committed. After the injustice has been dealt with, if you still think it's worthwhile and not an attempt to control the situation yourself, you can go back and discuss ways of expressing anger.

Often, because we are frequently complacent about injustice that doesn't affect us directly, it takes a lot of anger and aggressive action to bring attention to a problem. If we were more proactive about identifying and intervening in situations of injustice, people would not have to be so "loud" to get our attention in the first place.

Finally, part of the harm that racism does is that it forces people of color to be wary and mistrustful of all white people, just as sexism forces women to mistrust all men. People of color face racism every day, often from unexpected quarters. They never know when a white friend, co-worker, teacher, police officer, doctor, or passerby may discriminate, act hostile, or say something offensive. They have to be wary of all white people, even though they know that not all white people will mistreat them. They have likely been hurt in the past by white people they thought they could trust, and therefore they may make statements about all white people. We must remember that although we want to be trustworthy, trust is not the issue. We are not fighting racism so that people of color will trust us. Trust builds over time through our visible efforts to be allies and fight racism. Rather than trying to be safe and trustworthy, we need to be more active, less defensive, and put issues of trust aside.

When people are discriminated against they may feel unseen, stereotyped, attacked, or as if a door has been slammed in their face. They may feel confused, frustrated, helpless, or angry. They are probably reminded of other similar experiences. They may want to hurt someone in return, or hide their pain, or simply forget about the whole experience. Whatever the response, the experience is deeply wounding and painful. It is an act of emotional violence.

It's also an act of economic violence to be denied access to a job, housing, educational program, pay raise, or promotion that one deserves. It is a practice that keeps economic resources in the hands of one group and denies them to another.

When a person is discriminated against it is a serious event and we need to treat it seriously. It is also a common event. For instance, the government estimates that there are over 2 million acts of race-based housing discrimination every year—20 million every decade. We know that during their lifetime, every person of color will probably have to face such discriminatory experiences in school, work, housing, and community settings.

People of color do not protest discrimination lightly. They know that when they do, white people routinely deny or minimize it, blame them for causing trouble, and then counterattack. This is the "happy family" syndrome described earlier.

People of color are experts in discrimination resulting from racism. Most experience it regularly and see its effects on their communities. Not every complaint of discrimination is valid, but most have some truth in them. It would be a tremendous step forward if we assumed that there was some truth in every complaint of racial discrimination, even when other factors may also be involved. At least then we would take it seriously enough to investigate fully.

How could the teacher in the above scenario be a better ally to Roberto? We can go back to the guidelines suggested earlier for help. First, he needs to listen much more carefully to what Roberto is saying. He should assume that Roberto is intelligent, and if he says there was racism involved then there probably was. The teacher should be aware of his own power and position, his tendency to be defensive, and his desire to defend other white people or presume their innocence. It would also be worthwhile to look for similar occurrences because racism is usually not an isolated instance but a pattern within an organization or institution.

Let's see how these suggestions might operate in a replay of this scene.

Teacher: Hey, Roberto, what's happening?

Roberto: That son of a bitch! He wasn't going to give me no job. He was messin' with me.

Teacher: You're really upset. Tell me what happened.

Roberto: He was discriminating against me. Wasn't going to hire me cause I'm Latino. White folks are all alike. Always playing games.

Teacher: This is serious. Why don't you come into my office and tell me exactly what happened.

Roberto: Okay. This company is advertising for computer programmers and I'm qualified for the job. But this man tells me there aren't any computer jobs, and then he tries to steer me toward a janitor job. He was a racist bastard.

Teacher: That's tough. I know you would be good in that job. This sounds like a case of job discrimination. Let's write down exactly what happened, and then you can decide what you want to do about it.

Roberto: I want to get that job.

Teacher: If you want to challenge it, I'll help you. Maybe there's something we can do.

This time the teacher was being a strong, supportive ally to Roberto.

An Ally Makes a Commitment

Nobody needs fly-by-night allies, those who are here today and gone tomorrow. Being an ally takes commitment and perseverance. It is a lifelong struggle to end racism and other forms of social injustice. People of color know this well because they have been struggling for generations for recognition of their rights and the opportunity to participate fully in our society. The struggle to abolish slavery took over 80 years. Women organized for over 60 years to win the right to vote. I was reminded about the long haul recently when my sister sent me a news clipping about my old high school in Los Angeles, Birmingham High.

The clipping was about the 17-year struggle to change the "Birmingham Braves" name and caricatured image of an "Indian" used by the school teams to something that did not insult Native Americans. I was encouraged to hear that the name and mascot were now being changed, but was upset to read that there was an alumni group resisting the change and filing a lawsuit to preserve the old name.

Soon after receiving the article I had the good fortune to talk with a white woman who had been involved with the struggle over the mascot. The challenge had originated with a group of Native Americans in the San Fernando Valley. This woman decided to join the group—the only white person to do so. She started attending meetings. For the first two or three years all she did was listen, and the group hardly spoke to her. After a time, members of the group began to acknowledge her presence, talk with her, and include her in their activities. This woman learned a tremendous amount about herself, the local Native cultures, and the nature of white resistance during the 15 years she was involved with this group. They tried many different strategies and eventually, because they met with so much intransigence at the high school, they went to the Los Angeles school board.

When the school board made its decision to eliminate Native-American names and logos in school programs, it affected every school in the Los Angeles area. Subsequently the decision became a model for the Dallas school district's policy and is being considered for adoption in other school districts across the country.

This was a long struggle, but much public education was accomplished in the process. This work is part of a national effort by Native Americans and their allies to get sports teams and clubs to relinquish offensive names and mascots.

If the woman I talked with had been discouraged or offended because nobody welcomed her or paid her special attention during those first meetings, or if she felt that after a year or two nothing was going to be accomplished, or if she had not listened and learned enough to be able to work with and take leadership from the Native American community involved in this struggle, she would have gone home and possibly talked about how she had tried but it hadn't worked. She would not have been transformed by the struggle the way she had been; she would not have contributed to and been able to celebrate the success of this struggle for Native-American dignity and respect. Her work as an ally reminded me of what commitment as an ally really means.

SOURCE: Excerpts from *Uprooting Racism: How White People Can Work for Racial Justice* by Paul Kivel. Published by New Society Publishers, revised edition 2002. Reprinted with permission.

COMMITMENT TO COMBAT RACISM

Judith Katz

SHEET 1

Indicate whether you have taken action on the items listed below. Check appropriate box.

Yes	No	
☐	☐	Have I aggressively sought out more information in an effort to enhance my own awareness and understanding of racism (talking with others, reading, listening)?
☐	☐	Have I spent some time recently looking at my own racist attitudes and behavior as they contribute to or combat racism around me?
☐	☐	Have I reevaluated my use of terms or phrases that may be perceived by others as degrading or hurtful?
☐	☐	Have I openly disagreed with a racist comment, joke, or action among those around me?
☐	☐	Have I made a personal contract with myself to take a positive stand, even at some possible risk, when the chance occurs?
☐	☐	Have I become increasingly aware of racist TV programs, advertising, news broadcasts, etc.? Have I complained to those in charge?
☐	☐	Have I realized that White Americans are trapped by their own school, homes, media, government, etc., even when they choose not to be openly racist?
☐	☐	Have I suggested and taken steps to implement discussions or workshops aimed at understanding racism with friends, colleagues, social clubs, or church groups?
☐	☐	Have I been investigating political candidates at all levels in terms of their stance and activity against racist government practices?
☐	☐	Have I investigated curricula of local schools in terms of their treatment of the issue of racism (also textbooks, assemblies, faculty, staff, administration)?
☐	☐	Have I contributed time and/or funds to an agency, fund, or program that actively confronts the problems of racism?
☐	☐	Have my buying habits supported nonracist shops, companies, or personnel?
☐	☐	Is my school or place of employment a target for my educational efforts in responding to racism?
☐	☐	Have I become seriously dissatisfied with my own level of activity in combating racism?

SOURCE: Developed by James Edler, University of Maryland.

SHEET 2

1. Educating roommates, close friends.

2. Raising issues in the dorm with heads of residence, resident directors, counseling staff, students, student government.

3. Providing information services—changing what normally appears on bulletin boards and walls to provocative posters, handouts, and other materials relevant to racism.

4. Being a referral resource—directing others to people or groups who might be of assistance.

5. Acting as a race model, questioning the White power structure.

6. Establishing discussion groups, colloquia.

7. Finding films to expose racism, developing new directions and strategies.

8. Finding out how dorm money is spent, using it to demonstrate meaningful concern about racism.

9. Working as a counselor with people who are genuinely interested in making sense of racial issues.

TOOLS FOR WHITE GUYS WHO ARE WORKING FOR SOCIAL CHANGE

Chris Crass

1. Practice noticing who's in the room at meetings—how many gender privileged men (biological men), how many women, how many transgendered people, how many white people, how many people of color, is it majority heterosexual, are there out queers, what are people's class backgrounds? Don't assume to know people, but also work at being more aware—listening to what people say and talking with people one on one who you work with.

2a. Count how many times you speak and keep track of how long you speak.

2b. Count how many times other people speak and keep track of how long they speak.

3. Be conscious of how often you are actively listening to what other people are saying as opposed to just waiting your turn thinking about what you'll say next. Keep a notebook so that you can write down your thoughts and then focus on what other people are saying. As a white guy who talks a lot, I've found it helpful to write down my thoughts and wait to hear what others have to say (frequently others will be thinking something similar and then you can support their initiative).

4. Practice going to meetings or hanging out with people focused on listening and learning—not to get caught in the paralysis of whether or not you have anything useful to say, but acting from a place of valuing other people's knowledge and experiences.

5a. Pay attention to how many times you put ideas out to the group you work with.

5b. Notice how often you support other people's ideas for the group.

6. Practice supporting people by asking them to expand on ideas and get more in-depth.

7a. Think about whose work and what contributions to the group get recognized.

7b. Practice recognizing more people for the work they do and try to do it more often. This also includes men offering support to other men who aren't recognized and actively challenging competitive dynamics that men are socialized to act out with each other.

8. Practice asking more people what they think about events, ideas, actions, strategy and vision. White guys tend to talk amongst themselves and develop strong bonds that manifest in organizing. These informal support structures often help reinforce informal leadership structures as well. Asking people what they think and really listening is a core ingredient to healthy group dynamics, think about who you ask and who you really listen to. Developing respect and solidarity across race, class, gender and sexuality is complex and difficult, but absolutely critical—and liberating. Those most negatively impacted by systems of oppression have and will play leading roles in the struggle for collective liberation.

9. Be aware of how often you ask people to do something as opposed to asking other people "what needs to be done": logistics, child care, making phone calls, cooking, providing emotional support and following up with people are often undervalued responsibilities performed by people who are gender oppressed (biological women and trans folks).

10. Struggle with the saying, "you will be needed in the movement when you realize that you are not needed in the movement."

11. Struggle with and work with the model of group leadership that says that the responsibility of leaders is to help develop more leaders, and think about what this means to you: how do you support others and what support do you need from others. This includes men providing emotional and political support to other men. How can men work to be allies to each other in the struggle to develop radical models of anti-racist, class conscious, pro-queer, feminist manhood that challenges strict binary gender roles and categories. This is also about struggling to recognize leadership roles while also redefining leadership as actively working to build power with others rather than power over others.

12. Remember that social change is a process, and that our individual transformation and individual liberation is intimately interconnected with social transformation and social liberation. Life is profoundly complex and there are many contradictions. Remember that the path we travel is guided by love, dignity and respect—even when it brings us to tears and is difficult to navigate. As we struggle let us also love ourselves.

13. This list is not limited to white guys, nor is it intended to reduce all white guys into one category. This list is intended to disrupt patterns of domination which hurt our movement and hurt each other. White guys have a lot of work to do, but if we white guys support and challenge each other, while also building trust and compassion we can heal ourselves in the process.

14. Day-to-day patterns of domination are the glue that maintain systems of domination. The struggle against capitalism, white supremacy, patriarchy, heterosexism and the state, is also the struggle towards collective liberation.

15. No one is free until we are all free.

Thanks and love to my comrades in the Bay Area gender privileged men's group of the Ruckus Society and the men's group (biological and transgendered men) of the Challenging White Supremacy Collective.

For more reading, check out:

On the Road to Healing: A Booklet for Men Against Sexism

P.O. Box 84171, Seattle, Washington 98124 or plantingseeds@tao.ca http://colours.mahost.org/org/whiteguys.html.

SOURCE: Reprinted with permission of the author.

DISCUSSION QUESTIONS

1. Why does Williams state that color blindness is a fiction? If a truly color-blind society is the eventual goal, why do scholars like Williams, Bell, and others advocate color-conscious policies for ending inequality? Is it possible to create feasible solutions for racism that do not acknowledge race, knowing that modern racism occurs often without mentioning race? Which type of approach do you think would be more effective for ending racism (color-blind or color-conscious policy) and why?

2. Do you think overt or covert racism is easier to fight, and why? Since our legal structure deals mainly with overt racism, what policy suggestions can you offer for dealing with covert racism, including that which is perpetuated unintentionally? Should people be punished similarly whether they intended to be discriminatory or not, if the effect is the same on the victim? (Hint: think of how the law treats other crimes.)

3. The Bell and Steinberg readings both point to how resistant dominant culture is to change, whether racism or sexism is the target of those social change efforts. If it is our natural human tendency to respect and gravitate more toward the talents of those similar to us, should efforts to change people's thinking occur before attempting policy change, or vice versa? Can one occur without the other?

4. How often do you see groups concerned with ending racism working together with groups concerned with ending sexism on particular issues or events (a) on your campus and (b) in larger society? What issues would you expect them to be working together on? What challenges exist for coalition-building across these two groups?

5. Do you think whites' energies are better spent working with other whites (that is, being "race traitors," challenging whites who give them privileges) or as allies to people of color? Similarly, should male pro-feminists work with other men, or as allies to women? What are the benefits and drawbacks of each approach? If you are a person of color, what would you prefer whites to do and why? Women, which would you prefer to see men do and why? If you are a white person, which would be easier and which would be harder for you and why? Men, which approach would be easier and which would be harder for you? Why?

6. What kinds of activities do you think you can do in your own life to end oppression? Are there things that you do already or that you would like to do more of? Think of the last time you witnessed racism or sexism and were pleased with how you handled the situation. Consider what you would have done differently. What kinds of things can you do, even in the absence of such overt incidents, to help reduce oppression in society? If you cannot think of anything that you would be willing to do, what is it that holds you back?

INDEX

About the Editors

Joseph F. Healey is Professor and Chair of Sociology and Anthropology at Christopher Newport University. He is the author of *Race, Ethnicity, Gender, and Class* (4th edition, 2006), *Statistics: A Tool for Social Research* (7th edition, 2005), and several other textbooks. He received A.B. and M.A. degrees from the College of William and Mary (Sociology and Anthropology) and a Ph.D. from the University of Virginia (Sociology and Anthropology). In his spare time, he reads and plays the banjo and hammer dulcimer.

Eileen O'Brien is Assistant Professor at the University of Richmond, where her teaching and research interests range from introductory sociology to courses on race, ethnicity, gender, social class, and theory. She authored *Whites Confront Racism* (2001) and has coauthored *White Men on Race* (2003) with Joe Feagin, a preeminent scholar on race and ethnic relations. She received her Ph.D. from the University of Florida in 1999 and an M.A. from Ohio State University in 1996, both degrees in Sociology.